CAPITAL IN
THE AMERICAN ECONOMY

Its Formation and Financing

NATIONAL BUREAU OF ECONOMIC RESEARCH

STUDIES IN CAPITAL FORMATION AND FINANCING

Capital in the
American Economy

ITS FORMATION AND FINANCING

BY

SIMON KUZNETS
HARVARD UNIVERSITY

ASSISTED BY
ELIZABETH JENKS

A STUDY BY THE
NATIONAL BUREAU OF ECONOMIC RESEARCH

PUBLISHED BY
PRINCETON UNIVERSITY PRESS
1961

This monograph is part of a larger investigation of trends and prospects in capital formation and financing made possible by a grant from the Life Insurance Association of America. The Association, of course, is not to be held responsible for statements made or views expressed.

RELATION OF THE DIRECTORS
TO THE WORK AND PUBLICATIONS
OF THE NATIONAL BUREAU OF ECONOMIC RESEARCH

1. The object of the National Bureau of Economic Research is to ascertain and to present to the public important economic facts and their interpretation in a scientific and impartial manner. The Board of Directors is charged with the responsibility of ensuring that the work of the National Bureau is carried on in strict conformity with this object.

2. To this end the Board of Directors shall appoint one or more Directors of Research.

3. The Director or Directors of Research shall submit to the members of the Board, or to its Executive Committee, for their formal adoption, all specific proposals concerning researches to be instituted.

4. No report shall be published until the Director or Directors of Research shall have submitted to the Board a summary drawing attention to the character of the data and their utilization in the report, the nature and treatment of the problems involved, the main conclusions, and such other information as in their opinion would serve to determine the suitability of the report for publication in accordance with the principles of the National Bureau.

5. A copy of any manuscript proposed for publication shall also be submitted to each member of the Board. For each manuscript to be so submitted a special committee shall be appointed by the President, or at his designation by the Executive Director, consisting of three Directors selected as nearly as may be one from each general division of the Board. The names of the special manuscript committee shall be stated to each Director when the summary and report described in paragraph (4) are sent to him. It shall be the duty of each member of the committee to read the manuscript. If each member of the special committee signifies his approval within thirty days, the manuscript may be published. If each member of the special committee has not signified his approval within thirty days of the transmittal of the report and manuscript, the Director of Research shall then notify each member of the Board, requesting approval or disapproval of publication, and thirty additional days shall be granted for this purpose. The manuscript shall then not be published unless at least a majority of the entire Board and a two-thirds majority of those members of the Board who shall have voted on the proposal within the time fixed for the receipt of votes on the publication proposed shall have approved.

6. No manuscript may be published, though approved by each member of the special committee, until forty-five days have elapsed from the transmittal of the summary and report. The interval is allowed for the receipt of any memorandum of dissent or reservation, together with a brief statement of his reasons, that any member may wish to express; and such memorandum of dissent or reservation shall be published with the manuscript if he so desires. Publication does not, however, imply that each member of the Board has read the manuscript, or that either members of the Board in general, or of the special committee, have passed upon its validity in every detail.

7. A copy of this resolution shall, unless otherwise determined by the Board, be printed in each copy of every National Bureau book.

(Resolution adopted October 25, 1926
and revised February 6, 1933 and February 24, 1941)

Contents

Contents

Contents

Contents

Tables

Tables

Tables

Tables

Tables

Tables

REFERENCE TABLES

Appendix A

Tables

Tables

Appendix C

Tables

Figures and Charts

Figures and Charts

Acknowledgments

My greatest indebtedness for assistance in the research reported here and in the preparation of this monograph is to Elizabeth Jenks. Without her painstaking, patient, and skillful handling of both major problems and minor details over a number of years, the work could not have been completed.

In the earlier stages of the study, Lillian Epstein rendered valuable assistance, and she also undertook the initial editing of the manuscript. The final editor was Margaret T. Edgar, who did a thoughtful and critical job. The charts were expertly drawn by H. Irving Forman.

The manuscript profited from review by the members of the National Bureau's reading committees, particularly Moses Abramovitz, Gary S. Becker, Melvin G. de Chazeau, Solomon Fabricant, and Raymond W. Goldsmith.

The monograph is largely the outcome of a cooperative enterprise, drawing upon the work of a number of scholars many of whom were responsible for the other monographs in the series. My obligation to them is great, and is certainly not fully acknowledged in the references to their work as cited in this volume.

Throughout the broad inquiry of which this volume is the last and summary monograph—and particularly in the early years—the Advisory Committee on the Study of Capital Formation and Financing gave generous and valuable help. The Committee was composed of Leo Wolman, Chairman; Sherwin C. Badger, Donald R. Belcher, Claude L. Benner, Percival F. Brundage, Arthur F. Burns, W. Braddock Hickman, Edgar M. Hoover, DeLong H. Monahan, and Geoffrey H. Moore.

I enjoyed and benefited by the cooperation and keen interest of James J. O'Leary of the Life Insurance Association of America, all during the years from the initiation of the study in 1950 to its completion here.

To all these co-workers, advisers, and friends I hereby express my sincere thanks.

SIMON KUZNETS

xxix

CAPITAL IN
THE AMERICAN ECONOMY

Its Formation and Financing

Introduction

I

THIS is the last in a series of monographs resulting from an inquiry initiated by the National Bureau of Economic Research in 1950, with the financial assistance of the Life Insurance Association of America.[1] The inquiry examines long-term trends in capital formation and financing in the United States, and is organized primarily around the principal capital using sectors of the economy—agriculture, mining and manufacturing, the regulated industries (public utilities), nonfarm residential real estate, and governments. The analysis for each sector summarizes the major trends in real capital formation from 1870 (or the earliest year for which data are available) and in financing

[1] The others, all published by Princeton for the National Bureau of Economic Research, are: *Capital Formation in Residential Real Estate: Trends and Prospects*, by Leo Grebler, David M. Blank, and Louis Winnick (1956); *Capital in Agriculture: Its Formation and Financing since 1870*, by Alvin S. Tostlebe (1957); *Financial Intermediaries in the American Economy since 1900*, by Raymond W. Goldsmith (1958); *Capital in Transportation, Communications, and Public Utilities: Its Formation and Financing*, by Melville J. Ulmer (1960); *Capital in Manufacturing and Mining: Its Formation and Financing*, by Daniel Creamer, Sergei Dobrovolsky, and Israel Borenstein (1960); and *Trends in Government Financing*, by Morris A. Copeland (1961).

Some of the findings had previously been presented in part or in preliminary form in a series of occasional and technical papers published by the National Bureau: Leo Grebler, *The Role of Federal Credit Aids in Residential Construction*, Occasional Paper 39 (1953); Daniel Creamer, *Capital and Output Trends in Manufacturing Industries, 1880–1948*, Occasional Paper 41 (1954); Raymond W. Goldsmith, *The Share of Financial Intermediaries in National Wealth and National Assets, 1900–1949*, Occasional Paper 42 (1954); Melville J. Ulmer, *Trends and Cycles in Capital Formation by United States Railroads, 1870–1950*, Occasional Paper 43 (1954); Alvin S. Tostlebe, *The Growth of Physical Capital in Agriculture, 1870–1950*, Occasional Paper 44 (1954); Israel Borenstein, *Capital and Output Trends in Mining Industries, 1870–1948*, Occasional Paper 45 (1954); David M. Blank, *The Volume of Residential Construction, 1889–1950*, Technical Paper 9 (1954).

from 1900 (the earliest practicable date), and the factors determining those trends; and, so far as possible, suggests the significance of those factors for the future. In addition to the five sector studies, the inquiry comprises two others. The first deals with trends in financing channeled through intermediate financial institutions and attempts to link the major types of institutions with the various groups of capital users. This, the second, utilizes the results of all the other studies within a framework provided by countrywide estimates of national product and its relevant components and of assets and debts, and draws upon estimates and findings not covered in the other monographs.

II

A proper view of trends in capital formation and in its major components requires comparison with national product, from which the savings embodied in capital formation are drawn, and for the production of which capital investment is made. Although the five sector monographs—on agriculture, manufacturing and mining, the regulated industries, nonfarm residential real estate, and governments—do not cover the whole economy, the capital investment and output of those sectors account for a substantial part of the national totals of capital formation and product. Yet it was necessary in this summary monograph to provide a set of continuous and comparable estimates of national capital formation and national product, covering the decades since the 1870's. Of capital formation, several components are distinguished: construction, further subdivided into nonfarm residential, government, and all other; producers' durable equipment; net changes in inventories; and net changes in claims against foreign countries. Within national product, in addition to the distinction between capital formation and flow of goods to consumers, there is the distribution of the latter among services and commodities of differing durability. The task involved the preparation of a fairly elaborate framework of estimates: both capital formation and national product were estimated with and without allowance for consumption of durable capital; these totals and their components were expressed in both current and constant prices; for some of the totals several statistical variants were calculated; and important related series such as population and labor force had to be estimated. In addition, in order to distinguish between the long-term trends and the swings or alternations in the rate of growth, we needed continuous estimates for successive periods short enough to permit study of changes in the rate of growth.

4

Introduction

A similar task was involved in securing a nationwide view of trends in financing—even though the statistical picture of that aspect extends back only to 1900. The sector monographs on capital formation and financing do not cover the entire economy, and, furthermore, the differing supply of data available results in varying degrees of detail and coverage. The monograph on financial intermediaries presents a more comprehensive picture, but it stresses external financing and the changing shares of various groups of intermediaries in the latter. Consequently, it was necessary to organize and supplement the data on financing by countrywide estimates covering both internal and external financing, a task for which Raymond Goldsmith's monumental study of saving in the United States and his work at the National Bureau in recent years were invaluable.

Thus, much of the material for this summary monograph, other than that drawn from the monographs that preceded it, was estimated, and the need to present the estimates and describe the sources and methods used accounts for much of the bulk of the present volume. Indeed, the appendixes are really a statistical supplement, which sets out in detail the series on national product and capital formation, as well as the related series on population and labor force. But even in the body of the report a fair amount of space is devoted to the estimates and their derivation. Because of the detail in presentation and description throughout, the volume can be used for reference as a compendium of estimates which can be employed for a great variety of analytical purposes.

Having at hand the national estimates and the wealth of series in the preceding monographs on various sectors and on the financial intermediaries, the next task—in logical if not historical sequence—was to order and classify these data so that they would reveal the levels of and movements in capital formation and its financing. Because our concern was with long-term movements, the process of classification and arrangement called for the grouping of the data in space—distinguishing, comparing, and combining various components of capital formation and financing by type, by grossness and netness, by industrial user—and relating some of these groups to the appropriate product, population, and labor force totals. It was necessary also to group the data in time, by periods long enough to cancel the effects of short-term fluctuations associated with business cycles and to reveal, if possible, the underlying long-term movements. This task of classifying was rendered all the more difficult because we were compelled to distinguish within the long-term movements two components: the long swings or alternations in the rate of growth, and the secular trends that underlie and transcend those swings.

Most of the discussion is devoted to the results of this ordering of the data on national product and on capital formation and its financing. The aim was to observe the long-term movements in these important aspects of the economy since the 1870's or since the beginning of this century, and to present the findings in a systematic sequence that would help us absorb this segment of experience into the background of our thinking. This apparently simple task is beset with numerous pitfalls: the component categories available in any set of estimates are often too broad to permit distinction of significantly different groups or processes, and the changes over time are often so violent and erratic that the underlying trends can be discerned only with difficulty. The major reason for space-consuming alternative groupings and discussion of them is to minimize the danger of overstating the findings, of attributing a degree of simplicity and firmness to them that is not justified by the evidence. But prone as we all are to oversimplification and generalization, this weakness may not have been entirely avoided here.

With the ordered empirical findings at hand, the next task in logical sequence was that of explanation—of attempting to show with what patterns of established generalizations a specific finding could be associated, of what general law it was a specific case. Since there are few such generalizations or laws in the field of economic knowledge, and since any linking of a given set of findings to some established theoretical tenets requires more precise knowledge of the mechanism involved than is available, adequately tested explanations are not now feasible—at least for the findings of the present inquiry. Our explanatory discussions are, perforce, only suggestions of the factors that were likely to have been operative in producing the trends and long swings found, and where practicable, the findings were reduced to the next set of immediate quantitative determinants. The result is, at best, a sketch of a possible but untested association between the findings and a set of known or reasonably acceptable general patterns of economic behavior, an indication of the directions in which specific tests of the suggested associations are to be sought, not a demonstration of the existence of such links. In short, the explanations are conjectural rather than tested, partial rather than complete, suggestive rather than definitive.

Introduction

Conjectural as the explanations must be, they are essential if we wish to speculate, in a systematic fashion, on the bearing of past trends upon the prospects for some projected future. For the trends in the past are never so persistent and stable as to permit a purely statistical extrapolation into the future, even if one were willing to accept the mechanical projection of patterns of human behavior without attempting to understand why and how such patterns have come about. It is thus indispensable to identify at least some of the factors that may have produced the past trends and to evaluate their possible continuation into the future. We face the problem of projection only in the last chapter. This is, essentially, a task of controlled speculation, but one which, to be done properly, requires a systematically organized sequence of steps that could not be encompassed within this inquiry. There are, in consequence, no quantitative projections given. Instead, Chapter 10 lists the conditions for the future that would have to be carefully examined in any systematic projection, and discusses briefly some aspects of these conditions that seem relevant on the basis of general observations rather than intensive examination.

The study reported here is thus largely a compound of estimation and classification, seasoned at different levels of empirical findings with conjectural explanation, and topped off with a frosting of impressionistic speculation. But this description should be amplified in two respects.

First, the distinction drawn above between the different phases of the work is too neat, and, as everyone who has ever engaged in research knows, the logical sequence is never followed in reality. One begins an examination of the available data, already full of notions as to the important groupings and classifications that are to be followed, which in turn are guided by some explanatory hypotheses, that have been either explicitly formulated or only adumbrated, and by some ideas as to the significant persistent factors. Then, in the process of organizing the data called for by this complex of the half known and half conjectured, revisions of the initial mixture of knowledge and conjecture occur, which may—and usually do—call for more data, different classifications, and different hypotheses. Then, with the additional data and new groupings, still another revision may occur. The actual work is thus a continuous interplay of estimation, classification, explanation, and speculation—not a concentration on each successive phase in accordance with the logical sequence.

Second, the relative weight of untested judgment—of tentative choice

7

—increases as we move from estimation to classification to explanation and to speculation. But this element of untested judgment is also present in the results most closely connected with the observational data. The very term estimation, as distinct from measurement, indicates that untested judgment is involved in fitting the primary data— themselves subject to error—into the categories of the framework of economic analysis, from which such concepts as national product and capital formation are drawn. Moreover, the way in which we order and classify the estimates, in itself, reflects some hypotheses concerning the relations of the underlying processes: we do not attempt to exhaust all possible ways of combining the data. Conversely, explanatory hypotheses concerning the past and speculative conjectures about the future obviously carry a heavy load of empirical observation— even if we sometimes have difficulty in distinguishing and identifying it when the formulation is too general. And yet, the argument must not be carried too far. There is a clear distinction between stating that the past records reveal this or that trend or level and arguing that there is a causal association between a given finding and, say, changes in distribution of income by size or relative prices of debt and equity funds. There is an even greater distinction between statements concerning trends in the observable past and their projection into the unobservable future. We hope that these distinctions are sufficiently clear in the discussion to minimize the danger of misunderstanding.

III

An attempt to summarize here the empirical findings of the study, and the explanatory hypotheses relevant to them, would run the danger of overstatement and repetition. Chapter 9 has been expressly designed as an effective summary, and readers who do not care to go systematically through the entire volume are advised to begin with Chapter 9, and then dip into the earlier chapters or into the other monographs of the series, whenever some specific finding or hypothesis invites closer attention and scrutiny.

It may be useful, however, to list what seem to be the more important empirical findings, without attempting a complete coverage or touching upon the explanatory hypotheses suggested. As in Chapter 9, the findings are those observed for Variant III, excluding the military; and, except where noted, 1946–1955 is the terminal period.

1. Over the period since the 1870's gross capital formation (the sum of gross construction, producers' durables, net changes in inventories,

and net changes in foreign claims) accounted for a fairly constant proportion of gross national product in current prices—somewhat over a fifth. The long-term trend in the gross capital formation proportion based on volumes in constant prices was slightly downward.

2. The consumption of durable capital (construction and equipment), a measure largely of economic obsolescence rather than of physical wear and tear, grew at higher rates than did gross capital formation; and its ratio to the latter rose from about four-tenths in the early decades to almost two-thirds in the recent decade (for volumes in constant prices).

3. The proportion of net capital formation in net national product declined, for volumes in constant prices, from somewhat less than 15 per cent in the early decades to 7 per cent in the most recent; for volumes in current prices, it declined from 13 per cent to somewhat less than 9 per cent.

4. Within gross capital formation, the share of construction declined, from almost two-thirds in the early decades to over one-half in the most recent; and so did the share of net changes in inventories, from about one-seventh to about one-nineteenth. The share of producers' durable equipment increased from somewhat above one-fifth to over four-tenths, while the rather minor share of net changes in foreign claims shifted from negative to positive. These trends relate to totals in current prices, but the trends in the shares in constant prices are fairly similar.

5. In the distribution of domestic capital formation (construction, producers' durables, and net changes in inventories) by category of user, we find that, in the gross totals in constant prices, the share of governments increased, from less than one-twentieth to almost one-eighth; that of households (nonfarm residential construction) declined, from well over one-quarter to about one-sixth; and that of business firms rose, although only slightly. The movement of the shares of governments and households in gross volumes in current prices was similar to that in constant prices, but the share of business firms declined.

6. Among the major divisions of the business sector—agriculture, manufacturing and mining, and the regulated industries (public utilities)—the share of the first in net durable capital formation in constant prices showed no distinct trend, that of manufacturing and mining rose, and that of the regulated industries declined. These movements of shares in net durable capital formation do not correspond to the

trends in growth of output of these sectors: agriculture's share in their combined output (also in constant prices) declined, and those of manufacturing and mining and of the regulated industries rose.

7. The ratio of net capital stock (net of depreciation) to net national product (both in constant prices) first rose, from 3.2 in the early decades to 3.6 in the 1920's, and then declined, to 2.9 in 1939–1955 or to 2.5 in 1946–1955. The movement of the ratios for the various sectors of the economy differed: for agriculture, and mining and manufacturing there was also a rise through the 1920's and then a decline; for the regulated industries there was a continuous decline from the high levels of the earlier decades.

8. For the economy as a whole, the ratio of internal financing (gross retention) to total uses declined, but moderately, from 0.60 in the first decade of the century to 0.56 in the recent decade. There was an even slighter decline in the ratio of internal financing to gross capital formation, from 0.78 to 0.77.

9. The stability or slight decline in the ratio of internal financing for the country as a whole was due largely to the effects of the household (nonfarm residential construction) and federal government sectors, in both of which the ratio declined and that of external financing rose. By contrast, the trend in the ratio of internal financing in the business sector—the combined total of agriculture, nonfarm unincorporated enterprises, and business corporations—was upward, although mildly so, the ratio of internal financing to total uses of funds rising from 0.59 to 0.64. The latter trend was naturally dominated by the corporate component, by far the largest in the business sector. For nonfinancial corporations the ratio of internal financing to total uses rose from 0.55 to 0.61.

10. The rise in the ratio of internal funds was particularly marked for corporations in the regulated industries, but for mining and manufacturing corporations there was no rise when internal funds were related to total uses (rather than to gross capital formation).

11. In total external financing, the share of the federal government rose markedly and the share of the private component declined. Within the latter, however, the share of households increased substantially, that of agriculture declined appreciably, while those of nonfarm unincorporated enterprises and corporations showed only a slight decline, or stability.

12. The share of equity financing in total external financing for nonfinancial corporations declined somewhat, from about three-tenths

at the beginning of the century to about one-fifth in the recent decade. But the trend was neither marked nor consistent.

13. The share of financial intermediaries in total external financing in the country increased, from somewhat less than one-half early in the century to about two-thirds in recent years. The share of financial intermediaries in total financing in the country also rose, from about one-fifth to about three-tenths in 1946–1955 or four-tenths in 1931–1955.

14. Among financial intermediaries, the share of the banking sector in total assets declined, from an average of well over six-tenths in the first two decades of the century to somewhat less than four-tenths in recent years. The share of the insurance sector rose from less than one-eighth in the first two decades to almost four-tenths in recent years. The share of government institutions (Federal Reserve Banks, government lending institutions, government pension and security funds) rose over this period from well below one-tenth to somewhat over one-fifth.

15. The statements above refer to secular trends that underlie the long swings, the alternations in rates of growth. These long swings, about twenty years in duration on the average, are clearly observable in additions to population, immigration, gross nonfarm residential construction, gross durable capital expenditures by railroads, net changes in claims against foreign countries (capital imports and exports), and indexes of stock market prices for some groups of securities (particularly utility). We find them also in other components of national product, capital formation, and financing; but the results do not lend themselves to brief summary.

IV

In concluding this introduction, we consider a question suggested by the description in section II of the kind of compound the present study is, and by the results listed in section III. Granted that the inquiry manages to establish a number of empirical findings of the type illustrated, if they are not accounted for by a testable theory that can provide a firm basis for projections into the future or policy decisions in the present, is the study of much practical use? If we do not succeed in establishing a reliable, generally persistent pattern backed by a valid theory, that is, an association with other invariant patterns of behavior on whose persistence we can rely, do the few additional empirical findings have any value except as a matter of idle antiquarian curiosity?

Introduction

The answer to such a broad question can, within the present context, be only a matter of judgment; and the question would not have been raised except that, to my mind, it reflects a common misunderstanding concerning the relation between research on social processes and its applicability to social action. In particular, the misunderstanding rests upon an inadequate view of the links between knowledge and policy; and it may not be out of place to comment upon this problem here.

We begin with the simple statement that any tested empirical knowledge, relating as it does to observable natural or social processes, is by definition potentially useful. For usefulness means exploitability of the patterns of behavior of nature and society for ends deemed positive by us as human beings. And it is difficult to see how additional knowledge about observable patterns of behavior of either nature or society can fail to be potentially useful—since every aspect of such patterns is relevant to some positive aim of mankind.

The failure to recognize this ingrained potential usefulness of all tested knowledge is due partly to the wide gap in some cases between knowledge and its specific application to ends other than idle curiosity, and the links involved in bridging the gap are almost inconceivably complex. Consider the leap of imagination required of an observer who could have glimpsed the value of the application of Hertzian short waves to the electronic industry of today, or of non-Euclidean geometry (although that is not empirical knowledge pure and simple) in its later uses in applied physics.

These examples are taken from the natural sciences by design, for it is in them that the distance between knowledge and use is often great; and this may well be one of the sources of their strength. In the field of social study, unlike the others, additions to knowledge have two types of use. One is similar to the application of knowledge in the natural sciences: thus, measures of the price elasticity of demand for a commodity may be employed to estimate the likely effects of an excise tax, in consideration of tax policy, just as knowledge of resistance of materials, prospective weights, and theoretical mechanics can be used in calculating the requirements for a bridge. The other use has much less in common with the application of findings of the natural sciences, but it is pervasive in the social processes: additions to knowledge in that field become absorbed into the background of a wide variety of people, and it is against this background, professional and lay, that discussion and consideration of broad policy issues occur.

Introduction

New theories and discoveries in physics and astronomy concerning cosmogony no longer agitate us, as they did our forebears in the times of the Copernican and Galilean revolutions; but the changing knowledge of the behavior patterns of society colors both the continuous succession of social doctrines and the whole milieu within which social problems are discussed and solutions decided upon.

Thus, in addition to the purely technical application of findings of the study of economic and social patterns when possible, there is the more pervasive use of those findings as a framework within which the social problems of the present and the future are considered. The time lag may be long between establishment of empirical findings and their absorption into a tested theory of reliably invariant patterns for practical technical use in projections or in estimating calculable effects under alternative policy actions (as illustrated above in connection with short-term price elasticity of demand). But the time lag is short between new findings and their use to enrich the background against which broad current problems are considered. Indeed, the danger is not that such findings will not be used for practical purposes, but rather that the results will be eagerly seized upon to yield a spate of hypotheses that claim too much generality, of new theoretical positions which have vitality because they lead to policy consequences that seem more adequate than the old. Yet, granting this ever-present danger that new empirical findings may provide a starting point for distorted use or for unwarranted dogmatic generalizations, there is a clear need for more, not less, such empirical knowledge; for a longer, not shorter historical perspective; for a more detailed, not a more aggregated, structuring of the empirical evidence; for wider interspatial and intertemporal comparisons rather than concentration on a single country and period.

In short, the most important practical use of the type of findings the present study provides, coupled with the related suggestive explanations, is to enrich the stock of tested knowledge which provides the background for much of the theorizing and decisive discussion of broad policy issues. Without such findings, the background is inadequate—one against which, for example, recent short-term changes could not be set in their longer historical perspective, and against which some extrapolation could not be fully tested, and consequently might be erroneously projected into the future. I do not mean to argue that additions to tested knowledge and to relevant hypotheses are a sufficient condition for more effective theorizing and better decisions on broad policy issues, but they are surely necessary. And if it is true, as Lord Keynes once said, that the political leaders of today usually operate with the obsolete economic theories of yesterday, then there is surely immense value in additions to tested economic knowledge that contribute to economic theories with broader and longer validity, and thus reduce the deleterious effects of that type of cultural lag.

This potential contribution of the present study can best be visualized if it is remembered that no inquiry stands by itself. It is but another item in a whole sequence, and in a wide range of related inquiries. Its results should be utilized not in isolation, but together with all else that is known in the field—either in the way of empirical data or theoretical hypotheses linked to such data. The optimum use of the present study is as an *addition* to the economic history and analysis of the United States and of other countries, to the stock of already known hypotheses, and in as full conjunction with these other data and hypotheses as any particular problem warrants.

To put it another way: like any other empirically oriented inquiry, this one has no true beginning and no sharp end. It has no beginning because it is rooted in a variety of past studies, and is in a sense unintelligible unless it is added to much of what is already known or conjectured in the more comprehensive literature on the broad aspects of modern economic life. It has no clear end because, while we hope that it advances our knowledge a notch, its contribution can be tested only when its results have been absorbed and revised in a more extensive framework in which they will find their proper niche as well as eventual oblivion in the loss of their identity. But only in such building upon the past complex of knowledge was the study feasible; and only in its absorption in the next phase of work in the field can it make an effective contribution.

CHAPTER 1

Capital Formation, Saving, and Financing:
Definitions and Relations

Capital Formation

IN modern society, capital is the stock of means, separable from human beings and legally disposable in economic transactions, intended for use in producing goods or income. These means must be separable from human beings because our society, unlike slave societies, does not permit ownership of or trade in persons and hence in the skills embodied in them. They must exclude means not legally disposable in economic transactions, that is, the many natural resources vital to the economy but not subject to ownership, and the most important resource of all—empirically tested knowledge. And if we distinguish production by economic units from ultimate consumption within households, the capital stock limited to means of production must exclude other stock often included in national wealth—for instance, consumer goods in households.

Capital in the hands of various units within a country—households, business firms, nonbusiness associations, governments—may take the form of goods (tangible assets) or claims (financial assets or intangibles). The claims may be domestic, against residents of the country, or foreign, against residents of other countries. In totaling the stock of capital of the country, domestic claims are exactly offset by domestic obligations, and only the net balance of foreign claims remains. Nationwide capital, by definition, therefore, consists of the stock of goods within the country and the net balance (positive or negative) of foreign claims.

Capital Formation, Saving, and Financing

Capital formation, strictly speaking, denotes *additions* to the stock of tangible goods within the country or to foreign claims. These additions are usually taken on a net basis, which means that for some owner or user groups, for some periods, or for some types of goods or claims, there may be subtractions rather than additions, declines rather than rises. We should, then, speak of capital dissolution or reduction. But it has become customary to use the term capital formation for all changes in the stock of goods or claims, whether positive or negative, and to use the latter as qualifying adjectives. Thus, nationwide capital formation is a sum of the net changes in the stock of goods within the country and in the net balance of foreign claims. For some purposes, changes in the stock of durable (long-lived) capital goods are estimated on a gross basis: capital goods consumed are not subtracted from the total additions to stock. And gross capital formation is distinguished from net in that it, too, is gross of the allowance for current consumption.

Of the numerous questions of inclusion and exclusion that arise in defining capital and capital formation, two deserve note here. The first, already alluded to, is the treatment of goods within households. The measures used below exclude such goods (food, clothing, furniture, passenger cars, and so on, in the hands of individuals and families), but include dwellings, whether rented or owner occupied. The case for excluding the former rests upon the basic distinction between ultimate consumption and economic production, which defines the former as the disposal of goods by households and the latter as the use of goods to produce other goods, largely for the market—that is, for units other than the producing one. Since capital is conceived as a *productive* factor, the stock of consumer goods within households must be excluded. Otherwise the disposition of these goods within households would have to be classified as economic production. On the other hand, the wide choice between ownership and rental of dwellings, and the very magnitude of the outlays involve decisions that are akin to economic behavior in business capital investment; and in its disposition of the owned residence, a household can, in a sense, be viewed as an economic producer. We therefore treat all dwellings as capital goods, and include the yield of all, rented and owner occupied, in production and income.

The other question relates to the stock of goods in the hands of governments. In some estimates, those of the Department of Commerce for instance, the stock of goods in the hands of governments is not included in capital and additions to it are not included in capital formation, since governments are treated as ultimate consumers. This view does not seem acceptable. It is true that governments do not operate for the market as business firms do. However, they do yield both final services (health, education, recreation, etc.) and intermediate services (protection, administration, business information, etc.), which cannot be regarded as finished output but which do enter into the value of that output and are similar to the services rendered by legal and accounting firms to business and society. Like business firms, governments should be viewed as producers, since production is their economic reason for existence. The only ultimate consumers in society are the human beings who comprise it. For this reason, the concept of capital followed here includes the entire stock of goods in the hands of governments no matter how remote it may seem to be from embodiment in final product, although for statistical reasons the estimates of that stock are often incomplete.

Relation to Saving

How does nationwide capital formation—changes in the stock of goods and in claims against the rest of the world—originate? Such changes may come from current production of the economy or from other sources. If some current product is not consumed, it must be added to the stock of goods within the country or exported to the rest of the world—positive capital formation. Conversely, if households, business firms, governments, and other units absorb more than the current net output, such overspending (more commonly called dissaving) necessitates a draft upon the existing stock of goods or upon the net claims against foreign countries—negative capital formation. To the extent that this is true, savings or dissavings, which may be defined as the difference, positive or negative, between current net output and consumption, are the source of capital formation; and on a nationwide scale, savings obviously equal capital formation.

But additions to or drafts upon the nationwide stock of goods, and net changes in claims against foreign countries may arise from sources that we hesitate to define as savings, because we hesitate to treat them as part of economic production and current net output. Two such sources may be suggested: (1) additions to the stock of natural resources by territorial expansion or scientific discovery, in which the rise in economic value far exceeds any calculable costs of exploration, or reductions in such stock due to unforeseen natural calamities; and (2) political changes and war. The former is exemplified by the peaceful expansion of the territory of the United States, the discovery of its natural resources, and the appreciation in the value of the resources associated with the discovery of new uses (such as oil and uranium deposits); and on the calamitous side, by earthquakes, major epidemics of man, animals, and crops, by storms, floods, and forest fires. The latter is illustrated by additions to territory as a result of armed aggression, and by destruction or complete devastation in war. Should we include in economic production unforeseen and, in a sense, unearned results of exploration and discovery? Should we include in income the sudden appreciation in the value of possessions, and include in savings the monetary equivalent of that appreciation not spent by the lucky owners? Should we classify wars of aggression as economic ventures similar to rather risky business projects? Should we treat the ruin suffered from bombing as capital consumed in the process of economic production?

In the concept followed here, such changes in the stock of capital goods are excluded from capital formation; and their underlying sources are excluded from economic production, income, and savings. The reason is obvious. Even if the meaning of economic processes were stretched to include acquisition of natural resources by geographic exploration or by scientific discovery, by war or other manipulations of political power, the resulting "economic product," "net income," "savings," and "capital formation" would be very different from those that occur under relatively peaceful and normal political conditions. To avoid confusion, it is perhaps best to treat only the latter as the results of economic processes, and to regard the other sources of change in the stock of capital as noneconomic.

Two important aspects of this decision should be stressed here. First, however one defines economic and noneconomic sources of change in the stock of capital, and whether one does or does not include both under capital formation, the identity of savings and capital formation on a nationwide scale is the result of defining both of them equally narrowly or widely. That uniformity in definition is insisted upon because the resulting identity is useful in both measurement and analysis. Yet capital formation can be defined broadly as the total change in the stock of goods and in claims, that is, the change in all national wealth whether due to economic or other processes, and savings and economic product can be defined more narrowly. Second, any limitation of the definition of economic product, income, savings, capital formation, and so on must be recognized for what it is—deliberate restriction of the field of measurement and analysis in the hope that better understanding and more tenable generalizations will thereby be attained. Even if the hope is justified, there is some loss in validity: for example, any generalization concerning economic processes from which wars and political changes are excluded will be useful only so long as wars and political changes do not dominate reality. And limitation of capital formation to changes in *reproducible* capital alone and exclusion of changes in the supply of natural resources is restrictive, in that it may mean neglect of the importance of those resources in a country's long-term past.[1]

The Problem of Financing

Robinson Crusoe's decisions regarding capital formation were simply orders to himself (and to his man Friday) as to the number of hours of work to be devoted to producing consumer goods and to producing tools and housing. Disposition of income between consumption and savings coincided with distribution of the product between flow of goods to consumers and capital formation. There was no financing problem because there was no money, and no possible discrepancy in identity between the saver and the capital user. In a completely planned authoritarian economy, orders concerning saving—diversion of current product from consumption or of current income from expenditure on consumer goods—can be assumed to be matched by orders concerning capital formation; and here again there is no financing problem.

Modern economic society organizes its extensive division of labor by the use of money and other means of payment, and by the interlocking of hosts of legally independent and free economic units through the ties of the market place. In such a society, only in exceptional cases

[1] The limitation of savings and capital formation to the difference between current product and ultimate consumption—product defined to exclude discovery, territorial expansion, and political gains—means the exclusion also of other changes in capital values (realized or unrealized capital gains or losses). Such changes have considerable effect on the structure of production and consumption processes, on the distribution of economic power, on the patterns of behavior of economic units. Their disregard here is due to a designed concentration upon the real side of production and capital formation and, as in the case of the exclusions discussed above, the limitation of coverage is attended by loss of some explanatory factors.

(as a farmer using his free time to mend fences) does capital formation take place without the use of money. The overwhelming proportion of additions to the stock of capital goods is ordinarily purchased by their users from their producers, and would-be users of the capital goods face the problem of financing, the problem of securing the means of payment. The purchase may be made with the user's current or past savings (internal financing), or with somebody else's savings (external financing). Since, as a matter of course, there are disparities in time and place between the need for capital goods and the ability to save for them, external financing is common. For instance, it may be most advantageous to an individual to own a house in the early years of family life, when savings cannot be accumulated easily because raising children increases current consumption. Business units often have opportunities requiring capital investment much greater than the savings they can withhold from current profits. Governments may be under pressure for additions to capital equipment on a scale that far exceeds their ability to collect revenues by taxation or other means. Consequently, a fairly elaborate institutional machinery is needed to channel the savings generated among some units in the economy into the opportunities for capital formation elsewhere. For the would-be capital users, this is the problem of financing; for the savers, it is the problem of investing advantageously; and for the community, it is the problem of utilizing savings to enhance the prospects of economic growth and minimize the dangers of economic instability.

Because of the variety of capital users and savers, and because of the complexity of the institutional framework set up to facilitate solution of their problems, we present several graphical illustrations—at the risk of oversimplifying the picture. In Figure 1 we distinguish three groups of capital users—business corporations, individuals (including unincorporated firms), and governments—and we assume that savings are used to finance capital formation only. To each group we assign hypothetical net changes in the stock of goods and claims it holds. These changes are not actual figures for any given year, but their relative magnitudes have been chosen for their approximation to reality. By and large, barring the exceptional periods of major wars, business corporations not only add to their stock of goods but also increase their domestic obligations (in Figure 1 this increase appears as a net decrease in domestic claims). Governments operate similarly, although on a much smaller scale. Individuals, however, add to both their stock of capital goods and their domestic claims. As already in-

FIGURE 1

Capital Formation and Savings, No Financial Intermediaries, Savings Not Used for Current Expenditures

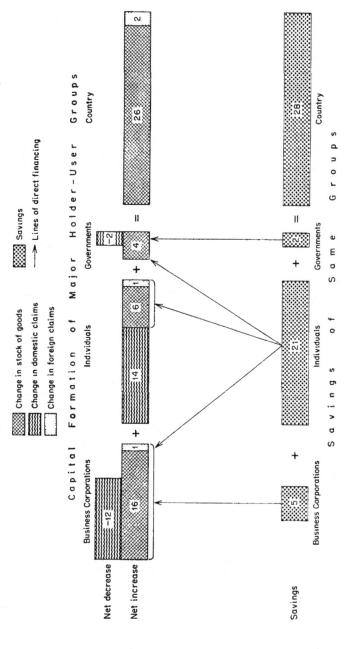

dicated, changes in domestic claims among various groups within the country must offset each other (as they do in Figure 1); hence no changes in domestic claims appear under the capital formation total for the country.

The capital holder-user groups are assumed to account fully for all economic units and must, therefore, be the saver groups also. By definition, savings and capital formation for each are identical if the latter includes not only changes in the stock of goods and in foreign claims but also changes in domestic claims. But if we apportion the nationwide total of capital formation among the user groups and consider their shares in this total, it becomes apparent that, with identity of savings and capital formation for the country as a whole, the amounts of capital additions of the several groups and their shares in nationwide capital formation do not coincide with the amounts of their savings and their shares in nationwide savings. The shares of some user groups in nationwide capital formation are larger and the shares of other user groups smaller than their shares in savings.

If we assume, as we do here, that the savings of any group should be assigned first to its share in nationwide capital formation—that is, to the increase of its stock of goods or foreign claims—we can draw one line of financing between the savings and the capital formation of business corporations and of governments; but we must allow three lines to stem from the savings of individuals, which finance capital formation of all three groups of users.

Now let us consider what happens when savings are used to finance current expenditures, not capital formation (Figure 2). Total savings of business corporations and individuals in Figure 2 are 26 units, the amount assigned to the savings of these two groups in Figure 1. But here the governments are assumed to have added to their domestic obligations far more than was added to the stock of tangible goods in their possession—a situation that prevails during a major war when war outlay, classified by us as current expenditure, is financed by the sale of government bonds to corporations and individuals resident in the country. During the emergency, the purchasers not only refrain from making net additions to their stock of capital goods and foreign claims, but actually convert some of the existing stock and claims into money with which to purchase government bonds. The lines of financing in Figure 2 all run in one direction—toward the government sector—not in three directions, as in Figure 1; and they stem not only from the savings of business corporations and individuals, but from

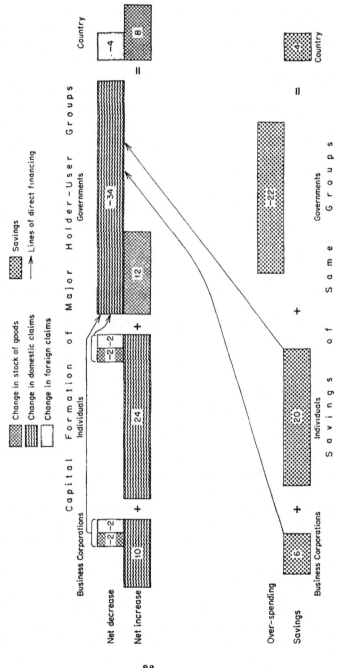

FIGURE 2

Capital Formation and Savings, No Financial Intermediaries, Savings Used for Current Expenditures

23

their stock of goods and claims as well. If we were to replace net savings by gross—that is, add the money spent for government bonds representing the conversion of already existing capital goods and foreign claims—there would be just two lines of financing in Figure 2, one each from business corporations and individuals toward the government sector.

The pictures just presented are, of course, starkly oversimplified, and we can get a better approximation to reality by listing the major points affected by the oversimplification.

1. We do not show the changes within the stock of capital goods and domestic claims and are therefore ignoring these changes, differences in which might help us understand the processes of capital formation, saving, and financing. For example, no distinction is made within domestic claims between long-term and short-term claims, and within the former, between bonds and stocks. Thus, the increase of 12 units in domestic obligations of business corporations in Figure 1 (shown as a net decrease in domestic claims) may be a combination of an increase of 8 in short-term debt and of 6 in common stocks, and of a decline of 2 in bonds. Such a decline in bonds, which would be entered as a net increase in domestic claims of corporations, might mean a reduction in holdings by individuals and appear as a decrease in their domestic claims. The implied process of conversion and shifting of funds in the financial channels is completely concealed in Figure 1. We make this point to emphasize the fact that demand for long-term funds may arise not only out of nationwide capital formation but also out of shifts from the short-term to the long-term domestic claims category.

2. An even more obvious aspect of oversimplification in Figures 1 and 2 is the small number of groups of capital users and savers into which the millions of individuals, thousands of business corporations, and hundreds of government units have been aggregated. To understand the factors that account for the accumulation of capital goods, the origin of savings, and the channeling of savings into capital formation, each of the three groups would have to be subdivided. Various industrial categories among business corporations, and social and economic groups among individuals would certainly have to be distinguished; entrepreneurs would have to be segregated from other individuals, and some industrial distribution of the former given; nonprofit, nongovernment associations would also have to be recognized;

and governments would have to be subdivided in accordance with their different characteristics as capital users and potential savers.

If the number of groups were multiplied beyond the original three, there would be that many more boxes in Figures 1 and 2 and obviously many more lines of financing connecting shares of these groups in savings with their shares in nationwide capital formation. What may not be so obvious is that, even when we follow the principle that the savings of a group are used first to finance its own capital expenditures, any excess of savings over capital formation being used to finance an increase in foreign assets or in domestic claims, many of the lines cannot be drawn without additional information (or, for lack of information, additional assumptions). For example, if we distinguish three industries among business corporations, all of which increase their stock of capital goods but finance the increase by issuing bonds (i.e., by increasing their domestic obligations), and if we distinguish three groups of savers among individuals, all of whom add, in varying amounts, to their claims against business corporations, how do we connect the three individual-saver groups with the three industrial groups of business corporations? Do we draw a line from each of the three groups of savers to each of the three groups of business corporations? Or do we reduce the possible 9 lines of financing to a smaller number by additional assumptions? This difficulty was avoided in Figure 1 by having only one group whose share in savings exceeded its share in nationwide capital formation, and in Figure 2 by having only one group whose share in nationwide capital formation exceeded its share in savings.

3. No matter how detailed the classification of capital users and savers, there is no practical way of distinguishing and handling each economic unit in a country separately, and most groups in any classification would include many units.

Consequently, the net change in the stock of capital goods of any one group is the sum of changes of different magnitude and sign. Thus, one industrial group of business corporations may—and most probably will—include some corporations with an increase in the stock of capital goods financed out of current undistributed profits; some with an increase in stock financed by net borrowing; some with a decline in stock but with an increase in domestic claims; and even some with a decline in both stock of capital goods and domestic claims.

Such possible variety of behavior concealed by a single net change figure for a group emphasizes the artificiality of the assumption followed in Figure 1: that savings of a group are the primary source of financing of its share in nationwide capital formation. For a single economic unit (such as a firm or an individual) this assumption is quite plausible. But it is unrealistic to assume that any firm would use its savings to finance the capital formation of another firm in the same industry; indeed, it might prefer to invest its money in a firm in another industry. Hence, even if the share of a group in nationwide capital formation exceeds its share in savings, we have no right to assume that none of its savings finances capital formation of another group in the economy. It is more realistic to assume in Figure 1 that lines of financing run from every group of savers to every group of capital users. Even governments may and do (if sometimes only indirectly) finance the capital formation of other groups in the economy.

The need to alter our assumption, combined with the need for a more detailed grouping of capital users and savers (point 2), obviously means a vast multiplication of the lines of financing if we are to analyze the country's economy effectively. With three groups, there should be 9 lines of financing, not 5 as shown in Figure 1. In general, the number of lines should equal the square of the number of groups of capital users-savers distinguished. If one were to take account also of the possible distinctions within the stock of capital goods and among various types of claims the picture would indeed become complex.

4. Figures 1 and 2 depict net changes that have occurred over some period—say, a month, a year, a decade. Within that period there may have been, and probably were, flows and counterflows. Even for a single economic unit, say an individual, a net increase in claims against business corporations during a year may result from the reduction of one batch of claims held and a more than offsetting increase in another (for example, the use of proceeds from redeemed bonds and net savings to buy another block of bonds). This is all the more likely for *groups* of units in any practical classification of savers and capital users, unless the net changes are for an infinitesimally short period. Thus an industrial group of business corporations is likely to have, during a year, both retirements of claims and additions to them, regardless of type of claim—even long-term. Hence the net increase may be the result of a large inflow and a smaller outflow in the way of repayment. In studying the whole process of channeling savings into capital formation, the connection between *net* changes and the combinations of gross inflows and outflows that underlie them would have some importance. Therefore, 3 lines should replace each of those now shown in Figure 1: a gross flow line, with an arrow pointed upward; a re-

payment line, with an arrow pointed downward; and a net flow line, with an arrow pointed in whatever direction the net balance lies. Of these 3 lines, only the last is now shown. Thus, the number of net financing lines suggested at the end of point 3 must be multiplied by 3 to yield the number of lines of financial flow, and to reveal how net changes are derived from gross.

5. We have been assuming so far that savings flow directly from the saver to the capital user; and this assumption was reflected in Figure 1 by a line (or lines) drawn directly from a box at the lower level to a box (or boxes) at the upper level. But the preceding discussion, suggesting the complexity of the process, also indicates that direct connection between each group of savers and each group of would-be capital users is next to impossible, and, if attempted, would result not only in pools of savings failing to flow into adequate investment opportunities, but also in vast areas of unsatisfied demand for funds. In reality, a large and constantly evolving body of financial intermediaries has grown up, essentially to facilitate the channeling of savings into capital formation. Once these financial intermediaries come into existence, savings can flow not only directly from saver to user, as in Figures 1 and 2, but also through the financial intermediaries.

Role of Financial Intermediaries

Figures 3 and 4 follow the pattern of Figures 1 and 2 but introduce financial intermediaries, and provide a convenient way of considering their role in the processes of saving and capital formation.

We did not increase the number of lines of direct flow of savings, which should be 9; nor did we allow for gross flows and repayments. But provision had to be made for savings flowing indirectly, via the financial intermediaries. To the solid lines representing direct net flows of savings into capital formation, we assigned arbitrary numbers that indicate the amount of net savings channeled directly. For example, in Figure 3, the left-hand solid line drawn from the box of 21 savings units of individuals is marked 3, meaning that individuals' net direct investment in business corporations (say in the form of net acquisition of stocks and bonds) amounted to 3 units. The same procedure was followed in Figure 4, and, in addition, numbers were attached to the solid lines at the upper level that represent conversion of goods and foreign claims of business corporations and individuals into claims against governments.

27

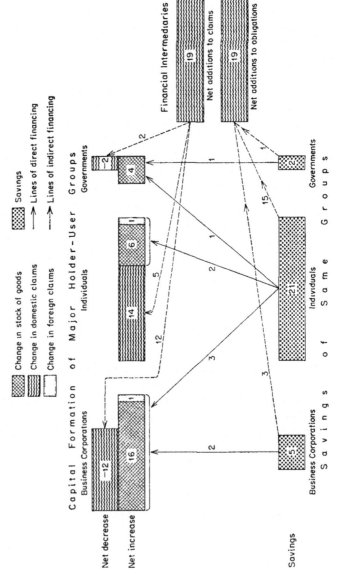

FIGURE 3

Figure 1, but with the Introduction of Financial Intermediaries

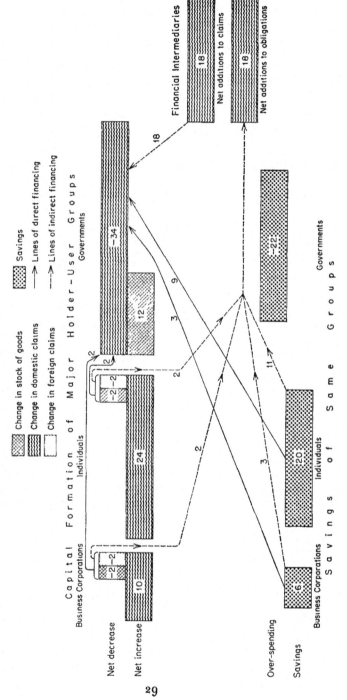

FIGURE 4

Figure 2, but with the Introduction of Financial Intermediaries

29

Capital Formation, Saving, and Financing

Whatever savings are not channeled directly into capital formation must flow through the financial intermediaries. For simplicity's sake, we treat these intermediaries in Figures 3 and 4 as one body that operates without any stock of goods (buildings, equipment, etc.) and provides a completely fluid passage of savings from the ultimate savers to the capital users. On these assumptions we transfer all the numbers assigned to savings and capital formation in Figures 1 and 2 to Figures 3 and 4, respectively, and using the numbers assigned to direct flows in Figures 3 and 4, we derive for each group the flow of savings through the financial intermediaries. These flows to and from financial intermediaries are depicted by broken lines. Given the numbers representing savings and capital formation by type in each of the three groups, we can also derive as residuals the units of savings flowing from each group of savers to the financial intermediaries (see numbers attached to the broken lines at the lower level of Figure 3); and the units of savings flowing from the financial intermediaries to each of the three groups of capital users (numbers attached to the broken lines at the upper level). In Figure 3 the total residual is a flow of 19 units of savings *to* the financial intermediaries, a net addition to their domestic obligations, and an identical flow *from* the intermediaries to capital users, a net addition to the former's claims (the corresponding number of units in Figure 4 is 18).

The introduction of financial intermediaries further complicates the picture. In addition to the direct lines of financing, we now have the indirect. Thus, in Figure 3, we have, in addition to the 9 possible (5 shown) solid lines of *net* financing (one from each group of savers to each group of capital users), 6 broken lines representing 3 flows to and 3 flows from intermediaries. We have 6 rather than 3 broken lines, because the lines of inflow and outflow cannot be paired: the savings of various groups channeled into the financial intermediaries form a common pool and it is impossible to tell which group's savings flow to which group of capital users.

Actually, there is not one body of financial intermediaries, but a host of them—banks, life insurance companies, investment houses, building and loan associations, and so on, and among them there are primary and secondary intermediaries, the latter borrowing from the former. If we distinguish the various financial intermediaries, we increase the number of lines of financial flows. Thus, allowing for another set of intermediaries in Figure 3 would mean an additional set of 6 broken lines, plus still another line to connect the two groups of financial intermediaries. The possible number of lines of net financial flows in a hypothetical chart allowing for several groups of financial intermediaries is the sum of: (1) the square of the number of groups of savers-capital users (lines of *direct* financing); (2) double the number of groups of savers-capital users, multiplied by the number of intermediaries distinguished; (3) the number of combinations of financial intermediaries taken two at a time. Thus, if we distinguish ten groups of savers-capital users, and five groups of financial intermediaries, the potential number of lines of net flow is: [2]

$$(10)^2 + [(10 \times 2) \times 5] + \frac{5!}{2!(5-2)!}, \text{ or } 210.$$

If we distinguish gross flows and repayments, the number of lines has to be further multiplied by 3, yielding 630. Of course, many of these lines will in fact not be important because direct financing of some groups of capital users by some groups of savers is negligible. Since intermediaries specialize, some would be tapping only selected groups of savers and supplying only selected groups of capital users. Nevertheless, the picture of financial flows is complex, and much information would obviously be required to select and trace the most important channels. A certain amount of aggregation is indispensable if one is not to get completely lost in the maze.

But while the introduction of financial intermediaries complicates the picture by multiplying the number of financial flows to be considered, it also simplifies the problem. For financial intermediaries obviate the need for each group of savers to seek out and choose among the wide variety of capital users, and conversely, for each group of capital users to seek out and choose among the wide variety of savers. As already indicated, attempts at such direct connections would often fail and cause inefficiency in the use of savings. By eliminating the need for direct financing, by allowing savings from various sources to flow into a common pool and by channeling funds from this common pool to various groups of capital users, the whole system of financial intermediaries makes it not only impossible but also unnecessary for the analyst to determine which groups of savers finance which groups of capital users. Financial intermediaries reduce significantly the number of important lines of direct financing. In terms of Figure 3, of a possible 100 lines (for ten groups of savers-capital users distinguished)

[2] A figure followed by ! is a *factorial*, defined by the equation
$$n! = n(n-1)(n-2) \cdots 1.$$

only 10 may be important. By mobilizing and effectively channeling savings, financial intermediaries also reduce drastically the number of important lines of connection between ultimate savings and capital formation. However, the distinctive characteristics of savers, reflected in the type and form of their savings, may still impose limits upon the type of capital use into which these savings can be channeled. In such cases, the structure and direction of specialization among financial intermediaries are revealing.

Another major effect of the introduction of financial intermediaries has not been touched upon and is not reflected in the oversimplified schemata in Figures 3 and 4. Some intermediaries—for example, commercial banks—have the power to "create" credit, i.e., to extend credit to an amount greater than that of claims deposited with them in the form of capital shares or of deposits originating outside the banking system proper. Insofar as credit thus created can finance capital formation, it may be viewed as "forced" saving, which does not stem from decisions of individuals, business corporations, or governments. Likewise, under certain conditions, governments can issue money claims that can be used to finance capital formation, in which case the latter is financed not out of taxes collected from individuals and corporations but out of new money creation.

This complication is omitted from Figures 3 and 4 because they are designed to describe an observable *ex post facto* situation, rather than some imagined *ex ante* one; and correspondingly, we have assumed that net additions to obligations of financial intermediaries (including governments) equal the net additions to claims by them. In a strictly formal sense, this is true *ex post facto* under any circumstances: if the financial intermediaries make additions to their credit advances greater than the claims that originate in savings of stockholders or depositors, such assets are assignable, in the final count, to the stockholders and depositors in those institutions. Likewise, an addition to money issue by the federal government means, in its further use, an addition to claims on the part of the corporations, individuals, and government agencies which appear at the lower level of Figures 3 and 4. Were we to try to represent the imaginary *ex ante* situation, we would have to split the savings assigned at the lower level of Figures 3 and 4 between voluntary—those that cannot be associated with credit creation or nonneutral money issue policy (on the part of the government)—and forced—those that can be associated with the latter. It would also mean that we would have to allow room at the lower level of the savings groups for the financial intermediaries themselves, alongside the business corporations, and that for governments we would allow savings not only out of taxes and fees but also out of money creation. The difficulty is that our observable records of savings and of capital formation do not permit us to make that distinction. Insofar as credit creation or financing through new money issues takes place, voluntary and forced savings are intermixed. And voluntary savings under conditions of credit creation or new money inflation can never be assumed to be the same as voluntary savings under conditions of no credit creation or of neutral money issue policy. Yet in discussion of the factors determining the supply of savings and their flow into capital formation, the existence and development of the power of credit and money creation represent an important complex that has to be borne in mind. We shall return to this point in Chapter 3.

The Guiding Thread

In our preceding comments we have defined the commonly used terms *capital formation, saving, financing*—which stand for fundamental processes in the economy—and have pointed to the lines of relation among them in a situation similar to the complex institutional network of a modern economic society. The past performance of this country's economy with respect to capital formation and financing cannot be studied in adequate detail, because of lack of data. The limited data now available or obtainable by practicable effort make it imperative that an inquiry like the present have a guiding thread that will direct us to rational relations among past trends. Since we are interested in determining the factors that have affected past use of capital funds as a basis for more intelligent consideration of their future use, should we try to trace the origin and flow of such funds in the hundreds of channels through which savings move into capital formation? It must be remembered that the labyrinth is even more intricate than was suggested above because the flow of capital may involve shifts among types and forms of savings and among various levels of financial intermediaries only hinted at in the comments above. Clearly, we need some guide to give direction to the inquiry and set up priorities for the choices that inevitably have to be made.

The basic assumptions that provide the guiding thread can only be indicated, not elaborated. To avoid misunderstanding, it should be said in advance that these are assumptions designedly accepted here to provide criteria by which analysis can be guided. Thus, when we refer below to purposes served by the complex economic system under study, they are the broad social purposes *as we see them*. This is not as arbitrary as it may seem; and it is far more illuminating than if we were to interpret economic processes in the light of the individual goals of each of the various economic units—entrepreneurs, employees, capital owners, and so on—in the thousands of sectors that can be distinguished. For a country's economy is a system of interrelated parts, which can be understood only if some broad set of purposes is assigned to it. Its functioning in the short and long run makes sense only if related to such broad goals as can be discerned; and they can be discerned if only because failure to meet them (for example, failure to provide enough for subsistence and growth) will be seen to set up a chain of policy reactions and adjustments to overcome such failure. Granted the existence of such broad purposes and the lack of any overt record of them (we have no economic charter or constitution that specifies them), it is the task of the investigator to formulate them as best he can—that is, with the closest approximation to what, from his preliminary observation and study, is suggested by the operation of the economy.

1. The fundamental purpose of the complex economic system of modern society is to increase the economic welfare of the country's inhabitants—that is, to provide more goods to satisfy their material wants, present and future. This purpose is pursued within a given social and legal framework which society maintains.

2. The pursuit of the basic purpose requires an increasing stock of capital goods within the country for the extension of the volume of production by the application of technological knowledge or even without any technical changes. Such nationwide capital formation is indispensable for economic growth—that is, for increased economic production, total and per capita, and, hence, economic welfare.

3. To a given economic unit, savings may be essentially a provision for economic security. But unless such savings are channeled into capital formation and serve to increase production, that unit's security will be at the expense of another unit's economic welfare. From the nationwide standpoint the rationale for saving is capital formation; and that rationale, if realized, contributes to the economic security of the given unit, at no cost to others.

4. The main social purpose of the complicated and elaborate structure of financial institutions, practices, and so forth, is to facilitate

greater production. Its more immediate purpose is the channeling of savings into nationwide capital formation to ensure an effective use of savings. This complex and ramified structure of claims and counter-claims, of gross and net flows—discussed only briefly in the comments above—originated as a means of increasing economic production through additions to the stock of capital goods.

5. The institutional practices developed in various sectors of a country's economy, even though originating in response to basic needs and purposes, have a momentum of their own which may make them persist after the needs have passed or may deflect them from the very needs they were meant to satisfy. But it seems best, as a working hypothesis for the study of long-term trends, to assume that a rough con-silience prevails between the major economic institutions and practices and the basic purposes of the economy. Guided by this hypothesis, we try to interpret the major changes that have come about as adaptations to changing needs and forms within the basic purpose.

It follows from the premises just stated that, since our interest is in the uses of and demand for capital funds, we should begin with nationwide capital formation, inasmuch as it is the immediate major purpose for which savings are generated and the major use to which capital funds are put. For this reason, both in this report and in the inquiry as a whole, our foremost consideration is the trends in na-tionwide capital formation and the factors that may have affected them. From this the thread leads on to consideration of uses of capital funds other than nationwide capital formation—for example, capi-tal formation for distinct groups of capital users in the major produc-tive sectors of the economy, or the extension and acquisition of natural resources, or financing current expenditures of such institutions as governments. It leads next to the distinction between internal and external financing, then to the distinction among various types within external financing, and finally, to the structure of financial inter-mediaries in their holdings of claims. In short, the direction of analysis is from the use to the source, from the purpose to the means, from the operation to the mechanism by which it is performed.

CHAPTER 2

The Meaning of Long-Term Trends

THE present analysis emphasizes long-term trends in capital formation and financing, as distinct from short-term changes associated with business cycles. Clarification of the meaning of long-term trends is, therefore, in order.

This is facilitated by a study of Chart 1, which portrays the volume of gross national product, in constant prices, in the United States annually from 1869 through 1955. We disregard for the moment questions as to the coverage of gross national product or as to the reliability of the series as a measure of the annual volume. The main point for the present is that the chart shows the movement over time in an economic flow that is a major topic of our analysis—a movement combining short-term, long-term, and all other kinds of change.

Looking at the chart, we may therefore ask what we mean by a long-term trend in the gross national product of the United States. The entries on the vertical scale show that the annual volume was below $8 billion in 1869–1871, and hovered close to $190 billion in 1955. Over this eighty-seven-year span there was a rise to almost 25 times the initial level. But are we justified in comparing national product in the 1870's with that in the 1950's, as if they were both of the same universe? Would we be as sure that this rise in gross national product represented a long-term trend if, instead of the rather gradual climb, Chart 1 showed an annual level close to $8 billion all the way from 1869 through 1954 and then a jump to $190 billion in 1955? And assuming that the answers to these two questions help us define long-term trends, what is the rationale for distinguishing the latter from short-term changes? Finally, if some worthy purpose justifies the cost

CHART 1

Gross National Product, Variant I, Regression Series, 1929 Prices, United States, 1869–1955

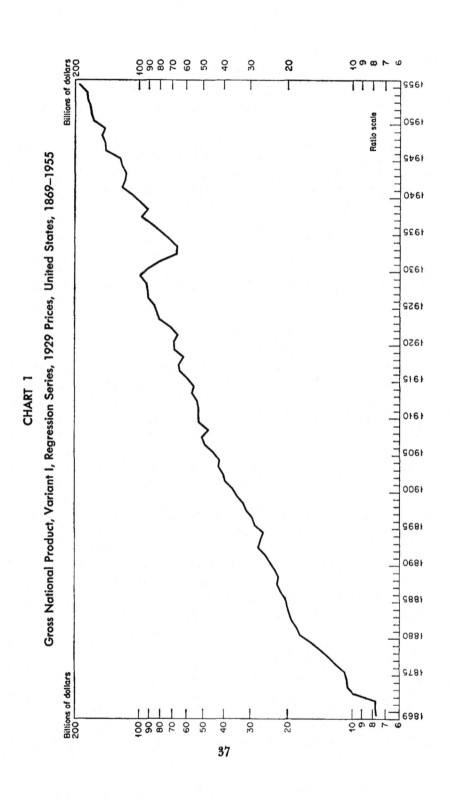

of distinguishing between long-term trends and short-term changes, how, precisely, do we make the distinction to ensure reasonably useful results?

Some of these questions may sound simple to the point of fatuity. But it is dangerous to assume that any aspect of social processes is simple. It may seem simple, but only because of our familiarity with it—the kind of familiarity that makes it impossible to see the forest for the trees. We must, therefore, deal with these questions explicitly. This chapter is devoted to a discussion of the following points needed to clarify the meaning of long-term trends: (1) comparability over the period; (2) continuity or persistence of trend; (3) rationale for distinguishing between long-term trends and short-term changes; (4) the general lines of the statistical procedures used to draw the distinction between them, and the variety of long-term change patterns.

Comparability over the Period

The central question here can be stated most strikingly by assuming that the record in Chart 1 runs not from 1869 but from 1569 to 1955, portraying the annual changes for the span of 387 years in the gross national product of societies inhabiting what is the present continental United States. (This is not out of the realm of possibility: one can never tell what some intrepid statistician may be able to accomplish some day!) Would we then draw a continuous line on the chart, and talk of the increase in the product from, say, $1 million per year to $190 billion? And if so, would it make sense to assume that the national product of the sixteenth-century Indians is comparable with that of twentieth-century United States?

The answer to the question is not as obvious as it may seem. We deal here, in this span of over three centuries, with human beings who belong to the same species and have the same elemental needs, instincts, and aspirations. And since we also deal with one territory, where climate and other natural conditions may have remained constant over the centuries, at least insofar as they have determined total economic product, there are grounds for treating the Indian society of the sixteenth century and the United States society of the twentieth as if they were links within one homogeneous period extending from 1569 to 1955.

Yet the balance of judgment is against it—not against comparing the economic product of the society of the Indians with that of the

United States on the ground that we are dealing with two distinct types of economic and social organization, but against treating the volumes as points on a single line of long-term trend. The judgment is based essentially on the conclusion, from whatever knowledge we have, that the size, technological levels, social institutions, and international relations of the sixteenth-century Indian society were vastly different from those of the United States economy during the last century, and the latter cannot therefore be regarded as a continuation or later expression of the forces that molded the former. By contrast, we assume that no such gulf separates the United States economy of the 1950's from that of the 1870's, and that the former can be better understood as the result of a process of growth from the 1870's than as a "new" era in the literal sense of that term—that is, without deep roots in the historical past stretching back a century or more.

This assumption is a kind of operating premise, the validity of which can be tested only by the effectiveness of the analysis it makes possible; and there is no assurance that a somewhat different assumption would not lead to even more effective analysis. Perhaps beginning our series in 1839—had it been statistically feasible—would have provided not only a longer and still relatively homogeneous period, but also one in which measurement of the long-term trends and analysis of the factors that determined them would have yielded richer and operationally more tenable conclusions. On the other hand, it may well be that limiting the single line of the long-term trend to a period extending back only to the 1890's would have led to a clearer view and better understanding of the long-term trends in national product prevailing today and of the factors that may determine them in the proximate future.

Given the data, these various alternatives are possible, and are, in fact, explored in any adequate analysis. But the major point to be noted is that in dealing with long-term trends we must determine the time span to be studied and establish homogeneous periods within it. The assumption that the processes under study are comparable throughout the period or periods is based essentially upon—and implies—some preliminary knowledge of those processes and some preliminary theory of the factors that mold them. It is the incompleteness of our knowledge and possible differences in theoretical hypotheses concerning the factors at play that lead to differences in the limits set to the period or periods in question, within the coverage of the data available for analysis.

Meaning of Long-Term Trends

Specifically, why do we, in this report, take the decades back to 1869 as a single period for study—subject to possible distinction of phases within it that may be revealed by further analysis? Presumably, we do so because whatever knowledge we have of this period suggests that the institutions and factors that we consider important in determining the levels of national product and its components have persisted throughout. Technological skills, domestic institutions, and international conditions prevailing today are of course different from those in the 1870's. But we still have the republican form of government, and even the same two major political parties. Our economy still operates under the aegis of free enterprise, and we still have the rights of private property extending to both consumer goods and tools of production. We still have individual freedom—no one is compelled to slave in labor camps. And the list of basic institutions still persisting could be extended through the money and credit mechanisms, distribution patterns, and so on. True, a good many examples of the differences between the 1870's and the 1950's could be cited—ranging from the income tax to the H-bomb. The judgment is then necessarily a matter of weighing the likenesses against the differences, and we assume that the balance is in favor of treating the 1870's and the 1950's in this country as belonging to the same historical epoch. To repeat, this is a working assumption, and its proof is in the results, just as the proof of the pudding is in the eating. All we attempted, and could achieve, in the preceding discussion was to bring the assumption into the light for explicit formulation.

Continuity of Trend

The assumption that a given period is homogeneous throughout may be regarded as applying equally to the long-term trend, in the sense that we can draw a single line for it, and to the short-term changes, in the sense, say, that business cycles at the beginning and end of the period are viewed as parts of the same universe. For while the assumption of homogeneity may have greater bearing upon long-term than upon short-term changes, the close relationship among the forces that affect the two, gives us, prima facie, a case for assuming that a period homogeneous with respect to one is likely to be homogeneous with respect to the other—although this is not necessarily so. But the point of this comment is that the arguments concerning the definition of homogeneity of a period apply *pari passu* to short-term changes.

Meaning of Long-Term Trends

We come now to the distinction between long-term trends and short-term changes. By the former, in terms of quantitative operation, we mean a change *in one direction,* over a period of time that is "long enough" in comparison with short-term changes. Thus, when we refer to a long-term rise, we usually mean a rise that extends over a period of time long enough to transcend the temporary rises occurring during cyclical expansions; and likewise, in referring to a long-term decline, we mean a decline distinct from a cyclical contraction. There are, therefore, two elements in the operational definition of long-term trends: (1) the unidirectional character of the movement; and (2) the extension of this movement over a period that is viewed as long enough. Both elements require further exploration. The second—what we mean by long enough—is best taken up later, when we deal more closely with the statistical procedures from which it will become evident that the *relative* meaning of long enough results in a variety of types of long-term movement. In the present section, we concentrate on what we mean by movement in one direction.

The problem involved can be illustrated by two questions. The first has already been stated: had Chart 1 shown a level of $8 billion from 1869 to 1954, and then a jump to $190 billion in 1955, would we still consider the rise evidence of a long-term trend? The second question is: had the average volume of national product shown successive rises over the successive decades, but violently fluctuating annual levels within each decade—say, from a lower limit of zero to an upper limit five to six times the average—would we assign much significance to the long-term rise in the decade averages?

The two questions are distinct, and each brings out a significant aspect of long-term trends. Each question has only one answer: the movement over any long period can be regarded as unidirectional only if it is sustained, i.e., occurs repeatedly within shorter segments of the period; and it is significant only if the short-term deviations from it do not dwarf the magnitude of the long-term rise or decline. These answers bear upon much that follows; but they can perhaps be perceived more clearly if we analyze the series in Chart 1 not only for the continuity of the long-term trend, but for the amplitude of the short-term changes as well.

In Table 1, part A, we deal with the continuity or steadiness of the long-term trend as reflected in levels for successive periods, each long enough for the average to be free from short-term changes. We use decade averages here, and with the 87 years in the series can calcu-

TABLE 1

MEASURES OF CONTINUITY OF LONG-TERM TREND IN GROSS NATIONAL PRODUCT, VARIANT I, REGRESSION SERIES, 1929 PRICES, 1869–1955

| CLASSES BY SIZE OF PER CENT CHANGE OVER PRECEDING DECADE | PART OF PERIOD | | | | | |
| | First Half | | Second Half | | Total | |
	Num-ber (1)	Per Cent of Total (2)	Num-ber (3)	Per Cent of Total (4)	Num-ber (5)	Per Cent of Total (6)
A. FREQUENCY DISTRIBUTION OF DECADE AVERAGES						
Decline						
0 to 5	0	0	1	2.9	1	1.5
Rises						
0–5	0	0	3	8.8	3	4.4
5–10	0	0	2	5.9	2	2.9
10–15	0	0	1	2.9	1	1.5
15–20	0	0	2	5.9	2	2.9
20–25	0	0	2	5.9	2	2.9
25–30	0	0	1	2.9	1	1.5
30–40	7	20.6	13	38.2	20	29.4
40–50	14	41.2	2	5.9	16	23.5
50–60	9	26.5	7	20.6	16	23.5
60–80	2	5.9	0	0	2	2.9
80–100	2	5.9	0	0	2	2.9
Total	34	100.0	34	100.0	68	100.0
B. FREQUENCY DISTRIBUTION OF ANNUAL DATA						
Declines						
15–20	0	0	1	2.6	1	1.3
10–15	0	0	1	2.6	1	1.3
5–10	0	0	2	5.3	2	2.6
0–5	0	0	2	5.3	2	2.6
Rises						
0–5	0	0	1	2.6	1	1.3
5–10	0	0	1	2.6	1	1.3
10–15	0	0	0	0	0	0
15–20	0	0	1	2.6	1	1.3
20–25	0	0	2	5.3	2	2.6
25–30	2	5.1	1	2.6	3	3.9
30–40	10	25.6	7	18.4	17	22.1
40–50	9	23.1	10	26.3	19	24.7
50–60	6	15.4	4	10.5	10	13.0
60–80	5	12.8	5	13.2	10	13.0
80–100	4	10.3	0	0	4	5.2
100–125	1	2.6	0	0	1	1.3
125–150	2	5.1	0	0	2	2.6
Total	39	100.0	38	100.0	77	100.0

Because of rounding, detail will not necessarily add to total.
SOURCE: Calculated from the series given or described in Tables R-22 and R-26.

late 78 such averages, each removed from the next by one year. To test the steadiness we use the rate of secular change per decade—the minimum period over which to measure it. With 78 decade averages we can calculate the decade rate of change for 68 intervals; and it is these that are classified in Table 1, part A, by size of percentage change.

Of the 68 decade intervals there is just one with a decline in the secular levels, and there are only 5 with a rise of less than 10 per cent, which may be considered a minimum rise (columns 5 and 6). In other words, if during this historical period an observer had been continuously present, and had compared each decennial level of the economy's product with that ten years before, he would have found, 62 times out of 68, a rise of 10 per cent or more; and in only one case would he have observed a decline.

Interestingly enough, the series differs in its behavior between the first and the second half of the period (columns 1 and 3). In the first 34 decade intervals there is not a single decline, nor even a rise of less than 30 per cent; in the second group of decade intervals, there are one decline and several small rises. But even in the second half only 6 out of 34 intervals show changes algebraically less than +10 per cent.

A similar procedure is followed in part B of the table to test for the effects of short-term changes of the kind associated with business cycles. The latter are presumably reflected in annual data. If they were very prominent relative to the long-term trends, to the point of dominating the latter, the decennial intervals in the annual series would reveal a large number of declines or of slight rises. With really dominant short cycles, decennial interval changes calculated from annual data would not reveal many declines and other deviations from a consistent long-term rise unless the cycles were strictly periodic and the periods or phases a simple multiple of 10 (e.g., if the cycles were exactly ten or five years in duration). This condition is clearly not true of our series.

If we inspect the distribution of the 77 decade interval changes in the annual data, classified by size of percentage change, we find, as would be expected, more with declines or decennial rises of less than 10 per cent than we find in part A: the declines number 6, and the rises of less than 10 per cent, another 2, making 8 deviations in the total of 77. As in part A, these deviations are concentrated in the second half of the period. But, all in all, the consistency of the long-term rise in gross national product is high—despite the short-term fluctuations in the annual data. Our observer, recording the level of the product each year and comparing it with the level ten years earlier, would have found, 69 times out of 77, that there had been a substantial rise over the preceding decade—a rise of 10 per cent or more (in fact, in excess of 15 per cent).

It can now be stated briefly why the continuity of successive changes, either in secular levels (as reflected in decennial averages) or in annual data (which reflect short-term changes), is necessary to give meaning and significance to the concept of long-term trends.

1. If, in successive decade intervals or in any other reasonably acceptable succession of intervals, the direction of the change is relatively constant and the magnitude of the change persists above a certain minimum, we can argue that the measures relate to a truly long-term process—a movement that has continued through a succession of periods. It is this continuity through different historical periods that lends significance to the established long-term trend. To come back to our illustration: gross national product increased at least 10 per cent per decade in almost every decade. During some of those decades the administration was Republican, and during some, it was Democratic; during some we had free immigration, during others we did not; during some the general price level was rising, and during others it was declining; and so on. Had our chart shown a level of $8 billion per year through 1954 and then a jump to $190 billion in 1955, we would have been forced to suspend judgment regarding the significance of that rise until we saw what happened for a large number of years after 1955.

2. Likewise, the fact that short-term changes in general, and business cycles in particular, rarely, if at all, cause the series to fall to levels low enough to wipe out the preceding rise (or to rise to levels high enough to wipe out the preceding decline, if the long-term trend is downward) lends significance to the long-term trend, in two ways. First, it implies that the forces that mold and determine the long-term trend resist, as it were, any counterforces that tend to alter the trend. Or, to put it differently, the forces that determine the long-term trend also provide, over any given short period, a kind of floor and ceiling, and tend to control the extent of deviations from the current secular level. Second—and related to the point just made—limited amplitude of the short-term disturbances will, in turn, tend to minimize the variability over time in the rate of secular change calculated over any successive, not too long intervals. This conclusion assumes a

lack of strict periodicity or regularity in the short-term disturbances, whether or not associated with business cycles. With this lack of regularity, averages covering one or even two decades might still reflect some short-term changes since they would not completely offset each other. And short-term changes of wider amplitude than the rate of long-term trend might be reflected in decadal or even bi-decadal averages and thus introduce a lack of continuity in the rate of long-term rise or decline. This last point shows clearly that the two aspects of continuity of long-term changes discussed in this section are, in fact, interrelated—provided the short-term changes are not so regular as to permit one to determine the precise minimum period for which the averages would cancel these changes completely and thus yield secular levels unaffected by them.

Rationale for Distinguishing between Long-Term and Short-Term Movements

The preceding comments have already suggested the reason for distinguishing between long-term trends and short-term changes. If long-term trends are a persistent component of change over time, and in their cumulative effect produce movements that dwarf the short-term variations, they may well be due to some identifiable group of factors different from those that determine short-term changes. If so, it may be that the relations among various aspects of economic processes that come to light when we compare long-term trends are quite different from those found when we compare short-term changes. Consequently, distinguishing the two types of movement may be a more fruitful way of analyzing the total complex of economic change, because—being based upon a distinction between groups of operating determinants—it should lead more easily and directly to generalizations and proper bases for extrapolation and prediction than would the ostensibly more direct way of studying economic change as a whole.

The several links in the chain of argument just presented must be clearly differentiated. The first is the finding that long-term trends— movements characterized by persistent change in one direction over a "long enough" period—exist. The second link is the assumption, not proved and not fully provable, that the factors that determine a persistent change in one direction may perhaps be quite distinct from those that determine short-term changes; and correspondingly, relations among various aspects of the economy characteristic of long-term trends may differ from those revealed by a study of short-term variations. Third, if this assumption is valid, a separate study of long-term trends should shed light on the factors determining them and on relations among long-term trends in various aspects of a living and growing economy. It should lead to a better understanding of the forces at play than would be attained without distinguishing between long-term and short-term changes. Fourth, if the promise indicated in the third link is fulfilled even in part, it should mean a better basis for generalization and extrapolation, at least of the long-term trends—and also of the short-term changes, if a similar analysis were carried through for them. The "better" is relative to what could be learned by trying to analyze the statistical record without distinguishing between long-term trends and short-term changes.

The first link in this argument can be proved for various long series, by devices like those employed in Table 1 (and many others can be contrived). It is the second link, the assumption upon whose validity everything that follows hinges, that cannot be demonstrated. But it is strongly supported by two considerations. One is quite general: if we observe different patterns of change, different patterns of behavior, we should proceed upon the assumption that the forces, factors, or whatever name we wish to assign to the determinants of these different types of observed results, are also different. Certainly, it is safer to start with such an assumption than with the opposite—that despite differences in the patterns of change, i.e., differences in results, the antecedent factors are the same. We may eventually come to the latter conclusion, possibly in the sense that the one set of forces in the background works through different sets of conditions to produce different patterns of change over time. Even then the analysis would have to show some differentiation of the antecedent factors to account for differences in the resulting patterns of movement.

The second consideration supporting that link in our argument—and, in the present connection, the more telling one—is that we know that certain institutions in our society operate in full recognition of the difference between long-term trends and short-term changes. They thus directly "produce" much of the former, in ways in which they do not, at least consciously, produce the latter. Even an individual, short as the span of his life may be compared with that of a country, considers the long-term trend of his active life, prepares for it, and allows for it, distinguishing it as best he can from transitory, short-term changes which must be expected but usually cannot be forecast. And an individual's active life, including professional or other preparation for it, may last over forty years, which is not an insignificant segment in the long stretch we consider in this report. If one also takes into account the plans of parents for their children, and the succession of generations of family units cognizant of the long-term trend as distinct from the short-term variations, we can see that, insofar as economic change is a matter of decisions by family units, the considerations behind those decisions—and hence the determining factors—are quite different from those involved in producing or responding to short-term changes.

A similar argument can be advanced, with even greater force, regarding decisions and actions by individuals in their capacity as members of business enterprises, or of other institutional units (nonprofit, or government). It should be noted at once that in theory, and often in actual practice, these nonfamily institutions act as if endowed with eternal life. Their time horizon, therefore, can be, and often is, much wider than that of individuals acting as members of family units; they are even more cognizant of the difference between the long and the short run; and they can, at least to some extent, weigh differently the costs and returns of decisions that are temporary and of decisions that are more lasting in effect.

The argument is reinforced by the fact that relations among many aspects of the economy observed in long-term trends have already been found to differ from those observed in short-term changes. Thus, in short-term changes associated with business cycles, increases in aggregate income per capita are usually accompanied by increases in the countrywide savings-income proportion, whereas, in the long run, an increase in aggregate income per capita is not necessarily followed by a secular rise in the countrywide savings-income proportion. In the short run, changes in prices and in quantity of output tend to be positively associated—at least where entrepreneurs have technical control over output, that is, excluding agriculture. In the long run, a downward movement in prices may be associated with an extraordinarily high rate of secular growth, as in this country from the 1870's to the 1890's—growth in the output of all products, not just agricultural.

One reason for these perhaps obvious remarks is the fact that since the distinction between long-term trends and short-term changes, like any other abstraction, is a distortion of reality, it involves certain costs, and must, therefore, be justified. But the main reason here is to challenge the inclination, not uncommon among observers of current events, to view anything beyond the immediate yesterday as having little relevance, and to look forward only to tomorrow, and not to the day after. Both tendencies were given support by the late Lord Keynes in an unfortunate remark to the effect that in the long run we are all dead. Justified as it may have been by the urge for immediate short-term action, this less-than-half-truth overlooks the obvious fact that, if long run means more than the next few years, a good many of us will still be alive, and even more of our children will be. In any case, even if one is interested in only the next short run, the understanding of it will be dangerously incomplete unless, currently, one can distinguish the secular level from the shorter-term changes, which cannot be done without adequate knowledge of the long run of the past. In view of the quantitatively dominant effects of cumulative long-term trends in modern economies, and of the importance of better knowledge of their characteristics and implications for decisions by the many economic institutions that are, and must be, concerned with the longer future, the value of properly distinguishing the long-term trends from the short-term variations can hardly be gainsaid.

The Statistical Distinction

In drawing the statistical distinction between long-term movements and short-term variations, we must specify what we mean by long and short. As we do so, it becomes apparent that the terms are relative. If by a long-term trend we mean movement in one direction over a period "long enough" to transcend temporary rises (or declines) in the short-term variations, the meaning of long enough obviously depends upon the meaning of short-term. If by the latter we mean business cycles, ranging in duration from, say, 4 to 11 years, then long enough means a period that substantially exceeds in duration any single expansion or contraction, and preferably covers several of them so that the direction and magnitude of the trend can be ascertained. In this case, a period of 20 years or longer is sufficient. If by short-term changes we mean cycles of, say, 20 years, then for statistical analysis the period is long enough only if it contains several 20-year units. And if we think of the major historical epochs as themselves being variations around the long-term trend of history, then the medieval economy, merchant capitalism, and industrial capitalism in Western Europe must be viewed as long historical waves, and the trend can be determined only if the period analyzed covers many centuries.

By definition, the "long" in a long-term trend must exceed the time span of the longest unit of change viewed as short term. But in the statistical practice of measuring long-term trends, even this is not enough, for we must cover more than one unit of short-term change (i.e., more than a single upturn and downturn) to be able to measure the magnitude of a long-term trend reliably. In economic and social statistics particularly, the pattern of short-term changes is so irregular that a single unit will not suffice to establish and measure the underlying movement with any degree of reliability.

Given the relative element in the definition of long-term movements, the specification of what *long* means may be approached in one of two ways. In the first, the analyst may already know, on the basis of some information concerning the processes that shape the long-term movement, not only the length of the period over which it extends, but even some of its characteristics which he can embody in a mathematical equation. For example, in the study of the processes of human growth, biologists may have found the steady increase from birth in weight and height to reach its optimum within a fairly narrowly defined span of time—but long, compared with short-term fluctuations that may occur because of disease, nutritional variations, and so on. It may follow a pattern easily expressible by a simple mathematical curve which, in its characteristics, embodies the requirement of a unidirectional sustained movement.

In the other approach, the analysis begins with a specification of what short-term changes are, a specification based either upon some theory and the general characteristics of the changes (for example, that they are periodic cycles), or upon observation of the specific features of the short-term changes in the record being analyzed. Next, the short-term changes, being by definition variations that offset each other, are canceled by an appropriate procedure, usually by taking some type of moving average. This moving average, therefore, represents changes that are not short-term: by definition it approximates the long-term movements.

It is the second approach that we adopt in this report, because we do not have sufficient knowledge to attempt a direct description of the long-term movements in the form of simple mathematical curves. This is particularly true since we are interested, not just in those movements that, for one reason or another, perhaps could be described by

49

such curves, but rather in long-term changes in both quantity volumes and financial flows—that is, in a wide variety of the aspects of a growing economy. Besides, it is a matter of advisable caution, in our emphasis on the study of long-term movements, to begin with the most complete description of them, including everything except the elements directly identifiable as short-term variations. And so we follow the procedure that attempts to eliminate the latter by some type of moving average.

The results of two such attempts are shown in Chart 2. In one, we use the reference chronology of business cycles in this country, prepared at the National Bureau of Economic Research, and convert the annual series of gross national product to averages representing complete reference cycles (either peak to peak or trough to trough). It might have been better to use the periods secured by identifying the specific cycles in the series. But changes in gross national product conform quite closely to the reference cycle chronology, as is indicated in Appendix C; and there is an advantage in using the standard chronology for all our series. Each average is then plotted as a line (*b*) extending from the mid-point of the first phase of the cycle to the mid-point of the second, and another line (*c*) connects the mid-point of the cycle with that of the next cycle. Since the points represent averages for complete cycles, line *c* connecting them is presumably free from the effects of the latter and of other short-term changes, and thus approximates the long-term movements.

Line *a* in Chart 2 represents a 5-year moving average of the annual estimates. Since the cycles in general business conditions and in gross national product average during the period somewhat under 4 years in duration, a 5-year moving average should remove almost all the cyclical element and any other short-term changes (of less than 5 years' duration). Even when the cycle is longer than 5 years, which occurs once or twice, the moving averages are free from most of the amplitude of these cycles—retaining and reflecting only a minor portion of them. A more complicated moving average would cancel more completely the short-term variations and yield a more precise description of long-term movements; but the additional labor involved in attaining greater precision is not warranted here.

Chart 2 shows that most of the up-and-down movements associated with the short-term changes observed in Chart 1 have been eliminated; and some of the declines or irregularities that remain would have been removed by a more elaborate moving average. But, even if we

CHART 2

Averages for Successive Peak-to-Peak and Trough-to-Trough Reference Cycles and Five-Year Moving Averages of Annual Data,
Gross National Product, Variant I, Regression Series, 1929 Prices, 1869–1955

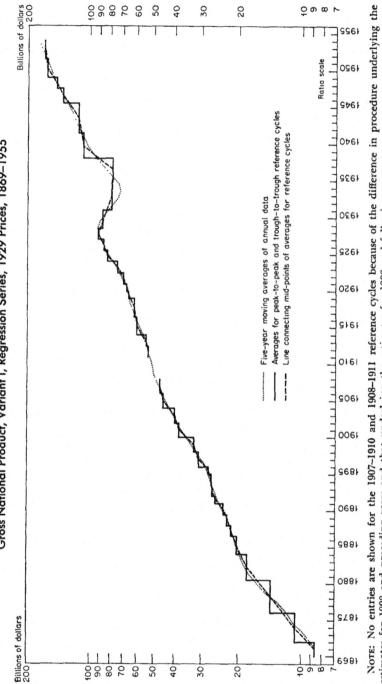

Five-year moving averages of annual data

Averages for peak-to-peak and trough-to-trough reference cycles

Line connecting mid-points of averages for reference cycles

Ratio scale

NOTE: No entries are shown for the 1907–1910 and 1908–1911 reference cycles because of the difference in procedure underlying the estimates for 1908 and preceding years and that underlying the estimates for 1909 and following years.

were to assume the complete removal of short-term changes, i.e., that the changes would cancel each other within a period of some 5 to 13 years, variations in the rate of change would still be noticeable in the residual lines descriptive of the long-term movements. Since distances on the vertical scale in Chart 2 measure relative or percentage changes, any conspicuous oscillations or swings in the slope of the lines mean correspondingly conspicuous alternations in the percentage rate of growth. And it is clear that, in addition to the sweep of the rise in gross national product, there are long swings or alternations in its rate of secular growth.

To point up the components of the long-term movement of the series in Chart 2, we use a simple device that yields the results presented in Chart 3. From the averages for reference cycles we calculate the rate of change per decade, for intervals approximating decades. Beginning with the average for the first cycle, 1869–1873, we calculate the rise to the average about a decade later (it happens to be the cycle for 1878–1885, 11.5 years later, but we reduce the increase proportionately to 10 years). We then follow with the change per decade from the average for the next cycle, 1870–1878, to that for 1882–1887, and so on, computing the intercycle rate of growth for a number of decade intervals. It is these rates, reduced to a decade basis and centered at the mid-points of the intervals from which they were calculated, that are plotted as line *a* in the upper part of Chart 3.

If the intercycle rates of change were constant, or steadily accelerating or decelerating, line *a*, described in the preceding paragraph, would fluctuate irregularly around either a horizontal line or an upward or downward sloping straight line. That the line in fact oscillates in long up-and-down movements is a clear indication that the rate of growth moves in long swings of fairly wide amplitude; it goes through alternations, which—judging at least by Chart 3—are over 20 years in duration.

A similar result emerges when we calculate the rate of change from each ordinate in the series of 5-year moving averages to the ordinate 10 years later. This decadal rate of change, centered at the mid-points of the intervals from which it was calculated, is plotted as line *a* in the lower part of Chart 3, and exhibits the same long swings as the decadal rate of change calculated from reference cycle averages.

Lines *b* and *c* in Chart 3 represent *the* underlying long-term trend. The horizontal line *c* (identical in both parts of Chart 3) is the average rate of growth per decade for the period as a whole; it was calculated

CHART 3

Percentage Change Per Decade in Averages for Reference Cycles and in Five-Year Moving Averages of Annual Data, Gross National Product, Variant I, Regression Series, 1929 Prices, 1869–1955

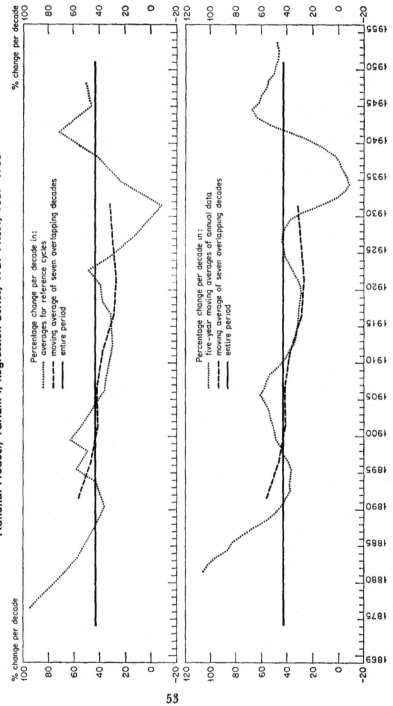

from the values for the first and last decades, 1869–1878 and 1946–1955. This is a geometric mean, and represents the rate in a simple compound interest line. Line *b* (also identical in both sections of Chart 3) is the decadal rate of change shown by successive ordinates of a seven-item moving average (geometric) of decade values overlapping by 5 years. Each ordinate covers a period of 45 years (but with different weights for the items within it) and should, therefore, be free from effects of any alternations in the rate of growth extending over 20 to 25 years. The percentage change per decade between successive ordinates should show whether there is, in general, acceleration, retardation, or constancy in the long-term trend. Chart 3 clearly reveals that the decadal rates of change in reference cycle averages and in 5-year moving averages describe long swings around a steadily declining rate of growth constituting the long-term trend—although this retardation in the rate of growth cannot be found after the 1920's.

We thus find at least two components in the long-term movements within our records: (1) the underlying movement, which for convenience we designate "long-term trend," and which may be constant, or continuously accelerating, or decelerating; and (2) long alternations in the rate of growth, which we designate "long swings"—not cycles, since we are far from sure that these are even a roughly recurrent type of variation. The finding of two such components is an unmitigated nuisance, because it complicates both our statistical analysis and our explanatory task. It would be much simpler if we could limit the description and analysis of long-term movements to what we designate long-term trend, but unfortunately it is only one component in the complex of long-term movements.

We retain this distinction throughout the discussion in the subsequent chapters. Those that follow immediately are limited to measurement and analysis of the long-term trends in capital formation and financing, and indeed, the major emphasis of this report is on long-term trends. The reason is twofold. First, in terms of magnitude, it is the long-term trend that is dominant—the long swings, though significant, being in a sense only qualifications of the long-term trend. Second, our data yield a much more detailed picture of the long-term trends than of the long swings. Study of the long swings requires records both continuous over time and available over a long period, while continuity of data over short intervals is not as important in measuring long-term trends. Nevertheless, we will turn later to the long swings to learn as much about them as we can from our limited records.

CHAPTER 3

Trends in Total Capital Formation, 1869–1955

Rate of Growth in Gross and in Net Capital Formation

THIS chapter deals with the long-term trends in total capital formation—that is, in total current additions to the country's reproducible capital. The relevant data are summarized in Table 2.

As measured in this table, capital formation comprises: construction of all types including residential, but excluding repairs and maintenance; flow to domestic users of producers' durable goods—machinery and other equipment but excluding small tools; net changes in inventories of business and, insofar as data permit, of governments; and net changes in claims against foreign countries. Neither consumers' durable commodities nor changes in inventories within households are included. In gross capital formation, the annual volumes of construction and of the flow of producers' durables are taken before deduction of current consumption of fixed durable capital; in net capital formation, the latter is deducted. Capital formation, gross or net, is a component of national product, gross or net. It represents withdrawals from aggregate product for the purpose of adding to the stock of material capital within the country or to claims against other countries, and it is thus identical with national savings, gross or net.

Since our primary interest is in the volume of capital formation unaffected by changes in price levels, the totals in Table 2 are in constant prices. And to eliminate not only the shorter business cycles but also the long swings discussed in Chapter 2, the series were averaged for periods of at least twenty years. The only exception is the average

TABLE 2

RATE OF GROWTH IN CAPITAL FORMATION, GROSS AND NET, 1929 PRICES, 1869–1955
(amounts in billions of dollars, averages per year)

Periods	Gross Capital Forma- tion (1)	Capital Consump- tion (2)	Net Capital Forma- tion (3)	Ratio of (2) to (1) (4)	Capital Retire- ments (5)	Ratio of (5) to (1) (6)
VOLUMES						
Total						
1. 1869–1888	3.48	1.46	2.02	0.42	0.87	0.25
2. 1889–1908	8.68	4.03	4.65	0.46	2.18	0.25
3. 1909–1928	15.5	8.39	7.12	0.54	4.72	0.30
4. 1929–1955	22.7	17.3	5.44	0.76	14.5	0.64
5. 1946–1955	33.0	25.1	7.88	0.76	21.4	0.65
Total, excluding military						
3a. 1909–1928	15.0	8.0	7.00	0.53	4.33	0.29
4a. 1929–1955	19.1	14.4	4.69	0.75	11.6	0.61
5a. 1946–1955	29.7	19.3	10.5	0.65	15.6	0.52
PERCENTAGE RATE OF GROWTH PER DECADE, TOTAL PERIOD						
Total						
6. Line 1 to line 4	34.4	47.6	16.9		55.8	
7. Line 1 to line 5	36.7	48.4	20.8		56.1	
Total, excluding military						
6a. Line 1 to line 4a	30.8	43.5	14.2		50.5	
7a. Line 1 to line 5a	34.7	43.1	25.7		49.4	
PERCENTAGE RATE OF GROWTH PER DECADE, SUBPERIODS						
Total						
8. Line 1 to line 2	58.0	66.1	51.8		58.7	
9. Line 2 to line 3	33.7	44.3	23.8		47.1	
10. Line 3 to line 4	17.7	36.1	−10.8		61.1	
11. Line 3 to line 5	26.6	40.9	3.2		60.4	
Total, excluding military						
8. Line 1 to line 2	58.0	66.1	51.8		58.7	
9a. Line 2 to line 3a	31.5	40.9	22.7		40.9	
10a. Line 3a to line 4a	10.9	28.6	−15.7		52.2	
11a. Line 3a to line 5a	23.8	31.6	13.3		49.1	

SOURCE: Lines 1–5: Cols. 1, 2, and 3 calculated from Table R-29; col. 5 calculated by procedure described in the text.
Lines 3a–5a: Lines 3–5 minus military, calculated from Table R-7.

for the decade after World War II, shown to reveal the recent level of peacetime capital formation in the country. The averages in Table 2 are arithmetic means, although the underlying secular trends would have been more accurately portrayed by geometric means. But we felt that the additive relation between net capital formation, capital consumption, and gross capital formation retained by using arithmetic instead of geometric means justified the minor error involved.

The findings suggested by Table 2 may now be listed:

1. The annual volume of gross capital formation increased markedly. From 1869–1888 to 1929–1955, it rose to almost seven times its original level; and during the most recent period, 1946–1955, was at a level over ninefold that prevailing during 1869–1888. The average rise per decade over the period was 34 per cent, if we use 1929–1955 as the terminal period; or 37 per cent, if we use the post-World War II years as terminal.

2. Military construction and other military durables swelled the volume of total capital formation in recent decades. For many purposes, it may be better to limit capital formation to peacetype goods. When this is done, the rate of secular growth in gross capital formation is reduced somewhat, but not appreciably: the rise per decade from 1869–1888 to 1929–1955 is 31 per cent; from 1869–1888 to the post-World War II decade, about 35 per cent.

3. The secular rise in capital consumption was greater than that in gross capital formation. The former increased almost elevenfold from 1869–1888 to 1929–1955, if we include military capital; slightly less than ninefold, if we exclude military goods. The rise was even greater from the average for 1869–1888 to that for the post-World War II years. The percentage rate of growth per decade ranged, for the different definitions of the terminal period and including or excluding consumption of military capital, from 43 per cent to somewhat over 48 per cent.

4. With the higher rate of growth in the volume of capital consumption than in gross capital formation, there was a secular rise in the proportion of the former to the latter. The ratio of capital consumption to gross capital formation rose from somewhat over four-tenths in the early decades to over three-quarters (for total capital) or almost two-thirds (for capital excluding military) in the latest period. Correspondingly, the proportion of net capital formation to gross declined from somewhat less than six-tenths to almost a quarter (for total capital) or over one-third (for capital excluding military). To put

57

it differently, in the earlier decades it took about 1.7 dollars of gross capital formation to yield 1 dollar of net addition to capital stock; in the recent period it took from less than 3 to somewhat over 4 dollars of gross capital formation to yield 1 dollar of net addition to capital stock.

5. The volume of net capital formation also grew significantly, but at a rate lower than that for either gross capital formation or capital consumption. From 1869–1888 to 1929–1955, it rose to over 2.5 times the initial level, and by the post-World War II years had risen to almost 4 times the initial level, for total capital including military. If we exclude military capital, the level in the post-World War II years is more than 5 times as high as that in 1869–1888. But whether for total or peacetype capital, the net capital formation level in 1929–1955 is well below that in 1909–1928; and when we use 1929–1955 as the terminal period, the average rate of growth over the entire period is reduced considerably. The average percentage rate of growth per decade shown in Table 2 thus varies from 14 to almost 26, depending upon the terminal period used; but in either case it is appreciably lower than the rate for gross capital formation, which is over 30 per cent, and that for capital consumption, which is over 40 per cent per decade.

6. When three intervals within the total period are distinguished (lines 8–11), the percentage rate of growth declines—even when we terminate the last interval with the post-World War II years, with their relatively high levels of capital formation and consumption. This retardation in the percentage rate of growth is observed in all three totals, including or excluding military capital. The decline in the rate of growth is most marked for net capital formation, and least marked for capital consumption.

The rest of this chapter is devoted to an attempt to suggest some of the factors that may account for the growth of capital formation over the period. But first it may be useful to discuss the meaning of capital consumption. Little mystery attaches to the meaning of gross capital formation: it is largely a flow of tangible and observable commodities into identifiable channels, and while there are many statistical difficulties in its estimation, the conceptual difficulties are those of scope, i.e., of inclusion and exclusion (for example, whether we should include consumers' durables and military capital) and of valuation (primarily allowance for quality changes). Capital consumption, however, is not a directly observable, but rather an imputed, process; and in view of the magnitudes involved, it should be clearly defined. Any ambiguity in the meaning of capital consumption, of course, affects the meaning of net capital formation since the latter is the residual after we deduct capital consumption.

The estimate is described briefly here, the details being provided in the notes to the basic reference tables in the appendixes. In calculating capital consumption we assumed a useful life span for the durable capital involved—that reflected in the depreciation charges of business firms or, in the case of residential housing, that reflected by diminution in the market value of a house as it ages. Given these life spans, annual consumption is approximated either on a straight-line principle or by some simple curve suggested by market experience, the values being converted from original cost to a 1929 price basis or to a current replacement cost basis.[1] But what do these life spans mean? What is the meaning of the continuous reduction in the value of a structure or of a machine from 100 per cent of its value to zero?

An approximate answer to the question would be that the reduction is intended to reflect the loss in earning power: in the case of business capital, the loss associated largely with obsolescence because of technical progress; in the case of residential housing, the loss associated perhaps more with changes in taste, neighborhood, and other elements determining desirability. The essential physical productive power of the capital good may remain unaffected for quite a number of years after its installation or construction; with proper repairs and maintenance (which are assumed but not included in depreciation charges), the machine or the house is as good as new for a number of years—in

---

[1] This is not an accurate description. In fact, for our capital consumption series for the years since 1929, we accept the Department of Commerce estimates of business capital consumption, including accidental damage and charges to current account, and add to them estimates of depletion, and of capital consumption of nonfarm residential construction and government construction. The components (except nonfarm residential construction) are then carried back by totals derived from the application of the assumption of a constant life span and of straight-line allocation. But the resulting estimates, despite the use of Department of Commerce totals for recent years, approximate for long periods the levels that would be derived on the basis of the assumed life spans. For example, for 1929–1955, total capital consumption (in 1929 prices) for producers' durables (excluding military), the component for which the comparison can be made most directly, was $178 billion in the series incorporating the Department of Commerce totals, $173 billion in the series based on 13-year life applied to gross producers' durables (including the nonmilitary equipment going to governments). Thus for long periods, the description in the text is roughly true; and there is essential statistical comparability between the capital consumption estimates in column 2 and the capital retirements estimates in column 5.

fact may be somewhat better after initial adjustments and "settling." But with the passage of time, new machines become available, which, per dollar in constant prices, can produce at lower costs; or new types of houses in new neighborhoods emerge, which, again per dollar in constant prices, are more desirable—in the sense of suiting better the housing needs of a given economic or social group. A business firm must allow for the effects of progress-induced obsolescence on its earning power if it is to compete in the long run—or, more generally, if it is to maintain the value of its capital. A house owner must likewise allow for the erosive effect of changes in tastes, neighborhoods, and so forth on the value of his house once built and unmodifiable without further capital expenditures. Simple calculation would demonstrate that, all other conditions being equal, it would pay an entrepreneur to use the older machines at lower rates of capacity, and purchase new ones (to be operated at maximum rates), even though he could still produce the same volume of goods without increased costs (but *not* without foregoing the lower costs possible with the new machines); and that it would pay a house owner to trade the old house for a new one long before the physical deterioration of the former reduced its value to a level close to zero.[2]

To the extent that it represents obsolescence, capital consumption does not signify reduction in the absolute level of productive capacity, nor an increase in absolute cost per unit, but rather the opportunity cost of *not* utilizing the more efficient newer capital items. Insofar as this is true, net capital formation acquires a highly specific meaning: it is net in the sense of being over and above not merely replacement of productive capacity but over and above the stock of old capital built up to the productive capacity which it could have in terms of *current* efficiency of a dollar's worth of capital goods. Zero net capital formation does not, therefore, mean failure to increase the productive capacity of the capital stock. It only means limiting the increase to the sum represented by the product of the annual rate of secular obsolescence and the already existing capital stock.

[2] I have discussed this problem on different occasions, originally in connection with the acceleration principle, in *Economic Essays in Honor of Wesley Clair Mitchell* (New York, Columbia University Press, 1935), particularly pp. 228–248, reprinted in my *Economic Change: Selected Essays in Business Cycles, National Income, and Economic Growth* (New York, Norton, 1952), pp. 66–85; and most recently in a comment on Edward F. Denison's paper in *Problems of Capital Formation: Concepts, Measurement, and Controlling Factors*, Vol. 19, Studies in Income and Wealth (Princeton for NBER, 1957), pp. 271–280.

Trends in Total Capital Formation

Short of detailed technical studies of specific capital goods, it would be impossible to measure the relative weight in capital consumption of such obsolescence, as distinct from the physical deterioration which eventually does come about. And increasing obsolescence would lead to retirement of a capital good—since, if economic conditions do not warrant its use, the cost of retaining it, no matter how slight, is still a cost. A rather speculative estimate of the volume of retirements, as distinct from capital consumption, is provided in column 5 of Table 2. Durable goods are assigned the life span implicit in the capital consumption figures, but they are "retired" only at the very end of their life. We make no deduction in its value while a capital item still has any useful life; but its full value is deducted at the end, on the presumption that with completion of its useful life the item is retired and is no longer available as a productive tool.

The estimate is quite tentative because it depends heavily upon an estimate of total useful life. But the order of magnitude it suggests is not without interest. Capital retirements averaged about 0.5 to 0.6 of total capital consumption, until the more recent periods—largely because they reflect capital formation in the more distant past, while capital consumption reflects the more recent levels of capital formation. With a generally upward trend in the volume of capital formation, retirements will be consistently lower than capital consumption— the difference being largely a function of the rate of secular rise in the volume of capital formation. Additions to capital stock, net of retirements but gross of depreciation on stock still in use, averaged, in the early periods, about three-quarters of gross capital formation, retirements averaging about a quarter. It took about one and one-third dollars of gross capital formation to provide a dollar's addition to capital stock net of retirements, but gross of accumulated depreciation on capital items still in use.

The relation changed drastically in recent decades—a reflection primarily of the sharp decline in the rate of growth of gross capital formation, and partly of the emergence of military capital for which we equated current consumption and retirement. Retirements rose to between eight- and nine-tenths of total capital consumption, or between one-half and two-thirds of gross capital formation. Hence, the trend in additions to capital stock, net of retirements and gross of other current depreciation charges, resembles the trend in net capital formation in column 3, showing a sharp decline in the rate of growth.

Trends in Total Capital Formation

Two corollaries follow. First, in considering how much additional capital is needed to turn out more product, we must take into account not only net capital formation (column 3) but also at least the part that represents the balance of current depreciation over retirements. For the "replacement" of this balance, as well as of the retirements themselves, means an addition to capital capacity—greater power to produce. Second, the totals are obviously interrelated, and not merely in an additive sense. Capital consumption and retirements of today are the gross capital formation volumes of yesterday. Given the depreciation rates—which change slowly and reflect a rough approximation to wear, tear, and particularly obsolescence—current gross capital formation, the most inclusive of the processes in which we are interested, is a sum of *past* gross capital formation in the form of either capital consumption or retirements and net capital formation which presumably looks toward the *future*. It is this combination of past and future that has to be kept in mind in explaining any aspect of capital formation that takes place currently, that is, within any period whose trend we are trying to analyze.

Relation to Growth of Population and Labor Force

In considering why capital formation grew at the rates and in the pattern suggested by Table 2, we may begin with the obvious point that during the period covered the population and labor force of this country also grew. If we accept this growth as a datum, it is easy to argue that the annual volume of capital formation had to increase to meet the demands of the larger number of people who are the direct users of at least some of the capital goods (residential and related construction, in particular) and to equip the larger number of workers with tools of production. Of course, the relation of growth in population and in labor force to capital formation is not that simple: population and labor force can increase without an increase in capital formation, and vice versa. But the least that can be said is that growing numbers of consumers and workers mean both increasing need and increasing productive power, which in turn make more capital formation necessary and feasible; and unless major obstacles bar the way, the growth in population and in labor force will increase the volume of all production, including capital formation.

Another way of expressing the connection between capital formation and the growth in population and in labor force can be suggested.

Trends in Total Capital Formation

An increase in population enjoying constant income per capita can induce additions to the stock of houses and related structures without a decline in the yield of capital so embodied, which would otherwise be the effect of an increase in housing capital per head. Growth in labor force can induce enlarged capital stock without a reduction in yield per dollar of capital which, in the absence of technological progress and perhaps even with its advance, would otherwise be the effect of a rise in the ratio of capital to labor. Conversely, growth in population and in labor force unaccompanied by additions to capital stock should raise the yield of capital and stimulate capital formation.

How should we compare growth in population and in labor force with growth in capital formation? The latter represents additions to the already existing stock. We could (1) compare the stock of capital, growing as a result of current capital formation, with the human stock, i.e., total population or labor force; or (2) compare *additions* to capital stock—current capital formation—with additions to the stock of population or labor force. Of the two comparisons the former is to be preferred. The latter involves the artificial assumption that additions to capital stock are necessarily closely related to additions to population and to labor force. We use this assumption for a specific purpose later, but the most relevant comparison between growth in capital and growth in population and in labor force rests on the view that the total stock of capital is a tool in the hands of, and for the service of, the total stock of population and workers.

Table 3 brings together the data needed for this comparison. The net capital stock figure (column 3) is the value, in constant prices, of the accumulated capital formation, net of current depreciation. But there are, in addition, two gross capital stock figures. In one—gross, net of retirements (column 2)—we subtract retirements, but not the accumulated depreciation of stock that is still extant because it is assumed not to have been retired. In the other (column 1), no deduction for capital consumption is made. This series in column 1, unrealistic because it exaggerates the volume of capital goods available at any given time, nevertheless serves the purpose of a kind of upper level.

With these comments, and a note to the effect that the labor force includes all gainful workers, whether or not employed at the time of reporting, we summarize the findings suggested by Table 3.

1. As expected, the stock of capital, both net and gross, grew at high rates. From 1869 to 1955, net capital stock increased to about 16 times its initial level; gross capital stock net of retirements, to 18

TABLE 3

RATE OF GROWTH IN CAPITAL STOCK, GROSS AND NET, 1929 PRICES, IN POPULATION, AND IN LABOR FORCE, 1869–1955

Years [a]	Total Capital Stock ($ billions)			Population (millions)	Capital Stock Per Capita ($ thousands)			Labor Force (millions)	Capital Stock Per Member of Labor Force ($ thousands)		
	Gross (1)	Net of Capital Retirements (2)	Net of Capital Consumption (3)	(4)	Gross (5)	Net of Capital Retirements (6)	Net of Capital Consumption (7)	(8)	Gross (9)	Net of Capital Retirements (10)	Net of Capital Consumption (11)
Total stock				VOLUMES							
1. 1869	45	36	27	40.0	1.12	0.90	0.68	12.8	3.52	2.82	2.11
2. 1879	71	56	42	49.7	1.42	1.12	0.85	17.0	4.16	3.27	2.49
3. 1889	116	89	68	62.5	1.86	1.43	1.09	22.3	5.22	4.01	3.06
4. 1899	190	143	108	75.1	2.53	1.90	1.44	28.5	6.66	5.01	3.79
5. 1909	296	224	165	90.9	3.25	2.47	1.82	37.4	7.90	5.99	4.41
6. 1919	430	323	227	105.9	4.06	3.04	2.15	41.6	10.32	7.75	5.46
7. 1929	607	440	306	122.3	4.96	3.60	2.50	48.4	12.54	9.09	6.33
8. 1939	727	480	319	131.8	5.52	3.64	2.42	52.8	13.77	9.08	6.04
9. 1946	895	547	374	142.0	6.30	3.85	2.63	58.0	15.44	9.43	6.45
10. 1955	1,191	649	442	165.9	7.18	3.91	2.66	65.6	18.15	9.89	6.74

Total stock, excluding military

7a. 1929	597	437	304	122.3	4.88	3.58	2.49	48.4	12.33	9.04	6.28
9a. 1946	820	501	328	142.0	5.77	3.53	2.31	58.0	14.13	8.63	5.65
10a. 1955	1,085	626	419	165.9	6.54	3.78	2.53	65.6	16.54	9.54	6.39

PERCENTAGE RATE OF GROWTH PER DECADE, TOTAL PERIOD

1869 to 1955

11. Total stock	46.4	40.0	38.4	18.0	24.1	18.6	17.3	21.0	21.0	15.7	14.4
11a. Total stock, excluding military	44.8	39.4	37.6	18.0	22.7	18.1	16.6	21.0	19.7	15.2	13.7

1869 to 1929

12. Total stock	54.3	51.8	49.9	20.5	28.1	26.0	24.4	24.9	23.6	21.5	20.1
12a. Total stock, excluding military	53.9	51.6	49.7	20.5	27.7	25.9	24.3	24.9	23.2	21.4	19.9

PERCENTAGE RATE OF GROWTH PER DECADE, SUBPERIODS

Total stock

13. 1869 to 1889	60.8	57.6	58.9	25.1	28.6	26.1	27.0	32.1	21.7	19.3	20.3
14. 1889 to 1909	59.4	58.4	55.7	20.6	32.2	31.3	29.2	29.6	23.0	22.2	20.1
15. 1909 to 1929	43.3	40.1	36.2	16.0	23.5	20.7	17.4	13.8	26.0	23.2	19.8
16. 1929 to 1955	29.6	16.1	15.1	12.4	15.3	3.3	2.4	12.4	15.3	3.3	2.4

Total stock, excluding military

13. 1869 to 1889	60.8	57.6	58.9	25.1	28.6	26.1	27.0	32.1	21.7	19.3	20.3
14. 1889 to 1909	59.4	58.4	55.7	20.6	32.2	31.3	29.2	29.6	23.0	22.2	20.1
15a. 1909 to 1929	42.1	39.7	35.7	16.0	22.5	20.4	17.0	13.8	24.9	22.8	19.3
16a. 1929 to 1955	25.9	14.8	13.2	12.4	11.9	2.1	0.7	12.4	12.0	2.1	0.7

ᵃ Mid-year date for absolute volumes.

(Notes on following page)

65

Trends in Total Capital Formation

TABLE 3 (concluded)

SOURCE: The capital stock figures in col. 3 are net of accumulated depreciation. The basic figure is that for 1880, taken from Raymond W. Goldsmith, "The Growth of Reproducible Wealth of the United States of America from 1805 to 1950," *Income and Wealth, Series II* (International Association for Research in Income and Wealth, Cambridge, England, Bowes and Bowes, 1952), Table II, p. 310. It includes reproducible durables (excluding consumer durables), inventories, gold and silver, and the net balance of foreign claims. To derive the series for the other years, we added to or subtracted from the basic 1880 figure our annual estimates of net capital formation.

The gross capital stock figure in col. 1 begins with an estimate of the net capital stock of wealth in 1805, also from Goldsmith's series. This, in terms of the concept mentioned above, amounts to $0.9 billion in 1929 prices. If we assume a ratio of gross stock to net of about 1.67 (corresponding to a long-term ratio of net capital formation to gross of 0.60), the gross stock of capital in 1805 is $1.5 billion. The ratio of net to gross capital formation of 0.6 was based on Table 2; but even a major error in that figure or in the ratio applied to the 1805 figure for net capital stock to derive gross capital stock would have minor effects on the totals beginning in 1869.

Goldsmith's figures yield net capital formation from 1805 to 1880 (derived as first differences in the net stock of capital between the two dates). On the assumption that net capital formation is 0.6 of gross, we can then estimate gross capital formation for 1805–1880. Adding this total to gross capital stock in 1805 yields the gross capital stock in 1880. The ratio of the latter to the net capital stock (Goldsmith's total) is, as should be expected, 1.67. We applied this ratio to our net capital stock total for 1869 to derive the initial estimate of gross capital stock for 1869 in col. 1. With this figure and our estimates of gross capital formation at hand, we derived the figures for later dates by successive addition.

The series on gross capital stock net of retirements (col. 2) was derived along lines similar to those described for gross capital stock in col. 1. The major difference lies in the ratio of net capital formation to gross, in this case gross net of retirements. On the basis of the life spans (13 years for producers' durables and 50 years for construction, the terminal years or decades given half weight) and the earlier levels of construction and producers' durable equipment underlying the capital consumption estimates, we set the ratio at 0.75; which yields a ratio, in the long run, of gross capital stock net of retirements to net capital stock of 1.33. With these ratios set, and with the application of constant life spans, the initial estimate for 1869 in col. 2 was derived and the subsequent totals estimated by successive addition. These calculations were applied to nonmilitary construction and equipment alone; for military we assumed retirements to be equal to consumption.

The population and labor force estimates are the annual series underlying Tables R-37 and R-39.

times; and the somewhat unrealistic capital stock gross of all consumption, to about 26 times its initial level. The exclusion of military capital reduces these rates of growth slightly.

2. If the growth of capital stock were caused by growth in numbers— of total population and of the labor force—and returns to scale were constant, capital per head and per member of the labor force would have remained constant during the period. Instead, we observe a marked growth in capital per person and per member of the labor force. Net capital stock per head rose, over the period as a whole, to

about 4 times its initial level, whether or not we include military capital, i.e., at a rate of about 17 per cent per decade. The rate of growth for gross capital net of retirements per head was slightly higher. That for total gross capital per person was materially higher, but the element of exaggeration must be borne in mind. Since labor force grew at somewhat higher rates than total population, the rate of growth of capital stock per member of the labor force was somewhat lower than that of capital per person. But even its lowest rate of growth per decade, for the period as a whole, was 14 per cent (for net capital stock).

3. The rate of growth declined significantly. This is apparent from the entries in lines 11 and 12, which show the rate of growth for the period as a whole, from 1869 to 1955, and for the period terminating in 1929. In every comparison, the rate of growth for the period including the last twenty-seven years was distinctly below that for the first six decades covered, not only for each total capital stock series, but also for capital stock per person and per member of the labor force.

Retardation in the rate of growth of the aggregates is found also when we study successive wide intervals, not shorter than twenty years, within the period (lines 13–16). Even for gross capital stock, the rate of growth in the third interval (from 1909 to 1929) was significantly lower than in the first two.

4. The retardation in the rate of growth of total capital stock is to some extent accounted for by a decline in the rate of growth of population and of the labor force. The entries in columns 4 and 8 record the familiar and well-established fact that the percentage rate of growth in numbers in the country has been tending downward. Consequently, the retardation in the rate of growth of capital stock per capita and per member of the labor force is not as continuous as that of total stock. The decrease in the rate of growth of stock per capita—whether net, gross excluding retirements, or gross of all consumption—is not evident until after 1909; and for two of the variants of stock per member of the labor force, retardation in the rate of growth does not set in until after 1929. Neither date should be given too much weight. The important finding is that with the exception of net capital stock the supply of capital goods per worker grew at a slightly increasing rate through most of the period, the decline in the rate of growth emerging only in the most recent interval, 1929 to 1955.

Trends in Total Capital Formation

5. This last finding is of particular interest. Over some sixty years of the period, capital stock per worker grew at high rates, and except in the case of net capital stock, at slightly rising rates. It is only after the 1920's that the growth of capital per worker declined. And the decline was quite drastic. In the two most realistic series, net capital and gross capital excluding retirements, the level of capital per member of the labor force shows very little growth after 1929. It is true that the period beginning in 1929 includes the Great Depression; but on the other hand, it includes also the expansion years of World War II and a decade of particularly high levels of capital formation following the conclusion of that war. If we view the average in 1929–1955 as an approximation to long-term secular levels, we can hardly escape the conclusion that substantial changes have occurred in the factors that determine capital formation—a point to be explored further as we proceed.

With the data in Table 3 it is possible to allocate the growth in total capital between that part which can be ascribed merely to the increase in population or in the labor force—on the assumption of a constant supply of capital per person or per worker—and that which can be ascribed to the growth in stock per capita or per member of the labor force. The results of the calculations are given in Table 4. We assume that the stock per capita or per member of the labor force remained constant at the 1869 level in the decades that followed, and that the growth in capital stock was due merely to growth in population or labor force. Lines 1 and 1a, covering the total period, show that, under such conditions, the growth in total capital stock would have been only a small fraction of the actual increase. In the case of stock gross of all consumption, the increase in population accounts for between one-eighth and one-seventh of the total addition that occurred. In other words, gross capital formation cumulated over the period would have been only 12 to 14 per cent of its actual volume. The increase in the labor force, under the conditions assumed, would have contributed a somewhat greater increase to gross capital stock—about one-sixth of the increase that occurred. In other words, gross capital formation under these conditions would have been from 16 to 18 per cent of its actual volume. In the case of net stock, the hypothetical contribution of the increase in numbers is somewhat greater—about one-fifth due to the rise in population, and over one-quarter due to the rise in labor force. In the case of gross stock, net of retirements, the percentage contributions are slightly lower.

Trends in Total Capital Formation

TABLE 4

ALLOCATION OF RISE IN CAPITAL STOCK BETWEEN RISE IN POPULATION OR LABOR
FORCE AND RISE IN CAPITAL STOCK PER UNIT, 1869–1955

| | PROPORTION OF RISE IN: | | | | | |
| | Gross Capital Stock Due to Rise in: | | Stock Net of Capital Retirements Due to Rise in: | | Stock Net of Capital Consumption Due to Rise in: | |
PERIODS	Population (1)	Labor Force (2)	Population (3)	Labor Force (4)	Population (5)	Labor Force (6)
	TOTAL PERIOD					
1869–1955						
1. Total capital stock	0.12	0.16	0.18	0.24	0.20	0.27
1a. Total capital stock, excluding military	0.14	0.18	0.19	0.25	0.22	0.28
	SUBPERIODS, TOTAL CAPITAL STOCK					
2. 1869–1888	0.36	0.47	0.38	0.50	0.37	0.49
3. 1889–1908	0.29	0.44	0.30	0.45	0.32	0.48
4. 1909–1928	0.33	0.28	0.36	0.31	0.40	0.34
5. 1929–1955	0.37	0.37	0.75	0.75	0.80	0.80
Geometric means, lines 2–5	0.34	0.38	0.42	0.48	0.44	0.50
	SUBPERIODS, TOTAL CAPITAL STOCK, EXCLUDING MILITARY					
2. 1869–1888	0.36	0.47	0.38	0.50	0.37	0.49
3. 1889–1908	0.29	0.44	0.30	0.45	0.32	0.48
4a. 1909–1928	0.34	0.29	0.36	0.31	0.41	0.35
5a. 1929–1955	0.44	0.43	0.83	0.82	0.94	0.94
Geometric means, lines 2–5a	0.35	0.40	0.43	0.49	0.46	0.53

SOURCE: Calculated from the data underlying Table 3.

Naturally, the relative contribution of growth in numbers increases as we shorten the period, largely because the weight of the other factor—the increase in stock per capita or per member of the labor force—is cumulated over a shorter period. When we average the results for the four intervals, each covering twenty years or more, the contribution of the increase in numbers to the increase in capital stock ranges from slightly more than one-third to about one-half.

These findings for the intervals, however, are less significant in the present connection than those for the period as a whole, which indicate quite clearly that the direct arithmetic contribution of increase in numbers to capital formation is quite moderate. It is true that growth of population and of the labor force may have many indirect influences, which are extremely important in explaining the volume and growth of capital formation. For example, the wider division of labor made possible by greater numbers permits specialization, increased productivity, and consequently greater capital formation. But there are better measures of these ramified effects than the growth in numbers. The latter, in itself, has contributed too little directly to capital formation in this country since 1869 to merit much weight in any explanatory hypotheses, and we must turn to some other proximate determinants.

There is, however, one significant exception to this statement. The retardation in the growth of population and of labor force is quite marked. According to columns 4 and 8 of Table 3, the rate of growth of population in 1929–1955 was less than half the rate in 1869–1889; and the retardation in the rate of growth of the labor force is even more striking—the rate in 1929–1955 being somewhat over one-third of that in 1869–1889. Considerable significance could be attributed to such slowing down in the rate of growth of population and of labor force in explaining, if only in part, the retardation in the rate of growth of capital stock, and via the latter, the decline in the rate of growth of capital formation. We must, therefore, bear in mind that, while the increase in numbers alone may be quantitatively of little importance in accounting for the volume and rate of growth of capital formation, the *retardation* in the rate of growth of population and of labor force may be of much greater importance in accounting for the retardation in the rate of growth of gross capital formation, and thus—for reasons that will become clearer in subsequent discussion—for the increased proportion of capital consumption, and for the even greater retardation in the rate of growth of net capital formation.

Rate of Growth in Gross and in Net National Product

If increase in population and labor force contributes little, directly, to the growth of capital stock and to the trends in capital formation, we may find a more important proximate determinant in national product. However, since national product is an aggregate of which capital formation is a component, there is a tautological relation between the two in the sense that, all other conditions being equal, changes in capital formation mean identical changes in national product. One could argue that to try to explain trends in capital formation on the basis of their relation to trends in national product is like explaining a phenomenon by the phenomenon itself. And yet we feel that there is some meaning in relating capital formation, either directly or in the form of the cumulated stock, to national product. The reason for this "feeling" can be easily stated. Capital formation represents additions to capital stock, which is an important tool in producing national income, output, or product. Capital formation also represents national savings, and is thus a fraction of national product. Hence changes in capital stock will affect national product, and these expected effects may be the *raison d'être* for capital formation and may, therefore, explain it. In turn, changes in national product, the pool from which capital formation is drawn, will naturally affect the magnitude of capital formation. In this two-way relation between capital formation and national product the tautological element is conceptually removed by the introduction of a disparity in the time reference, although in the statistical estimates used here, the time periods are far too long and the data too crude for the lag and lead allowances to be significant and feasible. When capital formation is viewed as additions to tools for turning out national product, the latter is conceived as being produced in the future and capital formation as taking place in the present—governed, as it were, by future product expectations. When capital formation is viewed as the saved portion of national product, the latter is regarded as having been produced in the past, and capital formation as taking place in the present, since it is only realized product that can give rise to real savings. Much of the discussion in the rest of this chapter will deal with these two relations between capital formation and national product.

As a prelude to that discussion, it will be helpful to observe the long-term trends in national product—total, per capita, and per member of the labor force (Table 5). These summary measures, shown in several variants, distinguish gross and net national product, the net differing from the gross in that current capital consumption has been deducted. In Appendixes A and B we present three variants of gross and net national product (or national income, the two terms being used interchangeably here), each variant including identical estimates of gross and net capital formation but each differing in its estimate of flow of goods to consumers. Variant I is based on the original estimates

TABLE 5

Rate of Growth in National Product, 1929 Prices, Gross and Net, Total, Per Capita and Per Member of Labor Force, 1869–1955

Periods	Gross National Product			Net National Product		
	Total (billions) (1)	Per Capita (2)	Per Member of Labor Force (3)	Total (billions) (4)	Per Capita (5)	Per Member of Labor Force (6)
Variant I						
	VOLUMES, AVERAGES PER YEAR					
Total						
1. 1869–1888	$ 14.4	$ 288	$ 854	$ 13.0	$ 261	$ 772
2. 1889–1908	34.0	454	1,196	30.0	401	1,057
3. 1909–1928	67.3	636	1,594	59.0	558	1,398
4. 1929–1955	115.3	832	2,034	99.0	714	1,746
5. 1946–1955	161.7	1,052	2,605	136.6	888	2,201
Total, excluding military						
3a. 1909–1928	66.7	631	1,582	58.8	556	1,394
4a. 1929–1955	112.1	809	1,977	98.2	708	1,732
5a. 1946–1955	158.4	1,030	2,553	139.2	905	2,242
	PERCENTAGE RATE OF GROWTH PER DECADE, TOTAL PERIOD					
Total						
6. Line 1 to line 4	38.8	18.2	14.6	37.7	17.2	13.7
7. Line 1 to line 5	40.0	19.7	16.8	38.7	18.5	15.7
Total, excluding military						
6a. Line 1 to line 4a	38.2	17.6	14.1	37.5	17.0	13.6
7a. Line 1 to line 5a	39.6	19.3	16.4	39.0	18.8	16.0
	PERCENTAGE RATE OF GROWTH PER DECADE, SUBPERIODS					
Total						
8. Line 1 to line 2	53.8	25.5	18.4	52.1	24.0	17.0
9. Line 2 to line 3	40.7	18.3	15.4	40.1	17.9	15.0
10. Line 3 to line 4	25.8	12.1	10.9	24.7	11.1	9.9
11. Line 3 to line 5	31.5	17.0	16.6	30.0	15.6	15.2
Total, excluding military						
8. Line 1 to line 2	53.8	25.5	18.4	52.1	24.0	17.0
9a. Line 2 to line 3a	40.1	17.9	15.0	39.9	17.7	14.8
10a. Line 3a to line 4a	24.7	11.2	10.0	24.4	10.9	9.7
11a. Line 3a to line 5a	31.0	16.6	16.1	30.9	16.5	16.0

(continued)

TABLE 5 (continued)

Periods	Gross National Product			Net National Product		
	Total (billions) (1)	Per Capita (2)	Per Member of Labor Force (3)	Total (billions) (4)	Per Capita (5)	Per Member of Labor Force (6)
Variant III						
VOLUMES, AVERAGES PER YEAR						
Total						
12. 1869–1888	$ 14.7	$ 296	$ 874	$ 13.3	$ 267	$ 792
13. 1889–1908	34.9	466	1,226	30.9	412	1,087
14. 1909–1928	69.7	659	1,652	61.4	580	1,456
15. 1929–1955	122.3	882	2,158	106.0	765	1,870
16. 1946–1955	172.3	1,121	2,777	147.2	957	2,372
Total, excluding military						
14a. 1909–1928	69.1	654	1,639	61.2	578	1,451
15a. 1929–1955	119.1	860	2,101	105.2	759	1,855
16a. 1946–1955	169.1	1,099	2,724	149.8	974	2,414
PERCENTAGE RATE OF GROWTH PER DECADE, TOTAL PERIOD						
Total						
17. Line 12 to line 15	39.6	18.8	15.3	38.6	18.0	14.5
18. Line 12 to line 16	40.7	20.3	17.4	39.6	19.4	16.5
Total, excluding military						
17a. Line 12 to line 15a	39.0	18.3	14.8	38.5	17.9	14.3
18a. Line 12 to line 16a	40.4	20.0	17.1	39.9	19.7	16.7
PERCENTAGE RATE OF GROWTH PER DECADE, SUBPERIODS						
Total						
19. Line 12 to line 13	53.9	25.5	18.5	52.2	24.2	17.2
20. Line 13 to line 14	41.4	18.9	16.0	41.0	18.6	15.7
21. Line 14 to line 15	27.1	13.3	12.0	26.2	12.5	11.2
22. Line 14 to line 16	32.7	18.1	17.6	31.4	16.9	16.5
Total, excluding military						
19. Line 12 to line 13	53.9	25.5	18.5	52.2	24.2	17.2
20a. Line 13 to line 14a	40.9	18.5	15.6	40.8	18.4	15.5
21a. Line 14a to line 15a	26.1	12.3	11.1	25.9	12.3	11.0
22a. Line 14a to line 16a	32.2	17.6	17.2	32.3	17.7	17.2

(continued)

TABLE 5 (concluded)

	Gross National Product			Net National Product		
	Total (billions) (1)	Per Capita (2)	Per Member of Labor Force (3)	Total (billions) (4)	Per Capita (5)	Per Member of Labor Force (6)
Periods						

Commerce Concept

VOLUMES, AVERAGES PER YEAR

23. 1869–1888	$ 14.7	$ 296	$ 876	$ 13.4	$ 269	$ 794
24. 1889–1908	35.5	475	1,250	31.5	422	1,110
25. 1909–1928	72.0	681	1,707	63.7	603	1,511
26. 1929–1955	136.8	987	2,414	120.5	870	2,126
27. 1946–1955	190.3	1,237	3,066	165.2	1,074	2,662

PERCENTAGE RATE OF GROWTH PER DECADE, TOTAL PERIOD

28. Line 23 to line 26	42.0	20.9	17.3	41.4	20.3	16.8
29. Line 23 to line 27	42.7	22.0	19.0	41.8	21.2	18.3

PERCENTAGE RATE OF GROWTH PER DECADE, SUBPERIODS

30. Line 23 to line 24	55.3	26.7	19.5	53.7	25.3	18.3
31. Line 24 to line 25	42.4	19.7	16.8	42.1	19.6	16.7
32. Line 25 to line 26	31.4	17.1	15.9	31.2	16.9	15.6
33. Line 25 to line 27	35.5	20.5	20.1	34.7	19.8	19.4

SOURCE:

Columns 1 and 4

Lines 1–3 and 12–14. Geometric means of successive decade averages in Table R-12.
Lines 4 and 15. Weighted geometric means of decade averages for 1929–1938 and 1939–1948 (from Table R-12) and of the average for 1949–1955 (from Table R-2).
Lines 5 and 16. From Table R-2 (arithmetic means of annual estimates).
Lines 3a–5a and 14a–16a. For military, see notes to Table 2.
Lines 23–27. Average value of gross national product is given for 1929–1938 and later years in Table A-6, col. 2 and extrapolated for earlier years by applying to Variant III the ratio of the Commerce series to Variant III in 1929–1938, and assuming a 0.8 per decade decline in the ratio (as suggested by the movement of the ratio since 1929 in Table A-3). The net national product series is calculated by deducting from the gross national product estimates the difference between cols. 1 and 4, lines 1–5.

Columns 2, 3, 5, and 6

For estimates of population and labor force see notes to Table 3. The decade averages of national product were divided by the decade averages of population and of labor force, and then geometric means of the decade averages of per-capita or per-worker product were calculated for the longer periods in the same fashion as for total national product.

derived by the income-payments method in *National Income and Its Composition, 1919–1938*.[3] Services (and hence total flow of goods to consumers) are approximated by subtracting from national income independently derived estimates of cost of commodities to consumers and of net capital formation. Variant I is extrapolated forward from the 1930's by the appropriate items in the national income accounts of the Department of Commerce. Variant II retains all the commodity flow series of Variant I, but the services component is measured directly, not as a residual. Variant III is based upon the commodity flow and services estimates of the Department of Commerce for the years beginning with 1929, but only those that reflect the concepts underlying Variants I and II. These components of flow of goods to consumers are then extrapolated back to 1919 by the commodity components of Variant I and the services component of Variant II.[4]

Table 5 shows Variants I and III, but to reduce detail, Variant II, which is fairly close to I and III, is omitted. Conceptually all three variants are identical: they are intended to exclude the intermediate product of government activities. They differ only in respect to the estimating procedures. A more important feature of Table 5 is the inclusion of measures for another concept of national product—that used presently by the Department of Commerce. Its chief difference from Variants I and III (and II) lies in the treatment of all government expenditures on commodities and services as final product, and hence the inclusion of those expenditures in national product along with private capital formation and flow of goods to ultimate consumers.

This profusion of variants of national product may be embarrassing, and it certainly does not make for easy discussion and understanding. The retention of these variants and different concepts is not due to a capricious desire to befuddle the unwary reader, but rather serves a purpose. Use of Variants I and III is warranted because it indicates that, even for one definition of national product, justifiable differences in statistical procedure may result in different rates and patterns of growth. Use of the Commerce national product total serves as a reminder of the important differences in judgment of what constitutes net or gross output. It shows that these differences inevitably mean different levels and patterns of long-term trends in the volume of output and, for that matter, of capital. In the attempt to arrive at some ac-

[3] Simon Kuznets, assisted by Lillian Epstein and Elizabeth Jenks (New York, NBER, 1941).

[4] For more detailed discussion and comparison see Appendix A.

ceptable record of long-term trends in such aggregative totals as national income or capital it is important to bear in mind the possible effects of differences in concept and statistical procedures, lest we assign too much weight to the results of a specific conceptual or statistical decision.

With these cautions in mind, we can now list the major findings suggested by Table 5 on rate of growth of national product.

1. For the period as a whole—from the first two decades, 1869–1888, to either the last long period, 1929–1955, or to the post-World War II years—the rise in national product has been impressive. From 1869–1888 to 1946–1955 the volume rose to ten or more times its initial level. The rate of growth per decade ranges from 37.5 to almost 43 per cent—depending upon the terminal period chosen, the inclusion or exclusion of military items (in this case only military capital formation), the deduction or inclusion of capital consumption, and the concept followed. The differences in statistical procedure and even in scope have relatively little effect on the average rate of growth over the period as a whole.

2. Much of this impressive growth in national product can be directly associated with growth in population and in labor force. For product per capita and per member of the labor force, the average percentage rate of increase was from about one-third to one-half of that for the total: that in product per capita ranged from 17 to 22 per cent per decade; that in product per member of the labor force, from somewhat under 14 to 19 per cent. But the cumulation of such rates over more than six or seven decades produces a marked rise in product per capita or per worker. Thus, net national product per capita in 1929–1955 was about three times its 1869–1888 level; and net national product per worker grew almost as much. A tripling of the average standard of living per head in slightly over six decades—and this is essentially what is implied—is an extraordinary performance, in that there are few equally long historical periods when it could have occurred, and there are almost no countries in which such a rise occurred from levels that, in the initial period, were already so high.

3. In observing the rates of growth for successive intervals within the period, the last interval terminating in 1929–1955 or 1946–1955, we find that for total product, whether gross or net and whatever the variant, the rate of growth declined. Invariably, the average level for the post-World War II decade, 1946–1955, reflects a higher rate of growth per decade from 1909–1928 than that for the longer period

1929–1955. But even if we use this more favorable showing of the post-World War II decade, the rate of growth per decade is lower than in the interval from 1889–1908 to 1909–1928. And there is room for argument as to whether the average for 1946–1955 represents a long-term secular level, rather than a position above it reflecting some transiently favorable conditions of the immediate post-World War II years. This problem of interpretation of the secular significance of the recent decade requires careful examination, best undertaken at a later stage in the analysis.

4. As might have been expected from our earlier discussion, much of the retardation in the rate of growth of total product can be directly associated with retardation in the rate of growth of population and of labor force. As a consequence, for product per capita or per member of the labor force, no sweeping conclusion concerning retardation in the rate of growth can be made; and the evidence must be summarized with careful attention to detail.

5. If 1929–1955 is taken as the terminal period, we find a consistent decline in the rate of growth of product per capita and per member of the labor force—for Variants I and III and the Commerce concept, gross and net product, including and excluding military. The only qualification is that for the Commerce concept, in which the expansion of government activities is tantamount to an increase in final product, the decline from the rate of growth of product per capita and per worker for the interval 1889–1908 to 1909–1928 to that for the interval 1909–1928 to 1929–1955 is rather moderate (see lines 31 and 32).

6. If we use the high level of the 1946–1955 decade as the terminal datum, the results change. The decline in the rate of growth of product per capita and per worker between the first and the second intervals is not affected, of course. But the retardation over the interval between 1909–1928 and 1946–1955 (i.e., when we skip the intervening depression and war years) disappears. In other words, from the secular level in 1909–1928 to the level in 1946–1955, treated here as secular, the rate of growth in product per capita and per worker is almost as high as, or higher than, the rate of growth from 1889–1908 to 1909–1928.

7. The conclusions suggested just above may be restated somewhat more vividly. If we assume that the depression of the 1930's is canceled by the expansions that preceded and followed it, and regard the longer-term averages as truly representative secular levels, we find retardation in the rate of growth not only of total income, but also of product per head and per worker. If, however, we omit the depres-

sion and the war years, and regard the 1946–1955 averages as secular levels, there is no clear case for retardation in the rate of growth of product per capita or per worker.

The emphasis above on ascertaining the existence or absence of retardation in the secular rate of growth may at first seem puzzling. But it should be no more puzzling than our interest in the absolute level of income or in its percentage rate of growth. Given an initial level of product or income, it makes a difference whether, in the process of secular growth, the average rate over a long period is 5 or 15 per cent per decade: a higher rate not only means much greater volume with the passage of time, but, in the present connection, it may also be associated with the volume of capital formation, and may in turn have an effect on it. But given an average rate of growth per decade over a long period, we must also know whether this is an average of relatively constant rates—about the same at the beginning and at the end of the period—or whether it is an average of rates that systematically decline or rise. For consistent retardation or acceleration is a signal that some process is continuously at work modifying the factors that determine the average rate of growth; and this calls for an investigation of these factors to see whether the consistency observed in the past is likely to continue into the future.

Relation of Capital to Output

If capital formation is necessary to maintain or increase the stock of capital goods required to produce desired output, the possibilities of explaining the level of and trend in capital formation lie in a comparison of capital stock with output—on either an aggregative or component basis. The line of reasoning, following the Harrod-Domar model, can be briefly stated. Assume that technological and other requirements call for a given ratio of capital stock to desired annual output, say the ratio of 3 to 1. Then if population and its desired level of per capita output both increase, the required rate of growth of total output or national product (i.e., increased population multiplied by increased per capita product) is, let us say, x per cent per year. To maintain the required ratio of capital to output of 3 to 1 with the x per cent of growth of output calls for a growth in capital stock equal to $3x$ per cent of annual aggregate output. Hence, under the assumptions just stated, capital formation—additions to the stock of capital—equals $3x$ per cent of national product (which determines the level of the capital formation proportion to national product), and the rate of percentage growth in capital stock equals the rate of growth in national product. In turn, the percentage rate of growth of capital stock, if observed over successive periods, will reveal the rate of growth of capital formation, i.e., of additions to capital stock. If we can either explain or assume the level and rate of growth of population and of product per capita, we can, given a constant (or changing) capital-output ratio, derive the level and rate of growth of capital formation.

While this is obviously a highly oversimplified view, it is sufficient to indicate the broad rationale for our interest in the capital-output ratio as a measure that may advance our understanding of the factors that determine the volume of and rate of growth in capital formation. But in trying to apply the schema to the estimates, we are immediately confronted with specific questions. Should we use gross capital stock or stock adjusted for actual retirements as the numerator of the ratio we wish to study? Or should we take capital stock net of all accumulated depreciation? What measure of aggregate output should we use as the denominator—national product, as we define it or as the Department of Commerce defines it, and should it be gross or net of depreciation? These specific questions have wider implications that bear upon the whole meaning and usefulness of the capital-output ratios in the analysis; but these implications can be discussed more effectively after studying the statistical value of the ratios. For the present therefore, the purpose of these questions is merely to indicate the reason for the several sets of capital-output ratios given in Table 6.

In one set, gross capital stock is related to gross national product, Variant I, and the Department of Commerce concept. We shall henceforth omit Variant III to reduce detail; besides, Variant I and the Commerce totals show the widest differences, whereas those among our three variants do not affect the findings significantly. In another set, gross capital stock, net of retirements, is related to net national product. It might have been more justifiable to relate it to gross national product, net of retirements, but the resulting ratios would have differed only slightly from those shown. In the third set of ratios net capital stock is related to net national product.

The capital-output ratios are calculated for the successive decades, the numerator being the geometric mean of the capital stock at the beginning and end of the decade, and the denominator, the annual average of national product during that decade. Both numerator and denominator are in constant prices, to avoid the effect of the greater

79

TABLE 6

RATIO OF CAPITAL STOCK TO AVERAGE ANNUAL NATIONAL PRODUCT PER DECADE, BASED ON VOLUMES IN 1929 PRICES, 1869–1955

Intervals for Capital Stock, Geometric Mean of Terminal Years	Periods for National Product, Annual Averages	Ratio of Gross Capital Stock to Gross National Product		Ratio of Gross Capital Stock Net of Retirements to Net National Product		Ratio of Net Capital Stock to Net National Product	
		Variant I (1)	Commerce Concept (2)	Variant I (3)	Commerce Concept (4)	Variant I (5)	Commerce Concept (6)
Total stock and product							
1. 1869 & 1879	1869–1878	5.4	5.3	4.7	4.6	3.6	3.5
2. 1879 & 1889	1879–1888	4.6	4.5	4.0	3.8	3.0	2.9
3. 1889 & 1899	1889–1898	5.4	5.2	4.7	4.5	3.6	3.4
4. 1899 & 1909	1899–1908	5.6	5.3	4.8	4.5	3.5	3.4
5. 1909 & 1919	1909–1918	6.2	5.9	5.4	5.0	3.9	3.6
6. 1919 & 1929	1919–1928	6.5	6.0	5.4	5.0	3.8	3.5
7. 1929 & 1939	1929–1938	8.1	7.3	6.4	5.7	4.4	3.9
8. 1939 & 1949	1939–1948	6.8	5.4	5.0	3.8	3.3	2.5
9. 1946 & 1955	1946–1955	6.4	5.4	4.4	3.6	3.0	2.5
Total, excluding military							
5a. 1909 & 1919	1909–1918	6.2		5.4		3.8	
6a. 1919 & 1929	1919–1928	6.4		5.3		3.7	

7a. 1929 & 1939		7.9	6.4		4.3
8a. 1939 & 1949		6.9	5.0		3.3
9a. 1946 & 1955		6.0	4.0		2.7
Longer Intervals (arithmetic means)					
Total stock and product					
10. Lines 1 & 2	1869–1888	5.0	4.4	4.9	4.2	3.2
11. Lines 3 & 4	1889–1908	5.5	4.8	5.2	4.5	3.4
12. Lines 5 & 6	1909–1928	6.4	5.4	6.0	5.0	3.6
13. See note a	1929–1955	7.2	5.3	6.1	4.5	3.0
14. See note b	1939–1955	6.6	4.7	5.4	3.7	2.5
Total, excluding military					
10. Lines 1 & 2	1869–1888	5.0	4.4		3.3
11. Lines 3 & 4	1889–1908	5.5	4.8		3.6
12a. Lines 5a & 6a	1909–1928	6.3	5.4		3.8
13a. See note a	1929–1955	7.0	5.3		3.5
14a. See note b	1939–1955	6.5	4.6		3.1

a Weighted average of line 7 (or 7a), 8 (or 8a), and geometric mean of 1949 and 1955.

b Weighted average of line 8 (or 8a) and geometric mean of 1949 and 1955.

SOURCE: The capital stock series are from Table 3; the national product series are those underlying Table 5.

sensitivity of price movements of current output than of reported valuation of capital stock. The decadal ratios thus obtained are averaged over longer periods to convey some idea of the long-term trends. The results of these calculations are now summarized.

1. The ratios of net capital stock to net national product range from 2.5 to close to 4 (disregarding the levels over 4 in the decade of the 1930's when output and rates of utilization of capital were distinctly below the secular levels). The capital-output ratios are somewhat higher if we take capital stock net of retirements but gross of depreciation on assets still in existence: they range from slightly over 3.5 to almost 5.5, again excluding the abnormal decade of the 1930's. Naturally, if we deal with capital stock gross of all consumption, the ratios tend to be still higher, even though we use gross national product rather than net as the denominator: they range from 4.5 to almost 7.

2. Of greatest interest here are the movements in the capital-output ratios over time. Have they been constant in the long run, suggesting the existence of some deep-seated and persistent forces? Or if there have been marked trends, what have been the direction, timing, and magnitude of these trends?

In answering these questions, the longer period averages are of most bearing. Over periods as short as decades, the effects of business cycles and similar short-term disturbances may still be marked—on the numerator and perhaps more so on the denominator. If, then, we concentrate attention on lines 10–14, we find that the net capital stock ratios tended to rise from the first long subperiod, 1869–1888, to the third, 1909–1928, and then declined, regardless of whether the terminal period is 1929–1955, or 1939–1955, that is, omitting the decade of the 1930's. Two aspects of this long rise and subsequent decline in the net capital-output ratios should be noted. First, this movement is observed in both variants. Second, although the capital-output ratio for the last subperiod, 1929–1955, is bolstered by the abnormally low level of the denominator in the 1930's, it is still lower than that for 1909–1928.

An almost identical pattern is observed for the ratios of gross capital, excluding retirements, to net national product: the same distinct rise from 1869–1888 to 1909–1928, the same distinct decline to 1929–1955, even more distinct if we limit the last subperiod to 1939–1955. The somewhat unrealistic gross capital-gross national product ratios, however, reveal a different long-term pattern. These ratios continue to rise throughout, if we use 1929–1955 as the last subperiod. But even here, the rise from 1909–1928 to 1929–1955 is negligible when the "grosser" Commerce concept product total is used as the denominator; and it disappears or becomes negligible for both variants when we omit the depressed 1930's and use 1939–1955 as the last subperiod.

3. This reversal in the long-term movement of the capital-output ratios is but a result of differential changes in the rate of growth of capital stock and of national product, commented upon in connection with Tables 3 and 5. The rate of growth of both capital stock and national product declined over the long period beginning with 1869. But until the end of the 1920's the growth of capital stock more than kept pace with the growth of national product, whereas in recent decades the sharp decline in the proportional volume of capital formation reduced the growth of capital stock far more than it did the long-term level of national product. Both numerator and denominator were still rising during the last subperiod, as they were during the earlier ones; but the retardation in the growth of capital was much greater than that in the growth of product.

The measures in Table 6 are average ratios, relating total capital stock to total national product. But we are interested in capital formation, i.e., additions to or changes in capital stock; and these are perhaps more directly affected by *changes* in national product. It may be helpful, therefore, to calculate the marginal capital-output ratios, i.e., the ratios of changes in capital stock to changes in national product. In this calculation, the results of which are shown in Table 7, we use capital stock at the mid-point of a decade and average annual national product for each decade, dividing the change in the successive intervals in the capital stock totals by the change in the successive decadal levels of national product.[5] The variants parallel those in Table 6; but in grouping the decadal intervals into longer ones, we have intentionally

[5] As already suggested, it would have been more defensible to allow some lag between additions to capital stock and those to output, on the premise that some time may elapse between installation of additional capital equipment and its initial contribution to additional output. In the present calculations no significant time lag is allowed for.

The reason is that no data for any acceptable estimate of the lag are available. Furthermore, unless the lag is substantial—and we have no basis for such an assumption—the extension of the interval over which changes are being compared would reduce to insignificance the proportional effect of the lag on the capital-output ratio. Since we are interested in the long-term capital-output ratios, the lag problem is of little importance here, unless it is of the type discussed in Chapter 4, i.e., of a long-term character observed in some industries in the early periods of their growth.

TABLE 7

RATIO OF CHANGES IN CAPITAL STOCK ᵃ TO CHANGES IN AVERAGE ANNUAL NATIONAL PRODUCT PER DECADE, BASED ON VOLUMES IN 1929 PRICES, 1869–1955

| Intervals ᵇ | Ratio of Changes in Gross Capital Stock to Changes in Gross National Product | | Ratio of Changes in Capital Stock Net of Retirements to Changes in Net National Product | | Ratio of Changes in Net Capital Stock to Changes in Net National Product | |
	Variant I (1)	Commerce Concept (2)	Variant I (3)	Commerce Concept (4)	Variant I (5)	Commerce Concept (6)
Total						
1. 1873–1883	3.7	3.6	3.1	3.0	2.4	2.3
2. 1883–1893	7.7	7.2	6.9	6.4	5.2	4.9
3. 1893–1903	5.8	5.4	4.8	4.5	3.5	3.2
4. 1903–1913	8.1	7.4	7.2	6.4	4.8	4.3
5. 1913–1923	7.1	6.3	5.7	5.0	3.7	3.2
6. 1923–1933	45.0	25.6	33.9	16.2	20.0	9.6
7. 1933–1943	4.4	2.8	1.9	1.1	1.2	0.7
8. 1943–1952 (mid-year)	5.2	5.3	2.3	2.4	1.7	1.8

Total, excluding military

4a. 1903–1913	8.2		7.3		4.8	
5a. 1913–1923	6.7		5.3		3.4	
6a. 1923–1933	44.2		40.4		24.3	
7a. 1933–1943	4.3		1.7		0.9	
8a. 1943–1952 (mid-year)	3.9		1.8		1.2	

Longer Intervals

Total

9. 1873–1893	5.5	5.2	4.7	4.5	3.6	3.4
10. 1893–1913	6.9	6.4	5.9	5.4	4.1	3.8
11. 1903–1923	7.5	6.7	6.3	5.5	4.1	3.7
12. 1923–1952 (mid-year)	6.4	4.9	3.2	2.4	2.1	1.5

Total, excluding military

9a. 1873–1893	5.5		4.7		3.6	
10a. 1893–1913	7.0		6.0		4.1	
11a. 1903–1923	7.3		6.0		3.9	
12a. 1923–1952 (mid-year)	5.7		2.8		1.7	

a Changes in capital stock represent capital formation.

b The interval for capital stock is the difference between successive mid-decade dates indicated in Table 6. The decadal flow figures for national product cover the period from the mid-point of one decade to the next in Table 6. The dates for capital stock and for product flow are the same, and hence the resulting intervals coincide. Dates are for end of year unless otherwise noted.

SOURCE: Calculated from the capital stock and national product estimates underlying Table 6, and summarized in Tables 3 and 5.

assembled them in such a way as to distinguish the period after the 1920's from the earlier ones.

4. The marginal ratios for the decadal intervals are quite variable. Even if we disregard the extreme results for the intervals affected by the depression of the 1930's and the decade immediately following, the variations in the marginal ratios are far wider than those in the average ratios. This was to be expected.

5. Of more importance here are the ratios for the longer intervals. These reflect the pattern of movement over time already shown by the average ratios in Table 6—the rise to the 1920's and the decline thereafter. The only modification here is in timing: for net capital stock, the marginal ratios cease to rise, or show a decline, after the second interval, and this is true also for gross capital stock, net of retirements, excluding the military. But of more interest is the fact that the recent decline is much greater in the marginal than in the average ratios. In other words, the downturn in the capital-output ratios in the recent period, that is, after the 1920's, is much more prominent in the marginal ratios—a mathematical necessity, since reversal in the direction of a line means a greater change in the first differences. But this again points up the question how we can evaluate such a marked turn in the relation between changes in national product and in capital formation.

After this brief summary of the statistical evidence on nationwide capital-product ratios, we address ourselves to the wider implications of the measures, and ask what ratios of this type can contribute to our understanding of the factors that determine levels of and trends in capital formation. Such a broad question can hardly be treated exhaustively; but we touch upon a few major points that should guide us in further analysis.

1. One of the apparently important aspects of the ratio is the underlying notion of technological necessity or constraint—the indispensability of capital in the production of goods, and hence the implied indispensability of capital formation in the production of additional quantities of goods. If this notion is valid, further analysis should stress the technological factors that may have determined the levels of the capital-product ratios indicated in Tables 6 and 7, and the technological changes that may have accounted for the indicated movement of the ratios over time.

This element of technological necessity or constraint actually does exist, as is evident if we consider some specific product. For instance, transportation services of the speed and convenience and at the price that railroads provide cannot be supplied unless there is antecedent capital accumulation in the form of railroad stock, rolling equipment, and so on. The same is true of thousands of products that cannot be turned out by direct labor alone. If we envisage national output as a congeries of specific products and assume that some or many of these specific products literally cannot be produced by direct labor alone, without some reproducible capital, it can be argued that the pre-existence of some capital stock is a necessary condition. In this sense some minimum positive capital-output ratio must exist. But even this conclusion is contingent upon the assumption that national output or product is not limited to items that are producible by natural resources and labor alone.

2. The minimum capital-output ratio assumed above, however, tells us little concerning the actual level of the capital-output ratio except that it is above zero. How large it would or should be is less a matter of technology than of economics; and the greater the economic element, the greater the doubt that the capital-output ratio is an illuminating approach to the analysis of capital formation.

Our reasons for discounting the purely technological constraints are numerous, but one should serve to illustrate our point. To provide railroad services requires some minimum of capital stock: but the track can be of solid and heavy construction or it can be two streaks of rust over the plain; the rolling equipment can be brand-new and modern, or it can be purchased secondhand and boast no new features whatever. In short, wide variations in the real value of the numerator are possible—naturally above some rock bottom minimum—and these variations will be largely governed by economic considerations. Likewise, there may be appreciable variations in the denominator. Under certain conditions, it may be advantageous to run the equipment—the capital—continuously, and the total product (say, during a year) to which the capital stock is related may thus be quite large, and the capital-output ratio low. Under others, it may be more advantageous to run the equipment at lower capacity and, with a correspondingly lower output, the capital-output ratio will be high. Thus, even for a specific product, and even disregarding cyclical fluctuations, it is perfectly possible, indeed quite realistic, to expect that different economic conditions (say, in different countries and epochs, and without regard to any technological changes) will cause a wide range in capital-output

87

ratios, all above the minimum dictated by purely technological constraints.

3. It is because of the possible dominance of these economic elements in the determination of the capital-output ratios that those in which the net capital stock is the numerator have more meaning. When we deduct depreciation we allow the economic elements of opportunity cost to operate in determining the rate of utilization of capital that may still be physically present: the proportion of net to gross capital stock is the economically rational long-term rate of utilization of gross capacity. Hence in relating net capital stock to output we are, in fact, relating capital stock weighted by its rational rate of capacity utilization, whereas, in relating gross capital stock to output the stock is treated as a congeries of physical units whose total capacity is not utilized. For this reason, the behavior of the resulting net capital stock ratios may be explained more easily than the gross ratios.

4. If, with a given technology, economic factors may produce wide variations in the ratio of capital to output for a single product, the economic—as distinct from purely technological—factors must have even greater effects when we deal with a wide congeries of products, among which there can be substitution. If, to continue the earlier illustration, we consider freight transportation services, there is a choice among railroads, trucks, and sometimes water transport, and in this choice the different capital-output ratios, or rather the implied differences in relative cost of capital, may play a part. Thus, if national product is regarded as response to a basket of broadly defined needs—sustenance, clothing, shelter, transportation, and so forth—with specific goods substitutable for each other in satisfying each major category of needs, the existing technology admits of wide differences in the minimum ratio of capital stock to output; and related economic factors widen the range of these differences.

It follows that technology, as a constraining factor, accounts for but a minor part of our problem. To put it simply: given a current level of national income and a stock of technological knowledge, the "required" capital—the stock indispensable for the production of that national income total, broadly subdivided into major final product categories—would be but a small part of the actual capital stock except in the most underdeveloped countries. Even if we coupled the given total national product with some minimum level of product per capita, reference to existing technology would yield—under different economic conditions—a wide range of possible capital-product ratios. This can be

88

clearly seen when one observes the framework of the "engineering" estimates of capital-output ratios: they are calculable only on the basis of detailed specifications of economic conditions—costs of labor, transportation, etc. In short, technological considerations do little to explain why the nationwide ratio of capital to output should be 3 to 1, and not 1 to 1, or 10 to 1. And insofar as the explanation lies in economic rather than technological constraints, the direction of further search may be more clearly suggested by other statistical relations, which do not acquire their meaning from technological implications.

5. What has just been said about the bearing of technological factors on capital-output ratios at a point of time applies also to trends over time. True, technological considerations may provide some hypotheses as to the probable course of long-term movements in capital-output ratios, and hence of volumes of capital formation. Thus, all other conditions being equal, the long-term trend in net capital-output ratios should be downward: "replacement" being substitution of more efficient tools, it should be continuously possible to produce greater output with the same or even smaller *net* capital stock. On the other hand, many technological changes that result in the creation of new products and new tools may raise—at least for a while—the nationwide capital-output ratio, either by requiring more elaborate tools which embody resources that are in a higher ratio to current annual output, or by stimulating expansion of durable capital which for some time is in advance of the growth of final output. In fact, in subsequent discussion of the patterns of capital formation in the major industrial sectors of the economy, we shall use hypotheses based largely on technological considerations.

But granting the usefulness of these hypotheses, one may still doubt that technological factors are dominant in determining the long-term trends in *nationwide* capital formation, or nationwide capital-output ratios, if by technology we mean inventions and improvements associated with the stock of engineering and other knowledge. For economic and other considerations—changing pressures and forms of organization—exercise a major influence on the trends as well as on the levels of the capital-output ratios. Repeatedly in the past, great improvements have been effected in utilization of capital under conditions in which the technological framework has remained unchanged—as in the United States during the 1930's. In the course of its long-term economic growth, a nation can choose between high and low capital-output industries, and its choice will be made in the light of availabilities of resources for capital formation, that is, largely in terms of the costs of withdrawing them from current consumption. With such a choice, and the changing conditions that affect it, long-term trends in nationwide capital-output ratios may well reflect trends in the supply of savings much more than trends in capital presumably required technologically by some pattern of relations between specific baskets of final products and capital indispensable for producing them.

6. The comments above are not meant to minimize the importance of technological processes and changes, and of considerations and hypotheses based upon them, in the analysis of capital formation and economic growth. In fact, we hope they will prove fruitful at a later stage in the analysis when, having dealt as best we can with the determinants of the over-all nationwide rate of capital formation, and of the long-term trends in the nationwide levels, we deal with the separate capital using sectors. At that point, the time sequence of technological change in these sectors, and their different levels of capital-output ratios may help to explain the changing apportionment of nationwide capital formation among major user sectors. Also, if we were concerned with the explanation of trends in total national product, technological changes (additions to the stock of knowledge) would play a major part in the explanation. But in the problem before us here—the attempt to explain the levels of and trends in nationwide capital formation—we find the technological factors overlaid and dominated by a variety of economic and social factors. More specifically, we doubt that pushing the analysis into consideration of the capital-output ratios for types of industries or products would add much to the explanation of the levels and trends in countrywide volumes of capital formation. This conclusion, which reflects the view that the observed capital-output ratios are economic rather than technological measures, leads to the inference that the ratios are radically incomplete in their rationale, in that they do not lead to proper emphasis on the supply of savings—a major factor determining them. In view of the importance of this factor, the technologically colored plausibility of the capital-output ratios is likely to lead us away from rather than toward the forces that determine—at least on a nationwide basis—the levels and trends in capital formation. To direct our attention to these forces, we must restate the relation between capital formation and national product, and regroup our totals.

Trends in Total Capital Formation

Capital Formation and Savings-Income Proportions

The discussion above has indicated the possible importance of viewing capital formation as the saved part of current product, and of directing attention to the factors that govern savings-income proportions and may determine, with changes in income, the levels of capital formation and its trends. This obviously involves calculating the share of gross capital formation in gross national product, and of net capital formation in net product. The shares for the several variants of national product are shown in Table 8. Again, for continuity with the preceding discussion, the underlying totals are in constant prices.

Over the successive decades the proportion of gross capital formation to gross national product shows a fair degree of stability through the decade of the 1920's. It ranges from somewhat over 20 per cent to 26 per cent in the two variants, and, when averaged for periods of not less than twenty years, shows no significant trend before the 1930's. This constancy for some six decades at a level averaging somewhat below one-quarter is one of the few unchanging trends in our analysis so far.

After the 1920's the movement in the proportion of gross capital formation to gross national product is more erratic. In both variants there is a significant drop during the depressed decade of the 1930's, and the subsequent movement is greatly affected by military capital formation. If we include the latter, the proportion after the 1930's is only slightly lower than that preceding the 1930's—at least in Variant I. If we exclude the military, the proportion of gross capital formation even after the 1930's is distinctly lower than that prevailing from 1869–1878 through 1919–1928. On the whole, we can conclude that after some six decades of relative stability, the gross capital formation proportion declined, particularly noticeably if we exclude military capital formation.

The stability in the gross capital formation proportion can be seen as a combination of two opposite trends: in both variants the proportion of capital consumption to gross national product rises, and that of net capital formation declines, the latter particularly after 1908. Net capital formation tends to decline not only as a proportion of gross national product but also as a proportion of net national product. However, the decline is not conspicuous until the 1909–1918 decade. From about 15 per cent of net national product during the first four decades,

91

TABLE 8

PERCENTAGE SHARES OF CAPITAL FORMATION IN NATIONAL PRODUCT, BASED ON
VOLUMES IN 1929 PRICES, 1869–1955

	Per Cent of Gross National Product			Per Cent of Net National Product
Periods	Capital Consumption (1)	Net Capital Formation (2)	Gross Capital Formation (3)	Net Capital Formation (4)
VARIANT I				
Total				
1. 1869–1878	9.5	13.9	23.4	15.4
2. 1879–1888	9.8	13.1	22.9	14.5
3. 1889–1898	12.1	14.0	26.0	15.9
4. 1899–1908	11.3	12.9	24.2	14.6
5. 1909–1918	12.3	11.2	23.4	12.7
6. 1919–1928	12.3	9.9	22.3	11.3
7. 1929–1938	13.0	1.8	14.8	2.1
8. 1939–1948	14.2	6.1	20.3	7.1
9. 1946–1955	15.5	4.9	20.4	5.8
Total, excluding military				
5a. 1909–1918	12.3	10.3	22.6	11.7
6a. 1919–1928	11.5	10.4	21.9	11.8
7a. 1929–1938	12.6	1.8	14.4	2.1
8a. 1939–1948	12.1	3.7	15.9	4.3
9a. 1946–1955	12.2	6.6	18.8	7.5
Longer Periods (averages of percentages)				
Total				
10. 1869–1888	9.6	13.5	23.2	15.0
11. 1889–1908	11.7	13.4	25.1	15.2
12. 1909–1928	12.3	10.6	22.8	12.0
13. 1929–1955	14.1	4.2	18.3	4.9
Total, excluding military				
10. 1869–1888	9.6	13.5	23.2	15.0
11. 1889–1908	11.7	13.4	25.1	15.2
12a. 1909–1928	11.9	10.4	22.2	11.8
13a. 1929–1955	12.4	3.6	16.0	4.1

(continued)

Trends in Total Capital Formation

TABLE 8 (concluded)

Periods	Per Cent of Gross National Product			Per Cent of Net National Product
	Capital Consumption (1)	Net Capital Formation (2)	Gross Capital Formation (3)	Net Capital Formation (4)
	COMMERCE CONCEPT			
Total				
14. 1869–1878	9.3	13.7	22.9	15.1
15. 1879–1888	9.5	12.7	22.2	14.0
16. 1889–1898	11.6	13.5	25.1	15.2
17. 1899–1908	10.7	12.3	23.0	13.8
18. 1909–1918	11.5	10.5	22.1	11.9
19. 1919–1928	11.4	9.2	20.6	10.4
20. 1929–1938	11.8	1.6	13.4	1.9
21. 1939–1948	11.2	4.8	16.0	5.4
22. 1946–1955	13.2	4.1	17.3	4.8
Longer Periods (averages of percentages)				
23. 1869–1888	9.4	13.2	22.6	14.6
24. 1889–1908	11.2	12.9	24.0	14.5
25. 1909–1928	11.4	9.8	21.4	11.2
26. 1929–1955	11.9	3.4	15.3	3.9

Because of rounding, detail will not necessarily add to total.

SOURCE: *Gross and net national product:* Decade averages given in or calculated from Tables R-2 and R-12 (see also notes to Table 5).

Capital consumption and capital formation: Decade averages given in or calculated from Tables R-5, R-8, R-15, and R-17.

For each decade, the percentage was calculated from the arithmetic mean of absolutes, not as the arithmetic mean of the percentage for each year in the decade.

The averages of percentages in lines 10–13, 10a–13a, and 23–26, were derived from the decadal entries in the lines above. For 1929–1955 we computed the weighted mean of the percentage for 1929–1938, 1939–1948, and the seven-year period 1949–1955.

the proportion of net capital formation drops to between 11.2 and 12 per cent in 1909–1928, is catastrophically affected by the depression of the 1930's, and in the prosperous decade, 1946–1955, constitutes only 4.8 to 5.8 per cent.

If we view these capital formation shares as savings proportions, there is one obvious limitation to the evidence in Table 8: it relates to volumes in constant prices. Conversion to constant prices is useful if our interest lies in the allocation of real resources between flow of goods to consumers and additions to capital stock. Our interest here lies, however, in the allocation of money income (including the proportionately small amount of income in kind) between that used for consumption purchases and that constituting savings. Since decisions by individuals and firms between spending and saving are perhaps more closely related to money income, it may be more useful to study capital formation or nationwide savings proportions for totals in current prices. For this reason we include here, for the first time in our discussion, estimates based on totals in current prices (Table 9).

The proportions based on the totals in current prices show movements somewhat different from those in the proportions based on the constant price totals, the reason being that the price trend in capital formation (affected largely by construction) shows a somewhat greater long-term rise than that in national product as a whole. We now list the findings based on values in current prices.

1. The proportion of gross capital formation to gross national product is relatively constant, at a level close to or somewhat above 20 per cent in both Variant I and the Commerce series. For the longer terminal period, 1929–1955, there is some decline in Variant I if we exclude the military, and in the Commerce estimates even in the total. For the decade 1946–1955, however, the level in each set of estimates is about the same as that prevailing before the 1930's. Thus, by and large, one can conclude that, for totals in current prices, there has been a rough long-term constancy in the gross capital formation proportion—at about or somewhat over 20 per cent.

2. The proportion of capital consumption to gross national product rises, both in Variant I and in the Commerce series. For the longer periods, the rise is from somewhat over 8 to 13.3 or 15.6 per cent. As we shall see in the next chapter, it is a reflection partly of the retardation in the rate of growth of capital formation itself, partly of the shift from the longer-lived construction to the shorter-lived producers' equipment.

3. The proportion of net capital formation to net national product is fairly constant until 1909–1918: between 13 and 13.9 per cent in Variant I and between 12.4 and 13.2 per cent in the Commerce series. It drops down to either 11.8 or 10.8 per cent in 1909–1928, and declines drastically thereafter. The highest recent rate, 9.0 per cent, is for

Trends in Total Capital Formation

TABLE 9

PERCENTAGE SHARES OF CAPITAL FORMATION IN NATIONAL PRODUCT, BASED ON
VOLUMES IN CURRENT PRICES, 1869–1955

Periods	Per Cent of Gross National Product			Per Cent of Net National Product
	Capital Consumption (1)	Net Capital Formation (2)	Gross Capital Formation (3)	Net Capital Formation (4)
VARIANT I				
Total				
1. 1869–1878	8.0	12.3	20.3	13.4
2. 1879–1888	8.7	11.8	20.6	13.0
3. 1889–1898	10.7	12.5	23.1	13.9
4. 1899–1908	10.5	12.4	22.8	13.8
5. 1909–1918	11.5	10.6	22.1	12.0
6. 1919–1928	12.1	10.3	22.4	11.7
7. 1929–1938	13.8	2.1	15.9	2.5
8. 1939–1948	15.7	6.1	21.8	7.3
9. 1946–1955	17.6	6.0	23.6	7.2
Total, excluding military				
5a. 1909–1918	11.5	9.4	20.9	10.7
6a. 1919–1928	11.3	10.8	22.0	12.1
7a. 1929–1938	13.4	2.1	15.5	2.5
8a. 1939–1948	13.2	3.9	17.1	4.5
9a. 1946–1955	14.2	7.7	21.9	9.0
Longer Periods (averages of percentages)				
Total				
10. 1869–1888	8.4	12.0	20.4	13.2
11. 1889–1908	10.6	12.4	23.0	13.8
12. 1909–1928	11.8	10.4	22.2	11.8
13. 1929–1955	15.6	4.7	20.2	5.6
Total, excluding military				
10. 1869–1888	8.4	12.0	20.4	13.2
11. 1889–1908	10.6	12.4	23.0	13.8
12a. 1909–1928	11.4	10.1	21.4	11.4
13a. 1929–1955	13.7	4.2	17.9	4.9

(continued)

TABLE 9 (concluded)

Periods	Per Cent of Gross National Product			Per Cent of Net National Product
	Capital Consumption (1)	Net Capital Formation (2)	Gross Capital Formation (3)	Net Capital Formation (4)

COMMERCE CONCEPT

Total

14. 1869–1878	7.8	11.9	19.8	12.9
15. 1879–1888	8.4	11.4	19.8	12.4
16. 1889–1898	10.2	11.8	22.0	13.2
17. 1899–1908	9.8	11.6	21.4	12.9
18. 1909–1918	10.7	9.9	20.5	11.0
19. 1919–1928	11.2	9.5	20.6	10.7
20. 1929–1938	12.6	1.9	14.5	2.2
21. 1939–1948	12.6	4.9	17.5	5.6
22. 1946–1955	15.1	5.1	20.2	6.0

Longer Periods (averages of percentages)

23. 1869–1888	8.1	11.6	19.8	12.6
24. 1889–1908	10.0	11.7	21.7	13.0
25. 1909–1928	11.0	9.7	20.6	10.8
26. 1929–1955	13.3	3.9	17.2	4.5

Because of rounding, detail will not necessarily add to total.

SOURCE: *Gross and net national product:* Decade averages given in or calculated from Tables R-1, R-6, and R-11. The Commerce series was estimated by converting the gross national product series in constant prices (see Table 8) to current prices by an index calculated by extrapolating the implicit price index for 1929–1938 by the implicit price index in our Variant III series for the earlier years. From the resulting estimates of gross national product in current prices we subtracted our estimate of capital consumption (see below).

Capital consumption and capital formation: Decade averages given in or calculated from Tables R-4, R-8, R-14, and R-16. For procedure used in calculating the percentages for decades, and the averages of percentages for longer periods, see notes to Table 8.

Variant I for 1946–1955, for the share of net capital formation in net national product, both excluding net military investment.

We may now ask how the view of capital formation as the saved portion of national product helps us understand the factors that determine the volumes of and trends in capital formation. It would be impossible here, and for that matter anywhere—with our limited knowledge—to develop a cogent theory that would connect the saving process with capital formation, and would explain why the levels and trends of capital formation are of the order suggested by our estimates. But it is possible and useful to sketch the lines of connection and influence and thus point the way for further analysis.

In this outline we begin with net capital formation, try to connect it with the net saving process, and then deal with capital consumption, the other component of gross capital formation, treating it as a function of the long-term cumulation of past net capital additions.

1. Our initial observation is that net capital formation may be financed out of personal savings (including those of unincorporated enterprises, whether farm or nonfarm), out of undistributed profits or net income of corporations, and out of government funds (the excess of current revenues over current expenditures). Goldsmith's monumental study of saving helps us to see roughly the relative importance of these three sources of financing in total net savings or total net capital formation since 1897. During the two periods unaffected by war and major depressions, 1899–1908 and 1919–1928, personal savings accounted for over 70 per cent of all net savings or net capital formation; corporate savings, for about 21 per cent; and government savings, for almost 7 per cent.[6] During the war-affected decades, 1909–1918 and 1939–1948, governments incurred substantial dissavings, and total personal savings were either close to or far exceeded total net capital formation. With total net savings or net capital formation averaging in nonwar and nondepression decades between 12 and 13 per cent of net national product, personal savings contributed between 8.5 and slightly over 9 per cent of net national product, corporations almost 3 per cent of national product, and governments somewhat less than 1 per cent of national product. In terms of disposable personal income, personal savings in the "normal" periods were about 10 per cent.

These rough orders of magnitude—which would have to be modified if we carried the estimates back to the nineteenth century when net savings or net capital formation proportions were somewhat higher—indicate that we must pay most attention to the factors that determine personal savings. In a country with an economic and social structure

[6] See Raymond W. Goldsmith, *A Study of Saving in the United States*, Vol. I (Princeton University Press, 1955), Table T-1, p. 345. In Table S-12, p. 271, Goldsmith shows the shares of major saver groups in the "normal" period to be about 72 per cent for personal, 20.4 per cent for corporate, and 7.4 per cent for government.

such as ours, the proportion of net savings that can be contributed either by corporations or by governments will necessarily be limited. The executive branches of the government are not permitted to use large proportions of current revenues—let alone large proportions of total national product—for capital investment. There is little justification for levying taxes upon individuals and the private business sector to permit the government to finance capital undertakings without interest charges, except in a major war when the government is forced to make huge military capital investments. Under such conditions current expenditures are likely to exceed current revenues, so that not only military capital formation but even part of current expenditures may be financed out of savings of individuals and corporations. In other words, the secular level of government capital formation financed out of current revenues rather than borrowing, in nonauthoritarian societies like the United States, is bound to be a minor fraction of national product and, indeed, of total net savings or capital formation.[7]

The limits on the net savings contributed by corporations are not as narrow as those on governments' contributions, but they are confining nevertheless. To begin with, net income originating in corporations is only a fraction of the country's national income: since 1929 the share has been somewhat more than one-half, and it was probably lower in the earlier decades.[8] The share of national income originating in corporations that could be classified as total net profits, after all expenses but before payment of taxes and dividends, is limited by competition of other corporations and by noncorporate enterprises engaged in business. It is limited also by taxes, which increase as net profits increase whether the profits are paid out as dividends or retained as undistributed earnings. And, finally, even disregarding the large corporate sector in public utilities that is subject to special limiting regulations, most corporate business is carried on by units whose shares are traded on public investment markets. Any tendency to keep the level of undistributed profits unduly high exposes such corporations—if their

---

[7] This statement is, of course, too simplified and rigid. Changing technology may increase the share of government savings, by permitting the use of taxes for capital investment, such as construction of highways. Changing demand may induce governments to use taxes for construction of hospitals, and changing political views may well enlarge the share of governments in savings and capital formation even in times of peace. The statement in the text is a capsule summary of limitations on the share of governments in the saving process as they characterized most of the period before World War II.

[8] See *U.S. Income and Output* (Supplement, *Survey of Current Business*, 1958), Table I-12, pp. 134–135.

shares are widely held—to possible "capture" by outsiders, since the price of their shares may be more affected by the level of their dividend payments than by that of their net profits. All these circumstances combined would tend to keep corporate savings at limited proportions of net profits, at even lower proportions of net income originating in the corporate sector, and, finally, at quite low proportions of national income or net national product. These comments should, of course, be supplemented by analysis showing the quantitative limits in actual operation—a task beyond the scope of this study. However, although the comments do not indicate why the share of corporate savings in recent decades is less than 3 per cent of net national product or only about one-fifth of all net savings, they do suggest the variety of factors that limit rather narrowly the share of corporate savings.

2. Turning to the main source of net savings, individuals, we begin by suggesting that the indicated savings proportions—about 10 per cent of their disposable income in "normal" times, and perhaps 11 or 12 per cent in the decades from 1870 to 1900—seem quite low. It should be remembered that according to our estimates, per capita income, and presumably also per capita disposable income, was rising over the period at a rate of about 17 per cent per decade. Such a rate means that in just two decades per capita income in real terms would rise from an assumed initial level of 100 to 136.9. Assume for the sake of illustration that, with a constant population, consumption was 100 in the first decade (i.e., no savings) and that by the third decade consumption rose only 10 per cent. Then in that third decade individuals' savings would be 26.9 out of 136.9 or close to 20 per cent. The illustration is unrealistic in several ways, but it serves to stress the major point: the persistence of a limited ratio of personal savings to income, under conditions of a relatively high rate of growth in real per capita income, means that all but a small fraction of the gain in income is absorbed in increased consumption. It follows that one major factor in explaining the rate of personal savings, under such conditions of growth as occurred in the United States, is the great responsiveness of consumption, as evidenced by its capacity to absorb all but 10 per cent (slightly more in the earlier decades) of the gain in per capita income.

This is hardly the place to deal with the aspects of the economic and social structure of the United States that explain this pressure for ever-rising levels of consumption per capita. Many come easily to mind: the relative freedom of individuals and consumers; the widespread

social mobility that has characterized our society; the increasing concentration of population in cities, where the practice of imitation (the
so-called "demonstration effect") is so natural, making higher consumption levels necessary if only to offset the increasing discomforts
of urban life. Indeed, the fact that economic growth has been attained so largely by technological discovery and improvement—creating new products for ultimate consumers—and that this technological
change has been further impelled by imbalances created in the past
(with more cars creating the need for more roads, and the like), suggests that rising consumption levels are a built-in feature of the whole
process of economic growth in this country.[9]

With the pressure for high-level consumption in mind, any consideration of why the personal savings-income proportion was at a
given level, would involve analysis of the factors that impel such savings, despite the pressure for use of current income for current consumption. Such analysis would proceed most effectively from the oversimplified but nevertheless useful dichotomy between the vast majority
of people whose income position is below the very top and whose
savings, therefore, have to be tailored to the indispensable needs which
such savings must satisfy, and the very top group of income recipients
who can afford a much higher savings-income rate without limiting
their consumption standards. Our current data on savings-income patterns are unfortunately affected too much by the use of annual income as the basis for classification by size, and the transient elements
in such income make for an exaggerated contrast between savings in
the top brackets and dissavings in the lower brackets. We might divide
the whole body of personal savers into two groups: the overwhelming
majority—say, the lower 95 per cent classified by their relatively permanent income position—who perhaps account for 80 per cent of income and 50 per cent of total personal net savings; and the top 5 per
cent who account for the other 50 per cent of total personal savings.
A countrywide savings-income rate of 10 per cent under these conditions implies a savings-income ratio of about 6 per cent (or 5:80) for
the lower 95 per cent, and of 25 per cent (5:20) for the top 5 per cent.
The figures are illustrative, intended only to suggest the broad lines of
the dichotomy.[10]

[9] See Ruth P. Mack, "Trends in American Consumption and the Aspiration to
Consume," *American Economic Review*, May 1956, pp. 55–68.
[10] Much of the discussion that follows was presented in Kuznets, "Economic Growth
and Income Inequality," *American Economic Review*, March 1955, pp. 1–28, par-

3. For the lower group of income recipients, hereafter referred to as the L group, savings are geared to minimum needs, which may arise from many considerations: cash balances against sudden emergencies; saving for future bulk purchases or expenses; and saving for retirement. We know too little about practices with respect to these savings needs, but the dominant one—saving for retirement—lends itself to a simple illustration that indicates the major demographic and economic forces involved.

Assume for simplicity that the working, income-earning life of an individual is 40 years, from, say, age 20 to age 60; the expected retirement period is 10 years, from 60 to 70; and no allowance is made for any legacy or the like. Assume also that the income needs during retirement are one-half the total annual income during active life. Then if we disregard interest accumulation, savings needed for retirement would equal one-eighth of the average annual income during the 40 years of active life ($\frac{10}{40}$ multiplied by $\frac{1}{2}$), a savings-income ratio of 12.5 per cent. An allowance for interest, which would depend upon the rate that is assumed, the time pattern of earnings, and the time pattern of retirement expenditures, would presumably bring the savings-income ratio well below 12.5 per cent.

However, if population, other demographic variables, and per worker income are constant, and the retirement savings scheme out-

---

ticularly pp. 7–12. See also Appendixes C and D of *idem,* "International Differences in Capital Formation and Financing," *Capital Formation and Economic Growth* (Special Conference Series, No. 6, Princeton for NBER, 1955), pp. 82–106.

This chapter was written before I read Milton Friedman's *A Theory of the Consumption Function* (Princeton for NBER, 1957). His analysis would lead me to qualify the magnitude of difference in the savings-income ratios suggested, although it is already much narrower than that suggested by statistical data for pre-World War II years. But these would be largely qualifications, for two reasons. First, I am dealing here with permanent income more in the sense of lifetime income than with the distinctive concept that Friedman employs—the empirical counterpart of which appears to be a level characterizing a period of about three years. For lifetime income, I see no escape from the conclusion that units whose average income is near the subsistence level would have a savings-income ratio of close to zero; and that units whose lifetime income is high in the scale, and who would presumably wish to preserve that position for themselves and their descendants, would have fairly high savings-income ratios. Second, even Friedman finds that his permanent savings-income ratios for entrepreneurs are double those for employees; and while he ascribes the difference to a greater income dispersion for the former, the association with the difference in permanent income levels is not denied. It is quite possible that further differentiation among socio-economic groups distinguished by different lifetime income levels (or even Friedman's permanent income levels) would yield a further variation in the savings-income ratio.

lined above is actually followed, total dissavings of retired persons would exactly equal the current savings of people still in the active labor force, and aggregate savings would be zero, not 12.5 per cent or less of total income of the population. But population and per capita income do grow. In the United States the income mass or total income in real terms grew at the rate of about 37.5 per cent per decade. In the illustration above, the average time span between active and retired life is something like 25 years. Hence the income level and savings of active workers exceed the expenditure-dissavings level of the retired group by the ratio of (1.375 raised to the power of $2\frac{1}{2}$) to 1, or 2.217. The aggregate savings then are 12.5 per cent multiplied by 1.217, or roughly 15 per cent of an income mass which in relation to the actual is as 1 is to 2.217. The implicit aggregate net savings-income fraction is then 15 per cent divided by 2.217, or slightly less than 7 per cent.

The illustration is, of course, hypothetical: the empirical coefficients are roughly realistic, but the assumption of retirement needs is purely notional. Its importance, however, is that it suggests the major factors that determine the aggregate savings-net income ratio for the overwhelming proportion of the income earning population: not only their savings plans but also the relative magnitudes of the active and the retired population, and the differences between their expenditure levels. It would be relatively easy to shape the empirical coefficient to yield an aggregate savings-income proportion of some 5 to 6 per cent. While this would be partly a matter of arbitrary design, one should note that many of the coefficients used—the relative duration of active and of retirement life, the rate of growth in numbers of population and of active workers, and in per capita real income—are fairly realistic. One can legitimately argue that in this direction lies the promise of explaining why the personal savings-income proportions in the United States were 10 to 12 per cent, and not 2 to 3, or 20 to 30. Such an explanation would also bring us close to understanding why the net capital formation proportions in net national product before the 1930's ranged from 11 to 14 per cent, and not from 2 to 4, or from 20 to 30.[11]

[11] The analysis in the text, which deals with savings and dissavings associated with retirement, can be applied to savings connected with or in anticipation of any future expenditures (dissavings). Thus, in the early years of marriage before the arrival of children, funds may be saved as a reserve against expenditures on children; and then, with their arrival, a period of dissaving may ensue. The pattern of analysis of such expenditure-oriented savings, and the problem of weighting the individual life-cycle patterns into aggregates in a growing population with growing per capita income would be the same as those suggested in the text.

4. This outline of the factors involved in determining the personal savings-income rate for the L group at a given point of time, is useful also in suggesting the possible long-term trends. In general, the rapid rise in real income per capita suggests the possibility of an upward movement in the savings-income ratio. That movement may be offset to some extent by such counteracting factors as the desire and need for higher consumption occasioned partly by changing conditions of life (urbanization, need for greater education and training, and the like) and partly by the stimulus of new products. The more interesting implication of the scheme outlined above, however, lies in the demographic and income-growth factors. All other conditions being equal, retardation in the rate of growth of population and of per capita income would produce a lower aggregate net savings-income ratio. Thus, if in the illustrative example we had assumed that the population and per capita income grew at the rate of 5 per cent per decade, yielding a decadal rate of growth of total income of 10.25 per cent (rather than the 37.5 per cent shown in our Variant I estimates and used in the illustration), the aggregate net personal savings rate derived for the L group would have been only 2.7 per cent instead of about 7. (With a decadal rate of growth of 10.25 per cent, the cumulation over twenty-five years yields an income mass of 1.276, and the savings rate equals 12.5 per cent multiplied by 0.276, divided by 1.276.)

It follows that, with the retardation in the rate of growth of national income observed in the United States, the factors suggested above as determining savings would make for a secularly lower personal savings-income ratio—provided the other assumptions of the hypothetical scheme remained constant. But they need not remain constant: the duration of retirement life relative to that of active life may become longer than that assumed in the calculation; the proportion of active-life income desired for retirement life may rise. Moreover, other needs for savings—emergencies or bulk purchases—though minor, may be subject to trends of their own. Clearly, we are dealing here with a complex situation in which forces of vast variety are operating, some making for a higher savings-income ratio for the L group, others tending to produce a lower ratio as time goes on. All we can do here is indicate the factors that seem important, and that would therefore suggest directions in which further research could fruitfully be undertaken. It seems particularly useful, also, to indicate in such an outline the relations by which one aspect of economic growth, such as the retardation in the rate of growth of total income, is connected—in ways that may not have been stressed heretofore—with another, such as the possible constancy of the savings-income ratio in the face of a rising per capita income, or even some tendency for the savings-income ratio to drop.

5. Minimum needs can play only a limited role in determining the savings patterns of the upper group of income recipients (the U group), and consequently, the problem of explaining the level of the savings-income ratio for this group is more difficult. Why, for instance, did we assume, in our illustration of the dichotomy, that the savings-income ratio for the U group was 25 per cent? It could, presumably, have been 50 per cent, since consumption per capita of the U group would still have been over twice that of the L group. Yet if the savings-income ratio of the U group had been 50 rather than 25 per cent, the countrywide personal savings-income ratio would have been 15 rather than 10 per cent.

What, then, limits the savings-income ratio for the U group? It is difficult even to suggest an answer, in our general ignorance of the economics of the small upper groups in society. The only complex of relevant factors that comes to mind is suggested by the continuous gradation of per capita consumption levels and savings proportions that one finds in cross-section studies of family income and expenditures. In these arrays of families grouped in increasing order of income position, there is always a continuous and gradual rise in consumption per head, in savings per head, and in the proportion of savings to income. Particularly in a society like that of the United States, there is no dichotomy of the oversimplified type suggested in our illustration. There is no clear line of division and contrast between the "poor" masses and the "rich" elite, but a great range of "middle" classes forming a continuous bridge from the lowest to the highest levels of the income distribution. The implication of this gradation is that patterns of social and economic life produce—i.e., make possible, and to some extent compel—ever-rising consumption and expenditure standards with rises in relative position in the long-term income scale.

This implication has direct bearing upon our question in the sense of setting some upper limits to the savings-income fraction. To illustrate: at the upper reaches of the L group, before we pass into the U group, the savings-income fraction may be as high as, say, 12 per cent (compared with the average for the L group of about 6 per cent). The next group in the array, in the lower reaches of the U group, may have a per capita income, say, 10 per cent higher; but it would tend to have a consumption level per capita that would also be somewhat higher. Even if its consumption level were not higher but merely equal to that of the upper segment of the L group, its savings-income ratio could not exceed (12 + 10): 110, or 20 per cent. If, then, consumption levels rise with a rise in the income level, that is, if differentials in consumption persist in response to differentials in income, either because human beings naturally adjust themselves to higher standards of living or because they regard consumption as a symbol of higher social position and thus a means of setting themselves above their neighbors, there are definite limits to the savings-income ratio of the U group. These limits are in fact determined by the desire and need to maintain consumption levels above those of the lower neighboring economic groups.[12]

The precise working out of this hypothesis in quantitative terms, demonstrating why the savings-income ratio for the U group happens to be x rather than y, or s times the ratio for the L group rather than t, would involve analysis of the whole income and consumption structure of the population of this country. Here again all we can do is point out the connecting links—this time between the factors that motivate high-level consumption and the limits set upon the savings-income ratio. But even this is of value, if it directs our attention into the proper channels.

6. What bearing have the savings-income proportions upon long-term trends? For the U group it lies partly in the trend in their savings-income ratio, partly in the trend in their share in total income. An increase in either means a secular rise in the ratio of aggregate savings to total income; a decline means a secular decline in the ratio.

Little new can be said here relative to long-term trends in the savings-income ratio for the U group proper: given the linking of their consumption patterns with the consumption levels of the rest of the population, their savings-income ratio would be subject to the same growth factors as the ratio for the rest of the population would be. And what we have said above about the pressures for high and rising levels of consumption expenditures would apply *pari passu* to the U group, so far as the effects of technical progress in the way of new products and the continuous desire for groups to differentiate themselves from those immediately below would produce a rise in the

[12] In this connection see the emphasis on the demonstration effect and the interdependence of the tastes of consumer units in James S. Duesenberry, *Income, Saving, and the Theory of Consumer Behavior* (Harvard University Press, 1949).

consumption levels of the U group and thus prevent its savings-income ratio from rising.

In dealing with the trends in the income shares, we encounter a new problem. The inequality in the distribution of savings may well be greater, and in fact was greater, in recent decades in the United States, than that in the distribution of property incomes, and hence of assets. This is because of the frequency of a combination of large service incomes with large property incomes. All other conditions being equal, persistence of a higher share of savings than of property in the hands of the U group should result in an even greater concentration of property, hence of property incomes, hence of total incomes. In other words, in the greater concentration of savings in the U group there is a built-in tendency to produce increasing concentration of income—and, to that extent, even further concentration of savings. It is important, *therefore, to consider whether any factors tend in the long run to* counteract the concentration of savings, and the inferred effect—the secular rise in the income share of the U group.

These counteracting factors can be briefly listed. The most obvious is, of course, intervention on the part of society, in the form of economic legislation relating to both inheritance and income. Just as inheritance taxation was introduced to break up the cumulation of large property holdings—the mechanism by which the tendency suggested above operates—so, in recent decades, progressive income taxation was introduced to limit the relative excess of the per unit incomes of the U group over the per unit incomes of the L group.

But there are more important if less obvious factors. In the demographic growth of a country like the United States, with natural increase much lower in the U group than in the L group, and immigration swelling the numbers in the L group, the relative numerical increase in an initially top group is smaller than in that of the rest of the population. Consequently the U group of the 1870's comprising the top 5 per cent cannot, with its descendants, account for the top 5 per cent of the population in the 1920's. It follows that on this account alone the U group of the 1920's includes a fairly substantial proportion of units that have come up from the lower ranks and the cumulation of whose wealth may not lead to as much concentration of income. An even more important factor lies in the dynamism of the economy of the United States, in the shift of focus of growth, and hence of sources of wealth, from one industry to another, from one area to another. With such shifts, the successful entrepreneurs of a generation ago or their descendants are rarely among the ranks of the successful today. This change in identity of successful entrepreneurs means continuous turnover in the composition of the top group and prevents persistent accumulation of wealth in the same hands. Finally, one must also consider the service income component of the income of the U group. Already high and tending to be concentrated in the high per capita earnings sectors, it is not likely to rise as rapidly as the per capita service income of the L group, which is affected both by increases within industrial sectors and by shifts in the distribution of the gainfully occupied from sectors with lower per capita earnings to those with higher per capita earnings.

These comments, which suggest the factors that counteract any possible concentration of income in the hands of the U group, in and of themselves tell nothing about the possible trends in its income share. The continuous entry of new economically successful units may be accompanied by a rising share of income for the U group, if the new units capture more of the growing income than was captured by the successful units of preceding generations. Or the share of the U group in income may decline, if the sources of new wealth are not as large proportionately as they were in earlier times. All one can say is that prima facie there is no case for expecting the trend in the income share of the U group to be upward; and that in more recent times factors operated to reduce that share.

7. With the income share and savings-income ratio constant, the savings contribution of the U group, as a percentage of net national product, would also tend to be constant in the long run; or would diminish if, under legislative and other pressures, property yields were to decline and progressive income taxation rates increase. There are also a variety of factors that could keep the savings-income ratio of the L group constant, and this constant ratio, combined with retardation in the rate of growth of total income, could result in a downward turn of the long-term savings-income proportion. While the comments above are far short of an explanation of the trends in the aggregate personal savings-income proportion, they do point to and emphasize the directions in which the explanatory hypotheses might be found and the fields in which further data could be mobilized for specifying and testing them.

In the present connection, an additional factor should be noted. The preceding discussion suggested that there is no firm ground for expecting a secular rise in the proportion of personal savings to income, and that in fact some factors would make for a downward trend in this proportion. However, it must be remembered that we are discussing money savings here, whereas countrywide net capital formation proportions, even in current prices, reflect real processes. It is quite possible for the money savings-income proportion for all individuals and even for all corporations to rise, while the countrywide net capital formation proportion declines, because governments may absorb savings for uses that are not additions to capital stock. This is, in fact, what happened during World War II and in some of the postwar years when military expenditures were unusually large.

This points to an additional factor that in recent decades contributed to a downward trend in the net capital formation proportion— a factor that comes from the uses side, rather than from the savings side, although technically it can be expressed as a decline in the contribution of government savings. There is no need to stress the possible weight of this factor in the present and foreseeable future, considering the major shifts that have occurred in international relations and the greater burdens that governments have had to assume to preserve the security of their countries.

8. The comments so far have borne directly upon the net capital formation levels and trends, viewing the levels as savings proportions of net national product and linking both levels and trends with the factors that determined levels of and trends in personal savings-income ratios. We conclude with a brief outline of the relations between the net capital and gross capital proportions or—what amounts to the same thing—the relations between net capital formation and capital consumption.

In the simplest model, which is adequate for our purposes, capital consumption is a straight-line function of past capital formation, and it is at any given time equal to some fraction of the gross value of capital stock, net of retirements. Given the life span of capital equipment, the ratio of depreciable capital (fixed durable) to nondepreciable (inventories and foreign claims), and the past rate of growth of net capital formation, it is possible to derive capital consumption and hence gross capital formation.

To illustrate: assume that, in the past, net fixed (subject to depreciation) capital formation and the useful life of capital equipment remained constant. Capital consumption would then equal net fixed capital formation, and in fact retirements would equal total capital consumption. For under these conditions, the sum of the fractions representing current depreciation can be shown to equal one-half the constant annual gross fixed capital formation, or a full year's net fixed capital additions. In this case, net fixed capital formation would be 50 per cent of gross fixed capital formation; and the size of the proportion of gross fixed capital formation to gross national product would be a direct function of net fixed capital formation. Thus, if the latter is 15 and net national product 100, then the gross fixed capital formation proportion would be 30 divided by 115, or roughly 26 per cent.

The illustration can be modified to allow for the growth of net fixed capital formation at a certain percentage rate. With such growth, the earlier levels of capital accumulation, which affect current depreciation, are below those of current net additions; fixed capital stock gross of depreciation and net of retirements, the base that determines depreciation charges, will not be twice net fixed capital stock but somewhat less; capital consumption charges, instead of being equal to net fixed capital formation, will be smaller; and net fixed capital formation will be more than 50 per cent of gross. In general, the higher the rate of growth of net fixed capital formation and the longer the period of life from entry into use to retirement, the lower the ratio of capital consumption to net fixed capital formation, the higher the ratio of the latter to gross fixed capital formation, and the smaller the relative excess of the gross fixed capital formation proportion over the net. The lower the rate of growth of net fixed capital formation and the shorter the life of capital goods, the higher the ratio of capital consumption to current net fixed capital formation, the lower the ratio of the latter to gross fixed capital formation, and the greater the relative excess of the gross fixed capital formation proportion over the net.[13]

This simple model can serve as an outline for explaining both the levels of and the long-term trends in the capital consumption and

---

[13] For an algebraic analysis of these relations see Appendix B of my paper, "International Differences in Capital Formation and Financing," in *Capital Formation and Economic Growth*, pp. 76–81. The analysis there is in terms of gross national product and the gross capital formation proportion, but can be restated in terms of rates of growth of net national product and assumed constancy of the net capital formation proportion.

The formulation in the text is limited to depreciable capital. Total capital also includes inventories and claims against foreign countries, neither of which is subject to depreciation. Hence the relations indicated in the text apply to gross and net *total* capital formation only if the trends in the shares of the nondepreciable components are of limited magnitude and do not offset the effects of retardation in the rate of growth of fixed—depreciable—capital formation.

gross capital formation proportions, given the levels of and trends in the net capital formation share in net national product. Additional data are needed on the period of useful life of durable capital goods subject to depreciation, the method of apportioning depreciation over time (whether along a straight line or by some curve), and the proportion of total capital subject to depreciation. Such additional data are, to be sure, reflections of a variety of factors: the rapidity of obsolescence induced by technological progress and changes in taste (the latter being to some extent a function of the former); and the factors that determine the share in total capital of fixed durable assets, and the shares of inventories and of claims against foreign countries. Some light may be shed on these factors in the next chapter when we consider the distribution of total capital formation by type of capital good. For the present it is sufficient to indicate the identity of the empirical coefficients and the factors they represent, in passing from the net capital formation proportion to the gross.

The bearing upon long-term trends is also clear. In particular, if as suggested above, the net capital formation proportion in the long run tends to be constant at best, while there is retardation in the rate of growth of net national product, it follows that the rate of growth of net capital formation must decline. And indeed we found such retardation in discussing the long-term movement of net capital formation shown in Table 2. Given such retardation, it follows from the simple model above—which assumes constancy of useful life of durable capital and of the proportion of total capital subject to depreciation— that the proportion of capital consumption to net capital formation is bound to show an upward trend; the proportion of net capital formation to gross capital formation, a declining trend; and the gross capital formation proportion, less of a declining trend than the net capital formation proportion and, if the latter proportion is declining, the gross capital formation proportion may fail to show a decline. Thus, the various lines of connection outlined above do in fact promise an explanation of the results in Tables 8 and 9 insofar as they reveal a long-term decline in the net capital formation proportion coincident with rough stability in the gross capital formation proportion.

Savings and Capital Formation

The discussion in the two preceding sections elaborates our view that the explanation of the levels of and trends in capital formation in this country is to be sought in the saving process—in the factors that govern the supply of savings rather than the demand for capital funds. It is in the economic and social constraints on the savings contribution of governments and of private corporations, and in the factors that govern the consumption and savings patterns of individuals—the main source of savings—that we may find the basis for a theory that would cogently account for the levels of and trends in at least the *proportion* of capital formation to national product. This would leave the explanation incomplete in that we would still have to account for the levels of national product itself and its trends. But even so, a valid explanation of the capital formation proportion would link the latter closely with the basic processes of economic growth. It would also permit, given some basis for projection or assumption of future trends in national product, an estimation of the probable course of capital formation.

The suggested basic importance of the saving process tempts one to argue that it was the supply of savings that limited capital formation in the past, and that it was not limited by demand for capital created by technological change and investment opportunities. But no such inference can be drawn from our discussion and, for reasons set forth below, no firm inference can really be drawn as to whether it was the supply or demand side that limited capital formation in the past.

To begin with, the explanatory hypotheses above, as indicated repeatedly, did not, and in the present state of analysis cannot, yield specific coefficients. We did not and could not demonstrate that the economic and social conditions under which governments and private corporations operate make it impossible for them to contribute savings of more than 1 and 3 per cent, respectively, of net national product. We did not and could not demonstrate that the factors governing saving by individuals make it impossible or at least exceedingly difficult for them to contribute savings that, in the long run, amount to more than 10 to 12 per cent of net national product. And since it was not feasible to demonstrate that the factors on the supply-of-savings side could not have permitted significantly higher net capital formation proportions, or even significantly different trends, it is possible that the levels and trends that were in fact attained were lower than the savings potential alone could have generated. It is possible also that reduction to levels below the savings potential was produced by some constraining factors on the demand side.

An even more important qualification of our results is that the whole discussion so far has dealt with the demand for savings and supply of savings separately; and the reasoning has been in terms of demand, as suggested by capital-output ratios, and of supply, as suggested by capital formation proportions. But the actual capital formation proportions and capital-output ratios cannot be fully explained by factors that deal with *ex ante* demand by users of savings and *ex ante* supply by the savers. Savings are generated by individuals or corporations in specific forms and offered for use only on certain conditions—yield, security, duration of loan, and so forth. There may be demand for these funds, but from sources and on conditions that do not match those of the offer. It is the basic function of financial intermediaries to deal with this problem of matching the demand and supply of savings; and the actually observed capital formation volumes are not equal either to *ex ante* demand or to *ex ante* supply, but to some balancing of the two. We have yet to consider the mechanism for such balancing.

Once we introduce the financial intermediaries, defined most broadly as the institutional mechanism for bringing together supply of and demand for savings, and set the basic lines of the money and credit system as a framework within which such meshing can effectively and continuously occur, two major groups of questions arise. The first is suggested by the credit-creating powers of some financial intermediaries, and by the money policy power of governments and of those agencies to which such power may be delegated. In the long run, could not the creation of credit or attempts at financing through issuance of new money be the dominant factor in setting the capital formation proportion in the country? Assume, as suggested above, that factors that determine *voluntary* savings ratios by private economic agencies and even by governments limit the proportion of product that can be devoted to capital formation. Could not credit creation or money inflation be used to force diversion of larger proportions to capital users? The answer to this question would lie in examination of the limits to such "forced" saving set by the reaction of voluntary saving. Such limits can be clearly seen if we assume that credit creation or financing with new money will raise prices (or keep them constant, whereas they might otherwise decline). Under such conditions, the units whose economic power has been reduced by the rise in prices (or by their failure to decline) may react by continuing to consume as much as before, and hence reduce their actual voluntary savings below the level that could otherwise have been expected. If this happens, the total volume of savings actually realized may not be any larger than it would have been without credit creation or new money issue. Indeed, under certain circumstances the effort to accelerate saving by excessive credit creation or new money issues may have the opposite effect, if, for example, it undermines the faith of the would-be savers in the stability of purchasing power of the money claims that embody their savings. Under different conditions, a controlled development of the credit creating power of financial intermediaries, or the intelligent pursuit of an active money policy by the government, may result in a net increase in countrywide savings and the capital formation proportions—over and above what they might otherwise have been.

The questions just touched upon relate to the long-run effects of countrywide savings and the capital formation proportions. The second group of questions is connected with the short-run effects. We have discussed the processes in their long-term aspects because our interest is in long-term trends. But in reality everything takes place in the short run—from day to day—even though long-term considerations play an important part. Yet when we deal with the short-term aspects of economic life we may, and usually do, find that in the rather complex flow of savings into investment, the meshing of available savings with the demand for them is not simple and automatic. Granted that in the long run a country's economic institutions, particularly its financial intermediaries, are generally capable of resolving discrepancies in the conditions of supply of savings and of demand for capital funds. But such adjustments take time. At any one moment the offered supply of savings can exceed the real demand for them. In this sense, limitations on capital formation cannot lie entirely on the supply-of-savings side.

Note that this problem of short-term adjustment is, paradoxically, in itself a long-term problem. In any economy, particularly a rapidly growing one, there are ever-present shifts among groups in the distribution of income and within groups in the structure of their consumption and savings. The supply of savings is, therefore, flowing from ever-changing sources for ever-changing needs under ever-changing conditions; and the demand of would-be users for savings is subject to an equally varied and continuously changing set of circumstances. It is unlikely that the adjustments, assumed to take place eventually and thus resolve the failure of conditions of supply of and demand for savings to mesh, can ever catch up with these changes that continually create new maladjustments. One can, therefore, envisage actual capital formation as a process that continuously, in the long run, unfolds at levels below those that could be attained with the available supply of savings, because of the ever-present disparities in conditions of supply and demand. This view, in turn, has other implications, for capital formation is itself a tool of economic growth, and any shortfall in it may reduce the rate of growth of national product and thus affect the savings potential at the next stage. (We point out, in passing, that it is evident from the above that the capacity of the economic and social institutions to adapt themselves to the continuous adjustment problems of a growing society—the capacity for social invention—is a key to economic growth.)

While granting that the pressures are on both the supply and the demand side, and that the ways in which the mechanisms connecting them have affected the actual processes in economic life, we must also recognize that there is unfortunately no way of measuring the effects of these mechanisms. Available data give us no inkling of the extent to which the savings proportion in this country has been affected by the credit-creating power of the banks or by the money policy followed by the government. The preceding discussion, which stresses the high consumption propensity in the American economy, thereby suggests narrow limits upon the capacity of our credit and money system to effectuate a *net* rise in the savings proportion. This is a crude impression, however, and we are in no position to push this line of analysis further. Nor can we deny that one characteristic of the short-term but continuously present problems of balancing supply of savings and demand for savings is the extreme difficulty of measuring their quantitative effect on capital formation. We do not know how to establish, with reasonable firmness, the magnitude of the savings potential or, alternatively, the reduction effects of the imbalance of conditions of supply and demand. Measures such as we have are inadequate even for gauging the overt processes actually taking place. It would be oversanguine to expect that, without a long period of experimentation and testing, we could secure any measures of *potentials*, or of the effects of disparities between the supply that is being—or would be—offered under varying conditions, and the demand under matching conditions.

With these considerations in mind, all we can say is that our earlier discussion leaves us with the impression that it is the long-run factors on the supply-of-savings side that limit the potential levels and affect the potential trends of the capital formation proportions, even given the mechanisms of credit creation and money-issue financing; and that the limiting influence of the long-run factors on the demand or capital-use side seems less important. The impression is strengthened by the realization of the rapid increase, at least since the second half of the nineteenth century, in technological knowledge—the host of scientific discoveries, practical inventions, and production improvements—all of which have meant, in the long run, a high potential demand for capital. But this is, nonetheless, no more than an impression, and bears upon the potentials alone. The actual levels of the capital formation proportions are affected by continuous problems of short-term and long-term adjustment, in which, to repeat a famous analogy, demand and supply are like the two blades of a pair of scissors, and it is only in their combination that the explanation lies.

The impression of the dominance of long-term forces on the supply-of-savings side in setting limits to potential capital formation proportions is not, and cannot be, dispelled by consideration of interest rates. It is true that in the long run even riskless interest rates have declined; and one could presumably argue that such a decline precludes the claim that the factors on the supply side limit the level of capital formation. Yet the relevance of trends in interest rates to the question under discussion is only apparent. It is not just that these rates apply only to the part of the savings flow that takes the form of external funds seeking placement. Far more important, like all prices, they measure only the *relative* pressures of demand upon supply. The long-term decline in interest rates, whether in current or constant prices, means simply that the shortage of supply of savings relative to investment opportunities has become less acute. Or to put it differently: with the economic growth of the country and the increased supply of goods per capita, would-be savers give a relatively lower preference to present supply than to future supply. They are therefore willing to discount the future at a lower rate, whereas a comparable rise in investment opportunities over a period of the same duration has not occurred. Thus, if the discount to be applied to a future twenty years hence is reduced on the supply-of-savings side (because of greater availability of goods for distribution between the present and the future), and if investment opportunities over the same time horizon do not rise in the same proportion, twenty-year term interest rates will decline. But the limiting pressure of the supply of savings is still there. The greater promise of a cogent explanation of intertemporal and international differences in the levels of and trends in capital formation proportions still lies, for reasons suggested in our earlier discussion, in the factors that determine the savings patterns of the country's population.

These comments should explain our earlier allusion to the impossibility, in the present state of knowledge, of providing a testable answer to the question whether in the past it was the supply of savings or the demand for capital funds that limited the levels of the actual capital formation proportions and determined their trends. We can have no more than impressions of the potentials on both sides, and we cannot measure the differences between the actual proportions and the potential. We shall return to this and related questions at the end of our analysis, for they are of obvious bearing upon the whole topic of the use of past experience in a prognosis of the future. It was necessarily touched upon here because the implications of this preliminary discussion are important in the more detailed analysis that follows.

It should be clear both from this preliminary answer and from much of the explanatory discussion preceding it that the forces determining the levels of capital formation and its trends are part of a complex that involves the full spectrum of demographic, economic, and social factors, which must be viewed in its entirety in considering the growth of the economy. It cannot be otherwise, since capital formation is an integral part of national product, affected by it and affecting it. Yet, if only because of the variety of the forces involved and the complexity of their interrelations, no simple scheme that would yield determinate and unequivocal answers is possible. The explanatory hypotheses outlined—although they are carried further perhaps than has been customary in economic literature—could just as easily have yielded answers different from those indicated by the statistical measures of past processes in this country. By using somewhat different assumptions and coefficients, we could have derived higher or lower levels of capital formation proportions, rising rather than constant trends in gross capital formation proportions, and constant rather than declining trends in net capital formation proportions. All we know at present is the directions in which further study should proceed—and it may be that more signposts are needed to lead us to the precise answers we are seeking.

Under these conditions, the channeling of analytical effort toward a close examination of the historical record is of the utmost importance. Such examination should help us avoid preliminary—and, by the nature of the case, dogmatic—hunches. It should compel us to scrutinize the more detailed parts and their interrelations as they can be observed in reality, so that the hypothetical links—which must remain hypothetical at least temporarily—are forged into a chain in which some other links are strengthened by the reasonably reliable records of what in fact has happened. What we shall be searching for in the chapters that follow is more of these sound links, to make sure that any explanation of the forces that determined capital formation in the past will be governed by more knowledge of the changing relative weights of types of capital, of categories of users, of sources and forms of financing.

CHAPTER 4

Trends in the Structure
of Capital Formation

IN the preceding chapter we dealt with capital formation as a total. Much can be learned also by studying its various components and distinguishing the domestic sector, that is, additions to capital located within the United States, from changes in claims against foreign countries; and by distinguishing not only the types of domestic capital formation—construction, producers' equipment, and inventories—but also the broad groups of eventual users—households, business firms, and governments, and even the business firms by their industrial affiliation. The present chapter is devoted to a summary of trends in the structure of capital formation, and to a discussion of factors that may have accounted for these trends.

Net Changes in Claims against Foreign Countries

Additions to the stock of buildings, plants, machinery, and inventories within the country may represent the current product of the economic activity of the members of the nation and their capital, or the product of the activity of members of other nations and their capital. The totals presented and analyzed in the preceding chapter were those of national capital formation, i.e., including additions to capital stock whether at home or abroad, so long as they belonged to the members of the community we call the United States. Such national capital formation may be smaller or larger than the total additions to capital located within the country—domestic capital formation: smaller if, on balance, the additions to claims by foreign countries against the United States are larger than the additions to claims by the United States against foreign countries; and larger if, on balance, the additions to claims by foreign countries against the United States are smaller than additions to claims by the United States against foreign countries. In the former case, the net balance of foreign claims is negative; and part of domestic capital formation is financed by foreign capital funds or by the reduction of United States claims through the loss of gold, which represents a stock of internationally acceptable claims. In the latter case, the net balance of foreign claims is positive, and to domestic capital formation we must add those additions to claims against foreign countries—in the form of a larger stock of gold or of other types of claims (foreign securities, direct ownership of real assets abroad, and the like).

We begin with this division of total national capital formation between the domestically located part and the changes in foreign claims partly because it bears most directly upon an important point in our discussion in Chapter 3. We argued there that a major limitation upon the long-term level of capital formation in the United States lay in the supply of savings that the economy could generate; and that, by and large, this limitation may have outweighed any long-term limits on the side of demand for capital funds, i.e., on the side of domestic investment opportunities. If so, could these limits on domestic capital formation be removed by drawing upon savings abroad? To test this possibility, we examine the extent to which shortages in the supply of domestic savings were relieved by the inflow of savings from foreign countries.

There is another reason for beginning with an examination of changes in claims against foreign countries. In a review of the mechanism by which such changes are brought about, much can be glimpsed of the factors that determine the flow of savings into capital formation, and these factors are not unlike those that govern the flow of savings into various types of domestic capital formation. Hence, whatever we learn about the forces that have determined the trend in the relative share of net changes in claims against foreign countries may contribute to the hypotheses that serve as preliminary leads in the analysis of trends in the distribution of domestic capital formation among its various components.

With these comments in mind, we turn to Table 10, which summarizes the flows to and from this country from 1850 to 1955, and the resulting net changes in claims against foreign countries. An examina-

TABLE 10

BALANCE OF INTERNATIONAL PAYMENTS OF THE UNITED STATES, 1850–1955
(annual averages, millions of dollars)

	Fiscal Years				Calendar Years			
	1850–1873 (1)	1874–1895 (2)	1896–1914 (3)	1914 a–1922 b (4)	1923–1928 (5)	1929–1940 (6)	1941–1945 (7)	1946–1955 (8)
Sources of foreign claims against U.S.								
1. Imports of merchandise	339	670	1,203	3,094	4,123	2,481	4,360	8,950
2. Imports of services	43	67	238	791	840	709	1,434	2,138
3. Military expenditures	—	—	—	—	—	5	1,459	1,411
4. Income on foreign investments in U.S.	38	85	200	118	192	216	178	354
5. Total, lines 1 to 4	419	822	1,642	4,003	5,155	3,411	7,431	12,853
6. Unilateral transfers (net)	−14	20	150	386	362	225	8,327	4,769
Private	−14	20	150	346	350	208	276	528
Government	—	—	—	40	12	17	8,051	4,241
Military	—	—	—	—	—	—	8,072 c	1,477
Other	—	—	—	40	12	17	−22	2,764
7. Total, lines 5 and 6	405	842	1,792	4,389	5,517	3,636	15,758	17,622
Sources of U.S. claims against foreign countries								
8. Exports of merchandise	277	783	1,691	5,748	4,861	3,048	11,817	13,000
9. Exports of services	27	7	5	482	456	432	2,739	2,612
10. Military transfers	—	—	—	—	—	—	n.s.s.	1,477
11. Income on U.S. investments abroad	n.a.	n.a.	40	392	921	642	546	1,656
Private	n.a.	n.a.	40	320	761	599	531	1,496
Direct	n.a.	n.a.	n.a.	n.a.	434	314	394	1,298
Other	n.a.	n.a.	n.a.	n.a.	326	285	137	198
Government	—	—	—	72	160	42	15	160
12. Total, lines 8 to 11	304	790	1,735	6,623	6,238	4,122	15,102	18,745

Balances of or net changes in claims on account of:

13. Merchandise, line 8 minus line 1	−62	113	488	2,654	738	567	7,457	4,050
14. Services, line 9 minus line 2	−16	−60	−233	−309	−384	−277	1,305	474
15. Military, line 10 minus line 3	—	—	—	—	—	−5	−1,459	66
16. Income on investments, line 11 minus line 4	−38	−85	−160	274	729	426	368	1,302
17. Total, line 12 minus line 5	−115	−32	93	2,620	1,083	711	7,671	5,892
18. Unilateral transfers, line 6, signs reversed	14	−20	−150	−386	−362	−225	−8,327	−4,769
19. Total, lines 17 and 18	−101	−52	−57	2,234	721	486	−656	1,123

Movement in claims

20. Gold sales (+), purchases (−)	46	5	−9	−213	−36	−1,265	392	−167
21. U.S. capital (inflow +; outflow −)	—	—	−53	−1,630	−973	163	−490	−2,232
Total private	—	—	−53	−438	−1,018	156	−96	−949
Direct	—	—	n.a.	n.a.	−310	−84	27	−642
Other long-term	—	—	n.a.	n.a.	−566	109	−108	−163
Short-term	—	—	n.a.	n.a.	−142	130	−15	−144
Government	—	—	—	−1,191	45	7	−394	−1,283
22. Foreign capital (inflow +; outflow −)	42	45	105	−269	470	297	660	785
Long-term	42	45	105	−278	222	138	−81	171
Short-term	—	—	n.a.	n.a.	248	159	740	614
23. Net capital flow, lines 21 and 22	42	45	53	−1,899	−503	460	170	−1,447
24. Errors and omissions, line 19, signs reversed, minus lines 20 and 23	14	2	13	−122	−182	320	95	490

Because of rounding, detail will not necessarily add to total. In this and the following tables, n.a. = not available; n.s.s. = not shown separately; — = nil, or negligible.

a July 1 of year.
b December 31 of year.

c Includes other grants.

SOURCE: 1850–1952: *Balance of Payments of the United States, 1919–1953* (Supplement, *Survey of Current Business,* July 1954).
1953–1955: *Survey of Current Business,* June 1956.

tion of the flows is indispensable to the understanding of the net changes.

The first group of entries (lines 1–7) records the flows to this country from abroad—the sources of gross additions to claims by foreign countries against the United States. The major item here is imports of merchandise (line 1), and to this we add purchases of services rendered by foreign resources—shipping, expenditures abroad by American tourists, insurance and other financial services, and the like. We must also add income earned by foreign capital invested in the United States. A plant located in the United States, but owned by a member of a foreign nation, must be viewed as part of foreign, not United States, resources, and the earnings on such an investment constitute an addition to claims against this country. Finally, a claim against the United States can arise without any antecedent import of a commodity from abroad, without any purchase of a service rendered by foreign resources, and without foreign ownership of resources located within the United States. A member or some collective body of the United States community can make a gift to a person or group abroad—and by its nature there is no tangible or overt *quid pro quo*. Such gifts, whether private remittances or government grants, are described as unilateral transfers, and are entered on a net basis (that is, net of any gifts from abroad to the United States) in line 6.

There is conceptually no duplication or overlapping among the five categories of additions to foreign claims against the United States. Imports of merchandise cannot, in the nature of the case, be included either under the purchase of services, military expenditures abroad, or under income on foreign investments. If the value of the import includes the charges for shipping by a foreign carrier, these charges are not included under services. If income originates in a plant located within the United States, it cannot appear under imports. And since unilateral transfers are direct additions to foreign claims, they cannot overlap imports from abroad, though they may be exports from the United States. Not only are the five categories nonduplicating, they are also comprehensive in that they comprise *all* current additions to foreign claims; and their sum is the total of all current additions to foreign claims against this country.

The second group of entries (lines 8–12) deals with the counterflows, the sources of additions to United States claims against foreign countries. Here the major item is exports of merchandise, supplemented by the sales of some services of United States resources to persons abroad and, in recent years, by military transfers. There is also, of course, income on United States investments abroad. Since, however, unilateral transfers are taken on a net basis in line 6 (such transfers to the United States have in any case been negligible), no entry for this item appears under additions to United States claims against foreign countries. Corresponding to the total of additions to foreign claims (line 7), there is the total of additions to claims by the United States against foreign countries (line 12).

It is the balances on these various accounts that are of particular interest (lines 13–19). Exports of merchandise can be balanced against imports of merchandise; exports of services against imports of services; and so on. However, such matching does not mean that claims against foreign countries derived from exports are in fact used to finance imports of merchandise but not to pay income on foreign investments. There is no reason for assuming that current additions to claims against foreign countries do not flow into a common pool in which their identity is lost, and from which drafts are made to finance any purchase from or payment abroad. Even if the sources retain their identity, it does not necessarily follow that a particular batch of claims originates as an export of a commodity rather than, say, as income on a United States investment abroad. The matching is just a simple classifying device, intended to show how each type of transaction—in commodities, in services, in income on investments, and so on—contributes to the net balance of or changes in total claims against foreign countries. This total (line 19) is of most interest to us, for it is a component of total capital formation and represents the difference between total and domestic capital formation.

This total net change in foreign claims, described in the current international balance of payments terminology as net foreign investment, can also, theoretically, be derived from movements in stocks of claims. In lines 20 to 23 these movements in stocks of claims are summarized, the claims being classified into two major categories—gold and capital assets. If the data on capital assets were complete and accurate, net changes in gold and capital assets (line 20 plus line 23) would agree with the total in line 19; but, since the estimates of capital assets are deficient, the item of errors and omissions (line 24) is introduced to provide the identity.

Two aspects of Table 10 should be noted before we comment on the findings. First, the periods distinguished were determined partly by the supply of data, partly by the desire to separate periods characterized by distinctive complexes of economic and other conditions. Thus, detailed estimates are available for 1850–1873, 1874–1895, 1896–1914, and 1914–1918, but not for the years or subperiods within each; and, while we were able to derive single-year estimates of total net changes in foreign claims for the years before 1919, it would have been impossible to calculate annual estimates of all the items in Table 10. We have, therefore, used the series for the periods as given, but extended the fourth through 1922, partly because the first few years after World War I were still much affected by it, partly because complete and reliable estimates by the Department of Commerce begin with 1923. Then we distinguish 1923–1928, a period of relative prosperity; 1929–1940, a period affected by the Great Depression; the years of World War II, most distinctive from the standpoint of conditions for flow of goods, services, and claims across the country's boundaries; and, finally, the post-World War II decade.

The second point to be noted is that the estimates for the periods before the 1920's are necessarily approximate, and we took advantage of the recent and detailed work by Goldsmith which contains revisions for 1897–1914 and 1915–1922. These are summarized in Table 11, which can be regarded as an appendix to Table 10. It is important to emphasize that throughout our study we accepted Goldsmith's figures on savings, and they are, therefore, the basis for our estimates of net changes in foreign claims, and hence of national capital formation. His revisions are minor for the period 1915–1922, and not large absolutely even for 1897–1914. They show a positive balance for that period compared with a negative balance in the older estimates, although in both estimates net changes in claims are relatively small.

Among the findings suggested by Tables 10 and 11, there is, as expected, a substantial rise in the flows to and from this country. Total imports of goods and services per year rose from less than one-half billion dollars during 1850–1873 to close to $13 billion in 1946–1955 (Table 10, line 5). Total exports of goods and services per year rose from less than one-third billion dollars during the first period to almost $19 billion during the post-World War II decade (Table 10, line 12). Even the net balance rose considerably in volume, signs disregarded—from between $50 million and $100 million per year in the early periods to over $1 billion per year in the latest (Table 10, line 19); or to almost $6 billion, excluding unilateral transfers (line 17). All these volumes are in current prices and affected by price changes, but even when adjusted for price changes, both gross and net flows would

Trends in Structure of Capital Formation

TABLE 11

REVISION OF BALANCE OF INTERNATIONAL PAYMENTS ITEMS, 1897–1922
(annual averages, millions of dollars)

	1897–1914 (1)	1915–1922 (2)
Balances of or Net Changes in Claims On Account of:		
1. Commodities	571	2,810
2. Services	−201	−414
3. Income on investments	−78	346
4. Total, lines 1 to 3	291	2,742
5. Private remittances	−147	−372
6. Total, lines 4 and 5	144	2,370
Changes in Stocks of Claims		
7. Gold stocks (increase −)	−68	−265
8. U.S. foreign assets (increase −)	−102	−1,888
Total private	−102	−622
Direct	−76	−64
Other long-term	−26	−558
Government	—	−1,266
9. Foreign assets in U.S. (increase +; decrease −)	82	−240
Long-term	57	−213
Short-term	25	−26
10. Net balance of assets, lines 8 and 9	−20	−2,128
11. Errors and omissions, line 6, signs reversed, minus lines 7 and 10	−56	23

Because of rounding, detail will not necessarily add to total.

SOURCE: Raymond W. Goldsmith, *A Study of Saving in the United States*, Vol. I (Princeton University Press, 1955), pp. 1078–1085.

still show a sharp secular rise. This is hardly surprising in view of the country's prodigious growth during the century covered by the estimates. One cannot attach much significance to these movements, unless they are compared with the movements in other countrywide totals to reveal whether the *proportional* weight and contribution of international flows, gross and net, have changed materially.

Even the absolute figures in Tables 10 and 11 clearly suggest three important, if familiar, findings. First, during periods of major wars, there is an acceleration in outflows—in exports of commodities and services to other participants in the conflict (excluding any flows representing direct participation by this country). Such marked rise in exports sets up other movements, not only in balances and stocks of claims, but on the import side as well. Thus during World War I the huge rise in exports from the United States was offset partly by a rise in imports, but largely by an outflow of capital funds, some of which represented repatriation of foreign investments in this country, some, advances in capital loans by the United States. During World War II, the large rise in exports was offset partly by a rise in imports, but largely by unilateral transfers—government grants of various kinds to our allies.

Second, unilateral transfers have become of major importance in the whole network of international flows, to an extent unparalleled in the past. Their increase during the quinquennium of World War II was mentioned above. It continued through the post-World War II decade, and is obviously a factor that must be considered in the future. With this growing importance of unilateral transfers, net changes in claims against foreign countries can now be negative not because of greater investment of foreign capital in the United States, but because of greater grants by the United States to other countries.

Third, the balance of changes in claims against foreign countries has shifted from negative to positive. It was negative in the first two periods, covering 1850 to 1895, although even as early as 1874–1895 the net balance of merchandise and services was positive (see Table 10, lines 13 and 14). The country was exporting more commodities and services than it was importing, and capital imports were financing interest payments to foreigners, and gifts. According to the older set of estimates, that situation continued through 1896–1914, but Goldsmith's revisions for 1897–1914 suggest a small positive balance. Certainly World War I saw a sharp reversal, and since that time positive balances have been the rule with the single exception of the World War II quinquennium when huge unilateral transfers were made. With this exception, by and large since the late 1890's, there has been no period of net imports of foreign capital; and only during the first five years of the total period covered in our study—from 1869 to the mid-1870's—was capital formation located within the United States assisted by net inflow of capital funds from abroad.

The picture becomes more distinct when we relate exports, imports, and other sources of foreign claims to countrywide totals. The first comparison is presented in Table 12, where the various flows summarized in Tables 10 and 11 are expressed as percentages of gross national product in current prices.

Trends in Structure of Capital Formation

Table 12 excludes the period 1850–1873, because we have no reliable estimates of gross national product for those years. But more important is the question whether gross national product is the proper base of reference. It might be more logical to use gross national product plus imports of goods, i.e., including imports of commodities, services, and income on foreign investments in the United States. Theoretically, net imports can exceed domestically produced output, in which case national product, gross or net, will be negative; and any reference to a negative base would be illogical. However, the total of gross national product and all imports of goods, which could be described as the total of all available resources, would be, as Table 12 clearly indicates, not much larger than gross national product, because in no period have imports constituted as much as 10 per cent of total national output. Percentages of total available resources would therefore differ only slightly from percentages of gross national product, and the trends in the two would practically parallel each other. We decided, therefore, to let the comparison stand, since gross national product is the base of reference for all other comparisons.

With this qualification, the major trends can be briefly summarized. First, the proportion of imports of all goods, including income on foreign investments, was at its highest during 1874–1895: almost 8 per cent of gross national product. It declined thereafter, and in the last period, the post-World War II decade, it was only 4.9 per cent of gross national product. This percentage is somewhat higher than that in the depressed period 1929–1940 but distinctly below the level of 5.9 per cent in 1923–1928.

Second, the share of unilateral transfers tended to increase, but it was minor—below 1 per cent of gross national product—until the World War II quinquennium, when it rose markedly. But even in the post-World War II decade, when it was somewhat less than 2 per cent of gross national product, it was distinctly higher than during any other period except that of World War II, keeping the proportional level of total additions to foreign claims higher than at any period since World War I. Despite this bolstering effect of unilateral transfers, the share of all additions to foreign claims in gross national product in 1946–1955 was lower than before the 1920's.

Third, the share of all exports in gross national product, disregarding the two world war periods, drifted downward—from 7.5 per cent in 1874–1895 to 7.2 per cent in 1946–1955. But this decline in the proportional importance of outflows is less pronounced than that in the

TABLE 12

INTERNATIONAL FLOWS AS PER CENT OF GROSS NATIONAL PRODUCT, BASED ON VOLUMES IN CURRENT PRICES, 1874–1955

	Fiscal Years			Revised Estimates Calendar Years		Calendar Years			
	1874–1895 (1)	1896–1914 (2)	1914[a]–1922[b] (3)	1897–1914 (2a)	1915–1922 (3a)	1923–1928 (4)	1929–1940 (5)	1941–1945 (6)	1946–1955 (7)
1. GNP, Variant I, annual averages, in current prices ($ billions)	10.56	23.81	61.24	25.01	62.96	87.27	73.70	129.06	259.97
Percentages of GNP									
Sources of Claims									
2. Imports of goods	7.0	6.1	6.3			5.7	4.3	5.6	4.8
3. Income on foreign investments	0.8	0.8	0.2			0.2	0.3	0.1	0.1
4. Unilateral transfers	0.2	0.6	0.6			0.4	0.3	6.5	1.8
5. Total sources of foreign claims	8.0	7.5	7.2			6.3	4.9	12.2	6.8
6. Exports of goods	7.5	7.1	10.2			6.1	4.7	11.3	6.6
7. Income on investments abroad	n.a.	0.2	0.6			1.1	0.9	0.4	0.6
8. Total sources of U.S. claims	7.5	7.3	10.8			7.1	5.6	11.7	7.2

Balances of or Net Changes in Claims
  On Account of:

9. Goods	0.5	1.1	3.8	1.5	3.8	0.4	0.4	5.7	1.8
10. Income on investments	−0.8	−0.7	0.4	−0.3	0.5	0.8	0.6	0.3	0.5
11. Unilateral transfers	−0.2	−0.6	−0.6	−0.6	−0.6	−0.4	−0.3	−6.5	−1.8
12. Total net balance	−0.5	−0.2	3.6	0.6	3.8	0.8	0.7	−0.5	0.4
Derived Combinations									
13. Flow of goods	14.5	13.2	16.5			11.8	9.0	16.9	11.4
14. Flow of goods and investment income	15.3	14.2	17.3			13.1	10.2	17.4	12.1
15. Exports of goods minus unilateral transfers	7.3	6.5	9.6	1.2		5.7	4.4	4.8	4.8
16. Total net balance, excluding unilateral transfers	−0.3	0.4	4.2		4.4	1.2	1.0	6.0	2.2

Because of rounding, detail will not necessarily add to total.
a July 1 of year.
b December 31 of year.

SOURCE, BY LINE

1. Calculated from the annual estimates underlying Table R-25.
2. Table 10, lines 1, 2, and 3.
3. Table 10, line 4.
4. Table 10, line 6.
5. Lines 2, 3, and 4.
6. Table 10, lines 8, 9, and 10.
7. Table 10, line 11.
8. Lines 6 and 7.
9. Table 10, lines 13, 14, and 15; or Table 11, lines 1 and 2.
10. Table 10, line 16; or Table 11, line 3.
11. Line 4, signs reversed; or Table 11, line 5.
12. Lines 9, 10, and 11.
13. Lines 2 and 6.
14. Lines 3, 7, and 13.
15. Line 6 minus line 4.
16. Line 12 minus line 11.

proportional weight of inflows, and it might be safer to infer that no significant decline in the relative share of outflows has occurred. The absence of a significant decline is associated with the rise in the proportional weight of unilateral transfers, which induces a greater flow of exports. However, it is not quite legitimate to argue that without the unilateral transfers exports from the United States would have declined. Had the large government grants not been made in 1946–1955, foreign countries might still have been able to purchase some of the United States exports that were in fact financed by those grants. But if we do assume a direct connection between the two, total exports of commodities and services in 1946–1955 would have amounted to 4.8 per cent of gross national product (line 15), and the addition of income on investments abroad would have meant an outflow of goods equivalent to 5.4 per cent of gross national product, compared with percentages of about 7 per cent in 1874–1895, 1896–1914, 1923–1928, and 5.3 per cent in the depressed period 1929–1940. In other words, the proportion of total exports to gross national product may have failed to decline largely because of the increase in the relative weight of unilateral transfers, particularly during the post-World War II decade.

Fourth, the total net balance was a minute fraction of gross national product—below 1 per cent—except during the period dominated by World War I; but small as the balance was, we find a clear reversal from negative balances, indicating foreign capital imports, in the earlier periods, to positive balances, indicating United States capital exports, in the later periods. These positive balances, prevailing since the end of the nineteenth century, are particularly evident when we adjust for the effects of unilateral transfers (line 16). But even with this adjustment, they range from less than 1 to slightly over 2 per cent of gross national product, except during the world war periods.

However, our major interest here is the relation of net changes in foreign claims not to national product but to capital formation; for we are concerned with the level of and trend in this component as part of total capital formation. The relevant percentages are given in Table 13. In part A the percentages are for the periods distinguished in Tables 10 through 12; in part B they are for overlapping decades from 1869 to 1955.

Two conclusions stand out. First, except for the years associated with World War I, net changes in claims against foreign countries constituted large percentages of net capital formation alone, and only for periods in which depressed economic conditions lowered the absolute level of net capital formation appreciably. If we were to group the years, as we should for secular analysis, to avoid the marked effects of depressions or major wars, we would find that net changes in claims against foreign countries never averaged more than 10 per cent of net capital formation, and distinctly less than that as a per cent of gross capital formation. In other words, quantitatively, net foreign additions to or drafts upon domestic capital formation, particularly gross, have not been a secularly important component of capital formation in this country.

Second, we naturally find here the reversal in sign noted above. In the earlier periods, domestic capital formation was larger than the total, the former being financed in part by a net inflow of capital from abroad. In the later periods, the opposite was true: domestic capital formation was smaller than the total, the latter being accounted for in part by net additions to capital investments abroad by the United States.

This necessarily summary account of the long-term trends in the balance of international payments of this country, and in the importance of outflows, inflows, and their net balance relative to national product and capital formation, raises three questions. (1) Why, during the second half of the nineteenth century, when this country enjoyed extraordinary growth, were not the inflows of foreign capital proportionately more substantial? (2) Why have the net changes in foreign claims shifted from negative to positive, from net capital imports to net capital exports, although the rapid growth that continued through the twentieth century could presumably have absorbed net capital imports from abroad? (3) Given the factors that make for net capital exports, which would presumably provide at least part of the answer to question (2), what limits the proportional level of capital exports? Clearly, these questions involve consideration of conditions not only in this country but in the rest of the world, and data and knowledge at our command are hardly sufficient for well founded and tested answers. Yet some attempt to deal with them must be made, if only to penetrate below the surface of the overt flows that have been summarized statistically, and to suggest the lines of direction that might lead to a tentative explanation.

1. The first question is especially puzzling when we consider that by the late 1870's the United States had recovered from the Civil War, and its capacity for growth had become an established fact. That increasing numbers of people immigrated in search of economic op-

TABLE 13

NET CHANGES IN CLAIMS AGAINST FOREIGN COUNTRIES AS PER CENT OF NATIONAL PRODUCT AND OF CAPITAL FORMATION, BASED ON VOLUMES IN CURRENT PRICES, 1869–1955

(amounts in billions of dollars)

Periods	Net National Product (Variant I) (1)	Gross Capital Formation (2)	Net Capital Formation (3)	Net Changes in Claims as Per Cent of:			
				Gross National Product (4)	Net National Product (5)	Gross Capital Formation (6)	Net Capital Formation (7)
A. PERIODS IN TABLE 12, 1874–1955							
Fiscal Years							
1. 1874–1895	9.58	2.27	1.28		−0.5	−2.3	−4.0
2. 1896–1914	21.27	5.28	2.74		−0.3	−1.1	−2.1
3. 1914 (July 1) to 1922 (Dec. 31)	53.53	13.98	6.27		4.2	16.0	35.6
Revised Estimates, Calendar Years							
4. 1897–1914	22.33	5.49	2.81		0.6	2.6	5.1
5. 1915–1922	55.02	14.52	6.58		4.3	16.3	36.0
Calendar Years							
6. 1923–1928	77.17	19.19	9.10		0.9	3.8	7.9
7. 1929–1940	63.59	12.43	2.32		0.8	3.9	20.9
8. 1941–1945	109.40	28.66	9.00		−0.6	−2.3	−7.3
9. 1946–1955	214.18	61.29	15.50		0.5	1.8	7.2

B. OVERLAPPING DECADES, 1869–1955

Decades				
10. 1869–1878	−1.3	−1.4	−6.5	−10.7
11. 1874–1883	a	a	−0.1	−0.2
12. 1879–1888	−0.4	−0.4	−1.8	−3.1
13. 1884–1893	−0.6	−0.7	−2.8	−5.2
14. 1889–1898	0.1	0.2	0.6	1.1
15. 1894–1903	1.2	1.3	4.9	8.8
16. 1899–1908	1.0	1.1	4.3	8.0
17. 1904–1913	0.3	0.3	1.2	2.3
18. 1909–1918	2.4	2.8	11.1	23.1
19. 1914–1923	3.1	3.6	13.7	30.2
20. 1919–1928	1.6	1.8	7.2	15.7
21. 1924–1933	0.6	0.8	3.9	11.7
22. 1929–1938	0.5	0.6	3.0	22.8
23. 1934–1943	0.4	0.4	1.8	5.3
24. 1939–1948	1.0	1.2	4.7	16.8
25. 1944–1953	0.4	0.5	1.8	8.1
26. 1949–1955	−0.2	−0.3	−0.9	−3.6

a Less than 0.05 per cent.

SOURCE:

Part A

Col. 1.   Calculated from the annual estimates underlying Table R-25.

Cols. 2 and 3. Calculated from the annual estimates underlying Table R-29.

Cols. 5–7.   Entries in line 19 of Table 10, and line 6 of Table 11, as per cent of entries in columns 1–3.

Part B

The averages of the absolutes underlying the entries are given in Tables R-11 and R-14, or are calculated from Tables R-1 and R-4.

133

portunity is evidence enough that the economic potential of the United States was held to be one of the brightest. Why, under such circumstances, was the inflow of foreign capital, at its highest, only one-tenth of *net* capital formation and a small percentage of the national product?

Part of the answer lies in the size of the would-be lender countries compared with that of the would-be borrowers—even if we limit the latter to those countries where expectations would warrant the prognosis of favorable and vigorous economic growth. Before World War I the major creditor countries were the United Kingdom, France, and Germany, with the Netherlands, Belgium, and Switzerland providing limited additional funds. The would-be borrowers comprised not only the United States, the largest and in many ways most promising country, but also some countries in northwestern Europe (Denmark, Sweden, and Norway), Japan, several Latin American countries, Canada, and other British dominions. Even on the extreme assumption that all the savings generated in the would-be creditor countries were available for investment abroad, the supply to the would-be borrower countries, while much larger than the amount actually borrowed, would not be much larger relatively—given conditions in those countries that favored a vigorous flow of domestically originated savings. It must be remembered also that even where conditions were not very favorable to vigorous growth, as in some of the would-be borrower countries listed above, conditions for foreign investment established through special privileges encouraged some, and perhaps substantial, foreign investment. Although the economic prospects in India were, by and large, less favorable than those in the United States, the special relation of Great Britain to India warranted and required a flow of capital funds from the British Isles to India, leaving fewer British funds for investment elsewhere. In other words, the channeling of foreign capital is affected not only by the economic conditions, referred to above as the prospects of economic growth, in the would-be borrower country, but also by the noneconomic factors of political dominance and political expediency. The distribution of foreign capital investments by recipient areas, even before and especially after World War I, reveals the extent to which such investments followed not merely the economic prognosis of the long-term growth potential of the borrower country but the political factors. In fact, a substantial proportion of the foreign capital flow was a matter of political necessity, for instance, the large volumes of capital invested in Russia (by France), in the Balkan countries, and in colonies dominated by the European powers.

But what limited the share of total savings originating in the lender countries that could be diverted to investment abroad? This question applies not only to the countries that in fact were creditors, but even to those that were not. Consider Russia as a specific illustration: it could be argued that any possessor of investment funds, even located within that country, would have concluded, upon a careful appraisal of prospects, that by the end of the nineteenth century and certainly by the twentieth it would be, in the long run, far safer to shift the funds into investment in the United States or Canada than keep them in Russia. The same argument applies even to an underdeveloped country like China. One may ask why Britain failed to invest all its current savings in foreign countries, where the prospects of economic growth were distinctly brighter than at home. One may also ask why possessors of funds in underdeveloped countries, confronted with difficult and recalcitrant economic and social problems at home, with dim prospects of successful solution and with the dangers of a breakdown fairly obvious, failed to channel their funds abroad—particularly to such promising areas as the United States.

This question, artificial and rhetorical as it may seem, points directly to one obvious but nevertheless important factor in the situation: all the savings of a country are not available for investment abroad. Assume that an English—or a Russian, or a Chinese—merchant realizes a total net income on his enterprise substantially in excess of withdrawals for use in ultimate consumption, and that he has, therefore, a net profit available for investment. Even if the net profit emerges in the form of easily disposable funds rather than larger inventory or larger stock of fixed capital, the very profitability of the enterprise makes attractive the reinvestment of the funds in the enterprise in the form of increased equity. This additional investment will then be under the control of the merchant and, combined with his continued participation and other already invested assets, will promise a substantial return. The yield on such accumulated savings invested in fixed-return foreign securities, while viewed as "safe," could hardly match the expected profits in one's own business. In addition, investment in foreign equities would either require active participation—and thus mean, in effect, migration of the investor as an active entrepreneur—or call for the exercise of judgment in the choice of equity stocks under conditions of comparative ignorance. And what is true of the illustrative case of savings originating in a private trading firm is true of a wide variety of savings closely connected with the activities and desires of the individual saver and therefore far from free to flow abroad—savings generated by ultimate consumers in preparation for bulk outlays (such as residential housing), gross savings arising out of depreciation allowances in going enterprises, and the like.

The development of the elaborate complexes of intermediate financial institutions has, of course, facilitated the mobilization of savings and made possible diversion of at least part of such flow into foreign investment and, for that matter, into investment elsewhere within the domestic economy. Indeed, this is an important strand of modern economic growth. One major difference between developed and underdeveloped countries lies precisely in the capacity of the former to develop the financial institutions that mobilize savings, amassed at various points for various purposes, and pool them in funds in which they have much greater fluidity, permitting them to be channeled into uses that are likely to be economically more productive in the long run. All that is argued here is that in any given country a large part of the savings originates with a specific destination in the mind of the saver; that this condition may—and most likely will—restrict the savings to the uses the savers intended; and that such uses, being often indissolubly associated with the desire to combine the savings with other domestic resources, will keep them from flowing freely abroad.

To put it differently: the yield of savings or capital funds is conditioned by their combination with other resources. The potential growth of the United States means one thing to an investor who would accompany his savings to this country and add to the participation of his savings his own active participation in the process of growth. It means something different, and much less lucrative, to an investor who would limit his participation to the purchase of fixed-interest securities. And there are many gradations between the active participation of the former and the coupon clipping of the latter. The basic reason for the far from complete flow of savings, gross and net, from countries with low growth prospects to countries with high economic growth potentials has to be sought in the very factors that would explain the lack of complete mobility of people between two countries (which would equalize their current and prospective real income per capita): ignorance of foreign conditions as against familiarity with conditions at home; the large margin of error that necessarily attaches to any long-range forecast, and such a forecast is involved in the movement of people and capital funds; and the heavy cost of dislocation and re-adaptation to new economic and social conditions. People migrate only when the pressures at home become exceedingly great, and savings migrate only when the supply of funds exceeds that needed for investment at home.

It is this complex of factors that explains why even in the major creditor countries, and even in the most favorable periods as, for example, from the late nineteenth century to World War I, only part of gross savings originating at home became available for investment abroad. In the United Kingdom, funds flowing into foreign investment in 1870–1913 averaged somewhat less than one-half of domestic gross capital formation.[1] It also explains why practically no capital funds flow abroad from underdeveloped countries. The reason is not so much the low rate of savings in these countries as the emergence of savings in forms not accessible to free flow. Those savings that are accessible can often be used at home, by users familiar with domestic conditions, in ways that yield exceedingly high returns—temporary though they may prove to be if the pressing weight of domestic economic and social problems causes a radical change in the country's political and social framework.

All these factors help to explain why the flow of capital funds into the United States was not greater than it was, and some of them apply not only to the distribution of savings among countries, but also to the apportionment of savings among various uses within a country. They will, therefore, bear upon the analysis of the distribution of domestic capital formation that follows. Finally, some of the points relate also to the next question: why, in the course of our development, the net changes in foreign claims have shifted from negative to positive, from net capital imports to net capital exports.

2. The reversal from net capital inflows to outflows and, eventually, from net debtor to net creditor position occurred in this country, as in many others, partly as specific historical events occasioned by transient circumstances such as wars, and partly as results of trends in economic growth. Even the war-conditioned circumstances of the shift in capital flows may be viewed as part of a wider complex of trends, and it is these that are of particular interest here.

Insofar as a greater potential for economic growth and prospects of

[1] See Simon Kuznets, "International Differences in Capital Formation and Financing," *Capital Formation and Economic Growth*, Special Conference Series, No. 6 (Princeton for NBER, 1955), Table II-4, Part B, p. 70.

higher yields in a country induce a flow of capital funds into it, that flow is likely to originate in countries that have already attained a high level of economic development and maturity where the needs for capital are less acute and the expected returns on it are lower. The differences among countries in the potential for economic growth during the last one to two centuries are to some extent a function of the time differences among them in adopting the new industrial technology and in equipping themselves with modern capital and attaining higher levels of economic productivity. Certainly the industrial revolution in Britain preceded that in the United States by one-half to three-quarters of a century. The point to be stressed, however, is that the complex of circumstances that brought about the early industrialization and modern economic growth of Great Britain also made it inevitably an active participant in World War I. That became a world war and involved large economic magnitudes precisely because by that time modern economic growth had spread to France and particularly to Germany. The complex of circumstances that delayed industrialization in the United States—its distance from the seat of the old economic civilization of Western Europe and the abundance of its land relative to population, which made agriculture the dominant economic activity for so long—also minimized its active participation as a belligerent in World War I. In that sense, the large positive change in the net balance of foreign claims in World War I in the United States was not an historical accident. It was part of the complex of trends that accounted for the difference in stage of economic growth between the United States and Great Britain through the nineteenth century, and that set earlier the conditions for net capital imports from Britain to the United States. Somewhat similar reversals in the flow of capital occurred during World War I in several Scandinavian countries and in Japan. And the following general proposition may be argued: insofar as net capital imports characterize countries with the large economic growth potentials associated with a late entry into the phase of modern industrialization, and insofar as the late entry determines their position in the "new" world, outside the area of the "older" economic units, world wars—which involve the major advanced and thus older economic units—are usually accompanied by major reversals in the flow of capital funds. Such reversals are partly a matter of repatriation by the older creditor countries, partly advances by the younger debtor countries. It may well be that such an outflow would also have occurred in the United States in World War II, except that by that time the relevant foreign capital balances in the United States were small relative to the demands of the conflict, and the position of the United States as a world power subject to direct threat warranted the liberal use of its resources for assistance to its allies, largely in the form of unilateral transfers. It is this pattern rather than that of World War I that is likely to persist in any major war that may arise in the future.

Even if there had been no world wars, other forces would have produced a shift in this country from net capital imports to exports, although it might have occurred less precipitously. First, in the process of modern economic growth and industrialization, accompanied as it was by improvements in means of transportation and communication, reliance on imports of raw materials increased markedly. The United States used far more raw materials from abroad in the mid-twentieth century than it did in the mid-nineteenth century, even proportionately to the much greater volume of commodity production. Whereas imports of manufactured goods lead eventually to an attempt to produce them at home, imports of raw materials often lead to direct purchases of their sources and to an attempt to control their production to assure their supply in the form and at the rate most suitable for domestic needs. The well-known trends in the composition of exports and imports of a country as it becomes industrialized are away from the dominance of raw materials in exports to dominance of manufactured goods, and away from the dominance of manufactured goods to dominance of raw materials in imports. These trends induce parallel trends in direct investment abroad. Dependence upon imports of raw materials is conducive to direct investment in the production of raw materials abroad, whereas dependence upon imports of manufactured products is conducive to attempts to start their production at home. Dependence upon exports of raw materials does not lead to branch plants abroad, but dependence upon exports of manufactured products does. There was, consequently, a second group of reasons for this country to increase its direct investments abroad (and this would be true of any industrialized country)—the setting up of branch plants of manufacturing and industrial enterprises. This enhanced its creditor position except in those instances where investment abroad was disguised as a native unit with no indication of its control or ownership from the outside. Given these pressures for raw materials ownership and industrial branch plants abroad, it is significant that already by 1900 private United States assets abroad amounted to about $0.9 billion, of which over 80 per cent were in the form of direct investment, and that even by 1946, of $17 billion of total private assets abroad, almost one-half were direct investments.[2] One need not stress the obvious fact that the economic growth of a country that provides these stimuli to *direct* investments abroad also increases its knowledge and political prestige, both of which render such foreign investments more attractive to the country's economic units.

There is a third group of factors—the growth of a system of financial institutions and practices that mobilizes savings, making them more accessible to foreign portfolio investment, if the latter is warranted. As part and parcel of modern economic growth, an increasing proportion of the country's economic community becomes involved in and habituated to the network of developed financial institutions. Clearly, large sales of foreign bonds and securities like those in the United States in the 1920's would not have been possible at the end of the nineteenth century, when the banking system and other financial institutions were far less developed, when the proportion of individual savers that dealt in securities and other financial instruments was far lower. The greater externalization of savings, which accompanies economic growth, obviously facilitates the flow of funds abroad provided the conditions are favorable, just as it facilitates the flow of funds into large-scale economic investment at home.

Finally, the role of the federal government, at least in the historical period with which we are dealing, is not to be overlooked. Much of the capital flow abroad that led to the reversal in net changes in foreign claims was due to government transactions and decisions, and not exclusively in connection with armed conflicts. The growth in the economic power of this country permitted the government, when national interests were involved, to force a flow of funds abroad in the form of loans (which, unlike unilateral transfers, affected both the net capital position and subsequent current flows) that might not have occurred merely in response to the stimulus of market conditions on private business enterprises. But even though these foreign loans stemmed from government decisions, they were still a function of the country's economic growth. Clearly their contribution to the reversal in net changes in claims against foreign countries was conditioned, or at least made possible, by the rise in the country's economic resources and power.

[2] See Raymond W. Goldsmith, *A Study of Saving in the United States*, Vol. I (Princeton University Press, 1955), Table K-7, p. 1093.

3. The preceding comments make it unnecessary to deal at length with the last question—what factors limited the net capital outflow from the United States to small proportions of national product and even of capital formation. In a way, the question is easily answered by pointing to the successive periods distinguished in Tables 10 through 13. Capital exports during World War I were substantial, amounting to over one-third of net capital formation and about one-sixth of gross capital formation. During 1923–1928, investments abroad obviously had to compete with large capital needs at home for reconstruction equipment and expansion of domestic output. During the depressed period 1929–1940, absolute volumes of net capital exports were kept down by unfavorable economic conditions, but they were large relative to total or domestic net capital formation. During World War II, the huge outflows of resources abroad did not add to claims against foreign countries only because they were gifts, not loans. And after World War II, despite the great domestic need for capital goods, capital flow abroad was substantial, particularly if we take account of unilateral transfers. If we treat the latter as negative items, net changes in claims in this recent period amount to 7 per cent of net capital formation, but if we treat them as positive items, the proportion mounts to well over one-third of net capital additions.

If we disregard political and unilateral transfers, capital exports are obviously limited by the forces that make for direct investment abroad and those that set the feasible amount of portfolio foreign investment. The former are partly technological and partly economic functions of economic growth and of the change in industrial structure accompanying such growth. Little can be said about them, except that the inducements to control foreign supplies of raw materials or facilitate exports by setting up branches of manufacturing and other plants can necessarily account for only a small fraction of national output, and of total capital formation. Portfolio foreign investment is limited by domestic competition for savings. The whole question of the demand for savings in the United States versus savings abroad is involved. This problem was touched upon in Chapter 3 and will be discussed further in Chapter 10. All that need be said here is that the long-run opportunities for further investment in this country, associated with continuous technological progress and its effects on the structure of demand and production, will probably preclude a large margin for flow of savings abroad—especially since domestic needs for capital are likely to receive a higher priority on many economic grounds. It is, therefore, difficult to say whether, even if the political and social conditions abroad in the recent past had been as favorable as they were in the second half of the nineteenth century, net capital exports from this country would have constituted higher proportions of capital formation and national product than they actually did. For it must be remembered that while unfavorable political conditions reduced the flow of capital abroad under private auspices, they forced the flow of this country's resources abroad, either as grants or loans, under government auspices. And one would be hard put to guess whether, with favorable political conditions and without the government-sponsored flows of resources abroad, net capital exports of a purely business character would have been proportionally greater. Neither the United Kingdom nor France can be used as an example in this connection, since this country is much larger, and capital-demanding technological potentials have changed, so that the proportion of United States savings flowing abroad cannot be expected to equal the proportions that flowed from the United Kingdom and France. It must also be remembered that in the latter countries, politically motivated capital exports loomed quite large. We must, therefore, conclude—rather unsatisfactorily—that net changes in claims or net balances of flows of resources across the boundaries are a component which, if determined by purely economic forces, would not be proportionately large in a country like the United States. But that component is greatly affected by political and other noneconomic elements, and its importance in our analysis and prognosis depends largely upon the weight we wish to assign to those elements.

Structure of Capital Formation, by Type of Capital Good

Having considered that part of capital formation in this country financed from abroad or constituting net additions to claims against foreign countries, we turn to the distribution of domestic capital formation—gross and net additions to stock of commodities within the country that may be considered tools of production, and hence, capital.

One customary distribution that will be discussed in the present section distinguishes construction (buildings, roads, and other construction), producers' durables (machinery and equipment), and net changes in inventories. The basic reason for this classification lies in the span of economic life of units in the three categories. Buildings, roads, bridges, and so on continue in use for a long time, and the conversion of their original value into current product extends over decades. Producers' equipment or machinery has a much shorter economic life span, but is also measured in years, the standard life assumed in our calculations being thirteen years. Inventories are sold or "turned-over" relatively quickly, the inventory-annual output ratio varying from 0.2 to about 0.3 in manufacturing,[3] and averaging about the same in many branches of retail trade. Presumably, such differences in the span of economic life—the period during which the value of the capital item is translated into finished product and its cost recouped—are of major importance in the problem of financing, since funds for a capital investment that will not be fully amortized for fifty years will be tied up that long, whereas funds for inventories can presumably be viewed as a short-term investment. There are also consequential differences on the demand side in the economic factors that determine the rate of long-term versus short-term capital investment.

Two aspects of this customary classification warrant stressing. First, the basis of the classification is the *economic*, not the physical, life of the capital item. A disk harrow in the hands of a firm selling agricultural machinery is part of inventory, and its economic life is assumed to be brief, since the average period during which it will remain in stock is at most a year or two, and once it is sold, the firm's funds will no longer be tied up in that item. The same disk harrow in the hands of the farmer who purchases it will last ten to fifteen years and is a producers' durable item. Its economic life is assumed to be fairly long, because the user is expected to charge its depreciation and amortization to cost of annual product for years to come. Economic life is largely a matter of the intent and practice of the economic unit that disposes of the capital item in question, rather than a matter of physical properties, although the latter naturally exercise a permissive or limiting effect. Where physical life is short, it is impossible to have long economic life—eggs *as* eggs cannot become an item of producers' durable equipment.

Second, the distinction by length of economic life is valid for each physically identifiable capital item, not for the total economic value of the complex. We think of inventory as relatively short-lived because we expect the physically identifiable items to be sold more or less promptly, their value to be converted into cash, the firm to have the option to replace them or not, and the creditor to have the opportunity

[3] See Moses Abramovitz, *Inventories and Business Cycles, with Special Reference to Manufacturers' Inventories* (New York, NBER, 1950), Table 114, p. 569.

to renew the loan or not. But when we think of inventory as a whole—its economic magnitude—we realize that a minimum volume is indispensable in the life of the firm. To operate, the firm will require x million dollars of inventory, just as it will require y million dollars of buildings and machinery, and in this sense the economic life of inventory as a whole is the same as the life of the firm.

As a consequence, one can easily envisage a situation in which long-term credit is legitimately advanced to finance additions to inventory, so long as that credit goes to a firm with a growing market and is used for additions that constitute the indispensable minimum in long-term expansion. One can also envisage short-term funds being advanced to finance a long-lived machine or building, so long as the firm makes a depreciation charge allowance that can, within the year, be used toward repayment of the loan, rather than being economically mortgaged to the financing of some indispensable replacement.

Yet these are exceptional cases. By and large, the short economic life of inventories, on the *margin*—that is, the additions to them—does permit a check upon the profitability of investment in them, a check that is impossible with the complex of capital equipment tied up in a railroad, for example, or in a house. Granted that the physical and technological characteristics of capital items act largely as permissive or limiting conditions rather than determining factors, the economic forces operating through the decisions of firms and other economic units follow patterns that reflect these underlying differences in physical and technological characteristics—if only obliquely. And we should not neglect the customary distinctions that mirror these patterns, for from them we should be able to learn what factors guided capital formation in the past and are likely to affect it in the future.

After these introductory remarks we turn to the statistical evidence in Table 14—percentage distributions of countrywide capital formation. The distribution that is of most interest to us here is that of domestic capital formation classified into construction, producers' durables, and net changes in inventories. For the sake of completeness we also present the percentage distribution of total capital formation, which includes net changes in claims against foreign countries, discussed in the preceding section; and finally, the distribution of durable capital alone (construction and producers' durables), to bring out more clearly the difference in trend movements between the two.

For guidance among the five parts of Table 14, the following notes may be useful:

Trends in Structure of Capital Formation

First, let us indicate the scope of the items. Construction represents the value of construction work put in place, including the installed value of equipment, which is an integral part of a structure—house, plant, bridge, road, harbor installation, and the like—and including what are usually designated major repairs and alterations, but excluding ordinary repairs and maintenance. Producers' durable equipment includes machinery and similar items of considerable size, but excludes hand tools and minor types of equipment often chargeable to current expense. Inventories are stocks of commodities that are held for sale or for further fabrication, or are in process of fabrication. Construction comprises both private and public—including military construction unless specifically excluded—and that done under contract as well as that done on force account. Producers' durable equipment covers both private and public, including munitions unless military capital formation is specifically excluded. Inventories are, for conceptual reasons, limited to those in the hands of business and government agencies and exclude stocks within households; for statistical reasons they are limited to business inventories (including farm), there being no data on government inventories for the early years. However, the available series show the latter to be quite small, except for stocks of expendable (nondurable) munitions—which were enormous during the war years.[4] We excluded them because their inclusion would produce gyrations in the inventory item that would dwarf and conceal any economic movements in inventory levels.

Second, the structure by type of capital good is shown for four countrywide totals of capital formation: gross capital formation, in current and in constant prices; and net capital formation, also in current and in constant prices. In addition, since the inclusion or exclusion of military construction and munitions affects the distributions, particularly for the decades beginning with World War I, we show the

[4] At the end of 1949, public inventories in 1929 prices amounted to $2.4 billion, accounting for almost 5 per cent of the total of $50.4 billion. This high level of public inventories may be due largely to recent accretions, because before 1934 (except in the few years associated with World War I) and back to 1897, public inventories were well below $100 million, while total inventories grew from $16 billion to $38 billion. The only noticeable modification in the estimate of net changes in inventories that would be introduced by the addition of public inventories would be in 1929–1938, when the item would add $0.11 billion per year to our total. For the estimates, see R. W. Goldsmith, Dorothy S. Brady, and Horst Mendershausen, *A Study of Saving in the United States,* Vol. III (Princeton University Press, 1956), Table W-3, pp. 20–21.

TABLE 14

STRUCTURE OF CAPITAL FORMATION, BY TYPE OF CAPITAL GOOD, 1869-1955

(amounts in billions of dollars)

A. GROSS CAPITAL FORMATION, CURRENT PRICES

PERIODS	TOTAL CAPITAL FORMATION					DOMESTIC CAPITAL FORMATION				DURABLE CAPITAL FORMATION		
	Average Volume Per Year (1)	Percentage Distribution of (1)				Average Volume Per Year (6)	Percentage Distribution of (6)			Average Volume Per Year (10)	Percentage Distribution of (10)	
		Construction (2)	Producers' Durables (3)	Net Changes in Inventories (4)	Net Changes in Claims against Foreign Countries (5)		Construction (7)	Producers' Durables (8)	Net Changes in Inventories (9)		Construction (11)	Producers' Durables (12)
Total												
1. 1869–1898	2.23	63.9	22.9	14.9	−1.8	2.27	62.8	22.5	14.7	1.93	73.6	26.4
2. 1879–1908	3.44	64.4	23.8	9.9	1.9	3.37	65.7	24.3	10.1	3.03	73.0	27.0
3. 1889–1918	5.67	57.0	27.5	8.3	7.2	5.26	61.4	29.6	9.0	4.79	67.5	32.5
4. 1899–1928	10.81	53.2	29.9	9.1	7.8	9.96	57.7	32.5	9.8	8.98	64.0	36.0
5. 1909–1938	12.89	52.9	33.8	6.5	6.9	12.00	56.8	36.3	6.9	11.17	61.0	39.0
6. 1919–1948	20.38	45.6	43.9	5.3	5.2	19.33	48.1	46.3	5.6	18.24	50.9	49.1
7. 1929–1955 a	37.01	47.6	47.3	4.0	1.1	36.62	48.2	47.8	4.1	35.13	50.2	49.8
8. 1946–1955	61.29	48.3	45.0	4.9	1.8	60.17	49.2	45.8	5.0	57.15	51.8	48.2
Total, Excluding Military												
3a. 1889–1918	5.48	57.6	26.3	8.6	7.5	5.07	62.3	28.4	9.3	4.60	68.7	31.3
4a. 1899–1928	10.48	53.7	28.9	9.4	8.1	9.63	58.4	31.4	10.2	8.65	65.0	35.0

5a. 1909–1938	12.44	53.7	32.5	6.7	7.1	11.56	57.8	35.0	7.2	10.72	62.3	37.7
6a. 1919–1948	17.42	50.7	37.0	6.2	6.0	16.37	54.0	39.4	6.6	15.29	57.8	42.2
7a. 1929–1955 ª	31.91	53.1	41.0	4.7	1.2	31.52	53.7	41.6	4.7	30.03	56.4	43.6
8a. 1946–1955	55.78	51.8	40.7	5.4	2.0	54.65	52.9	41.6	5.5	51.64	56.0	44.0

B. GROSS CAPITAL FORMATION, 1929 PRICES

Total

9. 1869–1898	4.68	70.5	20.8	9.9	−1.2	4.74	69.6	20.6	9.8	4.28	77.2	22.8
10. 1879–1908	7.29	68.2	22.9	7.1	1.8	7.16	69.5	23.3	7.2	6.64	74.9	25.1
11. 1889–1918	10.26	62.6	25.2	6.2	6.0	9.64	66.6	26.9	6.6	9.00	71.3	28.7
12. 1899–1928	13.76	57.4	28.6	6.6	7.4	12.75	62.0	30.9	7.1	11.84	66.7	33.3
13. 1909–1938	14.42	55.0	33.2	4.8	7.0	13.42	59.2	35.7	5.1	12.73	62.3	37.7
14. 1919–1948	18.32	45.9	43.7	5.4	5.0	17.40	48.4	46.0	5.7	16.42	51.3	48.7
15. 1929–1955 ª	23.90	43.1	50.3	5.0	1.6	23.52	43.8	51.2	5.1	22.32	46.1	53.9
16. 1946–1955	32.98	41.5	49.2	6.8	2.6	32.14	42.6	50.5	7.0	29.89	45.8	54.2

Total, Excluding Military

11a. 1889–1918	10.04	63.0	24.5	6.3	6.2	9.42	67.2	26.1	6.7	8.79	72.0	28.0
12a. 1899–1928	13.42	57.9	27.8	6.7	7.6	12.41	62.6	30.1	7.3	11.50	67.6	32.4
13a. 1909–1938	13.95	55.9	32.0	4.9	7.2	12.95	60.2	34.5	5.3	12.26	63.6	36.4
14a. 1919–1948	15.87	50.6	37.4	6.2	5.8	14.95	53.7	39.7	6.6	13.97	57.5	42.5
15a. 1929–1955 ª	20.27	48.4	43.8	5.9	1.9	19.88	49.4	44.6	6.0	18.69	52.5	47.5
16a. 1946–1955	29.72	45.0	44.6	7.6	2.9	28.87	46.3	45.9	7.8	26.62	50.2	49.8

Percentages, except those for 1946–1955, are based on three-decade moving totals of absolute volumes. ª 1949–1955 given the weight of a decade.

(continued)

TABLE 14 (continued)

	TOTAL CAPITAL FORMATION					DOMESTIC CAPITAL FORMATION				DURABLE CAPITAL FORMATION		
		Percentage Distribution of (1)					Percentage Distribution of (6)				Percentage Distribution of (10)	
PERIODS	Average Volume Per Year (1)	Construction (2)	Producers' Durables (3)	Net Changes in Inventories (4)	Net Changes in Claims against Foreign Countries (5)	Average Volume Per Year (6)	Construction (7)	Producers' Durables (8)	Net Changes in Inventories (9)	Average Volume Per Year (10)	Construction (11)	Producers' Durables (12)
Total												
17. 1869–1898	1.26	63.9	12.8	26.4	−3.1	1.30	62.0	12.4	25.6	0.96	83.3	16.7
18. 1879–1908	1.88	64.7	13.8	18.0	3.5	1.82	67.1	14.3	18.6	1.48	82.4	17.6
19. 1889–1918	2.88	53.9	15.6	16.4	14.2	2.47	62.7	18.2	19.1	2.00	77.5	22.5
20. 1899–1928	5.16	47.3	17.4	19.0	16.3	4.32	56.5	20.8	22.7	3.34	73.1	26.9
21. 1909–1938	4.75	37.9	25.9	17.5	18.6	3.86	46.6	31.8	21.6	3.03	59.4	40.6
22. 1919–1948	6.26	25.2	40.7	17.3	16.8	5.21	30.2	48.9	20.8	4.13	38.2	61.8
23. 1929–1955 a	9.38	51.4	28.5	15.9	4.2	8.98	53.7	29.7	16.6	7.49	64.4	35.6
24. 1946–1955	15.50	67.1	6.2	19.5	7.2	14.38	72.3	6.7	21.0	11.36	91.5	8.5
Total, Excluding Military												
19a. 1889–1918	2.71	54.6	12.9	17.4	15.1	2.30	64.3	15.2	20.5	1.83	80.9	19.1
20a. 1899–1928	5.10	46.9	17.4	19.2	16.5	4.26	56.1	20.8	23.0	3.28	72.9	27.1
21a. 1909–1938	4.69	38.3	25.1	17.8	18.9	3.80	47.2	30.9	21.9	2.97	60.4	39.6

C. NET CAPITAL FORMATION, CURRENT PRICES

22a. 1919–1948	5.21	27.0	32.0	20.8	20.2	4.16	33.9	40.0	26.1	3.07	45.8	54.2
23a. 1929–1955 [a]	9.14	52.0	27.4	16.3	4.3	8.74	54.3	28.7	17.0	7.26	65.4	34.6
24a. 1946–1955	19.57	55.4	23.4	15.4	5.7	18.45	58.8	24.8	16.4	15.43	70.3	29.7
D. NET CAPITAL FORMATION, 1929 PRICES												
Total												
25. 1869–1898	2.62	73.4	11.1	17.8	−2.2	2.67	71.8	10.8	17.4	2.21	86.9	13.1
26. 1879–1908	3.96	70.6	13.1	13.1	3.3	3.83	73.0	13.5	13.5	3.31	84.4	15.6
27. 1889–1918	5.23	62.2	13.9	12.1	11.8	4.61	70.5	15.7	13.7	3.98	81.7	18.3
28. 1899–1928	6.58	54.0	16.8	13.8	15.4	5.56	63.8	19.9	16.3	4.66	76.2	23.8
29. 1909–1938	5.25	42.4	25.4	13.1	19.1	4.25	52.4	31.4	16.2	3.56	62.5	37.5
30. 1919–1948	5.63	24.5	41.6	17.5	16.3	4.71	29.3	49.8	20.9	3.72	37.1	62.9
31. 1929–1955 [a]	5.70	34.2	38.1	21.0	6.7	5.32	36.7	40.8	22.5	4.12	47.4	52.6
32. 1946–1955	7.88	55.3	5.5	28.5	10.8	7.03	62.0	6.1	31.9	4.79	91.0	9.0
Total, Excluding Military												
27a. 1889–1918	5.04	62.9	12.2	12.6	12.3	4.42	71.7	13.9	14.3	3.79	83.7	16.3
28a. 1899–1928	6.50	53.7	16.8	13.9	15.6	5.48	63.6	19.9	16.5	4.58	76.2	23.8
29a. 1909–1938	5.17	42.8	24.5	13.3	19.4	4.17	53.1	30.4	16.5	3.48	63.6	36.4
30a. 1919–1948	4.69	26.3	33.1	21.0	19.6	3.77	32.7	41.2	26.1	2.78	44.3	55.7
31a. 1929–1955 [a]	5.19	35.5	34.1	23.1	7.4	4.81	38.3	36.8	24.9	3.61	51.0	49.0
32a. 1946–1955	10.45	43.9	26.5	21.5	8.1	9.60	47.8	28.8	23.4	7.36	62.4	37.6
D3. NET CAPITAL FORMATION, 1929 PRICES, USING THE ALTERNATIVE ESTIMATE OF CAPITAL CONSUMPTION [b]												
Total												
33. 1869–1898	2.69	75.4	9.5	17.3	−2.2	2.75	73.8	9.3	16.9	2.28	88.8	11.2
34. 1879–1908	4.08	72.8	11.3	12.7	3.2	3.95	75.2	11.7	13.1	3.43	86.5	13.5
35. 1889–1918	5.40	65.0	11.8	11.7	11.5	4.78	73.4	13.3	13.3	4.15	84.7	15.3

(continued)

TABLE 14 (concluded)

| | TOTAL CAPITAL FORMATION | | | | | DOMESTIC CAPITAL FORMATION | | | | DURABLE CAPITAL FORMATION | | |
| | Percentage Distribution of (1) | | | | | Percentage Distribution of (6) | | | | Percentage Distribution of (10) | | |
PERIODS	Average Volume Per Year (1)	Construction (2)	Producers' Durables (3)	Net Changes in Inventories (4)	Net Changes in Claims against Foreign Countries (5)	Average Volume Per Year (6)	Construction (7)	Producers' Durables (8)	Net Changes in Inventories (9)	Average Volume Per Year (10)	Construction (11)	Producers' Durables (12)
36. 1899–1928	6.64	57.9	13.2	13.6	15.3	5.63	68.3	15.6	16.1	4.72	81.4	18.6
37. 1909–1938	4.84	53.8	11.3	14.2	20.7	3.84	67.9	14.2	17.9	3.15	82.7	17.3
38. 1919–1948	5.63	33.3	32.9	17.5	16.3	4.71	39.8	39.3	20.9	3.73	50.3	49.7
39. 1929–1955 a	6.88	39.6	37.4	17.4	5.5	6.50	42.0	39.6	18.4	5.30	51.4	48.6
40. 1946–1955	10.88	49.5	22.1	20.6	7.8	10.03	53.6	24.0	22.4	7.78	69.1	30.9
Total, Excluding Military												
35a. 1889–1918	5.21	65.9	10.1	12.2	11.9	4.59	74.7	11.5	13.8	3.96	86.7	13.3
36a. 1899–1928	6.56	57.6	13.1	13.8	15.5	5.55	68.2	15.5	16.3	4.64	81.5	18.5
37a. 1909–1938	4.76	54.5	10.1	14.4	21.1	3.76	69.0	12.7	18.3	3.07	84.4	15.6
38a. 1919–1948	4.69	36.8	22.6	21.0	19.6	3.77	45.8	28.1	26.1	2.79	62.0	38.0
39a. 1929–1955 a	6.37	41.1	34.1	18.8	6.0	5.99	43.7	36.3	20.0	4.79	54.6	45.4
40a. 1946–1955	13.45	41.7	35.2	16.7	6.3	12.60	44.6	37.6	17.8	10.35	54.2	45.8

Because of rounding, detail will not necessarily add to total.

Percentages, except those for 1946–1955, are based on three-decade moving totals of absolute volumes.

a 1949–1955 given the weight of a decade.

b For a description of the alternative estimate of capital consumption—for producers' durables (excluding military) and for "other" construction—see text.

SOURCE: Calculated from the series given in, or underlying, Tables R-6, R-7, R-29, R-30, R-32, R-33, and R-34.

150

percentage distribution for each of the four totals including and excluding those military items.

Third, our interest here is in the long-term trends in the structure of capital formation, not in its changes during business cycles, not even (until we reach a later stage in our analysis) in the changes during the long swings that have characterized the rate of economic growth in this country. We therefore need averages for periods of at least twenty-five to thirty years.

Those averages can be calculated in two ways. In one, the percentage shares of construction, producers' durables, etc., in the countrywide total can be calculated for each decade and then the decade shares averaged for the longer periods. In the resulting average all decades are weighted equally, although the absolute volumes of capital formation—the bases to which the percentage shares are computed—may differ markedly from decade to decade.

Such averages, when calculated, proved to be erratic, as they would be if the absolute volume of capital formation in any decade was low and if any large component was negative. That was true for net capital formation in the 1929–1938 decade, and it distorted the three-decade averages toward the end of the period. We therefore adopted the alternative procedure: the absolute volumes were averaged for successive periods of three decades each and the percentage shares were calculated from those averages. Such averages are weighted by the volume of capital formation in each decade, and they therefore assign the heaviest weights to the decades in which capital formation is largest. We used arithmetic means to preserve the additive relation of the components.

Fourth, scrutiny of the movements of percentage shares in *net* capital formation for recent decades suggested the possible value of a series based upon an alternative set of capital consumption estimates—for producers' durables (excluding munitions) and for construction other than nonfarm residential and government. For the former component, our present estimates of capital consumption for the decades since 1919 are based essentially on business depreciation shifted to a cost of replacement basis and supplemented by estimates of capital charged to current account. We link those totals with estimates for the earlier decades based upon straight-line depreciation and the assumption of a thirteen-year economic life. Comparison for the years since 1919 of consumption estimated on this basis with that based on business accounts indicates that (as mentioned in footnote 1 of Chapter 3) the average volumes for long periods are about the same, but the estimate based on business accounts is more variable, more responsive to changing business conditions, than that based on straight-line depreciation. Thus, the business accounts measure of depreciation falls markedly short of the straight-line life total during the depressed decade 1929–1938 and exceeds it substantially in the 1940's and 1950's. To secure better continuity in our estimate of consumption of producers' durables we used as an alternative for the entire period an estimate based directly on the assumption of a thirteen-year economic life. The second modification in our standard estimate of capital consumption—for construction other than nonfarm residential and government—was to exclude the charge for depletion. As indicated in Appendix A, we consider the charge for depletion a proper deduction from current capital formation. But there may be disagreement concerning such treatment, and depletion volumes have risen rapidly in recent years. It seemed advisable, therefore, to consider an alternative that would exclude this charge. The totals of *net* capital formation based upon these alternative estimates of depreciation of producers' durables and "other" construction and the resulting percentage shares of components are shown for volumes in 1929 prices in part Da of Table 14. The modifications have only a minor effect on the trends in the aggregates, but they affect more significantly the movement in some components in the recent decades.

We now list the findings suggested by Table 14, seriatim.

1. The percentage share of net changes in claims against foreign countries in gross capital formation, whether in current or in 1929 prices, rose to a peak in the thirty-year period centered on 1909–1918, and then declined (parts A and B). The share was not large, varying from −1.8 per cent to +8.1 per cent. As already indicated, the level was held down in the recent decades by huge unilateral transfers made abroad on government account. But we can say that the proportional importance of private foreign investment in total gross capital formation has declined significantly from the peak levels in the period from 1915 to 1929.

Net changes in foreign claims loomed much larger as shares in net capital formation, ranging—even for the thirty-year periods used here—from −3.1 per cent to +21.1 per cent (parts C, D, and Da). The rise in the share of net changes in foreign claims in net capital formation continued almost to the end of the period, the peak being in the period centered on 1919–1928 or on 1929–1938, combining the decades of the 1920's and the 1940's. We can say, in general, that relative to net capital formation, capital investment abroad continued at comparatively high levels until quite recently when world conditions and the emergence of large unilateral transfers by government—as well as a huge expansion of domestic capital formation—brought the percentage share down.

2. The share of net changes in inventories in domestic gross capital formation varied for the thirty-year periods from 4.1 per cent to about 15 per cent. The trend in the share was generally downward: a decline is observed in both parts A and B of Table 14, that is, whether based on current or constant price values, whether for totals including or excluding military capital formation. And the decline was quite marked. On the basis of the totals in current prices, the share of net changes in inventories in domestic gross capital formation shrank from 14.7 per cent to 4.1 per cent, or to less than three-tenths its original level. When the components of domestic gross capital formation are adjusted for price changes (part B), the drop in the share of net changes in inventories is reduced somewhat, but even then it is from roughly 10 per cent at the beginning to 5 per cent at the end (for totals including military), or to 6 per cent (for totals excluding military).

No such clear-cut decline is evident in the movement of the share of net changes in inventories in domestic net capital formation (parts C, D, and Da). For the totals in current prices, the share declined from almost 26 per cent and then rose again, and toward the end of the period, particularly when we exclude the military, it is no lower than at the beginning. Hence, for the totals in current prices, it is safest to conclude that there is no significant evidence of a major long-term decline in the share of net changes in inventories in net capital formation. With the adjustment for price changes, the picture is altered somewhat: the share is slightly higher in the later periods than in the earlier—well over 20 per cent as against 17 per cent, the rise being even more marked for the totals excluding military capital formation.

This effect of the adjustment for price changes is clearly due to the differential price movement. Prices of the goods constituting inventories must have risen less or declined more (obviously the former, because over the period as a whole the trend in prices has been upward) than have the prices of the sum of the other two components of domestic capital formation—construction and producers' durables. This was caused largely by the construction component (although for totals including military, the high price of munitions also had some effect in recent decades), in which a lesser rise of productivity than in most other sectors of the economy made for a differentially higher price level at the end of the period than at the beginning. With prices of goods entering inventories rising less than other prices, their 1869 prices are a higher fraction and their post-1929 prices a lower fraction of 1929 levels than are the comparable prices of construction plus producers' durables. Because the multiplicand in the conversion to 1929 prices is the reciprocal of this fraction, it would be lower before 1929 and higher after 1929 than that for construction plus producers' durables. For this reason the share of net changes in inventories in constant prices (parts D and Da) is lower than that in current prices (part C) in the earlier periods and higher in the later periods.

3. The share of construction in gross durable capital formation declined, and that of producers' durable equipment rose (parts A and B). The decline in the share of construction when we include military capital formation—from about three-quarters to about one-half—is more pronounced than when we exclude it, because the addition of munitions to producers' durables is relatively greater than the addition of military construction to construction.

The same trend is observable in the distribution of net durable capital formation between net construction and net producers' durables (parts C, D, and Da). The levels of the shares and the slopes of the trends are somewhat different, however. Thus, in general, in the early periods the share of net construction in net durable capital formation tended to be higher than that of gross construction in gross durable capital formation. And the decline in the share of construction in the net totals in 1929 prices was somewhat more precipitous than the decline in its share in the gross total in constant prices. But all these differences are in the nature of details. For the present it can be stated that in current or in constant prices, including or excluding the military items, for gross or net volumes, the share of construction in durable capital formation declined, which means that the rate of growth of construction was significantly lower than that of producers' durable equipment.

Several questions suggested by these findings warrant further discussion. (a) Why did the share of net changes in inventories in *gross* domestic capital formation decline? (b) Why did the share of net changes in inventories in *net* domestic capital formation either remain stable or rise? (c) Why did the share of construction in total durable capital formation decline? (d) Why did the share of construction in durable capital formation totals move differently from its share in the net, and did this difference have any bearing on the ratio of countrywide net capital formation to gross?

a. In dealing with the first question, we begin by assuming that net changes in inventories and net capital formation embodied in construction and producers' durables serve the same broad purpose inasmuch as they both measure additional equipment for the production of an increment of goods. This assumption is not implausible: inventories are used in the extraction, manufacture, and distribution of commodities, as well as in the provision of services. Construction and machinery are also used to produce commodities and services. The product-mix for any specific complex of structures and machinery will differ from that for any other, and it will differ from that associated with specific groups of inventories. But it can be argued that countrywide inventories and the countrywide stock of structures and equipment service the same product—the countrywide aggregate.

Let us assume also, pending further discussion, that the ratios of inventories and of net durable capital to output are constant, and so, therefore, are the marginal ratios—the ratios of net changes in inventories and of net durable capital formation to net additions to output. Under these conditions the average and the marginal ratios will be the same. It follows from this assumption that the share of net changes in inventories in net domestic capital formation is also constant.

But we are interested here in the share of net changes in inventories in gross domestic capital formation. If their share in net domestic capital formation is constant, their share in gross domestic capital formation will be constant only if the proportion of capital consumption (or of net capital formation) to gross capital formation is constant. This can be seen from the following equations:

DCF (domestic capital formation)
= DC (durable capital formation) + Inv (net changes in inventories)
DGCF (domestic gross capital formation) = DCG (durable capital formation, gross) + Inv
DNCF (domestic net capital formation) = DCN (durable capital formation, net) + Inv

If Inv/DCN is constant and equal to a, Inv = aDCN. DCG = DCN + B (capital consumption), and if B is a constant fraction of

DCN, say k, it is also a constant fraction of DCG, and the equation will read $\text{DGCF} = \text{DCN} + \text{DCN}k + \text{Inv} = \text{Inv}(k/a) + \text{Inv} = \text{Inv}(1 + k/a)$, and with k and a constant, Inv will be a constant fraction or multiple of DCG, or of DGCF.

As will be seen later, however, the proportion of capital consumption to gross durable capital formation is not constant but increases, partly because of the retardation of growth in the total of gross construction and producers' durables, partly because of the growing importance of the producers' durable component, which has an economic life span shorter than that of construction. It follows that if the ratio of net changes in inventories to net domestic capital formation is constant and the proportion of durable capital consumption to gross durable capital formation increases (or the proportion of net durable capital formation to gross declines), the ratio of net changes in inventories to *gross* domestic capital formation must decline—and this is the finding indicated in Table 14.

As noted above, this explanation is based on the assumption that the ratios of net investment in inventories and of net investment in durable capital to additions to output are constant (and that consequently the average ratios involved are also constant). But is this assumption valid? Should we expect that each dollar of new output will necessitate a constant number of dollars of net changes in inventories and a constant, although possibly different, number of dollars of net capital formation in construction and producers' durable equipment? This brings us to the second question listed above—that relating to the movement in the share of net changes in inventories in *net* domestic capital formation.

b. Changes in inventories and in durable capital can be related to changes in the aggregate product presumably made possible by the former. The relevant comparisons are provided in Table 15, and a few notes will explain the calculations involved.

Column 1 represents additions to the annual output of finished commodity product, in 1929 prices. It includes the commodity components of flow of goods to consumers (perishables, semidurables, and durables) at cost to consumers (because the distribution and transportation services involved in bringing commodities from producers to consumers require both inventories and plant and equipment). It also covers gross construction and gross producers' durables, including military items—since the latter may be and are produced in any plant serviced by the stock of construction and equipment the net changes

TABLE 15

RATIO OF NET DURABLE CAPITAL FORMATION AND OF NET CHANGES IN INVENTORIES TO NET CHANGES IN FLOW OF FINISHED COMMODITY PRODUCT, BASED ON VOLUMES IN 1929 PRICES, 1869–1955

(amounts in billions of dollars)

Periods	Net Changes in Finished Commodity Product (1)	Net Durable Capital Formation (2)	Ratio of (2) to (1) (3)	Net Durable Capital Formation, Excluding Nonfarm Residential and Government Construction (4)	Ratio of (4) to (1) (5)	Net Changes in Inventories (6)	Ratio of (6) to (1) (7)
		A. USING STANDARD DEPRECIATION ESTIMATE					
1. 1869–1898	19.6	66.2	3.38	33.5	1.71	13.9	0.71
2. 1879–1908	26.9	99.4	3.70	56.6	2.10	15.5	0.58
3. 1889–1918	26.4	116.0	4.39	67.4	2.55	19.0	0.72
4. 1899–1928	41.6	139.2	3.34	74.3	1.78	27.1	0.65
5. 1909–1938	31.7	104.8	3.31	43.3	1.37	20.6	0.65
6. 1919–1948	61.8	88.0	1.42	25.3	0.41	29.6	0.48
7. 1929–1955	68.1	87.5	1.28	23.6	0.35	30.4	0.45
8. 1946–1955	43.1	71.2	1.65	34.4	0.80	22.5	0.52
		B. USING ALTERNATIVE DEPRECIATION ESTIMATE					
9. 1869–1898		68.5	3.50	35.8	1.83		
10. 1879–1908		102.9	3.83	60.1	2.23		
11. 1889–1918		121.2	4.59	72.6	2.75		
12. 1899–1928		141.2	3.39	76.3	1.83		
13. 1909–1938		92.6	2.92	31.0	0.98		
14. 1919–1948		88.1	1.42	25.4	0.41		
15. 1929–1955		112.9	1.66	49.0	0.72		
16. 1946–1955		101.2	2.35	64.4	1.49		

SOURCE:

Part A

Col. 1. Sum of changes in flow of goods to consumers (Variant I), gross construction, and gross producers' durables. The changes are obtained from the annual series underlying Tables R-28, R-30, and R-33, at thirty-year intervals—1899 minus 1869, 1909 minus 1879, and so on, except for lines 7 and 8: 1955 minus 1929; and 1955 minus 1945.

Col. 2. Sum of net construction including military, and net producers' durables excluding military, calculated from the annual series underlying or given in Tables R-7, R-32, and R-33.

Col. 4. Column 2 minus nonfarm residential and government construction, calculated from the annual series underlying Table R-32.

Col. 6. Calculated from the decade averages in Table R-15 and the annual series in Table R-5.

Part B

For description of alternative depreciation estimate, see text.

in which we are attempting to measure.[5] From the annual series of finished commodity output we derived changes for thirty-year periods corresponding to the three-decade periods used in measuring net durable capital formation and net changes in inventories. Thus we obtained the growth in annual output of finished commodity product from 1869 to 1899, to compare with net durable capital formation and net changes in inventories for 1869–1898; from 1879 to 1909, to compare with 1879–1908; and so on.

Two variants of net durable capital formation are studied in Table 15. The first covers all net construction, including military (because the latter can be used to produce the military items in construction and producers' durables), and all net producers' durables except munitions (because munitions, by definition, cannot be used to produce other commodities). This first total, appearing in column 2, includes nonfarm residential construction which cannot be conceived directly as a tool in the production of finished commodities. It also includes government construction, some of which may be in the form of munition- and other commodity-producing plants, but most of which can be assumed to produce services not embodied in commodities. The second variant of net durable capital formation (column 4) excludes nonfarm residential and government construction, and is perhaps more directly relevant to our purposes. For both variants of net durable capital formation, we have the alternative estimate based upon the alternative series of capital consumption for producers' durables and "other" construction, discussed in connection with Table 14. Finally, net changes in inventories are shown in column 6. All the entries are in 1929 prices; and the thirty-year cumulative totals of net capital formation in columns 2, 4, and 6, are compared with the additions to the annual output of finished commodities in column 1.

The results can be stated simply. The ratio of net changes in inventories to net additions to finished commodity output, while fluctuating, remained at roughly the same level through most of the period

---

[5] We exclude services not embodied in finished commodities, i.e., the services component of flow of goods to consumers, although some inventories and some durable capital are used to produce these services. For example, medical practitioners use both inventories and durable capital and so do cleaning and dyeing establishments. But the construction, equipment, and inventories employed in this sector of the economy must be relatively small, and their ratio to total net output much lower than that for commodity output. It seemed to us that a much clearer picture of the ratios of changes in inventories and in durable capital to output would emerge if services not embodied in commodities were excluded from output.

covered, with a distinct decline only in the periods that include World War II and the subsequent decade. The movements of the ratios of net durable capital formation to additions to finished commodity product are quite different. These marginal capital-output ratios rose perceptibly to a peak in the thirty-year period centered on the first decade of this century, and then declined precipitously. This sharp decline is observed whether we deal with net durable capital formation including or excluding nonfarm residential and government construction, and whether we employ the standard depreciation estimate or the alternative. Even during the 1946–1955 decade, the ratio of net durable capital formation to net additions to commodity output, as shown in part A, was considerably less than one-half that reached at the peak, 1889–1918, and, as shown in part B, it was only slightly more than one-half. Clearly, greater commodity output could be produced with a smaller net addition to construction and producers' equipment.

This is a trend already observed, in somewhat different form, in Chapter 3. It is associated partly with the change in technology and in the rate of growth, and partly with the fact that a larger proportion of capital consumption and replacement to total gross durable capital formation means greater opportunity for introducing more efficient equipment, and this reduces the need for net durable capital formation. In the present connection, it is the change in technology and particularly the utilization of capital replacement to increase efficiency (a factor that is not present in the case of inventories) that may have caused the greater decline in the marginal net durable capital-output ratio than in the marginal inventory-output ratio. And as a result— at least in the calculations using the weighted averages—the share of net changes in inventories in total net domestic capital formation rose.

One cardinal qualification of this finding must be introduced at this point. The estimates of construction and the flow of producers' durable equipment, like all economic estimates, are based on imperfect data. But we do have at decennial or shorter intervals back to 1869 the basic census data that permit us to distinguish construction materials, and machinery and equipment, and a variety of subsidiary data to provide a relatively firm foundation for the estimates. No such anchorage in basic data is available for the estimates of some of the major components of inventories before the 1920's, particularly manufacturing and trade. For these we assumed that net changes were a constant ratio of changes in output or activity—the ratio prevailing in the 1920's. This assumption may have introduced a false stability into the marginal ratios of inventories to output in Table 15, which, of course, is the reason for the secular rise in the share of net changes in inventories in total domestic net capital formation.

Agricultural inventories are estimated on the basis of census data, and their secular movements are different from those of nonfarm inventories. It may therefore be of interest to distinguish farm from nonfarm and to observe the long-term trends in the structure of net changes in total inventories by groups (Table 16). Our estimates run through 1938, but for the distinction between farm and other inventories we can extend the record another decade by means of Goldsmith's estimates.

Net changes in farm inventories (which include changes in livestock) were a rapidly declining proportion of total inventory change. Regardless of the validity of the estimates of nonfarm inventories, this trend is beyond question. For one thing, agriculture constituted a diminishing fraction of the total commodity output of the economy, and it would be surprising if farm inventories did not likewise account for a declining share of the country's inventories. Second, the substitution of machinery for animals resulted in an absolute diminution of the number of horses and mules on farms, and the growth in other livestock was far slower than could have been true of inventories either in manufacturing or in trade. For the present purpose the important consequence is that, if we consider net changes in nonfarm inventories alone, they would presumably account for an even more rapidly rising proportion of net domestic capital formation than would net changes in total inventories. In part B of Table 16, where the share of changes in nonfarm inventories in both gross and net domestic capital formation is calculated, the rise of the share in net domestic capital formation is striking, more than doubling from 1869–1898 to 1919–1948. But even the share of changes in nonfarm inventories in gross domestic capital formation fails to show any significant decline, the difference in movement between the marginal ratio of nonfarm inventories to output and the marginal ratio of durable capital to output almost completely offsetting the effects of the increasing proportion of capital consumption to gross durable capital formation.

The calculation in part B of Table 16 is not quite logical, however. Changes in nonfarm inventories are compared with durable capital formation, which includes construction and equipment designed to service the farm sector. We therefore attempted to recalculate the

160

TABLE 16

Structure of Net Changes in Inventories, 1929 Prices, 1869–1948

A. Percentage Distribution of Total Net Changes in Inventories [a]

Periods	Total Farm (1)	Livestock (2)	Total Nonfarm (3)	Mining, Manufacturing, and Construction (4)	Trade (5)	All Other (6)
			BASED ON KUZNETS ESTIMATES			
1. 1869–1898	27.3	22.0	72.7	33.1	22.9	16.6
2. 1879–1908	20.8	15.7	79.2	37.0	25.0	17.2
3. 1889–1918	12.9	9.7	87.1	37.1	33.7	16.3
4. 1899–1928	2.1	1.1	97.9	43.5	40.8	13.7
5. 1909–1938	-1.2	-1.1	101.2	35.0	46.8	19.4
			BASED ON GOLDSMITH ESTIMATES			
6. 1889–1918	18.3	12.0	81.7			
7. 1899–1928	4.4	2.2	95.6			
8. 1909–1938	2.0	-1.9	98.0			
9. 1919–1948	0.5	-4.5	99.5			

(continued)

TABLE 16 (concluded)

B. ESTIMATED EFFECT OF EXCLUSION OF FARM INVENTORIES

Periods	Net Changes in Nonfarm Inventories as % of Total (1)	Net Changes in Inventories as % of Gross Domestic Capital Formation (2)	Net Changes in Nonfarm Inventories as % of Gross Domestic Capital Formation (1) × (2) (3)	Net Changes in Inventories as % of Net Domestic Capital Formation (4)	Net Changes in Nonfarm Inventories as % of Net Domestic Capital Formation (1) × (4) (5)	Alternative Estimate of (4) (6)	Alternative Estimate of (5) (1) × (6) (7)
10. 1869–1898	72.7	9.8	7.1	17.4	12.6	16.9	12.3
11. 1879–1908	79.2	7.2	5.7	13.5	10.7	13.1	10.4
12. 1889–1918	87.1	6.7	5.8	14.3	12.5	13.8	12.0
13. 1899–1928	97.9	7.3	7.1	16.5	16.2	16.3	16.0
14. 1909–1938	101.2	5.3	5.4	16.5	16.7	18.3	18.5
15. 1919–1948	102.4	6.6	6.8	26.1	26.7	26.1	26.7

a Percentages are based on three-decade moving totals of absolute volumes.

SOURCE, BY LINE

1–5. Absolutes calculated from Simon Kuznets, *National Product since 1869* (New York, NBER, 1946), Tables II-10 and II-11, pp. 108 and 111.

6–9. Absolutes calculated from Goldsmith, *A Study of Saving,* Vol. I, pp. 797 and 903.

10–15. Col. 1 from part A, above, line 15 being extrapolated from 1909–1938 to 1919–1948 by the movement in the Goldsmith ratio, with allowance for the difference in movement between his series and ours from 1899–1928 to 1909–1938. Cols. 2, 4, and 6 from Table 14, parts B, D, and Da, respectively.

marginal ratios of durable capital and inventories to output, excluding the farm or agricultural sector from all terms of the comparison.

Exclusion of the farm sector can be only approximate, and yet the results have sufficient validity to merit examination. In Table 17, net changes in finished commodity product are those shown in Table 15, reduced by an estimate of net income originating in agriculture. This reduction excludes the contribution of agriculture proper, without eliminating further fabrication, transportation, and distribution of the products of agriculture and without eliminating the products other industries may have contributed to agriculture. The totals in columns 2 and 4 are net durable capital formation (the former including, the latter excluding, residential and government construction, and both excluding munitions) minus the estimated construction and producers' durable equipment channeled into the agricultural sector. Finally, net changes in nonfarm inventories are derived from Table 16 and, being net of farmers' inventories, are dominated by two categories—manufacturers' and trade stocks.

The movements of the marginal ratios of durable capital and of inventories to output are not unlike those in Table 15. For net durable capital formation excluding residential and government construction, the ratio in Table 17 rises from 1.81 to 2.53 and declines to 0.36, whereas that in Table 15 (for a comparable period) moves from 1.71 to 2.55 and then to 0.41. The similarity persists for the ratio based upon values derived from the alternative estimate of depreciation. In Table 17, the marginal ratio for inventories declines from between 0.6 and 0.7 to 0.5; that in Table 15, from between 0.7 and 0.8 to below 0.5. But the decline in the marginal ratio for inventories is still far smaller than that in the marginal ratio for net durable capital; and in any calculation using as a base net domestic capital formation, excluding the agricultural sector, the share of net changes in inventories will show a secular rise, and that of net durable capital formation, a decline.

But how plausible is the basic assumption underlying this trend? Is it likely that the marginal ratio of inventories to output in manufacturing and in trade remained constant from the 1870's to the 1920's and at the level prevailing in the 1920's? Here, for lack of specific evidence, conjecture can run rampant. It can be argued that technological improvements in transportation and communication would in general make for a lower marginal ratio of inventories to output or sales, because it would not be necessary to hold as much inventory against possible shortages resulting from delays in delivery. It can be argued

TABLE 17

RATIO OF NET DURABLE CAPITAL FORMATION AND OF NET CHANGES IN INVENTORIES TO NET CHANGES IN FLOW OF FINISHED COMMODITY PRODUCT, EXCLUDING AGRICULTURE, BASED ON VOLUMES IN 1929 PRICES, 1869–1948

(amounts in billions of dollars)

Periods	Net Changes in Finished Commodity Product (1)	Net Durable Capital Formation (2)	Ratio of (2) to (1) (3)	Net Durable Capital Formation, Excluding Nonfarm Residential and Government Construction (4)	Ratio of (4) to (1) (5)	Net Changes in Inventories (6)	Ratio of (6) to (1) (7)
		A. USING STANDARD DEPRECIATION ESTIMATE					
1. 1869–1898	16.28	62.2	3.82	29.5	1.81	10.1	0.62
2. 1879–1908	23.78	93.3	3.92	50.5	2.12	12.3	0.52
3. 1889–1918	23.33	107.6	4.61	59.0	2.53	16.6	0.71
4. 1899–1928	37.81	132.5	3.50	67.6	1.79	26.6	0.70
5. 1909–1938	30.75	104.0	3.38	42.4	1.38	20.8	0.68
6. 1919–1948	60.52	84.4	1.39	21.8	0.36	30.3	0.50
		B. USING ALTERNATIVE DEPRECIATION ESTIMATE					
7. 1869–1898		64.5	3.96	31.8	1.95		
8. 1879–1908		96.8	4.07	54.0	2.27		
9. 1889–1918		112.8	4.83	64.2	2.75		
10. 1899–1928		134.5	3.56	69.6	1.84		
11. 1909–1938		91.8	2.99	30.2	0.98		
12. 1919–1948		84.5	1.40	21.9	0.36		

For description of estimates, see text. Agriculture is excluded from cols. 1, 2, 4, and 6.

that improvements in manufacturing processes, insofar as they reduce the time required to produce a given item, would lower the ratio of inventories constituted by stock in process to the total finished output of the plants. It can be argued that improved efficiency in trade, particularly in the form of larger units with a high stock-turnover ratio, would reduce the marginal ratio of trade inventories to sales. On the other hand, several arguments can be adduced for expecting an upward trend in the inventory-output or inventory-sales ratio: the greater detail in manufacturing production may make for a longer production process; the higher standard of living and the demand for wider selection may force trade units to hold stocks that are larger relative to sales volume; the greater dispersion of consumer markets, combined with greater concentration of producer centers, may make for large inventory holding at various focal points to bridge the gap between producer and consumer. Finally, there is the whole question of the changing product-mix. Different branches of manufacturing and trade are characterized by different inventory-output or inventory-sales ratios; and intersector shifts within manufacturing or within trade might produce trends in the aggregate ratios, even though the ratios within each sector of manufacturing or trade remained constant.

For lack of specific information, it is not easy to appraise these several conjectures. By and large, if, as we would have expected, the marginal ratio of inventories to output declined in the long run, net changes in inventories in the earlier decades are underestimated in our measures; and their share in total net domestic capital formation should show a decline rather than constancy or a rise. But this hypothesis is doubtful, if only because the marginal ratio of net durable capital to output was increasing through the thirty-year period terminating in 1918. The factors making for this rise, particularly the establishment of new large plants and units that were built for the long run and which in the early years of their use were operated at a rate below their maximum capacity, would also make for a high rate of inventories to current output. And the interindustry shift within manufacturing and the interbranch shift within trade would also militate against a decline in the inventory-output or the inventory-sales ratio. For, in this long-term change in structure, the durable goods sectors with their higher inventory-output or inventory-sales ratios were becoming more important relatively than the perishable goods sectors with their low inventory-output or -sales ratios. When we calculate the over-all ratio for manufacturing for 1899 and 1929, using Abramovitz's inventory-sales ratios for 1919–1938, by major branches,[6] and Fabricant's estimates of value added in the same branches for 1899 and 1929,[7] we find that it rises from 22.7 per cent to 22.9 per cent. This is a small rise indeed, but a rise nevertheless; and from 1869 to 1899 there might well have been an even greater rise. In trade also, the recession in importance of wholesale trade, and particularly of products that flowed directly from producers to consumers without going through trade channels,[8] as well as the shift within retail trade in favor of the more durable types of commodities, would tend to sustain the ratio of trade inventories to total finished output in the economy.

While it is impossible, therefore, to come to firm conclusions, it is perhaps not unwarranted to infer that the marginal ratio of inventories to finished output, if it did decline from the 1870's to the 1920's, could not have declined appreciably; and that there is some validity to our finding that the share of net changes in inventories in total net domestic capital formation in constant prices has risen over the long period from the 1870's to the post-World War II decade.

c. In dealing with the trends in the structure of durable capital proper—specifically the decline in the share of construction and the rise in the share of producers' durable equipment—the first relevant observation is that construction is a much more heterogeneous total than producers' durable equipment. As measured here, construction includes nonfarm residential and related housing, and other structures above ground and underground—roads, bridges, streets, sewers, and many more. It thus includes capital items designed directly for the use of ultimate consumers (such as residences); those designed for the use of both ultimate consumers and business producers (such as roads and other common carrier installations); those designed for the exclusive use of governments and other public institutions; and finally, those intended for use as tools of commodity production in the hands of business firms (including farmers). There is considerable variety also in the type and user of producers' durable equipment: it includes equipment for farmers as well as for nonfarm enterprises, for government installations as well as for private firms. But it is narrower and more homogeneous than construction in that it excludes con-

---

[6] See *Inventories and Business Cycles,* Table 30, p. 133.

[7] See Solomon Fabricant, assisted by Julius Shiskin, *The Output of Manufacturing Industries, 1899–1937* (New York, NBER, 1940), p. 635.

[8] See Harold Barger, *Distribution's Place in the American Economy since 1869* (Princeton for NBER, 1955), Table 20, p. 70.

sumer durable commodities and, particularly in the variant excluding munitions, is heavily dominated by machinery and equipment destined for use by producing firms in the private business sector.

Consequently, any reasons for the slower growth in the volume of construction than in the volume of producers' durables can be more easily established if we distinguish at least the major categories of structures. The classification in Table 18 is based upon detailed estimates given in the reference tables (see Appendix C). It distinguishes nonfarm residential construction and construction on government account. "Other" construction is a residual still too mixed for our purposes. For example, it includes institutional construction, which could be separated for recent decades only. It is nevertheless a useful category, because it is predominantly construction used by producing enterprises in the business sector and, hence, much more comparable in scope with producers' durables than is total construction.

The trends in the distribution of the gross volume of construction are clear and conspicuous. The share of government construction rose, whether or not we include military construction, from considerably less than one-tenth in the first thirty-year period to about one-third in the last. The shares of nonfarm residential and "other" construction both declined—the former from about four-tenths to about three-tenths, the latter from well over one-half to somewhat above one-tenth. And the share of "other" construction, dominated by industrial plant and office buildings, declined more than the share of nonfarm residential. Thus the share of nonfarm residential construction in gross non-government construction would rise, and that of "other" construction would decline.

The trends in the distribution of the net volume of construction are affected by the estimate of depreciation for "other" construction. If we use the standard estimate, net "other" construction is negative in 1919–1948 and 1929–1955. If we use the alternative estimate of depreciation for "other" construction, the net volume of "other" construction is still negative in 1919–1948, but the decline is not so sharp, and the distorting effects on the percentage distributions, not so great.

Despite the differences between these variants of net construction, we can still come to fairly firm conclusions. First, the share of governments in net construction shows a conspicuous upward trend, whether or not we include military construction. It rises from about 6 per cent in the period 1869–1898 to 50 per cent or more in 1929–1955; and

TABLE 18

Distribution of Gross and Net Construction by Type, 1929 Prices, 1869-1955

(amounts in billions of dollars)

PERIODS	GROSS CONSTRUCTION				NET CONSTRUCTION				NET CONSTRUCTION, USING ALTERNATIVE ESTIMATE OF DEPRECIATION FOR "OTHER" CONSTRUCTION [a]			
	Average Volume Per Year (1)	Percentage Distribution of (1)			Average Volume Per Year (5)	Percentage Distribution of (5)			Average Volume Per Year (9)	Percentage Distribution of (9)		
		Nonfarm Residential (2)	"Other" (3)	Government (4)		Nonfarm Residential (6)	"Other" (7)	Government (8)		Nonfarm Residential (10)	"Other" (11)	Government (12)
Total												
1. 1860–1898	3.30	40.1	53.1	6.8	1.92	50.7	43.2	6.1	2.03	48.0	46.3	5.8
2. 1879–1908	4.97	35.9	56.1	7.9	2.80	43.0	48.9	8.1	2.97	40.5	51.9	7.6
3. 1889–1918	6.42	31.5	56.8	11.7	3.25	35.6	50.2	14.2	3.51	33.0	53.9	13.1
4. 1899–1928	7.94	33.0	51.4	15.6	3.55	41.7	39.0	19.3	3.85	38.5	43.7	17.8
5. 1909–1938	7.94	31.2	44.2	24.5	2.23	48.4	7.9	43.8	2.61	41.3	21.3	37.4
6. 1919–1948	8.41	30.0	37.3	32.7	1.38	67.1	−51.3	84.1	1.88	49.4	−11.3	61.9
7. 1929–1955 [b]	10.29	28.8	35.2	36.0	1.95	60.0	−33.7	73.7	2.73	42.9	4.3	52.8
8. 1946–1955	13.68	33.3	38.4	28.3	4.36	60.9	15.6	23.5	5.38	49.3	31.6	19.1
Total, Excluding Military												
3a. 1889–1918	6.33	32.0	57.5	10.5	3.17	36.6	51.5	12.0	3.43	33.8	55.2	11.0
4a. 1899–1928	7.77	33.6	52.3	14.2	3.49	42.4	39.8	17.8	3.78	39.1	44.4	16.4
5a. 1909–1938	7.80	31.8	45.0	23.2	2.21	48.6	7.9	43.5	2.59	41.5	21.4	37.1
6a. 1919–1948	8.03	31.4	39.1	29.5	1.23	75.2	−57.4	82.2	1.73	53.6	−12.3	58.6
7a. 1929–1955 [b]	9.82	30.2	36.9	32.9	1.84	63.7	−35.8	72.1	2.62	44.8	4.5	50.7
8a. 1946–1955	13.37	34.1	39.3	26.6	4.59	57.8	14.8	27.5	5.61	47.2	30.3	22.5

Because of rounding, detail will not necessarily add to total.

Percentages, except those for 1946-1955, are based on three-decade moving totals of absolute volumes.

[a] For description of the alternative estimate of depreciation used in columns 9 and 11, see text.

[b] 1949–1955 given the weight of a decade.

SOURCE: Calculated from Tables R-7, R-30, and R-32.

even in 1946–1955, when private construction was high, the share of governments was about one-fifth or more.

The share of nonfarm residential construction in net construction does not decline. It is roughly stable if we use the alternative estimate of depreciation; and rises if we use the standard estimate. This trend is different from that of the share of nonfarm residential construction in gross construction. The two trends differ because capital consumption of nonfarm residential construction grew at a lesser rate than capital consumption of "other" construction. This, in turn, is because the retardation in the rate of growth of nonfarm residential construction was less than the retardation in the rate of growth of "other" construction.

It follows that the share of "other" construction in net construction declined, whatever variant of depreciation we use and whether or not we include military construction. Indeed, the marked decline in the share of "other" construction in total construction—whether gross or net—is the major conclusion from Table 18.

We are thus led to the following inference. In the decline of the share of gross construction in gross durable capital formation, the lower rate of growth of nonfarm residential construction was a contributing factor, but the major factor was the even lower rate of growth of gross "other" construction. In the decline of the share of net construction in net durable capital formation, the lower rate of growth of nonfarm residential construction was a contributing factor but with less weight; and the major and dominant factor was again the even lower rate of growth of net "other" construction. Government construction, since it grew rapidly, did not contribute to the decline in the share of construction in total durable capital formation. In short, it is the much slower growth of "other" construction relative to that of producers' durables (with which it is most comparable in scope) that accounts for most of the shift in the distribution of durable capital in favor of producers' equipment.

"Other" construction is predominantly for the strictly business sectors—mostly nonagricultural plant, roadway (for railroads), utility, and office construction. It is a tool, therefore, for much the same commodity product that is served by producers' durable equipment, despite the minor differences in scope of the aggregate output turned out by these two complexes of capital items. The much slower rate of growth in "other" construction than in producers' durables means that the ratio of changes in the former to changes in output has declined more, or risen less, than the ratio of changes in the latter to changes in output. The movements of these ratios can be observed directly (Table 19).

The comparisons in Table 19 are similar to those in Tables 15 and 17, except that "other" construction and producers' durables, including or excluding agriculture, are related to net changes in finished commodity output, including or excluding the contribution of agriculture. But here we have gross volumes of construction and producers' equipment as well as net volumes. The former are included in the analysis to reveal whether the trends in the marginal capital-output ratios are substantially affected by the allowance for capital consumption.

The movements in the marginal capital-output ratios are quite similar for the several variants. The ratio of "other" construction to changes in output rose to a peak in the period 1889–1918, and then declined sharply: the gross ratio dropped to less than one-third of the peak level, and the net ratio turned negative. If the middle decade can be taken as the more exact date of the secular level of a thirty-year average, the peak ratio of "other" construction to changes in output can be said to have been reached in the 1899–1908 decade; and the drop since then has been particularly sharp in the periods including the World War II and postwar years.

The ratio of producers' durables to changes in commodity output follows a different secular pattern. The gross ratio, and the net ratio based on the standard depreciation estimate, rose to a peak in the period 1909–1938, while the net ratio based on the alternative depreciation estimate reached a peak in the period 1899–1928. But despite a decline from those peak levels, the ratios in the later periods are substantially above their levels in the early periods or above their previous peak levels. Thus the ratio for gross producers' equipment is over 3.0 both in 1929–1955 and 1946–1955, compared with less than 2.0 in 1869–1898 and 1879–1908; whereas the ratio for gross "other" construction is 1.4 in 1929–1955 and 1.2 in 1946–1955, compared with 2.7 and 3.1 in the first two thirty-year periods. Likewise, the net producers' durables ratio (standard depreciation series) is well above 0.6 in the most recent periods (over 0.7 in 1919–1948), compared with less than 0.6 in the first two periods. But the recent net "other" construction ratio is either negative or a small fraction of the level that prevailed in 1869–1898.

In short, the shift in the structure of total durable capital formation away from construction toward producers' durables can be largely accounted for by the shift away from "other" construction toward pro-

TABLE 19

Capital-Output Ratios: Ratios of Gross and Net Volumes of "Other" Construction and Producers' Durables to Net Changes in Flow of Finished Commodity Product, Based on Volumes in 1929 Prices, 1869–1955

(amounts in billions of dollars)

Periods	Net Changes in Finished Commodity Product (1)	Gross Volumes				Net Volumes				Net Volumes, Using Alternative Depreciation Estimate			
		"Other" Construction (2)	Ratio of (2) to (1) (3)	Producers' Durables, Excluding Munitions (4)	Ratio of (4) to (1) (5)	"Other" Construction (6)	Ratio of (6) to (1) (7)	Producers' Durables, Excluding Munitions (8)	Ratio of (8) to (1) (9)	"Other" Construction (10)	Ratio of (10) to (1) (11)	Producers' Durables, Excluding Munitions (12)	Ratio of (12) to (1) (13)
Total													
1. 1869–1898	19.6	52.6	2.68	29.3	1.49	24.9	1.27	8.7	0.44	28.1	1.43	7.7	0.39
2. 1879–1908	26.9	83.7	3.11	50.0	1.86	41.0	1.52	15.5	0.58	46.2	1.72	13.9	0.52
3. 1889–1918	26.4	109.3	4.14	73.8	2.80	49.0	1.86	18.5	0.70	56.8	2.15	15.8	0.60
4. 1899–1928	41.6	121.9	2.93	111.9	2.69	41.6	1.00	32.7	0.79	50.4	1.21	25.8	0.62
5. 1909–1938	31.7	105.3	3.32	133.9	4.22	5.2	0.16	38.0	1.20	16.6	0.52	14.4	0.45
6. 1919–1948	61.8	94.1	1.52	178.1	2.88	−21.2	−0.34	46.5	0.75	−6.4	−0.10	31.8	0.51
7. 1929–1955	68.1	91.9	1.35	224.0	3.29	−22.4	−0.33	46.0	0.68	−2.5	−0.04	51.5	0.76
8. 1946–1955	43.1	52.5	1.22	132.5	3.07	6.8	0.16	27.7	0.64	17.0	0.39	47.4	1.10
Total, Excluding Agriculture													
1a. 1869–1898	16.3	n.a.	n.a.	n.a.	n.a.	21.8	1.34	7.8	0.48	25.0	1.53	6.8	0.42
2a. 1879–1908	23.8					36.3	1.53	14.1	0.59	41.5	1.74	12.5	0.53
3a. 1889–1918	23.3			n.a.		42.9	1.84	16.2	0.70	50.7	2.18	13.5	0.58
4a. 1899–1928	37.8					37.0	0.98	30.6	0.81	45.8	1.21	23.7	0.63
5a. 1909–1938	30.8					5.4	0.18	37.0	1.20	16.8	0.55	13.4	0.44
6a. 1919–1948	60.5					−21.2	−0.35	42.9	0.71	−6.4	−0.11	28.2	0.47

Ratios, except those for 1946–1955, are based on three-decade moving totals of absolute volumes.

n.a. = not available.

SOURCE, BY LINE

1–8. Col. 1: Table 15, col. 1.
Cols. 2, 6, and 10: Calculated from the series given in, or underlying, Tables R-30 and R-32. For the alternative estimate of depreciation, see notes to Table 14, part Da. Cols. 4, 8, and 12: Calculated from Table 14, parts B, D, and Da.

1a–6a. Col. 1: Table 17, col. 1.
Cols. 6, 8, 10 and 12: Calculated from the series underlying the estimates in Table 17.

ducers' durables. The latter shift, in turn, means that after roughly the first decade of this century the marginal capital-output ratio for "other" construction declined far more precipitously than did that for producers' durables. The greater decline in the ratio for "other" construction is evident even when we use gross volumes, that is, gross rather than net capital formation. In other words, during recent decades it has become increasingly possible to produce more finished commodities with absolutely and proportionately smaller gross or net additions to the stock of "other" construction than to the stock of producers' durable equipment.

The explanation of the difference between the movement in the capital-output ratio for "other" construction and that for equipment requires an examination of output and capital formation for major industry sectors, and a brief discussion along these lines is to be found in a later section of this chapter. It may be said here that the explanatory model would have to distinguish trends in the relation between construction and equipment and output within industries from trends in the weights of different industries, characterized by different ratios of construction to output and equipment to output. Thus, in a given industry, say steam railroads, the records might suggest that in the early stages of its growth the construction of track, stations, and so on formed a large part of its durable capital formation, and the ratio of construction to output was high and rising. Later, after the basic network had been completed, the need for new construction, gross or net, lessened, while technical progress stimulated the demand for new producers' equipment. If the suggestion holds, the pattern for the railroad sector may be described as an early rise in the marginal capital-output ratios, for both construction and equipment, succeeded by a marked decline in the ratio for construction, and a lesser decline, stability, or even a rise in the ratio for producers' equipment. This pattern may have typified not only railroads but also other utilities, many manufacturing industries, and so forth. However, there may also have been simultaneously interindustry shifts. We are dealing here with aggregates of "other" construction and producers' durable equipment, even if we exclude agriculture. Within the total complex of nonagricultural industries, sectors characterized by higher than average ratios of construction to output may have predominated during the early periods; and it may be that the decrease in their importance brought about the precipitous decline in the marginal ratio of "other" construction to output—even though within each industry no significant decline occurred.

We can advance beyond such conjectures only after we consider the more detailed evidence on the industrial distribution of durable capital. The present remarks are intended merely to indicate the lines that a complete explanation would have to follow. And we now turn to the last question raised above—the effect of the changes in structure of capital formation by type of capital good on the ratio of capital consumption to gross capital formation.

d. Our estimates of capital consumption are based largely on an assumption of constant economic life and straight-line depreciation, although for some components (nonfarm residential construction, for example) and for recent decades somewhat different procedures were followed. It can be demonstrated that if constant economic life and straight-line depreciation are assumed, trends in the ratio of capital consumption to gross capital formation will depend upon three variables: first, the movement of the rate of growth in gross capital formation (retardation in the rate increases the ratio of capital consumption to gross capital formation and acceleration in the rate decreases it); second, trends in the relative weight in gross capital formation of the several categories subject to different economic life (e.g., an increase in the weight of gross producers' durables relative to construction will raise the ratio of capital consumption to gross durable capital formation); and third, trends in the weight in capital formation of items subject to depreciation relative to those, already net, that are not (net changes in inventories and in foreign claims). Clearly, a rise or decline in the share of the nondepreciable items in gross capital formation would mean, all other conditions being equal, a decline or rise in the ratio of capital consumption to gross capital formation.[9]

All three relations indicated above operated in part to raise the proportion of capital consumption to gross capital formation. We have already observed that the share of net changes in inventories in gross domestic capital formation declined. For a while, the share of net changes in foreign claims in total capital formation rose, but after reaching a peak during World War I and in the 1920's, it fell. Thus, the share of the nondepreciable components in gross capital formation declined. We have also pointed out that the rate of growth of gross

[9] For an algebraic analysis of these relations see Appendix B, in Kuznets, "International Differences in Capital Formation and Financing," in *Capital Formation and Economic Growth*, pp. 76–81.

construction was slower than that of gross producers' durables, which means that the share of the latter, with its shorter economic life span and higher depreciation ratio, increased. Now, in Table 20, we observe the movement in the rates of growth in the volumes (in constant prices) of gross construction, gross flow of producers' durables, and their total (columns 1, 2, and 3).

The period covered in Table 20 is too short for our purposes. It should extend about fifty years further back for construction, and about a decade and a half further back for producers' durables, since current capital consumption is affected by earlier rates of growth in gross capital formation. Nevertheless, it is clear even from the truncated period covered that the rate of growth in construction shows a sharp retardation, whereas retardation in the rate of growth in producers' durable equipment is not nearly so marked. The effects on the movement of the ratio of capital consumption to gross capital formation for these two categories of durable capital (columns 4 and 5, or 9 and 10) are conspicuous—particularly if we exclude the military items from both categories. For construction (column 4), the ratio of capital consumption to gross capital formation rose from less than one-half to over eight-tenths. For producers' durables (column 5) it fluctuated around seven-tenths, the only noticeable rise being in the period including World War II and later years.

The most interesting item of evidence in Table 20, however, relates to the ratio of capital consumption to gross capital formation for the more comprehensive totals. Thus, for total durable capital formation, the sum of construction and producers' durables, the ratio of capital consumption to total gross volume, rose almost as much as did the ratio for construction, even though there was no such rise in the ratio for producers' durables. But it was the increasing weight of the latter that served to sustain the rise in the proportion of capital consumption to gross durable capital formation, from almost one-half to over eight-tenths (column 6). We find similar rises in the ratio of capital consumption to domestic and total capital formation—i.e., when capital formation includes the nondepreciable components of net changes in inventories and in foreign claims (columns 7, 8, 12, and 13).

Structure of Capital Formation, by Category of User

The ultimate purpose of capital formation is that of all economic activity—to provide goods for the satisfaction of wants of the human

TABLE 20

RATE OF GROWTH IN GROSS CONSTRUCTION AND IN GROSS PRODUCERS' DURABLES, AND RATIO OF CAPITAL CONSUMPTION TO GROSS CAPITAL FORMATION, BASED ON VOLUMES IN 1929 PRICES, 1869–1955

Periods	% Rate of Growth, Per Decade			Ratios of Capital Consumption to Gross Totals					Ratios of Capital Consumption to Gross Totals, Using Alternative Estimate of Depreciation [a]				
	Gross Construction (1)	Gross Producers' Durables (2)	Gross Durable Capital Formation (3)	Construction (4)	Producers' Durables (5)	Durable Capital Formation (6)	Domestic Capital Formation (7)	Total Capital Formation (8)	Construction (9)	Producers' Durables (10)	Durable Capital Formation (11)	Domestic Capital Formation (12)	Total Capital Formation (13)
Total													
1. 1869–1898				0.42	0.70	0.48	0.44	0.44	0.39	0.74	0.47	0.42	0.43
2. 1879–1908	50.6	70.9	55.2	0.44	0.69	0.50	0.46	0.46	0.40	0.72	0.48	0.45	0.44
3. 1889–1918	29.0	55.2	35.6	0.49	0.72	0.56	0.52	0.49	0.45	0.75	0.54	0.50	0.47
4. 1899–1928	23.1	52.3	31.5	0.55	0.72	0.61	0.56	0.52	0.51	0.78	0.60	0.56	0.52
5. 1909–1938	0.5	21.6	7.5	0.72	0.72	0.72	0.68	0.64	0.67	0.89	0.75	0.71	0.66
6. 1919–1948	6.0	66.9	28.9	0.84	0.71	0.77	0.73	0.69	0.78	0.77	0.77	0.73	0.69
7. 1929–1955 [b]	22.3	50.3	36.0	0.81	0.82	0.82	0.77	0.76	0.73	0.79	0.76	0.72	0.71
8. 1919–1928 to 1946–1955, or 1946–1955	13.6	49.5	28.5	0.68	0.97	0.84	0.78	0.76	0.61	0.85	0.74	0.69	0.67
Total, Excluding Military													
3a. 1889–1918	27.3	47.5	32.4	0.50	0.75	0.57	0.53	0.50	0.46	0.79	0.55	0.51	0.48
4a. 1899–1928	22.8	51.6	30.9	0.55	0.71	0.60	0.56	0.52	0.51	0.77	0.60	0.55	0.51
5a. 1909–1938	0.3	19.7	6.6	0.72	0.72	0.72	0.68	0.63	0.67	0.89	0.75	0.71	0.66
6a. 1919–1948	3.0	33.0	13.9	0.85	0.74	0.80	0.75	0.70	0.78	0.82	0.80	0.75	0.70
7a. 1929–1955 [b]	22.3	49.4	33.8	0.81	0.80	0.81	0.76	0.74	0.73	0.75	0.74	0.70	0.69
8a. 1919–1928 to 1946–1955, or 1946–1955	13.2	41.1	24.3	0.66	0.79	0.72	0.67	0.65	0.58	0.64	0.61	0.56	0.55

Rates of growth and ratios, except those in lines 8 and 8a, are based on three-decade moving totals of absolute volumes.

[a] For "other" construction and producers' durables, excluding military.

[b] 1949–1955 given the weight of a decade.

SOURCE: Calculated from the series underlying Table 14 and those underlying Tables R-7, R-31, and R-33.

beings who comprise society, in whatever institutional and organizational framework society sets up. Viewed in that light it does not matter whether a capital item is bought directly by the ultimate consumer for his own use (a house, for instance), is purchased by a business firm to produce finished goods, or is procured by governments for needs that are the responsibility of government agencies. In all these cases, the three groups of users of capital equipment can be viewed as delegates of society for the performance of identical functions. The house owner, business firm, and government unit can all be viewed as business units, either purchasing and planning the use of a capital item in an economic calculus, or supplying the ultimate needs of society, directly or indirectly.

While the function involved in capital formation is the same no matter who the ultimate user of the capital item may be, the identity of the user does make a difference—in the institutional arrangements by which capital formation decisions are made, in the patterns of behavior with respect to these decisions, modes of financing, and the like. While for some purposes we have to apply conventions to impose uniformity, it would be misleading to let those conventions guide our analysis. Thus in estimating national income, an owner-occupant of a dwelling is treated as an entrepreneur, in the business of supplying residential services to himself; and net income originating is calculated just as for a business firm, all relevant expenses, actual or imputed, being charged against an imaginary gross rent. Likewise, in some approaches, governments are treated as huge business enterprises, whose income is from tax receipts and other charges, and whose expenses are in the form of factor payments or payments to other industries. But such conventions should not lead us to assume that decisions by individuals on house purchase or construction, or by governments on capital acquisition or construction, are similar in all major respects to decisions by business firms; that the channels of financing are the same; or that the lines of distinction between gross capital formation, capital consumption, and net capital formation have quite the same meaning.

It is of interest, therefore, to classify capital formation by the three main groups of final users of capital items—households, business firms, and government agencies. The percentage distributions in Table 21 suggest the levels of and trends in the shares of these three major groups of final users in domestic capital formation.

Trends in Structure of Capital Formation

Unfortunately, the classification permitted by the available data suffers from many limitations, some stemming from conceptual difficulties, but most of them due to the scarcity of relevant statistics. The first set of difficulties relates to capital formation for households. Assuming that we exclude consumers' durable commodities, for reasons already discussed in Chapter 1, we should cover all residential housing, whether farm or nonfarm. But the distinction between the farm residence and the part of the farm that serves productive purposes is difficult and artificial—particularly when the estimates are extended to the early decades. We have, therefore, included farm residences with the rest of farm capital and limited residential construction to nonfarm. The omission of farm residences is not important quantitatively: Goldsmith's very rough estimates suggest an annual average gross volume, in 1929 prices, ranging from somewhat over $30 million to almost $300 million, and averaging less than $150 million for the period 1897–1949.[10] For the same period the gross totals of nonfarm residential construction averaged almost $2.5 billion, or almost sixteen times farm residential construction. A somewhat different question arises with respect to nonfarm residential construction proper: some of it is owner occupied, some is rented. Should we treat both parts as household capital formation, or only the former—classifying the latter as business because it is handled chiefly by business firms? We decided to treat all of it as household capital formation, on the grounds that the distance to the ultimate household user is quite short, and that renting part of a two-family or multifamily house by an individual owner is often little different from owner occupancy of a single family dwelling. Defined as nonfarm residential construction (excluding nonhousekeeping units), the estimate of household capital formation is fairly complete.

The difficulties in estimating the government component are somewhat different: they all lie in the scarcity of data. First, as previously indicated, changes in inventories do not include government inventories; and, to the extent that inventories in the hands of governments have increased, their total capital formation and share in the aggregate are underestimated. Second, all producer equipment except munitions is allocated to business, because we have no basis for a long-term estimate of the share going to government agencies. Here again, the flow of producers' durables to governments may have increased more than the flow to business firms; and if so, the levels of and trends in the gov-

[10] *A Study of Saving*, Vol. I, Table A-7, p. 761.

TABLE 21

Structure of Domestic Capital Formation, by Category of User, 1869–1955

(percentages)

Periods	Gross, Current Prices			Gross, 1929 Prices			Net, Current Prices			Net, 1929 Prices			Net, 1929 Prices, Using Alternative Estimate of Depreciation		
	House-holds [a] (1)	Busi-ness Firms (2)	Govern-ments (3)	House-holds [a] (4)	Busi-ness Firms (5)	Govern-ments (6)	House-holds [a] (7)	Busi-ness Firms (8)	Govern-ments (9)	House-holds [a] (10)	Busi-ness Firms (11)	Govern-ments (12)	House-holds [a] (13)	Busi-ness Firms (14)	Govern-ments (15)
Total															
1. 1869–1898	22.6	73.2	4.3	27.9	67.4	4.7	29.0	67.2	3.8	36.4	59.2	4.4	35.4	60.3	4.3
2. 1879–1908	21.4	73.3	5.3	25.0	69.5	5.5	26.6	67.9	5.6	31.4	62.7	5.9	30.4	63.8	5.7
3. 1889–1918	17.5	72.2	10.3	21.0	69.9	9.1	20.3	64.9	14.8	25.1	62.5	12.4	24.2	63.8	11.9
4. 1899–1928	18.9	68.7	12.4	20.5	68.2	11.3	25.2	61.9	12.9	26.6	60.8	12.6	26.3	61.2	12.5
5. 1909–1938	17.3	65.2	17.5	18.5	64.5	17.0	23.7	52.2	24.2	25.4	50.1	24.5	28.1	44.8	27.1
6. 1919–1948	14.3	57.0	28.8	14.5	57.8	27.7	19.8	40.0	40.2	19.7	38.8	41.5	19.7	38.9	41.5
7. 1929–1955 [b]	15.1	57.3	27.6	12.6	58.2	29.2	30.0	44.3	25.7	22.0	43.4	34.6	18.0	53.7	28.3
8. 1946–1955	16.9	61.7	21.4	14.2	64.6	21.2	41.7	67.1	−8.8	37.7	80.9	−18.6	26.4	86.6	−13.1
Total, Excluding Military															
3a. 1889–1918	18.1	74.9	7.0	21.5	71.5	7.1	21.9	69.8	8.4	26.2	65.2	8.6	25.2	66.5	8.3
4a. 1899–1928	19.6	71.1	9.4	21.0	70.1	8.9	25.6	62.8	11.6	27.0	61.7	11.3	26.7	62.1	11.2
5a. 1909–1938	17.9	67.7	14.3	19.2	66.9	13.9	24.0	53.0	23.0	25.8	51.1	23.1	28.7	45.7	25.6
6a. 1919–1948	16.8	67.3	15.9	16.9	67.3	15.9	24.8	50.2	25.1	24.6	48.5	26.9	24.6	48.6	26.9
7a. 1929–1955 [b]	17.5	66.6	15.9	14.9	68.8	16.3	30.8	45.5	23.7	24.4	48.0	27.6	19.6	58.3	22.2
8a. 1946–1955	18.6	68.0	13.4	15.8	71.9	12.3	32.5	52.3	15.2	27.6	59.3	13.1	21.0	68.9	10.0

Because of rounding, detail will not necessarily add to total. Percentages, except those for 1946–1955, are based on three-decade moving totals of absolute volumes.

[a] Nonfarm residential construction.

[b] 1949–1955 given the weight of a decade.

SOURCE: Calculated from the total in col. 6 of Table 14, and from the components either in or derived from Tables R-6, R-7, R-30, R-32, and R-33. Shares of business firms are derived as residuals.

ernment share in capital formation are understated. Finally, it would have been desirable to include the nonprofit public institutions with the government sector rather than with the business sector, which is necessary because of lack of detailed data for long periods back. The share of such institutions in the capital formation total has very likely increased; and if they were included in the share of the total public sector, the latter would be larger and might show greater growth. On all these counts, the share of governments in capital formation is understated. However, it appears from some alternative distributions presented below that the magnitude of the understatement may be exaggerated.

It follows that the share of the business sector in total capital formation is overstated and may have an upward trend bias. But all these qualifications are relatively unimportant, and certainly do not materially affect the clear long-term movements in the structure of capital formation by category of user.

Before summarizing the findings, it should be noted that the distribution in Table 21 is of domestic capital formation, because net changes in claims against foreign countries cannot be allocated by category of user. The users in this case in this country (rather than abroad) would presumably be the holders of the claims—households as individual owners of some claims against foreign countries, business firms as direct or portfolio investors, and governments as owners either of debt claims or of some material assets located abroad. No data indicating such a distribution are available for the years before the 1920's; and the significance of such a distribution is questionable.

The movement that dominates the picture is the rise in the share of the government sector. It is found whether we deal with gross or net capital formation, in constant or current prices, and on either basis of capital consumption. Furthermore, the rise is conspicuous. From less than 5 per cent in the early period, the share rose—even when military items are excluded—to about 16 per cent in the gross totals, and to considerably more than 20 per cent in the net totals (1929–1955, line 7a). We emphasize here 1929–1955 as the terminal period, since the distribution for 1946–1955 may be too much affected by transient elements. The broad findings would not, however, be much changed by the use of 1946–1955 as the terminal period.

As noted above, the share of governments tends to be understated in our estimates. To evaluate the effects of the understatement, alternative estimates based on Goldsmith's series on net changes in reproducible wealth (in constant prices) are presented. Inventories and producer equipment in the hands of governments are included, but all military goods are excluded. The results, for the broad periods that can be distinguished, appear in Table 22.

The table, a supplement, in a way, to Table 21, not only confirms the rise in the share of the government sector, but also indicates that the allowance for inventories and equipment produces little change in the percentages. The shift from 6 per cent in 1880–1900 to somewhat over 25 per cent in 1922–1948 (lines 8 and 10) is similar to the change from 6 per cent in 1879–1908 to almost 27 per cent in 1919–1948 (Table 21, column 12 or 15, lines 2 and 6a). In other words, the direction and

TABLE 22

STRUCTURE OF NET DOMESTIC CAPITAL FORMATION, EXCLUDING MILITARY, BY CATEGORY OF USER, BASED ON WEALTH ESTIMATES, 1929 PRICES, 1850–1948

	Percentage Shares of:		
		Business	
Dates or Periods	Households [a]	Firms	Governments
	(1)	(2)	(3)
	WEALTH, END OF YEAR		
1. 1850	21.7	75.0	3.3
2. 1880	24.9	71.5	3.6
3. 1900A [b]	29.3	65.5	5.2
4. 1900B [c]	31.8	61.1	7.2
5. 1922	29.9	60.5	9.5
6. 1948	29.6	55.5	14.9
	CHANGES IN WEALTH		
	(NET CAPITAL FORMATION)		
7. 1850–1880	25.7	70.5	3.7
8. 1880–1900A [b]	32.1	61.7	6.2
9. 1900B–1922 [c]	28.0	60.0	12.0
10. 1922–1948	29.1	45.5	25.4

[a] Nonfarm residential construction.

[b] Entries for 1900A are comparable with entries for earlier years.

[c] Entries for 1900B are comparable with entries for later years.

SOURCE: Raymond W. Goldsmith, "The Growth of Reproducible Wealth of the United States of America from 1805 to 1950," *Income and Wealth, Series II* (International Association for Research in Income and Wealth, Cambridge, England, Bowes and Bowes, 1952), p. 307.

magnitude of the rise in the share of the government sector in capital formation would remain much the same even if our series included equipment and inventories (excluding military items) in the hands of governments.

The share of the business sector in capital formation declined in all the variants, whether gross or net, whether in constant or current prices, whether including or excluding military—with one interesting exception. For the gross totals in 1929 prices (Table 21, column 5), excluding military, the moderate rise in the share of the business sector after the turn of the century was followed by only a slight decline. On the whole, therefore, the share of the business sector in those totals shows no significant long-term decline. However, in the gross totals in current prices the share declined, and in the net totals, whether in current or in constant prices, it declined even more sharply.

The share of the household sector in total *gross* domestic capital formation, whether in constant or in current prices, declined. Its share in net totals in current prices was fairly stable, but in net totals in constant prices, the share again showed a downward trend. In other words, the share of the household sector declined in all variants except that of net totals in current prices.

Since the rise in the share of governments dominates the percentage distributions in Tables 21 and 22, we also analyze the private sector alone and observe the shares of the household and the business sectors (Table 23).

The share of the household sector (nonfarm residential construction) in gross private domestic capital formation declined—only slightly for volumes in current prices, but quite appreciably for volumes in 1929 prices. The business sector, therefore, accounted for a somewhat rising proportion of all gross private domestic capital formation. With the shift to a net basis, the share of the household sector in volumes in current prices rose, and fairly appreciably. The trend in the share in net volumes in constant prices was, on the whole, downward. In short, within private domestic capital formation proper, the business sector tended to hold its own or even to rise, except in net volumes in current prices.

The findings just summarized have already been explained in part in the discussion of the trends in the structure of capital formation by type of capital good. Nevertheless, it may be useful to deal briefly with two points: (1) the reasons for the rise in the share of the government

TABLE 23

STRUCTURE OF PRIVATE DOMESTIC CAPITAL FORMATION, BY CATEGORY OF USER, 1869–1955

(percentages)

Periods	Gross, Current Prices		Gross, 1929 Prices		Net, Current Prices		Net, 1929 Prices		Net, 1929 Prices, Using Alternative Estimate of Depreciation	
	Households [a] (1)	Business Firms (2)	Households [a] (3)	Business Firms (4)	Households [a] (5)	Business Firms (6)	Households [a] (7)	Business Firms (8)	Households [a] (9)	Business Firms (10)
1. 1869–1898	23.6	76.4	29.3	70.7	30.1	69.9	38.1	61.9	37.0	63.0
2. 1879–1908	22.6	77.4	26.4	73.6	28.1	71.9	33.4	66.6	32.3	67.7
3. 1889–1918	19.5	80.5	23.1	76.9	23.9	76.1	28.7	71.3	27.5	72.5
4. 1899–1928	21.6	78.4	23.1	76.9	28.9	71.1	30.4	69.6	30.0	70.0
5. 1909–1938	20.9	79.1	22.3	77.7	31.2	68.8	33.6	66.4	38.5	61.5
6. 1919–1948	20.0	80.0	20.0	80.0	33.1	66.9	33.6	66.4	33.6	66.4
7. 1929–1955 [b]	20.8	79.2	17.8	82.2	40.4	59.6	33.7	66.3	25.1	74.9
8. 1946–1955	21.5	78.5	18.0	82.0	38.3	61.7	31.8	68.2	23.4	76.6

Percentages, except those for 1946–1955, are based on three-decade moving totals of absolute volumes.

[a] Nonfarm residential construction.

[b] 1949–1955 given the weight of a decade.

SOURCE: Calculated from Table 21.

182

sector in total capital formation; and (2) the reasons for the rising share of the business sector in gross private domestic capital formation, and its declining share in net in current prices.

1. The rise in the share of the government sector in total capital formation is a finding beyond doubt or qualification, and would be observed even with alternative definitions of capital accumulation (for example, one including consumers' durable commodities). While it cannot be explained in full here, an effective approach would be to view it as a product of two trends: the rise in the share of governments in the total economic activity of the nation, and the relation between this rise in activity under government auspices and the accumulation of material capital needed to effect it.

The rise in the share of governments in total economic activity can be demonstrated in various ways: by measuring the share of factor payments originating in the government sector in national income; by gauging the share of employment under government auspices in the country's labor force; by estimating the share of the total finished product of the economy purchased by government agencies; by appraising the extent to which the activity of the whole economy, including the private sector, is determined by decisions, acts, and policies of the governments—whether in their regulating, inducing, or limiting capacities. Each of these approaches would yield a clear picture of the rising weight of governments in the functioning of the national economy.

These trends, and the factors underlying them, have been discussed elsewhere.[11] There is little need here to repeat the discussion, except by way of a capsule summary. One point to be stressed is that the very pattern of the country's internal economic growth—the increasing density of population in urban conglomerates, the growing scale and complexity of the forms of economic organization, the increasing importance of overhead capital that cannot be financed under private auspices—has meant an increasing need for services and functions that cannot be left to private business. The satisfactory operation of private markets and private enterprise requires that the discrepancy between returns to business and returns to society, particularly in the long run, must not be large. For if the expected returns to business exceed the

---

[11] Notably in the following National Bureau studies: Solomon Fabricant, *The Trend of Government Activity in the United States since 1900* (New York, 1952); George Stigler, *Trends in Employment in the Service Industries* (Princeton, 1956); and Morris A. Copeland, *Trends in Government Financing* (Princeton, 1961).

social returns by too wide a margin, some resources will be diverted to uses that are not justified by the interests of society and that, therefore, diminish the potential social product in the long run. If the prospective returns to private business are smaller than they should be from the standpoint of society, then too few resources with high social priority will be employed.

With this general formula there may be far-reaching disagreement in specific cases about what constitutes the social as against the private net returns. Yet many illustrations may be cited. For example, with the increasing density of population, and the consequently greater need to protect public health, it would clearly be quite unsatisfactory to leave epidemic control and other public health measures to private concerns. They could not be expected to provide the necessary goods and services at prices within the means of all groups in the population. It would be dangerous not to employ the compulsive powers of government agencies in fields in which a few failures to conform (milk, mosquito, water control) would endanger entire communities. If—to use another example—a private enterprise expands to such a size that the preponderance of fixed costs in its financial structure makes competition impossible, whereas the importance of its product makes monopoly socially dangerous, only the government can intervene to regulate such a potential monopoly and reduce the discrepancy between private and public costs and returns. As the structure of the economy grows in complexity and as its parts are more closely interrelated, an increasing proportion of activities in the private sector assumes dominating public importance—in the sense that failure to perform is a graver threat to the efficiency of the economy as a whole than in earlier times when the various parts of the economy were more self-sufficient. The continuous development of social and economic institutions, which has been fundamental in permitting this country's economy to tap the increasing potential of economic productivity inherent in the growing stock of useful knowledge, requires an increasing role by the government in regulating, adjusting, and complementing those institutions, whenever there is evidence that, left to themselves, they may develop bottlenecks or misallocate resources from the point of view of society as a whole.

Just as the economic growth of the country produced internal pressure for greater activity by governments, so economic growth on an international scale had similar effects within the historical period covered by our estimates. It was the spread of the modern industrial system to an increasing number of large national units or empires that provided, at least in the permissive sense, conditions in which international discord could have economic effects and exercise economic pressures. Before the emergence of new industrial powers (Germany, Japan, and Russia), when Great Britain was the leading—in fact the only—major industrial power and could enforce *Pax Britannica* throughout a large part of the world, the threat to the United States of major international conflicts was small. Since the last quarter of the nineteenth century, however, that threat has increased steadily.

Given the growing share of governments in the country's total economic activity, their share in countrywide capital formation would increase if government activity required material capital, and if that requirement—as expressed by the capital-output ratio for the government sector—were not subject to a downward trend offsetting the upward trend in the government share in total economic activity. We have no evidence on the capital-output ratio for government activity. For some major areas of government operation such a ratio would be difficult to secure, because the activities served by the capital (streets, roads, and so on) are not those of government proper. Unlike business firms, which acquire capital goods to service their own productive operations exclusively, or households, which gear acquisition of capital to their own specific needs, many of the capital goods acquired by government agencies serve the broader purposes of society as a whole. The capital-output ratio would therefore have a clear meaning only for that part of government capital stock designed to service its own operations (office buildings, military construction, and munitions).

It is reasonable to suggest, nevertheless, that, aside from the special case of durable military material, the capital-output ratio associated with government capital formation is certainly not lower than the ratio prevailing for construction and equipment items elsewhere in the economy; and that the trend movement in the government ratio is at least not likely to show a greater decline or a lesser rise than that in the capital-output ratio for the economy at large. What might be called the utilities component of government capital formation, which bulked quite large in the nonmilitary totals of government capital, is in general characterized by a fairly high capital-output ratio. The same is true of the construction component, such as office buildings, associated directly with government operation. And as for the long-term trends in the capital-output ratio for the government sector, it might be reasonably argued that, because of the absence of those continuous pressures to economize and raise the rates of utilization of equipment that characterize use of capital in the private business sector (and to some extent even the household sector), we should not expect the capital-output ratio for the government sector to decline more or rise less than that for the economy at large. If this conjecture is accepted, the rise in the share of governments in the country's total economic activity would necessarily be accompanied by a similar, or perhaps even greater, rise in their share in countrywide capital formation.

In connection with the rise in that share it may be useful to distinguish between capital formation of local and state governments and that occurring under the auspices of the federal government. The former would, by and large, be almost exclusively in response to internally generated needs associated with the domestic aspects of the country's economic growth. Capital formation under direct federal auspices, a mixed category, can reflect both internal and external pressures, both domestic and foreign factors.

The distributions in Table 24 are quite suggestive. If the military items are excluded, capital formation under state and local government auspices (excluding federal aid) accounted for a dominating share of government capital formation—between 80 and 90 per cent—until the period covering the decade of the 1930's. It dropped below 80 per cent only when the Great Depression necessitated increased federal government financing of state and local capital formation, and again when World War II and the postwar years led to a far greater volume of federal construction, even nonmilitary (as housing). It is war, beginning with World War I, and the increasing demands it makes that change the picture radically. One can distinguish two quite different phases in the long record of government capital formation in this country. In the early phase, urban services—road building, education, public health, and other peacetime functions of government—grew apace and required capital formation largely under the auspices of state and local governments. In the later phase, problems of war and defense became dominant and, in turn, exacerbated internal problems—of stability and depression (for clearly, the depression of the 1930's was partly a post-world-war phenomenon), of internal migration, of regional disparities—calling for multiplication of activities and capital formation under federal auspices, both military and nonmilitary. Because wars are violent phenomena, one can hardly

TABLE 24

DISTRIBUTION OF GOVERNMENT GROSS CAPITAL FORMATION, CURRENT PRICES, BETWEEN
FEDERAL, AND STATE AND LOCAL, 1869–1955

| Periods | Percentage Shares in Total Nonmilitary | | | Military as Percentage of Nonmilitary (4) | Percentage Share of Federal in Total, Including Military (5) |
	State and Local, Including Federal Aid (1)	Federal Aid (2)	Direct Federal (3)		
1. 1869–1898 ᵃ	84.5	0	15.5	0	15.5
2. 1879–1908 ᵃ	83.9	0	16.1	0	16.1
3. 1889–1918 ᵃ	87.0	0.3	13.0	54.1	43.6
4. 1899–1928 ᵃ	92.6	3.1	7.4	36.5	32.2
5. 1909–1938 ᵃ	87.2	14.0	12.8	27.1	31.4
6. 1919–1948 ᵃ	72.2	15.4	27.8	113.7	66.2
7. 1929–1955 ᵃᵇ	72.5	11.4	27.5	101.7	64.1
8. 1946–1955	77.1	7.2	22.9	75.2	56.0
Decades (except line 17)					
9. 1869–1878	82.3	0	17.7	0	17.7
10. 1879–1888	87.0	0	13.0	0	13.0
11. 1889–1898	83.2	0	16.8	0	16.8
12. 1899–1908	83.5	0	16.5	0	16.5
13. 1909–1918	89.5	0.3	10.5	93.8	53.8
14. 1919–1928	95.2	4.6	4.8	23.2	22.7
15. 1929–1938	81.1	23.8	18.9	13.9	28.8
16. 1939–1948	53.7	14.7	46.3	234.9	84.0
17. 1949–1955	77.2	6.6	22.8	75.7	56.1
18. 1946–1955	77.1	7.2	22.9	75.2	56.0

Flow of nonmilitary producers' durables to governments is excluded.
ᵃ Percentages based on three-decade moving totals of absolute volumes.
ᵇ 1949–1955 given the weight of a decade.

SOURCE, BY COLUMN

(1) and (3) Calculated from unpublished estimates underlying Table R-30.
(2) Underlying absolutes from *Construction and Building Materials, Statistical Supplement, May 1954*, Table 5; and *Economic Report of the President*, January 1957, Table E-30.
(4) For military construction and munitions, see Table R-6.

call the movements associated with them trends. Therefore, lest the thirty-year periods give a false impression of gradual and continuous change, we provide decade distributions in the lower part of Table 24. Yet, by and large, the last four to five decades of this century may be considered "war dominated," compared with the "peaceful" decades from 1870 to 1910.

2. While it is not difficult to explain the upward trend in the share of governments in countrywide capital formation, the distribution within the private sector between households (in our measures, nonfarm residential construction) and the business sector (including farms) is more complicated. The reason lies in the fact that the determinants of household capital formation and of business capital formation are such different complexes. All we can do here is discuss further the relations between these two sectors of private capital formation, and the groups of variables to which they can be reasonably linked.

A detailed and thorough analysis of the factors that determine the demand for nonfarm residential construction, and their effect on the trends in that construction, is presented elsewhere.[12] Clearly, growth in population, change in the number of households, internal migration, the price of housing, and levels of income are all important elements in determining demand for residential housing in nonfarm areas. Of this complex of factors, we analyze here only the growth in nonfarm population, and in part A of Table 25 we relate to it the gross and net volumes of nonfarm residential construction, in constant prices. The rate of growth in household capital formation is thus interpreted as a function of two trends—additions to the nonfarm population, and the ratio of construction to population additions. The movement of the first of these two variables is portrayed in column 2; the movement of the second is shown for gross construction (with volumes for 1869–1898 related to population additions for 1870–1900, and so on) in column 5, and for net construction in column 9. Thus the trend in volume of construction is a product of columns 2 and 5, or 2 and 9, and appears in column 6 or 10.

The model for business capital formation is somewhat more elaborate. We begin again with population, on the premise that its wants are the governing determinant, as they are for the household sector. But here (columns 1 and 2 of part B) we take changes in total rather

12 Leo Grebler, David M. Blank, and Louis Winnick, *Capital Formation in Residential Real Estate: Trends and Prospects* (Princeton for NBER, 1956), particularly pp. 76–133 and 143–155.

TABLE 25

DATA RELATING TO COMPARATIVE MOVEMENT OF HOUSEHOLD AND BUSINESS SECTORS IN PRIVATE DOMESTIC CAPITAL FORMATION, 1870–1950

(dollar amounts in 1929 prices)

A. HOUSEHOLD CAPITAL FORMATION [a]

Periods	Additions, Nonfarm Population (millions) (1)	Ratio of Successive Entries in (1) (2)	Gross Nonfarm Residential Construction				Net Nonfarm Residential Construction			
			(billions) (3)	Per Addition to Population (3) ÷ (1) (4)	Ratio of Successive Entries in (4) (5)	Ratio of Successive Entries in (3) (6)	(billions) (7)	Per Addition to Population (7) ÷ (1) (8)	Ratio of Successive Entries in (8) (9)	Ratio of Successive Entries in (7) (10)
1. 1870–1900	29.1		$3.98	$137			$2.92	$100		
2. 1880–1910	37.6	1.29	5.36	143	1.04	1.35	3.61	96	0.96	1.24
3. 1890–1920	40.6	1.08	6.07	150	1.05	1.13	3.48	86	0.90	0.96
4. 1900–1930	47.8	1.18	7.82	164	1.09	1.29	4.44	93	1.08	1.28
5. 1910–1940	41.6	0.87	7.44	179	1.09	0.95	3.23	78	0.84	0.73
6. 1920–1950	53.5	1.29	7.57	141	0.79	1.02	2.78	52	0.67	0.86

[a] Nonfarm residential construction.

SOURCE: Col. 1 for 1890–1950, from Leo Grebler, David M. Blank, and Louis Winnick, *Capital Formation in Residential Real Estate: Trends and Prospects* (Princeton for NBER, 1956), Table 23, p. 82, extrapolated to 1870 and 1880 by the movement of urban population in places up to 10,000 (Series B-156 and B-158, *Historical Statistics of the United States, 1789–1945*, p. 29).

(continued)

TABLE 25 (continued)

B. BUSINESS CAPITAL FORMATION

Periods	Additions, Total Population (millions) (1)	Ratio of Successive Entries in (1) (2)	Additions, Finished Commodity Product (billions) (3)	Per Addition to Population (3) ÷ (1) (4)	Ratio of Successive Entries in (4) (5)	Ratio of Successive Entries in (3) (6)	Gross Business Capital Formation (billions) (7)	Per Addition to Finished Commodity Product (7) ÷ (3) (8)	Ratio of Successive Entries in (8) (9)	Ratio of Successive Entries in (7) (10)
7. 1870–1900	37.4		$19.6	$ 524			$ 9.6	0.49		
8. 1880–1910	41.8	1.12	26.9	644	1.23	1.37	14.9	0.55	1.12	1.56
9. 1890–1920	42.8	1.02	26.4	617	0.96	0.98	20.2	0.77	1.40	1.36
10. 1900–1930	46.8	1.09	41.6	889	1.44	1.58	26.1	0.63	0.82	1.29
11. 1910–1940	39.7	0.85	31.7	798	0.90	0.76	26.0	0.82	1.30	1.00
12. 1920–1950	45.0	1.13	61.8	1,373	1.72	1.95	30.2	0.49	0.60	1.16

Net Business Capital Formation

Periods	(billions) (11)	Per Addition to Finished Commodity Product (11) ÷ (3) (12)	Ratio of Successive Entries in (12) (13)	Ratio of Successive Entries in (11) (14)
7. 1870–1900	$ 4.75	0.24		
8. 1880–1910	7.21	0.27	1.12	1.52
9. 1890–1920	8.65	0.33	1.22	1.20
10. 1900–1930	10.14	0.24	0.73	1.17
11. 1910–1940	6.38	0.20	0.83	0.63
12. 1920–1950	5.48	0.09	0.45	0.86

SOURCE: Col. 1 from *Historical Statistics and Continuation to 1952*, Series B-13.

(continued)

TABLE 25 (concluded)

C. RECONCILIATION WITH PERCENTAGE SHARES IN TABLE 23

Periods	Share, Gross Nonfarm Residential Construction (1)	Share in (1) x Ratio in (6), Part A (2)	Share, Gross Business Capital Formation (3)	Share in (3) x Ratio in (10), Part B (4)	Derived Share, Gross Nonfarm Residential Construction $\frac{(2)}{(2)+(4)}$ (5)	Share, Net Nonfarm Residential Construction (6)	Share in (6) x Ratio in (10), Part A (7)	Share, Net Business Capital Formation (8)	Share in (8) x Ratio in (14), Part B (9)	Derived Share, Net Nonfarm Residential Construction $\frac{(7)}{(7)+(9)}$ (10)
13. 1870–1900	0.293		0.707			0.381		0.619		
14. 1880–1910	0.264	0.39555	0.736	1.10292	0.264	0.334	0.47244	0.666	0.94088	0.334
15. 1890–1920	0.231	0.29832	0.769	1.00096	0.230	0.287	0.32064	0.713	0.79920	0.286
16. 1900–1930	0.231	0.29799	0.769	0.99201	0.231	0.304	0.36736	0.696	0.83421	0.306
17. 1910–1940	0.223	0.21945	0.777	0.76900	0.222	0.336	0.22192	0.664	0.43848	0.336
18. 1920–1950	0.200	0.22746	0.800	0.90132	0.202	0.336	0.28896	0.664	0.57104	0.336

SOURCE, BY COLUMN

(1) Table 23, col. 3.
(3) Table 23, col. 4.

(6) Table 23, col. 7.
(8) Table 23, col. 8.

than in nonfarm population, since it is the total increase in the number of inhabitants that has to be served by business capital. However, we cannot directly relate population numbers to business capital formation, as we do population numbers to residential construction; rather, the linkage is through finished commodity product, which business capital formation services. Hence, additions to total population are viewed as stimulating additions to finished commodity product (column 3), and we observe additions to commodity product per number added to total population (column 4). The movement in the per capita additions (column 5) multiplied by the movement in additions to total population (column 2) yields the trend in additions to finished commodity product (column 6). This trend, which characterizes the element of growth that additions to business capital service, is comparable with the trend in additions to nonfarm population, which characterizes the element of growth that new nonfarm residential construction services. It will be noted that the growth rate of this determinant of business capital formation tends to be higher than that of the immediate determinant of nonfarm residential construction. (Compare the entries in column 6 of part B with those in column 2 of part A.)

If additions to commodity product grow at a higher rate than additions to nonfarm population, business capital formation will grow at a higher rate than nonfarm residential construction if the marginal capital-output ratio for the former declines less or rises more than that for the latter. The comparison for gross marginal ratios is between column 9 of part B and column 5 of part A; and for net marginal ratios, between column 13 of part B and column 9 of part A. In the earlier periods, the ratio of business capital formation to finished commodity product additions is definitely higher than that of nonfarm residential construction to nonfarm population additions; but in the recent periods, the former declined much more drastically than the latter. On balance, however, the combination of these ratios with the movements in the basic determinants themselves yields a consistently higher rate of growth in business capital formation than in nonfarm residential construction for the gross volumes. But when we deal with the net volumes, the greater decline for business capital formation (column 12) than for nonfarm residential construction (column 8) offsets the other factors and produces a stability in the share of nonfarm residential construction in net private capital formation. Note, however, that this stability shown in Table 25 is for a period that omits the first decade (1869–1878) and the last quinquennium (1951–1955). Over the longer period covered in Table 23, the share of nonfarm residential construction in net private domestic capital formation declines, at least for 1929 price volumes.

In part C the calculations show how differences in the rates of growth are reflected in changes in the percentage shares of the household and business sectors in total private domestic capital formation. The algebra is quite simple. If for a given period the share of the household sector is h, that of the business sector is $(1 - h)$. If capital formation in the former grows by the ratio $(1 + a)$, while that in the latter grows by the ratio $(1 + b)$, the share in the next period will be: for the household sector, $[h(1 + a)] \div [h(1 + a) + (1 - h)(1 + b)]$; and for the business sector, $[(1 - h)(1 + b)]$ divided by the same denominator. Clearly, if $(1 + a)$ is smaller than $(1 + b)$, the case more or less consistently for gross volumes, the share of the household sector in private domestic capital formation will decline, as demonstrated in part C.

This translation of changes in the relative shares of the household and business sectors in total private domestic capital formation (in 1929 prices) into differences in rates of growth, reducible to differences in rates of growth of relevant population additions and other sources of demand, is of course not an explanation. It is merely another step in the analysis toward the point at which the operating factors can be more clearly discerned. But we still would have to answer several questions: Why were additions to nonfarm population changing at the rate indicated (column 2 of part A)—at a rate higher than additions to total population (column 2 of part B)? Why did gross or net nonfarm residential construction in constant prices per addition to nonfarm population move as it did (column 5 or column 9 of part A)? Why did additions to commodity product per addition to total population grow at the high rates indicated (column 5 of part B)? On the questions relating to the determinants and factors in the movement of nonfarm residential construction, we may refer again to the discussion by Grebler, Blank, and Winnick, just cited. On the questions relating to business capital formation, reference can be made to the material in the monographs that deal with agriculture, mining and manufacturing, and the regulated industries, some of which will be summarized in the next section of this chapter. At the present juncture all we do is pass from the percentage distributions of private domestic capital formation to the next stage, where the underlying rates of growth can be linked to the most obvious determinants.

If the distribution of private domestic capital formation in 1929 prices between the household and business sectors differs from the distribution in current prices, the discrepancy is assignable to differential trends in the price levels. As observed in Table 23, in the distribution of volumes in constant (1929) prices the share of the household sector (nonfarm residential construction) declined, and that of the business sector rose. If we do not observe the same trends in the distribution in current prices, it is clear that the prices of capital items in the two sectors moved differently.

This is brought out explicitly in Table 26. The price indexes in all columns were derived simply by dividing the volumes in current prices

TABLE 26

Price Indexes Implicit in Household and Business Sectors of Private Domestic Capital Formation, and in Consumer Commodities, 1869–1955

(1929 = 100)

	Gross Volumes		Net Volumes (standard depreciation)		
Periods	House-holds [a] (1)	Business Firms (2)	House-holds [a] (3)	Business Firms (4)	Consumer Commodities (5)
1. 1869–1898	38.6	51.9	38.6	55.1	56.2
2. 1879–1908	40.4	49.7	40.2	51.4	52.4
3. 1889–1918	45.4	56.3	43.4	55.7	60.8
4. 1899–1928	72.2	78.7	73.6	79.1	82.5
5. 1909–1938	83.6	90.4	84.9	94.7	88.5
6. 1919–1948	109.3	109.5	111.1	114.1	104.6
7. 1929–1955 [b]	185.9	153.4	230.1	172.2	131.4
8. 1946–1955	223.4	179.0	226.1	169.4	161.5

[a] Nonfarm residential construction.
[b] 1949–1955 given the weight of a decade.

Source, by Column

(1) to (4) Calculated from Table 23.
(5)   Calculated from Tables R-3, R-27, and R-28.

by those in 1929 prices. It will be observed immediately that prices implicit in the capital items in the household sector (nonfarm residential construction) rose more than those implicit in the capital items in the business sector—a total of construction, producers' equipment, and inventories. Whereas the prices implicit in the gross volumes in the most recent long period, 1929–1955 (with the last seven years given the weight of a decade), are, for the household sector, almost five times the level in the first thirty-year period, those for the business sector are not quite three times their level in the initial period. The greater rise in prices of nonfarm residential construction may well be due to a lesser rise in productivity and efficiency of the industries closely connected with that sector and thus reflect their backwardness relative to those engaged in producing the construction, equipment, and inventories that constitute business capital formation.

Such differences in the movement of prices can easily account for the differences between the trends in the distributions of volumes in constant and in current prices. Thus, looking back at Table 23, we find that in 1869–1898 the share of the household sector in gross private domestic capital formation, in 1929 prices, was 29.3 per cent. But its share in current price volumes was only 23.6 per cent. The reduction can be explained by the differences in the implicit prices for gross volumes shown in columns 1 and 2, line 1, Table 26. If we multiply 29.3 per cent (the share of the household sector) by 38.6 (the price index for the household sector), and 70.7 per cent (the share of the business sector) by 51.9 (its implicit price index), and divide the first product by the sum of the first and second, the ratio will be 0.236 or 23.6 per cent, the share of the household sector, in current price volumes. We can do that for every entry in Tables 23 and 26, translating the movement in the shares of the household and business sectors in gross or net private domestic capital formation in current prices into a product of the movements of the shares in constant prices and of the differential changes in implicit price levels.

This naturally does not mean that the changes in the structure of private domestic capital formation in constant prices are basic, and that the differential trends in the implicit price levels are a corollary with only an additive effect on the former. On the contrary, it may well be that the difference in the price trends partly determined the distribution of capital formation in constant prices—in the sense that the greater relative rise in prices of nonfarm residential construction decreased the relative demand for it in physical volumes, causing the share of nonfarm residential construction in total private domestic capital formation, in constant prices, to decline.

In this connection, the last column in Table 26 has much suggestive value. It contains the implicit price index of finished consumer commodities (perishables, semidurables, and durables). Those commodities form the preponderant part of finished commodity product, changes in which appear in column 3, part B of Table 25, as one of the basic determinants of business capital formation. In fact, we know that consumer commodities account, on the average, for well over 70 per cent of total finished commodity product (the rest being gross construction and gross producers' durables, including munitions), and that their share in the latter showed no distinct trend over the period. We found in Table 25 that additions to finished commodity product (in constant prices), largely consumers' commodities, per addition to total population, rose at a higher rate than did new nonfarm residential construction (also in constant prices) per addition to nonfarm population. (Compare column 5 of part A with column 5 of part B.) In other words, the demand for additional units of consumer commodities grew at a higher rate than the demand for new nonfarm residential construction did, both expressed in constant prices. In Table 26 we find that the rise in prices of consumer commodities was far less than the rise in prices of nonfarm residential construction. We may therefore infer that the higher ratio of secular additions to finished commodity product to total population additions, compared with the ratio of new nonfarm residential construction to nonfarm population additions is due, at least in part, to the rising prices of construction relative to prices of finished consumer commodities. If this inference is correct, the price differential is another factor in the greater rise in business capital formation in constant prices, that is, the rise in the share of the business sector in total private domestic capital formation in constant prices. The differentials in price trends not only provide a statistical account of differences in movement between the shares of the household and business sectors in private domestic capital formation in constant and in current prices; they also suggest an economic argument which goes part way toward explaining why, in volumes in constant prices, the share of nonfarm residential construction tended to decline and that of business capital formation tended to rise.

Shares of Selected Industry Sectors in Net Business Durable Capital Formation

We come now to the last aspect of the structure of capital formation, the distribution of net durable business capital formation among the industries using durable capital. It would have been valuable to study the distribution of all business capital formation—not only durable (which includes construction and equipment) but also inventories, not only net but also gross, and not for a few but for all industrial divisions that are likely to show different patterns of growth and different trends in their shares in total business capital accumulation. The available data, however, do not permit such an analysis even for recent years, let alone for decades back into the nineteenth century. We are limited to the distributions made possible by the basic monographs, in the series on capital formation and financing, dealing with agriculture, mining, manufacturing, and the regulated private industries (referred to below as public utilities).[13]

For these industrial sectors we can observe net durable capital formation, i.e., net construction and equipment, back to 1880. Table 27 presents a summary of the data, in comparable form, designed to reveal the long-term trends in the distribution of net durable business capital formation by these four major industrial sectors.

The comparison is limited to durable capital, that is, excludes inventories, because in some sectors, as the public utilities, long-term estimates of inventories cannot be secured; and in others, as manufacturing, estimates of inventories by subbranches are not possible over the long run. The estimates are limited to net volumes because, for the earlier decades, capital formation in agriculture, mining, and manufacturing, can be derived only as successive differences between estimates of stocks, and those stocks are net values. Only for the public utilities are both gross and net capital formation estimates available back to the 1870's. Finally, we deal with fairly long periods in Table 27, not only because our interest is in long-term trends, but also because the estimates for some sectors are derived as net differences between successive large totals (which are subject to marked trends), and the relative errors are likely to be smaller for long intervals than for short.

While Table 27 omits some sectors of the economy whose capital accumulation would be classified under business capital formation (e.g. contract construction, wholesale and retail trade, other business service), the missing sectors are not among the important users of

[13] See the following, published by Princeton for the National Bureau: Alvin S. Tostlebe, *Capital in Agriculture: Its Formation and Financing since 1870* (1957); Daniel Creamer, Sergei Dobrovolsky, and Israel Borenstein, *Capital in Manufacturing and Mining: Its Formation and Financing* (1960); and Melville J. Ulmer, *Capital in Transportation, Communications, and Public Utilities: Its Formation and Financing* (1960).

Trends in Structure of Capital Formation

TABLE 27

(amounts in billions of dollars)

	Agriculture (1)	Mining (2)	Manufacturing (3)	Regulated Industries (4)	Total, (1) to (4) (5)
	A. CAPITAL STOCK AND CAPITAL FORMATION				
1. Stock, June 1, 1880	6.57	0.37	1.88	11.80	20.62
2. Net capital formation, June 1, 1880– June 1, 1900	2.20	1.20	5.76	9.18	18.34
3. Stock, June 1, 1900	8.77	1.57	7.64 [a] 7.16 [b]	20.98	38.96 [a] 38.48 [b]
4. Net capital formation, June 1, 1900– Dec. 31, 1922	6.56	3.70	14.88	14.41	39.55
5. Stock, Dec. 31, 1922	15.33	5.27	22.04	35.39	78.03
6. Net capital formation, Dec. 31, 1922– Dec. 31, 1948	3.21	0.06	12.74	9.90	25.91
7. Stock, Dec. 31, 1948	18.54	5.33	34.78	45.29	103.94
	B. PER CENT DISTRIBUTION OF CAPITAL STOCK AND CAPITAL FORMATION				
8. Stock, June 1, 1880	31.9	1.8	9.1	57.2	100.0
9. Net capital formation, June 1, 1880– June 1, 1900	12.0	6.5	31.4	50.1	100.0
10. Stock, June 1, 1900	22.5 [a] 22.8 [b]	4.0 [a] 4.1 [b]	19.6 [a] 18.6 [b]	53.9 [a] 54.5 [b]	100.0 100.0
11. Net capital formation, June 1, 1900– Dec. 31, 1922	16.6	9.4	37.6	36.4	100.0
12. Stock, Dec. 31, 1922	19.6	6.8	28.2	45.4	100.0
13. Net capital formation, Dec. 31, 1922– Dec. 31, 1948	12.4	0.2	49.2	38.2	100.0
14. Stock, Dec. 31, 1948	17.8	5.1	33.5	43.6	100.0
	C. VOLUME OF OUTPUT				
15. 1880	5.53	0.35	8.82	0.76	15.46
16. 1900	8.99	1.13 [c]	23.18 [a] 21.98 [b]	3.16	36.46 [a] 35.26 [b]
17. 1922	10.55 [d]	2.56 [e]	50.57 [e]	9.60	73.28
18. 1948	18.02 [d]	5.81	128.12	27.65	179.60
	D. PER CENT DISTRIBUTION OF VOLUME OF OUTPUT				
19. 1880	35.8	2.3	57.1	4.9	100.0
20. 1900 [a] 1900 [b]	24.7 25.5	3.1 3.2	63.6 62.3	8.7 9.0	100.0 100.0
21. 1922	14.4	3.5	69.0	13.1	100.0
22. 1948	10.0	3.2	71.3	15.4	100.0

(continued)

TABLE 27 (concluded)

	Agriculture (1)	Mining (2)	Manufacturing (3)	Regulated Industries (4)	Total, (1) to (4) (5)
			E. RATIO OF CAPITAL STOCK TO OUTPUT		
23. June 1, 1880	1.19	1.06	0.21	15.53	1.33
24. June 1, 1900	0.98	1.39	0.33 [a]	6.64	1.07 [a]
			0.33 [b]		1.09 [b]
25. Dec. 31, 1922	1.45	2.06	0.44	3.69	1.06
26. Dec. 31, 1948	1.03	0.92	0.27	1.64	0.58
			F. RATIO OF NET CAPITAL FORMATION TO CHANGES IN OUTPUT		
27. 1880–1900	0.64	1.54	0.40	3.82	0.87
28. 1900–1922	4.21	2.59	0.52	2.24	1.04
29. 1922–1948	0.43	0.02	0.16	0.55	0.24
			G. APPROXIMATE NET PRODUCT		
30. 1880	3.78	0.22	2.41	0.50	6.91
31. 1900	5.82	0.71	6.07	2.09	14.69
32. 1922	6.71	1.60	13.99	6.26	28.56
33. 1948	9.16	3.62	35.50	18.08	66.36
			H. PER CENT DISTRIBUTION OF NET PRODUCT		
34. 1880	54.7	3.2	34.9	7.2	100.0
35. 1900	39.6	4.8	41.3	14.2	100.0
36. 1922	23.5	5.6	49.0	21.9	100.0
37. 1948	13.8	5.5	53.5	27.2	100.0
			I. RATIO OF CAPITAL STOCK TO NET PRODUCT		
38. June 1, 1880	1.74	1.68	0.78	23.60	2.98
39. June 1, 1900	1.51	2.21	1.26 [a]	10.04	2.65 [a]
			1.18 [b]		2.62 [b]
40. Dec. 31, 1922	2.28	3.29	1.58	5.65	2.73
41. Dec. 31, 1948	2.02	1.47	0.98	2.50	1.57
			J. RATIO OF NET CAPITAL FORMATION TO CHANGES IN NET PRODUCT		
42. 1880–1900	1.08	2.45	1.57	5.77	2.36
43. 1900–1922	7.37	4.16	1.88	3.46	2.85
44. 1922–1948	1.31	0.03	0.59	0.84	0.69

Because of rounding, detail will not necessarily add to total.

[a] Comparable with entry for 1880.

[b] Comparable with entry for later years.

[c] Extrapolated from 1902 or 1919 by NBER index (see Harold Barger and Sam H. Schurr, *The Mining Industries, 1899–1939*, New York, NBER, 1944, p. 14).

[d] Extrapolated from 1920 or 1950 by BAE index of farm production, *Statistical Abstract of the United States, 1951*, p. 507, and *Historical Statistics*, Series E-73.

[e] Extrapolated from 1919 by NBER index (see Solomon Fabricant, *The Output of Manufacturing Industries, 1899–1937*, New York, NBER, 1940, p. 44).

(Notes on following page)

and inventories. Whereas the prices implicit in the gross volumes in the most recent long period, 1929–1955 (with the last seven years given the weight of a decade), are, for the household sector, almost five times the level in the first thirty-year period, those for the business sector are not quite three times their level in the initial period. The greater rise in prices of nonfarm residential construction may well be due to a lesser rise in productivity and efficiency of the industries closely connected with that sector and thus reflect their backwardness relative to those engaged in producing the construction, equipment, and inventories that constitute business capital formation.

Such differences in the movement of prices can easily account for the differences between the trends in the distributions of volumes in constant and in current prices. Thus, looking back at Table 23, we find that in 1869–1898 the share of the household sector in gross private domestic capital formation, in 1929 prices, was 29.3 per cent. But its share in current price volumes was only 23.6 per cent. The reduction can be explained by the differences in the implicit prices for gross volumes shown in columns 1 and 2, line 1, Table 26. If we multiply 29.3 per cent (the share of the household sector) by 38.6 (the price index for the household sector), and 70.7 per cent (the share of the business sector) by 51.9 (its implicit price index), and divide the first product by the sum of the first and second, the ratio will be 0.236 or 23.6 per cent, the share of the household sector, in current price volumes. We can do that for every entry in Tables 23 and 26, translating the movement in the shares of the household and business sectors in gross or net private domestic capital formation in current prices into a product of the movements of the shares in constant prices and of the differential changes in implicit price levels.

This naturally does not mean that the changes in the structure of private domestic capital formation in constant prices are basic, and that the differential trends in the implicit price levels are a corollary with only an additive effect on the former. On the contrary, it may well be that the difference in the price trends partly determined the distribution of capital formation in constant prices—in the sense that the greater relative rise in prices of nonfarm residential construction decreased the relative demand for it in physical volumes, causing the share of nonfarm residential construction in total private domestic capital formation, in constant prices, to decline.

In this connection, the last column in Table 26 has much suggestive value. It contains the implicit price index of finished consumer com-

agriculture in total output, as evidenced by the data in part D of the table.

However, even though the share of agriculture in net durable capital formation failed to decline, it was at a level lower than that which must have prevailed in the past. For in 1880, agriculture accounted for 31.9 per cent of the total stock of durable business capital, which means that in the preceding decades the share of agriculture in the comparable total of current capital formation must have averaged at that level. By 1900, however, agriculture's share in durable business capital had declined to 22.5 per cent, a reflection of the decline in its share in output. By 1922 its share in durable capital had declined to 19.6 per cent, and by 1948, to 17.8 per cent.

2. The share of mining in net durable capital formation in the four sectors was 6.5 per cent in 1880–1900 and rose to 9.4 per cent in 1900–1922. For both periods the share was much larger than it must have been before 1880, since its share in the durable capital stock of the four sectors in that year was only about 2 per cent. With the much larger share of mining in current net capital formation, its share in total durable capital (of the four sectors) climbed from less than 2 to almost 7 per cent. However, during 1922–1948, the volume of its capital formation was so small that the share of mining in total capital stock had dropped to about 5 per cent by 1948.

3. The share of manufacturing in net durable capital formation of the four sectors in 1880–1900 was close to one-third, far larger than its share in the existing stock in 1880. The share in capital formation increased continuously and, consequently, its share in the accumulated stock increased. Whereas in 1880 the share of construction and equipment used in manufacturing in the total for the four sectors was barely 9 per cent, by the end of 1948 it had risen to 33.5 per cent.

4. The share of the public utilities sector in the combined total stock in 1880 was quite large—close to six-tenths. But from then on the share in current net durable capital formation declined continuously, particularly sharply in the interval 1900–1922. In 1948, the share of the sector in the total accumulated net durable capital was about 44 per cent, a drop of almost one-quarter from its 1880 level.

How can we account for these movements, shown in parts A and B, in the distribution of net durable capital formation? Granted that the estimates are subject to error, it seems clear that the broad trends are not likely to be negated or changed much by refinements, so long as we deal with net construction and equipment, and with these four sectors. Why, for example, should the share of manufacturing in the total for the four sectors increase, and that of public utilities decline?

The other parts of Table 27 help to resolve these trends into a combination of differential movements in the volume of output which the capital stock is to serve, and in the capital-output ratios, average and marginal.

In part C we have gross output—gross in that payments to other industries have not been deducted, although intraindustry duplication within agriculture is adjusted for. From our standpoint, it would have been preferable to use estimates of net output, specifically net income originating (or net plus capital consumption charges); and in part G we do have approximations to net output. But these approximations are quite rough, and the available data permit more accurate and detailed estimates of gross output. We should, therefore, emphasize the movement in capital, in gross output, and in the capital-gross output ratios, even though some inferences as to the movement in net output and in the capital-net output ratios are possible.

As might be expected, the share of agriculture in the total of gross output for the four sectors declined quite steadily; the shares of both the manufacturing and public utilities sectors rose quite steadily; and the share of mining rose until 1922 and then declined. On the basis of these trends in the structure of gross output, we would expect the share of manufacturing in net capital formation to rise continuously and that of mining to rise through 1922 and then decline, which is exactly what happened. We would also expect the share of agriculture in capital formation to decline, and that of public utilities to rise, but instead, the share of the former shows little change and that of the latter declined. Clearly, the capital-output ratio for agriculture must have moved quite differently from that for the public utilities sector, and both quite differently from those for mining and manufacturing.

This, an algebraic necessity, is what we find in part E. In agriculture, the ratio of capital stock (buildings, machinery, and implements) to output shows no definite trend over the period. In the public utilities sector, the capital-output ratio dropped precipitously, from a high of over 15.5 in 1880, to a low of 1.6 in 1948. The ratio in mining rose from 1.06 in 1880 to 2.06 in 1922, and then dropped sharply to 0.9 in 1948. The ratio in manufacturing more than doubled from 1880 to 1922, and then dropped markedly, but the trend over the period as a whole was upward. The weighted ratio for the four sectors combined dropped moderately from 1880 to 1922, and then appreciably from 1922 to 1948.

Part F, which shows the marginal ratios—i.e. the ratios of net capital formation to gross output additions—emphasizes the extreme variability in these ratios, even for huge sectors like manufacturing and the public utilities, in which conflicting movements among the various branches may be expected to cancel each other, at least in part. In general, the marginal ratios during the first two intervals were high and rising for agriculture, mining, and manufacturing, but were already declining for the public utilities sector. In the last interval, 1922 to 1948, there was a general drop in the marginal ratios, and this uniformity of direction in movement for the four sectors is reflected in the sharp break in the ratio for the total.

The picture suggested by Table 27 is clear: by and large the average capital-output ratios in agriculture, mining, and manufacturing did not decline significantly or at all, over the period as a whole. It is the ratio for the public utilities sector—very high initially—that showed the most consistent and largest decline. On the other hand, the manufacturing capital-output ratio—very low at the beginning of the period—showed a sizable rise, at least to 1922. As a result, the four ratios tended to converge: in 1880, the range was from 0.21 to 15.5; in 1948, from 0.27 to 1.64. When we omit the public utilities sector, the range narrows—that in 1880 being from 0.21 to 1.19, that in 1948, from 0.27 to 1.03.

In parts G to J we repeat the analysis, this time for the movement in net output and in the capital-net output ratios in the four sectors. The estimates are based essentially upon the sector shares in net national product in 1919–1928 (in current prices), extrapolated to earlier and later decades by the movement in rates of growth of gross output compared with that of net national product (both output and product series in 1929 prices). These estimates therefore assume constancy over time in the ratio of net to gross output within each sector, and for this reason can be viewed as only rough approximations. The only exception is for agriculture from 1910 on, for which we have direct estimates of both gross and net output, in constant prices.

The general conclusions suggested by parts G to J are the same as those suggested by parts C to F. In the movement of output, there is again the marked decline in the share of agriculture, the marked rise in the shares of manufacturing and public utilities, and the rise to 1922 in the share of mining and its slight decline thereafter. The capital-net output ratios are all significantly higher than those based on gross output, but their movement over time is similar except that the ratio for agriculture rises over the period as a whole. The marginal capital-net output ratios are even more variable than the marginal capital-gross output ratios.

Behind these movements in output and capital lie a variety of factors, many of which are discussed in the monographs from which the data are taken. It may not be amiss to consider some further detail, lest the simple story told by Table 27 leave a false impression. It is especially important to see whether the trends observed in the capital-output ratios remain the same when we vary the definition of capital and of output; and whether, by subdividing the major sectors, some light can be shed on the nature of the factors behind the trends.

We turn first to agriculture (Table 28) and consider two questions. (1) Is the movement in the ratio of net construction and equipment to net income originating the same as the movement in their ratio to gross income? (2) How does the movement of the capital-income ratio, when capital is limited to buildings and equipment, compare with the movement in the capital-income ratio when capital is defined more widely, or consists of other combinations of components?

The first question is answered simply by comparing the movement in line 7 with that in line 18. Considering only the period covered in Table 27, 1880–1950, we find that the ratio of net durable capital to gross income rose from 1.05 in 1880 to 1.27 in 1920 and then declined to 1.01 in 1950–confirming the movement already shown in Table 27. Over the period as a whole, there is no clear evidence of either an upward or downward trend in this ratio. But the ratio of net durable capital to net income originating moved from 1.22 in 1880 to 1.58 in 1920 and, after some decline, was again at 1.57 in 1950–clear evidence that the ratio over the period had, on the whole, risen. The reason, of course, lies in the fact that with increased mechanization, the use of inorganic fertilizers, and so on, the ratio of payments to other industries to gross income rose; or, in other words, the ratio of net income originating to gross income declined.

Why should the ratio of the value of buildings and equipment to net income (output) rise, and its ratio to gross income (output) remain constant in agriculture—although these ratios declined in some other sectors (as public utilities)? The answer is provided in part by the ratios for other major items of capital in agriculture, particularly land, and horses and mules (and to some extent, even other live-

TABLE 28

COMPONENTS OF CAPITAL RELATED TO GROSS AND NET FARM INCOME, AGRICULTURE, BASED ON VOLUMES IN 1910–1914 PRICES, 1870–1950

(amounts in billions of dollars)

	1870 (1)	1880 (2)	1890 (3)	1900 (4)	1910 (5)	1920 (6)	1930 (7)	1940 (8)	1950 (9)
1. Gross farm income	2.54	3.76	4.68	6.11	6.71	7.47	8.66	9.62	11.78
				RATIO OF CAPITAL TO GROSS FARM INCOME					
2. Total, including land	7.78	7.40	7.20	6.60	6.76	6.67	5.68	5.05	4.56
3. Land	5.36	5.08	4.90	4.59	4.50	4.27	3.75	3.45	2.93
4. Reproducible assets	2.41	2.31	2.30	2.01	2.26	2.40	1.93	1.60	1.63
5. Buildings	1.02	0.95	0.82	0.73	0.95	1.00	0.83	0.65	0.64
6. Equipment	0.10	0.10	0.11	0.14	0.19	0.27	0.26	0.20	0.37
7. Buildings and equipment	1.12	1.05	0.94	0.87	1.14	1.27	1.09	0.85	1.01
8. Horses and mules	0.41	0.39	0.44	0.38	0.40	0.38	0.25	0.17	0.07
9. Other livestock	0.57	0.52	0.54	0.42	0.38	0.40	0.32	0.32	0.28
10. Crops	0.31	0.35	0.39	0.34	0.33	0.34	0.27	0.26	0.27
11. Total inventories	1.29	1.27	1.36	1.14	1.12	1.12	0.84	0.74	0.62
12. Net farm income	2.23	3.22	3.90	4.98	5.33	6.02	6.74	7.27	7.61
				RATIO OF CAPITAL TO NET FARM INCOME					
13. Total, including land	8.86	8.64	8.64	8.09	8.51	8.28	7.29	6.68	7.06
14. Land	6.11	5.94	5.88	5.63	5.67	5.30	4.82	4.57	4.54
15. Reproducible assets	2.75	2.70	2.76	2.47	2.84	2.98	2.48	2.11	2.52
16. Buildings	1.17	1.11	0.99	0.90	1.20	1.24	1.07	0.86	0.99
17. Equipment	0.11	0.11	0.14	0.17	0.24	0.34	0.33	0.26	0.58
18. Buildings and equipment	1.28	1.22	1.12	1.06	1.44	1.58	1.40	1.13	1.57
19. Horses and mules	0.47	0.46	0.52	0.47	0.51	0.48	0.32	0.23	0.11
20. Other livestock	0.65	0.61	0.64	0.52	0.48	0.50	0.42	0.42	0.43
21. Crops	0.35	0.41	0.47	0.41	0.42	0.42	0.35	0.34	0.41
22. Total inventories	1.47	1.48	1.64	1.40	1.41	1.39	1.08	0.98	0.95

SOURCE, BY LINE

1. Tostlebe, *Capital in Agriculture*, Table 20. The BAE series is used through 1910 and is extrapolated to 1870 by the Strauss-Bean series. based on the gross income series. It is assumed that the difference between the gross and net series, as a percentage of the gross, rises—from 12.3 in 1870 to 14.4 in 1880, to 16.5 in 1890, and to 18.5 in 1900.

2–11 and 13–22. *Ibid.*, Table 9, related to line 1 or line 12.

12. *Ibid.*, Table 20. For 1870–1900, the estimates are

stock). The ratio of the value of land—improved land—to either gross or net farm income declined steadily, particularly sharply after 1920. The reason, of course, lies in the increasing difficulty of expanding the area of cultivated and improved land on farms. This puts a premium upon the capacity to increase output without additional land, a capacity in which the availability of equipment and many types of productive buildings is one factor. The ratio of the value of horses and mules to either gross or net income was fairly steady through 1920 and then declined sharply, clearly because of increasing substitution of mechanized equipment for power animals—another factor that tends to sustain the ratio of net durable capital to gross income or to raise its ratio to net income. Even for other livestock, there was a continuous decline in the ratio of the stock to gross or net income, apparent after 1890 and with another conspicuous falling off after 1920. Here also greater yield may have been possible through the input of products of other industries or of better capital (special types of chemically bolstered feed, new structures for milk cows, mechanical equipment for milking, and the like). In short, the estimates indirectly reflect the whole process of the industrialization of agriculture—the basis of the sustained ratio of net durable capital to gross or net income, coterminous with substantial declines in the ratios of other types of capital to gross or net income.

Another aspect of the process is revealed in Table 29. The ten regions into which the country is divided in the table are characterized by rather different types of agricultural complexes, and by differences in the time of entry upon sustained demographic and economic growth.[15] Of particular interest in the analysis of long-term trends in capital formation are two findings here regarding the relation between capital and output. One is the wide range of difference within one and the same "industry" (if agriculture can be called that) in the ratio of capital to income, whatever the variant. Thus in 1869, the ratio of total capital to gross income ranged from 3.45 to 16.87, that of reproducible capital, from 1.15 to 5.70 (and the range would presumably have been wider for ratios to net income originating); even by 1949, the range for the reproducible capital-income ratio was from 0.98 (in the Pacific region) to more than double that, 2.11 (in the Lake states). The second finding is that in the process of growth of various parts of an industry, or for a large part of the economy (as we observed

[15] For more detailed discussion see Tostlebe, *op. cit.*

TABLE 29

GROSS FARM INCOME AND CAPITAL-INCOME RATIOS, BY AGRICULTURAL REGION, BASED ON VOLUMES IN 1910–1914 PRICES, 1869–1950

(amounts in billions of dollars)

	United States (1)	North-east (2)	Appa-lach-ian (3)	South-east (4)	Lake States (5)	Corn Belt (6)	Delta States (7)	Great Plains (8)	Texas-Okla-homa (9)	Moun-tain (10)	Pacific (11)	Weighted Absolute Deviation of Capital-Income Ratios (12)	Weighted Relative Deviation, (12) as % of (1) (13)
						GROSS FARM INCOME							
1. 1869	2,254	584	323	183	178	690	153	34	45	10	54		
2. 1909	6,192	639	682	513	556	1,608	332	789	504	241	328		
3. Ratio, (2) to (1)	2.75	1.09	2.11	2.80	3.12	2.33	2.17	23.21	11.20	24.10	6.07		
4. 1909	6,598	681	726	547	593	1,713	354	841	537	257	349		
5. 1949	11,750	1,120	1,148	755	1,201	2,710	598	1,105	1,145	754	1,214		
6. Ratio, (5) to (4)	1.78	1.64	1.58	1.38	2.03	1.58	1.69	1.31	2.13	2.93	3.48		
						TOTAL CAPITAL-INCOME RATIO							
7. 1870 [a]	8.77	6.60	7.25	4.90	8.45	12.70	3.45	11.23	10.80	8.50	16.87	2.96	33.8
8. 1910 [a]	7.33	6.45	5.29	3.34	8.05	9.20	3.84	8.70	6.96	7.68	9.63	1.72	23.5
9. Ratio, (8) to (7)	0.84	0.98	0.73	0.68	0.95	0.72	1.11	0.77	0.64	0.90	0.57		
10. 1910 [a]	6.88	6.05	4.97	3.13	7.56	8.63	3.60	8.17	6.53	7.20	9.04	1.62	23.5
11. 1950 [a]	4.57	2.85	3.41	2.83	4.68	5.52	2.70	7.70	4.02	5.53	4.11	1.17	25.6
12. Ratio, (11) to (10)	0.66	0.47	0.69	0.90	0.62	0.64	0.75	0.94	0.62	0.77	0.45		
						REPRODUCIBLE CAPITAL-INCOME RATIO							
13. 1870 [a]	2.72	3.20	2.15	1.22	2.97	3.01	1.15	3.35	5.02	5.70	3.06	0.62	22.8
14. 1910 [a]	2.45	3.51	2.17	1.37	3.18	2.86	1.65	2.40	2.05	2.86	1.87	0.46	18.8
15. Ratio, (14) to (13)	0.90	1.10	1.01	1.12	1.07	0.86	1.43	0.72	0.41	0.50	0.61		
16. 1910 [a]	2.30	3.29	2.04	1.29	2.98	2.44	1.55	2.25	1.92	2.68	1.76	0.43	18.7
17. 1950 [a]	1.63	1.67	1.82	1.30	2.11	1.87	1.36	1.83	1.21	1.63	0.98	0.29	17.8
18. Ratio, (17) to (16)	0.71	0.51	0.89	1.01	0.71	0.77	0.88	0.81	0.63	0.61	0.56		

[a] Capital is for specified census year. Income is for year preceding census year.

SOURCE: Tostlebe, *Capital in Agriculture:* lines 1, 2, 4, and 5 from Table H-3, pp. 214–216; lines 7, 8, 10, and 11 from Table 22, pp. 108–109; lines 13, 14, 16, and 17 calculated as difference between Table 26, p. 117, and Table 22.

for the four sectors in Table 27), there is convergence—a reduction in the variability—in the capital-income (-output) ratios. When the ratios are initially high, the decline tends to be large or the rise small compared with the change in initially low or moderate ratios. The convergence is expressed statistically in columns 12 and 13 of Table 29. For the total capital-output ratios, the weighted absolute deviation—a proper measure of the variability of the ratios among the regions—drops from 2.96 in 1869 to 1.72 in 1909, and even as a relative of the mean, declines from 33.8 to 23.5. The average absolute deviation also declines, from 1.62 in 1909 to 1.17 in 1949, but that decline is about proportional to the drop in the countrywide mean ratio. A similar convergence, primarily during the first half of the total period, occurs in the regional ratios of reproducible capital to output.

Both the wide differences among regions in their capital-output ratios and the convergence of these differences by 1910 or 1920 were to be expected. In any major industry the various branches have different relations of capital to output, and as an industry grows the new areas tend to become more similar to the old, to the point where integration is completed and more intensive specialization and diversification begin. We shall observe the same two findings within each major sector covered.

Table 30 presents the detail we have for mining and manufacturing concerning the movement of capital-output ratios for the varying definitions of numerator and denominator. For mining we have capital excluding land, and fixed capital, that is, buildings and machinery. For each, the ratio to gross output moves in a similar pattern, rising more than threefold from 1870 to 1919 and then declining sharply. Over the period as a whole, the trend in each ratio is upward. One can only conjecture whether the results would be the same if net income originating were substituted for gross output in the denominator. There is no reason for assuming major long-term trends in the ratio of net to gross output for the branches of mining, but the internal shifts did probably tend to reduce the ratio of net income to gross output for total mining. In 1929, the ratio of total payments to individuals plus corporate savings to gross income in oil and gas was barely over 20 per cent, whereas it was over 65 per cent in anthracite coal and bituminous coal, and over 55 per cent in metals.[16] Since the share of

---

[16] See Kuznets, assisted by Epstein and Jenks, *National Income and Its Composition, 1919–1938* (New York, NBER, 1941), Vol. II, Tables Q1, Q7, and Q8, pp. 551 and 556.

TABLE 30

OUTPUT AND CAPITAL-OUTPUT RATIOS, MINING AND MANUFACTURING, BASED ON VOLUMES IN 1929 PRICES, 1870–1953
(amounts in billions of dollars)

CENSUS YEARS	MINING			MANUFACTURING					
						Ratio of Total Capital to:		Ratio of Fixed Capital to:	
	Output (1)	Ratio of Capital, Excluding Land, to Output (2)	Ratio of Plant and Equipment to Output (3)	Output (4)	Value Added Including Land (5)	Output (6)	Value Added (7)	Output (8)	Value Added (9)
1. 1870	0.18	0.72	0.61	n.a.	n.a.	n.a.	n.a.	n.a.	n.a.
2. 1880	0.35	1.16	1.02	8.82	3.20	0.55	1.51	0.27 a	0.75 a
3. 1890	0.67	1.36	1.19	15.27	6.76	0.73	1.65	0.36	0.82
4. 1900	1.13 b	n.a.	1.39 b	23.18 c	9.92 c	0.80 c	1.88 c	0.42	0.97
5. 1900	1.13 b	n.a.	1.39 b	21.98 d	9.28 d	0.79 d	1.88 d	0.41 a	0.97
6. 1909	1.93	1.80	1.52	32.65	13.67	0.97	2.31	n.a.	n.a.
7. 1919	2.44 c	2.30 c	2.00 c	45.09	18.04	1.02	2.55	n.a.	n.a.
8. 1919	2.51 d	2.27 d	1.97 d	45.09	18.04	1.02	2.55	n.a.	n.a.
9. 1929	3.98	2.14	1.57	71.22	31.20	0.88	2.02	0.43	0.99
10. 1937	4.21 c	1.59 c	1.10 c	74.69	30.58	0.74	1.81	0.35	0.85
11. 1948	5.81	1.34	0.92	128.12 c	50.33 c	0.61 c	1.55 c	0.29 c	0.73 c
12. 1948	5.81	1.34	0.92	128.60 d	n.a.	0.61 d	n.a.	0.29 d	n.a.
13. 1953	6.46	1.26	0.84	167.82	n.a.	0.59	n.a.	0.27	n.a.

a Based on the assumption of the same distribution between fixed and working capital as for 1890, or as for the preceding 1900 figure.

b See estimate in Table 27.

c Comparable with entries for preceding years.

d Comparable with entries for following years.

e Figure for 1940.

SOURCE: See Tables 31 and 32.

oil and gas in total mining output increased prodigiously—from a few percentage points in 1870 to over 60 per cent in 1953—the ratio of net to gross output in mining as a whole must have declined materially. If so, the capital-net output ratio in mining must have increased more markedly than the capital-gross output ratios shown in columns 2 and 3 of Table 30.

More information is available on the important sector of manufacturing. Both total and fixed capital can be related not only to gross output, but also to net value added—a closer approximation to net income originating than is gross output. (Net value added excludes the cost of fuel and raw materials but includes payments to other industries and capital consumption.) The striking feature of columns 6 to 9 is that the movement of the capital-output ratios over time follows the same pattern, whether the numerator is total or fixed capital, and whether the denominator is gross output or net value added. Here, there was apparently very little substitution of fixed capital (buildings and machinery) for other items in total capital (as there was in agriculture of fixed capital for livestock); and there was not much movement over time in the ratio of net value added to gross value of output. We find, therefore, that all the ratios rose to a peak in 1919, declined thereafter, and showed no significant rise or decline over the period as a whole.

Have the movements in the capital-output ratios observed for total mining and total manufacturing been the same for the branches that can be distinguished within these sectors? Table 31 answers this question for the five branches of mining for the period 1870–1953. The movements appear to follow the same pattern in all branches—a rise to a peak in 1919 and a subsequent decline—with the trend over the period as a whole being neither significantly up nor down. But there are some interesting exceptions. In anthracite, the sharp decline in output after 1919 not only kept the capital-output ratio (capital, excluding land) from dropping but actually tended to raise it. In metals, the peak capital-output ratio, whether for total or fixed capital, was reached in 1890. In oil and gas—an extremely interesting case because of its high rate of growth—the capital-output ratio, though higher in 1870 than that for any other branch of mining, rose quite rapidly and by 1919 was more than three times its 1870 level. Then it declined precipitously and by 1953 was significantly below its 1870 level, particularly so for fixed capital. But the oil and gas branch only reproduces in exaggerated form the pattern of movement observed in the

TABLE 31

OUTPUT AND CAPITAL-OUTPUT RATIOS, MAJOR BRANCHES OF MINING, BASED ON VOLUMES IN 1929 PRICES, 1870–1953

(amounts in millions of dollars)

Branches of Mining	1870 (1)	1890 (2)	1919ᵃ (3)	1919ᵇ (4)	1940 (5)	1953 (6)	Ratio, 1919 to 1870 (7)	Ratio, 1953 to 1919 (8)
				OUTPUT				
1. Metals	29	131	465	465	643	731	16.03	1.57
2. Anthracite coal	91	235	456	456	269	161	5.01	0.35
3. Bituminous coal	35	172	829	829	832	828	23.69	1.00
4. Petroleum and natural gas	7	65	535	535	2,051	3,939	76.43	7.36
5. Other nonmetals	n.c.	71	155	223	411	801	n.a.	3.59
6. Total	176ᶜ	673	2,439	2,507	4,206	6,460	13.86	2.58
			RATIO OF CAPITAL, EXCLUDING LAND, TO OUTPUT					
7. Metals	1.29	2.73	2.16	2.16	1.24	1.39	1.67	0.64
8. Anthracite coal	0.41	0.50	0.53	0.53	0.55	0.64	1.29	1.21
9. Bituminous coal	0.91	0.69	1.25	1.25	0.88	1.17	1.37	0.94
10. Petroleum and natural gas	1.75	3.78	5.86	5.86	2.26	1.41	3.35	0.24
11. Other nonmetals	n.c.	1.16	1.19	1.23	0.94	0.61	n.a.	0.50
12. Total	0.72	1.36	2.30	2.27	1.59	1.26	3.19	0.56
			RATIO OF FIXED CAPITAL, EXCLUDING LAND, TO OUTPUT					
13. Metals	1.14	2.37	1.49	1.49	0.59	0.77	1.31	0.52
14. Anthracite coal	0.35	0.45	0.45	0.45	0.34	0.32	1.29	0.71
15. Bituminous coal	0.66	0.59	1.07	1.07	0.53	0.72	1.62	0.67
16. Petroleum and natural gas	1.64	3.45	5.51	5.51	1.73	1.01	3.36	0.18
17. Other nonmetals	n.c.	0.88	0.95	0.98	0.43	0.33	n.a.	0.34
18. Total	0.61	1.19	2.00	1.97	1.10	0.84	3.28	0.43

n.c. = no comparable data available.
ᵃ Comparable with entries for preceding years.
ᵇ Comparable with entries for following years.
ᶜ Including an estimate for "other" nonmetals.

SOURCE: Israel Borenstein, *Capital and Output Trends in Mining Industries, 1870–1948* (Occasional Paper 45, New York, NBER, 1954), pp. 67, 34–35, and unpublished extensions.

others. Apparently increasing mechanization and technological complexity result first in an accumulation of capital, total or fixed, which means a higher rate of growth than in output; then, with the slowing down in the growth of the industries and with the technological base set, capital saving improvements can be introduced and attempts made to raise the rate of utilization of existing capacity.

Two aspects of the movement within mining deserve note. First, the relative importance of the oil and gas industry increased rapidly, its output accounting for less than 10 per cent of the total in 1890 but for over 60 per cent in 1953. With its capital-output ratio always well above the ratio for mining as a whole, this rise in relative importance of the industry contributed to an upward trend in the capital-output ratio for mining as a whole. The changes in the sector-mix therefore tended to raise the capital-output ratio throughout the period. Second, the capital-output ratios in the several branches converged, particularly between 1919 and 1953. Weighted absolute deviations of the branch ratios from the ratio for mining as a whole confirm that impression. For the ratios of total capital to output, these deviations were 0.99 for 1890, 1.57 for 1919 (or 1.53 comparable with the figure for the earlier year), and 0.21 for 1953. The weighted relative deviations for the relevant dates—the coefficients of variation—were 0.73, 0.69 (or 0.67 comparable with the figure for 1890), and 0.17, respectively. For the ratios of fixed capital to output, the absolute deviations were 0.89 for 1890, 1.51 for 1919 (or 1.54 comparable with the figure for the earlier year), and 0.20 for 1953. The coefficients of variation were 0.75, 0.77, and 0.24, respectively. The striking decline in the capital-output ratio for the oil and gas branch between 1919 and 1953, as well as the sharp drop in the ratio for metals from its peak in 1890—another branch with a high capital-output ratio—contributed to the greater equality in the branch ratios in the later periods than in the earlier periods.

For the manufacturing sector many more branches can be distinguished than for mining. Only the major industrial branches are shown in Table 32, but a more detailed analysis can be found in the monograph dealing with this sector. The main purpose of Table 32 is to reveal the similarity between the pattern of movement of the total capital-output ratio for manufacturing as a whole and that for the twelve major branches distinguished. In all branches—with the exception of rubber and its products, and transportation equipment (both of which showed a peak in 1900), and printing and publishing (which showed a peak in 1937)—the peak capital-output ratio was reached in 1919. In all of them (except printing and publishing) the movement in the ratio was downward after 1919. Some of the exceptions are illuminating: both rubber and its products, and transportation equipment (mainly automobiles) were going through periods of turbulent growth and mechanization somewhat later than the other branches, and their peak ratios in 1900 probably indicate that the high rates of new additions to plant and equipment reflected an expectation of growth exceeding the needs of current output.

For the other findings suggested by study of the major and minor branches of manufacturing we turn to the analysis in the relevant monograph (Creamer, Dobrovolsky, and Borenstein, *op. cit.*). Three conclusions merit emphasis here. The first concerns the effect of shifts in relative importance of various industries within total manufacturing. The finding, noted above, that the major branches display similar movements in their total capital-output ratios suggests that the shifts in weight among industries could not contribute greatly to the movement of the sector-wide ratio. And this suggestion is confirmed by direct calculations, which indicate that of the rise in the total capital-output ratio from 1880 to 1919, only one-sixth can be attributed to the altered composition of the manufacturing total. The downward movement from 1919 to 1937 occurred without any contribution from the changing industry-mix. The latter, in fact, would have made for a slight rise, rather than a decline, in the total capital-output ratio.

The second conclusion relates to the increasing convergence among the industry total capital-output ratios, similar to that observed among the ten regions in agriculture and the five divisions in mining. The coefficient of variation in the total capital-output ratios based on values in 1929 prices, in thirty-seven manufacturing industries, ranged from 63 to 70 per cent (of the mean ratio for manufacturing as a whole) from 1880 to 1900. It then dropped significantly and fairly consistently to slightly over 31 per cent in 1948. This means in essence that, in those industries for which the initial capital-output ratio was high, the decline was greater, or the rise smaller, than in those industries for which the initial capital-output ratio was low.

The third conclusion is that, while the relative changes in output and in total capital were positively correlated, the association between relative changes in output and in the total capital-output ratio was negative. For fifty or more industries distinguished in this calculation based on volumes in 1929 prices, the coefficient of correlation between relative changes in output and in capital was +0.85 for 1880 to 1919,

TABLE

OUTPUT AND CAPITAL-OUTPUT RATIOS, MAJOR BRANCHES OF

(amounts in mill

Branches of Manufacturing	1880 (1)	1900 [a] (2)	1900 [b] (3)
			OUT
1. Food and kindred products	2,452	6,794	6,513
2. Textiles and their products	1,553	3,822	3,279
3. Leather and leather products	1,013	1,569	1,435
4. Rubber products	17	37	37
5. Forest products	1,615	3,476	3,314
6. Paper, pulp, and products	90	334	332
7. Printing, publishing, and allied industries	225	965	965
8. Chemicals and allied substances	286	829	829
9. Petroleum refining	28	173	173
10. Stone, clay, and glass products	188	547	505
11. Metal and metal products	1,183	4,202	4,179
a. Iron and steel and products	459 } 619	1,434	1,452
b. Nonferrous metals and products	160 }	801	757
c. Machinery (except d)	513	1,658	1,658
d. Transportation equipment	51	309	312
12. Miscellaneous manufactures	170	434	423
13. Total	8,820	23,182	21,984
			RATIO OF TOTAL
14. Food	0.37	0.55	0.55
15. Textiles	0.64	0.82	0.88
16. Leather	0.32	0.57	0.56
17. Rubber	0.59	2.00	2.00
18. Forest products	0.52	0.82	0.68
19. Paper and allied products	1.00	1.36	1.36
20. Printing	0.64	0.83	0.83
21. Chemicals	0.72	1.05	1.05
22. Petroleum refining	1.32	1.13	1.13
23. Stone, clay, and glass	0.83	1.36	1.40
24. Metal products	0.86	1.07	1.07
a. Iron and steel	1.03 } 0.95	1.10 } 1.00	1.10 } 1.00
b. Nonferrous	0.72 }	0.81 }	0.81 }
c. Machinery	0.81	1.16	1.16
d. Transportation equipment	0.33	1.09	1.12
25. Miscellaneous	0.52	0.79	0.80
26. Total	0.55	0.80	0.79

	1890	1900 [a]	1900 [b]
			RATIO OF FIXED CAPITAL,
27. Food	0.21	0.25	0.24
28. Textiles	0.35	0.36	0.39
29. Leather	0.09	0.12	0.12
30. Rubber	0.90	1.27	1.19
31. Forest products	0.20	0.19	0.19
32. Paper and allied products	0.96	0.82	0.78
33. Printing	0.44	0.42	0.39
34. Chemicals } 35. Petroleum refining }	0.42	0.47	0.44
36. Stone, clay, and glass	0.50	0.64	0.65
37. Metal products	0.44	0.50	0.47
38. Miscellaneous	0.20	0.24	0.23
39. Total	0.29	0.33	0.33

[a] Comparable with entries for preceding years.
[b] Comparable with entries for following years.
[c] Calculated after adjustment of 1880 (or 1890) by ratio of entry for 1900 in col. 3 to that in col. 2.
[d] Calculated after adjustment of 1953 by ratio of entry for 1948 in col. 6 to that in col. 7.

MANUFACTURING, BASED ON VOLUMES IN 1929 PRICES, 1880–1953
ions of dollars)

1919 (4)	1937 (5)	1948ᵃ (6)	1948ᵇ (7)	1953 (8)	Ratio of 1919 to 1880ᵉ (9)	Ratio of 1953 to 1919ᵈ (10)
PUT						
11,240	18,346	26,196	26,196	34,153	4.8	3.0
6,530	10,286	14,735	14,735	15,968	4.9	2.4
1,854	1,510	2,008	2,008	1,979	2.0	1.07
459	1,089	2,743	2,743	3,241	27.0	7.1
2,710	2,398	4,161	4,161	4,269	1.76	1.58
966	1,834	3,242	3,242	4,082	10.9	4.2
2,054	2,871	3,725	3,725	3,898	9.1	1.90
2,128	4,911	9,054	9,054	11,515	7.4	5.4
910	6,150	12,532	12,532	16,221	32.5	17.8
982	1,622	2,885	2,885	3,814	5.6	3.9
14,282	21,983	42,868	43,194	62,362	12.1	4.3
4,747 } 6,777	6,630	13,833 } 17,510	17,356	20,733	11.0	3.1
2,030	3,265	3,677				
4,732	6,194	15,615	15,615	22,998	9.2	4.9
2,773	5,894	9,743	10,223ᵉ	18,631	54.4	6.4
975	1,687	3,975	4,129	6,320	5.9	6.2
45,090	74,687	128,124	128,604ᵉ	167,821	5.4	3.7
CAPITAL TO OUTPUT						
0.68	0.50	0.40	0.40	0.38	1.85	0.56
1.03	0.55	0.47	0.47	0.49	1.51	0.47
0.76	0.54	0.41	0.41	0.41	2.36	0.54
1.53	0.75	0.52	0.52	0.51	2.61	0.33
1.16	1.06	0.70	0.70	0.76	2.69	0.65
1.58	1.12	0.76	0.76	0.75	1.58	0.48
0.76	0.87	0.69	0.69	0.67	1.18	0.88
1.30	0.81	0.72	0.72	0.84	1.82	0.64
1.52	1.06	0.89	0.89	0.76	1.15	0.50
1.71	1.22	0.74	0.74	0.69	1.98	0.40
1.16	0.82	0.66	0.64	0.59	1.35	0.52
1.42 } 1.26	1.01 } 0.92	0.70 } 0.70	0.66	0.67	1.32	0.56
0.89	0.72	0.68				
1.18	0.85	0.66	0.66	0.60	1.46	0.51
0.89	0.62	0.58	0.59ᵉ	0.50	2.61	0.55
0.97	0.77	0.61	0.68	0.74	1.83	0.68
1.02	0.74	0.61	0.61ᵉ	0.59	1.89	0.58

1929	1937	1948ᵃ	1948ᵇ	1953	Ratio of 1929 to 1890ᵉ	Ratio of 1953 to 1929ᵈ
EXCLUDING LAND, TO OUTPUT						
0.26	0.18	0.15	0.15	0.12	1.30	0.46
0.30	0.19	0.16	0.16	0.14	0.79	0.47
0.16	0.11	0.09	0.09	0.07	1.78	0.44
0.39	0.23	0.17	0.17	0.14	0.46	0.36
0.58	0.54	0.37	0.37	0.36	2.90	0.62
0.69	0.63	0.45	0.45	0.46	0.76	0.67
0.28	0.25	0.28	0.28	0.28	0.68	1.00
0.55	0.49	0.47	0.47	0.47	1.41	0.85
0.86	0.69	0.38	0.38	0.34	1.69	0.40
0.39	0.35	0.27	0.27ᵉ	0.25	0.95	0.64
0.28	0.23	0.21	0.23	0.33	1.47	1.11
0.38	0.31	0.27	0.27ᵉ	0.26	1.31	0.68

ᵉ Includes shipbuilding, excluded in prior years.
SOURCE: Daniel Creamer, *Capital and Output Trends in Manufacturing Industries, 1880–1948* (Occasional Paper 41, New York, NBER, 1954), Table 2, p. 18; Table A-2, pp. 86–90; and unpublished worksheets.

and +0.68 for changes from 1919 to 1948. In other words, industries in which output increased more also showed greater proportional rises in their capital stock. However, the correlation between relative changes in output and in the capital-output ratio was negative, in the order of −0.39 for 1880–1919, and −0.37 for 1919–1948 (all coefficients were statistically significant). In other words, the greater the rise in output, the less the rise, or the greater the decline, in the total capital-output ratio.

The last two conclusions are, of course, interrelated. High capital-output ratios are likely to be found among industries in the early stages of growth, when extensive expansion is at a high rate and building is in advance of current needs. It is in these industries that the relative increase in output is also likely to be at a high rate, and it is in these industries, all other conditions being equal, that the capital-output ratio is likely to decline most precipitously. Thus, one and the same complex of factors—over-expansion in terms of current needs in "new" industries—would produce, as time goes on, a convergence of the ratios, that is, a situation in which the initially higher ratios would decline most or rise least, and the initially lower ratios decline least or rise most, yielding a negative correlation between the rate of relative growth in output and the relative change in the capital-output ratio.

It is in the capital-output ratios in the public utilities sector, a field that is of great importance in the history of industrialization and capital formation in this country and many others, that we observe the most rapid declines (Table 33). The contrast between the ratios for public utilities and the others discussed so far, particularly those for manufacturing, is, of course, much exaggerated by differences in the denominators used. Even net value added in manufacturing is a gross concept relative to net income originating: in 1929 the latter was less than 30 per cent of gross value of output, whereas net value added was well over 40 per cent. The gross income or output of the public utilities sector is, in a way, a far "netter" concept: in 1929, net income originating in steam railroads (including Pullman and express) accounted for over 70 per cent of gross income; that in electric light and power and gas, for well over 60 per cent; that in communications (telephone and telegraph), for somewhat over 70 per cent.[17] Hence the

[17] See Kuznets, assisted by Epstein and Jenks, *National Income and Its Composition, 1919–1938* (New York, NBER, 1941), Vol. II, Tables P1 and P2.

TABLE 33

OUTPUT AND CAPITAL-OUTPUT RATIOS, MAJOR COMPONENTS OF THE REGULATED INDUSTRIES, BASED ON VOLUMES IN 1929 PRICES, 1880–1950

(amounts in millions of dollars)

Components of Regulated Industries	1880 (1)	1890 (2)	1900 (3)	1910 (4)	1920 (5)	1930 (6)	1940 (7)	1950 (8)	Ratio of: 1900 to 1880 (9)	1910 to 1890 (10)	1920 to 1900 (11)	1930 to 1910 (12)	1940 to 1920 (13)	1950 to 1930 (14)
						OUTPUT								
1. Steam railroads	610	1,377	2,352	4,157	5,959	5,570	5,752	8,451	3.9	3.0	2.5	1.3	0.97	1.5
2. Electric railways		151	295	648	900	775	473	339		4.3	3.1	1.2	0.53	0.44
3. Electric light & power		7.2	46.8	196	685	1,874	3,024	6,806		27.2	14.6	9.6	4.4	3.6
4. Telephones		15	101	414	677	1,180	1,316	2,591		27.6	6.7	2.9	1.9 b	2.2
5. Local bus lines					26 a	155	245	411					9.4 b	2.7
6. All other		161	372	881	1,550	2,784	4,687	10,274		5.5	4.2	3.2	3.0	3.7
7. Total	757	1,712	3,167	6,297	9,792 c	12,339	15,497	28,872	4.2	3.7	3.1	2.0	1.6	2.3
					CAPITAL-OUTPUT RATIOS									
8. Steam railroads	16.0	9.9	6.5	4.4	3.6	4.4	4.0	2.7	0.41	0.44	0.55	1.00	1.11	0.61
9. Electric railways		3.3	6.8	5.8	4.1	3.4	3.4	2.3		1.76	0.60	0.59	0.83	0.68
10. Electric light & power		12.1	12.3	10.5	4.8	3.7	2.4	1.3		0.87	0.39	0.35	0.50	0.35
11. Telephones		5.0	3.9	2.6	1.6	1.9	1.8	1.8		0.52	0.41	0.73	1.12 b	0.95
12. Local bus lines					0.2 a	0.7	1.0	1.7					5.00 b	2.43
13. All other		12.6	7.2	4.3	3.7	2.9	1.7	0.9		0.34	0.51	0.67	0.46	0.31
14. Total	15.3	9.6	6.6	4.6	3.6 c	3.6	2.7	1.6	0.43	0.48	0.55	0.78	0.75	0.44

All entries in cols. 1–8, except the first and last of a series, are three-year averages centered on the second year.

a Estimate for 1922.

b Ratio of 1940 to 1922.

c Including an estimate for 1920 (instead of 1922) for line 5 (or line 12).

SOURCE: Ulmer, Capital in Transportation, Communications, and Public Utilities, Appendix I.

capital-output ratios in Table 33 are more properly compared with ratios to net income originating, or lacking the latter, ratios to net value added in manufacturing or to net farm income in agriculture. Yet even with this adjustment, there is little question that the capital-output ratios in the public utilities sector, particularly in steam railroads and in electric light and power, have for a long time been far higher than the comparable ratios—for fixed capital—in manufacturing, mining, and agriculture. It is also evident that these ratios were at very high levels in the early periods of the growth of these industries; and that they declined sharply, indicating remarkable progress in the efficiency of replacement and utilization of durable capital equipment.

The three conclusions concerning manufacturing, agriculture, and mining apply here, too. We find convergence among the capital-output ratios for the several components of public utilities—the initially high ratios move downward at a rate much greater than that of the initially lower ratios. We find this occurring in each component, and following a relatively similar pattern. And we find evidence of negative correlation between the relative increase in output and the relative change in the capital-output ratio, particularly conspicuous in recent decades when the resurgence of growth in output is accompanied by a decline in the capital-output ratios to record low levels.

For the public utilities sector there are two additional findings. First, in several components, where we can observe the early record of the industry, the initial period shows a rise in the capital-output ratios. This is observed for electric railways and for electric light and power in the rise from 1890 to 1900, and more recently for local bus lines. It may well be that in some industries, in which it is technologically possible, the very early phases witnessed an attempt to produce with only a small investment in fixed capital; and only somewhat later a big durable capital investment program became feasible, which resulted in a temporary but substantial rise in the capital-output ratio. In a sense, this parallels the rise in the ratios in agriculture, mining, and manufacturing that culminated in the 1920's. Agriculture, however, saw a long period of increasing mechanization and industrialization, whereas in the public utilities there were much shorter periods of transition from a makeshift, semi-experimental scale of operation to the building up of an elaborate fixed capital network.

The second additional finding is that the capital-output ratios declined at a decreasing rate, not only on an absolute, but even on a relative, basis. In other words, as time goes on and the efficiency in the use of capital increases, it becomes more difficult to reduce the ratio. This aspect of the long-term movement is clearly observable in lines 8 to 11 for the major components of the sector and for the sector as a whole. It is only in the recent decades that we see a break in that slowing down in the rate of utilization of capital, and it remains to be seen how transient or persistent the new and sizable reduction in the capital-output ratios will prove to be.

CHAPTER 5

Trends in Financing of Capital Formation:
Share of Internal Funds

Problems of Analysis

In modern economies, additions to and replacements of capital goods are, to an overwhelming extent, purchased by the would-be capital user. They are not the product of his own work. We must, therefore, consider the question of financing: where does the capital acquiring unit obtain the means for purchases? Here the important distinction between internal financing (by the user's own funds) and external (by somebody else's funds) arises. It is important because in internal financing only the capital user's decision matters, but in external financing others share in making the decision. Within external financing there are also significant distinctions: between equity funds, which carry no fixed obligation of interest and repayment, and debt moneys; and within debt, among loans of differing duration and conditions as to security. There are, finally, important differences in external financing between funds that flow directly from the owner-lender to the borrower-user, and those that are channeled through financial intermediaries.

In discussing the magnitudes of capital formation in the two preceding chapters, we dealt with part of the final product of economic activity and compared it directly with the over-all product represented by the relevant countrywide totals. In discussing financing, we deal with an aspect of the mechanism by which capital formation is brought about, not with the eventual result. This shift in the orientation of discussion raises several problems that must be clarified before we can deal meaningfully with the relevant statistical estimates.

Share of Internal Funds

The question of financing is realistic only when viewed from the standpoint of a single economic unit intending to acquire capital goods for replacement or additions. Only when we ask where it secures the means for such acquisition can we see clearly the distinction between external and internal funds. When we deal with the economy as a whole, external means are limited to foreign funds; and in a closed economy, there can be no external funds. Indeed, by definition, countrywide capital formation is financed by savings, and the two totals are identical; hence any distinction between investment and financing can begin only at the level of a subsector of the total economy. To put it differently, a countrywide total of capital formation financing, if it is to have more meaning than a tautology, should be built up from the records of each economic unit, with the distinctions among units recorded, rather than disregarded as they are in estimating total capital formation.

If, then, we view the process from the standpoint of the single economic unit—the house purchaser, the firm, the nonprofit or the government institution—the first important observation is that such units cannot operate with real capital assets alone. They also need financial assets: cash and near cash, to cover gaps between receipts and payments; accounts receivable as a means of easing sales; government securities as a way of keeping quick reserves without undue loss of interest; and so on. On a countrywide basis, these financial claims cancel all counterclaims except those on the foreign debts and claims account. But they are indispensable to the economic units within the country. Thus we find, particularly for business firms (most important for our purposes), that changes in real assets, representing capital formation, are almost always accompanied by changes in financial assets. Hence, except in those rare cases in which real assets are the only ones that rise over the period under study, the financing stream—the flow of funds on the sources side—must be related, not to capital formation alone, but to the acquisition of all assets, financial included. A business firm, especially, is a complex of both real and financial assets, and we can distinguish the financing of capital formation alone by assuming exceptional conditions in which it represents the only use of additional funds or by dint of other unrealistic assumptions.

The difficulty is solved but poorly by assigning certain sources of funds exclusively to certain uses. It is tempting to argue that depreciation allowances are assignable to the financing of gross capital formation alone, but the fact is that in industries with a limited growth horizon such funds can be, and are, put to other uses; and this may be true of all industries in times of depression. It seems plausible that short-term funds should be used to finance only quick assets; but it is rationally justifiable and not unusual for a growing industry to use them in part to finance long-term assets. The examples given refer to industries in the early and late stages of growth, because the fluidity among various sources of funds and uses is greatest in those transition phases. And one can argue that, "normally," long-term funds would be given priority in financing long-term assets, and short-term funds priority in financing quick assets. The exceptions are important, however, and it is necessary to stress in advance that many of the statistical comparisons to follow imply assumptions of too rigid a connection between specific sources and specific uses of funds.

There is a somewhat related difficulty. Granted an association between the character of the source of funds and the type of use, real and financial assets are interrelated and should be treated as a single complex. The point is important because levels of and trends in shares in financing of various types of sources are greatly affected. A simple illustration will suffice. Assume that a firm has gross real capital formation of $2 million, and an addition to its accounts receivable of $1 million— these being the only changes on the assets side. Assume further that there is a gross retention of $2 million, $1 million of which is depreciation allowances and $1 million retained profits, and that accounts payable increased $1 million—these being the only changes on the liabilities side. What was the share of capital formation financed by internal funds? If, as is often done, we net out accounts receivable and payable— which implies that this source of funds can finance only this use of funds—gross retention accounts fully for gross capital formation, and the share of internal funds in financing is 100 per cent. But if we say that the total $3 million of additions to assets was financed by $2 million of gross retention and $1 million of additions to accounts payable, the share of internal financing in total acquisition of assets is 66.7 per cent. We cannot say specifically, therefore, how gross capital formation was financed, except within a range of from $1 million to $2 million from internal funds, and from zero to $1 million from external funds.

I would be inclined to argue that the netting out of the receivables and payables in the example just cited (indeed, any netting out of this type) and the assignment of gross retention to gross capital formation exclusively represent an unwarranted oversimplification. For the problem of financing is essentially the problem of how effectively our economic institutions function in placing capital in the hands of would-be capital users. The fact that the firm in the example added to its accounts payable meant that the credit network had to be stretched to accommodate the change; and the fact that the firm, at the same time, advanced an equal amount of credit—while it affected the firm's net position—does not obviate the need for the services of the credit system with respect to the payables. Furthermore, additions to accounts receivable may be viewed as a means of making capital formation effective from the standpoint of the firm. We should, therefore, view the total addition to assets as a bundle of items that cannot be separated, either by netting out or by assigning gross retention to gross capital formation alone.

Even if we follow the rule of comparing all additions to assets with changes in all sources of funds, the result may be oversimplified from the standpoint of a proper study of the financing process. The above example is a simple case of the customary sources- and uses-of-funds analysis, based largely upon net changes in assets (uses) and in liabilities (sources), with some partial use of the income account (for such items as depreciation charges and net retention). But these are all net changes, and during the year (if that is the period under consideration) large inflows and outflows of funds may occur, which call for further services of financial and credit mechanisms. Thus, there may be no net change in long-term debt outstanding; but an old bond issue may have been repaid and a new one floated. Such transactions are not effortless acts that should be represented by a blank in the accounts. Many items on the uses and sources sides of funds—notably the short-term ones—are far more subject to cancellation of gross inflows and outflows than others. If we argue—not without reason—that it is the gross flows of funds that are indispensable to the firm's operation during the year, the picture of internal and external financing may change sharply again. Thus, if in the above example we assume that the net addition of $1 million to accounts receivable was the result of a gross extension of $5 million and repayment of $4 million; that the same was true of the net addition to accounts payable; and that no such gross flows could be associated with the movement of depreciation charges and net retention, then total gross uses of funds are $7 million, and the share of internal financing in gross uses of funds drops to 29 per cent. This percentage is an accurate reflection of the share of internal funds in the total financial operations during the year by the firm in question. The example could be pushed further to show also the effects on the calculation of the shares of internal and external financing.

If the argument above is valid, capital formation becomes a relatively small fraction of gross additions to total assets by the firm during the year, and the sources of its financing seem to become increasingly less identifiable. Yet it would be unrealistic to press the argument beyond its proper limit. It is useful only in indicating that capital formation financing is a small part of the total gross flow of funds financing economic activity. But if we treat financing in grosser terms, the distinction between long-term and short-term becomes stronger, and the rationale for assigning differing term funds to their corresponding term assets becomes more compelling. Net changes in short-term funds can be applied to long-term uses, up to a point; but this is not true of gross flows, which can be kept at their large volume only by frequent repayments. Conversely, long-term funds can be used for short-term assets and for their continuous circulation, but they are more appropriately employed when tied up in long-term assets; and if there is any need for the latter, long-term funds would have priority. In short, at the level of the single firm, we can get meaningful results by studying the financing of capital formation jointly with net changes in financial assets, setting against them the internal and external sources. If net changes in financial assets are not too large compared with additions to real assets, it may even be possible to discern movements in the financing of capital formation alone.

We rarely have data, however, for single economic units, and certainly not for enough of them to permit us to derive aggregates. Whatever data are available are already aggregates of units. This poses a new difficulty in the analysis of financing.

The difficulty is essentially that opposite movements among the units in the aggregate cancel each other. Assume that a firm employs its earned depreciation of $10 million to repay part of an outstanding bond issue, and has no other changes in assets and liabilities. Assume that another firm uses the same amount of earned depreciation plus $10 million derived from a bond issue to purchase $20 million in capital goods. For the aggregate—consisting of these two firms—total gross capital formation will be $20 million; the total debt outstanding will remain the same; and it will appear as if the $20 million in capital formation were financed by the earned depreciation, that is, entirely out of internal funds. But in reality, the firm that was responsible for this capital formation financed half of it from external funds; and the fact that the other firm made a net contribution to the capital market by redeeming $10 million of its bonds does not obviate the need for the services of the financial institutions. In particular, the fact that the firm providing the $10 million in bonds had a part in the acquisition of the $20 million in capital goods is concealed in the aggregated totals.

This difficulty is clearly additional to those illustrated by the case of a single economic unit. The essential point here is that what is internal to an industry may be external to some firms in it; and what is internal to an economy may be external to some industrial sectors in it. The whole concept of internality and externality is dependent, in an aggregated total, upon the size of the group involved in the aggregation. In general, the larger the number of units in the aggregate, the greater the likelihood of cancellation of the kind illustrated, and hence the greater the amount of external financing concealed. It follows that the practice of aggregating to a net total tends to exaggerate the share of internal financing and to understate the share of external financing, if the distinction between the two is, as it should be, in terms of the unit responsible for the decision—the firm, the individual, or the non-profit institution. It also tends to conceal any redistribution of liabilities and assets among the units in the aggregate, and hence the gross amount of external funds involved.

This bias and concealment could be obviated if, in the aggregation, units that had positive additions to a given type of asset could be separated from those that sustained net decreases in that asset. It could then be seen that the total additions were financed by corresponding changes on the sources-of-funds side (or by reduction of other assets); and that the total decreases were associated with corresponding reductions on the liabilities side (or with increases in other assets). But such totaling could be carried through systematically only for each type of asset separately (or for some specific combination of types), and would differ as the type of asset differed.

We could achieve the desired results if we divided all units into two groups—those whose gross capital formation was at least as large as their gross retention, and those whose gross capital formation fell short of the latter. Proceeding similarly for changes in financial assets, we could then observe the sources of financing separately for each group. But no such summations are available; and we are forced to operate with net aggregates of the type in our example.

The embarrassing consequence of this limitation is that it prevents us from observing trends in the proportion of concealment of external financing, which may run against or reinforce other trends suggested by a sources-and-uses analysis of funds based on industry or larger aggregates. To illustrate: assume that the ratio of gross retention to gross capital formation for an industry is rising, suggesting a rise in the share of internal funds in financing capital formation. Assume further that, in line with earlier discussion, gross retention is related not to gross capital formation alone but to total uses—the sum of gross capital formation and net changes in financial assets—and the share of internal funds still rises. Yet over the period, disparities in behavior, of the type suggested in the illustration, among individual firms within the industry may have increased. Whereas in earlier days all firms added to their capital stock and drew fully upon their retained funds for the purpose, in recent times some firms have continued to follow that course and have even expanded their capital assets through borrowing, but others have failed to expand and in a sense have shifted their resources out of the industry. If such a trend occurred, the external financing concealed in the aggregates would have increased proportionately, possibly to the point of offsetting the trend toward the decline in the share of external financing suggested above. Conversely, the trend in disparities among firms may have been in the opposite direction, reinforcing the trend toward the decline observed in the share of external financing in total asset acquisition.

Further problems in the analysis are bound to emerge as we attempt to deal with the estimates, but they can best be noted as they appear. For the present, the following conclusions may be stated, as qualifications upon any findings suggested by the statistical aggregates.

1. Financing of capital formation, as distinct from financing of all asset acquisition, can be measured only if we assign certain sources of funds to capital formation as a first priority. Such an assignment may be unrealistic.

2. It follows that financing of all asset acquisition must be studied, at least as a check; and if net changes in financial assets loom large compared with capital formation, statements concerning financing of the latter can be made only within wide limits.

3. Financing assumes full meaning only for a single economic unit because the distinction between external and internal funds and changes in various types of external obligations can be clearly stated only for a unit. In aggregating, on a net basis, the data for groups, the considerable cancellation that usually occurs conceals external financing and exaggerates internal (external and internal from the

standpoint of the unit). It naturally fails to reveal gross demands upon borrowing of various types.

Distribution between Internal and External Financing: the Industrial Sectors

We begin examination of the statistical evidence with the data that bear upon the long-term trends in the shares of internal and external financing. As already indicated, we cannot work with countrywide totals but must use data for groups of capital users, the number of groups being determined largely by the available material. We discuss first the financing of nonfarm residential construction, on which our data are most direct; then proceed to the financing of capital formation in agriculture and, insofar as data permit, in nonfarm unincorporated business; go on to the financing of capital formation by business corporations, distinguishing as many major industrial sectors as possible; and conclude with the rather distinctive pattern of financing by governments.

NONFARM RESIDENTIAL CONSTRUCTION

Thanks to the work by Grebler, Blank, and Winnick, the sources of funds can be linked directly with a given complex of real capital formation—in this case, nonfarm residential construction (excluding non-housekeeping units, which, however, are not a sizable proportion of the total).[1] The procedure involves direct, though approximate, data on the share of new construction (including cost of land) accounted for by transactions paid fully in cash; and then, within total housing expenditures financed by credit (largely mortgages), the share of purchase (or construction) costs accounted for by mortgage advances is distinguished (Table 34).

It should be noted at the start that cash purchases, which are described as internal financing, and whose share in total expenditures on nonfarm residential construction is shown in column 7, may exaggerate the true levels. If a person purchases a new house (or pays for its construction) with cash borrowed from a bank, external rather than internal financing is involved. It is fair to argue, however, that cash payments for residential construction can hardly be drawn to any significant extent from short-term credit sources; and if they repre-

[1] See Leo Grebler, David M. Blank, and Louis Winnick, *Capital Formation in Residential Real Estate: Trends and Prospects* (Princeton for NBER, 1956).

Trends in Financing of Capital Formation

TABLE 34

SHARES OF EXTERNAL FINANCING AND INTERNAL FINANCING, NEW NONFARM RESIDENTIAL
CONSTRUCTION, 1911–1955

(amounts in billions of dollars)

Periods	Total Expenditures for Nonfarm Residential Construction [a] (1)	Expenditures Financed by Mortgages and Contract Sales (2)	(2) as Per Cent of (1) (3)	Amount of Mortgages and Contract Sales (4)	(4) as Per Cent of (2) (5)	External Financing as Per Cent of Total (3) x (5) (6)	Internal Financing as Per Cent of Total 100 − (6) (7)
1. 1911–1920	13.41	9.60	71.6	6.50	67.7	48.5	51.5
2. 1921–1930	45.52	37.47	82.3	28.76	76.8	63.2	36.8
3. 1931–1940	14.23	12.10	85.0	8.68	71.7	60.9	39.1
4. 1941–1945	7.36	6.75	91.7	5.46	80.9	74.2	25.8
5. 1946–1955	105.49	93.32	88.5	76.96	82.5	73.0	27.0

[a] Including land.

SOURCE: Calculated from Leo Grebler, David M. Blank, and Louis Winnick, *Capital Formation in Residential Real Estate: Trends and Prospects* (Princeton for NBER, 1956), Table M-1, pp. 454–455, and Table 80, p. 320.

sent personal borrowing by the would-be capital user from relatives or friends, the sources of funds are still internal to the wider group of individuals joined by ties of blood or friendship. Yet, as measures of the share of internal financing, the entries in column 7 are over-estimates.

The distinction here between internal and external is, as it should be, with reference to a single unit—whether an individual or a corporation—that purchases or constructs new residential housing. This means that much of the external financing, i.e., a large share of the funds advanced, chiefly as mortgage money, is contributed by owners of residential housing paying back advances made in the past. Thus, even in the prosperous 1920's and the second half of the 1940's, repayments of mortgages accounted for between one-half and three-quarters of the mortgage loans made during a given year.[2] In poor years, repayments are likely to exceed new mortgage advances. Hence, if we viewed all owners of residential housing as constituting a single industry (including the new entrants or new purchasers) and offset new mortgages (or other credit advances) by repayments, the share of external financing would be far smaller than that shown in column 6 of Table 34. But the share as shown is far more relevant for our purpose.

[2] *Ibid.,* Table 49, p. 179.

Share of Internal Funds

Over the period covered by Table 34, the share of external sources in the financing of new nonfarm residential construction has risen markedly, and that of internal financing declined correspondingly. Even though the periods distinguished are, for the most part, discrete decades—no attempt having been made to cancel out the effects of long swings—the upward movement of the share of external financing is pronounced, consistent, and unmistakable.

The distribution within the table indicates that the upward trend is a composite of two subtrends. First, the proportion of new construction that involves external financing (i.e., that is not fully a cash transaction) has been rising (column 3). Second, the share of mortgages and contract sales in total expenditures financed by borrowing has also been rising (column 5). Indeed, the very high levels reached by the percentages in columns 3 and 5 suggest that they are not far from a limit. If we assume that, at most, 95 per cent of residential construction requires some financing (after all, some purchases will be made with cash), and that the ratio of the value of mortgages to the total expenditures financed by borrowing cannot appreciably exceed 80 per cent, then the upper limit of the share of external financing is 76 per cent—not much higher than the share prevailing since 1941.

While Table 34 covers only the period since 1911, there is evidence to suggest that the upward trend in the share of external financing is of longer duration—indeed, can be traced back to 1890. According to Grebler, Blank, and Winnick, the proportion of net change in mortgage debt to total nonfarm residential construction in 1910–1919 was about 38 per cent (compared with the 48.5 per cent share of external financing of total expenditures in 1911–1920, line 1 of Table 34), and the corresponding per cent was 15.5 in 1900–1909, and only 8.4 in 1890–1899.[3] Even if the rise in the ratio of new mortgage financing to new construction was not as rapid as that in the ratio of net changes in debt to new construction, it also must have risen appreciably between 1890–1900 and 1910–1920. Moreover, the proportion of mortgaged homes among owner occupied dwellings has increased (since 1890) and there is a tendency for the debt-to-value ratio of these mortgaged homes to rise.[4] It seems clear that the upward movement in the share of external financing in nonfarm residential capital formation is a trend that goes back at least to 1890.

[3] *Ibid.*, Table 45, p. 171.
[4] *Ibid.*, Table 44, p. 170.

During the same period, the ratio of depreciation or capital consumption allowances to gross capital formation represented by nonfarm residential construction was rising. This ratio, for volumes in current prices, rose from 37 per cent in 1889–1909 to 64 per cent in 1941–1950.[5] While the extension to 1955 lowers the ratio of depreciation charges to 44 per cent,[6] it is still higher than in 1889–1909; and through much of the period, when the share of internal financing was declining, the ratio of depreciation charges to gross value of new housing was rising. If we could assume that depreciation charges were "earned" by real estate owners, and that they were a source of financing internal to the whole group of owners, including the new, the share of internal sources would show an upward rather than a downward trend. But this is precisely what we cannot assume: the units that were earning and accumulating depreciation funds were least likely to be the units that were purchasing new construction.

Before we speculate about the reasons for the upward trend in the share of external sources in financing new nonfarm residential housing, three other relevant trends should be briefly noted. First, within this category there has been a steady rise in the share of owner occupied dwellings, and a decline in that of tenant occupied. The former rose from about 37 per cent in 1890 and 1900 to about 53 per cent in 1950; and the latter declined accordingly from about 63 per cent to about 47 per cent.[7] This means that owner occupied dwellings represented an increasing share of the net additions to the number of dwelling units. Between 1890 and 1910 the total increase in number of dwelling units reporting tenure was 5.7 million, the rise in owner occupied being 2.3 million or 40 per cent, and that in tenant occupied, 3.4 million or 60 per cent. The rise from 1910 to 1930 amounted to 9.2 million units, of which the rise in owner occupied was 5.3 million or 58 per cent and that of tenant occupied, 3.9 million or 42 per cent. From 1930 to 1950, the net addition to dwelling units was 14.2 million, of which the rise in owner occupied was 9.3 million or 65 per cent and the rise in tenant occupied, 4.9 million or 35 per cent. Thus the rise in the share of external financing was paralleled by an upward trend in the share of new dwellings that were owner occupied.

[5] *Ibid.*, Table 16, p. 66.

[6] *Ibid.*, Table 78, p. 313.

[7] By 1956 the share of owner occupied dwellings had risen to 59 per cent—see *Consumer Instalment Credit* (Board of Governors, Federal Reserve System, 1957), Part I, Vol. 1, Table 1, p. 10. See also *Historical Statistics of the United States, 1789–1945,* and *Continuation*, Series H-102 and H-104.

Share of Internal Funds

Second, during the last two to two and a half decades, the proportion of one-family dwellings in the total increased markedly.[8] The record extends back only to 1900. During the first three decades, one-family dwellings accounted for only about two-thirds of the total number of nonfarm housekeeping dwelling units started. Indeed, the proportion declined somewhat in the 1920's when it accounted for about 62 per cent, whereas two-family dwellings constituted almost 15 per cent, and three-family or multifamily units, almost 23 per cent. But in the period 1946–1955, one-family dwelling units accounted for 87 per cent of all dwellings, with two-family units constituting about 4 per cent, and multifamily units, somewhat over 9 per cent of all dwellings.

The third, and for the present purpose perhaps most important trend, was the decline in real capital investment per dwelling, relative to the general rise in per capita income. For the twenty years, 1889–1908, average expenditure per new private nonfarm housekeeping dwelling unit was $5,679, in 1929 prices, whereas in 1946–1955 it was only $3,894.[9] Net national product per worker, also in 1929 prices, rose from $1,057 in 1889–1908 to $2,242 in 1946–1955 (see Table 5, column 6, excluding military capital formation). This means that the ratio of average expenditure per dwelling unit to net national product per worker declined from 5.4 in 1899–1908 to 1.7 in 1946–1955. While one should not overrate the significance of the magnitudes just quoted, it is clear that the ratio of capital investment per dwelling unit to the average income of individuals has declined substantially.[10]

With these several trends in view, an explanation of the long-term rise in the share of external financing of new nonfarm residential con-

---

[8] See Grebler, et al., op. cit., Table B-2, pp. 333–334, and Historical Statistics.

[9] Grebler, et al., op. cit., Table J-1 and p. 315.

[10] Two factors may have made the decline somewhat smaller. One is the possible decline in the number of workers per family unit with the reduction in size of family, and a slightly lower ratio of labor force to total population in 1950 than in 1910. The other is the fact that national product per worker as shown relates to total labor force, not to nonfarm alone. The recent increase in the ratio of per-worker income in agriculture to per-worker income in the nonagricultural sectors means that product per worker in the nonfarm areas increased at a slightly lower rate than the countrywide level of product per worker. But both qualifications are quantitatively minor, and would reduce the decline in the ratio only slightly.

See also the recent discussion of the trend in average expenditure per dwelling unit in Margaret G. Reid, "Capital Formation in Residential Real Estate," Journal of Political Economy, April 1958, pp. 131–153, and the reply, "Once More: Capital Formation in Residential Real Estate," by Grebler, Blank, and Winnick, in that journal, December 1959, pp. 612–627.

struction can be suggested—particularly if we assume that the capital users are primarily individuals for whom house ownership and use is not a major occupation. We could, then, say that the rising trend in the share of external sources in financing new residential housing was a consequence of the increased willingness of would-be capital users—largely households—to borrow in order to acquire such assets, and of the increased willingness of lending agencies to extend credit. Although the factors involved in the demand for and supply of funds were somewhat interrelated, it is convenient to note them separately.

The increased willingness of the capital users to borrow was one manifestation of a broader movement that has emerged since 1900 and extended also to consumer durable goods.[11] It was partly an effect of the rising standard of living, of the increased output of goods per capita, which permitted consumers to satisfy their desire for superior goods, including owned houses rather than rented houses. It was partly an effect of technological changes, which permitted the extension of urban residential areas (and we deal here with nonfarm housing) away from the congested centers of cities, and made single-family dwelling economically more feasible. It was partly a result of the reduction in real capital invested per dwelling unit, a finding referred to above. The declining ratio of such capital investment to average income diminished the risk to the would-be capital user in acquiring ownership, even though investment meant the assumption of debt. The increasing stability of income over time, and the long-term rise in prices, which automatically brings about a decline in the ratio of fixed debt to the value of an asset, had similar effects. Finally, the terms of mortgage financing changed: interest rates were lowered and the average contract term was lengthened, which made the burden of borrowing easier.[12]

There were also changes on the supply side of funds, which increased the willingness of lending agencies to finance a rising share of new gross capital formation in this field. The very factors that reduced the risk to would-be capital users in assuming debt obligations in their purchase of new housing made the potential borrowers more credit worthy. The growth in the volume of mortgage financing meant, under normal conditions, a greater volume of repayments from which new housing could be financed. An increasing share of personal savings was flowing to such intermediate institutions as insurance companies

[11] See the discussion in *Consumer Instalment Credit*, Part I, Vol. 1, Chap. 2, pp. 7–21.
[12] See Grebler, *et al., op. cit.,* Chap. XV, pp. 220–237.

and building and loan associations, which found placement of funds in mortgages relatively attractive. Last, but not least, the attempt by the government, since the 1930's, to support residential mortgage credit has had considerable impact.[13]

AGRICULTURE

Turning now to trends in financing of capital formation in agriculture, we shift to capital users who must be treated more as business units than as households, although there is still an intimate connection between the farmer's business and his household.

Table 35 is based on the work of Tostlebe, presented in detail in his monograph, cited previously.[14] Data for 1950–1955 were extrapolated by the movement in the Department of Agriculture estimates. Because we deal here with a business unit, we are immediately confronted with some of the problems touched upon in the first section of this chapter. Should we relate the sources of financing to real capital formation alone, or to total additions to assets? And specific to farming (and other unincorporated business) is the question: should we view financial reserves (other than cash working balances) as internal to the business unit, or external?

The period of some fifty-five years covered by Table 35 is fairly long, as economic periods go. Yet it has been affected by violent changes in prices and in the market position of agriculture, which distort the ratios and make the establishment of long-term trends a rather hazardous undertaking. With this advance warning, we present some preliminary conclusions. We deal here with the financing of gross capital formation: the assignment of any sources of funds to net capital formation would be so arbitrary that inferences would be worthless.

1. In studying the movement of the ratio of borrowing to gross capital formation, we omitted the periods that cover the span from 1930 through 1944. In the depressed decade of the 1930's, capital formation was quite small, and market conditions restricted the supply of external funds. In the 1940–1944 quinquennium, on the other hand, funds were available but the supply of real capital goods was restricted. Both periods are, therefore, distorted either on the supply-of-funds side, or on the supply-of-assets side.

[13] *Ibid.*, Chapter XVI.
[14] Alvin S. Tostlebe, *Capital in Agriculture: Its Formation and Financing since 1870* (Princeton for NBER, 1957).

Trends in Financing of Capital Formation

TABLE 35

CAPITAL FORMATION FINANCING, AGRICULTURE, 1900–1955

(amounts in billions of dollars)

	1900–1909 (1)	1910–1919 (2)	1920–1929 (3)	1930–1939 (4)	1940–1944 (5)	1945–1949 (6)	1950–1955 (7)
Uses of Funds							
1. Net real capital formation	3.7	5.8	−1.6	−0.6	2.6	3.9	9.7
2. Capital replacement	5.2	9.0	13.2	9.7	7.3	13.3	20.1
3. Gross real capital formation, lines 1 and 2	8.9	14.8	11.6	9.1	9.9	17.2	29.8
4. Net increase in cash working balances	0.4	1.5	−0.5	0.6	2.9	2.4 ⎫	2.4
5. Net increase in financial reserves	0.5	3.8	−1.2	0.7	7.9	3.3 ⎭	
6. Total, lines 3, 4, and 5	9.8	20.1	9.9	10.4	20.7	22.9	32.2
Sources of Funds							
7. Capital consumption allowances	5.2	9.0	13.2	9.7	7.3	13.3	20.1
8. Net income, line 9 minus line 7	1.9	1.4	−4.7 (−6.7)	2.7 (−0.3)	15.4	6.6	5.8
9. Gross retention, line 11 minus line 10	7.1	10.4	8.5 (6.5)	12.4 (9.4)	22.7	19.9	25.9
10. Borrowing (net)	2.7	9.7	1.4 (3.4)	−2.0 (1.0)	−2.0	3.0	6.3
11. Total (equals line 6)	9.8	20.1	9.9	10.4	20.7	22.9	32.2
Ratios							
12. Capital consumption allowances to GCF, line 2 or 7 to line 3	0.58	0.61	1.14	1.07	0.74	0.77	0.67
13. Gross retention to GCF, line 9 to line 3	0.80	0.70	0.73 (0.56)	1.36	2.29	1.16	0.87
14. Borrowing to GCF, line 10 to line 3	0.30	0.66	0.12 (0.29)	—	—	0.17	0.21
15. Gross retention to total uses, line 9 to line 6	0.72	0.52	0.86 (0.66)	1.19	1.10	0.87	0.80

GCF = gross capital formation.

Figures in parentheses in cols. 3 and 4 are adjusted for estimated change in debt by foreclosure—see Tostlebe, *op. cit.*, pp. 142–144.

In this and the following tables in Chapters 5 and 6, a dash (—) indicates that the ratio was not computed because the numerator and/or the denominator was negative, zero, or close to zero.

SOURCE, BY COLUMN

(1)–(6) Tostlebe, *op. cit.*, Tables 34–36, pp. 135–138.
   (7) *The Balance Sheet of Agriculture, 1956*, Agriculture Information Bulletin No. 163, Nov. 1956.
   Line 1. Changes in volumes in constant prices, Table 2, p. 4, multiplied by the price index derived from Tables 1 and 2.
   Line 2. Depreciation and consumption of farm capital, Table 3, p. 6. The entry for 1951 is interpolated.
   Lines 4–5. Change in financial assets, Table 1.
   Line 10. Change in total debt, Table 1.

2. We can compare the experience of the three decades from 1900 through 1929 with that of the last eleven years of the period studied, 1945–1955. The share of borrowing, which was three-tenths of gross capital formation during 1900–1909, rose sharply in 1910–1919, when the increasing values of land and acquisitions of new farms were accompanied by extensive borrowing. The net change in debt in the 1920's should be corrected for the effects of reduction by foreclosure,

which obviously is not a reduction of debt by a draft upon income. With this approximate correction (see figures in parentheses in columns 3 and 4), the share of net borrowing in gross capital formation in the 1920's amounted to about three-tenths. The arithmetic mean share for the three decades is 42 per cent, compared with less than 20 per cent for the 1945–1955 period. One might say, then, that the share of borrowing in financing of new capital formation in agriculture declined appreciably.

3. A similar conclusion emerges if we relate borrowing to total uses of funds, that is, consider net increase in cash working balances and in financial reserves as part of the operating complex of agriculture. The share of borrowing in that larger total was 28 per cent in 1900–1909, 48 per cent in 1910–1919, and, with the correction for foreclosures, 34 per cent in 1920–1929, the arithmetic mean for the three decades being 37 per cent. The corresponding share was 13 per cent for 1945–1949 and 20 per cent for 1950–1955, an average of about 16 per cent for 1945–1955. Thus over the period the share of borrowing in total uses of funds declined to less than one-half its share in the early periods.

4. The conclusions remain unchanged if we exclude the decade of World War I as atypical. The share of borrowing in the financing of gross capital formation in 1900–1909 and in 1920–1929 (30 per cent) is higher than the share in 1945–1955 (below 20 per cent) and the same trend is evident in the share of borrowing in total uses of funds.

5. It follows that the share of internal financing—gross retention—in capital formation or in total uses rose over the period. But was this rise associated with the capital consumption allowances or the net income component of internal financing? In line 12 we show the ratio of capital consumption allowances to gross capital formation, based on current price values. Had this ratio been based on values in constant prices, we would expect to find a fairly continuous upward trend. There is some trace of such a trend even in the ratio shown, but it is not pronounced. True, during 1900–1919, the ratio of capital consumption allowances to gross capital formation was about 60 per cent, whereas the corresponding ratio for 1945–1955 was over 70 per cent. But when we include the 1920's, the average for the first three decades is almost 80 per cent.

6. One is more impressed by the role played by changes in the ratio of net income to gross capital formation in producing the upward trend in the ratio of internal financing to capital formation. Net in-

come was about two-tenths of gross capital formation in 1900–1909, less than one-tenth in 1910–1919, and was negative in 1920–1929. For 1945–1955, the ratio of net income to gross capital formation was over 26 per cent. The rise in the share of internal financing, indicated by the comparison of 1945–1955 with the period 1900–1929, may be ascribed, to a considerable extent, to the economic improvement in the position of agriculture, whereby it could earn sufficient net income, not only to increase its financial assets substantially, but to finance internally an increasing proportion of additions to its real assets—its gross capital formation.

In concluding this brief discussion of the findings suggested by Table 35, two major qualifications must be emphasized. First, a long-term "trend," derived by comparing the experience of eleven years at the end of a fifty-six year span with that of two or three decades at the beginning, may be subject to a wide margin of error. The rather wide changes in financial structure in agriculture from one decade to the next revealed in Table 35 make it unsafe to infer trends from such a comparison. Yet the data do not permit us to do much else.

The second qualification may be far-reaching. It results from the necessity of using data on outstanding debt to derive net borrowing, and of estimating net income as a residual. The implication of such a basis for our estimates—that net borrowing, i.e., net changes in debt outstanding, should be associated either with gross capital formation or with total additions to assets—may be unwarranted.

This point can be illustrated by a simple example. Assume that farmer Jones, having reached retirement age, sells his farm to young Smith, a new member of the farm community, and accepts a mortgage from Smith on the heretofore debt-free farm. Other conditions remaining the same, mortgage debt of the farming community increases, and we have a plus entry on the sources-of-funds side, and neither capital formation nor addition to financial assets on the uses-of-funds side. But the net income item on the sources-of-funds side, which is a residual, will be reduced to maintain the equality of sources and uses. Comparison over time will then show, other conditions being equal, a rise in the share of net borrowing in gross capital formation (or total uses) and a decline in the share of internal financing accounted for by a drop in the share of financing from net income. The example indicates the replacement of savings originally invested in agriculture (the equity of farmer Jones) by debt. Such shifts are quite common in a sector like agriculture, where exits and entries are frequent.

Share of Internal Funds

Another typical situation involves transfers within the body of capital users, disregarding entries and exits. If one farmer sells his land to another at a higher price than he paid—the buyer using funds borrowed from financial institutions to cover part of the purchase price—debt increases without any gross capital formation, as we measure it. However, in this case, the seller would be recorded—if he stays within agriculture—as a unit that added to its cash balances or financial reserves or to its real capital assets. If our data are complete, and we consider the capital users in agriculture a closed group, changes in debt (except through foreclosure) must be reflected in the uses of funds. But the lines of connection with real capital formation could not be distinguished from the lines of connection with additions to financial assets.

Because of these effects of transactions, either across the boundaries of agriculture or within agriculture, on the meaning of the net borrowing and net income items on the sources-of-funds side, it is important to recognize that the volume of such transactions is quite large. We have data on the number of voluntary sales of farms (as distinct from foreclosures) per thousand farms, from 1912 to date. The annual percentage of all farms passing through voluntary sales varied from a low of about 1.6 to 2 in the early 1930's (when sales were difficult and foreclosures ran high) to a peak of almost 6 in the late 1940's.[15] Cumulation of these percentages over a decade, assuming no repeats, would show that one-half of all farms changed hands within a decade. This is, of course, an exaggeration, but the point is that in agriculture, as in all sectors dominated by small business units, change in ownership is quite frequent. The transactions involving already existing complexes of assets must therefore be far greater than those involving new gross capital formation.

It follows that the evidence in Table 35 can be interpreted as shedding light on trends in internal and external financing of capital formation (real and financial) in agriculture only under the highly restrictive assumption that the proportion of changes in debt (and of the residual item, net income invested) that financed acquisition of real and financial assets, as distinct from the proportion that financed entries and exits, showed no definite trend over time. And any statement concerning trends in the shares of financing of gross real capital formation is based upon the further assumption that the proportion of

[15] See Tostlebe, *op. cit.*, Table 37, p. 144.

changes in debt (and the proportion of net income) that financed acquisition of real assets showed no distinct trend over time. We have no data by which to test the validity of these assumptions. But it is relevant to note that, while the number of farms increased from 5.7 million in 1900 to 6.8 million in 1935, it declined to 5.4 million in 1950, and the reduction may have continued beyond that year. Insofar as the reduction toward the end of the period meant a larger number of exits, and to the extent that these were accompanied by withdrawal of savings from agriculture and their replacement, if only partly, by assumption of debt, such additions to debt should not be assigned to financing of new capital formation (gross or net). If the inference just made is valid, it only reinforces the conclusion suggested by Table 35, that the ratio of internal financing to capital formation rose.

NONFARM UNINCORPORATED BUSINESS

Data on capital formation and financing for this sector of the economy are meager and unreliable. We are fortunate to have the estimates derived by Goldsmith.[16] These estimates, as Goldsmith emphasizes, are based upon a rough allocation between the corporate and unincorporated sectors, and must be interpreted with caution.

The relevant data are summarized in Table 36. It would have been possible, using Goldsmith's estimates, to distribute gross savings, or retention, between capital consumption allowances and net income (with all estimates on an original cost basis of depreciation, with net income unadjusted for effects of inventory revaluation and for the difference between original cost and replacement bases of depreciation, and with capital formation including changes in inventory in current valuation). But the basis for this distribution would be too tenuous to yield significant results.

The table runs only through 1949. But one may assume that, as for agriculture (see Table 35), the share of borrowing in total uses of funds in the period 1950–1955 would show a rise over that in 1945–1949. In both cases, the great volumes of financial assets accumulated during the war years, when the supply of capital goods was restricted, were the major source of funds during 1945–1949; and in the later years, greater reliance was placed on external funds.[17]

16 Raymond W. Goldsmith, *A Study of Saving in the United States*, Vol. I (Princeton University Press, 1955).

17 That net *additions* to cash and government securities of nonfarm unincorporated business were recorded for 1945–1949 is due largely to the inclusion of 1945. For

TABLE 36

GROSS CAPITAL FORMATION FINANCING, NONFARM UNINCORPORATED BUSINESS, 1897–1949

(amounts in billions of dollars)

Share of Internal Funds

	1897–1914	1915–1919	1920–1929	1930–1934	1935–1939	1940–1944	1945–1949
				Volumes			
1. Gross real capital formation	6.68	4.67	16.20	0.96	4.63	6.32	14.50
2. Net change in cash and government securities	1.18	2.48	0.34	-1.37	0.85	13.00	2.00
3. Net changes in receivables	0.96	0.93	-0.42	-3.58	0.42	1.35	1.46
4. Total additions to assets, lines 1, 2, and 3	8.82	8.08	16.12	-3.99	5.90	20.67	17.96
5. Changes in debt	2.60	3.07	3.53	-3.09	-0.22	0.26	5.22
6. Gross retention or savings, line 4 minus line 5	6.22	5.00	12.59	-0.90	6.12	20.41	12.74
				Ratios			
7. Gross retention to GCF, line 6 to line 1	0.93	1.07	0.78	—	1.32	3.23	0.88
8. Gross retention to total additions to assets, line 6 to line 4	0.71	0.62	0.78	—	1.04	0.99	0.71
9. Changes in debt to GCF, line 5 to line 1	0.39	0.66	0.22	—	—	0.04	0.36

Security brokers and dealers, and the professions are excluded.

SOURCE: Raymond W. Goldsmith, *A Study of Saving in the United States*, Vol. I (Princeton University Press, 1955), Table U-11, p. 869.

239

With this assumption concerning the movement of the ratios in 1950–1955, the broad conclusion can be stated simply: there is little evidence of a long-term trend in the ratio of external (or internal) sources to either gross capital formation or total additions to assets. This conclusion is based largely upon the entries for three periods: 1897–1914, 1920–1929, and 1945–1949 extended on the basis of what probably happened during 1950–1955.[18] We exclude the quinquennium 1915–1919 as too much affected by World War I, and the period from 1930 through 1944 as too distorted by the depression of the 1930's and the effects of World War II.

The ratio of gross retention (internal funds) to gross capital formation was 0.93 in 1897–1914, 0.78 during the 1920's, 0.88 in 1945–1949, and either the same or somewhat lower in 1950–1955, showing no definite movement. Likewise, the ratio of gross retention to total additions to assets was 0.71 in 1897–1914, 0.78 in the 1920's, 0.71 in 1945–1949, and probably dropped in 1950–1955. This indicates rough stability in the ratio of internal sources, and hence of borrowing, to total additions to assets. Finally, the ratio of changes in debt to gross capital formation was 0.39 in 1879–1914, 0.22 in the 1920's, 0.36 in 1945–1949, and probably rose in 1950–1955—again indicating the absence of any significant long-term movement.

In the nonfarm unincorporated business sector, we find, then, long-term trends in the shares of external and internal financing different from those observed in nonfarm residential construction and in agriculture. As pointed out, the comparison with nonfarm residential construction is scarcely warranted in view of the basic difference in the measures used for these two sectors. The reason for movement different from that in agriculture can only be conjectured. Agriculture shifted from extensive expansion before 1930 to intensive growth after that. There was a marked rise, particularly during 1940–1955, in the ratio of its per capita income to the countrywide (or nonfarm) average income. No such major shifts took place in nonfarm unincorporated business, which in Table 36 is heavily dominated by distributive trades and (a distant second) the construction industry. While the unincorporated business sector was losing ground, in that its proportion of the

---

1946–1949, the net change would be −$2.0 billion, instead of +$2.0 billion, as shown in Table 36 for 1945–1949 (see Goldsmith, *op. cit.*, Table U-11, p. 869).

[18] We have, in fact, made rough estimates for 1950–1955, primarily to complete the summary in Tables 45 and 46, below. But these estimates are too rough for use in the discussion of the specific sector.

activity of either the whole nonfarm capital using field or of that within each respective industry was falling off, there is no evidence of change in its character and in its per capita income relative to other branches of the economy as great as that in agriculture.

It need hardly be stressed that the qualifications of the conclusions for agriculture from Table 35 apply equally to the conclusions for non-farm unincorporated business from Table 36. In this sector also, exits and entries are quite frequent; and, moreover, shifts from unincorporated to corporate status are common. There is no basis for evaluating the possible effects of continuous and large exits from and entries into the sector of nonfarm unincorporated business. It may be assumed, however, that the shift from noncorporate to corporate status, insofar as it withdraws the larger units which, because of their size, may exploit the advantages of incorporation, is partly responsible for the absence of significant trends in Table 36. To put it differently: if one could assume that units remained unincorporated no matter how large they grew, and if such larger units can and do rely on greater use of external funds, the trend toward larger size might have produced an upward trend in the share of external financing. In that sense, the movement toward corporate status makes for stability of structure, and hence of the type of financing practices, within the nonfarm unincorporated sector.

ALL CORPORATIONS

Here we deal with what is quantitatively and analytically the most important segment of capital formation inasmuch as business corporations provide the auspices, in times free from war pressures and restrictions, for most of the real capital formation in the country. The trend in the dependence of corporate financing on internal versus external sources is then a major factor in evaluating the degree to which business capital formation is subject to the test of the capital funds market. Of course, even internal sources must meet the test of the market. Depreciation allowances must be earned if they are to be available for financing, or to put it differently, net retained profits must be positive. Thus, the market passes upon a business firm by paying the price that yields positive net profits, and permits the firm to finance replacement or expansion from within. External financing must meet even more stringent tests, and it is of interest to observe the extent to which the financing of capital formation is subjected to those tests.

We observed in Chapters 3 and 4 that, in general, the ratio of capital consumption allowances to gross capital formation rose distinctly over the period from 1870, as shown by ratios based on long, two-decade to three-decade spans. This finding has little bearing upon the financing of residential housing, since, as already indicated, individual households are the main capital users, and we cannot expect the capital consumption charges to be earned and made directly available within the unit as an internal source of funds. In agriculture, we found some reflection of this trend in the rise in the ratio of capital consumption allowances to gross real capital formation. The data on nonfarm unincorporated business firms did not warrant separating capital consumption allowances from net retained income. However, for the aggregate of business corporations in the United States, we can expect that, assuming no distinct contrary trend in the share of corporate savings (net undistributed profits), the share of capital consumption allowances in real gross capital formation will show a rise. This, all other conditions being equal, should make for a rise in the share of internal financing.

It is this hypothesis that provides the rationale for Table 37. Through most of the period it is based on Goldsmith's estimates, capital consumption allowances and net undistributed profits (corporate savings) being adjusted for effects of inventory revaluation and the difference between original cost and replacement cost of depreciation reserves. The series are thus comparable with those on capital formation in Chapters 3 and 4. For the years since 1950, however, we cannot adjust for the difference between original and replacement cost of depreciation charges, although we can adjust for effects of changes in inventory valuation.

Table 37 suggests some conclusions, and also points to the difficulties of inferring long-term trends over the period since 1900. We can try to discern the long-term trends in two ways. First, following the procedure used earlier, we can eliminate the periods of war and distortion due to cyclical depressions, and observe the ratios over the periods marked by substantial capital formation under relatively prosperous conditions. Thus, if we concentrate our attention upon three periods—1897–1914, 1920–1929, and 1946–1956—we find that the ratio of capital consumption allowances to gross capital formation rose from about 0.39 in the first, to 0.56 in the second, and can be roughly estimated at 0.60 in the last.[19] This shows some rise in the ratio of capital con-

---

[19] The Goldsmith series were extrapolated to 1956 by the Department of Commerce estimates, by applying to the ratios in columns 6 to 8, line 8, the movement of the ratios from 1946–1949 to 1946–1956, i.e., from line 10 to 12. In averaging the ratios for longer periods the entries in column 1 were used as rough weights.

TABLE 37

COMPARISON OF GROSS AND NET CAPITAL FORMATION WITH GROSS AND NET RETAINED INCOME, ADJUSTED TOTALS, ALL CORPORATIONS, 1897–1956

(amounts in billions of dollars)

Periods	GCF (1)	Capital Consumption Allowances (2)	Savings (net retention) (3)	Gross Retention (2)+(3) (4)	NCF (1)–(2) (5)	Ratios of:		
						(4) to (1) (6)	(2) to (1) (7)	(3) to (5) (8)
				GOLDSMITH ESTIMATES				
1. 1897–1904	12.0	4.1	4.9	9.0	7.9	0.75	0.34	0.62
2. 1905–1914	24.3	10.1	7.0	17.1	14.2	0.70	0.42	0.49
3. 1915–1919	23.4	13.0	9.8	22.8	10.4	0.97	0.56	0.94
4. 1920–1929	72.4	40.4	20.4	60.8	32.0	0.84	0.56	0.64
5. 1930–1934	12.2	19.7	−16.9	2.8	−7.5	0.23	1.61	—
6. 1935–1939	22.2	19.0	−4.1	14.9	3.2	0.67	0.86	—
7. 1940–1945	35.3	28.5	17.2	45.7	6.8	1.29	0.81	2.53
8. 1946–1949	71.6	32.8	23.6	56.4	38.8	0.79	0.46	0.61
9. 1946–1956 a						0.81	0.60	0.55
				COMMERCE ESTIMATES				
10. 1946–1949	72.0	22.7	27.1	49.8	49.3	0.69	0.32	0.55
11. 1950–1956	180.5	83.6	46.1	129.7	96.9	0.72	0.46	0.48
12. 1946–1956	252.5	106.3	73.2	179.5	146.2	0.71	0.42	0.50
Longer Periods								
13. 1897–1914	36.3	14.2	11.9	26.1	22.1	0.72	0.39	0.54
14. 1915–1939	130.2	92.1	9.2	101.3	38.1	0.78	0.71	0.24
15. 1940–1956 b						0.88	0.63	0.66

Because of rounding, detail will not necessarily add to total.

GCF = gross capital formation; NCF = net capital formation.

a Extrapolated by the movement from line 10 to line 12.

b Weighted ratios. In cols. 6 and 7, the weights (from col. 1) are: 1940–1945, 0.04; 1946–1956, 0.25. In col. 8, the weights (from col. 5) are: 1940–1945, 0.007; 1946–1956, 0.12.

SOURCE, BY LINE

1–8. R. W. Goldsmith, *A Study of Saving*, Vol. I, Tables R-27, R-29, P-5, P-11, P-19, C-1, and C-41. All components are adjusted to correspond to the concept of capital formation.

10–12. *Economic Report of the President*, January 1957, Table E-53, p. 182, adjusted for changes in inventory valuation as shown in Table E-9, p. 132. Banks and insurance companies are excluded.

sumption allowances to gross capital formation. In the same periods, the ratio of gross retention to gross capital formation moved from 0.72 to 0.84, to 0.81. Here also the share of internal sources rose, but not consistently.

The other approach to establishing the long-term trends is by including all periods, even the exceptional ones of war or other unusual conditions. On the theory that those exceptional periods were the product of the antecedent years—which were consequently also exceptional because they gave rise to exceptional effects—and that those exceptional spans were in turn followed by periods that represent reactions and thus were also in some way unusual, we should include all periods. The problem is how to calculate averages that represent a balance of distorting elements. The three long periods in lines 13 to 15 are an attempt at such averaging. It may be deficient, particularly in that the span from 1940 through 1956 represents a less complete period than the preceding two. The ratio of capital consumption allowances to gross capital formation, thus derived, moved in about the same fashion as that based on the other procedure: it rose from 0.39 in 1897–1914 to 0.71 in 1915–1939, and declined to 0.63 in 1940–1956, but still showed a significant long-term rise. The proportion of total internal sources to gross capital formation rose fairly steadily over the three long periods—from 0.72 to 0.78 to 0.88. Even if we allow for exaggeration in the last period, for which the average might be reduced if more recent years were included, we may still conclude that there has been a long-term rise since 1900 in the ratio of corporate gross retention to corporate gross capital formation.

It is worth noting that the rise shown in Table 37 in the ratio of gross retention or internal funds to gross capital formation was due exclusively to the rise in the ratio of capital consumption allowances to the latter. The ratio of retained profits to gross capital formation did not show the long-term rise. Thus, in the three normal periods, 1897–1914, 1920–1929, and 1946–1956, the ratio of retained profits to gross capital formation was 0.33, 0.28, and 0.21, respectively, suggesting a decline rather than a rise. Likewise, in the three all-inclusive periods, 1897–1914, 1915–1939, and 1940–1956, the ratio of retained profits to gross capital formation was 0.33, 0.07, and 0.25, respectively—again indicating no long-term rise.

Table 37 also shows movements of the ratio of retained profits (corporate savings) to net capital formation. For reasons already indicated, corporate savings cannot be assigned to the financing of net real capital formation alone. Yet we may ask whether those savings were sufficient to finance net additions to capital, and whether there were any visible trends in the ratio of the one to the other.

The entries in column 8 indicate that, on the whole, the ratio of net retention to net capital formation did not rise—unless we include the war affected period, 1940–1945. The ratio was 0.54 in 1897–1914, 0.64 in 1920–1929, and 0.55 in 1946–1956. Only if we compare 1897–1914 with 1940–1956 does the proportion rise—from 0.54 to 0.66. Thus, while the ratio of gross retention to gross capital formation definitely rose, that of net retention to net capital formation showed no significant rise. This conclusion is compatible with our other findings of a rise in the share of capital consumption allowances in gross capital formation, and of a slight decline (or constancy) in the ratio of net retained profits to gross capital formation.

In Table 37 gross capital formation is adjusted for effects of inventory revaluation; net capital formation and retained net profits are adjusted for both the inventory revaluation effects and those due to the shift of depreciation to replacement from original cost basis; and capital consumption allowances are estimated on replacement rather than original cost basis. These adjusted totals differ from the totals recorded in corporate accounting and hence from those presumably recognized by entrepreneurs. Yet economic analysis warrants their use—for they do indicate what properly measured gross (and net) retention means relative to properly measured capital formation. It is of interest to study the ratios based on unadjusted totals, i.e., those reflecting changes in inventory in current valuation, and capital consumption allowances and net undistributed income as measured by customary accounting practices. Those ratios are given in Table 38.

Since the entries in this table reflect the fluctuations in prices more than do those in Table 37 (if prices were constant, the two sets of entries would be identical), the ratios show more conspicuous variations, and long-term trends are all the more difficult to discern. Yet some significant differences between Tables 37 and 38 with respect to long-term trends can be seen.

First, whereas when we use the adjusted totals the ratio of capital consumption allowances to gross capital formation shows a distinct upward trend, when we use the unadjusted totals the long-term rise is much reduced. Thus in Table 37, the ratio rose from 0.39 in 1897–1914 to 0.60 in 1946–1956 or to 0.63 in 1940–1956. In Table 38 the rise was only from 0.36 in the first period to either 0.39 for 1946–1956 or

TABLE 38

COMPARISON OF GROSS AND NET CAPITAL FORMATION WITH GROSS AND NET RETAINED INCOME, UNADJUSTED TOTALS, ALL CORPORATIONS, 1897–1956

(amounts in billions of dollars)

Periods	GCF (1)	Capital Consumption Allowances (2)	Savings (net retention) (3)	Gross Retention (2)+(3) (4)	NCF (1)−(2) (5)	Ratios of:		
						(4) to (1) (6)	(2) to (1) (7)	(3) to (5) (8)
GOLDSMITH ESTIMATES								
1. 1897–1904	12.6	3.9	5.4	9.4	8.7	0.75	0.31	0.62
2. 1905–1914	24.7	9.4	7.6	17.0	15.3	0.69	0.38	0.50
3. 1915–1919	31.4	9.3	19.9	29.2	22.1	0.93	0.30	0.90
4. 1920–1929	63.5	30.4	19.7	50.0	33.1	0.79	0.48	0.60
5. 1930–1934	8.3	18.9	−25.3	−6.4	−10.6	—	2.28	—
6. 1935–1939	23.0	17.2	−2.5	14.7	5.8	0.64	0.75	
7. 1940–1945	40.9	23.2	24.0	47.2	17.7	1.15	0.57	1.36
8. 1946–1949	82.3	22.3	42.2	64.5	60.0	0.78	0.27	0.70
9. 1946–1956 a						0.78	0.39	0.63
COMMERCE ESTIMATES								
10. 1946–1949	83.5	22.7	38.6	61.3	60.8	0.73	0.27	0.63
11. 1950–1956	191.3	83.6	56.9	140.5	107.7	0.73	0.44	0.53
12. 1946–1956	274.8	106.3	95.5	201.8	168.5	0.73	0.39	0.57
Longer Periods								
13. 1897–1914	37.3	13.3	13.0	26.4	24.0	0.71	0.36	0.54
14. 1915–1939	126.2	75.8	11.8	87.5	50.4	0.69	0.60	0.23
15. 1940–1956 b						0.83	0.41	0.71

Because of rounding, detail will not necessarily add to total.
a Extrapolated by the movement from line 10 to line 12.
b Weighted ratios. In cols. 6 and 7, the weights (from col. 1) are: 1940–1945, 0.04; 1946–1956, 0.27. In col. 8, the weights (from col. 5) are: 1940–1945, 0.02; 1946–1956, 0.17.

SOURCE: See notes to Table 37.

0.41 in 1940–1956. The much greater rise in prices of capital goods in the recent decades than that which preceded 1897–1914 reduced the ratio of capital consumption allowances at original cost to capital formation in current prices much more after 1940 than it did after 1897. There were similar effects of differences in movement of inventory values.

Second, while the shift from the adjusted to the unadjusted totals reduced the rise in the proportion of capital consumption allowances to gross capital formation, it had the opposite effect on the proportion of net retained profits to gross capital formation. In Table 37, the proportion declined from 0.33 in 1897–1914 to 0.21 in 1946–1956 (or 0.25 in 1940–1956). In Table 38, the corresponding ratio rose from 0.35 in 1897–1914 to 0.39 in 1946–1956 (or 0.42 in 1940–1956). The price movements that reduced the ratio of capital consumption charges raised the ratio of net profits.

Third, the opposite effects of the shift from the adjusted to unadjusted totals upon the trends in the proportions of capital consumption allowances and of net profits to gross capital formation largely offset each other. As a result, the movement in the ratio of total gross retention to gross capital formation in the unadjusted totals is about the same as in the adjusted. Thus in Table 37, this ratio rose from 0.72 in 1897–1914 to 0.81 in 1946–1956 (or 0.88 in 1940–1956); the corresponding ratio in Table 38 rose from 0.71 to 0.78 (or 0.83). The rise in the share of internal financing in the unadjusted totals is thus only slightly less than in the adjusted.

Finally, the unadjusted totals show a different movement in the ratio of retained profits to net capital formation. This ratio in Table 38 rose from 0.54 in 1897–1914 to 0.63 in 1946–1956 (or 0.71 in 1940–1956) in contrast to the stability in Table 37 (0.54 in 1897–1914, and 0.55 in 1946–1956, but 0.66 in 1940–1956).

Nonfinancial Corporations

We now consider the *total* uses and sources of corporate funds (Table 39). Here we use Goldsmith's series (extended through 1956 by the Commerce estimates). These series exclude financial corporations. (Their inclusion in Tables 37 and 38 did not matter because they account for minor fractions of the totals involved.) Inventories are taken at current valuation, and capital consumption allowances are on an original cost basis—with a corresponding effect on net retained profits—just as in Table 38. Our primary interest here is in the movement

TABLE 39

SOURCES OF FUNDS, NONFINANCIAL CORPORATIONS, 1901–1956

(amounts in billions of dollars)

Periods	Total Sources (1)	GCF (inventories at current valuation) (2)	Net Financial Assets (1) – (2) (3)	Internal Sources (4)	Capital Consumption Allowances (5)	Retained Profits (6)	Total Net Uses (1) – (5) (7)	External Sources (1) – (4) (8)	Ratios of: (4) to (1) (9)	(5) to (1) (10)	(6) to (7) (11)	(8) to (7) (12)
					GOLDSMITH ESTIMATES							
1. 1901–1912	40.0	26.1	13.9	22.1	13.4	8.7	26.6	17.9	0.55	0.34	0.33	0.67
2. 1913–1922	76.1	49.4	26.7	46.0	25.6	20.4	50.5	30.1	0.60	0.34	0.40	0.60
3. 1923–1929	86.1	51.1	35.0	47.1	32.1	15.0	54.0	39.0	0.55	0.37	0.28	0.72
4. 1930–1933	–0.6	5.2	–5.8	4.1	20.8	–16.7	–21.4	–4.8	—	—	—	—
5. 1934–1939	28.9	26.0	2.9	28.2	31.4	–3.3	–2.5	0.7	0.98	1.09	—	—
6. 1940–1945	75.4	40.9	34.5	60.5	36.6	23.9	38.8	14.9	0.80	0.49	0.62	0.38
7. 1946–1949	110.6	82.3	28.3	71.3	33.7	37.6	76.9	39.3	0.64	0.30	0.49	0.51
8. 1946–1956 a									0.61	0.38	0.37	0.63
					COMMERCE ESTIMATES							
9. 1946–1949	100.5	83.5	17.0	63.0	23.0	40.0	77.5	37.5	0.63	0.23	0.52	0.48
10. 1950–1956	254.8	192.4	62.4	142.0	83.4	58.6	171.4	112.8	0.56	0.33	0.34	0.66
11. 1946–1956	355.3	275.9	79.4	205.0	106.4	98.6	248.9	150.3	0.58	0.30	0.40	0.60
Longer Periods												
12. 1901–1922	116.1	75.5	40.6	68.1	39.0	29.1	77.1	48.0	0.59	0.34	0.38	0.62
13. 1913–1939	190.5	131.7	58.8	125.4	109.9	15.4	80.6	65.0	0.66	0.58	0.19	0.81
14. 1940–1956 b									0.64	0.40	0.40	0.60

Because of rounding, detail will not necessarily add to total. They are, therefore, slightly different from absolute volumes.
a Based on extrapolated absolute volumes calculated directly from the movement of the ratios from line 9 to line 11.
b Calculated from absolute volumes underlying the ratios in lines 6 and 8.

SOURCE: Raymond W. Goldsmith, *Financial Intermediaries in the American Economy since 1900* (Princeton for NBER, 1958), Table 53, pp. 222 and 223, extended by Department of Commerce data in *Survey of Current Business*, April 1954, Table 1, p. 15; October 1956, Table 1, p. 12; and February 1957, Table 11, p. 19.

of the ratio of all internal sources (gross retention) to total sources or uses of funds, the two totals being conceptually identical.

For short, relatively normal periods—1901–1912, 1923–1929, and 1946–1956—the ratio of capital consumption allowances to total uses of funds was 0.34, 0.37, and 0.38, respectively (column 10). Its movement is quite similar to that of the ratio of capital consumption allowances to gross capital formation in Table 38 from 1897–1914 to 1946–1956. There was also a rise—not large, but perhaps significant—in the averages over the long periods, 1901–1922, 1913–1939, and 1940–1956, the ratio moving from 0.34 to 0.58 to 0.40.

The upward trend is also slight when we compare total internal funds with total uses (column 9). The ratio was 0.55 in 1901–1912, 0.55 in 1923–1929, and 0.61 in 1946–1956. The change is equally slight in the ratio for the longer periods: from 0.59 in 1901–1922 to 0.64 in 1940–1956.

Just as in Tables 37 and 38 we studied the movement in the ratio of net retention (corporate savings) to net capital formation, so here we can observe the movement in the ratios of corporate savings and external sources to net total uses, i.e. total net of capital consumption allowances (see columns 11 and 12). The ratio of net savings to net total uses is stable, when we compare 1901–1922 (0.38) with 1923–1929 (0.28) and 1946–1956 (0.37); but the inclusion of 1940–1945 introduces a slight rise—to 0.40—in the ratio for 1940–1956. The ratio of external sources to net total uses also shows no marked trend: it was 0.62 in 1901–1922, 0.81 in 1913–1939, 0.63 in 1946–1956, and 0.60 in 1940–1956. Perhaps it is safest to infer that there were no significant long-term trends in the ratios of net retention and external financing to net total uses or sources.

Before passing on to major subgroups within the total body of corporations, it may be useful to recapitulate the findings.

1. For totals adjusted for effects of inventory revaluation and of the difference between original cost and replacement cost bases of capital consumption allowances, the ratios of both the latter and gross retention to gross real capital formation show a rise over the half century.

2. Again for adjusted totals, the ratio of net retention (corporate savings) to net real capital formation shows no significant rise over the period, unless we include 1940–1945 in the last period.

3. When we shift the analysis to unadjusted totals, more directly relevant to the study of financing flows, the rise in the ratio of capital consumption allowances to gross capital formation is greatly reduced.

By contrast, the shift to unadjusted totals produces a rise in the ratio of net retention (corporate savings) to gross capital formation. With these two effects of the shift from adjusted to unadjusted totals largely offsetting each other, the ratio of total gross retention to gross capital formation in the unadjusted totals still shows a rise.

4. The ratio of net retention (corporate savings) to net capital formation in the unadjusted totals shows a rise, whereas the corresponding ratio for the adjusted totals shows stability, unless we include the period 1940–1945.

5. Again for the unadjusted totals, the ratios of both capital consumption allowances and gross retention to total uses show but a minor rise, distinctly smaller than that in the ratios to gross capital formation.

6. The establishment of the trends suggested above was greatly affected by extremely wide variations in the ratios from period to period, even for periods as long as twenty years.

7. The moderate magnitude of the rise in the ratio of internal financing (gross retention) to total uses (in unadjusted totals) may be attributed to a combination of offsetting trends. One trend is the rise in the share of capital consumption allowances, when calculated on the basis of prices comparable with those underlying current capital formation (that is, in the adjusted totals). Offsetting this trend are: (a) the reducing effect, in depreciation accounting based on original cost, of the growing difference between the current and past prices of capital goods—an effect due to the greater rate of rise in those prices since the 1930's than in the periods preceding the 1920's and particularly before 1918; and (b) the proportional increase of nondurable assets in recent decades.

Mining and Manufacturing Corporations

For this major group we have a special analysis in Dobrovolsky's part of the joint monograph with Creamer and Borenstein.[20] Table 40 presents a comparison of plant and equipment expenditures (excluding inventory additions) with gross retention and its components.

The conclusions are briefly summarized.

1. The ratio of gross retention to plant and equipment expenditures shows an upward trend over the period 1900–1953. On an unadjusted basis (line 7b), the ratio was 0.88 in 1900–1914, 1.04 in 1920–1929

---

[20] Daniel Creamer, Sergei Dobrovolsky, and Israel Borenstein, *Capital in Manufacturing and Mining: Its Formation and Financing* (Princeton for NBER, 1960).

TABLE 40

COMPARISON OF GROSS RETENTION AND NET SECURITY ISSUES WITH PLANT AND
EQUIPMENT EXPENDITURES, MINING AND MANUFACTURING CORPORATIONS, 1900–1953
(amounts in millions of dollars, averages per year)

	1900–1914 (1)	1914–1919 (2)	1920–1929 (3)	1929–1937 (4)	1938–1946 (5)	1946–1953 (6)
Volumes						
1. Plant & equipment expenditures	1,014	2,041	2,461	1,736	3,171	9,345
2. Capital consumption allowances						
2a. Adjusted	484	1,366	2,291	1,890	2,769	5,866
2b. Unadjusted	432	1,170	2,065	2,018	2,763	5,332
3. Net retained profits						
3a. Adjusted	429	1,038	837	−824	1,447	3,284
3b. Unadjusted	459	1,968	503	−1,264	2,002	5,092
4. Gross retention						
4a. Adjusted, lines 2a and 3a	913	2,404	3,128	1,066	4,216	9,150
4b. Unadjusted, lines 2b and 3b	891	3,138	2,568	754	4,765	10,424
5. Net capital formation						
5a. Adjusted, line 1 minus line 2a	530	675	169	−154	402	3,479
5b. Unadjusted, line 1 minus line 2b	582	871	396	−282	408	4,013
6. Net security issues	314	488	870	10	206	2,032
Ratios						
7a. Line 4a to line 1	0.90	1.18	1.27	0.61	1.33	0.98
7b. Line 4b to line 1	0.88	1.54	1.04	0.43	1.50	1.12
8. Line 6 to line 1	0.31	0.24	0.35	0.01	0.06	0.22
9a. Line 2a to line 1	0.48	0.67	0.93	1.09	0.87	0.63
9b. Line 2b to line 1	0.43	0.57	0.84	1.16	0.87	0.57
10a. Line 3a to line 1	0.42	0.51	0.34	−0.47	0.46	0.35
10b. Line 3b to line 1	0.45	0.96	0.20	−0.73	0.63	0.54
11a. Line 3a to line 5a	0.81	1.54	4.95	—	3.60	0.94
11b. Line 3b to line 5b	0.79	2.26	1.27	—	4.91	1.27
12. Line 6 to line 5b	0.54	0.56	2.20	—	0.50	0.51

Because of rounding, detail will not necessarily add to total.

SOURCE: Based on estimates by Sergei Dobrovolsky in the joint monograph with
Daniel Creamer and Israel Borenstein, *Capital in Manufacturing and Mining: Its Formation and Financing* (Princeton for NBER, 1960), Tables 40 and 41, pp. 121 and 131.

The estimates by Dobrovolsky are annual average values for successive business
cycles. For the present table, we combined the averages without regard to the varying
duration of the cycles. The entries for 1900–1914 are arithmetic means of the annual
average values for the cycles, 1900–1904, 1904–1908, 1908–1911, and 1911–1914; those
for 1914–1919 are averages for a single cycle; those for 1920–1929 are means of averages
for three peak-to-peak cycles, 1920–1923, 1923–1926, and 1926–1929. The entries for
1929–1937 and 1938–1946 are averages for single cycles; those for 1946–1953 are
means of annual averages for two cycles, 1946–1949 and 1949–1953. In calculating the
cycle averages, Dobrovolsky gave the terminal year values half weight.

The estimate of capital consumption allowances is adjusted for the difference between original cost and replacement bases; the estimate of retained profits is adjusted
also for the effects of changes in inventory valuation.

and 1.12 in 1946–1953. While the inclusion of 1954–1956 and later years might reduce the last ratio somewhat, it would probably still be significantly above that in 1900–1914. The rise in the ratio of adjusted gross retention to plant and equipment expenditures (line 7a) was somewhat smaller, but still suggests an upward trend.

2. The ratio of capital consumption allowances to plant and equipment expenditures (lines 9a and 9b) also rose—from 0.43 or 0.48 in 1900–1914, to 0.57 or 0.63 in 1946–1953. The movement is quite similar to that of the ratio observed for all corporations in Table 37, but not in Table 38.

3. No such clear trends emerge in the ratio of net retained profits to plant and equipment expenditures (lines 10a and 10b). On an adjusted basis it was 0.42 in 1909–1914, 0.34 in 1920–1929, and 0.35 in 1946–1953. By contrast, when we use the unadjusted totals, the ratio declined from 0.45 in 1900–1914 to 0.20 in 1920–1929, but then rose to 0.54 in 1946–1953. Our judgment as to the trend in the contribution of net profits to the financing of plant and equipment expenditures depends upon the concept. If we adhere to estimates of capital consumption allowances and net profit corresponding to the economic accounting approach, the rise in the ratio of gross retention to gross plant and equipment expenditures can be seen to be due to ,the rise in the relative weight of capital consumption allowances, not of net retained profits. Here again the conclusions agree with those derived for all corporations, in Table 37.

4. The ratio of net security issues to plant and equipment expenditures (line 8) shows no rise, but rather some suggestion of a decline. This ratio was 0.31 in 1900–1914, 0.35 in 1920–1929, and 0.22 in 1946–1953. The inclusion of 1954–1956 and later years might raise the last ratio and reduce the decline substantially.

5. On both the adjusted and unadjusted bases, the ratio of net profit retention to net durable capital formation (lines 11a and 11b) rose: from 0.81 or 0.79 in 1900–1914 to 0.94 or 1.27 in 1946–1953. But in 1920–1929 it was either at the 1946–1953 level or much higher, and the movement therefore is not sufficiently consistent over time to be given much weight.

6. The latter is true also of the ratio of net securities issues to net durable capital formation (line 12): on an unadjusted basis it was 0.54 in 1900–1914, 0.51 in 1946–1953, but as high as 2.20 in 1920–1929.

We may now ask what the trends in the shares of total uses of funds were. The summary of the relevant data is provided in Table 41, also

Share of Internal Funds

TABLE 41

TOTAL, INTERNAL, AND EXTERNAL FINANCING,
LARGE MANUFACTURING CORPORATIONS, 1900–1953
(amounts in millions of dollars, averages per year)

	1900–1910 (1)	1915–1919 (2)	1920–1929 [a] (3)	1929–1937 (4)	1938–1946 (5)	1946–1953 (6)
Volumes						
1. Total financing	110	744	550	464	3,093	7,350
2. Expenditures on physical assets	n.a.	451	417	452	2,070	6,156
3. Other, line 1 minus line 2	n.a.	293	133	12	1,023	1,194
4. Internal financing	77	447	532	445	2,348	4,910
4a. Capital consumption allowances	34	125	270	409	1,265	2,117
4b. Undistributed earnings	43	322	262	37	1,083	2,793
5. External financing, line 1 minus line 4	32	296	18	19	745	2,440
Ratios						
6. Line 4 to line 1	0.70	0.60	0.97	0.96	0.76	0.67
6a. Line 4a to line 1	0.31	0.17	0.49	0.88	0.41	0.29
7. Line 4 to line 2	n.a.	0.99	1.28	0.98	1.13	0.80
7a. Line 4a to line 2	n.a.	0.28	0.65	0.90	0.61	0.34
8. Line 5 to line 2	n.a.	0.66	0.04	0.04	0.36	0.40

Because of rounding, details will not necessarily add to total.

n.a. = not available.

[a] Omitting one-half of 1923.

For sources and method of averaging cycle data, see notes to Table 40, and Creamer, *et al.*, *op. cit.*, Tables 44 and 46, pp. 142–143 and 148. There are three distinct samples: one collected by NBER, relating to 1900–1910; the second, also from NBER, used in cols. 2–4; and the third, from the Board of Governors, Federal Reserve System, used in cols. 5 and 6.

based on Dobrovolsky's analysis. But here serious qualifications attach to the representativeness of the data. They are for large manufacturing corporations alone, and the sample is quite small, particularly for the years preceding the 1920's when only 14 to 50 corporations were included. Whatever conclusions we derive from the estimates must be viewed as highly tentative. This table, like Table 39, is based upon business accounting, unadjusted totals.

7. The ratio of internal financing, i.e. gross retention, to total uses (line 6) fails to show any upward trend over the period. It was 0.70 in 1900–1910, 0.97 in 1920–1929, and 0.67 in 1946–1953. This relative constancy over the long period in the ratio of internal (and hence,

external) financing to all uses is to be compared with the slight rise in the internal financing ratio for all nonfinancial corporations in Table 39.

8. The ratios of the two components of gross retention—capital consumption allowances and undistributed earnings—to total uses were also relatively constant over the period (see line 6a). It is difficult to say whether the absence here of the trends observed in the ratios for all corporations in Table 39 represents a significant difference.

The Regulated Industries

A similarly brief exploration of the trends in financing of capital formation, or rather total uses, can be undertaken for four of the principal components of the regulated industries (all corporate) on the basis of the detailed analysis in Ulmer's monograph.[21] The relevant data are assembled in Table 42.

In contrast with the findings for all corporations, and for the mining and manufacturing sectors of the corporate group, there are pronounced trends here in the shares of internal and external financing in total uses and sources of funds. For steam railroads the share of gross retention (internal funds) in total uses rose from slightly over two percentage points in 1880–1890 to over 100 per cent in 1941–1949. The rise was less sharp for telephones, but here also the 40 per cent gross retention ratio in 1941–1950 was far greater than the 6 per cent ratio in 1891–1902. There is a similar movement in the financing of total uses in electric light and power, and street and electric railways.

Two comments are relevant. As Ulmer points out, the last period, 1941–1949, 1941–1950, or 1938–1950, combines two rather dissimilar periods: the war years, when gross retention was quite large in relation to total uses of funds, and the postwar years, when the ratio of gross retention to total uses must have dropped considerably. It follows that the ratio of gross retention to total uses for 1946–1956, if available, would be appreciably lower than that shown for the last period in Table 42. Yet it is almost certain that it would be higher than the very low ratio characterizing the early periods in the table.

Second, this upward trend in the ratio of gross retention to total uses of funds would persist even if we compared 1946–1956 with the first decade of the century—omitting the pre-1900 periods for greater comparability with the span studied for all the other sectors. A rough

---

[21] Melville J. Ulmer, *Capital in Transportation, Communications, and Public Utilities: Its Formation and Financing* (Princeton for NBER, 1960).

TABLE 42

Capital Formation Financing, Four Major Components of the Regulated Industries, 1880–1950
(amounts in millions of dollars)

Industrial Component and Capital Financing Item	Period I (1)	Period II (2)	Period III (3)	Period IV (4)	Period V (5)	Period VI (6)	Period VII (7)
Steam Railroads							
1. Dates	1880 [a]– 1890 [c]	1893 [a]– 1907 [c]	1907 [a]– 1916 [d]	1914 [a]– 1920 [d]	1921 [b]– 1930 [d]	1931 [b]– 1940 [d]	1941 [b]– 1949 [d]
2. Gross capital formation	2,687	2,978	5,280	3,021	8,088	2,874	7,020
Percentages of Total Uses (Sources)							
3. Gross capital expenditures [e]	86.5	76.7	111.1	93.4	115.3	117.6	84.9
4. Other assets	13.5	23.3	−11.1	6.6	−15.4	−17.7	15.0
5. Gross retention	2.4	9.5	42.9	52.7	94.8	97.4	101.6
6. Changes in liabilities	97.6	90.4	57.2	47.3	5.1	2.6	−1.6
Telephones							
7. Dates		1891 [b]– 1902 [d]	1903 [b]– 1912 [d]	1913 [b]– 1920 [d]	1921 [b]– 1930 [d]	1931 [b]– 1940 [d]	1941 [b]– 1950 [d]
8. Gross capital formation		382	905	948	3,708	2,092	7,083
Percentages of Total Uses (Sources)							
9. Gross capital expenditures [e]		87.0	86.5 [f]	96.3	88.6	110.8	93.5
10. Other assets		13.0	13.6 [e]	3.7	11.4	−10.9	6.5
11. Gross retention		6.3	19.6	58.3	43.1	99.8	40.5
12. Changes in liabilities		93.7	80.4	41.7	56.9	0.2	59.5
Electric Light and Power							
13. Dates		1881 [b]– 1912 [d]		1913 [b]– 1922 [d]		1928 [b]– 1937 [d]	1938 [b] 1950 [d]–
14. Gross capital formation		1,771		2,067		4,027	10,746
Percentages of Total Uses (Sources)							
15. Gross capital expenditures [e]		89.1 [f]		78.2 [f]		87.4 [f]	97.7
16. Other assets		10.9 [e]		21.8 [e]		12.6 [e]	2.3
17. Gross retention		7.6		15.5		23.6	50.3
18. Changes in liabilities		92.3		84.6		76.4	49.6
Street and Electric Railways							
19. Dates		1890 [a]– 1902 [c]	1902 [a]– 1912 [d]	1913 [b]– 1922 [d]			
20. Gross capital formation		1,134	1,410	1,087			
Percentages of Total Uses (Sources)							
21. Gross capital expenditures [e]		87.4	96.5 [f]	57.1 [f]			
22. Other assets		12.6	3.5 [e]	42.8 [e]			
23. Gross retention		1.4	5.4	13.6			
24. Changes in liabilities		98.7	94.6	86.4			

Because of rounding, detail will not necessarily add to total.
[a] July 1 of year.
[b] January 1 of year.
[c] June 30 of year.
[d] December 31 of year.
[e] Including inventories.
[f] Excluding inventories.

SOURCE: Melville J. Ulmer, *Capital in Transportation, Communications, and Public Utilities: Its Formation and Financing* (Princeton for NBER, 1960), Tables 46–49, pp. 150–153.

calculation indicates that the share of gross retention in total uses for, say, 1901–1910, would be at most 20 per cent for the combined total of the four regulated industries in Table 42; and the corresponding percentage for 1946–1956 would probably not be appreciably smaller than that for 1941–1950 (which works out to about 62).

Thus for these regulated industries there has been a marked upward trend in the ratio of gross retention (internal financing) to all uses of funds over the period (since 1900), during which all corporations and the mining and manufacturing sectors of the corporate group were characterized by only a slight rise in the ratio. The reasons for this trend in the regulated industries have been discussed by Ulmer, and there is no need to enlarge upon them here. The major explanation lies in the sharp slowing down in the rate of growth of these industries for which, in their early extensive growth, capital consumption allowances and income retention were insufficient to finance the needs for rapid expansion of plant and equipment. No such sharp deceleration in the rate of growth of all corporations or of the mining and manufacturing corporations occurred, if only because the historical period covered does not encompass the early phases of these groups, as it does those for the regulated industries.

One technical point, an apparent inconsistency, must be accounted for. How was it possible for one major component of all corporations, the regulated group, to show a significantly rising trend in the ratio of internal financing (gross retention) to total uses, and for all corporations not to show such a large rise in this ratio? The question seems particularly relevant since another big component of all corporations, the mining and manufacturing group, does not show any offsetting decline in the ratio.

The answer lies in the effect of combining groups whose ratios of internal-external financing to total uses differ, and whose weights change over time. A rough calculation will demonstrate the point. Using Table 42 and Ulmer's more detailed tables, we can set total gross capital formation in the four regulated industries for 1901–1912 at about $9.8 billion in current prices; and, if we assume that additions to other assets accounted for another 10 per cent, total uses would amount to roughly $10.8 billion. For 1941–1950 a similar calculation yields gross capital formation of about $25 billion, and an allowance of 7 per cent for changes in other assets brings total uses to about $26.8 billion. In Table 39, total uses for 1901–1912 were $40 billion, and for 1941–1950 they would be about $200 billion (they were $186 billion for 1940–1949). It follows that the share of total uses for the four regulated industries was 27 per cent in 1901–1912 and only 13.4 per cent in 1941–1950.

Also from Table 42 we can derive the ratio of gross retention to all uses for the four regulated industries—roughly 0.2 in 1901–1912 and 0.62 in 1941–1950. Gross retention in these industries amounted therefore to $2.2 billion in 1901–1912 and to $16.6 billion in 1941–1950. We know from Table 39 that the corresponding ratio for all corporations was 0.55 in 1901–1912 and about 0.70 in 1941–1950 (the latter is high because it includes the World War II period). If we apply these ratios to total uses for all corporations, we secure gross retention of $22 billion and $140 billion, respectively.

We can now subtract total uses and gross retention for the four regulated industries from the corresponding totals for all corporations in order to calculate the ratios for the large nonregulated industries residual. Total uses in the first period (1901–1912) amounted to $29.2 billion, the corresponding gross retention was $19.8 billion, and the ratio was 0.68. In 1941–1950 total uses amounted to $173.2 billion, gross retention to $123.4 billion, and the ratio was 0.71—not very different from the ratio for 1901–1912. The point is that the ratio for all corporations was kept from rising because the relative weight of the nonregulated industries increased from 1901–1912 to 1941–1950. And, because in the recent decades the gross retention-total uses ratio for these industries was generally lower than that for the regulated group, their increasing weight tended to depress the over-all ratio and thus offset the effects of the rise in the ratio for the regulated industries.

This calculation is necessarily crude, and applies to 1941–1950. But if we could repeat it for 1946–1956, we could demonstrate that the rise in the internal financing ratio for these regulated industries in that decade, compared with the pre-World War I period (and perhaps even with the 1920's), was offset by the shift in weight in total uses of funds between the regulated and the other sectors within all corporations, not by offsetting movements in the ratio within the nonregulated industry corporations.

GOVERNMENTS

In the discussion of the financing of governments, we deal with a group of institutions whose pattern in the use of borrowed funds and retained income is radically different from that of the major private sectors of the economy. Governments, particularly the federal, can and do borrow funds for what may be viewed as current consumption rather than addition to financial assets or real capital formation. This practice may be followed by some private economic units, e.g., households and business firms. But they are obviously a small proportion of the total private sector over any long period, and their borrowing for these purposes is necessarily limited. Unless the use of the borrowed funds improves the economic position of the private unit (returns it to solvency), further borrowing will cease. No such limitations, at least within similarly narrow confines, apply to borrowing by central government authorities. In times of emergency, such as a major war or depression, the governments can and are expected to borrow for defense or counter-depression types of expenditures, neither of which adds to the financial assets or real capital goods in the hands of governments proper—however beneficial the expenditures may be to the rest of the economy. We should, therefore, be prepared to find that in the case of governments the relation between internal funds, borrowing, and total uses of funds, and real capital formation bears no resemblance to that in the private sectors discussed so far.

However, in this respect, at least in this country, state and local governments differ substantially from the federal government, and their financing must be reviewed separately.

State and Local Governments

The relevant data, largely from Goldsmith's work, and extended through 1956 by rough extrapolation based on later sources, are summarized in Table 43.

Internal sources are estimated as the difference between current revenues of the governments and their current expenditures. This difference is the equivalent of funds from internal sources available for replacement of or net additions to real assets, and for net additions to financial assets, provided current expenditures do not include depreciation on already owned and used capital assets—an inclusion not customarily practiced in government accounting.

The trends suggested by Table 43 are distinctive and easily established. By and large, the ratio of internal sources to either total uses or capital outlay rose over the period since the turn of the century. The former ratio moved from 0.53 in 1901–1922 to 0.71 in 1913–1939, and on to 0.79 in 1940–1956. For the shorter periods and with those of war and depression disregarded, the ratio was 0.60 for 1901–1912, 0.68 for 1923–1929, and 0.72 for 1946–1956—the last necessarily a rough ap-

Share of Internal Funds

TABLE 43

CAPITAL FORMATION FINANCING, STATE AND LOCAL GOVERNMENTS, 1901–1956
(amounts in billions of dollars)

Periods	Total Uses (Sources) (1)	Capital Outlay (2)	Other Uses (1) − (2) (3)	Internal Sources (4)	Ratio of: (4) to (1) (5)	(4) to (2) (6)
1. 1901–1912	6.0	4.3	1.7	3.6	0.60	0.84
2. 1913–1922	11.9	7.0	4.9	5.9	0.50	0.84
3. 1923–1929	20.2	15.2	5.0	13.7	0.68	0.90
4. 1930–1933	6.6	8.7	−2.1	4.0	0.61	0.46
5. 1934–1939	14.6	9.9	4.7	14.3	0.98	1.44
6. 1940–1945	20.9	7.9	13.0	24.5	1.17	3.10
7. 1946–1949	22.4	14.3	8.1	16.4	0.73	1.15
8. 1950–1952	32.2	20.0	12.2	24.0	0.75	1.20
9. 1953–1956	60.5	37.8	22.7	42.8	0.71	1.13
Longer Periods						
10. 1901–1922	17.9	11.3	6.6	9.5	0.53	0.84
11. 1913–1939	53.3	40.8	12.5	37.9	0.71	0.93
12. 1940–1956	136.0	80.0	56.0	107.7	0.79	1.35
13. 1946–1956	115.1	72.1	43.0	83.2	0.72	1.15

SOURCE, BY LINE

Lines 1–6.   Raymond W. Goldsmith, *Financial Intermediaries*, Table 74, p. 260.
Lines 7 and 8. Daniel H. Brill, "Financing of Capital Formation," *Problems of Capital Formation* (Studies in Income and Wealth, Vol. 19, Princeton for NBER, 1957), Table 11, p. 171.
Line 9.   Capital outlay extrapolated from lines 7 and 8 by applying to state and local construction for 1953–1956 (*Economic Report of the President*, January 1957, Table E-30, p. 156) the ratio of capital outlay to that series for the earlier periods (the ratio assumed was 1.05). Likewise, total sources were estimated on the basis of the ratio to capital outlay (the latter was 1.61 for 1950–1952, and was set at 1.6 for 1953–1956). Finally, external sources were estimated for the recent period on the basis of the ratio of state and local government securities offered to net borrowing (for the series see *ibid.*, Table E-55, p. 184, and Table E-44, p. 173). This ratio, which was 1.36 for 1950–1952, was set at 1.35 for 1953–1956.

proximation. The ratio of internal funds to capital outlay shows an even greater upward trend: it rose from 0.84 in 1901–1922 to 0.93 in 1913–1939, and to 1.35 in 1940–1956. For the shorter periods it moved from 0.84 in 1901–1912 to 0.90 in 1923–1929, and to 1.15 in 1946–1956.

The movement of the ratio of internal funds to capital outlay (but not to total uses) can be observed for local and for state governments separately. This distinction suggests that the rise observed in Table 43 is due partly to an upward movement in the ratio within local governments, but even more to the greater relative rise of capital outlay and of gross savings by state governments than of those by local governments. Because in recent periods, specifically since 1934, the ratio of gross savings to capital outlay has been distinctly higher for state than for local governments, the rise in the relative weight of the former imparts an upward trend to the ratios in Table 43. It will be observed in this connection that the rise in column 6 is particularly sharp beginning with 1934–1939.

The ultimate explanation of these trends lies in the movement of gross savings and of capital outlay at the two levels of government. Apparently both, but particularly state, governments have managed since the late 1930's to tap sources of revenue increasingly in excess of current expenditures, enabling them to finance a greater proportion of capital outlay without additional borrowing. Exploration of the factors behind that trend would call for examination of the sources of current revenue in their relation to the needs for current expenditures as distinct from the needs for capital outlay. For instance, has such a major source of local government current revenues as taxes on real estate grown more rapidly in recent decades than have the current expenditures generated by the real estate tax base, and has this difference between current revenues and expenditures, that represents gross savings, made possible an increasing proportion of capital outlay financing without resort to new borrowing? Likewise, has such a major source of current revenues of state governments as the gasoline tax, for example, increased more rapidly than have the current expenditures connected with the expanded use of the automobile, with the excess contributing to a larger share of internal financing of capital outlay by the states? The answers to these questions would require a detailed examination of the major sources of current revenues, and an analysis that would link the factors responsible for trends in current revenues with those responsible for trends in current expenditures and in the needed capital outlay. Such an analysis is, unfortunately, beyond the scope of the present study.

The Federal Government

It is at the federal level that the peculiar pattern of government financing stands out most clearly (Table 44). Total uses here mean the additions to real capital goods (gross) in the hands of the govern-

Share of Internal Funds

TABLE 44

CAPITAL FORMATION FINANCING, THE FEDERAL GOVERNMENT, 1901–1955
(billions of dollars)

| Periods | Total Uses | | Real Capital Formation | | | Internal Funds | |
	Excluding Military (1)	Including Durable Military (2)	Excluding Military (3)	Including Durable Military (4)	Bor- rowing (5)	Excluding Military (6)	Including Military (7)
1. 1901–1912	1.8	1.8	0.94	0.94	0.8	1.0	1.0
2. 1913–1922	5.8	15.0	0.93	10.13	24.7	−18.9	−9.7
3. 1923–1929	1.7	2.6	0.76	1.7	−6.0	7.8	8.7
4. 1930–1933	3.7	4.7	1.29	2.3	7.8	−4.2	−3.2
5. 1934–1939	24.5	27.4	5.1	8.0	37.1	−12.6	−9.7
6. 1940–1945	55.5	128.7	11.7	84.9	240.6	−185.1	−111.9
7. 1946–1949	−9.6	0.3	4.1	14.0	−19.6	9.9	19.8
8. 1946–1955			15.6	70.8	2.0		
Longer Periods							
9. 1901–1922	7.6	16.8	1.9	11.1	25.5	−17.9	−8.7
10. 1923–1939	29.9	34.7	7.2	12.0	38.9	−9.0	−4.2
11. 1940–1949	45.9	129.0	15.8	98.9	221.0	−175.2	−92.1
12. 1940–1955			27.3	155.7	242.6		

SOURCE, BY LINE

1-7. Raymond W. Goldsmith, *Financial Intermediaries*, Table 76, p. 266. For military, see text.
8. By extrapolation as follows:
   Col. 3. Based on volume of nonmilitary construction ($14.7 billion for 1950–1955, see *Economic Report of the President*, January 1957, Table E-30), plus $2.0 billion for 1950–1955 for other capital goods, based on the 1946–1949 average volume.
   Col. 4. See Table 14, where military capital formation is $55.2 billion.
   Col. 5. Based on gross public debt of $278.7 billion at end of 1945, and $280.8 billion at end of 1955 (see *Economic Report of the President*, January 1957, Table E-45).

ment plus net additions to its financial claims. Goldsmith, from whose estimates Table 44 was derived, does not include either military construction or durable munitions among real capital goods, and this concept is reflected in column 1. By including our estimates of the gross additions of durable military goods (used in the corresponding variants in Chapters 3 and 4) we secure the more comprehensive entries in column 2.

Real capital formation represents, then, gross additions to durable goods and net additions to inventories, whenever the latter can be measured. Here again we can either exclude the gross volume of military construction and durable munitions (column 3) or include it (column 4).

The entries for net borrowing are independent of the others, in the sense that they are derived from data on debt outstanding, adjusted, when necessary, to a net basis with respect to the other sectors of the economy. Gross retention or internal funds as shown in columns 6 and 7 are residuals, derived by subtracting net borrowing (column 5) from total uses (column 1 or 2). Consequently, we have two variants of gross retention: one that treats durable military goods as capital assets (column 7); and another that treats them as current expenditures (column 6).

Whichever treatment is adopted, the federal government, over any long period that covers either a war or a major depression, borrows much more than is needed for additions to its assets. In such a period it borrows not only to finance asset acquisition but also to finance current expenditures. The entries in columns 6 and 7 for all the long periods (lines 9–11) are negative; and there is little question that the entries for 1940–1955, if we could have calculated them, would have been negative.

The reasons why the federal government resorts to borrowing rather than to taxation in periods of economic or military emergency are discussed at length in Copeland's monograph,[22] and need not be repeated here. One important element is the difference between the slowness inherent in the revenue collecting system and the speed with which current expenditures have to be expanded in an emergency. Another is public resistance, once the emergency is over, to continuance of the revenue collecting system in the high gear required not only to meet the greater burden of current expenditures but also to reduce appreciably the already established debt. Whatever the reasons, the results are clear: the federal government of this country, like the central governments of many other countries, has financed out of external funds, not merely additions to assets, but also current expenditures. In any true sense, the ratio of external financing to capital formation of the federal government is sharply upward when we compare the first half of the period since 1900—including World War I—with the second half, including the depression, World War II, and the cold war that has characterized the recent years.

[22] Morris A. Copeland, *Trends in Government Financing* (Princeton for NBER, 1961).

An Attempt at a Summary

Having reviewed the long-term movement in shares of internal and external sources of financing for the several sectors of the economy, we should combine the results in a summary for the economy as a whole. Several difficulties stand in the way. First, the data for the sectors do not cover the same periods, and some do not extend through 1950–1955 (or 1956). Second, we must decide on the form of the comparison of sources or uses, and not all the latter are available for the specific sectors. Finally, for some sectors, such as households, we may want to limit the concept of uses of funds more than for others, and the definition of sources may also differ among sectors.

Table 45 represents an effort to overcome these difficulties in order to secure a countrywide picture. The notes to the table contain a brief account of the statistical manipulations and short-cuts resorted to. More important is the fact that some lack of comparability remains—chiefly between the business sector (agriculture, nonfarm unincorporated business, and corporate business) where the sum of capital consumption allowances and undistributed profits is taken to represent internal sources, and households (represented by nonfarm residential construction) where no such assumption is made. Another source of discrepancy lies in the fact that gross retention of income in the case of governments, while analogous to that in the business sector with respect to accounting procedures, can hardly have the same meaning. All of these dissimilarities reflect the basic characteristics of the major segments of the economy, and in any attempt to bring those segments together some artificial element in the common conceptual structure imposed on them is inevitable.

In Table 45, gross capital formation is compared with gross retention or internal sources. Neither is adjusted for the effects of changes in inventory valuation or for the difference between original cost base and reproduction cost base of capital depreciation allowances. The main question is: did the ratio of gross retention to total real capital formation for the economy as a whole show any distinct trend?

We start with the business sector—agriculture, nonfarm unincorporated business, and all corporations (lines 7–9). For the discrete, relatively normal periods—the first decade of the century, the 1920's, and the post-World War II decade (columns 1, 3, and 6)—the ratio of internal funds to gross real capital formation was 0.82, 0.85, and 0.90,

TABLE 45

SUMMARY: RATIO OF GROSS RETENTION (INTERNAL FUNDS) TO GROSS CAPITAL FORMATION, BY CATEGORY OF USER, 1900–1956

(amounts in billions of dollars, averages per year)

Category of User	Periods				1940–44 or		Longer Periods				
	1900–09 or 1901–10 (1)	1910–19 or 1911–20 (2)	1920–29 or 1921–30 (3)	1930–39 or 1931–40 (4)	1940–45 or 1941–45 (5)	1945–55 or 1946–56 (6)	1900–19 or 1901–20 (7)	1920–39 or 1921–40 (8)	1940–55 or 1941–56 (9)	1900–29 or 1901–30 (10)	1930–55 or 1931–56 (11)
Agriculture											
1. Gross capital formation	0.89	1.48	1.16	0.91	1.98	4.27	1.18	1.04	3.51	1.18	2.47
2. Gross retention	0.71	1.04	0.65	0.94	4.54	4.16	0.88	0.80	4.29	0.80	2.95
Nonfarm Unincorporated Business											
3. Gross capital formation	0.35	0.71	1.62	0.56	1.26	3.60	0.53	1.09	2.82	0.89	1.92
4. Gross retention	0.27	0.75	1.26	0.52	4.08	2.53	0.51	0.89	3.05	0.76	2.04
Corporations											
5. Gross capital formation	2.05	4.44	6.35	3.13	6.82	24.7	3.24	4.74	18.74	4.28	12.50
6. Gross retention	1.73	4.10	5.82	3.23	10.08	22.6	2.92	4.52	18.43	3.88	12.35
Total Business											
7. Gross capital formation, lines 1, 3, and 5	3.29	6.63	9.13	4.60	10.06	32.57	4.96	6.86	25.07	6.35	16.89
8. Gross retention, lines 2, 4, and 6	2.71	5.89	7.73	4.69	18.70	29.29	4.30	6.21	25.77	5.44	17.34
9. Ratio, line 8 to line 7	0.82	0.89	0.85	1.02	1.86	0.90	0.87	0.91	1.03	0.86	1.03

Households [a]											
10. Gross capital formation	1.22	1.34	4.55	1.42	1.47	10.55	1.28	2.98	7.52	2.37	5.08
11. Internal sources	0.79	0.69	1.68	0.56	0.38	2.85	0.74	1.12	2.03	1.05	1.44
Total Private											
12. Gross capital formation, lines 7 and 10	4.51	7.97	13.68	6.02	11.53	43.12	6.24	9.85	32.59	8.72	21.97
13. Gross retention, lines 8 and 11	3.50	6.58	9.41	5.25	19.08	32.14	5.04	7.33	27.80	6.50	18.78
14. Ratio, line 13 to line 12	0.78	0.83	0.69	0.87	1.65	0.75	0.81	0.74	0.85	0.75	0.85
State and Local Governments											
15. Gross capital formation	0.30	0.53	1.84	1.86	1.32	6.55	0.42	1.85	4.81	0.89	3.63
16. Gross retention	0.20	0.40	1.42	1.83	4.08	7.56	0.30	1.62	6.40	0.67	4.57
Private plus State and Local Governments											
17. Gross capital formation, lines 12 and 15	4.81	8.50	15.52	7.88	12.85	49.67	6.66	11.70	37.40	9.61	25.60
18. Gross retention, lines 13 and 16	3.70	6.98	10.83	7.08	23.16	39.70	5.34	8.96	34.20	7.17	23.35
19. Ratio, line 18 to line 17	0.77	0.82	0.70	0.90	1.80	0.80	0.80	0.77	0.91	0.75	0.91
Federal Government											
20. Gross capital formation (excluding military)	0.07	0.11	0.09	0.64	1.95	1.56	0.09	0.36	1.69	0.09	1.27
21. Gross retention	0.10	−1.8	1.0	−1.68	−30.85	0	−0.85	−0.34	−10.28	−0.23	−6.84
Total including Federal Government											
22. Gross capital formation, lines 17 and 20	4.88	8.61	15.61	8.52	14.80	51.23	6.74	12.06	39.09	9.70	26.87
23. Gross retention, lines 18 and 21	3.80	5.18	11.83	5.40	−7.69	39.70	4.49	8.62	23.92	6.94	16.51
24. Ratio, line 23 to line 22	0.78	0.60	0.76	0.63	—	0.77	0.67	0.71	0.61	0.72	0.61

[a] Nonfarm residential construction. (Notes on following page)

Trends in Financing of Capital Formation

NOTES TO TABLE 45

SOURCE: Where the preceding tables cover the period through 1955 or 1956, there was no problem in bringing the estimates through that date. Also, even when the periods distinguished are different from those shown in the preceding tables (e.g. for nonfarm unincorporated business), the new totals could be calculated from the sources cited earlier.

The following additional estimates had to be made:

For nonfarm unincorporated business, we assumed that the movement from 1945–1949 to 1950–1955, in gross capital formation, in additions to other assets, and in the proportion of borrowing to total uses, was the same as for agriculture (in Table 35). This permitted us to bring the series for this sector through 1955.

For households, the estimates had to be extended back to 1901–1910. Expenditures on nonfarm housekeeping residential construction are available for that period in Grebler, Blank, and Winnick, *Capital Formation in Residential Real Estate*, Table B-3, p. 335. To them we added 33 per cent for the cost of land (see *ibid.*, Table M-1, p. 455, for the ratios used in 1911 and later years). We assumed that the percentage of external financing was 35 at most (it was less than 50 in 1911–1920), in view of the much lower ratio of debt to value in owner-occupied housing in the earlier of the two decades.

For the federal government we assumed that during 1946–1955 there was practically no retention. The small positive total for 1946–1949 ($9.9 billion) appeared to be offset by the cumulation of the deficits that followed.

The absolute values in columns 7 to 11 are arithmetic means of the entries in columns 1 to 6. Those in columns 7, 8, and 10 are unweighted; for columns 9 and 11, the entries in column 5 are given half weight. The ratios are derived directly from the absolute values, and are not arithmetic means of the ratios in columns 1 to 6.

respectively, showing a mild rise. For the three long periods, including major wars and depressions (columns 7 to 9), the ratio was 0.87, 0.91, and 1.03, respectively, showing a distinct rise. Finally, for the two long periods (columns 10 and 11), the ratio was 0.86 and 1.03, respectively, again a marked upward movement.

Then we add nonfarm residential construction to form the total private sector (lines 12 to 14). Adding it either cancels or reduces the rise in the ratio of internal funds to capital formation, for the simple reason that the ratio of internal funds to capital formation for households declined over time. For the three relatively short normal periods, the ratio was 0.78, 0.69, and 0.75, respectively—no evidence of either an upward or downward trend. For the three long periods, the ratio was 0.81, 0.74, and 0.85, respectively, a mild rise. Finally, for the two long periods, the ratio was 0.75 and 0.85, respectively, a distinct rise.

We next include state and local governments, and because that subsector is marked by a rather high and rising ratio of internal financing to gross capital formation, the new totals (lines 17 to 19) again suggest an upward movement in the ratio, especially for the longer periods. But without dwelling too long on this hybrid combination of the private sector with state and local governments, we pass to the comprehensive countrywide total, which includes also the federal government. Here there is a definite indication of constancy or slight downdrift in the ratio of internal funds to total gross real capital formation (line 24). The ratio moved from 0.78 in the first decade to 0.76 in the 1920's, then to 0.77 in 1946–1955. When we use longer periods, including wars and major depressions, the decline becomes more perceptible: the ratio rose slightly from 0.67 in the first two decades of the century, to 0.71 in the next two decades, and then dropped to 0.61 in the last decade and a half. For the two long subperiods of the full period, the ratio was 0.72 and 0.61, respectively. Thus, for the economy as a whole, the ratio of internal funds to gross real capital formation was either constant or declined, which means that the ratio of borrowing to gross real capital formation was either constant or increased.

Before we consider the significance of these findings, it may be well to compare internal funds or gross retention with total uses of funds rather than with gross real capital formation alone (Table 46). In the case of households we assume that new nonfarm residential construction represents total uses of funds. To treat it otherwise would necessitate consideration of the accumulation of cash and other financial assets by households, which would in turn call for distinguishing between households as investors in dwellings and households as the largest body of ultimate savers and spenders in the economy.

The results in Table 46 are not much different from those in Table 45, whatever differences there are being due to the greater weight of the business sector here, with its higher ratio of changes in financial assets to real capital formation. In the business sector proper, the ratio of internal funds to total uses (line 6) rose slightly, from 0.59 in each of the first three decades in the century to 0.64 in the post-World War II decade. The longer period averages in columns 7 to 9 and 10 to 11 confirm that upward trend. The inclusion of nonfarm residential construction eliminates or reduces the upward trend in the ratio of internal funds to total uses, as it reduces the ratio in Table 45. But while the movement in the ratio for the total private sector shows a decline if discrete periods are used—the ratio moving from 0.61 in column 1, to 0.53 in column 3, to 0.57 in column 6—we observe a rise in the ratio when wars and depressions are included—from 0.59 in the first two decades (column 7) to 0.62 in the last one and a half decades (column 9), or from 0.56 to 0.64 (columns 10 and 11).

TABLE 46

SUMMARY: RATIO OF GROSS RETENTION (INTERNAL FUNDS) TO TOTAL USES–SOURCES OF FUNDS, BY CATEGORY OF USER, 1900–1956

(amounts in billions of dollars, averages per year)

Category of User	Periods				1940-44		Longer Periods				
	1900-09 or 1901-10 (1)	1910-19 or 1911-20 (2)	1920-29 or 1921-30 (3)	1930-39 or 1931-40 (4)	1940-45 or 1941-45 (5)	1945-55 or 1946-56 (6)	1900-19 or 1901-20 (7)	1920-39 or 1921-40 (8)	1940-55 or 1941-56 (9)	1900-29 or 1901-30 (10)	1930-55 or 1931-56 (11)
Total Business											
1. Total uses, agriculture	0.98	2.01	0.99	1.04	4.14	5.01	1.50	1.02	4.72	1.33	3.25
2. Total uses, nonfarm unincorporated business	0.43	1.13	1.61	0.19	4.13	4.04	0.78	0.90	4.07	1.06	2.52
3. Total uses, corporations	3.15	6.83	10.58	2.83	12.57	36.92	4.99	6.70	28.80	6.85	18.41
4. Total uses, lines 1 to 3	4.56	9.97	13.18	4.06	20.84	45.97	7.26	8.62	37.59	9.24	24.18
5. Gross retention a	2.71	5.89	7.73	4.69	18.70	29.29	4.30	6.21	25.77	5.44	17.34
6. Ratio, line 5 to line 4	0.59	0.59	0.59	1.16	0.90	0.64	0.59	0.72	0.69	0.59	0.72
Total Private											
7. Total uses, line 4 plus households b	5.78	11.31	17.73	5.48	22.31	56.52	8.54	11.60	45.11	11.61	29.26
8. Gross retention a	3.50	6.58	9.41	5.25	19.08	32.14	5.04	7.33	27.80	6.50	18.78
9. Ratio, line 8 to line 7	0.61	0.58	0.53	0.96	0.86	0.57	0.59	0.63	0.62	0.56	0.64
State and Local Governments											
10. Total uses	0.43	0.88	2.52	2.12	3.48	10.46	0.66	2.32	8.13	1.28	5.73
Private plus State and Local Governments											
11. Total uses, lines 7 and 10	6.21	12.19	20.25	7.60	25.79	66.98	9.20	13.92	53.24	12.88	34.99
12. Gross retention a	3.70	6.98	10.83	7.08	23.16	39.70	5.34	8.96	34.20	7.17	23.35
13. Ratio, line 12 to line 11	0.60	0.57	0.53	0.93	0.90	0.59	0.58	0.64	0.64	0.56	0.67
Federal Government											
14. Total uses	0.13	0.55	0.20	2.82	9.25	3.47	0.34	1.51	5.40	0.29	4.37
Total Including Federal Government											
15. Total uses, lines 11 and 14	6.34	12.74	20.45	10.42	35.04	70.45	9.54	15.44	58.64	13.18	39.36
16. Gross retention a	3.80	5.18	11.83	5.40	-7.69	39.70	4.49	8.62	23.92	6.94	16.51
17. Ratio, line 16 to line 15	0.60	0.41	0.58	0.52	—	0.56	0.47	0.56	0.41	0.53	0.42

a From Table 45.   b Nonfarm residential construction, only.

Share of Internal Funds

NOTES TO TABLE 46

SOURCE: For nonfarm unincorporated business, we had to return to the original data in Goldsmith's *A Study of Saving*, because of differences between the periods in Table 36 and in the present table.

Because the periods in Tables 39, 43, and 44 for corporations, state and local governments, and the federal government, differ from those here, we computed the ratios of gross real capital formation to total uses for the periods in the earlier tables, and adjusted them roughly to correspond with the periods in the present table. Whereas for corporations they were 0.652 for 1901–1912, 0.649 for 1913–1922, and 0.593 for 1923–1929 (Table 39), we assumed 0.65 for 1900–1909, 0.65 for 1910–1919, and 0.60 for 1920–1929. For state and local governments, the three early periods in Table 43 yielded ratios of 0.72, 0.59, and 0.75; our estimates for the first three decades were 0.7, 0.6, and 0.73. For the federal government the ratios for the three early periods were 0.52, 0.16, and 0.45, respectively (Table 44, excluding military); we assumed those for the first three decades to be 0.52, 0.20, and 0.45, respectively. For 1946–1955 we assumed that the ratio of gross real capital formation to total uses was 0.45—the ratio that characterized the more "normal" span of 1921–1930.

With these ratios at hand, we could derive the estimated volumes of total uses from the volumes of gross capital formation in Table 45.

The absolute values and ratios in columns 7 to 11 were calculated in the manner described for Table 45.

The most interesting result is for the economy as a whole, i.e., for the private and public sectors combined (line 17). Here the discrete periods which skip the major wars and depressions show a slight decline; the ratio is 0.60 in column 1, 0.58 in column 3, and 0.56 in column 6. For the longer periods including wars and the depression of the 1930's, the ratio shows a somewhat more marked decline—from 0.47 in column 7 to 0.41 in column 9. And it moves from 0.53 in column 10 to 0.42 in column 11. It can thus be said, in general, that in the business sector we have an indication of an upward movement of the ratio of internal funds to either gross capital formation or to total uses; that in the private sector we have, on the whole, a slight decline on the basis of normal periods, and a rise if all periods are considered; and that in the economy as a whole we have a decline.

In the household sector and governments, especially the federal, the ratio of internal funds to either real capital formation or to total uses (narrowly defined) has declined significantly. It should be noted that in both Tables 45 and 46, government capital formation and total uses exclude durable military goods. Households had recourse to borrowing that constituted an increasing proportion of the value of the new dwellings they were buying or constructing. Governments, representing society as a whole, were borrowing increasingly for purposes that, at least in Tables 45 and 46, appear neither as gross capital formation nor as additions to financial assets (of the governments).

Within the business sector, however, the trend in the ratio of internal funds to uses was in the opposite direction. Obviously, the trend in any total depends upon the comprehensiveness of the total, the differences in the trends of its components, and the weights of the latter.

Two final observations should be made. First, we repeat the warning expressed in the first section of this chapter to the effect that aggregates of the type we had to use may conceal considerable financing external to each business unit, and hence exaggerate the relative share of internal funds in capital formation or in total uses. This is particularly true of large aggregates like all corporations; and it is not safe to conclude from the rise in the ratio of internal funds to uses, in Table 45 or Table 46, for this group or for the whole business sector that the dependence upon borrowing has decreased. As suggested earlier, increasing diversity in the use by corporations of their capital consumption allowances or of their net profits, may have meant greater concealment within aggregated totals of demands for external funds. On the other hand, the higher proportion of large corporations may have meant reduction in diversity of experience and a trend toward increased importance of internal funds far greater than is suggested by the ratios computed above. In short, the measures reflect only part of the process, and whatever trends they reveal are those at only one level of the process.

Second, there are obvious interrelations between the trends observed in the three sectors—business, household, and government. Indeed, at the risk of exaggerating, one can say that the upward trend in the ratio of internal funds to either capital formation or total uses in the business sector was associated with the downward trend of the ratios in the government and household sectors. It was government expenditures during the war and after, and the factors that determined them, that allowed (indeed, during the war years, actually forced) business units to follow a gross retention policy that yielded a very high ratio of internal funds to total uses. It was the sustention of consumer demand by the willingness of consumers to finance their purchases by borrowing that set the conditions for prosperity and favorable conditions in the business sector, permitting business units to earn both their capital consumption allowances and substantial retained profits, and to maintain a high ratio of internal funds to total uses, even when total uses were rising rapidly. These interrelations among the sectors are evidence of a mechanism that makes for stability in the countrywide ratio. This stability is not mechanically or inevitably assured; but the countrywide ratio of internal funds (and hence, of borrowing) to total real capital formation or to total uses (properly defined) is most likely to show a much less conspicuous trend than would the ratios for the subsectors of the economy.

CHAPTER 6

Trends in Financing of Capital Formation:
Structure of External Financing

In the preceding chapter we discussed long-term movements in the shares of internal and external funds in the financing of capital formation or of total uses. The main conclusions were that for the business sector as a whole the ratio of internal funds to either gross capital formation or total uses rose over the period; that, with the inclusion of nonfarm residential and related construction to make up the total private sector, the upward trend in the share of internal financing disappeared or was attenuated; and that, with the addition of governments, particularly the federal, the share of internal funds for the economy as a whole declined slightly and the share of external financing rose.

In the present chapter, we concentrate upon long-term movements in the structure of external financing. External funds may be secured through the issue of stock, which carries no specific debt obligations but represents an equity in the enterprise seeking funds; or by the assumption of debt by that enterprise. Within debt proper, a distinction can be drawn between long-term and short-term, the two differing in economic import. Finally, in the analysis of the mechanism of financing, we should attempt to separate funds flowing directly from owner to user (as when an individual buys securities newly issued by a corporation or advances mortgage money directly to a borrower) from funds flowing from owner to some financial intermediary (savings bank, building and loan association, life insurance company, or the like), which accepts responsibility for choosing the borrower to whom the funds will be loaned. These three aspects of the structure of external financing—the share of equity funds, the relative weight of short-term and long-term debt financing, and the share of financial intermediaries—are discussed in this chapter.

Distribution, by Category of User of Funds

First, we present the distribution of external financing, by category of user. Obviously, for some categories—households, unincorporated firms, and governments—equity financing is out of the question.[1] Then, too, the extent to which, by and large, the groups of users can and do have recourse to short-term or long-term debt differs, and the degree to which they rely upon financial intermediaries for supply of funds also differs. It is, therefore, useful to observe the shares of the groups of users in total external financing in the economy (Table 47).

Table 47 is derived directly from Tables 45 and 46 and the estimates are therefore subject to all the qualifications noted for those tables. These, however, do not affect the major conclusions now listed.

1. As one would expect, within the business sector, corporations accounted for the overwhelming proportion of external financing, ranging from about two-thirds to almost nine-tenths of the total (excluding the World War II period). More important, the long-term trend in corporations' share in the external financing of the total business group was upward—from about seven-tenths in the first two decades of the century to close to nine-tenths in the 1920's and in the post-World War II years. This trend resulted partly from the rise in the share of corporations in total business activity, and partly from the drop in the share of external in total financing—at least for agriculture—a decline not evident for corporations as a whole.

2. When we add external financing of households, represented by nonfarm residential construction, to derive the private sector as a whole, the picture changes. Then the long-term trends in the shares of agriculture and nonfarm unincorporated business are downward and even the share of corporations fails to rise, or shows a slight decline. The change is due to the sharp upward movement in the share of external financing of nonfarm residential construction commented upon in Chapter 5.

---

[1] Unincorporated enterprises are a special case. Part of the increase in the net worth of unincorporated business may represent new funds attracted from the outside; but we cannot separate them from the funds that represent reinvested earnings, and such outside funds are likely to be provided by contributors personally connected with the individual entrepreneur.

TABLE 47

SUMMARY: DISTRIBUTION OF EXTERNAL FINANCING, BY CATEGORY OF USER OF FUNDS, 1900–1956

(amounts in billions of dollars, averages per year)

Category of User	Periods						Longer Periods				
	1900–1909 or 1901–1910 (1)	1910–1919 or 1911–1920 (2)	1920–1929 or 1921–1930 (3)	1930–1939 or 1931–1940 (4)	1940–1944 or 1941–1945 (5)	1945–1955 or 1946–1956 (6)	1900–1919 or 1901–1920 (7)	1920–1939 or 1921–1940 (8)	1940–1955 or 1941–1956 (9)	1900–1929 or 1901–1930 (10)	1930–1955 or 1931–1956 (11)
					VOLUMES						
1. Agriculture	0.27	0.97	0.34	0.10	−0.40	0.85	0.62	0.22	0.43	0.53	0.30
2. Nonfarm unincorporated business	0.16	0.38	0.35	−0.33	0.05	1.51	0.27	0.01	1.02	0.30	0.48
3. Corporations	1.42	2.73	4.76	−0.40	2.49	14.32	2.08	2.18	10.38	2.97	6.07
4. Total business, lines 1, 2, and 3	1.85	4.08	5.45	−0.63	2.14	16.68	2.96	2.41	11.83	3.79	6.85
5. Households [a]	0.43	0.65	2.87	0.86	1.09	7.70	0.54	1.86	5.50	1.32	3.64
6. Total private, lines 4 and 5	2.28	4.73	8.32	0.23	3.23	24.38	3.50	4.28	17.33	5.11	10.49
7. State and local governments	0.23	0.48	1.10	0.29	−0.60	2.90	0.36	0.70	1.73	0.60	1.16
8. Federal government	0.03	2.35	−0.80	4.50	40.10	3.47	1.19	1.85	15.68	0.53	11.21
9. Total, lines 6, 7, and 8	2.54	7.56	8.62	5.02	42.73	30.75	5.05	6.82	34.74	6.24	22.86

				Ratios to Total in Line 4						
10. Agriculture	0.15	0.24	0.06	—	−0.19	0.05	0.21	0.09	0.04	0.14	0.04
11. Nonfarm unincorporated business	0.09	0.09	0.06	—	0.02	0.09	0.09	b	0.09	0.08	0.07
12. Corporations	0.77	0.67	0.87	—	1.16	0.86	0.70	0.90	0.88	0.78	0.89
					Ratios to Total in Line 6						
13. Agriculture	0.12	0.21	0.04	—	−0.12	0.03	0.18	0.05	0.02	0.10	0.03
14. Nonfarm unincorporated business	0.07	0.08	0.04	—	0.02	0.06	0.08	b	0.06	0.06	0.05
15. Corporations	0.62	0.58	0.57	—	0.77	0.59	0.59	0.51	0.60	0.58	0.58
16. Households ᵃ	0.19	0.14	0.34	—	0.34	0.32	0.15	0.43	0.32	0.26	0.35
					Ratios to Total in Line 9						
17. Agriculture	0.11	0.13	0.04	0.02	−0.01	0.03	0.12	0.03	0.01	0.08	0.01
18. Nonfarm unincorporated business	0.06	0.05	0.04	−0.07	b	0.05	0.05	b	0.03	0.05	0.02
19. Corporations	0.56	0.36	0.55	−0.08	0.06	0.47	0.41	0.32	0.30	0.48	0.27
20. Households ᵃ	0.17	0.09	0.33	0.17	0.03	0.25	0.11	0.27	0.16	0.21	0.16
21. State and local governments	0.09	0.06	0.13	0.06	−0.01	0.09	0.07	0.10	0.05	0.10	0.05
22. Federal government	0.01	0.31	−0.09	0.90	0.94	0.11	0.24	0.27	0.45	0.08	0.49

Because of rounding, detail will not necessarily add to total.   ᵇ Less than 0.005.

ᵃ Nonfarm residential construction.   Source: Based on Tables 45 and 46.

3. The addition of external financing by governments, particularly the federal, alters the picture even more. In total external financing by the economy, the rise in the share of the federal government is so marked that the shares of all other user groups necessarily decline (see, in particular, columns 10 and 11). When we examine the selected short periods, thus excluding the huge federal financing during World War II, the share of nonfarm residential construction in external financing exhibits some rise, while that of state and local governments appears stable. The share of nonfarm unincorporated business is either stable or shows only a very slight decline—but the estimates are too crude to be assigned much weight. Even these selected periods, however, indicate that the shares in total external financing accounted for by agriculture and, particularly important, by corporations declined. Thus the ratio for corporations was 0.56 in the first decade of the century, 0.55 in the 1920's, and 0.47 in the post-World War II years.

The general impression is one that could have been inferred from the summary in Chapter 5. With the business sector tending, more than the others, to show a rise in the share of internal financing and thus a decline in the share of external funds, a decline in the share of the business sector in total external financing was bound to occur unless total financing of the business sector accounted for a significantly rising share of total financing in the economy. But total uses in the business sector accounted for about 0.7 of total uses in the economy in the first decade of the century, and somewhat over 0.6 in the 1920's and the post-World War II years (see Table 46, lines 4 and 15). With the relatively constant weight of the business sector in the distribution of total uses (sources), the decline in the share of external financing within it, and the rise in the share of external financing in the other sectors in the economy, the share of the business sector in total external financing in the economy inevitably declined.

Share of Equity Financing

The issuance of stock (common or preferred) is a practice that can be followed by business corporations alone, and by only a selected group of them. The stock issues covered in the estimates include only those offered for public placement, and for obvious reasons exclude shares issued upon incorporation to former individual owners of assets, and stocks tendered upon consolidation in payment for existing assets. In order to place a new stock issue on the market with any reasonable hope of selling it, a corporation must have attained a certain size and maturity, with a record of past performance and evidence of continuity and stability. These preconditions necessarily limit the candidates to a relatively small fraction of all corporations, though the small number, because of individual size, may account for a large proportion of all corporate assets and sales.[2]

With this in mind, we turn to Table 48, which summarizes the available estimates on the structure of external financing by all nonfinancial corporations. We have to observe not only the net stock issues, but also the other major categories of external financing in order to compare the trends in the share of equity funds with other relevant changes in total external funds.

The movement of the ratio of net stock issues to all external funds is not consistent. Even if we consider only the shorter, normal periods, we find that it was 0.31 in the first period of the century, rose to 0.43 in the 1920's, and then dropped sharply to 0.21 in the post-World War II decade. Likewise, for the three long periods in lines 10 to 12, the ratio moved from 0.29 in 1901–1922, to 0.63 in 1923–1939, and then down to 0.22 in 1940–1955. For the two long periods, 1901–1929 and 1930–1955 (lines 13 and 14), the ratio was 0.35 and 0.27, respectively.

These are the shares of equity funds in total external financing. Changes in them can arise from either or both of two sources—the changing importance of long-term funds in the total of external funds, and the changing weight of equity funds in total long-term funds. We treat bonds and notes as long-term (notes and accounts payable as short-term),[3] and mortgage loans also as long-term; then we compare net stock issues with total long-term external funds (column 12). The ratio of net stock issues to total long-term external financing rose somewhat (column 12), from 0.38 in 1901–1912 to 0.48 in 1913–1922, then declined slightly to 0.47 in 1923–1929. Equity funds dominated all long-term external financing in 1930–1945, because both bonds and mortgage loans were being reduced rather than increased. But in

[2] This argument does not apply to sales of equity securities to insiders by new corporations without use of the investment banking machinery. Goldsmith's series in lines 1 to 6 of Table 48 includes a rough allowance for such sales.

[3] Short-term bonds and notes have been but a minor fraction (a few percentage points) of the total of bonds and notes for all years since 1919, with the exception of 1919, 1920, and 1932–1934 (see *Historical Statistics of the United States, 1789–1945*, and *Continuation*, Series N-225 and N-226). Likewise, long-term funds, i.e., funds whose length of life approximates that of goods included under durable capital formation, can be but a minute fraction of notes and accounts payable in column 6 of Table 48.

TABLE 48

STRUCTURE OF EXTERNAL FINANCING, NONFINANCIAL CORPORATIONS, 1901–1955

(amounts in billions of dollars)

Periods	Net Stock Issues (1)	Net Bonds and Notes (2)	Mortgage Loans (3)	Total Long-Term External Financing (1) + (2) + (3) (4)	Tax Accruals (5)	Notes and Accounts Payable (6)	Total Short-Term External Financing (5) + (6) (7)	Total External Financing (4) + (7) (8)	Ratio of: (1) to (8) (9)	(2) to (8) (10)	(4) to (8) (11)	(1) to (4) (12)	(2) to (4) (13)
GOLDSMITH ESTIMATES													
1. 1901–12	5.6	8.2	0.8	14.6	0.2	3.0	3.2	17.9	0.31	0.46	0.82	0.38	0.56
2. 1913–22	8.5	6.5	2.6	17.6	1.5	11.1	12.6	30.1	0.28	0.22	0.58	0.48	0.37
3. 1923–29	16.7	12.2	6.4	35.3	0.9	2.8	3.7	39.0	0.43	0.31	0.91	0.47	0.35
4. 1930–39	5.4	−0.3	−1.0	4.1	−0.4	−7.8	−8.2	−4.1	a	a	−0.02	1.32	−0.07
5. 1940–45	3.5	−3.8	0	−0.3	8.1	7.2	15.3	14.9	0.23	−0.26	a	a	a
6. 1946–49	8.1	12.1	6.5	26.7	3.2	9.3	12.5	39.3	0.21	0.31	0.68	0.30	0.45
7. 1946–55 b									0.21	0.27	0.63	0.34	0.43
COMMERCE ESTIMATES													
8. 1946–49	5.5	12.1	2.8	20.4	−0.8	17.9	17.1	37.5	0.15	0.32	0.54	0.27	0.59
9. 1946–55	19.8	35.7	8.4	63.9	8.4	56.6	65.0	128.9	0.15	0.28	0.50	0.31	0.56
Longer periods													
10. 1901–22	14.1	14.7	3.4	32.2	1.7	14.1	15.8	48.0	0.29	0.31	0.67	0.44	0.46
11. 1923–39	22.1	11.9	5.4	39.4	0.5	−5.0	−4.5	34.9	0.63	0.34	1.13	0.56	0.30
12. 1940–55 c									0.22	0.22	0.57	0.39	0.38
13. 1901–29	30.8	26.9	9.8	67.5	2.6	16.9	19.5	87.0	0.35	0.31	0.78	0.46	0.40
14. 1930–55 c									0.27	0.22	0.62	0.43	0.36

Because of rounding, detail will not necessarily add to total.

a Not shown because denominator is negative.

b Extrapolated from line 6 by the percentage change from line 8 to line 9.

c Weighted averages of the ratios for the subperiods included (lines 5 and 7 or 4, 5, and 7), the weights being the absolutes in cols. 1 to 8 or those implicit in the extrapolated ratios, line 7.

SOURCE, BY LINE

1 to 6. Raymond W. Goldsmith, *Financial Intermediaries in the American Economy since 1900* (Princeton for NBER, 1958), Table 53, p. 222.

8 to 9. *Survey of Current Business*, April 1954, p. 15, and October 1956, p. 12.

1946–1955, their ratio was down to 0.34—lower than for any earlier period distinguished in Table 48. The averages for the longer periods, lines 10 to 12 and 13 to 14, confirm the impression of a decline in the share of net stock issues in total long-term external financing, although the decline is mild and not consistent over time.

One can thus conclude: (1) the share of equity funds in total external financing of corporations (column 9) shows a downward trend, although not consistently—since the peak was in the 1920's and not early in the century; (2) the share of long-term external financing in total external financing (column 11) tended to decline, although not consistently; (3) the share of equity funds in total long-term external financing also declined, in that in the post-World War II decade it was distinctly lower than in any earlier period in the century. We emphasize again that trends based on only two of the six periods, or on movements that are not consistent over time, cannot be assigned much weight. They are meant to give only a general impression of the long record, not to suggest continuity of a dominating and persistent movement.

Before we deal with some general aspects of these findings, it will be helpful to consider the estimates for some important subgroups of corporations. Table 49 relates to mining and manufacturing corporations and summarizes Dobrovolsky's estimates.

While the periods distinguished here differ somewhat from those in Table 48, the similarity in movement is striking. The ratio of equity funds to total external financing shown in Table 49 also rose, from 0.37 in the first two decades of the century to 0.97 in the 1920's and the 1930's (if we compare 1900–1914 with 1920–1929, the movement is from 0.50 to 0.72); but then it declined in the post-World War II years to 0.15, appreciably below the level of the 1920's and even below the level at the beginning of the century. When equity funds are related to long-term external financing (in this case a simple sum of net stock and net bond issues), the ratio moves from 0.55 in 1900–1914, to 0.74 in 1920–1929, but then drops to 0.37 in 1946–1953. Clearly, for this major group of business corporations the relative movement in equity funds is almost identical with that for all nonfinancial corporations. Nor is this an algebraic necessity, because the group accounts for only a fraction of total or long-term or external financing by nonfinancial corporations.

In dealing with the other group of corporations covered in this study, the regulated industries, we are handicapped by the fact that

TABLE 49

STRUCTURE OF EXTERNAL FINANCING,
MINING AND MANUFACTURING CORPORATIONS, 1900–1953
(amounts in millions of dollars, averages per year)

| Periods | Net Stock Issues (1) | Net Bond Issues (2) | Total Long-Term External Financing (1) + (2) (3) | Total External Financing (4) | Ratio of: | | | |
					(1) to (4) (5)	(2) to (4) (6)	(3) to (4) (7)	(1) to (3) (8)
1. 1900–14	172	142	314	342	0.50	0.42	0.92	0.55
2. 1914–19	410	78	488	1,435	0.29	0.05	0.34	0.84
3. 1920–29	641	228	870	888	0.72	0.26	0.98	0.74
4. 1929–37	259	−249	10	11	—	—	—	—
5. 1937–44	133	−26	107	1,126	0.12	−0.02	0.10	1.24
6. 1946–53	750	1,281	2,031	5,078	0.15	0.25	0.40	0.37
Longer periods								
7. 1900–19	235	125	360	630	0.37	0.20	0.57	0.65
8. 1920–37	461	4	465	475	0.97	0.01	0.98	0.99
9. 1937–53	442	628	1,070	3,102	0.14	0.20	0.34	0.41

Because of rounding, detail will not necessarily add to total.

SOURCE: Based on Daniel Creamer, Sergei Dobrovolsky, and Israel Borenstein, *Capital in Manufacturing and Mining: Its Formation and Financing* (Princeton for NBER, 1960), Tables 51 and 44, pp. 162–163 and 142–143.

Cols. 1–3.   The estimates are those prepared by Dobrovolsky.

Col. 4.   Calculated by applying to col. 3 the ratio of long-term to total external financing for large manufacturing corporations. We used the ratio for 1900–1910 for line 1; that for 1915–1919 for line 2; that for 1923–1929 for line 3; that for 1929–1937 for line 4; that for 1937–1943 for line 5; and that for 1946–1953 for line 6.

Whenever the period involved several cycle averages (lines 1, 3, and 6), the latter were averaged with no allowance for differing durations.

The averages in lines 7, 8, and 9 are weighted by the duration of periods in lines 1 to 6.

none of Ulmer's estimates extends beyond 1950, and the periods he distinguishes for the several industries cannot be compared easily with those in Table 48. Nevertheless, some trends emerge, particularly when we look at the averages for the long periods (Table 50).

It should be noted that the long period in column 8 does not include the 1920's, i.e., the years during which the share of equity funds in total and long-term corporate external financing was high; in two cases, the 1920's are included in the later period (column 9). This division is favorable to showing a rise or at least constancy in the share of net stock issues or equity funds in total and in long-term external financing. But the result is quite the opposite in all four industries distinguished. Thus, for railroads, the ratio of net stocks to total external funds was 0.39 in the first of the longer periods (column 8) and only 0.16 in the second (column 9); their ratio to total net securities was 0.41 and 0.18, respectively. For electric light and power, the net

TABLE 50

STRUCTURE OF EXTERNAL FINANCING, FOUR MAJOR COMPONENTS OF THE
REGULATED INDUSTRIES, 1880-1950
(amounts in billions of dollars)

Industrial Component and External Financing Item	Periods							Longer Periods	
	I (1)	II (2)	III (3)	IV (4)	V (5)	VI (6)	VII (7)	(8)	(9)
Steam Railroads									
1. Dates	1880–1890	1893–1907	1907–1916	1914–1920	1921–1930	1931–1940	1941–1949	1880–1916	1914–1949
				VOLUMES					
2. Total uses [a]	3.36	5.52	6.44	5.04	8.51	1.77	7.71	15.32	23.03
3. Total external sources	3.28	5.13	4.35	3.00	2.11	−0.53	−1.18	12.76	3.40
4. Short-term external financing	0.23	0.67	−0.29	1.71	−1.39	−0.28	0.44	0.61	0.48
5. Net securities	3.06	4.47	4.64	1.29	3.50	−0.26	−1.62	12.17	2.91
6. Net stocks	1.35	1.90	1.71	−0.12	0.99	0.28	−0.62	4.96	0.53
7. Net bonds	1.71	2.57	2.93	1.41	2.51	−0.54	−0.99	7.21	2.39
				RATIOS					
8. Line 6 to line 3	0.41	0.37	0.39	—	0.47	—	—	0.39	0.16
9. Line 7 to line 3	0.52	0.50	0.67	0.47	1.19	—	—	0.57	0.70
10. Line 5 to line 3	0.93	0.87	1.07	0.43	1.66	—	—	0.95	0.86
11. Line 6 to line 5	0.44	0.43	0.37	—	0.29	—	—	0.41	0.18
Telephones									
12. Dates		1891–1902	1903–1912	1913–1920	1921–1930	1931–1940	1941–1950	1891–1920	1921–1950
				VOLUMES					
13. Total uses [a]		0.45	1.10	1.04	4.43	1.85	7.89	2.59	14.17
14. Total external sources		0.42	0.90	0.45	2.60	0.02	4.80	1.77	7.42
15. Short-term external financing		0.05	0.06	0.02	0.13	0.06	0.67	0.13	0.86
16. Net securities		0.37	0.84	0.43	2.47	−0.04	4.13	1.64	6.56
17. Net stocks		0.29	0.52	0.07	1.65	−0.13	0.65	0.88	2.17
18. Net bonds		0.08	0.32	0.37	0.82	0.09	3.48	0.77	4.39
				RATIOS					
19. Line 17 to line 14		0.69	0.58	0.16	0.63	—	0.14	0.50	0.29
20. Line 18 to line 14		0.19	0.36	0.82	0.32	—	0.72	0.44	0.59
21. Line 16 to line 14		0.88	0.93	0.96	0.95	—	0.86	0.93	0.88
22. Line 17 to line 16		0.78	0.62	0.16	0.67	—	0.16	0.54	0.33
Electric Light and Power									
23. Dates		1881–1912		1913–1922		1928–1937	1938–1950	1881–1922	1928–1950
				VOLUMES					
24. Total uses [a]		2.10		2.92		4.61	11.22	5.02	15.83
25. Total external sources		1.94		2.50		3.52	5.50	4.44	9.02
26. Short-term external financing		0.19		0.21		0.06	0.62	0.40	0.68
27. Net securities		1.75		2.29		3.46	4.88	4.04	8.34
28. Net stocks		0.98		0.98		1.68	2.05	1.96	3.73
29. Net bonds		0.77		1.31		1.78	2.83	2.08	4.61
				RATIOS					
30. Line 28 to line 25		0.51		0.39		0.48	0.37	0.44	0.41
31. Line 29 to line 25		0.40		0.52		0.51	0.51	0.47	0.51
32. Line 27 to line 25		0.90		0.92		0.98	0.89	0.91	0.92
33. Line 28 to line 27		0.56		0.43		0.49	0.42	0.49	0.45
Street and Electric Railways									
34. Dates		1890–1902	1902–1912	1913–1922				1890–1912	1902–1922
				VOLUMES					
35. Total uses [a]		1.30	1.67	2.07				2.97	3.74
36. Total external sources		1.28	1.59	1.82				2.87	3.41
37. Short-term external financing		0.14	0.16	0.37				0.30	0.53
38. Net securities		1.15	1.44	1.44				2.59	2.88
39. Net stocks		0.65	0.65	−0.10				1.30	0.55
40. Net bonds		0.50	0.79	1.54				1.29	2.33
				RATIOS					
41. Line 39 to line 36		0.51	0.41	—				0.45	0.16
42. Line 40 to line 36		0.39	0.50	0.85				0.45	0.68
43. Line 38 to line 36		0.90	0.91	0.79				0.90	0.84
44. Line 39 to line 38		0.57	0.45	—				0.50	0.19

Because of rounding, detail will not necessarily add to total.
[a] Including investments in affiliated companies.
SOURCE: Melville J. Ulmer, *Capital in Transportation, Communications, and Public Utilities: Its Formation and Financing* (Princeton for NBER, 1960), pp. 150–153.

stock issues accounted for 0.44 of total external financing in the first of the longer periods and 0.41 in the second; their ratio to total net securities was 0.49 and 0.45, respectively—mild declines but declines nevertheless. For telephones, the ratio of equity funds to total external financing dropped from 0.50 in the first of the longer periods to 0.29 in the second; their ratio to total net securities was 0.54 and 0.33, respectively. Even for street and electric railways, for which we have no estimates beyond 1922, the division into longer periods shows a decline in the ratio of net stock issues to total external financing, from 0.45 to 0.16; and in their ratio to all net securities, from 0.50 to 0.19.

The estimates for these regulated industries thus confirm the impression of a long-term decline in the shares of equity funds in total external financing and in long-term external financing suggested for all corporations in Table 48. Indeed, here the declines are much more conspicuous, although when we deal with the shorter periods they are not any more consistent.

Assuming that we accept the findings of long-term declines in the shares of equity funds in total external financing and in all long-term external financing, we may ask what factors could have accounted for them. The question is all the more relevant since we might have expected the shares to rise in the long run, for one important reason. If only relatively sizable, mature corporations can successfully appeal to the public capital markets for funds in the form of equity securities, one could argue that the proportion of such large, mature corporations to all corporations—in assets, in output, in total financing—must have increased over time. This is the natural consequence of the growth of the economy, the growing economies of scale of the firm, the continuous addition to the number of corporate giants. Assuming that other conditions remained equal, and also that large corporations draw upon the market for funds in proportion to their size, and that they are greater potential users of equity funds than smaller units, we would expect an upward long-term trend in their shares of equity funds in external financing and in total net security issues. Consequently, explaining the downward trend is all the more challenging a task.

As with many other major problems raised in this volume, the explanation can hardly go beyond indicating the possible identity of the factors involved and the directions in which further study may be warranted. But even such hints should be explicit.

The first possibility to be noted is connected with the rise in relative importance of the large, mature corporations that would presumably have access to money markets through the flotation of equity securities. It is true that these units have grown in relative importance among all corporations; but they are also the units which, because of their long past, may well have accumulated more fixed capital than others and therefore have less need for external financing, because they can draw more heavily upon capital consumption allowances and undistributed profits. In other words, the effect of the increasing weight of these large corporations on the possibly increasing share of equity funds in total external financing may be offset, or more than offset, by their greater reliance on internal funds.

We have no data readily available for testing this argument. Such information, which could be derived from a study of corporate financing practices by size of corporation, with the longest possible perspective, would be valuable but is not feasible within the limitations of this study. An illustrative calculation of the effect of shifts among large and other corporations must suffice. (In the tabulation, all stocks,

		Time Period I (1)	Time Period II (2)
		(per cent)	
	Share in Total Uses by		
1.	Large corporations	40	60
2.	Other corporations	60	40
	Share of External Financing in Total Uses		
3.	Large corporations	60	25
4.	Other corporations	60	60
5.	All corporations	60	39
	Structure of External Financing		
	Large Corporations		
6.	Share of stocks in total	50	50
7.	Share of bonds (or long-term debt) in total	40	40
8.	Share of short-term debt in total	10	10
	Other Corporations		
9.	Share of stocks in total	0	0
10.	Share of bonds (or long-term debt) in total	50	50
11.	Share of short-term debt in total	50	50
	All Corporations		
12.	Share of stocks in total	20	19
13.	Share of bonds (or long-term debt) in total	46	46
14.	Share of short-term debt in total	34	35
15.	Share of line 12 in line 12 + line 13	30	29

bonds, and debt refer to net issues.) Let us assume that the share of total financing by large corporations in total financing by all corporations increased from 40 to 60 per cent, and that the share of internal in total financing by those corporations rose from 40 to 75 per cent, while the share for the others remained at 40. We assume further that only the large corporations issue stocks, and that the structure of other external financing for both the large and the other corporations remained constant over time. All these specific ratios are, of course, hypothetical, but the basic trends and differences shown can be corroborated by observable data.

The illustration shows that even though the share of large corporations in total corporate financing increases, and even though within the large and the other corporations the structure of external financing remains constant, the greater shift to internal funds by the large corporations can produce a decline in the share of equity funds in total external financing (line 12) and in total net security issues (line 15). There is at the same time a rise in the share of short-term debt financing in external financing (line 14). All these effects accord with the long-term movements in Table 48 for all nonfinancial corporations.

The illustrative calculation also indicates, however, that the quantitative effect of the factor suggested is quite minor, indeed negligible when related to the assumptions made in the illustration or compared with the movements observed in the estimates. Despite the rather extreme assumptions underlying the illustrative calculation, the share of stocks in total external financing or in long-term external financing dropped by only one percentage point, and the effect on the share of short-term debt financing in total external financing was equally minor. The reason, of course, is that the change is the net product of two conflicting trends: the rise in the proportion of large corporations tends to raise the share of net stock issues and to reduce the share of net short-term debt; but we also assume that within large corporations the share of external financing declines. Only unrealistic assumptions concerning the movement of the share of external sources in total financing by large corporations could produce the downward trend we wish to explain.

While the illustration is useful in indicating that the rise in the proportion of large corporations has a double effect—on the share of equity funds in total external financing and in long-term external financing—it suggests that the explanation of any significant downward movement in the share of equity funds must be sought elsewhere. The explanation must deal with the possible reasons why in both large and other corporations the share of equity funds in total and long-term external financing declined. It should be noted that these trends have been observed within mining and manufacturing, so that the shifts in composition of the corporate body among the major economic sectors, while of possible influence, clearly cannot be dominant.

In considering the complexes of factors involved, one naturally tends to think of both the demand and the supply side. Were there factors that, other conditions being equal, made the corporations look less favorably upon stock issues than upon other sources of external financing as a means of obtaining funds? If this question is applied to corporations that, because of their size and maturity, have access to the markets for equity funds, and if "other conditions being equal" means that relative prices of funds remain the same—a designedly artificial assumption—we have to explore the reasons why, on the demand side, there would be a reduction in relative willingness to seek equity funds. There are several bases for analyzing the relative costs of equity and debt money under fixed conditions of interest rates, no taxation, and the like. But whatever approach we use, so long as we assume that the differential costs of equity and other money remain the same, only one argument can be suggested on the demand side to explain a decreasing willingness to obtain money by the issue of stock. It lies in the possibility that, as a corporation grows, the accumulation of past earnings and replacements adds to its equity and there is less danger and fear in assuming fixed debt obligations. If, then, the price differential between equity and debt money is assumed to remain the same, the lesser risk element involved in debt money would warrant greater reliance upon it. A similar effect might be produced by general upward movements in price levels. Under such conditions the prospective burden of fixed debt obligations would be progressively lighter, and other conditions being equal, a shift toward debt and away from equity is a rational response.

These arguments, which stress the evaluation, on the demand side, of the risks and costs of debt obligations compared with those of equity funds, have some relevance here. When prices were either stable, as during the 1920's, or declining, as during the 1930's, the proportion of equity funds was quite high, and that of debt money either relatively low or negative. Moreover, the rise in general price levels in recent decades was both proportionately greater and more generally expected than was that during the first decade of the century—a difference in line with the fact that the share of equity financing was lower in the post-World War II period than during 1900–1914. Finally, the trend over the period as a whole toward a more sizable equity position among the larger corporations made the assumption of debt less of a risk.

Yet these factors on the demand side can hardly be expected to account fully for the movements that have occurred. Our statement of the improved equity position of the larger corporations is but a plausible assumption. The argument concerning the effects of changes in price levels neglects the possibility that interest rates would be adjusted to take account of the expected fall in the purchasing power of the dollar. While institutional difficulties lie in the way of such an adjustment, the force of the argument is nevertheless reduced. Finally, it must be remembered that the public utilities, which relied more heavily on bond issues than other major groups of corporations did, have receded in importance in the capital markets since the beginning of this century. That shift, all other conditions being equal, would make for a reduction in the share of bonds and a rise in the share of stocks. In short, we must search for other relevant factors.

One group of factors heretofore omitted by design is reflected in the differential movement of rates charged for the different types of external funds. The real price, properly weighted, of equity funds or of bond credit or of short-term loans cannot be measured easily, and the available records are inadequate—particularly for the long period we cover. Table 51 presents a few indexes averaged for the periods distinguished in Table 48. Stock yields are the ratios of dividend payments to the market value of stocks during the period. Bond yields are, similarly, ratios of interest payments to market value, taken here for prime corporate bonds (Aaa) and extrapolated back by the yields of twenty-year maturities. As the cost of short-term loans, we took the interest on prime commercial paper, although a far better measure would have been the average interest rate charged by commercial banks on loans and notes. The measures are only rough approximations to what is needed, and yet the differences in their movement are striking enough to enable us to assume similar significant differences in more accurate approximations to the prices of different types of external funds.

In general, if the price of long-term external financing (line 3) rises in relation to the price of short-term funds (line 4), we would expect

Structure of External Financing

TABLE 51

MOVEMENT OF BOND AND STOCK YIELDS AND SHORT-TERM INTEREST
RATE COMPARED WITH RATIO OF EQUITY FUNDS TO TOTAL NET SECURITY
ISSUES, NONFINANCIAL CORPORATIONS, 1901–1955

(averages per year)

	1901–1912 (1)	1913–1922 (2)	1923–1929 (3)	1930–1939 (4)	1940–1945 (5)	1946–1955 (6)
Percentages						
1. Stock yield rate	4.577	6.256	5.124	4.746	5.353	5.373
2. Bond yield rate	3.904	4.844	4.732	3.893	2.752	2.822
3. Combined long-term rate, (line 1 + line 2) ÷ 2	4.240	5.550	4.928	4.320	4.052	4.098
4. Prime commercial paper rate	5.512	5.462	4.603	1.555	0.653	1.699
Ratios						
5. Line 3 to line 4	0.77	1.02	1.07	2.78	6.21	2.41
6. Long-term external to all external financing	0.82	0.58	0.91	∞	−0.02	0.63
7. Line 1 to line 3	1.08	1.13	1.04	1.10	1.32	1.31
8. Net stock issues to total net security issues	0.38	0.48	0.47	1.32	∞	0.34

SOURCE, BY LINE

1. *Economic Report of the President*, January 1957, Table E-40, p. 168 (common stock yields, Moody's), extrapolated back (1929–1936 overlap) by Series N-206, *Historical Statistics of the United States, 1789–1945*.
2. *Economic Report of the President*, January 1957, Table E-40, p. 168: corporate bonds, Aaa (Moody's), extrapolated by Series N-199 (corporate bonds, 20-year maturity), *Historical Statistics* (1929–1936 overlap).
4. Prime commercial paper, 4 to 6 months, from same sources as lines 1 and 2 (Series N-186 in *Historical Statistics*).
6 and 8. From Table 48, columns 11 and 12.

the ratio of all long-term to all external financing to decline, provided there were no offsetting movements on the demand side. Yet no such correlation is found. The ratio of the price of long-term financing to that of short-term credit (line 5) rises through the first five of the six periods covered in Table 51, but the ratio of long-term to all external financing (line 6) fluctuates. The only movement in accord with the hypothesis is found in the last two subperiods. The share of long-term external financing during 1940–1945 falls sharply from its level in 1930–1939 (or in any other preceding period), while the price of long-term money relative to short-term is at a peak. Then, in the shift to the post-World War II decade, the share of long-term in total external financing rises, while the relative price of long-term money falls. If we consider only the selected normal periods, we find some agreement with the hypothesis. In 1946–1955, when the ratio of the cost of long-term money to that of short-term was relatively high, the ratio of long-term external financing to total external sources was 0.63; in 1901–1912 and 1923–1929, when the former ratio was less than half that for 1946–1955, the latter ratio was 0.82 and 0.91, respectively. But the hypothesis is not supported by the movement from 1901–1912 through 1930–1939. Clearly, there are factors on the demand side that qualify the effects of differential changes in the price of financing. Reduction of the volume of activity and fear of declining prices will reduce short-term assets and short-term borrowing, no matter how cheap short-term money is relative to long-term. Conversely, war conditions accompanied by rising prices—during 1913–1922, for example—will make for an increase in short-term assets and a greater share of short-term borrowing, no matter how high the price of short-term credit relative to long-term money.

Of greater interest in the present analysis is the difference in movement between bond and stock yields. We would expect that, as the excess of stock yields over bond yields increases, corporations would rely less on stocks than on bonds, and vice versa. Comparison of the relevant estimates (lines 7 and 8) only partially confirms this expectation. During the first four periods, the average ratio of stock yields to the price of all long-term money did not vary appreciably—ranging from 1.04 to 1.13. The ratio of net stock to total net security issues showed wider variations and did not necessarily decline when stock yields rose relative to bond yields. The confirmation comes only at the very end: in the post-World War II decade, stock yields were greatly in excess of bond yields, and the ratio of net stock to total net security issues was at its lowest level.

The upshot of Table 51 is its bearing upon the post-World War II decade, when the decline in the share of long-term in total external financing and the decline in the share of equity funds in long-term external financing were particularly prominent. The table illustrates the well-known fact that interest rates on debt money in that period were far lower than those in the decades preceding the depression of the 1930's and, in the case of bond yields, lower than in the depression decade. Stock yields, on the other hand, were at about the same level as in the 1920's and distinctly higher than during 1901–1912. Insofar as stock yields can be viewed as the price of equity funds, the price of such funds relative to borrowing rose, and the reduction in the share of equity funds in total external financing and in total long-term external financing was a rational economic response.

This argument is further strengthened by consideration of differential tax burdens. With increased corporate income tax rates in recent decades and the deductibility (as costs) of interest payments on debt, the net cost of debt money to a corporation—relative to equity funds—was even lower than that indicated by the yield rates. The relevance of this factor is clear and need not be expatiated upon.

The account above is far from a complete explanation. In particular, no reasons have been advanced for the substantially different movement of bond yields and interest rates compared with stock yields. The action of governments in pegging their bond interest rates in many years in the post-World War II decade is only one obvious factor. But there are more elusive and intriging problems. Why, if the interest rate on bonds—government and other—was low, was the flow of funds from the fixed debt market into equity securities insufficient to raise the price of the latter and drive the yields down to a more normal (i.e. prevailing in earlier periods) ratio to bond yields? Disregarding the experience during the World War II years, which were affected by political pressures and noneconomic motives for investing money, how, during the more normal postwar decade, was such a differential between stock and bond yields maintained? Only toward the end of that decade was there the beginning of a break-through of funds leading to a greater equalization of yield levels, and it is apparently proceeding today. But why was there that delay in the equilibrating flows?

This is a question I do not feel competent to answer. But it seems to me that, in trying to deal with it, consideration must be given to the channels of supply of funds and the possibility that institutional shifts in these channels of savings affected the relative flows into the markets for fixed debt and equity securities. If this was so, the answer to the question would be readily at hand. But to ascertain whether it was, we would have to analyze the flow of savings through the financial intermediaries in relation to the practices of those institutions in investing in the different forms of external financing. Such an analysis falls outside the boundaries of the present volume, but some contributory information will be found later in the chapter when we deal with the shares of financial intermediaries and the major groups within them.

Trends in Financing of Capital Formation

Before we conclude the discussion of the share of equity funds, one more comment is relevant. Up to now, we have looked only at the share of equity funds in total external or long-term external financing of corporations. But business corporations alone issue stock and obtain equity funds on a systematic basis. Elsewhere in the economy, the nexus is usually family, friendship, or partnership, and no clear line between external and internal funds can be drawn. We can therefore view the issue of corporate stock as the only systematic way of obtaining equity funds as part of external financing, and hence measure the share of net stock issues in the external financing not only of corporations but also of the economy as a whole. Indeed, we can look at it as a share in the total financing of the economy, both internal and external.

The appropriate calculations appear in Table 52. The details being obvious, suffice it to say that just as we find a decline in the share of equity funds in external or total financing by corporations, so also we find a decline in the share of equity funds in external or total financing by all business, by the private sector, and by the economy as a whole. Indeed, the decline in the share of equity funds is proportionately greater when those funds are related to total financing by all business than when related to external financing by corporations alone (compare columns 4 and 5, lines 1 and 5). It is proportionately the same or greater when equity funds are related to external or total financing for the private sector as a whole than when related to external financing by corporations alone (compare columns 4 and 5, line 1 with lines 7 and 9). The decline is particularly marked when equity financing is related to total external financing by the economy (compare columns 4 and 5, lines 1 and 11). In this last case, the share of equity funds in 1930–1955 is about four-tenths its level in 1900–1929 (a drop from 0.17 to 0.07).

Long-Term and Short-Term Debt Financing

The distinction between short-term and long-term debt, customarily drawn at one-year maturity, is not consistently followed either in the estimates for corporations already shown in Tables 48–50 or in the tables that follow. It is often impossible to separate short-term notes from bonds or, for the longer period we cover, the long-term bank loans from others. Moreover, even in strictly short-term credit, a line of credit established in such a way that short maturities only mean fre-

Structure of External Financing

TABLE 52

Summary: Ratio of Net Stock Issues to External and to Total Financing,
Long Periods Only, 1900–1956

Ratios	1900–1919 or 1901–1920 (1)	1920–1939 or 1921–1940 (2)	1940–1955 or 1941–1956 (3)	1900–1929 or 1901–1930 (4)	1930–1955 or 1931–1956 (5)
1. Net stock issues to external financing, corporations	0.29	0.63	0.22	0.35	0.27
All Business					
2. External financing by corporations to that by all business	0.70	0.90	0.88	0.78	0.89
3. Net stock issues to external financing, line 1 × line 2	0.20	0.57	0.19	0.27	0.24
4. External financing to total financing	0.41	0.28	0.31	0.41	0.28
5. Net stock issues to total financing, line 3 × line 4	0.082	0.160	0.059	0.111	0.067
All Private					
6. External financing by corporations to that by all private	0.59	0.51	0.60	0.58	0.58
7. Net stock issues to external financing, line 1 × line 6	0.17	0.32	0.13	0.20	0.16
8. External financing to total financing	0.41	0.37	0.38	0.44	0.36
9. Net stock issues to total financing, line 7 × line 8	0.070	0.118	0.049	0.088	0.058
Over-All					
10. External financing by corporations to over-all external financing	0.41	0.32	0.30	0.48	0.27
11. Net stock issues to external financing, line 1 × line 10	0.12	0.20	0.07	0.17	0.07
12. External financing to total financing	0.53	0.44	0.59	0.47	0.58
13. Net stock issues to total financing, line 11 × line 12	0.064	0.088	0.039	0.080	0.042

Source: Based on Tables 46–48.

quent checks on the economic position of the borrower is different
from trade notes that have to be paid on time, lest not only the interest burden but also the credit standing of the borrower be affected.
Nevertheless, the distinction as it is drawn in the data is real and important and points up the differences in sources of funds that can and

cannot be used safely for financing capital investment of widely differing economic durability and liquidity.

The movement in the shares of long-term and short-term external financing for the most important business group, the nonfinancial corporations, was shown in Tables 48–50 and discussed in connection with those tables. But we summarize the findings here, where we concentrate on this aspect of the structure of external financing.

1. The ratio of short-term debt financing to total external financing by corporations increased from the earlier periods to the post-World War II decade. For 1901–1912, the ratio was 0.18; for 1923–1929, it was 0.09; for 1946–1955, it was 0.37 (see Table 48, column 11).[4] For longer periods, the ratio was 0.18 in 1901–1912, 0.12 in 1913–1939, and 0.43 in 1940–1955; or 0.22 for 1901–1929, and 0.38 for 1930–1955. The movement in the ratio for mining and manufacturing corporations was quite similar—from 0.43 in 1900–1919, to 0.02 in 1920–1937, to 0.66 in 1937–1953 (see Table 49, column 7). We can disregard the regulated industries in these comparisons because short-term debt financing is a negligible fraction of their total or external financing. The general conclusion is, then, that so far as the ratio of long-term to total external financing or its complement, the ratio of short-term to total external financing, is concerned, the downward or upward trend is largely a matter of comparing the post-World War II decade, or the 1940–1955 period, with the earlier periods. It is not a consistent trend, since the peak or trough comes in the 1920's.

2. What about the shares of long-term and short-term debt financing in total debt financing? The ratio for all nonfinancial corporations can be derived from Table 48 (columns 9 and 11). In 1901–1912, the ratio of long-term debt financing to total debt financing was 0.51 out of 0.69, or 0.73, leaving 0.27 for short-term debt financing; in 1923–1929, a similar calculation yields 0.84 for long-term and 0.16 for short-term debt financing; for 1946–1955, the ratios were 0.53 and 0.47, respectively. For the two long periods, 1901–1929 and 1930–1955, the ratio of long-term debt financing to total debt financing was 0.66 and 0.48, respectively, leaving the ratio of short-term at 0.34 and 0.52, respectively. In short, the movement of the ratios of long-term and short-

---

[4] Note should be taken of the increase in the proportion of bank loans (classified here as short-term debt) in the form of term loans after World War II (see Raymond W. Goldsmith, *Financial Intermediaries in the American Economy since 1900*, Princeton for NBER, 1958, pp. 145, 147–148). But such an extension of the average maturity is not sufficient to cancel the doubling of the share of short-term debt financing in total external financing.

term debt financing to total debt financing is roughly similar to that of their ratios to total external financing. There is a rise in the ratio of short-term debt financing, if we compare the post-1940 period with the earlier periods, but the rise is not consistent and the low point is in the 1920's. Similar conclusions can be derived from Table 49, columns 5 and 6, for mining and manufacturing corporations.

Some of the factors that might account for the decline in the share of long-term debt financing and the rise in that of short-term, either in total external financing or in total borrowing, were suggested in the preceding section—both in the illustrative calculation of the effects of the growth of large corporations and in the discussion of differential costs of equity, long-term, and short-term money. There is, however, another relevant variable to be noted here. One could argue that, in general, if the relative share of additions to quick assets in total uses or in uses financed by external funds is rising, the share of short-term debt financing in external financing should also rise. There should be some relationship between shifts in composition of additions to assets, by maturity, and the shifts in composition of debt, by maturity.

To test this proposition, the estimates for nonfinancial corporations given in earlier tables are used in a somewhat different form in Table 53. The only new entries, in column 1, are changes in short-term assets, the sum of inventories and financial claims, regardless of their character and maturity (since from the standpoint of the holding corporation they can be assumed to be liquid). Although the ratio of these changes to total uses (column 3) rose in some periods, the increase from 1901–1912 to 1946–1955 was barely perceptible. However, for our purposes the more relevant ratio is to external financing. To be sure, this comparison is based upon the assumption that all gross retention is allocated to durable capital assets, as the first priority, with the result that a minimum of external financing is associated with additions to durable assets. Although artificial, this assumption is not entirely unrealistic, because the durable assets whose conversion into income is delayed longest, could, from the standpoint of the business unit, be financed most safely out of internal funds, whereas the quicker assets could carry the burden that periodic obligations—the assumption of debt, or even equity financing—impose. At any rate, the results would not be very different if we assigned only the capital depreciation part of gross retention to the durable assets, and divided net undistributed profits proportionately among the various uses of funds.

The ratio of changes in short-term assets to external financing (col-

TABLE 53

RATIO OF CHANGES IN SHORT-TERM ASSETS (INVENTORIES AND FINANCIAL
CLAIMS) TO TOTAL USES AND TO TOTAL EXTERNAL FINANCING COMPARED
WITH RATIO OF SHORT-TERM DEBT FINANCING TO TOTAL EXTERNAL
FINANCING, NONFINANCIAL CORPORATIONS, 1901–1955

(amounts in billions of dollars)

Periods	Changes in Short-Term Assets (1)	Total Uses of Funds (2)	Ratio of (1) to (2) (3)	Total External Financing (4)	Ratio of (1) to (4) (5)	Ratio of Short-Term Debt Financing to Total External Financing (6)
	GOLDSMITH ESTIMATES					
1. 1901–1912	11.4	40.0	0.28	17.9	0.64	0.18
2. 1913–1922	38.9	76.1	0.51	30.1	1.29	0.42
3. 1923–1929	32.7	86.1	0.38	39.0	0.84	0.09
4. 1930–1939	−42.2	28.3	—	−4.1	—	—
5. 1940–1945	50.5	75.4	0.67	14.9	3.39	1.02
6. 1946–1949	30.9	110.6	0.28	39.3	0.79	0.32
7. 1946–1955 [a]			0.29		0.73	0.37
	COMMERCE ESTIMATES					
8. 1946–1949	36.1	100.5	0.36	37.5	0.96	0.46
9. 1950–1955	78.3	208.8	0.38	91.3	0.86	0.52
10. 1946–1955	114.4	309.3	0.37	128.9	0.89	0.50
Longer Periods						
11. 1901–1912	11.4	40.0	0.28	17.9	0.64	0.18
12. 1913–1939	29.4	190.5	0.15	65.0	0.45	0.12
13. 1940–1955			0.36 [b]		1.00 [c]	0.43 [c]

[a] Extrapolated from line 6 by the movement from line 8 to line 10.

[b] 1940–1945 weighted 0.075 (see col. 2, line 5); 1946–1955, 0.340 (col. 2, line 5 extrapolated by lines 8 and 10).

[c] 1940–1955 weighted 0.015 (see col. 4, line 5); 1946–1955, 0.135 (col. 4, line 5 extrapolated by lines 8 and 10).

SOURCE, BY COLUMN

(1)	Lines 1 to 6, from Goldsmith *et al., A Study of Saving,* Vol. III, Table W-31, p. 81.
	Lines 8 to 10, from *Survey of Current Business,* April 1954, p. 15; October 1956, p. 12; February 1957, p. 19.
(2) and (4)	From Table 39.
(6)	From Table 48.

umn 5) shows a definite upward trend: in 1946–1955 it was distinctly higher than in 1901–1912, and the impression is stronger if we compare 1940–1955 with the earlier segments. The movement of this ratio is quite similar to that of the ratio of short-term debt financing to total external financing (column 6). The correspondence clearly suggests that the long-term shift in the ratio of shorter-term or longer-term debt financing to all external financing of corporations is partly explained by the movement in the proportion of additions to short-term assets either to total uses or—more particularly—to total uses minus capital consumption allowances or minus gross retention.

The available data for agriculture allow us to distinguish mortgage loans, which can be classified as long-term debt, from debt to banks and federal agencies, and to others (merchants, other suppliers, and the like) (Table 54). "Debt to others" is probably exclusively or predominantly short-term, but some debt to banks and federal agencies may be long-term. However, for lack of data, we have assumed here that both are short-term.

By and large, the ratio of changes in long-term debt to total external financing declined (column 5). It was 0.51 in 1900–1914, very much larger in 1920–1929, but only 0.39 in 1945–1955. The movement was not consistent, but the long-term trend suggested was downward. This impression is confirmed by the averages for the three and two long subperiods (lines 9–11 and 12–13). Conversely, the trend in the ratio of changes in short-term debt to total external financing was upward. However, most of this rise was associated with debt to banks and governmental agencies. The ratio of changes in debt to others to total external financing (column 6) fluctuated from period to period, not displaying any distinctive long-term trend.

The rise in the share of debt to banks and government agencies in recent years is partly accounted for by CCC loans, which increased some $1.2 billion during 1945–1955. But even when we omit this item, the ratio of bank and agency borrowing to total external financing still rises—from 0.25 in 1900–1914 to about 0.30 in 1945–1955.

In Chapter 5 we found that in agriculture the ratio of total external financing to total uses declined. Thus the total studied in Table 54 accounts for a diminishing share of all additions to assets. Since the share of long-term debt financing in external financing declined, its share in total uses or sources declined even more. This can be seen by comparing columns 1 and 8. The ratio of mortgage loans to total sources or uses was 0.16 in 1900–1914; it rose sharply to 0.27 in 1915–

TABLE 54

Structure of External Financing, Agriculture, 1900–1955

(amounts in billions of dollars)

| | Changes in: | | | | | | Changes in Short-Term Assets (7) | Total Uses (8) | | | |
| | Mortgage Loans (1) | Debt to Banks and Federal Agencies (2) | Debt to Others (3) | Total External Financing (1) + (2) + (3) (4) | Ratio of (1) to (4) (5) | Ratio of (3) to (4) (6) | | | Ratio of (7) to (8) (9) | Ratio of (7) to (4) (10) | Ratio of [(2) + (3)] to (4) (11) |
Periods											
1. 1900–14	2.7	1.3	1.3	5.3	0.51	0.25	2.4	17.1	0.14	0.45	0.49
2. 1915–19	3.5	1.8	1.8	7.1	0.49	0.25	5.2	12.8	0.41	0.73	0.51
3. 1920–29	3.3 (5.3)	−0.9	−1.0	1.4 (3.4)	2.36 (1.56)	—	−3.2	11.8 (13.8)	0.08	—	−1.36 (−0.56)
4. 1930–39	−0.1 (2.9)	−1.0	−0.9	−2.0 (1.0)	—	—	1.1	13.1 (16.1)	0.51	—	—
5. 1940–44	−1.7	0.1	−0.4	−2.0	—	—	11.7	22.8		—	—
6. 1945–49	0.7 [a]	2.2 [b]	1.3	4.2 [a] [b]	0.17	0.31	4.2	22.9	0.18	1.00	0.83
7. 1950–55	3.4	1.8 [c]	1.1	6.3 [c]	0.54	0.17	4.6	32.2	0.14	0.73	0.46
8. 1945–55	4.1	4.0 [b] [c]	2.4	10.5 [b] [c]	0.39	0.23	8.8	55.1	0.16	0.84	0.61
Longer Periods											
9. 1900–14	2.7	1.3	1.3	5.3	0.51	0.25	2.4	17.1	0.14	0.45	0.49
10. 1915–39	6.7 (11.7)	−0.1	−0.1	6.5 (11.5)	1.03 (1.02)	—	3.1	37.7 (42.7)	0.08 (0.07)	0.48 (0.27)	−0.03 (−0.02)
11. 1940–55	2.4	4.1	2.0	8.5	0.28	0.24	20.5	77.9	0.26	2.41	0.72
12. 1900–29	9.5 (11.5)	2.2	2.1	13.8 (15.8)	0.69 (0.73)	0.15 (0.13)	4.4	41.7 (43.7)	0.11 (0.10)	0.32 (0.28)	0.31 (0.27)
13. 1930–55	2.3 (5.3)	3.1	1.1	6.5 (9.5)	0.35 (0.56)	0.17 (0.12)	21.6	91.0 (94.0)	0.24 (0.23)	3.32 (2.27)	0.65 (0.44)

Figures in parentheses allow for rough estimates of mortgage foreclosures.

[a] Line 8 minus line 7 and slightly different, therefore, from series in Table 35 (and Tables 45 and 46).

[b] Includes $1 billion of C.C.C. loans.

[c] Includes $0.2 billion of C.C.C. loans.

Source, by Line

1–6: Alvin S. Tostlebe, *Capital in Agriculture: Its Formation and Financing since 1870* (Princeton for NBER, 1957), Table 36, p. 137.

7: *The Balance Sheet of Agriculture, 1956*, Table 1, p. 2.

1919, and was either 0.28 or 0.38 in 1920–1929. Thereafter it dropped sharply, as mortgage debt was reduced during the 1930's and the period of World War II. Even in 1950–1955, when the ratio had regained its 1915–1919 level, it was only 0.11 of total uses.

Did changes in short-term debt, which grew in proportion to total external financing, also grow in proportion to total uses or sources? A comparison of the sum of columns 2 and 3 with column 8 provides the answer. In 1900–1914, changes in short-term debt were 0.15 of total uses, and rose to 0.28 in 1915–1919. The ratio dropped sharply thereafter, because the volume of short-term debt was reduced during 1920–1944. In 1945–1949, the ratio rose to 0.15 of total uses; in 1950–1955, it was about 0.09. The share at the end was thus somewhat lower than in 1900–1914 and distinctly lower than in 1915–1919. One can conclude that the ratio of changes in short-term debt to total sources declined in the long run.

Here too, we may ask whether the movement in the shares of short-term and long-term debt financing in total external financing was associated with changes in the ratios of short-term and long-term assets either to total uses or—still better—to that part of total uses not supplied from internal sources. The relevant data are assembled in columns 7 to 10.

Even the ratio of changes in short-term assets to total uses (column 9) rose somewhat over time. It was 0.14 in 1900–1914 and 0.16 in 1945–1955. It was higher only in the two world war quinquennia, and when we average all the entries into longer periods, the upward trend is more conspicuous (see lines 9–11 and 12–13). More relevant for our purpose is the ratio of changes in short-term assets to external financing (column 10), which increased from 0.45 in 1900–1914 to 0.84 in 1945–1955, and, when averaged for the long periods, shows a fairly sustained rise. Comparison of columns 10 and 11 again shows the expected association of movement in the structure of net additions to assets (net of financing by internal funds) with that in the distribution of external financing between long- and short-term.

Goldsmith's estimates for nonfarm unincorporated business allow us to distinguish between changes in real estate debt, which we regard as long-term, and changes in bank debt, which we classify as short-term (Table 55). The main difficulty here, in addition to the general crudity and error to which the estimates are prone, is that we have no information on the years since 1949, with the result that the position in the crucial post-World War II years, is not clear. The ratio of long-

TABLE 55

STRUCTURE OF EXTERNAL FINANCING, NONFARM UNINCORPORATED BUSINESS, 1900-1955
(amounts in billions of dollars)

	Changes in:		Total External Financing (1) + (2) (3)	Ratio of (1) to (3) (4)	Changes in Short-Term Assets (5)	Total Uses (6)	Ratio of:		
Periods	Real Estate Debt (1)	Debt to Banks (2)					(5) to (6) (7)	(5) to (3) (8)	(2) to (3) (9)
1. 1900–1914	0.76	1.51	2.27	0.33	1.75	7.50	0.23	0.77	0.67
2. 1915–1919	0.50	2.58	3.07	0.16	4.41	8.08	0.55	1.44	0.84
3. 1920–1929	3.83	−0.30	3.53	1.08	1.77	16.12	0.11	0.50	−0.08
4. 1930–1939	−0.33	−2.98	−3.31	—	−5.02	1.91	—	—	—
5. 1940–1944	−0.38	0.64	0.26	−1.46	16.04	20.67	0.78	61.69	2.46
6. 1945–1949	1.81	3.41	5.22	0.35	4.88	17.96	0.27	0.93	0.65
7. 1945–1955	6.64	9.97	16.61	0.4					
7a. 1945–1955 ª	8.30	8.31	16.61	0.5					
Longer Periods									
8. 1900–1914	0.76	1.51	2.27	0.33					
9. 1915–1939	4.00	−0.70	3.29	1.22					
10. 1940–1955	6.26	10.61	16.87	0.37					
10a. 1940–1955 ª	7.92	8.95	16.87	0.47					
11. 1900–1929	5.09	3.79	8.87	0.57					
12. 1930–1955	5.93	7.63	13.56	0.44					
12a. 1930–1955 ª	7.59	5.97	13.56	0.56					

ª Alternate estimates.

SOURCE, BY LINE

1–6. From Goldsmith, *A Study of Saving in the United States*, Vol. I (Princeton University Press, 1955), Table U-11, p. 869.

7. Cols. 1 and 2: calculated from cols. 3 and 4.
   Col. 3: as estimated in Tables 45 and 46.
   Col. 4: assumed roughly equal to line 6.

7a. Col. 4: assumed slightly higher than line 6. For other columns, see notes to line 7.

term to total external financing for 1945–1949 was about the same as for 1900–1914. (In agriculture the corresponding ratio for 1945–1949 was much lower than that for 1900–1914.) If we assume that the ratio for 1950–1955 was about the same as that for 1945–1949, the impression conveyed by Table 55 when we compare 1900–1914 with 1945–1955 is that there was no significant long-term trend in the distribution of external financing between long-term and short-term. However, when we compare the averages for the two long periods (lines 11–12), some semblance of a decline in the share of changes in long-term debt emerges; but it is robbed of significance when three long periods are distinguished (lines 8–10) and the average for 1900–1914 is compared with that for 1940–1955.

The only conclusion that can be derived from Table 55 is that, if there were any long-term trends in the distribution of external financing by nonfarm unincorporated business between long- and short-term, they cannot be discerned. The variations in the shares are too large, and the differences between presumably comparable periods too small, to support any claim of a long-term trend.

We have discussed so far the distribution between short-term and long-term debt in the structure of external financing of corporations, agriculture, and nonfarm unincorporated business. This distinction has little relevance to the financing of nonfarm residential and related construction, which, as defined here, includes the purchase or construction of new units and major alterations of old ones. The financing in this sector, largely by households, is so dominantly long-term that the data do not even refer to any short-term funds. There is perhaps more reason for the distinction in the case of governments, because they can and do borrow on notes and other instruments of relatively short maturity. The question is whether the distinction has much significance for governments as users of funds. To be sure, as a matter of technical procedure and from the standpoint of the suppliers, the distinction is important for governments also. At some conjunctures in the money and credit markets, or in the timing discrepancy between expenditures and receipts, it is expedient for governments to borrow on short-term notes to be liquidated promptly or to be funded later. Some sources of funds available for such short-term placement are not available for long-term financing of government issues. But we can also argue that the distinction between short- and long-term government debt has little to do with maturity of assets to be acquired, or with the need for periodic testing of the government's liquidity and solvency.

In any case, Goldsmith's data do not permit a clear distinction between short- and long-term government financing (the pure "borrowing" item is extremely small proportionately to "securities"), and for our purposes it is not straining too much to classify all government financing as long-term. This somewhat arbitrary classification of government financing permits us to derive countrywide totals of external financing (Table 56).

Three totals are used as bases in Table 56. The first is debt financing; the second is total external financing, i.e. debt financing and equity funds; and the most comprehensive is total financing, i.e. total sources or uses.

1. The ratio of changes in long-term debt to total debt financing declined for corporations and agriculture, and the long-term movement

TABLE 56

SUMMARY: RATIOS OF VARIOUS TYPES OF FINANCING TO DEBT FINANCING,
EXTERNAL FINANCING, AND TOTAL FINANCING, BY CATEGORY OF USER OF FUNDS, 1900–1955

(amounts in billions of dollars, averages per year)

		Periods			Longer Periods	
					1900–1929 or	
	1901–1912 or	1913–1939 or		1946–1955 or	1901–1929 or	
Category of User	1900–1914 (1)	1915–1939 (2)	1940–1955 (3)	1945–1955 (4)	1901–1930 (5)	1930–1955 (6)
A. RATIOS OF LONG-TERM DEBT FINANCING TO TOTAL DEBT FINANCING						
Debt Financing						
Corporations						
1. Total	1.02	1.27	7.13	10.27	1.94	4.02
2. Long-term	0.75	0.98	3.21	5.52	1.27	1.93
3. Ratio, line 2 to line 1	0.74	0.77	0.45	0.54	0.65	0.48
Agriculture						
4. Total	0.35	0.46	0.53	0.95	0.53	0.37
5. Long-term	0.18	0.47	0.15	0.37	0.38	0.20
6. Ratio, line 5 to line 4	0.51	1.02	0.28	0.39	0.72	0.54
Nonfarm Unincorporated Business						
7. Total	0.15	0.13	1.05	1.51	0.30	0.52
8. Long-term	0.05	0.16	0.39	0.60	0.17	0.23
9. Ratio, line 8 to line 7	0.33	1.23	0.37	0.40	0.57	0.44
Total Business						
10. Total, lines 1, 4, and 7	1.52	1.86	8.71	12.73	2.77	4.91
11. Long-term, lines 2, 5, and 8	0.98	1.61	3.75	6.49	1.82	2.36
12. Ratio, line 11 to line 10	0.64	0.87	0.43	0.51	0.66	0.48
Households [a]						
13. Total	0.54 (1900–1919)	1.86 (1920–1939)	5.50	7.70	1.32	3.64
Total Private						
14. Total, lines 10 and 13	2.06	3.72	14.21	20.43	4.09	8.55
15. Long-term, lines 11 and 13	1.52	3.47	9.25	14.19	3.14	6.00
16. Ratio, line 15 to line 14	0.74	0.93	0.65	0.69	0.77	0.70

[a] Nonfarm residential construction.

(continued)

TABLE 56 (continued)

| | Periods | | | | Longer Periods | |
| | | | | | 1900–1929 or | |
Category of User	1901–1912 or 1900–1914 (1)	1913–1939 or 1915–1939 (2)	1940–1955 (3)	1946–1955 or 1945–1955 (4)	1901–1929 or 1901–1930 (5)	1930–1955 (6)
A. RATIOS OF LONG-TERM DEBT FINANCING TO TOTAL DEBT FINANCING (concluded)						
Debt Financing						
Governments						
17. Total	0.27	2.93	17.41	6.37	1.13	12.37
Countrywide						
18. Total, lines 14 and 17	2.33	6.65	31.62	26.80	5.22	20.92
19. Long-term, lines 15 and 17	1.79	6.40	26.66	20.56	4.27	18.37
20. Ratio, line 19 to line 18	0.77	0.96	0.84	0.77	0.82	0.88
B. RATIOS OF LONG-TERM EXTERNAL FINANCING TO TOTAL EXTERNAL FINANCING						
External Financing						
Corporations						
21. Total	1.49	2.41	9.18	13.19	3.00	5.49
22. Long-term	1.22	2.11	5.26	8.44	2.33	3.39
23. Ratio, line 22 to line 21	0.82	0.88	0.57	0.64	0.78	0.62
Total Business						
24. Total, lines 21, 4, and 7	1.99	3.00	10.76	15.65	3.83	6.38
25. Long-term, lines 22, 5, and 8	1.45	2.74	5.80	9.41	2.88	3.82
26. Ratio, line 25 to line 24	0.73	0.91	0.54	0.60	0.75	0.60
Total Private						
27. Total, lines 24 and 13	2.53	4.86	16.26	23.35	5.15	10.02
28. Long-term, lines 25 and 13	1.99	4.60	11.30	17.11	4.20	7.46
29. Ratio, line 28 to line 27	0.79	0.95	0.69	0.73	0.82	0.74
Countrywide						
30. Total, lines 27 and 17	2.80	7.79	33.67	29.72	6.28	22.39
31. Long-term, lines 28 and 17	2.26	7.53	28.71	23.48	5.33	19.83
32. Ratio, line 31 to line 30	0.81	0.97	0.85	0.79	0.85	0.89

(continued)

TABLE 56 (concluded)

Category of User	Periods				Longer Periods	
					1900–1929 or 1901–1929	
	1901–1912 or 1900–1914 (1)	1913–1939 or 1915–1939 (2)	1940–1955 (3)	1946–1955 or 1945–1955 (4)	or 1901–1930 (5)	1930–1955 (6)

C. RATIOS OF LONG-TERM EXTERNAL FINANCING AND
SHORT-TERM DEBT FINANCING TO TOTAL FINANCING (TOTAL USES)

Various Types of Financing

Corporations

33. Total	3.33	7.06	26.51	34.88	6.97	17.40
34. Long-term external	1.22	2.11	5.26	8.44	2.33	3.39
35. Short-term debt	0.27	0.30	3.92	4.75	0.67	2.10
36. Ratio, line 34 to line 33	0.37	0.30	0.20	0.24	0.33	0.19
37. Ratio, line 35 to line 33	0.08	0.04	0.15	0.14	0.10	0.12

Total Business

38. Total	4.97	9.81	35.45	43.93	9.48	23.59
39. Long-term external	1.45	2.74	5.80	9.41	2.88	3.82
40. Short-term debt	0.54	0.26	4.96	6.24	0.94	2.56
41. Ratio, line 39 to line 38	0.29	0.28	0.16	0.21	0.30	0.16
42. Ratio, line 40 to line 38	0.11	0.03	0.14	0.14	0.10	0.11

Total Private

43. Total	6.25	12.79	42.97	54.48	11.85	28.67
44. Long-term external	1.99	4.60	11.30	17.11	4.20	7.46
45. Short-term debt	0.54	0.26	4.96	6.24	0.94	2.56
46. Ratio, line 44 to line 43	0.32	0.36	0.26	0.31	0.35	0.26
47. Ratio, line 45 to line 43	0.09	0.02	0.12	0.11	0.08	0.09

Countrywide

48. Total	6.90	16.08	56.61	68.41	13.48	38.83
49. Long-term external	2.26	7.53	28.71	23.48	5.33	19.83
50. Short-term debt	0.54	0.26	4.96	6.24	0.94	2.56
51. Ratio, line 49 to line 48	0.33	0.47	0.51	0.34	0.40	0.51
52. Ratio, line 50 to line 48	0.08	0.02	0.09	0.09	0.07	0.07

Notes to Table 56
Source, by Line

1 and 2. Calculated from the series given in or underlying Table 48.
4 and 5. Calculated from the series given in or underlying Table 54.
7 and 8. Calculated from the series given in or underlying Table 55.
13. Table 47.
17. Table 47 or the series underlying that table.
21 and 22. Calculated from the series given in or underlying Table 48.
33. Calculated from the series given in or underlying Table 53.
34 and 35. Calculated from the series given in or underlying Table 48.
38. Line 33 plus agriculture, calculated from Table 54, plus nonfarm unincorporated business, from Table 46 or calculated from Table 55.
39. Line 25.
40. Line 24 minus line 39.
43. Line 38 plus nonfarm residential construction (for dates indicated in line 13), calculated from Table 45.
44. Line 28.
45. Line 27 minus line 44.
48. Line 43 plus governments, calculated from the series given in or underlying Table 46, lines 10 and 14.

for nonfarm unincorporated business is indeterminate. Since corporations dominate the business sector total, we find for the latter a clear downward trend in the ratio of changes in long-term debt to total debt financing. And even the addition of nonfarm residential and related construction to form the total private sector leaves a downward trend in the ratio.

However, when we add the government sector to secure the countrywide totals, the picture changes (line 20). While the countrywide share of changes in long-term debt in total debt financing shows no consistent trend, there is a suggestion of stability or a rise rather than a decline.

2. The ratio of long-term external financing to total external financing shows a distinct decline for the business and the private sectors. This means that the share of short-term borrowing in total external financing has risen. But the inclusion of governments again changes the picture (line 32). For the three short periods, the share of long-term in total external financing moved from 0.81 in 1901–1912 to 0.85 in 1940–1955, or to 0.79 in the post-World War II decade. For the two long periods, however, the ratio rose from 0.85 to 0.89. Since we assume that government financing is all long-term, the level of and trend in the ratio of long-term external financing may be overstated, and a more accurate estimate might show a decline in the countrywide share of long-term external financing and a rise in the countrywide share of short-term borrowing in external financing. But the trend could not be marked or, in view of the lack of consistency over time, very significant.

3. The ratio of long-term external financing to total financing (total sources or uses) declined for corporations, the business sector, and the private sector. The trend in the countrywide ratio was upward (line 51). Comparison of the pre-World War I period with 1940–1955 shows a marked rise in the ratio—from 0.33 to 0.51; but its comparison with the more normal period, 1946–1955, shows a change only from 0.33 to 0.34. However, in the two long periods (columns 5 and 6) there was a distinct rise in the ratio of long-term external financing to total financing for the country as a whole.

The movement of the ratio of short-term borrowing to total sources or uses was upward. It rose for corporations, for the total business group, for the total private sector and, on the basis of the change from the pre-World War I period to 1940–1955 or 1946–1955, even for the country as a whole (line 52).

It should be remembered that practically all long-term movements and trends relating to the distribution between short- and long-term financing are subject to several major qualifications. First, none is consistent over time, there being a rise in the ratio of long-term until the 1920's and a decline thereafter (or a decline in the ratio of short-term until the 1920's and a rise thereafter). Second, the ratios are subject to marked fluctuations during wars, depressions, and even relatively normal periods. Third, in establishing the long-term trends we are forced to rely upon the ratios for the post-World War II years, and we are too close to those years to judge firmly.

Shares of Financial Intermediaries

In our consideration of the shares of financial intermediaries in external and total financing of the economy, three questions guide the presentation of data and the discussion. First, have there been any significant long-term movements in those shares? Second, if such movements are found, are there similar movements in the shares in total and external financing of the distinguishable capital user or borrower groups? Third, have there been significant shifts in the relative importance of the various types of financial intermediaries? These questions are answered here in summary fashion, because the detailed analysis is presented in Goldsmith's monograph.

Table 57 provides information relating to the first two questions. Changes in assets of financial intermediaries are compared first with external financing and then with total financing of the various sectors and of the economy as a whole. It should be noted that additions to the assets of a credit institution are not necessarily connected with current external or total financing of a group of capital users and fund borrowers. For example, financial intermediaries can buy or take over existing residential real estate mortgages from individuals, and they can buy notes from the nonfinancial firms that were the original holders. It is for this reason that, during some periods, the ratio of additions to assets of financial intermediaries associated with a given group of borrowers to external financing (or, theoretically, even total financing) can exceed 1.0; although a ratio of more than 1.0 can also be obtained if some components of external financing are negative (i.e., if a debt is reduced) and others are positive and are secured from or through a financial intermediary. More important is the possibility that, to the extent that financial institutions add to their assets by purchases of existing claims rather than by financing new borrowing, the ratios in Table 57 exaggerate the contribution of financial intermediaries to the external and total financing of the various sectors. But the bias introduced by this possibility can hardly be significant for long periods, and we can safely interpret major changes in the ratios as significant indications of changes in the share of intermediaries in the financing of capital formation or of total uses.

With this comment in mind, we can try to answer the first question—as to long-term trends in shares of financial intermediaries in external and total financing for the economy as a whole. The shares of financial intermediaries in financing did rise over the last half-century (lines 30 and 42). Goldsmith's data do not extend beyond 1949, but there is little ground for assuming that their shares in 1950–1955 were much lower than in 1946–1949—if lower at all. On this assumption, their share in the post-World War II years in external financing would be about two-thirds, compared with less than one-half during the decades preceding the 1930's, and their share in the two longer periods in columns 8 and 9 of line 30 confirms the rise. Their share in total financing rose from about two-tenths in the pre-1930 decades to three-tenths in the post-World War II years, and was much higher during the 1930's and during World War II (line 42).

In answer to the second question, it appears that the upward trend in the share of financial intermediaries in both external and total financing is not observed in all the sectors distinguished in Table 57. In agriculture, the share of financial intermediaries in external financ-

TABLE 57

Share of Financial Intermediaries in External and in Total Financing, 1900–1955

(amounts in millions of dollars)

	Periods							Longer Periods	
	1901–1912 (1)	1913–1922 (2)	1923–1929 (3)	1930–1939 (4)	1940–1945 (5)	1946–1949 (6)	1950–1952 (7)	1901–1929 (8)	1930–1949 (9)
A. SHARE OF FINANCIAL INTERMEDIARIES IN EXTERNAL FINANCING									
Agriculture									
1. External financing	5.4	10.6	−0.6	−4.2	−2.5	3.9		15.4	−2.8
Financial intermediaries									
2. Share	0.43	0.46	−0.15	0.42	0.74	0.48		0.47	0.64
3. Amount, line 1 × line 2	2.3	4.9	0.1	−1.8	−1.9	1.9		7.3	−1.8
Nonfarm Unincorporated Business									
4. External financing	1.9	3.4	3.4	−3.3	0.8	4.7		8.7	2.2
Financial intermediaries									
5. Share	1.67	0.99	0.29	−0.49	1.28	1.36		0.86	4.16
6. Amount, line 4 × line 5	3.2	3.3	1.0	1.6	1.0	6.4		7.5	9.0
Nonfinancial Corporations									
7. External financing	17.9	30.1	39.0	−4.1	14.9	39.3	61 (est.)	87.0	50.1
Financial intermediaries									
8. Share	0.36	0.30	0.40	0.88	0.16	0.53	0.48	0.36	0.39
9. Amount, line 7 × 8	6.5	9.0	15.7	−3.6	2.4	20.8	29.2	31.2	19.6
Total Business									
10. External financing, lines 1, 4, and 7	25.2	44.1	41.8	−11.6	13.2	47.9		111.1	49.5
Financial intermediaries									
11. Amount, lines 3, 6, and 9	12.0	17.2	16.8	−3.8	1.5	29.1		46.0	26.8
12. Share, line 11 ÷ line 10	0.48	0.39	0.40	0.33	0.11	0.61		0.41	0.54
Households [a]									
13. External financing [b]	2.2	5.9	15.9	−1.9	1.0	18.3		24.0	17.4

	Line									
Financial intermediaries										
Share, in long-term	14.	0.81	0.59	0.53	1.00	0.73	0.90		0.57	0.88
Amount, line 13 × line 14	15.	1.7	3.5	8.4	−1.9	0.8	16.4		13.6	15.3
Total Private										
External financing, lines 10 and 13	16.	27.4	50.0	57.7	−13.5	14.2	66.2		135.1	66.9
Financial intermediaries										
Amount, lines 11 and 15	17.	13.7	20.7	25.2	−5.7	2.3	45.5		59.6	42.1
Share, line 17 ÷ line 16	18.	0.50	0.41	0.44	0.42	0.16	0.69		0.44	0.63
State and Local Governments										
External financing	19.	2.4	6.0	6.5	2.9	−3.6	6.0	8.2	14.9	5.3
Financial intermediaries										
Share	20.	0.43	0.43	0.51	1.59	0.28	0.74	0.89	0.46	1.51
Amount, line 19 × line 20	21.	1.0	2.6	3.3	4.6	−1.0	4.4	7.3	6.9	8.0
Total Private plus State and Local Governments										
External financing, lines 16 and 19	22.	29.8	56.0	64.2	−10.6	10.6	72.2		150.0	72.2
Financial intermediaries										
Amount, lines 17 and 21	23.	14.7	23.3	28.5	−1.1	1.3	49.9		66.5	50.1
Share, line 23 ÷ line 22	24.	0.49	0.42	0.44	0.10	0.12	0.69		0.44	0.69
Federal Government										
External financing	25.	0.8	24.7	−6.0	44.9	240.6	−19.6		19.5	265.9
Financial intermediaries										
Share	26.	0.16	0.32	0.035	0.69	0.64	0.73		0.41	0.64
Amount, line 25 × line 26	27.	0.1	8.0	−0.2	31.0	154.0	−14.3		7.9	170.7
Countrywide										
External financing, lines 22 and 25	28.	30.6	80.7	58.2	34.3	251.2	52.6		169.5	338.1
Financial intermediaries										
Amount, lines 23 and 27	29.	14.8	31.3	28.3	29.9	155.3	35.6		74.4	220.8
Share, line 29 ÷ line 28	30.	0.48	0.39	0.49	0.87	0.62	.68		0.44	0.65

(continued)

TABLE 57 (concluded)

	Periods						Longer Periods	
	1900–1909 or 1901–1910 (1)	1910–1919 or 1911–1920 (2)	1920–1929 or 1921–1930 (3)	1930–1939 or 1931–1940 (4)	1940–1944 or 1941–1945 (5)	1945–1955 or 1946–1955 (6)	1900–1929 or 1901–1930 (7)	1930–1955 or 1931–1955 (8)
B. SHARE OF FINANCIAL INTERMEDIARIES IN TOTAL FINANCING (TOTAL USES)								
Total Business								
31. Share, financial intermediaries in external financing, line 12	0.48	0.39	0.40	0.33	0.11	0.61[c]	0.41	0.54
32. Share, external in total financing, Table 46	0.41	0.41	0.41	−0.16	0.10	0.36	0.41	0.28
33. Share, financial intermediaries in total financing, line 31 × line 32	0.20	0.16	0.16	−0.05	0.01	0.22	0.17	0.15
Total Private								
34. Share, financial intermediaries in external financing, line 18	0.50	0.41	0.44	0.42	0.16	0.69[c]	0.44	0.63
35. Share, external in total financing, Table 46	0.39	0.42	0.47	0.04	0.14	0.43	0.44	0.36
36. Share, financial intermediaries in total financing, line 34 × line 35	0.20	0.17	0.21	0.02	0.02	0.30	0.19	0.23
Total Private plus State and Local Governments								
37. Share, financial intermediaries in external financing, line 24	0.49	0.42	0.44	0.10	0.12	0.69[c]	0.44	0.69
38. Share, external in total financing, Table 46	0.40	0.43	0.47	0.07	0.10	0.41	0.44	0.33
39. Share, financial intermediaries in total financing, line 37 × line 38	0.20	0.18	0.21	0.01	0.01	0.28	0.19	0.23
Countrywide								
40. Share, financial intermediaries in external financing, line 30	0.48	0.39	0.49	0.87	0.62	0.68[c]	0.44	0.65
41. Share, external in total financing, Table 46	0.40	0.59	0.42	0.48	1.22	0.44	0.47	0.58
42. Share, financial intermediaries in total financing, line 40 × line 41	0.19	0.23	0.21	0.42	0.76	0.30	0.21	0.38

[a] Nonfarm residential construction.
[b] Mortgages only.
[c] Average for 1946–1949, that for 1946–1955 not being available.

SOURCE: Raymond W. Goldsmith, *Financial Intermediaries*, Table 46, p. 184; Table 48, p. 193; Table 51, p. 206; Table 53, p. 222; Table 74, p. 260; Table 76, p. 266. And *idem, A Study of Saving*, Vol. I, Table U-11, p. 869.

ing in the post-World War II years was higher than in 1901–1922, but the difference is very slight (line 2). Nor was there an upward trend in the share of financial intermediaries in the external financing by nonfarm unincorporated business (line 5). But for the most important group, corporations, there was a distinct rise in the share (line 8), and this carries over to the total for the business sector as a whole (line 12). But for the latter, the share rose only in the post-World War II years. Since for the business sector, external financing was a smaller fraction of total financing in recent decades than in the earlier, the share of financial intermediaries in total financing for the business sector in the post-World War II years (line 33) was only two points higher than in the first decade of the century. It is, therefore, safest to conclude that if there was any significant trend in the share of financial intermediaries in total financing of business, and perhaps even in their share in external financing, the trend is only barely perceptible.[5]

The share of financial intermediaries in external financing connected with nonfarm residential construction fluctuated widely, and for the discrete periods, no clear upward trend is found; the longer periods, however, do show an appreciable rise (line 14). More important, since the share of external financing in total financing for this sector has risen markedly over time, it follows that the share of financial intermediaries in total financing associated with nonfarm residential construction also rose over the period. It is for this reason that the share of financial intermediaries in total financing for the private sector (line 36) shows a distinct rise—although again largely because of the high level in the post-World War II years.

It is for the state, local, and federal governments that the share of financial intermediaries in external financing shows an unmistakable upward trend (lines 20 and 26). For the former, the share rose from about one-half in the pre-1930's to almost three-quarters in the post-World War II years, and the rise in the share for the federal government was even greater. It is, therefore, government financing that produces the distinct upward trend in the shares of financial intermediaries in countrywide external financing and total financing (lines 30 and 42). This effect of the government sector is particularly marked beginning with the 1930's, when the share of financial intermediaries in

[5] The shares in the post-World War II years are affected by the treatment of corporate tax accruals as external funds. Their exclusion would raise the share of financial intermediaries in the external financing of corporations, giving it a more marked upward trend.

financing the government sector reached a much higher level than the share of intermediaries in financing the private sector. This higher level of the shares of intermediaries in financing the government sector, together with the increase in the weight of governments in external and total financing for the economy would have raised the shares of financial intermediaries in the countrywide totals, even if their shares within the private and government sectors taken separately had remained constant following that date.

Data bearing upon the third question, concerning shifts among various types of intermediaries, are assembled in Table 58. They are based on Goldsmith's estimates, discussed in detail in his monograph. Only two changes were made: substitution of a National Bureau estimate for government lending institutions; and omission of sales finance and personal finance companies, because these companies finance consumer durable goods and other consumer purchases not classified by us under capital formation.

The trends in the structure of financial intermediaries, weighted by value of assets, are quite clear. First, the shares of commercial banks, savings banks, and personal trust departments declined significantly (lines 19, 20, and 33). It is the decline in the first two that reduced the share of the banking sector from over six-tenths in the first two decades of the century to less than four-tenths in the post-World War II years. Second, the shares of the various groups of insurance and retirement funds increased—particularly, life insurance, private pension funds, and the government retirement and social security funds (lines 23–27). The insurance sector as a whole rose from almost one-sixth of the total before the 1930's to almost four-tenths in the post-World War II years. Third, the fluctuations in the shares of the various groups of miscellaneous financial intermediaries are quite marked, and it is not easy to establish significant trends (lines 28–32). The shares of land banks and of the combined group of investment companies, stock brokers, investment holding trusts, and factors appear to decline; that of government lending institutions appears to rise. But only the last of these trends is significant. Finally, there is the rise in the share of all government institutions. The Federal Reserve Banks, while legally not part of the government structure, can be viewed as an arm of the government. Their share (line 18), combined with those of government funds (line 25) and government lending institutions (line 30), rose from 7 per cent in 1901–1922 to 21 per cent in 1913–1939, and to 27 per cent in 1930–1955. Even in 1946–1955, when the share dropped because of the net liquidation of assets by government lending institutions, it was still 22 per cent, or about three times that in 1901–1922.

The causes of these shifts among the various groups of financial intermediaries and their effects are clear enough in some cases, but quite obscure in others. Thus the rise in the share of government institutions among financial intermediaries is naturally part and parcel of the rise in the share of governments in many aspects of economic activity. In the present context, the connection with the increasing share of governments in the total and external financing of the economy is particularly to be noted. If governments are drawing heavily upon the money and credit markets in the community, part of the demand is for uses for which it is more expedient to channel the funds through the governments' own intermediaries. And the effects of the governments' practice of placing funds in debt obligations rather than in equity issues would, obviously, be pronounced.

The causes and effects of shifts among financial intermediaries in the private sector are, however, more complex. Was the growth of large corporations and their financial power a factor in reducing the share of commercial banking, limited as it was primarily to short-term business credit? What were the roles of the decreasing inequality in the distribution of income and of the steadily growing income per capita, both of which make for increased contributions to the pool of individual savings by the lower- and middle-income groups? Were the savings of these groups, directed toward security and retirement, more likely to flow to such growing sectors of financial intermediaries as life insurance companies, pension and retirement funds, and savings banks and associations? What was the impact of increasing progressivity in personal income taxes on the shift of upper-income-class savings from a type of income that might flow through financial intermediaries to capital gains, a growing type of direct equity participation? These and many other questions that could be raised suggest that the changing structure of financial intermediaries—even in the private sector alone—reflects a vast variety of changes in income levels and income distribution, which in turn lead to changes in patterns of demand for different types of savings by various groups of individuals and households as well as changes in the economic structure and patterns of behavior of the business units proper.

TABLE 58

DISTRIBUTION OF CHANGES IN ASSETS, BY GROUPS OF FINANCIAL INTERMEDIARIES, 1901–1955

(amounts in billions of dollars)

Financial Intermediaries	Periods						Longer Periods			
	1901–1912 (1)	1913–1922 (2)	1923–1929 (3)	1930–1939 (4)	1940–1945 (5)	1946–1955 (6)	1901–1922 (7)	1913–1939 (8)	1930–1955 (9)	1901–1929 (10)
A. VALUES										
1. Federal Reserve Banks	0	5.3	0.2	13.5	26.1	7.2	5.3	19.0	46.8	5.5
2. Commercial banks	11.8	25.7	18.7	0.1	94.0	50.4	37.5	44.5	144.5	56.2
3. Mutual savings banks [a]	1.6	2.7	3.4	3.3	7.0	15.6	4.3	9.4	25.9	7.7
4. Savings and loan associations	0.5	1.8	4.6	−2.0	3.2	29.1	2.3	4.4	30.3	6.9
5. Total banking, lines 1 to 4	13.9	35.5	26.9	14.9	130.3	102.3	49.4	77.3	247.5	76.3
6. Private life insurance companies [b]	2.9	4.6	9.1	12.1	16.1	46.7	7.5	25.8	74.9	16.6
7. Private noninsured pension funds	0	0.1	0.4	0.5	1.9	12.0	0.1	1.0	14.4	0.5
8. Government funds [c]	0	0.2	1.3	4.8	19.3	31.8	0.2	6.3	55.9	1.5
9. Fire, marine, casualty, etc., insurance	0.5	1.3	2.4	0.1	2.9	14.0	1.8	3.8	17.0	4.2
10. Total insurance, lines 6 to 9	3.3	6.2	13.2	17.6	40.2	104.4	9.5	37.0	162.2	22.7
11. Mortgage companies	0.2	0.2	0.2	−0.4	−0.2	1.6	0.4	0.0	1.0	0.6
12. Land banks	0	1.0	0.9	0.5	−1.2	0.4	1.0	2.4	−0.3	1.9
13. Government lending institutions	0	0.2	0.0	7.1	−1.2	20.8	0.2	7.3	26.7	0.2
14. Investment companies, etc. [d]	0.4	3.1	13.4	−12.2	2.9	14.3	3.5	4.3	5.0	16.9
15. Total, lines 11 to 14	0.6	4.5	14.5	−5.0	0.3	37.1	5.1	14.0	32.4	19.6
16. Personal trust departments	4.0	11.0	12.0	5.0	10.0	29.9	15.0	28.0	44.9	27.0
17. Total included, lines 5, 10, 15, and 16	21.8	57.2	66.6	32.5	180.8	273.7	79.0	156.3	487.0	145.6

B. PERCENTAGE SHARES

18. Federal Reserve Banks	0	9.3	0.3	41.5	14.4	2.6	6.7	12.2	9.6	3.8
19. Commercial banks	54.1	44.9	28.1	0.3	52.0	18.4	47.5	28.5	29.7	38.6
20. Mutual savings banks [a]	7.3	4.7	5.1	10.2	3.9	5.7	5.4	6.0	5.3	5.3
21. Savings and loan associations	2.3	3.1	6.9	−6.2	1.8	10.6	2.9	2.8	6.2	4.7
22. Total banking, lines 18 to 21	63.8	62.1	40.4	45.8	72.1	37.4	62.5	49.5	50.8	52.4
23. Private life insurance companies [b]	13.3	8.0	13.7	37.2	8.9	17.1	9.5	16.5	15.4	11.4
24. Private noninsured pension funds	0	0.2	0.6	1.5	1.1	4.4	0.1	0.6	3.0	0.3
25. Government funds [c]	0	0.3	2.0	14.8	10.7	11.6	0.3	4.0	11.5	1.0
26. Fire, marine, casualty, etc., insurance	2.3	2.3	3.6	0.3	1.6	5.1	2.3	2.4	3.5	2.9
27. Total insurance, lines 23 to 26	15.1	10.8	19.8	54.2	22.2	38.1	12.0	23.7	33.3	15.6
28. Mortgage companies	0.9	0.3	0.3	−1.2	−0.1	0.6	0.5	0.0	0.2	0.4
29. Land banks	0	1.7	1.4	1.5	−0.7	0.1	1.3	1.5	−0.1	1.3
30. Government lending institutions	0	0.3	0.0	21.8	−0.7	7.6	0.3	4.7	5.5	0.1
31. Investment companies, etc. [d]	1.8	5.4	20.1	−37.5	1.6	5.2	4.4	2.8	1.0	11.6
32. Total, lines 28 to 31	2.8	7.9	21.8	−15.4	0.2	13.6	6.5	9.0	6.7	13.5
33. Personal trust departments	18.3	19.2	18.0	15.4	5.5	10.9	19.0	17.9	9.2	18.5
34. Total included, lines 22, 27, 32, and 33	100.0	100.0	100.0	100.0	100.0	100.0	100.0	100.0	100.0	100.0

Because of rounding, detail will not necessarily add to total.

[a] Including Postal Savings System and credit unions.

[b] Including fraternal organizations and life insurance departments of savings banks.

[c] Pension, retirement, and social security.

[d] Including investment holding companies, brokers and dealers, and factors.

SOURCE: Goldsmith, *Financial Intermediaries*, Table 10, p. 73, extended through 1955 and revised for government lending institutions by NBER.

To establish the effects of changes in the structure of financial inter-mediaries on the availability of funds to different sectors among the potential capital users in the economy is not easy. Some financial institutions may, because of restrictions imposed upon them by the kind of savings entrusted to them and because of legal regulations, direct their funds into fixed debt obligations; and there might be some lag in their adjustment, or in the adjustment of the corpus of statutes and administrative rules, to the need to channel an increasing proportion of their funds into equity uses. This is particularly true of the insurance intermediaries, whose shares in external and total financing of the economy have increased markedly. Perhaps there is some association, also, between trends in the distribution of long-term external financing between equity and debt funds in recent decades, the related differentials in stock and bond yields, and the rapid growth in recent years of the shares of financial intermediaries in the insurance category (to which we may also add governments).

It would be an oversimplification to rely on such an association, however, for two important reasons. First, because within each group of intermediaries changes in investment policy may provide adequate flexibility, it may be incorrect to classify a given group of financial intermediaries by any one kind of investment policy for a long period. Second, the assignment of an independent effect to financial inter-mediaries is based on the assumption that the practices of such institutions introduce a constraint into the flow of funds that would not otherwise exist—for example, the larger rise in assets of certain types of financial institutions than of other types means a greater flow into corresponding instruments of financing and, hence, even into certain types of capital formation. But it is quite possible that, even if individuals had continued to channel their savings directly rather than increasingly through financial intermediaries, they might have shifted toward the types of investment made by the intermediaries. It is also possible that, if an increasingly large proportion of new savings is placed by individuals with certain types of financial intermediaries, the rise in value of corresponding assets (such as bonds) might induce some individuals who already hold those assets to shift to others (such as equities). The adjustment can be made not only by the allocation of new savings to various uses, but also by the redistribution of existing claims. Thus, because financial intermediaries may be merely responding to the wishes of primary savers, and because of elasticity in the response of markets for both new and existing financial assets, no hard and fast statements can be made concerning the specific effects of the differential growth of financial intermediaries on the channeling of funds into various instrumentalities or various types of capital investment.

CHAPTER 7

Long Swings in Population Growth, Capital Formation, and National Product

---

IN Chapter 2 we discussed the existence of long swings in the rate of growth, a component of change that has to be recognized when we distinguish long-term trends from the shorter fluctuations. If long-term trends mean movements that persist in one direction over periods as long as twenty-five to thirty years, and if we describe those long-term trends and remove them, the residuals reveal that in addition to the shorter fluctuations associated with business cycles there are longer up-and-down movements. Their amplitude is not insignificant and an analysis of long-term changes—longer than business cycles—must take them into account. Charts 2 and 3 illustrated such long swings in gross national product, in constant prices. It was to eliminate those long swings that the analysis in Chapters 3 and 4 was based largely on thirty-year averages, and that in the analysis in Chapters 5 and 6 we studied the longer periods, or shorter periods selected to represent possibly similar levels in the long swing.

We now consider directly these up-and-down movements in the volume or rate of growth of the economic variables of importance in connection with past and prospective trends in capital formation and financing. In the discussion that follows, we cannot hope to give a complete picture of the prevalence of long swings in the movement over time of the various aspects of the country's economy. For this purpose the data should cover a much longer period and should relate, on a continuous, almost annual, basis to many more aspects of the economy than they do. The analysis requires laborious statistical manipulation, the application of which to a large number of series becomes a forbidding chore. An even greater difficulty lies in the fact that the analytical literature on this topic is only in its very beginnings, and we have no large stock of accumulated findings to draw upon.[1] Under the circumstances, we can only suggest the broad outlines of the long swings as they can be observed in the countrywide aggregates with which we deal, to provide at least an indication of the magnitude of this particular pattern of change over time, the mechanism of relations among various components in the economy during these swings, and the importance to be assigned to them in any consideration of the bearing of past trends upon the future.

The present chapter is devoted to an attempt to describe the long swings in the real flows, that is, in capital formation, national product, and the related components and variables. Chapter 8 will deal with the long swings in financial flows.

Population Movements

Population offers the best way of breaking into the chain of interconnections among the several economic variables that is involved in any pattern of movement over time—long swings included. Population estimates also happen to be one of our best series, independent of the sources from which capital formation and national product estimates are derived, and they are less subject to imaginative piecing out and to limiting theoretical assumptions than the more synthetic economic totals.

Additions to population are clearly an important factor in the demand for new housing and for additional consumer goods, and in eventually providing additions to the labor force. We begin therefore

[1] An early survey of the problem of long swings is given in Wesley C. Mitchell, *Business Cycles: The Problem and Its Setting* (New York, NBER, 1927), pp. 226–230. Later discussions include Simon Kuznets, *Secular Movements in Production and Prices* (Houghton Mifflin, 1930), pp. 200–267; Arthur F. Burns, *Production Trends in the United States Since 1870* (New York, NBER, 1934), pp. 174–252; and more recently, Brinley Thomas, *Migration and Economic Growth* (Cambridge, England, 1954), and W. Arthur Lewis, "Secular Swings in Production and Trade" (*Manchester School of Economic and Social Studies,* May 1955).

Since this chapter was written, Moses Abramovitz has initiated a comprehensive analysis of long swings in the growth of the American economy, with particular emphasis on capital formation. Some preliminary results of the analysis appear in the following annual reports of the National Bureau: 38th, May 1958, pp. 47–56; 39th, May 1959, pp. 23–27; and 40th, May 1960, pp. 19–21. It has not been possible here to take advantage of Abramovitz' suggestive findings, which may lead to analytical hypotheses somewhat different from those suggested in the text.

by observing the rate of additions to the population of the United States (Chart 4).

The measures of population growth used here are the changes between quinquennial averages ten years apart. The only exception is the use at each end of the series, when quinquennial averages are not

CHART 4

Decadal Additions to Native Born, Foreign Born White, and Total Population, 1870–1955

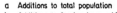

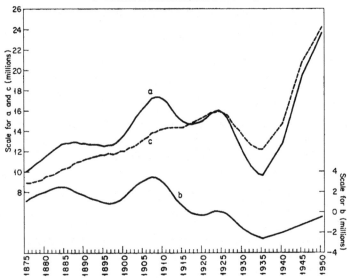

available, of changes over ten-year spans between single years (one entry at each end) and between three-year averages (one penultimate entry at each end). The use of quinquennial averages tends to smooth out the rather mild short-term changes in the annual population figures. Since we use the increment over ten-year periods, the absolute growth is large relative to any short-term fluctuations that may still remain in the five-year moving averages—provided, of course, that long-term growth has been substantial, as it has been in this country's population. Hence these measures of absolute additions to population, over decennial intervals taken successively with an overlap of one year, are largely free from effects of short-term changes of the kind associated with business cycles.[2]

The long swings in additions to population are clearly shown in Chart 4. Thus for total population, the additions rise to a peak in the mid- or late 1880's (each addition is centered in the middle of the decade for which it is calculated), decline to a trough in the mid-1890's, rise to another peak in 1909, decline again to a trough in 1917, rise moderately to another peak in the mid-1920's, show a sharp dip in the mid-1930's and then a sharp rise with its crest not yet in sight. Similar long swings can be observed not only in additions to the foreign born white population—in which they are quite prominent before the legal limitations on immigration that began in the 1920's and continued with progressing severity—but also in additions to the native born population, in which they tend to be less pronounced.

Nothing in the procedure used to calculate the additions to population would, in and of itself, produce the long swings. In fact, we know that immigration, for which annual data are available, did fluctuate in highly pronounced twenty-year swings,[3] and it is their effect that is reflected in the additions to the foreign born white population. These up-and-down movements in the volume of immigration and the stock of foreign born would themselves produce swings in additions to native born children of foreign born. Moreover, available data on the native born children of native parentage give evidence of long swings in the additions to their numbers.[4] So far as the procedure is concerned, the additions to population in Chart 4 could look like roughly straight lines, or lines with continuous acceleration or deceleration. Whatever swings are shown must be in the original data.[5]

---

[2] Of the reference cycles in the United States from 1869 through 1955, counting from trough to trough or peak to peak, only 7 were longer than five years. The alternative procedure, using average values for successive reference cycles, would not change the results significantly, as was illustrated in Chart 2. Nor would the results be very different if seven-year or nine-year moving averages—also a decade apart—were used.

[3] See Simon Kuznets and Ernest Rubin, *Immigration and the Foreign Born*, Occasional Paper 46 (New York, NBER, 1954), particularly Table 4 and Chart 3, pp. 28–29.

[4] See Kuznets, "Long Swings in the Growth of Population and in Related Economic Variables," *Proceedings of the American Philosophical Society*, February 1958, pp. 25–52. Much of the following discussion relating to population can be found in greater detail in that paper.

[5] In fact, the danger is not that the procedure introduces swings where they did not exist, but that it fails to reveal swings of a specified character. Assume that there was a highly symmetrical and regular ten-year swing in population additions

Long Swings

Granting the existence of these long up-and-down movements in additions to population, we record some of their quantitative characteristics (Table 59). In part A we attempt to date the troughs and peaks of the long swings by inspection of Chart 4. Precise dating is not always easy or necessarily meaningful, because each entry represents a decadal average. Furthermore, there is the problem of establishing the turning points at the ends of the series. In general, to avoid losing too much of the available record, we assumed that the first and the last year represented turning points—even though the phases may have begun earlier or ended later. In any case, we cannot provide accurate and specific measures but only suggest rough orders of magnitude.

The swings average about twenty years in duration, and their amplitude can be seen clearly from changes in the values entered in part B of the table. Thus, in column 1, additions to the foreign born white population are 1.1 million for the decade centered in the first trough (from 1870 to 1880, inclusive), but are more than double that, 2.5 million, for the decade centered in the following peak (from 1879 to 1889, inclusive). The alternations in additions from trough to peak and from peak to trough, on a per year basis, are entered in part C. Finally, the most complete measure of amplitude, the difference in the rate of change in additions between successive phases, is entered in part D.

The additions are measured on an absolute, not a percentage, basis. If a population is growing at a constant (or systematically accelerating or decelerating) percentage rate, we would expect the absolute additions per year to increase (or decrease) steadily. However, the actual additions per decade for total population rise and decline in swings of roughly twenty years' duration (column 3). The alternations in additions are quite substantial. In the first observed swing, the rate of additions increased from 10.0 to 12.9 million per decade, then declined to 12.5 million, and after the first swing the up-and-down movements were even more pronounced.

reflected in the annual data. A five-year moving average would not eliminate such a swing completely; but additions over successive ten-year intervals would not reflect it, because the differences would be taken between points representing identical phases within the ten-year cycle. And what is true of a regular ten-year cycle would be roughly true of a cycle of approximately the same duration. This means that the procedure cannot reveal long swings with a duration of about a decade or less—a limitation that is not serious, because a distinction between swings of that duration and business cycles could not be drawn easily.

TABLE 59

TIMING AND AMPLITUDE OF LONG SWINGS IN ADDITIONS TO NATIVE BORN,
FOREIGN BORN WHITE, AND TOTAL POPULATION, 1870–1955

(numbers in millions)

		Additions to:		
		Foreign Born White (1)	Native Born (2)	Total Population (3)
A. DATES OF TURNING POINTS				
1 First trough		1875	1876	1875
2. Peak		1884	1888	1888 (1885)
3. Trough		1896	1897	1895 (1897)
4. Peak		1907	1911	1909
5. Trough		1920	1915	1917
6. Peak		1923	1924	1924
7. Trough		1935	1935	1935
8. Peak		1950	1950	1950
B. VOLUMES PER DECADE AT DATES INDICATED				
9. First trough	(line 1)	1.1	8.9	10.0
10. Peak	(line 2)	2.5	10.9	12.9 (12.8)
11. Trough	(line 3)	0.8	11.7	12.5 (12.6)
12. Peak	(line 4)	3.4	14.3	17.3
13. Trough	(line 5)	−0.3	14.3	14.6
14. Peak	(line 6)	0.1	15.9	16.0
15. Trough	(line 7)	−2.6	12.2	9.6
16. Peak	(line 8)	−0.4	24.1	23.6
C. CHANGES PER YEAR DURING SUCCESSIVE PHASES				
17. Trough to peak	(line 9 to line 10)	+0.16	+0.17	+0.22 (0.28)
18. Peak to trough	(line 10 to line 11)	−0.14	+0.09	−0.06 (−0.02)
19. Trough to peak	(line 11 to line 12)	+0.24	+0.19	+0.34
20. Peak to trough	(line 12 to line 13)	−0.29	0.00	−0.34
21. Trough to peak	(line 13 to line 14)	+0.13	+0.18	+0.20
22. Peak to trough	(line 14 to line 15)	−0.22	−0.34	−0.58
23. Trough to peak	(line 15 to line 16)	+0.15	+0.79	+0.93
D. CHANGES BETWEEN SUCCESSIVE PHASES				
24. Trough to trough	(line 17 to line 18)	−0.30	−0.08	−0.28
25. Peak to peak	(line 18 to line 19)	+0.38	+0.10	+0.40
26. Trough to trough	(line 19 to line 20)	−0.53	−0.19	−0.68
27. Peak to peak	(line 20 to line 21)	+0.42	+0.18	+0.54
28. Trough to trough	(line 21 to line 22)	−0.35	−0.52	−0.78
29. Peak to peak	(line 22 to line 23)	+0.37	+1.13	+1.51

In this and the following tables and accompanying charts, the title dates cover the earliest and latest years in the moving averages underlying the computations.

The turning points are dated by inspection of Chart 4 and the underlying series.

Entries in parentheses, here and in the following tables, are alternative estimates, shown because there is no clear indication of when a given phase ends and another begins.

SOURCE: The series used are the five-year moving averages of population from Table R-37 and the underlying annual estimates. For the years beyond 1939 for which no five-year averages are available we used the estimates for 1940, 1945, 1950, and 1955 given in the paper referred to in text footnote 4. The entries in lines 9 to 16 are changes between moving averages (or single years) ten years apart, centered in the middle of the decade. Entries in lines 24 to 29 are derived directly from those in lines 17 to 23.

Two further findings of interest are suggested by the entries in Table 59. First, the amplitude of the swings has increased, and more substantially than the base. Thus for total population the differential movement (part D) was at the rate of some 0.3 or 0.4 million per year (3 or 4 million per decade), when additions were between 10 and 13 million per decade—a ratio of about a third. In the last two swings, the differential amplitude was at a rate of either 8 or 15 million per decade and the average additions were between 10 and 24 million—ratios of from 0.6 to 0.8 and far higher than those for the earliest swings.

Second, the relative contributions of the foreign born white and the native born components to the long swings in additions to total population have shifted continuously. The differential amplitude in additions to native population relative to that in additions to foreign born white population rose steadily—from about one-fourth to over three times the latter (lines 24 and 29). To put it differently, before the 1920's the long swings in additions to the foreign born white population accounted for most of the long swings in additions to total population, and after the 1920's the relationship was reversed—long swings in additions to native born population dominating the swings in total population growth.

Above all, it must be stressed that these long up-and-down movements in additions to this country's population have not been due exclusively to the long swings in immigration. The rate of natural increase of the native born, i.e., if we disregard the direct effects of immigration, appears to be subject to long swings reflected largely in the birth rates. In other words, conditions that produced the movements in immigration produced similar movements (although of narrower amplitude) in the number of native born children of native born parents. These swings in native births to native born parents have certainly been the dominating component in recent swings in additions to total population, and they were not insignificant even before World War I.

Another aspect of population movements to consider here is internal migration within the country—shifts in residence, particularly long term rather than brief and temporary. Population may be constant in numbers but, if there are extensive shifts in residence, the demand for housing will grow in areas that gain from internal migration, even though there may be unoccupied houses in areas that lose. Internal migration may thus have an effect on demand for residential construction and related facilities not unlike that of additions to total population, especially if the movement is from areas of low capital investment per head (as the countryside) to high (as urban communities). Likewise, if internal migration is a response to differential economic opportunities it may be tantamount to an increase in the supply of labor, since labor is flowing to higher-income and, presumably, more productive uses. In this sense, too, internal migration may be like net additions to population, in that it contributes to an increase in the effective labor supply.

The available data permit estimates of internal migration in the United States only for the native born, for the approximate decade intervals between the successive population censuses. Furthermore, the estimates show only the net surviving balance of migrants, not the total migration into and out of various areas within the country. It is impossible here to describe the calculations in detail.[6] For interstate migration the general procedure was to allow for the deaths of native born in a given decade for each state, for whites and nonwhites separately, by age and sex, and compare the number of survivors with the number shown in the state at the next census. The difference is the number of survivors of the total to-and-fro migration that occurred over the period, on the valid assumption that few native born left the country. For the rural-urban migration the general procedure was to assume, quite crudely, that the natural increase in native born over the census interval was the same for the rural and urban populations enumerated at the beginning of each census decade. The application of that rate of increase to the rural and urban bases separately shows the deficiency in the rural population matched by the excess in the urban, and the deficiency was used as an approximation to the rural-urban net migration.

Both types of estimates understate the volume of internal migration by substantial fractions. The first, interstate migration, omits all migration within state boundaries. It is a measure of net shift, whereas a measure of gross in-migration to an area and one for the offseting out migration would have been far more useful. The second, rural-urban migration, is an understatement because the true rates of natural increase tend to be significantly higher for the rural than for the urban sector, and because migration within the rural and, more importantly,

[6] See the parts dealing with population redistribution in *Population Redistribution and Economic Growth, United States, 1870–1950*, Vol. I, by E. S. Lee, A. R. Miller, C. P. Brainerd, and R. A. Easterlin, prepared under the direction of Simon Kuznets and Dorothy S. Thomas (Memoirs Volume 45, American Philosophical Society, 1957).

within the urban is not recorded. Understatement of the volume of internal migration is probably accompanied by an understatement of the amplitude of any long swings in that volume, not only because long, decadal intervals are used, but also because some of the more sensitive components of migration are not properly reflected.

CHART 5

Decadal Additions to Total Population Compared with Internal Migration of Native Born Per Decade, 1869–1955

a   Additions to total population
b   Interstate migration, native born
c   Rural-urban migration, native born
d   Total internal migration, native born (b+c)

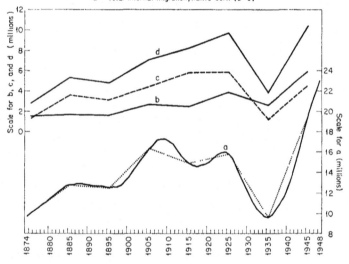

These qualifications must be kept in mind when we compare internal migration with additions to total population (Chart 5). Internal migration (lines *b*, *c*, and *d*) had to be plotted in decadal units (with pro rata adjustments for the slight inequalities in the census decade intervals); and for additions to total population (line *a*), we added the line connecting the mid-points of the decadal intervals.

It is immediately apparent that even these rough measures of internal migration are subject to long swings, synchronous, on the whole, with those in additions to total population. There is one exception: during the decade including World War I, when additions to total population declined, the volume of rural-urban migration increased—an expected and easily explained difference in movement. The impact of a great war, with the shift in production and population induced by military production and mobilization, intensifies internal migration, regardless of the movement in additions to total population. If the decade including World War II had fallen in the downward phase of a long swing in total population growth (as did the decade including World War I), we might have observed a second exception. But as the record stands, the synchronism appears significant.

As already indicated, our internal migration measures relate to native born population alone, while additions to total population include foreign born, and in fact the earlier long swings in total population were dominated by the long swings in immigration. Hence, in summary of the finding in Chart 5, the conditions that increased or retarded the pace of immigration and of additions to total population also increased or retarded the pace of internal migration of the native born population (largely adult, because the proportion of infant migrants is exceedingly low).

The comparison of internal migration with total additions to population is given in Table 60. The entries are for intercensal intervals, adjusted, when necessary, to precise decades.

Obviously, there is some overlap between interstate and rural-urban migration. Movement from one state to another may involve a shift from a rural to an urban area and, to that extent, adding the two totals leads to duplication. On the other hand since, for reasons indicated, each measure understates the true migration by a substantial fraction, there is little doubt that even the total of the two is an underestimate of the amount of net nontransient internal migration of the native born in each decade.

It is this observation that makes column 4 so impressive. Even these underestimates of decadal migration range from almost three-tenths to over six-tenths of the total additions to population. And I would not be surprised if the true volume of nontransient migration during any decade was at least equal to the total additions to population.

Several other findings are suggested by Table 60. (1) As part C shows, the changes between successive decades in total internal migration (column 4) and in interstate migration (column 2)—but not in rural-urban migration (column 3), because of the effect of World War I—are synchronous with changes in additions to total population (column 1). (2) The amplitude of long swings in internal migration is

TABLE 60

Additions to Total Population Compared with
Internal Migration of Native Born, 1869–1952
(numbers in millions)

| | Additions to Total Population (1) | *Native Born Migration* | | |
		Interstate (2)	Rural-Urban (3)	Total Internal (2) + (3) (4)
A. VOLUMES PER DECADE				
1. 1870–1880	10.0	1.52	1.30	2.82
2. 1880–1890	12.8	1.72	3.58	5.30
3. 1890–1900	12.5	1.64	3.13	4.77
4. 1900–1910	16.3	2.70	4.38	7.08
5. 1910–1920	14.9	2.48	5.78	8.26
6. 1920–1930	15.8	3.90	5.83	9.73
7. 1930–1940	9.6	2.63	1.26	3.89
8. 1940–1950	19.4	5.88	4.52	10.40
B. INTERDECADE CHANGES, SUCCESSIVE PHASES				
9. Line 1 to line 2	2.8	0.20	2.28	2.48
10. Line 2 to line 3	−0.3	−0.08	−0.45	−0.53
11. Line 3 to line 4	3.8	1.06	1.25	2.31
12. Line 4 to line 5	−1.4	−0.22	1.40	1.18
13. Line 5 to line 6	0.9	1.42	0.05	1.47
14. Line 6 to line 7	−6.2	−1.27	−4.57	−5.84
15. Line 7 to line 8	9.8	3.25	3.26	6.51
C. CHANGES BETWEEN SUCCESSIVE PHASES				
16. Line 9 to line 10	−3.1	−0.28	−2.73	−3.01
17. Line 10 to line 11	+4.1	+1.14	+1.70	+2.84
18. Line 11 to line 12	−5.2	−1.28	+0.15	−1.13
19. Line 12 to line 13	+2.3	+1.64	−1.35	+0.29
20. Line 13 to line 14	−7.1	−2.69	−4.62	−7.31
21. Line 14 to line 15	+16.0	+4.52	+7.83	+12.35

Source, by Column

(1) Calculated from the five-year averages in Table R-37. For line 1, the entry was calculated as the difference between the five-year average centered at 1880 and the three-year average for 1869–1871, centered at 1870.

(2) Calculated from the study referred to in text footnote 6. Entries cover native white (from Table 1.11) and Negroes or nonwhites (from Table 1.14).

(3) Calculated from *ibid.*, Table P-4B, by method described in the text. Entries cover native whites and Negroes.

quite wide—indeed, wider on a relative basis than that in additions to total population (columns 4 and 1 in part C compared with the same columns in part A). With additions to total population running from about 1.6 to 3.5 times as large as total internal migration, the same relative amplitude of long swings should yield for column 4 of part C entries about three-tenths or six-tenths of those in column 1. Instead, the differential change for internal migration is in two cases (lines 16 and 20) either larger than or close to that in additions to total population; and in two other cases (lines 17 and 21), from about seven-tenths to over three-quarters as large. When population growth accelerates or decelerates, the volume of internal migration is affected even more, relatively.

Population and Capital Formation

Additions to population and its redistribution within the country obviously have far-reaching effects, direct and indirect, on the volume and structure of economic activity. Residential construction and many related types of capital formation are directly affected. True, the gross volume of residential construction is influenced even on the demand side by needs for replacement and by rising standards of living. On the supply side, in addition to the lag in the building industry's response to deficits and surpluses in supply, there are speculative excesses and financial ups and downs. Yet one may reasonably assume that population growth and internal migration are the major direct forces, and that long swings in population growth are probably followed by long swings in the volume of residential construction and related capital formation components.

This assumption provides the rationale for Chart 6, in which we compare decadal additions to total population, as plotted in Charts 4 and 5, with corresponding totals in the two long series (among the few available to us) that might be said to represent population-sensitive capital formation—nonfarm residential construction, and gross capital expenditures (construction and equipment) by railroads, both in 1929 prices. (If our long series were more detailed, we might have been able to distinguish within capital formation other population-sensitive components, particularly within the large, miscellaneous "other" construction.) We assumed that railroad capital expenditures would be directly affected by population growth, and particularly by internal migration because expenditures for new construction and equipment would be responsive to demands created by additional population, in the country as a whole and in areas gaining rapidly from internal migration. Conversely, once railroad construction was accelerated, it would in turn affect internal migration.

In Chart 6 the decadal volumes of gross nonfarm residential construction and of railroad construction and equipment expenditures are

CHART 6

Decadal Levels of Population-Sensitive Gross Capital Formation, 1929 Prices, Compared with Decadal Additions to Population, 1869–1955

a   Additions to population
b   Capital expenditures by railroads
c   Nonfarm residential construction
d   Population-sensitive capital formation (b+c)

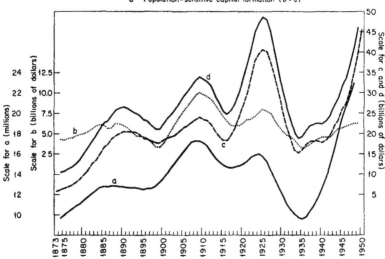

compared with decadal additions to total population. More logically, net totals of capital formation might have been compared with net additions to population, but the former are estimated by deducting from the gross totals a rather approximate estimate of depreciation, and in trying to establish long swings, there is some advantage in using series that are not affected too much by crude statistical approximations. Needless to say, the long swings in the net volumes of nonfarm residential construction and of railroad capital expenditures would be even more marked than those in the gross series, and would perhaps have slightly earlier turning points.

The decadal totals of the capital formation components in Chart 6 are centered in the fifth year. Thus, additions to population from 1869 to 1879 inclusive, centered in 1874, are plotted against total nonfarm residential construction covering the years 1870 through 1879, centered in 1874. Because the population totals are mid-year figures, the exact center of the ten-year interval falls in the middle of 1874. Because the capital formation figures are for calendar years, the exact center of the ten-year period falls at the end of 1874. As plotted in Chart 6, the series allow for a lag of one-half year in capital formation behind the additions to population.

The series are statistically independent. The estimates of nonfarm residential construction for the years since 1884 are based largely on building permits and, for the earlier years, on crude breakdowns between residential and other construction, with the over-all construction totals derived largely from the flow of construction materials into domestic use. The capital expenditures by railroads were estimated on the basis of a large sample of reports by individual railroads. And the total additions to population are based on the decennial censuses and their age, sex, and other breakdowns.[7]

Both nonfarm residential construction and capital expenditures by railroads are subject to long swings, approximately the same in timing and duration as the long swings in additions to total population. The existence of these long up-and-down movements has been fairly firmly established, and is discussed in detail in the Grebler and Ulmer monographs.

The statistical measures relating to these swings in what we term population-sensitive capital formation are assembled in Table 61. The following findings are clearly indicated:

1. The timing of the long swings in nonfarm residential construction and in railroad capital expenditures is quite similar to that in the long swings in additions to population. During the nineteenth century, the turning points in the capital formation series tended to lag (see lines 2 and 3) (if there was such a lag in the 1870's, the record does not go back far enough to permit us to see it). The residential con-

---

[7] For details on the construction series, see Leo Grebler, David M. Blank, and Louis Winnick, *Capital Formation in Residential Real Estate: Trends and Prospects* (Princeton for NBER, 1956), pp. 34–37, and Appendixes A to F, pp. 327–386. The present study should also be consulted, particularly the notes to Tables R-14 and R-15, column 1, and Table R-30, columns 1 and 6. For the railroad series and its derivation, see Melville J. Ulmer, *Capital in Transportation, Communications, and Public Utilities: Its Formation and Financing* (Princeton for NBER, 1960), Appendixes A and C.

TABLE 61

TIMING AND AMPLITUDE OF LONG SWINGS IN ADDITIONS TO POPULATION AND IN
POPULATION-SENSITIVE CAPITAL FORMATION, 1869–1955
(numbers in millions; amounts in billions of dollars, in 1929 prices)

		Additions to Population (1)	Gross Nonfarm Residential Construction (2)	Gross Capital Expenditures by Railroads (3)	Gross Population-Sensitive Capital Formation (2) + (3) (4)
A. DATES OF TURNING POINTS					
1. First trough [a]		1874	1874	1875	1874
2. Peak		1888 (1885)	1890	1889	1890
3. Trough		1895 (1897)	1899	1899	1899
4. Peak		1909	1909	1909	1909
5. Trough		1917	1916	1918	1916
6. Peak		1924	1925	1925	1925
7. Trough		1935	1934	1935	1934
8. Peak [b]		1948	1948	1948	1948
B. VOLUMES PER DECADE AT DATES INDICATED					
9. First trough	(line 1)	9.7	6.2	4.2	10.5
10. Peak	(line 2)	12.9 (12.8)	20.6	6.2	26.6
11. Trough	(line 3)	12.5 (12.6)	17.7	3.3	21.0
12. Peak	(line 4)	17.3	23.9	10.0	33.9
13. Trough	(line 5)	14.6	18.3	5.9	24.8
14. Peak	(line 6)	16.0	40.7	8.0	48.7
15. Trough	(line 7)	9.6	15.2	3.2	18.8
16. Peak	(line 8)	23.0	34.9	6.3	41.2
C. CHANGES PER YEAR DURING SUCCESSIVE PHASES					
17. Trough to peak	(line 9 to line 10)	+0.23 (0.28)	+0.90	+0.14	+1.01
18. Peak to trough	(line 10 to line 11)	−0.06 (−0.02)	−0.32	−0.29	−0.62
19. Trough to peak	(line 11 to line 12)	+0.34	+0.62	+0.67	+1.29
20. Peak to trough	(line 12 to line 13)	−0.34	−0.80	−0.46	−1.30
21. Trough to peak	(line 13 to line 14)	+0.20	+2.49	+0.30	+2.66
22. Peak to trough	(line 14 to line 15)	−0.58	−2.83	−0.48	−3.32
23. Trough to peak	(line 15 to line 16)	+1.03	+1.41	+0.24	+1.60
D. CHANGES BETWEEN SUCCESSIVE PHASES					
24. Trough to trough	(line 17 to line 18)	−0.29	−1.22	−0.43	−1.63
25. Peak to peak	(line 18 to line 19)	+0.40	+0.94	+0.96	+1.91
26. Trough to trough	(line 19 to line 20)	−0.68	−1.42	−1.13	−2.59
27. Peak to peak	(line 20 to line 21)	+0.54	+3.29	+0.76	+3.96
28. Trough to trough	(line 21 to line 22)	−0.78	−5.32	−0.78	−5.98
29. Peak to peak	(line 22 to line 23)	+1.61	+4.24	+0.72	+4.92

Because of rounding, detail will not necessarily add to total.

[a] For first year included in all series.

[b] For last year included in all series.

Population Growth and Countrywide Aggregates

NOTES TO TABLE 61

SOURCE, BY COLUMN

(1) See notes to Table 59.

(2) Ten-year moving totals calculated from the annual series underlying Table R-30. The totals are centered in the fifth year.

(3) Ten-year moving totals calculated from the annual series given through 1950 in Melville J. Ulmer, *Capital in Transportation, Communications, and Public Utilities: Its Formation and Financing* (Princeton for NBER, 1960), Table C-1, col. 4, p. 257. Ulmer's series on gross capital expenditures in current prices was extrapolated through 1954 by expenditures for new plant and equipment by railroads (*Statistical Abstract of the United States, 1956*, p. 498). His index of cost of road and equipment was extrapolated by the index implicit in railroad construction (*ibid.*, pp. 757 and 758). From these two series it was possible to calculate an extension of the 1929 price series on gross capital expenditures.

struction estimates before 1889 are rather crude, but the series on railroad capital expenditures is not. Offhand one might expect a lag in the response of construction and capital equipment expenditures to population increase, but its length would depend upon conditions of the productive system over the period—with which we are not familiar.

2. The amplitude of the long swings in both residential construction and railroad capital expenditures is far wider than the amplitude of the swings in additions to total population. This is not unexpected because increase in numbers is only one of several temporally correlated factors (internal migration, per capita income changes, and others) that would produce long swings in residential construction and in railroad capital expenditures.

3. The amplitude of the long swings in the capital formation components would have been far wider had we used net rather than gross volumes.

4. The amplitude of those long swings, relative to the average volume, widened over the period, as did the amplitude of long swings in additions to population. While this finding should be qualified in view of the crudity of the estimates of nonfarm residential construction during the first two decades, it has been established over the shorter period in the Grebler monograph, and merits consideration at least as a tentative finding.

5. Association in time is not causation, and the association found is no proof that the swings in population growth and internal migration produce swings in residential and railroad construction. Indeed, it may well be that other factors produce at the same time swings in population growth and internal migration, as well as those in residential and railroad construction; and that if the former swings induced the latter

swings the lags would have been longer and the synchronism less conspicuous. The mechanism of connection is still to be explored.

We now turn to the other components of capital formation and ask how they move when the population-sensitive components display long swings of rather wide amplitude that are synchronous with the long swings in population growth and in internal migration. The answer to this question is provided in Chart 7, in which the successive ten-year totals of population-sensitive capital formation are plotted alongside ten-year totals of residual (that is, "other") capital formation, the latter including or excluding government. The residual is a miscellaneous category which, in line *b* comprises "other" construction including government, "other" producers' durable equipment including munitions, changes in inventories, and changes in claims against foreign

CHART 7

Population-Sensitive Capital Formation Compared with Other Gross Capital Formation and Other Private Gross Capital Formation, Decadal Levels in 1929 Prices, 1870–1954

a Population-sensitive capital formation
b Other gross capital formation
c Other private gross capital formation

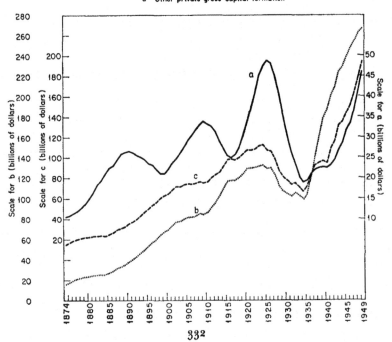

countries. In line *c* government is excluded and we deal with "other" private capital formation alone, i.e., a sum of "other" private construction, "other" producers' durables exclusive of munitions, changes in inventories, and changes in foreign claims. In both cases there is a *semblance* of negative association until the 1920's, and positive association thereafter between long swings in population-sensitive capital formation and in "other" capital formation.

Table 62 provides a check on this impression. Here we record the standings, changes per year during successive phases, and differential changes between successive phases for total and other capital formation, during the phases of long swings in population-sensitive capital formation. To use the National Bureau terminology, we employ the dates of turning points in long swings in population-sensitive capital formation as a reference chronology for observing changes in total and private gross capital formation (columns 2 and 4) and other capital formation, inclusive and exclusive of government (columns 3 and 5). By comparing column 1 with columns 3 and 5, lines 16 to 19, we find that through the first four swings (trough to trough and peak to peak) the differential change in other capital formation moved inversely to the differential change in population-sensitive capital formation. This suggests that when population-sensitive capital formation was increasing more rapidly, other capital formation was increasing less rapidly, and vice versa. It suggests also that there were limits to total capital formation with the result that acceleration (or deceleration) in the population-sensitive components left so much less (or so much more) room for the growth of other capital formation. This restraining influence of a limit on total capital formation appears to have been removed in the 1920's, and synchronism has prevailed since then.[8]

---

[8] This is only one possible interpretation, for much depends upon the mechanism of response. In his comments on this chapter, Abramovitz argued an alternative interpretation, based largely upon a positive association between population-sensitive and other capital formation, with a long lag (not assumed here) of the population-sensitive components behind other capital formation, particularly at the peak. In other words, with other capital formation more closely keyed to the rate of change in output and income than are the population-sensitive components (which are more closely associated with population growth), the negative association observed before World War I may have arisen because the rate of growth of output reached its peaks and troughs long before population growth did, and because of the sluggish response of railroad construction and house building to deficits and surpluses in the supply of railroad facilities and houses.

At the present juncture, we cannot say which interpretation is the more likely. But the point to be stressed here is that, given the possibility of varying leads and lags among the variables in the response of one to the other (for instance, of resi-

TABLE 62

<small>Changes in Population-Sensitive and Other Gross Capital Formation during Phases of Long Swings in Population-Sensitive Capital Formation, 1870–1954</small>

(billions of dollars, in 1929 prices)

		Gross Capital Formation			
	Population-Sensitive (1)	Total Including Military (2)	Other (2) − (1) (3)	Total Private (4)	Other Private (4) − (1) (5)
A. VOLUMES PER DECADE AT DATES OF TURNING POINTS IN COLUMN 1					
1. Trough, 1874	10.5	26.6	16.1	25.3	14.8
2. Peak, 1890	26.6	64.4	37.8	61.5	34.9
3. Trough, 1899	21.0	88.6	67.6	83.9	62.9
4. Peak, 1909	33.9	118.3	84.4	108.7	74.8
5. Trough, 1916	24.8	142.0	117.2	122.4	97.6
6. Peak, 1925	48.7	177.5	128.8	155.7	107.0
7. Trough, 1934	18.8	118.0	99.2	85.1	66.3
8. Peak, 1948	41.2	302.5	261.3	219.8	178.6
B. CHANGES PER YEAR DURING SUCCESSIVE PHASES					
9. Trough to peak (line 1 to line 2)	+1.01	+2.36	+1.36	+2.26	+1.26
10. Peak to trough (line 2 to line 3)	−0.62	+2.69	+3.31	+2.49	+3.11
11. Trough to peak (line 3 to line 4)	+1.29	+2.97	+1.68	+2.48	+1.19
12. Peak to trough (line 4 to line 5)	−1.30	+3.39	+4.69	+1.96	+3.26
13. Trough to peak (line 5 to line 6)	+2.66	+3.94	+1.29	+3.70	+1.04
14. Peak to trough (line 6 to line 7)	−3.32	−6.61	−3.29	−7.84	−4.52
15. Trough to peak (line 7 to line 8)	+1.60	+13.18	+11.58	+9.62	+8.02
C. CHANGES BETWEEN SUCCESSIVE PHASES					
16. Trough to trough (line 9 to line 10)	−1.63	+0.33	+1.95	+0.23	+1.85
17. Peak to peak (line 10 to line 11)	+1.91	+0.28	−1.63	−0.01	−1.92
18. Trough to trough (line 11 to line 12)	−2.59	+0.42	+3.01	−0.52	+2.07
19. Peak to peak (line 12 to line 13)	+3.96	+0.55	−3.40	+1.74	−2.22
20. Trough to trough (line 13 to line 14)	−5.98	−10.55	−4.58	−11.54	−5.56
21. Peak to peak (line 14 to line 15)	+4.92	+19.79	+14.87	+17.46	+12.54

SOURCE, BY COLUMN

(1) See Table 61, col. 4.
(2) Ten-year moving totals, calculated from the annual series underlying Table R-29, centered on fifth year.
(4) Col. 2 minus ten-year moving totals of government construction and munitions, calculated from the annual series underlying Table R-30, or given in Table R-7.

Population Growth and Countrywide Aggregates

To test the probability of the inverse correlation in long swings between population-sensitive and other capital formation, we first distinguish the major subcomponents of other capital formation and observe the characteristics of their long swings. In Chart 8 we have the

CHART 8

Decadal Levels of Components of Private Gross Capital Formation Other Than
Population-Sensitive, 1929 Prices, 1869–1955

a Private gross capital formation other than population-sensitive
b Net changes in inventories
c Net changes in foreign claims
d "Other" private gross capital formation excluding net changes in
inventories and foreign claims [a−(b+c)]

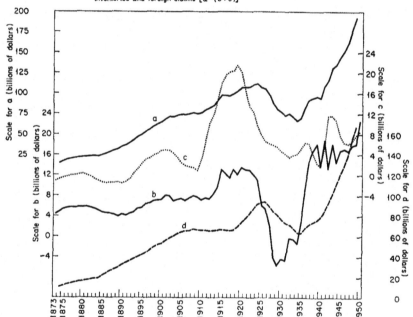

successive decade totals, in 1929 prices, for private gross capital formation excluding nonfarm residential construction and railroad capital expenditures; other private construction plus other private producers'

dential construction to population growth), an interpretation of the association in movements over time depends upon the lead and lag allowed. If time discrepancies in response are substantial, synchronism may in fact mean absence, rather than presence, of significant association. This problem is particularly acute with long-term changes, because the time variance of the leads and lags can be much wider than in the short-term fluctuations associated with business cycles.

TABLE 63

TIMING AND AMPLITUDE OF LONG SWINGS IN COMPONENTS OF GROSS CAPITAL FORMATION OTHER THAN POPULATION-SENSITIVE, 1869–1955

(billions of dollars, in 1929 prices)

	Gross Capital Formation Other Than Population-Sensitive				
	Total (1)	Private (2)	Private Construction and Producers' Durables (3)	Net Changes in Inventories (4)	Net Changes in Foreign Claims (5)
A. DATES OF TURNING POINTS					
1. First peak	1877	1876	1876	1881	1880
2. Trough	1884	1884	1884	1889	1890
3. Peak	1902	1902	1906 (1908)	1901	1901
4. Trough	1909	1909	1917	1912	1909
5. Peak	1924	1924	1926	1920	1919
6. Trough	1934	1934	1935	1929	1932 (1940)
7. Peak (for last year included in all series)	1948	1948	1948	1941	1942
B. VOLUMES PER DECADE AT DATES INDICATED					
8. Peak (line 1)	21.4	18.7	13.3	5.87	0.22
9. Trough (line 2)	25.4	23.1	19.1	3.97	−1.63
10. Peak (line 3)	77.2	71.3	64.8 (66.7)	8.07	4.89
11. Trough (line 4)	84.4	74.8	65.4	7.30	0.92

336

			(1)	(2)	(3)	(4)	(5)
12.	Peak	(line 5)	131.9	111.9	93.5	13.47	21.56
13.	Trough	(line 6)	99.2	66.3	63.1	−5.74	3.54 (1.57)
14.	Peak	(line 7)	261.3	178.6	154.2	18.72	11.52

C. CHANGES PER YEAR DURING SUCCESSIVE PHASES

			(1)	(2)	(3)	(4)	(5)
15.	Peak to trough	(line 8 to line 9)	+0.57	+0.55	+0.72	−0.24	−0.18
16.	Trough to peak	(line 9 to line 10)	+2.88	+2.68	+2.08 (+1.98)	+0.34	+0.59
17.	Peak to trough	(line 10 to line 11)	+1.03	+0.50	+0.05 (−0.14)	−0.07	−0.50
18.	Trough to peak	(line 11 to line 12)	+3.17	+2.47	+3.12	+0.77	+2.06
19.	Peak to trough	(line 12 to line 13)	−3.27	−4.56	−3.38	−2.13	−1.39 (−0.95)
20.	Trough to peak	(line 13 to line 14)	+11.58	+8.02	+7.01	+2.04	+0.80

D. CHANGES BETWEEN SUCCESSIVE PHASES

			(1)	(2)	(3)	(4)	(5)
21.	Peak to peak	(line 15 to line 16)	+2.31	+2.13	+1.36 (+1.26)	+0.58	+0.77
22.	Trough to trough	(line 16 to line 17)	−1.85	−2.18	−2.03 (−2.12)	−0.41	−1.09
23.	Peak to peak	(line 17 to line 18)	+2.14	+1.97	+3.07	+0.84	+2.56
24.	Trough to trough	(line 18 to line 19)	−6.44	−7.03	−6.50	−2.90	−3.45 (−3.01)
25.	Peak to peak	(line 19 to line 20)	+14.85	+12.58	+10.39	+4.17	+2.19

SOURCE, BY COLUMN

(1) Calculated from the sources and by the procedure shown for Table 62, col. 3.

(2) Calculated from the sources and by the procedure shown for Table 62, col. 5.

(3) Series underlying col. 2 minus series underlying cols. 4 and 5.

(4) and (5) Based on ten-year moving totals calculated from the annual series underlying Table R-34, centered on fifth year.

durables; net changes in inventories; and net changes in claims against foreign countries.

On the whole, the dating of the long swings in these four totals is fairly similar. Of particular interest are the prominent swings in the net changes in claims against foreign countries, a series that is statistically independent of the others and has an adequate basis. The series on net changes in inventories is less significant, because before 1919 it was estimated largely as a function of changes in total commodity flow. All one can say about it is that if changes in inventories can reasonably be estimated as such a function, the timing of their long swings is fairly similar to that of the long swings in net changes in foreign claims and in other private capital formation. The series on other construction and producers' durables (line *d*), quantitatively a major component of total or of private capital formation, shows swings that are a bit different in timing from the others—reaching a peak late rather than early in the first decade of this century. But the similarity of long swings in the several totals—excluding government construction and munitions which we would not expect to follow the same pattern—is clear.

Table 63 presents the usual measures of the long swings for the four totals in Chart 8 and, in addition, for the widest total of "other" capital formation—gross, including government. It indicates the rather marked amplitude of the long swings, not only in the net change components (inventories and foreign claims), but also in the gross components in column 3. And it shows, particularly in parts A and D, that, given the rough similarity in dating of the long swings, there is a fair correlation among the long swings in the components of other capital formation. Long swings with approximately the same dating can be found in all of them.

In our final test of the probability of the inverse correlation in long swings between population-sensitive and "other" capital formation, we turn to Table 64. Here we use the dates of turning points of the long swings in population-sensitive capital formation as a reference chronology (as in Table 62) and measure standings and changes for the resulting reference phases in the total and the three components of other private capital formation (excluding the government component, because it may be affected by many other factors).

In lines 16 to 19, we would expect to find a series of +, −, +, −, an exact inversion of the sequence of differential changes between successive phases of population-sensitive capital formation (which runs

TABLE 64

CHANGES IN COMPONENTS OF PRIVATE GROSS CAPITAL FORMATION OTHER THAN
POPULATION-SENSITIVE DURING PHASES OF LONG SWINGS IN
POPULATION-SENSITIVE CAPITAL FORMATION, 1870–1954

(billions of dollars, in 1929 prices)

		Private Gross Capital Formation Other Than Population-Sensitive		
	Total (1)	Construction and Producers' Durables (2)	Net Changes in Inventories (3)	Net Changes in Foreign Claims (4)

A. VOLUMES PER DECADE AT DATES OF TURNING POINTS IN POPULATION-SENSITIVE CAPITAL FORMATION				
1. First trough, 1874	14.8	10.7	4.9	−0.8
2. Peak, 1890	34.9	32.2	4.3	−1.6
3. Trough, 1899	62.9	51.5	7.1	4.2
4. Peak, 1909	74.8	66.2	7.7	0.9
5. Trough, 1916	97.6	65.8	12.2	19.6
6. Peak, 1925	107.0	92.9	6.2	8.0
7. Trough, 1934	66.3	63.5	−1.4	4.1
8. Peak, 1948	178.6	154.2	17.7	6.6

B. CHANGES PER YEAR DURING SUCCESSIVE PHASES				
9. Trough to peak (line 1 to line 2)	+1.26	+1.34	−0.04	−0.05
10. Peak to trough (line 2 to line 3)	+3.11	+2.14	+0.31	+0.64
11. Trough to peak (line 3 to line 4)	+1.19	+1.47	+0.06	−0.33
12. Peak to trough (line 4 to line 5)	+3.26	−0.06	+0.64	+2.67
13. Trough to peak (line 5 to line 6)	+1.04	+3.01	−0.67	−1.29
14. Peak to trough (line 6 to line 7)	−4.52	−3.27	−0.84	−0.43
15. Trough to peak (line 7 to line 8)	+8.02	+6.48	+1.36	+0.18

C. CHANGES BETWEEN SUCCESSIVE PHASES				
16. Trough to trough (line 9 to line 10)	+1.85	+0.80	+0.35	+0.69
17. Peak to peak (line 10 to line 11)	−1.92	−0.67	−0.25	−0.97
18. Trough to trough (line 11 to line 12)	+2.07	−1.53	+0.58	+3.00
19. Peak to peak (line 12 to line 13)	−2.22	+3.07	−1.31	−3.96
20. Trough to trough (line 13 to line 14)	−5.56	−6.28	−0.17	+0.86
21. Peak to peak (line 14 to line 15)	+12.54	+9.75	+2.20	+0.61

Because of rounding, detail will not necessarily add to total.

For dates of turning points, see Table 61, col. 4. For source, see notes to Table 63, cols. 2, 3, 4, and 5, respectively.

−, +, −, +). We do find such complete negative association for net changes in inventories and net changes in claims against foreign countries (columns 3 and 4). Before the 1920's, upswings in population-sensitive capital formation were accompanied by downswings in inventory accumulation and in capital exports (upswings in capital imports); and, conversely, downswings in population-sensitive capital formation were accompanied by upswings in inventory accumulation and in capital exports (downswings in capital imports). Of these associations the most interesting is that with capital imports. When population-sensitive capital formation was in the up-phase of the long swing—presumably in response to an upswing in immigration, native population growth, and internal migration—capital imports were also in the up-phase of the long swing; and the same association persisted in the downswing.

The results for other private construction and producers' durables are not so clear (lines 16 to 19, column 2). There are only two agreements out of the four expected, and the case of negative association is not proved as it stands. But one qualification of this finding must be taken into consideration. Nonfarm residential construction and capital expenditures by railroads are not the only components of capital formation that can be regarded as directly and positively affected by additions to population and by internal migration. There are a variety of others—construction of stores, local transportation facilities, service establishments, and so on—which, being directly geared to the provision of services to ultimate consumers, could be expected to reflect the long swings in the additions to population and in the extent of migration to new areas. All these population-sensitive components of capital formation are included in the category labeled "other" private construction and producers' durables (column 2 of Table 64). This, therefore, is a mixed category, and may include substantial components whose long swings are positively, rather than negatively, associated with the long swings in population growth. If we could draw a finer line of distinction, and remove more of the population-sensitive components, column 2 might show the same sequence of signs in lines 16 through 19 as columns 3 and 4 show, indicating negative association with the measures for additions to population.

We conclude this section with the tentative findings that the long swings in additions to population and in internal migration are synchronous with long swings in population-sensitive components of capital formation (nonfarm residential construction and capital expenditures by railroads, which can be segregated in our estimates, and probably in several other components which cannot be segregated); until the 1920's these long swings in population growth and in population-sensitive capital formation are coterminous with *opposite* swings in "other" private capital formation (total, net changes in inventories, net changes in foreign claims, and possibly the "other" construction and producers' durables components). But the association between the long swings in population-sensitive and other capital formation shifted from negative to positive, beginning with the 1920's. This suggests that whatever factors tended to prevent synchronous acceleration in the population-sensitive and the other components of capital formation before the 1920's ceased to be operative after World War I.

Population Movements and Additions to Product

In the preceding discussion of the possible effects of long swings in population growth and internal migration on demand for certain population-sensitive components of capital formation, we found, in addition to the expected positive association, a negative association with long swings in "other" capital formation before the 1920's. The question naturally arises whether these associations have affected total output.

A first, rather tentative, answer to this question is suggested by the comparisons in Chart 9. Line *a* relates to private construction and producers' durables, excluding the population-sensitive components. This is a measure of gross additions to durable capital stock within the country, excluding stock serving primarily needs for housing and railroad transportation (its inclusion would not change the picture materially). We might have included also changes in inventories but, in view of the rough basis of the estimates before 1919, it seemed best to omit that component.

Line *b* measures decadal additions to the labor force. It would have been desirable to limit the series to additions to the labor force not engaged in nonfarm residential construction or in producing construction materials, but that was impossible with the existing data. Another desirable exclusion would have been the labor force engaged in provision of services not embodied in commodities. We can only hope that the long swings in the labor force excluding those engaged in construction, production of construction materials, and provision of serv-

CHART 9

Decadal Levels of Private Gross Construction and Producers' Durables Excluding Population-Sensitive Capital Formation, and Decadal Additions to Labor Force, Compared with Decadal Additions to Gross National Product Excluding Services, 1870–1955

a   Private gross construction and producers' durables excluding population-sensitive capital formation, 1929 prices
b   Additions to labor force
c   Additions to gross national product excluding services, 1929 prices

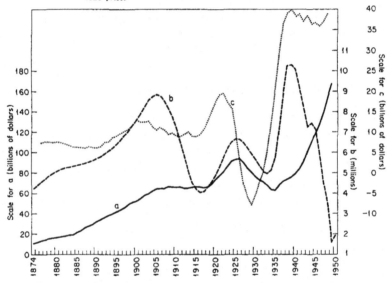

ices are not unlike the swings in the total labor force portrayed in Chart 9.

The two lines just described, which represent additions to factors of production, are compared with additions to gross national product excluding services (line c). Services are excluded because two major components are the net yield of residential housing, and government services (and we wish to exclude the latter from the analysis). The comparison is thus quite crude, and yet the results merit consideration.

There is fair consilience between the combined movements of "other" private durable capital formation and additions to the labor force, on the one hand, and additions to what might be called gross commodity product, on the other. There is a downswing in capital formation from the mid-1870's to the early 1880's, and in additions to the labor force from the late 1870's to the late 1880's; and there is a similar downswing in additions to gross commodity product from the late 1870's to the late 1880's. There is an upswing in capital formation from the early 1880's to about the middle of the first decade of the twentieth century, and an upswing in additions to the labor force from the late 1880's also to the middle of the first decade of this century; and an upswing in additions to commodity product from the late 1880's to about 1900. There follows a downswing in capital formation from about the middle of the first decade of this century to about 1917, and a marked downswing in additions to the labor force from about 1905 to about 1916; and a similar downswing in additions to gross commodity product from about 1900 to about 1915. Beyond World War I the similarity continues—provided we combine the movements of capital formation and additions to labor force.

The association just described is measured in Table 65 which records the standings, the changes per year during successive phases, and the differential changes between successive phases, for all the series during the phases of the long swings in additions to gross national product excluding services. Lines 16 to 21 are particularly instructive. If the changes in capital formation and labor are weighted equally (the latter should be given greater weight, but the labor force totals used here are more comprehensive than they should be for our purposes), the sum of the differential changes in columns 2 and 3 agrees in sign with those in column 1 in five out of six cases. The implication is that long swings in additions to gross national product, excluding services, are associated with long swings in private gross durable capital formation, excluding the population-sensitive components, and with long swings in additions to the labor force.

It should be remembered that long swings in additions to population were associated, at least until the 1920's, with opposite swings in capital formation other than population-sensitive. If this other capital formation contributed to swings in additions to commodity product (national, excluding services), there should have been, at least until the 1920's, a negative association between long swings in population growth and in additions to commodity product. This is confirmed, if only partly, in column 4 of Table 65, where we measure changes in additions to total population during phases of long swings in additions to commodity product. During the first two phases (lines 16 and 17), the differential change in long swings of population growth (column 4)

TABLE 65

Changes in Private Gross Construction and Producers' Durables Excluding Population-Sensitive Capital Formation, and in Additions to Labor Force Compared with Changes in Additions to Gross National Product Excluding Services during Phases of Long Swings in the Latter, 1870–1955

(dollars in billions, in 1929 prices; numbers in millions)

	Additions to GNP Excluding Services (1)	Private Gross Construction and Producers' Durables Excluding Population-Sensitive Capital Formation (2)	Additions to Labor Force (3)	Additions to Population (4)
A. VOLUMES PER DECADE AT DATES OF TURNING POINTS IN COLUMN 1				
1. First peak, 1880	7.46	15.8	5.07	11.5
2. Trough, 1890	6.09	32.2	5.68	12.8
3. Peak, 1900	12.85	52.6	7.61	13.6
4. Trough, 1915	8.88	66.4	4.19	14.9
5. Peak, 1922	19.60	81.6	5.78	15.7
6. Trough, 1929	−7.73	80.7	5.94	12.7
7. Peak, 1939	39.91	75.6	10.29	11.7
8. Trough[a] 1946	36.01	127.7	6.01	20.7

B. CHANGES PER YEAR DURING SUCCESSIVE PHASES

		(1)	(2)	(3)	(4)
9. Peak to trough	(line 1 to line 2)	−0.14	+1.64	+0.06	+0.13
10. Trough to peak	(line 2 to line 3)	+0.68	+2.04	+0.19	+0.08
11. Peak to trough	(line 3 to line 4)	−0.26	+0.92	−0.23	+0.09
12. Trough to peak	(line 4 to line 5)	+1.53	+2.17	+0.23	+0.11
13. Peak to trough	(line 5 to line 6)	−3.90	−0.13	+0.02	−0.43
14. Trough to peak	(line 6 to line 7)	+4.76	−0.51	+0.44	−0.10
15. Peak to trough	(line 7 to line 8)	−0.56	+7.44	−0.61	+1.29

C. CHANGES BETWEEN SUCCESSIVE PHASES

		(1)	(2)	(3)	(4)
16. Peak to peak	(line 9 to line 10)	+0.81	+0.40	+0.13	−0.05
17. Trough to trough	(line 10 to line 11)	−0.94	−1.12	−0.42	+0.01
18. Peak to peak	(line 11 to line 12)	+1.80	+1.25	+0.46	+0.02
19. Trough to trough	(line 12 to line 13)	−5.44	−2.30	−0.20	−0.54
20. Peak to peak	(line 13 to line 14)	+8.67	−0.38	+0.41	+0.33
21. Trough to trough	(line 14 to line 15)	−5.32	+7.95	−1.05	+1.39

[a] Last year included in all series.

SOURCE, BY COLUMN

(1) Changes between five-year moving averages ten years apart, centered on the fifth year. The averages are calculated from the annual estimates underlying the series in Tables R-26 and R-28.

(2) See Table 64, notes to col. 2.

(3) Changes between five-year moving averages ten years apart, centered in the middle of the decade. The averages are calculated from the annual estimates underlying the series in Table R-39.

(4) See Table 59, notes to col. 3.

bears a sign opposite to that for additions to commodity product (column 1). The correlation would be more significantly negative if column 1 were based on additions to commodity product per capita.

The associations indicated in Chart 9 and Table 65 suggest a mechanism by which long swings in population growth produced, at least before the 1920's, opposite swings in additions to product. The acceleration or retardation in growth of population numbers, by producing similar swings in population-sensitive capital formation, resulted in opposite swings in all other capital formation. At the same time, those swings in population growth, even if largely dominated by immigration, did not result immediately in similar swings in additions to the labor force. The reasons may be that there were other movements in labor force participation by the population already resident in the country, and also that—insofar as swings in population growth were produced by up-and-down movements in the rate of natural increase— additions to the labor force would come much later. Hence the inverted swings in other than population-sensitive capital formation, not offset by any positive swings in additions to the labor force, tended to produce swings in additions to product that were, until the 1920's, negatively associated with swings in population growth.

Another facet of this association is portrayed graphically in Chart 10. Here we have decadal additions to total population compared with decadal additions to flow of goods to consumers, total and per capita. All three measures are calculated in identical fashion—as changes between five-year moving averages, ten years apart, and centered in the middle of each decade interval.

Total flow of goods to consumers includes services not embodied in new commodities but does not include capital formation. In these two respects it differs from the gross commodity product changes plotted in Chart 9. But because flow of goods to consumers is such a large fraction of gross national product, and because the movement of services in the short run was estimated for the earlier years as a function of commodity movement, the movement of additions to total flow of goods to consumers in Chart 10 is more or less like that of additions to total commodity product in Chart 9. The similarity indicates that the factors suggested earlier as determinants of the long swings in additions to total commodity product also determine the long swings in additions to flow of goods to consumers. It is these factors that produce a semblance of negative association between long swings in population

CHART 10

Decadal Additions to Population Compared with Decadal Additions to Flow of Goods to Consumers, 1869–1955

a Additions to population
b Additions to flow of goods to consumers, 1929 prices
c Additions to flow of goods to consumers per capita, 1929 prices

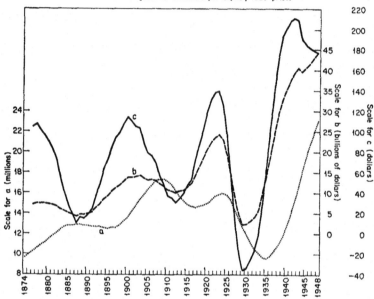

growth and those in additions to total flow of goods to consumers, until the period of World War I.

As a result, the long swings in additions to flow of consumer goods *per capita* are inverted to those in additions to population in the years before World War I—and quite prominent. Yet they suggest one explanation of the swings in additions to population, if we allow for a long lag that would, in a sense, turn negative into positive association. It must be remembered that an important component of additions to population was immigration. Immigration, particularly in its timing, could be assumed to be responsive to the pull—that is, largely to conditions in this country rather than in the country of origin. This assumption of responsiveness to the pull is clearly indicated by the fact that *net* additions were affected not only by gross inflow but also by emigration, which clearly reflected conditions in this country. It is indicated also by the fact that the long swings in emigration from various countries of origin were fairly similar.[9] One could, then, argue that a sizable reduction in additions to per capita flow of goods to consumers (with some lag), all other conditions being equal, would represent a discouragement to immigration, while a sizable rise in additions to per capita flow of goods to consumers would represent an encouragement. This is not to contend that additions to per capita

CHART 11

Decadal Additions to Population Compared with Decadal Levels of Unemployment and Bank Earnings Ratio, 1870–1955

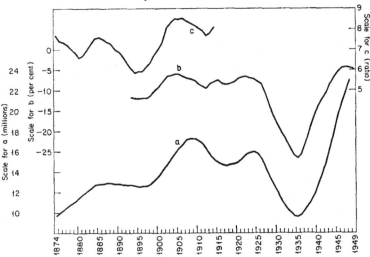

a   Additions to population
b   Unemployment, per cent of nonfarm employees (signs reversed)
c   Bank earnings ratio

flow of goods to consumers were necessarily a major element in producing swings in immigration, and thus in additions to population (as well as in internal migration and natural increase), but they may have contributed to them. The importance of additions to per capita flow of goods to consumers in the present connection lies in the fact that, at least before World War I, they can be identified as after-effects of long swings in population growth.

That the swings in additions to per capita flow of goods to consumers do not tell the whole story is suggested by Chart 11. We tried, in this

[9] On these points see further evidence in Kuznets, "Long Swings in the Growth of Population."

chart, to compare the long swings in population growth with some measures of the state of the economy that would indicate changes in degree of engagement of resources and profitability—conditions of pull that would affect not only net immigration but also internal migration and the rate of natural increase. We found only two relevant measures for the long period to be covered, although a further search might unearth more. One is an index of unemployment taken as a percentage of nonfarm employees. Even pieced out in various ways, this index could be carried back only to the early 1890's. The other index is the profit earning record of national banks (the ratio of profits to total capital accounts). The indexes, shown as lines *b* and *c* in Chart 11, are decadal averages centered on the fifth year.

In both series, the long swings reflecting general economic conditions, while similar to those in population additions, precede them by significant periods varying from two to five years. The indexes have turning points that, in consequence, are fairly close in timing to those in additions to per capita flow of goods to consumers in Chart 10. They add to the impression that there may be some validity in assuming that the lag in response of population movements to changes in economic conditions in the United States contributed in some measure to the inverted long swings in additions to product per capita, which set the stage for the next long swing in population growth.

If there was such a self-perpetuating mechanism of long swings before World War I, it disappeared thereafter. The reasons for the change are not far to seek. To begin with, immigration was greatly restricted. Second, the two world wars made for a change in timing that brought about a coincidence of the long swings in residential construction and in other components of capital formation. Finally, the productive capacity of the country after World War I was such that the earlier limits that prevented synchronous upswings in population-sensitive capital formation and in other capital formation ceased to operate. This is clearly indicated by the shift from debtor to creditor position in the international capital markets, by the ease with which expansions were attained after World War I without running into the capacity bottlenecks that were a common feature of the cyclical expansions in this country before that war, and by the tremendous reserve capacity revealed during World War II in contrast with our experience in World War I.

Long Swings

The Countrywide Aggregates

We conclude the discussion of long swings in the output flows by observing those in the countrywide aggregates. Chart 12 presents decadal averages of gross national product excluding military, flow of goods to consumers, total and per capita, and gross capital formation excluding military. The inclusion of military output would alter the picture only slightly, affecting the standing from about 1913 through 1922 and from about 1937 through 1950, but without changing the timing of the long swings observed.

CHART 12

Decadal Levels of Gross National Product, Flow of Goods to Consumers, Gross Capital Formation, and Flow of Goods to Consumers Per Capita, 1929 Prices, 1869–1955

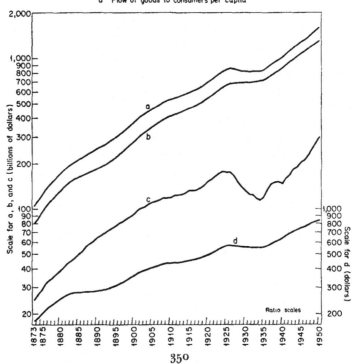

a   Gross national product excluding military
b   Flow of goods to consumers
c   Gross capital formation excluding military
d   Flow of goods to consumers per capita

Population Growth and Countrywide Aggregates

Because the totals in Chart 12 have a pronounced long-term upward rise, they have been plotted on a ratio scale to reveal more sharply the long swings in rate of growth. The long swings in gross national product, in flow of goods to consumers, and in flow of consumer goods per capita are quite clear. In gross capital formation, however, the movement up to World War I reveals no marked long swings. Apparently the difference in timing between the long swings of population-sensitive components and of other capital formation, which prevailed until World War I, resulted in so much cancellation that the comprehensive capital formation totals fail to reveal distinct long swings.

In lines 1 to 5 of Table 66 we attempt to date the turning points of long swings in the major countrywide aggregates. As in all other cases discussed so far, the dating is based on a close inspection of the charts of decadal averages and on calculation, if necessary, of successive changes. The dating follows the rule of regarding a phase as terminated only when the beginning of a new phase is clearly indicated. The results are naturally subject to error, but they suffice to outline the broad timing of the swings.

The long swings in gross national product, including or excluding military, and in flow of goods to consumers, total or per capita, were quite similar in timing. There was an upswing from 1873 (the earliest year that can be covered in the procedure followed here) to the early 1880's; a downswing to about 1893 (somewhat earlier in flow of consumer goods per capita); another upswing to 1908 (although the peak came earlier in flow of consumer goods per capita); a downswing to 1915 or 1916 (with flow of consumer goods per capita again reaching a trough earlier); an upswing to the middle of the 1920's; a marked downswing to the early or mid-1930's; and then a sharp rise to 1950, the most recent year covered by our averages.

The long swings in gross capital formation are discernible beginning with the peak in the 1920's, and from that date on they follow closely those for gross national product and flow of goods to consumers. Since, as stated above, it is extremely difficult to discern the long swings in total capital formation before World War I, the dates in line 5, columns 3 to 5, are quite problematical.

The dates of turning points in long swings in the various components of gross capital formation, discussed in the preceding sections, are also entered in Table 66. Three general impressions are suggested by these entries, in comparison with those for long swings in gross national

TABLE 66

DATES OF TURNING POINTS IN LONG SWINGS OF GROSS NATIONAL PRODUCT AND ITS COMPONENTS, 1869–1955

(based on decadal levels in 1929 prices)

	Trough (1)	Peak (2)	Trough (3)	Peak (4)	Trough (5)	Peak (6)	Trough (7)	Peak (8)
1. Gross national product	1873	1882	1893	1908	1916	1926	1934	1950
2. Gross national product, excluding military	1873	1882	1893	1908	1916	1926	1934	1950
3. Flow of goods to consumers	1873	1882	1893	1908	1915	1926	1932	1950
4. Flow of goods to consumers, per capita	1873	1882	1889	1904	1912	1924	1934	1950
5. Gross capital formation			1884	1902	1909 (1916)	1924	1934	1950
6. Nonfarm residential construction	1874	1890	1899	1909	1916	1925	1934	1948 [a]
7. Gross capital expenditures by railroads	1875	1889	1899	1909	1918	1925	1935	1948 [a]
8. Private construction & producers' durables excluding nonfarm residential construction and capital expenditures by railroads		1876	1884	1906 (1908)	1917	1926	1935	1948 [a]
9. Net changes in inventories		1881	1889	1901	1912	1920	1929	1941
10. Net changes in foreign claims		1880	1890	1901	1909	1919	1932 (1940)	1942

[a] Last year for which series are available for lines 6, 7, and 8.

SOURCE, BY LINE

1 to 5. Decadal totals were calculated from the annual series underlying the five-year averages in Tables R-26, R-29, and R-40, and from the annual series in Table R-7.

6 and 7. See Table 61, cols. 2 and 3, respectively.

8 to 10. See Table 63, cols. 3, 4, and 5, respectively.

product and flow of goods to consumers, which can be used as a reference chronology. First, the timing of the long swings among the various components of capital formation is different, particularly before the 1920's, and for some components (net changes in inventories and in foreign claims) there are differences even in recent decades. Second, before World War I, the long swings in many components of capital formation were neither positively nor negatively correlated with swings in gross national product and in flow of goods to consumers, but were in between—their peaks and troughs falling within the phases of the reference chronology. Third, the partly inverted relation between long swings in the population-sensitive and in other components of capital formation accounts for the mild character of long swings in total gross capital formation before World War I (and during the latter, if we include military production). It explains also the difficulty of discerning clearly marked turning points.

Using the dates of long swings in gross national product as a reference chronology, we can measure the amplitude of the long swings in all major countrywide totals (Table 67). In addition to providing the usual measures of standings at troughs and peaks, the rate of change per year during the up-and-down phases, and the differential change from one phase to the next, we attempt here to measure relative amplitude. The base is the average volume of the specific series during the swing for which the differential change is measured. To simplify calculations, the average volume is derived from the standings in part A; and, in calculating the ratio of the differential change over the long swing to the average volume, we first convert the differential change to a per decade rather than a per year basis.

Several findings, some already indicated, are clearly suggested by Table 67.

1. Gross national product, including and excluding military, and flow of goods to consumers, total and per capita, reflect the long swings as dated, without exception. This is not true of gross capital formation, including or excluding military. It shows a rise in rate of growth from 1873–1882 to 1882–1893, instead of a decline as expected by the reference chronology; and for totals including military the decline in line 18 is too mild to be significant.

2. When converted to percentages of the base, the differential change in decadal rates of growth during the long swings varies, even in the conforming series (gross national product and flow of goods to consumers, total and per capita) from −4 per cent to 52 per cent. However,

TABLE 67

CHANGES IN MAJOR COUNTRYWIDE AGGREGATES DURING PHASES OF LONG SWINGS IN GROSS NATIONAL PRODUCT, 1869–1955

(in billions of dollars, except per capita in dollars; in 1929 prices)

	Gross National Product (1)	Gross National Product Excluding Military (2)	Flow of Goods to Consumers (3)	Flow of Goods to Consumers, Per Capita (4)	Gross Capital Formation (5)	Gross Capital Formation Excluding Military (6)
A. VOLUMES PER DECADE AT DATES OF TURNING POINTS IN COLUMN 1						
1. First trough, 1873	105.0	105.0	80.3	179	24.7	24.7
2. Peak, 1882	188.9	188.9	145.6	267	43.3	43.3
3. Trough, 1893	273.7	273.7	201.8	294	71.8	71.8
4. Peak, 1908	506.6	506.6	388.4	430	118.3	118.3
5. Trough, 1916	615.2	605.8	473.2	459	142.0	132.6
6. Peak, 1926	857.3	855.8	680.0	574	177.3	175.7
7. Trough, 1934	824.7	820.5	706.7	553	118.0	113.8
8. Peak, 1950	1,617.1	1,584.4	1,287.2	835	329.8	297.2
B. CHANGES PER YEAR DURING SUCCESSIVE PHASES						
9. Trough to peak (line 1 to line 2)	+9.32	+9.32	+7.26	+9.8	+2.07	+2.07
10. Peak to trough (line 2 to line 3)	+7.71	+7.71	+5.11	+2.5	+2.59	+2.59
11. Trough to peak (line 3 to line 4)	+15.53	+15.53	+12.44	+9.1	+3.10	+3.10
12. Peak to trough (line 4 to line 5)	+13.58	+12.40	+10.60	+3.6	+2.96	+1.79
13. Trough to peak (line 5 to line 6)	+24.21	+25.00	+20.68	+11.5	+3.53	+4.31
14. Peak to trough (line 6 to line 7)	−4.08	−4.41	+3.34	−2.6	−7.41	−7.74
15. Trough to peak (line 7 to line 8)	+49.53	+47.74	+36.28	+17.6	+13.24	+11.46

C. CHANGES BETWEEN SUCCESSIVE PHASES

16. Trough to trough (line 9 to line 10)	−1.61	−1.61	−2.15	−7.3	+0.52	+0.52
17. Peak to peak (line 10 to line 11)	+7.82	+7.82	+7.33	+6.6	+0.51	+0.51
18. Trough to trough (line 11 to line 12)	−1.95	−3.13	−1.84	−5.5	−0.14	−1.31
19. Peak to peak (line 12 to line 13)	+10.63	+12.60	+10.08	+7.9	+0.57	+2.52
20. Trough to trough (line 13 to line 14)	−28.29	−29.41	−17.34	−14.1	−10.94	−12.05
21. Peak to peak (line 14 to line 15)	+53.61	+52.15	+32.94	+20.2	+20.65	+19.20

D. VOLUMES PER DECADE DURING LONG SWINGS [a]

22. Average, lines 1 to 3	189.1	189.1	143.3	252	45.8	45.8
23. Average, lines 2 to 4	310.7	310.7	234.4	321	76.3	76.3
24. Average, lines 3 to 5	475.5	473.2	363.0	403	112.6	110.2
25. Average, lines 4 to 6	648.6	643.5	503.7	480	144.9	139.8
26. Average, lines 5 to 7	788.6	784.5	635.0	540	153.6	149.4
27. Average, lines 6 to 8	1,031.0	1,020.3	845.2	629	185.8	175.1

E. CHANGES BETWEEN SUCCESSIVE PHASES (MULTIPLIED BY 10) AS PER CENTS OF AVERAGE VOLUMES

28. Line 16 ÷ line 22	−9	−9	−15	−29	+11	+11
29. Line 17 ÷ line 23	+25	+25	+31	+21	+7	+7
30. Line 18 ÷ line 24	−4	−7	−5	−14	−1	−12
31. Line 19 ÷ line 25	+16	+20	+20	+16	+4	+18
32. Line 20 ÷ line 26	−36	−37	−27	−26	−71	−81
33. Line 21 ÷ line 27	+52	+51	+39	+32	+111	+110

[a] Calculated by averaging the terminal standings (trough or peak—each weighted 1) and the middle turning point (peak or trough—weighted 2).

SOURCE: Same as in notes to Table 66, lines 1 to 5.

because the secular trend in these series is upward, the negative changes tend to be smaller than the positive. The average of the two changes (disregarding signs), taken as a fair representation of the amplitude of each long swing, varies from 10 to 44 per cent of the base for the gross national product series, and from about 12 to 33 per cent for the flow of goods to consumers series.

3. The relative amplitude of the long swings tends to widen—a result largely of the long sharp depression of the 1930's and of the recovery thereafter.

4. If we were to take the differential change over the long swings as a percentage not of the absolute volume of the series, but of the average change per decade during the swing, the relative amplitude would be much wider; and the trend toward widening the relative amplitude would be much sharper. To put it differently, the long swings affect the cumulative volumes of gross national product and its components in the manner indicated in part E of Table 67; but they affect the rate of change in those volumes in much more violent fashion.

One final inference should be stressed. If the long swings in gross capital formation differ in timing from those characterizing gross national product, it follows that the ratio of gross capital formation to gross national product—the gross national savings fraction—must display long swings of its own. Indeed, the same result would follow even if the swings in the numerator (gross capital formation) and the denominator (gross national product) of the fraction were identical in timing but differed in relative (proportional) amplitude.

Chart 13 shows four measures of the relation between capital formation and national product (both excluding military because, as before, we wished to eliminate it from the analysis). In line *a* we have the proportion of gross capital formation to gross national product—both in terms of ten-year moving averages and in constant prices. This ratio describes three peak-to-peak swings, on the assumption that the initial year in the series is a peak. The dates of these swings are quite different from those in gross national product recorded in Table 66. There is a peak in the mid-1870's at about the time of the trough in gross national product; there is a trough in the early 1880's, when there is a peak in gross national product; and there is a marked peak in the early 1890's, when there is a trough in national product. It is only starting with World War I that the swings in the ratio of gross capital formation to gross national product begin to coincide with those in gross national product.

CHART 13

Decadal Level of Gross Capital Formation as Per Cent of Gross National Product, and Marginal Capital-Output Ratios, Based on Volumes in 1929 Prices, 1869–1955

a   Decadal level of GCF excl. military as per cent of decadal level of GNP excl. military
b   Decadal level of GCF excl. military as ratio to decadal change in GNP excl. military
c   Decadal level of NCF excl. military as ratio to decadal change in NNP excl. military
d   Decadal level of private NCF excl. nonfarm residential construction as ratio to decadal change in NNP excl. military and services

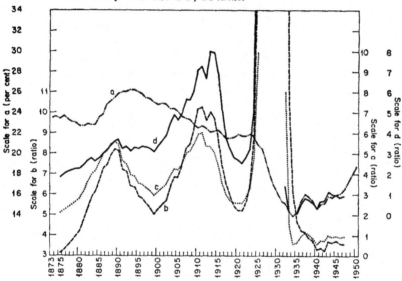

The other lines in Chart 13 can be described as marginal capital-output ratios. Two of them (lines *b* and *c*) represent the ratio of capital formation (gross or net), in the form of a ten-year moving average, to the increment in national product (gross or net), over essentially the same ten-year period. In these ratios both capital formation and national product exclude military. Furthermore, the increment in national product is derived from quinquennial averages in order to reduce short-term variations. Thus, the first entry in line *b* (or *c*) of the chart is the ratio of the decennial average of gross (or net) capital formation for 1871–1880, centered in the fifth year (1875), to the difference between two quinquennial averages of gross (or net) national product, one centered in 1871 and the other in 1881. There is a slight discrepancy in timing: the increment in national product should be centered at the middle of 1876, whereas capital formation for the period is centered at the end of 1875. But the discrepancy would not affect the long swings in the ratios materially. Line *d* portrays perhaps the most interesting marginal capital-output ratio: the ratio of private net capital formation excluding nonfarm residential construction to the increment in net national product excluding services (the method of relating capital formation to additions to product is the same as that followed for lines *b* and *c*). All the underlying volumes are in constant prices.

In some periods capital formation is positive and the decadal change in product is negative, in which case the marginal capital-output ratio is infinitely large (as happened during the severe depression of the 1930's). In some periods net capital formation is negative, and the change in net national product is positive, in which case the marginal capital-output ratio is negative. Both contingencies could be eliminated by the use of longer periods for both numerator and denominator. But this would have resulted in a substantial damping of the long swings in the marginal capital-output ratios, and we are interested in their magnitudes unreduced by such damping.

It is clear from Chart 13 that the swings in the marginal capital-output ratios are extremely wide, even when the periods in which the ratios drop below zero or become infinitely large are omitted. Table 68, which records the standings and approximate dates of the turning points of the series in Chart 13, confirms this impression, but the calculations are impeded by the occurrence of infinitely large values.

There is some similarity between the long swings in the capital formation proportion (line *a*) and in the marginal capital-output ratios (lines *b*, *c*, and *d*). However, the latter are affected not only by the former, but also by the varying rate of growth of national product itself. Three long swings and the beginning of a fourth are conspicuous; but the dissimilarity in timing between the swings in the marginal capital-output ratios and those in the proportion of capital formation to national product is also quite marked.

With this general indication of the wide amplitude of the long swings, the evidence in Chart 13 and Table 68 leads to one important inference. The long-term trend in the gross capital formation proportion is somewhat downward, as can be seen if we calculate the average ratio for each swing by the procedure followed for the entries in panel D of Table 67. But the long swings in the standings are obviously an important qualification of this long-term trend, and must be considered in any interpretation of the past as a basis for the

TABLE 68

DATES OF TURNING POINTS AND STANDINGS IN LONG SWINGS OF GROSS CAPITAL FORMATION AS
PER CENT OF GROSS NATIONAL PRODUCT, AND OF MARGINAL CAPITAL-OUTPUT RATIOS, 1869–1955

	GCF [a] as % of GNP [a] (1)	Ratio of GCF [a] to Additions to GNP [a] (2)	Ratio of NCF [a] to Additions to NNP [a] (3)	Ratio of Private NCF, Excluding Nonfarm Residential Construction, to Additions to NNP [a] Excluding Services (4)
		A. DATES OF TURNING POINTS		
1. First peak	1876			
2. Trough	1884	1875	1875	1875
3. Peak	1894	1889	1889	1890
4. Trough		1899	1899	1899
5. Peak		1911	1911	1913
6. Trough	1917	1921	1921	1921
7. Peak	1923	————————Late 1920's————————		
8. Trough	1934	1942	1934	1934
9. Peak	1950	1947 (1945) [b]	1947 (1943) [b]	1947 (1943) [b]
		B. STANDINGS AT DATES INDICATED, BASED ON DECADAL LEVELS		
10. First peak (line 1)	23.7			
11. Trough (line 2)	22.8	3.12	2.07	1.83
12. Peak (line 3)	26.2	8.20	5.57	3.68
13. Trough (line 4)		5.02	2.95	3.08
14. Peak (line 5)		10.27	6.01	8.01
15. Trough (line 6)	21.5	5.21	2.56	2.52
16. Peak (line 7)	21.9	∞	∞	∞
17. Trough (line 8)	13.9	3.27	0.60	∞
18. Peak (line 9)	18.8	3.59 (3.74)	0.97 (1.02)	0.93 (1.12)

Percentages and ratios are based on values in 1929 prices.
GCF = gross capital formation; GNP = gross national product.
NCF = net capital formation; NNP = net national product.
[a] Excluding military.
[b] 1947 is the latest year available for all series in cols. 2 to 4. The peak appears to fall somewhat earlier, as indicated by the entries in parentheses.
SOURCE: See text for derivation of entries.

future. This is more conspicuously true of the marginal capital-output ratios, especially that in line *d*, which climbs during the first half of the period, from 1875 to 1913, and then declines sharply during the second half. One must conclude that the long-term trend in the relation between additions to capital and additions to output is not persistent, and that any extrapolation into the future must take account of the variability of the marginal capital-output ratios, not only within the span of shorter business cycles, but also over the decades that mark the long swings.

CHAPTER 8

Long Swings in Financing of Capital Formation

Introduction

IN the preceding chapter we discussed the alternations in the rates of additions to or growth of real flows (capital formation, national product) and population. The procedures employed were simple, and the significance of the findings should not be exaggerated. In particular, no claim is made that these alternations are periodic, or that we know the mechanism that produces them. But whether we use moving averages or averages for reference or specific cycles to eliminate the effects of fluctuations associated with business cycles, the resulting totals do not display uniformly constant, uniformly accelerating, or uniformly decelerating rates of growth. The growth rates are for a period above or for a period below the underlying long-term trend, and the magnitude of these deviations above or below the underlying trend line is too large to be disregarded. Hence the need for segregating these alternations in rates of growth for separate study, and their designation as long swings is a semantic facility that should not mislead us into ascribing to these movements an unwarranted connotation of regular periodicity.

Two arguments against treating this component separately should be faced. The first points to the fact that over the last forty to fifty years the timing and characteristics of the long swings were much affected by the two world wars. The latter caused the deep troughs in residential construction and materially affected the structure of both capital formation and national product. Furthermore, while the major depression of the 1930's was an even more important factor in setting the trough of the last long swing, it in turn reflected in good part the dislocations World War I produced in this country and elsewhere. It may, therefore, be argued that, at least since 1914, long swings have been largely a result of world wars; and it is hardly justifiable to treat these long swings as an aspect of economic growth dissociated from what are major incidents in international relations. In considering this argument, we cannot deny that world wars put a distinctive stamp on the long swings in rate and structure of economic growth. But this means only that when such wars occur, they modify the dates and affect the amplitude of the long swings compared with what they might have been otherwise. It does not mean that had there been no world wars there would have been no long alternations in the rate and structure of growth. They occurred in this country between the 1880's and 1914, and for some aspects of the economy can be seen in the record of economic growth between the 1830's and the Civil War. Any consideration of the bearing of the analysis of past trends upon even a future assumed to be warless must take account of the finding that, over the period covered by the record, the rates of secular growth for some major aspects of the economy (construction, additions to population, internal migration, and others to be discussed below) have been subject to long alternations even during decades of peace.

The second argument relates to the statistical procedure employed in Chapter 7 and to be followed here. The use of moving averages covering a long period—such as a decade—introduces a semblance of long continuous swings even when no such continuity characterizes the underlying data. A big change, such as a pronounced cyclical expansion followed by a mild contraction, or an especially severe depression, or a large annual bulge or trough—each transient in the sense that it may characterize just one or two or three years—will, in the calculation of a ten-year moving average, raise or depress the ordinates of that average over the ten successive items in which it is included. The continuous swings in our charts may, therefore, be statistical illusions. Given the procedure employed, all that is needed to produce those swings, apparently, is the occurrence, at roughly equal intervals, of an exceptionally large transient change, upward or downward.

The formal validity of this argument cannot be denied: transient changes of unusual magnitude may, when smoothed by a long-period average, produce apparent long swings. But it does not follow that, where moving averages reveal long swings, the latter are necessarily due to the "stretching out" of a few large transient changes. The underlying detailed data may, in fact, without any averaging, reveal long swings which, with their wide amplitude, dominate the shorter-term fluctuations associated with business cycles. In such cases the moving averages yield a picture of long swings less affected by the short-term fluctuations in the more detailed data, but they in no sense create the continuous long-term alternations in the rate of growth. And for several important components of economic activity the annual data do reveal the long swings suggested above: gross and net immigration to this country; annual increments in population for the recent periods (since 1930), when they are not derived by linear interpolations between census dates; nonfarm residential construction; expenditures on durable capital equipment (construction and producers' durables) in many of the regulated industries; additions to capital in manufacturing industries; and changes in the annual balance of international payments.

Even when the amplitude of long swings relative to that of short-term fluctuations is not so dominant that such swings can be observed clearly in the annual (or more detailed) time series, the emergence of long swings after the series have been averaged for successive cycles or smoothed by means of long-period moving averages is not necessarily a statistical illusion. Two somewhat distinct cases can be considered.

In the first case we assume that the economic process measured in the series fluctuates within a fairly narrow range, the fluctuations being combined with an underlying secular movement of any magnitude. If, then, a sharp upward change occurs during a given year, and no offsetting change follows immediately, the smoothing of the underlying data by, say, a ten-year moving average will lift the level of the average over a ten-year period. The rise will be followed by a drop in the sixth year following that of the assumed large upward change (if the average is centered at the mid-point). The semblance of a continuously high level for ten years, followed by a continuously lower level—the effects of the underlying long-term trend being allowed for—is, then, an illusion, in that the series was above the secular level for one year, not ten. But is such a hypothetical example consistent with what we must assume concerning the operation of the economic system? We would ordinarily expect the economic process to respond to a sharp disturbance by canceling it, if that disturbance does not correspond to the underlying determinants. If, by some accident, the output of a commodity rises steeply above its secular level, we would expect, all other conditions being equal, a relative decline in prices of that commodity, a subsequent fall in output in response to the price decline, and the emergence of deviations below the secular level that would offset the original upward disturbance. The inference would apply to an equal degree in the case of a sharp downward break in output. And if the economic process reacts to this annual bulge or trough, either would affect a moving average for only a year—not for the full decade involved in the period of cumulation. It is only if we conceive the transient changes as purely random, that is, assume independence among successive values, that the moving average will produce the statistical illusion we are considering. In the case of economic time series, in which we expect a deviation from an underlying secular movement to produce an offsetting effect, there is no such independence among successive deviations (i.e., the serial correlation coefficient among irregular changes should be significantly negative). Therefore, the emergence of long swings in a decadal moving average cannot be reduced to what is essentially a stretching out of random transient changes. In a situation in which at intervals there is an upward or downward change not offset by an immediate reaction in the opposite direction, the long-term swings in the original data may be viewed as genuine because of the very absence of an immediately offsetting reaction.

The same logic applies to the other case—a more realistic one—where we recognize the existence of cyclical fluctuations in the underlying detailed data, but assume that one of the cycles is exceptionally severe or exceptionally mild. To produce the effect of a long swing, such severity or mildness must refer to an imbalance between expansion and contraction. In other words, because of a contraction exceptionally severe in relation to the preceding or following expansion or an expansion exceptionally pronounced in relation to the preceding or following contraction, the average for the cycle as a whole is below or above the long-term secular level. If we can conceive successive cycles as units of a random universe—assume no significant correlation between the deviation of a given cycle average from the underlying secular trend and the deviation of the preceding or next cycle from that trend—a moving average may generate long swings that are statistical illusions because of the stretching out of a single deviation of a cycle average from the long-term level.

Here again, however, assuming such independence—randomness— of successive cycle averages means an implicit denial of the significance of the underlying secular trend as a reflection of forces setting a path of movement for the economic process, to which it will tend to return when disturbed. If a given cycle is above the secular average, we would expect the next cycle to be below the secular average, and vice versa. This does not mean that the negative serial correlation should be perfect; but it does mean that, in the absence of significant forces working to the contrary, negative correlation should be the rule, and disturbances capable of generating a long swing through moving averages should be few and far between.

The major point for both cases can be put somewhat differently. The responsiveness of economic processes to short-term disturbances, which bars conceiving them as purely random changes (whether such randomness be applied to annual or cycle-average values), means a significant negative correlation between the successive values. Given such negative correlation, the probability that moving averages will generate long swings as statistical illusions becomes much less than in cases where we deal with truly random changes. This must be taken into account in considering the justification for segregating the long swings for separate study, along with the fact, noted previously, that in many important components of national product and capital formation the long swings are conspicuous even before short-term fluctuations are reduced by means of cycle averages or moving averages.

These somewhat technical arguments having been dealt with, we now consider long swings in the financing of capital formation. The financing processes are far more volatile than the real flows discussed in the preceding chapter, and the effects on them of wars and business cycles are far more prominent. It may seem at times that long swings are statistical artifacts far removed from reality, which fluctuates so widely in the short run. In a sense this impression is true: if the annual or cyclical ups and downs are violent, the resulting averages and trends are more in the nature of fiction than they are if the short-term fluctuations are within a narrow compass and the long-term movement dominates the picture. But this does not render completely unreal the movements that transcend in duration the more violent cycles or other short-term fluctuations—so long as we have institutions (and there are many) that survive the cycles and that adjust in their response and planning to periods beyond the next cyclical expansion or contraction. Therefore, just as we attempted to establish the long-term trends in financing (in Chapters 5 and 6), despite the fact that those trends are quantitatively limited relative to the short-term fluctuations of the financing ratios in the course of business cycles or of war periods, so we must consider the long swings in at least some financing ratios.

Unfortunately, few direct data are available except for recent decades in which wars dominate the picture and when the conclusions are too obvious to warrant discussion. The two world wars, of course, had an immediate effect on the structure of countrywide financing, with the major shifts from equity to debt and from private to government debt. Just as clearly, the postwar prosperity periods affected the ratio of internal to external financing, and of debt to equity financing. Much of the material in Chapters 5 and 6, where we had to select periods similar with respect to position in the long swings in order to make inferences concerning underlying trends, is in fact relevant here, and need not be repeated. Our main interest should be in the earlier decades, which were not so markedly affected by wars and their aftermath, but for which direct information on financing of capital formation is quite scarce.

Under the circumstances, we must resort to indirect evidence. The next two sections present several types of such indirect evidence. The final section gives actual examples relating to swings in financing ratios for selected sectors of the economy—examples borrowed from the monographs in this series that deal with the capital using sectors.

The Structure of Capital Formation, in Current Prices

One type of indirect evidence on long swings in financing is provided by the data on changes in the components of capital formation, in current prices. The bearing of those changes may be stated as follows. We assume that, by and large, it is capital formation that gives rise to financing—particularly external—and in fact we are interested in how capital formation was financed, not in the general use of credit funds. If, then, there are distinct and persistent differences in the way the several components of capital formation are financed, changes in the proportional share of such components in total capital formation should give rise to changes in the proportional magnitude of various types of financing. For example, if we assume that, by and large, inventory accumulation is financed by short-term borrowing, whereas accumulation of fixed durable capital is financed either by internal funds or by long-term external funds with the proportions of the two assumed constant, shifts in the distribution of capital formation between inventory accumulation and accumulation of fixed capital will produce corresponding changes in the apportionment of total financing between internal and external, and within external, between short-term and long-term.

The qualifications attached to such tying of types of capital formation to distinctive sources of financing were discussed in Chapter 5. For the present it suffices to say that the connections between types of capital formation and their financing, while not close and absolutely

CHART 14

Structure of Gross Capital Formation in Current Prices, by Category of User, 1869–1955

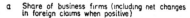

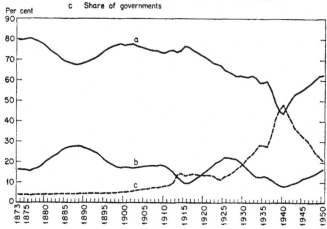

a   Share of business firms (including net changes in foreign claims when positive)
b   Share of households (nonfarm residential construction)
c   Share of governments

invariant, are sufficiently realistic so that if there are marked long swings in the distribution of capital formation among its components (all in current prices, because the current price volumes are more directly tied in with financing than the constant price volumes are), and if the components are marked by persistent differences in the structure of financing, there will result long swings in the distribution of total financing of capital formation among different sources.

It is this rationale that underlies the presentation of the data in Charts 14 through 16. In Chart 14, we show the percentage apportionment of total gross capital formation (including military construction and munitions, and excluding net changes in foreign claims when negative) among the three major user categories: nonfarm residential construction (used preponderantly by private households), government capital formation (comprising government construction and munitions), and business capital formation (which, being a residual, includes farm and nonfarm, corporate and noncorporate, as well as net changes in claims against foreign countries when positive). Chart 15 shows the percentage apportionment of gross domestic business capi-

CHART 15

Structure of Gross Domestic Business Capital Formation in Current Prices, by Type of Capital Good, 1869–1955

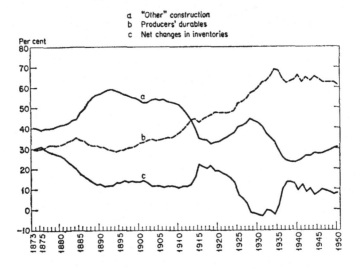

a   "Other" construction
b   Producers' durables
c   Net changes in inventories

tal formation, by type of capital good: construction, which in this case excludes nonfarm residential and government construction; producers' durable equipment; and net changes in inventories. Chart 16 shows, for durable domestic business capital formation, the proportion of estimated capital consumption to gross volumes. In all three charts, the percentage shares are based on ten-year moving averages of totals in current prices, centered on the fifth year.

The first point to be noted is that long swings in the various aspects of the structure of capital formation in current prices are quite prominent, even before the second half of the period, which is marked by world wars and their aftermath. This is what we would have expected from the discussion, in Chapter 7, of the volumes in constant prices.

But relative price movements might well have exhibited long swings inversely related to those in real volumes, i.e., to those in constant prices. If they had, the distributions of the totals in current prices would not have shown long swings. That the swings do emerge means either that the swings in relative prices were not inverted to those in real volumes or, if inverted, were of far narrower amplitude.

CHART 16

Capital Consumption as Per Cent of Gross Durable Domestic Business Capital Formation, 1869–1955

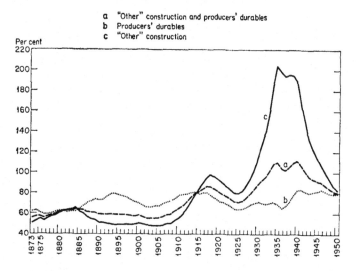

a   "Other" construction and producers' durables
b   Producers' durables
c   "Other" construction

To illustrate the implications of Charts 14–16 for long swings in the structure of financing, we give, for selected years, the actual percentage shares shown in the three charts (Table 69). The basis for selecting the years differs somewhat from chart to chart, but in general, the intent was to choose those that marked the points of greatest difference in the structure of capital formation—the years in which the lines shown in the charts either converged most or diverged most. For Chart 14 this end was attained by choosing the turning points in the share of nonfarm residential construction; for Chart 15 the choice was based largely on the turning points in the shares of construction and of net changes in inventories; for Chart 16 the dates are those of turning

TABLE 69

STRUCTURE OF CAPITAL FORMATION, CURRENT PRICES, SELECTED YEARS, 1871–1955

A. PERCENTAGE SHARES IN TOTAL GROSS CAPITAL FORMATION,[a] BY CATEGORY OF USER

Year	Households [b] (1)	Governments (2)	Business Firms [a] (3)
1. 1876	15.7	3.8	80.4
2. 1888	27.9	4.2	67.8
3. 1902	16.8	5.6	77.6
4. 1909	18.5	7.9	73.6
5. 1915	9.6	13.4	77.0
6. 1926	22.1	13.6	64.2
7. 1940	8.1	48.2	43.7
8. 1950	16.5	20.8	62.8

B. PERCENTAGE SHARES IN GROSS DOMESTIC BUSINESS CAPITAL FORMATION, BY TYPE OF CAPITAL GOOD

Year	Durables "Other" Construction (1)	Producers' Durables (2)	Net Changes in Inventories (3)
9. 1875	39.0	30.0	31.1
10. 1884	44.4	35.5	20.1
11. 1892	58.8	29.5	11.7
12. 1901	52.6	33.1	14.3
13. 1910	51.7	37.7	10.6
14. 1918	32.4	46.3	21.3
15. 1928	44.4	57.3	−1.6
16. 1938	23.3	63.1	13.7
17. 1950	30.7	61.2	8.1

C. RATIO (%) OF CAPITAL CONSUMPTION TO GROSS DOMESTIC BUSINESS CAPITAL FORMATION

Year	"Other" Construction (1)	Producers' Durables (2)	Total Durables (3)	Total (4)
18. 1875	54.4	60.9	57.2	39.5
19. 1884	65.8	62.3	64.2	51.3
20. 1902	48.5	65.3	55.1	47.7
21. 1917	94.1	80.1	86.1	68.7
22. 1925	79.7	64.4	71.1	66.0
23. 1940	189.5	83.2	111.4	100.6
24. 1950	82.1	79.8	80.6	74.0

Percentages and ratios are based on ten-year moving averages of annual volumes centered on the fifth year.

[a] Including net changes in foreign claims when positive.

[b] Nonfarm residential construction.

(Notes on following page)

Financing of Capital Formation

NOTES TO TABLE 69

SOURCE: Based on the annual series underlying, or shown in, the following tables:

PART A

Gross capital formation: Table R-29, col. 1, and Table R-34, col. 3.
Households (nonfarm residential construction): Table R-30, col. 1.
Governments: Table R-30, cols. 2 and 3, and Table R-6, col. 4.
Business firms: gross capital formation minus nonfarm residential construction and government capital formation.

PART B

Gross domestic business capital formation is the sum of the following:
"Other" construction: from Table R-30, col. 1.
Producers' durables: from Table R-33, col. 1 and Table R-6, col. 4.
Net changes in inventories: Table R-34, col. 1.

PART C

Gross domestic business capital formation is the same as for part B.
Capital consumption:
"Other" construction: Table R-31, col. 4.
Producers' durables: Table R-33, col. 2, and Table R-6, col. 6.

points in the long swings in the ratio of capital consumption to the total of construction and producers' durables.

Using the percentage shares in Table 69, we attempted some calculations that would illustrate the effects on the structure of financing. In Tables 45 and 46, total uses for the business sector for the first decade of this century were about 1.4 times gross capital formation, the corresponding ratio for government was 1.5, and that for nonfarm residential construction, 1.0. For the same decade, the proportion of internal financing (gross retention) to total uses was 0.59 for business, about 0.5 for government, and 0.65 for nonfarm residential construction. Let us assume that the ratio of total uses to gross capital formation for the earlier decades was the same as that for 1901–1910 (or 1900–1909), but that the ratio of internal financing to total uses was 0.5 for business, 0.5 for government, and 0.7 for nonfarm residential construction. On this assumption the countrywide proportion of gross retention to total uses for 1876 would be $[(80.4 \times 1.4) \times 0.5] + [(3.8 \times 1.5) \times 0.5] + [(15.7 \times 1.0) \times 0.7]$ divided by $(112.6 + 5.7 + 15.7)$, or 0.52. A similar calculation would show a fraction of 0.54 for 1888, and 0.53 for 1902. In other words, the proportion of internal financing to total uses increased somewhat from the trough of the nonfarm residential construction cycle to the peak and then declined again to the trough. If, in general, nonfarm residential construction is characterized by a high ratio of internal financing to total uses, the long swing of its share in the total will, *ipso facto*, mean a corresponding long swing in the share of internal financing in the countrywide total of uses of funds.

The changes in the share of internal financing (gross retention) in total sources (uses) derived above to illustrate the implication of the first long swing in Chart 14 may seem quite small. But it must be remembered that we deal here with large sectors, and that the assumed difference among them in the share of internal financing in total sources is not large. If we had assumed that the share for nonfarm residential construction was 0.8 instead of 0.7, and that for business was 0.4 instead of 0.5, the long swing in the proportion of internal financing to total would have been more prominent.

Similar illustrations can be devised for the other aspects of the structure of capital formation in current prices in Charts 15 and 16. If we assume that net changes in inventories are all financed by short-term borrowing, and that the other elements in gross domestic business capital formation are financed half by external long-term financing and half by gross retention, the ratio of total internal financing to gross business capital formation would rise from 0.345 in 1875 to 0.44 in 1892; and of the 0.655 share of external financing in 1875, 0.344 would be long-term and 0.311 short-term; whereas in 1892, of the 0.56 of external financing, 0.44 would be long-term and 0.12, short-term. (All of the figures are calculated from part B of Table 69 relating to Chart 15.) Finally, if we can assume that, by and large, capital consumption charges are earned, the entries in part C of Table 69 show the swings in one major component of the share of internal financing in total.[1]

The purpose here is not to assign precise values to the links between the long swings shown in the three charts (and in the underlying data) and the implicit long swings in the structure of financing (total or business alone). It is rather to suggest the links by which the observed long swings in the distribution of capital formation in current prices among components can generate long swings in the structure of financing. Given the hypotheses concerning the association between type of

[1] The totals of capital consumption underlying Chart 16 and part C of Table 69 should be not reproduction values (as they are) but original cost—if they are to correspond to customary practices of business accounting. But one may argue that when, because of price rises, reproduction cost is higher than original cost, the use of the former allows for the associated rise in accounting net profits, with an opposite allowance in periods of declining prices and of replacement cost below original cost. At any rate, for illustrative uses the difference is not important, and the extra calculations involved in securing capital consumption charges based on original cost did not seem worth while.

asset and uses and type of financing, such long swings will be generated unless there are offsetting movements in the proportions of various sources of financing for each sector distinguished. There is, however, no reason to expect such offsetting movements.

Price and Yield of Securities

Another body of indirect evidence that can shed some light on long swings in financing, and indeed on those in real flows, is the price and yield of securities. In Chart 17 we show nine-year moving averages of the longest available series on the price of stocks, for major industrial groups and for all stocks, and in Table 70 we record the turning points of the long swings in the index for all stocks, and measure within these phases the changes in each of the four stock-price indexes.

Three observations are suggested by the evidence. First, for at least two of the stock groups (railroad and utility) prices show marked long swings, of sizable amplitude, and averaging about twenty years in duration. The swings in the index of prices of industrial stocks are

CHART 17

Nine-Year Moving Averages of Indexes of Stock Prices, Total and Major Groups, 1871–1956

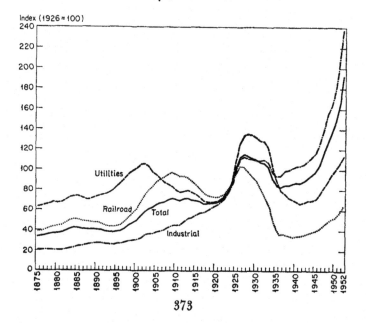

TABLE 70

CHANGES IN STOCK PRICES DURING PHASES OF LONG SWINGS
IN THE PRICE INDEX FOR ALL STOCKS, 1871–1956

(index, 1926 = 100)

	Total (1)	Railroad (2)	Utilities (3)	Industrial (4)
A. INDEXES OF STOCK PRICES AT DATES OF TURNING POINTS IN COLUMN 1				
1. First trough,[a] 1875	33.6	38.8	63.0	20.2
2. Peak, 1885	42.6	50.7	73.6	24.1
3. Trough, 1894	38.0	43.7	79.2	25.8
4. Peak, 1909	70.9	96.9	82.7	44.3
5. Trough, 1917	65.5	75.9	68.5	57.4
6. Peak, 1927	114.9	103.4	134.5	112.8
7. Trough, 1936	81.8	35.8	79.4	93.4
8. Last peak,[a] 1952	191.9	64.2	113.2	238.0
B. CHANGES PER YEAR DURING SUCCESSIVE PHASES				
9. Trough to peak (line 1 to line 2)	+0.90	+1.19	+1.06	+0.39
10. Peak to trough (line 2 to line 3)	−0.51	−0.78	+0.62	+0.19
11. Trough to peak (line 3 to line 4)	+2.19	+3.55	+0.23	+1.23
12. Peak to trough (line 4 to line 5)	−0.68	−2.62	−1.78	+1.64
13. Trough to peak (line 5 to line 6)	+4.94	+2.75	+6.60	+5.54
14. Peak to trough (line 6 to line 7)	−3.68	−7.51	−6.12	−2.16
15. Trough to peak (line 7 to line 8)	+6.88	+1.78	+2.11	+9.04
C. CHANGES BETWEEN SUCCESSIVE PHASES				
16. Trough to trough (line 9 to line 10)	−1.41	−1.97	−0.44	−0.20
17. Peak to peak (line 10 to line 11)	+2.70	+4.33	−0.39	+1.04
18. Trough to trough (line 11 to line 12)	−2.87	−6.17	−2.01	+0.41
19. Peak to peak (line 12 to line 13)	+5.62	+5.37	+8.38	+3.90
20. Trough to trough (line 13 to line 14)	−8.62	−10.26	−12.72	−7.70
21. Peak to peak (line 14 to line 15)	+10.56	+9.29	+8.23	+11.20

[a] First or last year included in all series.

Indexes are based on nine-year moving averages of annual series and are centered on the fifth year.

SOURCE, ANNUAL SERIES

1871–1937: Historical Statistics of the United States, 1789–1945, Series N-215–N-218.
1938–1956: Extrapolated from 1937 by the Standard and Poor series, splicing by the average ratio for 1935–1937. Series are given in *Business Statistics, 1957 Biennial Ed.* (Supplement, *Survey of Current Business*), p. 101.

much less clearly marked, and are not apparent until the early 1880's. The index for all stock prices (weighted by the volume of all stock issues) shows clear and prominent swings. In other words, we find long alternations in the rate of movement, not only in the real volume of some types of productive activity and in additions to population, but also in stock prices, where they presumably reflect the general estimate of the long-term prospects of growth and growth profits.

Second, the timing of the long swings in the index of prices for all stocks is close to that in gross national product, flow of goods to consumers, and population-sensitive capital formation (see Table 66). The first observable trough was in 1875 (and it may well have been in 1873, as was the case with gross national product); the first peak was in 1885, between that for gross national product (1882) and that for population-sensitive capital formation (1890); the next trough was in 1894, a year after the trough in gross national product but in advance of the trough in population-sensitive capital formation. From then on the coincidence has been quite close.

Third, Table 70 suggests and Chart 17 confirms the impression that before World War I there was significant divergence in the long swings among the three groups of stocks. The railroad stock prices moved in closest conformity with the general index, and hence in closest conformity with the real flows represented by national product. The utility stock prices moved somewhat differently in that they showed a trough in 1886–1887 (whereas the general index did not reach a trough until 1894), and a peak in 1902 (much earlier than the peak in the general index), perhaps reflecting the phase of the fastest growth of the nonrailroad utilities. We have already noted that the industrial stock prices failed to show a significant upswing until the early 1880's, and that upswing extended to the early 1890's rather than to the middle 1880's (the trough in the index of prices for all stocks). Departures from the common pattern during the period affected by World War I can be explained by the differential effect of war and inflation on the prices of stocks in sectors like railroads and utilities which were restricted by price regulation, compared with the industrial group in which profits were unrestricted. The discrepancies in timing of the long swings in the earlier periods must have been associated with differences in the timing of the swings in rates of growth of the sectors involved. In other words, just as in Chapter 7 we found that before World War I the long swings in the components of national product differed in timing (particularly as between the population-sensitive and other elements in capital formation), so we find here the long swings in stock prices for various sectors diverging before World War I. The data, however, do not permit us to trace specific associations between long swings in stock prices and in real flows for individual sectors.

All of this, while of some interest for what it adds to the picture of long swings in economic activity, has only a remote bearing upon financing. Alternations in the prices of stocks do not necessarily mean similar movements in the use of new stock issues for purposes of financing, either in absolute terms or relative to the use of other credit instruments or of internal financing.

There is, however, a way to suggest the bearing upon financing. From series on stock prices and on dividend payments we can calculate stock yields--the ratio of dividend payments to the current price of stocks. This ratio does not necessarily reflect the actual cost of new stock issue money to corporations that use this means of financing their capital expenditures, because the price at which a new security can be marketed may be different from that of extant issues, and the current payment of dividends is not necessarily the minimum price that has to be paid for marketability of a new issue. However, barring disturbances such as wars (when other circumstances affect the yield of stocks and its relation to prices of new stock money), we can assume that the long-term movements in stock yields do approximate fluctuations in the cost of equity money to corporations. We may, then, compare stock yields with bond yields and argue that if the difference in favor of bond yields increases (if bond yields are increasingly lower than stock yields), there should be, other conditions being equal, a shift in the distribution of new issues in favor of bonds, and the opposite effect should be found if the difference in favor of bonds decreases. Hence, if there are long swings in the stock-bond-yield differentials, there should be corresponding long swings in the distribution of new issues between stocks and bonds.

This is the rationale for the comparison in Chart 18. Line *a* is a nine-year moving average of the difference between yields of railroad stocks and of high-grade twenty-year bonds, adjusted for maturity. It does not go beyond 1937, because the subsequent averages begin to reflect the abnormal interest rates and bond yields of World War II, and also because for the last decade for which we have data on new railroad security issues (1940–1949), both stocks and bonds declined.

If we had an annual series on net bond and stock issues of railroads from which we could compute the nine-year moving average of the ratio of the former to the latter, we would expect it to move as the ratio in line *a* moves. However, our data on net bond and stock issues for railroads are easily available only for the long periods covered in Ulmer's monograph. In Table 71 we have taken them gross of invest-

CHART 18

Average Differential between Yields of Bonds and of Railroad Stocks Compared with Average Ratio of Net Bonds to Net Security Issues of Railroads, 1871–1941

a   Difference between yields of bonds and of railroad stocks
    (9-year moving averages)
b   Difference between yields of bonds and of railroad stocks
    (annual averages, selected periods)
c   Ratio of net bonds to net security issues, railroads
    (selected periods)

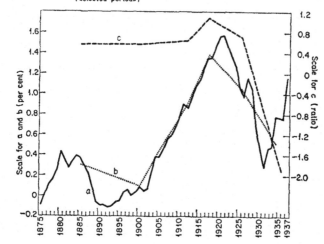

ment in affiliated companies (because such investment is not apportioned between stocks and bonds) and we also show the ratio of net bond issues to total net security issues (line *c* in the chart, drawn by connecting the mid-points of the six periods distinguished). To facilitate comparison, we also calculated annual averages of the stock-bond-yield differential for the same periods (line *b* in the chart).

With one exception—the movement from 1880–1890 to 1893–1907—the correspondence is what we would have expected. The differential in favor of bonds (column 1) rises from 1893–1907 to 1907–1916 and further to 1914–1920, and over these two intervals the ratio of bonds to total issues (column 5) rises from 57 per cent to well over 100 per cent. The differential declines from 1914–1920 to 1921–1930 and still further to 1931–1937 (which we take to represent the decade of the 1930's, excluding the effects of World War II), and the ratio of net bonds to total net security issues declines precipitously. The only exception is the failure of the bond ratio to decline when the differential

377

TABLE 71

AVERAGE DIFFERENTIAL BETWEEN YIELDS OF BONDS AND OF RAILROAD STOCKS
COMPARED WITH AVERAGE SHARE OF NET BONDS IN NET SECURITY
ISSUES OF RAILROADS, SELECTED PERIODS, 1880–1940

		Per Cent of Total Sources (*Uses*)			
Period	Average Yield Differential (%) (1)	Net Stock Issues (2)	Net Bond Issues (3)	Total Net Issues (2) + (3) (4)	(3) as % of (4) (5)
1. 1880–1890	0.30	43.0	54.9	97.9	56.1
2. 1893–1907	0.10	47.5	63.8	111.3	57.3
3. 1907–1916	0.89	35.0	60.1	95.1	63.2
4. 1914–1920	1.38	−3.0	36.5	33.5	109.0
5. 1921–1930	1.05	14.8	37.1	51.9	71.5
6. 1931–1940	0.52	11.9	−22.6	−10.7	−189.9 [a]

[a] Col. 3 as percentage of col. 2 (because col. 4 is negative).

SOURCE, BY COLUMN

(1)   Obtained by subtracting bond yields from railroad stock yields, and then averaging (weighting terminal years according to number of months covered by census data) for the years indicated. For line 6, the average relates to 1931–1937 only, because later ordinates of the nine-year moving averages reflect the World War II years with their artificially low bond-yield rates. The bond and stock yield series are from the following sources:

Bond Yield Series: 1900–1952, from *Historical Statistics of the United States, 1789–1945*, and *Continuation to 1952*, Series N-199. Extension through 1955 is by the series of corporate bonds, 20-year maturity, given in *Statistical Abstract of the United States, 1956*, Table 551, p. 466. Extension back through 1880 is from Frederick R. Macaulay, *Some Theoretical Problems Suggested by the Movements of Interest Rates, Bond Yields and Stock Prices in the United States since 1856* (New York, NBER, 1938), Table 5, col. 3, pp. A111-112. The series for best five bonds is used without splicing, inasmuch as the difference between the series in 1900–1902 is too small to call for any adjustment.

Stock Yield Series: 1880–1937, from *Historical Statistics*, Series N-208. 1938–1955 is the Standard and Poor series in *Statistics; Security Price Index Record, 1957*, pp. 100–103. The series were not spliced inasmuch as the overlapping figures for 1937 were close, although those for 1936 differed considerably.

(2) to (4) Gross of investment in affiliated companies. The data are from Melville J. Ulmer, *Capital in Transportation, Communications, and Public Utilities: Its Formation and Financing* (Princeton for NBER, 1960), Table 46, p. 150.

in favor of bonds declined from 1880–1890 to 1893–1907. While the comparison is necessarily crude, because so few long periods can be used, it does corroborate the responsiveness of the bond-stock ratios to bond-stock-yield differentials. The long swings in the latter can be assumed, therefore, to produce long swings in that aspect of the structure of financing.

A somewhat more telling comparison can be made for mining and manufacturing corporations, but only for the years since 1900. Here we calculate the differential between the yields of industrial stocks and those of high-grade twenty-year bonds (the bond yield index used in the comparison for railroads). Nine-year moving averages of this differential appear in Chart 19, in this case through World War II and later years. We compare this series with the ratio of net bond issues to net stock issues (stocks are used as the denominator rather than total net security issues to minimize the number of periods with negative

CHART 19

Average Differential between Yields of Bonds and of Industrial Stocks Compared with Average Ratio of Net Bond to Net Stock Issues of Manufacturing and Mining Corporations, 1896–1955

a   Difference between yields of bonds and of industrial
     stocks (9-year moving averages)
b   Ratio (%) of net bond to net stock issues
     (averages for successive business cycles)

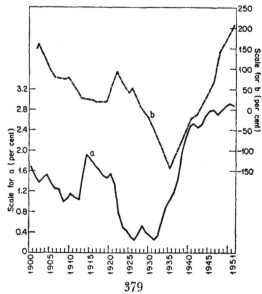

bases), the ratio being averaged for the successive business cycles, positive and inverted. The underlying entries, for the mid-point of each cycle, appear in Table 72. Both lines in Chart 19 describe long cycles: a downward phase from 1900 (or 1902) to either 1912 or the end of 1916; then an upswing to a peak either in the middle of the 1910–1920 decade or at the beginning of the 1920's; a trough in either the early or the mid-1930's; and an upswing to the 1950's. Also, there is rough positive correspondence between the two lines—in accordance with the hypothesis advanced here—although the bond-stock ratio tends to lag behind the bond-stock-yield differentials. The major exception occurs during the years of World War I which are marked by exceedingly large excesses of stock over bond yields, the war having caused a rise in profits and dividend payments of industrial corporations far beyond the rise in market prices of the securities. One could argue that in those years stock yields were far above the minimum needed to attract more money into new securities, and—in terms of our hypothesis—the yield differentials were substantially exaggerated. If one were to lower correspondingly the nine-year moving averages of the yield differentials centered in 1913–1917, the trough in the differentials might well come closer in time to the trough in the bond ratios, and the peak in the differentials would be in 1920. But whether or not such *ad hoc* reasoning is justified, the conclusion remains that there is broad similarity in the long swings in the stock-bond-yield differentials and in the distribution of new issues between stocks and bonds.

It would have been useful to apply the same kind of analysis to the cost of all external financing relative to internal, to ascertain whether there were long swings in the differentials and corresponding long swings in the distribution of total financing between internal and external. But we would need measures of the possible yields on funds from internal sources if invested elsewhere relative to the possible costs of external funds. Even if we had adequate measures of the latter, the estimation of the former would be extremely hypothetical. All we can do at present is to indicate the susceptibility of differentials in yields of various types of credit instruments to long swings, and to suggest that they may be productive of similar swings in the structure of financing, given no offsetting movements on the demand side. And with this suggestion we turn to the limited direct evidence on long-term alternations in financing ratios for selected capital using sectors.

TABLE 72

AVERAGE DIFFERENTIAL BETWEEN YIELDS OF BONDS AND OF INDUSTRIAL STOCKS
COMPARED WITH RATIO OF NET BOND TO NET STOCK ISSUES OF
MANUFACTURING AND MINING CORPORATIONS, SUCCESSIVE BUSINESS CYCLES, 1900–1953

(amounts in millions of dollars)

Dates of Successive Business Cycles (Positive and Inverted)	Mid-Point of Business Cycle (1)	Net Issues Per Year		Ratio (%) (3) to (2) (4)	Average Yield Differential Centered on Year Shown in (1) (%) (5)
		Stocks (2)	Bonds (3)		
1. 1899–1903 ᵃ	1901.5	167	249	149.1	1.98
2. 1900–1904	1902	158	254	160.8	2.05
3. 1903–1907	1905	132	124	93.9	1.24
4. 1904–1908	1906	143	113	79.0	1.07
5. 1907–1910	1908.5	164	124	75.6	0.84
6. 1908–1911	1909.5	177	140	79.1	0.75
7. 1910–1913	1911.5	224	104	46.4	1.32
8. 1911–1914	1912.5	212	59	27.8	1.35
9. 1913–1918	1915.5	295	70	23.7	2.24
10. 1914–1919	1916.5	410	78	19.0	2.29
11. 1918–1920	1919	878	182	20.7	1.00
12. 1919–1921	1920	815	427	52.4	0.41
13. 1920–1923	1921.5	442	406	91.9	0.53
14. 1921–1924	1922.5	385	283	73.5	0.60
15. 1923–1926	1924.5	529	224	42.3	0.53
16. 1924–1927	1925.5	569	304	53.4	0.53
17. 1926–1929	1927.5	953	55	5.8	0.07
18. 1927–1932	1929.5	733	−146	−19.9	0.38
19. 1929–1937	1933	259	−249	−96.1	0.58
20. 1932–1938	1935	174	−249	−143.1	0.72
21. 1937–1944	1940.5	133	−26	−19.5	2.71
22. 1938–1946	1942	234	−28	−12.0	2.54
23. 1944–1948	1946	798	548	68.7	1.99
24. 1946–1949	1947.5	810	1,125	138.9	2.66
25. 1948–1953	1950.5	707	1,394	197.2	3.52
26. 1949–1953	1951	691	1,437	208.0	3.55

ᵃ Average covers 1900–1903.

SOURCE, BY COLUMN

(2) and (3) From Daniel Creamer, Sergei Dobrovolsky, and Israel Borenstein, *Capital in Manufacturing and Mining: Its Formation and Financing* (Princeton for NBER, 1960), Table 51, pp. 162–163.

(5)   Obtained by subtracting bond yields from industrial stock yields and then averaging for the business cycles indicated, terminal years being given half weight. The series on bond yields is identical with that used for col. 1 of Table 71, and the stock yield series is from the sources indicated in the notes to that table.

Long Swings

Financing Ratios for Selected Capital Using Sectors

Agriculture is the first sector for which we can observe fluctuations over time in the ratios of various sources of funds to capital formation (in this instance comprising not only fixed capital and inventories but also changes in cash working balances). The question to be explored is whether the proportions of various sources of funds to the total of

CHART 20

Ratios of Various Sources of Funds to Real Capital Formation Plus Cash Working Balances, Agriculture, Successive Quinquennia, 1900–1949

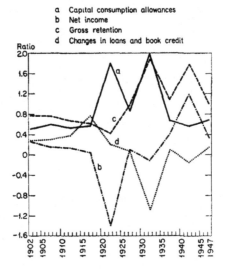

capital formation so financed exhibit any long swings. The relevant ratios are presented in Chart 20 and in Table 73.

One major difficulty with the data for agriculture is that they are for quinquennia—time units too long and too crude for an adequate portrayal of long swings whose duration may average not more than twenty years. But even with this qualification, the ratios in question do not change uniformly in one direction, although on balance there is a strong indication of an underlying trend. Thus, by and large, the trend in the proportion of gross retention (internal financing) to capital formation is upward, and in that of loans and book credit downward—conclusions suggested in our discussion in Chapter 5. But the

Financing of Capital Formation

TABLE 73

Ratios of Various Sources of Funds to Real Capital Formation
Plus Cash Working Balances, Agriculture, Successive Quinquennia, 1900–1949

	Capital Consumption Allowances (1)	Net Income (2)	Gross Retention (1) + (2) (3)	Changes in Mortgage Credit (4)	Changes in Debt to Banks and Federal Agencies (5)	Changes in Other Debt (6)	Changes in Total Loans and Book Credit (4)+(5)+(6) (7)
1. 1900–1904	0.51	0.26	0.77	0.09	0.09	0.09	0.28
2. 1905–1909	0.60	0.16	0.76	0.10	0.10	0.10	0.30
3. 1910–1914	0.53	0.14	0.67	0.26	0.06	0.06	0.37
4. 1915–1919	0.57	0.04	0.61	0.38	0.19	0.19	0.76
5. 1920–1924	1.79	−1.38	0.41	0.59	−0.18	−0.21	0.21
6. 1925–1929	0.86	0.10	0.96	0.14	−0.03	−0.03	0.08
7. 1930–1934	2.00	−0.12	1.88	−0.08	−0.67	−0.33	−1.08
8. 1935–1939	0.67	0.41	1.08	0.01	0.08	−0.01	0.08
9. 1940–1944	0.57	1.20	1.77	−0.13	0.01	−0.03	−0.16
10. 1945–1949	0.68	0.34	1.02	0.03	0.06	0.07	0.15

Because of rounding, detail will not necessarily add to total.

Source: Alvin S. Tostlebe, *Capital in Agriculture: Its Formation and Financing since 1870* (Princeton for NBER, 1957), Table 36, pp. 137 and 138. Real capital formation is the sum of fixed capital and changes in inventories.

ratio of gross retention to capital formation, which declined slightly from 1900–1904 to 1920–1924, thereafter appears to have gone through two swings with peaks in the first half of the 1930's and in the quinquennium affected by World War II. In both these periods capital formation was relatively small, and reliance on internal financing was forced either by tightness in the supply of external funds (during the depression) or by abundance of earned funds (during World War II) or by lack of need for net additions to capital.

Long swings in the ratio of gross retention to total capital formation become more prominent when we distinguish between the capital consumption and net income components of gross retention, with the ratio of capital consumption inverted to that of net income. Finally, for the proportion of external financing to capital formation we find one long swing with a peak during World War I and a trough in the early 1930's, and what appears to be the beginning of another long swing.

To be sure, the world wars and the major depression of the 1930's put their marks on the fluctuations we have been noting, through their effects on prices, on the availability of credit funds, and on the supply of capital goods. But long swings in prices, in output, and in cost and ease of credit funds existed even during the periods when there were no world wars. According to Table 73, there was an up-and-down swing in the ratio of capital consumption to capital formation even from 1900–1904 to 1910–1914. Moreover, war and threats of war, if they affect the financing ratios so profoundly and over such long periods, should not be neglected in consideration of the future.

One other point concerning the movement of the financing ratios is to be noted. The ten quinquennia covered in Table 73 permit us to observe nine changes. For real capital formation plus cash working balances, seven of these are rises and two declines. By and large, the change in the ratio of gross retention to capital formation tends to be inverted to the change in capital formation: the signs differ in six of the nine comparisons. A downward movement in capital formation brings with it a rise in the internal financing proportion, and vice versa. The opposite is true of external financing, with seven agreements in sign out of the possible nine. In other words, an upward swing in capital formation is accompanied by a rise in the external financing proportion, and a downward swing, by a decline. This is what we would expect in the course of the short-term fluctuations associated with business cycles, and there is no reason for the association to be different in the longer swings. While the data on agriculture hardly permit us to test this hypothesis thoroughly, they do suggest it; and we should refer to it in considering the other sectors.

The data on financing ratios for all corporations in mining and manufacturing, which also extend back only to 1900, are somewhat better, because—though rough—they are annual, and we can calculate the averages for successive business cycles.[2] The ratios based on these averages are plotted in Chart 21 and given in Table 74. The difficulty here is that on the uses side of funds, continuous estimates are available for plant and equipment expenditures alone (excluding net changes in inventories and financial assets).

The ratio of gross retention (unadjusted for changes in inventory valuation and differences between original cost and replacement bases of capital consumption allowances) to plant and equipment expendi-

---

[2] Here we omit the overlapping inverted units (peak to peak) and use only the positive business cycles (trough to trough), which are sufficient to reveal the long swings.

CHART 21

Financing Ratios for Manufacturing and Mining Corporations, Successive Business Cycles, 1900–1953

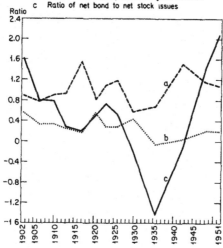

a Ratio of gross retention to plant and equipment expenditures
b Ratio of net security issues to gross retention
c Ratio of net bond to net stock issues

tures for averages for successive business cycles (centered at the midpoint of each cycle) reveals two long swings with peaks in the two world wars. And yet other changes (as the peak in the 1920's) clearly suggest such swings even for periods without wars.

The average volume of plant and equipment expenditures by mining and manufacturing corporations, unlike the average volume of capital formation in agriculture, shows such a strong upward trend that only three of twelve changes are declines. However, if we count as a decline any change of less than a given minimum (in this case 20 per cent from cycle to cycle), we can distinguish five declines and seven rises. With this we can compare changes in the ratios of gross retention (internal financing) and of net security issues to plant and equipment expenditures.[3] In eight of the twelve changes, the movement in the ratio of gross retention is opposite to that in capital ex-

[3] The ratio of net security issues to plant and equipment expenditures is given in Daniel Creamer, Sergei Dobrovolsky, and Israel Borenstein, *Capital in Manufacturing and Mining: Its Formation and Financing* (Princeton for NBER, 1960), Table 40, p. 121; and its movement is somewhat similar to that shown in Chart 21 and Table 74 for the ratio of net security issues to gross retention.

TABLE 74

FINANCING RATIOS FOR MANUFACTURING AND MINING CORPORATIONS, SUCCESSIVE BUSINESS CYCLES, 1900–1953

Dates of Successive Business Cycles	Mid-Points of Business Cycles (1)	Gross Retention as Per Cent of Plant and Equipment Expenditures (2)	Net Security Issues as Per Cent of Gross Retention (3)	Net Bond Issues as Per Cent of Net Stock Issues (4)
1. 1900–1904	1902	89.5	57.3	160.8
2. 1904–1908	1906	77.9	32.8	79.0
3. 1908–1911	1909.5	90.2	33.0	79.1
4. 1911–1914	1912.5	92.8	24.6	27.8
5. 1914–1919	1916.5	153.7	15.6	19.0
6. 1919–1921	1920	82.4	55.7	52.4
7. 1921–1924	1922.5	108.8	29.3	73.5
8. 1924–1927	1925.5	118.3	28.9	53.4
9. 1927–1932	1929.5	57.7	44.5	−19.9
10. 1932–1938	1935	68.4	−6.2	−143.1
11. 1938–1946	1942	150.3	4.3	−12.0
12. 1946–1949	1947.5	116.6	19.8	138.9
13. 1949–1953	1951	107.5	19.2	208.0

SOURCE: Given in or calculated from Creamer, Dobrovolsky, and Borenstein, *Capital in Manufacturing and Mining*, Tables 40 and 51, pp. 121 and 162–163.

penditures; in nine of the twelve, the movement in the ratio of net security issues is positively associated with that in capital expenditures. As in agriculture, but in application to what might be called long-term financing relative to long-term capital expenditures, the long swings in internal financing ratios are negatively associated with, and the long swings in external financing ratios positively associated with, the long swings in capital formation volumes.

The data in Chart 21 and Table 74 relate to net security issues and fixed capital investment alone. But the finding of positive association between long swings in the external financing ratios and those in the volume of total uses (and negative association of the latter with long swings in the internal financing ratios) is confirmed by Dobrovolsky's analysis of the data for samples of large manufacturing corporations, for which reference cycle averages can be computed for years beginning with 1914.[4] Of eight changes in cycle-to-cycle (positive cycles only)

[4] *Ibid.*, Table M-1, pp. 454 and 455, and Table 80, p. 320.

averages of annual volume of total financing, six are rises and two declines; and the changes in the ratio of external financing (short-term and long-term) to total uses are in agreement seven times out of eight. Thus, one may conclude that the associations suggested above between the long swings in external-internal financing ratios and in volumes of total financing hold not only for long-term funds relative to fixed capital investment but also for total funds relative to total financing.

Line *c* in Chart 21 (column 4 in Table 74) relates to the distribution of external financing between stocks and bonds, discussed in connection with Chart 19. The ratio of net bond issues to net stock issues reveals a long swing, roughly similar to the swing in the ratio of net security issues to either internal financing or durable capital expenditures: a drop to the World War I cycle, a rise to the 1920's, a sharp decline to the 1930's, and then another rise to the recent period. The explanation of this movement, in its connection with the industrial bond-stock-yield differentials, was suggested above.

The last sector for which we can observe long swings in the financing ratios is nonfarm residential construction. The data for Chart 22 are annual series taken directly from the Grebler, Blank, and Winnick

CHART 22

Expenditures on New Nonfarm Residential Construction Compared with Ratio of Equity Funds to Total Expenditures, Annually, 1911–1955

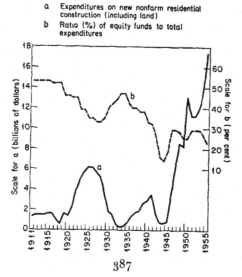

a Expenditures on new nonfarm residential construction (including land)

b Ratio (%) of equity funds to total expenditures

monograph.[5] The two series are new residential construction expenditures, and the ratio of equity funds to total expenditures. The complement of the latter ratio is, of course, the ratio of external funds (predominantly mortgages) to total expenditures, in this case, total uses (sources) of funds.

To be sure, the proportion of equity funds is an estimate based on scattered sources, and is not an exact record (in the usual sense of the word) of the flow of funds. Nevertheless, the evidence of long swings in this ratio of equity funds to total financing, combined with its generally downward trend, is quite significant. Furthermore, the swings are directly inverted to those in the volume of total expenditures—gross capital formation in this sector. During the 1920's when the long swing in nonfarm residential construction was in the up-phase, the ratio of equity funds declined and that of external financing rose; the same happened during the rise from 1933 to 1941 and during the recent rise (since World War II). By contrast, during the decline from the mid-1920's to the mid-1930's, the ratio of equity funds rose and that of external financing declined. The only exception to this inverse correlation between swings in internal financing ratios and in capital formation (or positive correlation of the latter with swings in external financing ratios) occurred during the few years of World War II, when a greatly reduced volume of nonfarm residential construction was accompanied by a decreasing ratio of equity funds and hence a rising ratio of external financing. This resulted from the special character of residential construction during those years (only housing needed for war workers being permitted), which warranted extension of credit and militated against the use of equity funds.[6]

[5] Leo Grebler, David M. Blank, and Louis Winnick, *Capital Formation in Residential Real Estate: Trends and Prospects* (Princeton for NBER, 1956).

[6] "Only during World War II, when new residential construction was limited to housing for war workers and practically all of its debt financing was under the special liberal terms for FHA-insured mortgages, did the ratio fall below 25 per cent." *Ibid.*, p. 182.

CHAPTER 9

Summary of Findings

In the hope that the major findings can be so presented that an attentive reader can follow them without referring to the detailed discussion, it seems useful to provide a summary—if only to bring the threads of the analysis together in a conveniently brief account. In the process of summarizing, however, it is difficult to avoid oversimplifying and, in omitting evidence and qualification, claiming too much. The critical reader should, therefore, turn to the substantive chapters.

The Central Topic (Chapters 1 and 2)

By capital formation we mean diversion of part of the current product for use as capital, that is, goods to produce other goods or income. Specifically, it is defined here to include current construction, flow of producers' durable equipment to users, net additions to inventories of business units and other agencies (but not households), and—in order to allow for this country's position among others—net changes in claims against foreign countries. Gross capital formation is the sum of these four components before deduction of current consumption of fixed capital—construction and producers' durables. Net capital formation is the sum of these four components after deduction of current consumption of fixed capital. In the concepts used here, the sum of gross capital formation and flow of goods to ultimate consumers (households or associations of these) is gross national product. The sum of net capital formation and flow of goods to ultimate consumers is net national product or national income—the two terms being used interchangeably here.

Summary of Findings

Two aspects of this definition of capital formation must be noted even in a brief summary. First, we exclude additions to or drafts upon the stock of capital that result from forces extraneous to economic processes proper. Manna from heaven and fire from hell, fortuitous legacies of nature and the destruction of war, may affect the stock of capital at the disposal of a nation. These effects are not included in capital formation, inasmuch as our interest is in economic processes and in the way they operate to augment or reduce productive wealth at our disposal. This interest is justified, in that additions to capital from current product have been by far the major component of the change in capital stock. If we lived in a world in which productive wealth was greatly and frequently affected by other means, our interest in capital formation as part of current economic product would be far less intense.

The second exclusion from our totals is much more important. The greatest factor in economic capacity to produce is the stock of knowledge—not measured by the commodities (or foreign claims) that enter our capital formation totals. Indeed, there is a question whether such stock can be measured directly in a meaningful fashion. However, among the items that we include in flow of goods to ultimate consumers, some distinctly measure inputs that add to our stock of knowledge, as for example, outlays on education and research; and others contribute to an increase in the productive capacity of human beings by making them healthier and happier, as for example, outlays on medical care and recreation. These items, if identifiable, could be assigned economic magnitudes. But there are two reasons for excluding such uses of current product from capital formation. First, it is hard to draw the line between uses of such goods for the purpose of adding to productive capacity and their uses for a richer life. Second, these investments by ultimate consumers, unlike the components of capital formation defined here, are not part and parcel of the complicated mechanism of capital investment and financing. Yet for many purposes—particularly the study of economic growth over long periods and among widely different societies—the concept of capital and capital formation should be broadened to include investment in the health, education, and training of the population itself, that is, investment in human beings. From this point of view the concept of capital formation followed here is too narrow.

Why, then, do we study capital formation made up of additions to the stock of tangible capital goods? Simply because this stock is indispensable to adequately high levels of economic productivity. Granted that, without the accumulated body of knowledge and a healthy and educated labor force, such stock of capital is useless. Yet, if knowledge does exist and human labor is available to apply it, effective use of those resources requires material capital goods. Major additions to our technology—the mechanization of spinning or weaving, the introduction of coal and coke for smelting iron and making steeel, the invention of the stationary steam engine and its use for transportation, the discovery of electric power and its production in giant hydroelectric plants, and the brilliant promises of power and automation from applications of atomic energy—each has called for large inputs of resources into construction and equipment. One persistent bottleneck in the use of knowledge in economic production has been the scarcity of the resources for the production of capital goods needed for the application of new knowledge. Furthermore, since efficient production requires some minimum of capital goods per worker, the growth of population and the labor force requires accumulation of more capital. This is so even if no capital-demanding innovations are introduced, provided that capital-saving inventions do not swing the balance in favor of the same or higher efficiency with a lower supply of capital per worker.

Capital formation is, therefore, our primary interest because it is essential to economic productivity and economic growth. And since capital formation is diversion from current product, on a countrywide scale it represents the real savings of the nation. In a society such as ours, the basic decisions that determine capital formation are those made by households, business units, and governments, in the disposition of their income between current expenditures and savings. It is these savings that finance capital formation, i.e., permit the would-be users of capital to secure funds for the purchase of capital goods. The relations between national capital formation and the savings of various groups within the nation, which fall under the title of financing, are complex. The question that provides the guiding thread in our study is what determines the volume, composition, and industrial destination of capital formation, and financing is treated as a mechanism, the analysis of which is needed to illuminate approaches to that question.

Capital formation and its financing are strategic not only for long-run economic change—as one group of conditions for economic growth—but also for the short-term fluctuations that affect the course of a country's economic activity—its business cycles. As long known, capital formation fluctuates during business cycles with a far wider amplitude than does flow of consumer goods; and a similarly high sensitivity to business cycles is characteristic of the savings of individuals, business firms, and even governments. For these reasons, the role of capital formation and financing in business cycles, in connection with the problem of economic stability, has long been a subject of economic analysis—of direct bearing upon economic policy. But here our interest lies in the long-term aspects, the trends in capital formation that are of more direct bearing upon economic growth than upon stability, although the two are interrelated.

Long-term trends are sustained movements in one direction, movements that dwarf any fluctuations around or deviations from them. While their measurement requires statistical tools for distinguishing them from the short-term fluctuations, neither the long-term trends nor the short-term cycles are mere statistical artifacts. Life may impress us with its day-to-day ups and downs, and we may often feel that a persistent long-term trend is an illusion. But individuals, business firms, and governments do plan for the longer-range future—a range transcending a month, a year, or even a decade; and, with due allowance for partial failure, the plans are carried through. There is continuity in society, within generations and between generations. And the quantitative data for many aspects of economic production, with no statistical manipulation whatever, display impressive and sustained rises, on which the short-term fluctuations appear as mere ripples. Long-term trends might have been illusory in both the Old World and the New when, for lack of knowledge of natural processes and means of controlling them, the rate of population increase was very low with correspondingly low economic growth potentials. Populations were preoccupied with survival and subsistence, with many a setback (disease, natural calamities, massacres, famines) in the struggle. The last one and a half to two centuries have witnessed, in many now developed countries, long-term trends that far surpassed those of the past in both magnitude and the sustained character of the rise.

In measuring long-term trends in capital formation and financing in this country, we find, however, in addition to short-term fluctuations of some four to nine years' duration—associated with business cycles—long swings in the rate of growth, spanning roughly twenty years. These long swings are particularly prominent in nonfarm residential and related construction, and in durable capital investment by railroads; and they are sufficiently marked in many other components of capital formation and financing to merit attention. Both the statistical treatment and the analytical discussion are, therefore, complicated by the distinction between the long-term trends and the long swings—the former being sustained movements that transcend even the latter in duration.

Trends in Total Capital Formation (Chapter 3)

The measures of capital formation used here extend back to 1869, thus covering a period of over eight and a half decades. It may be asked whether it is realistic to view this long period as framing a continuous process, in which the economy almost ninety years ago is regarded as comparable with the economy today. The treatment is a working assumption, hardly susceptible of definitive proof. All that can be said here is: the period covers not much more than three generations; numerous economic actions initiated even in the 1870's—on railroads and other investments, on expansion to the West, on corporate organization and regulation, to mention but a few—are still influencing us today. Even if many material trappings of the 1950's are the results of inventions and innovations that were unknown in the 1870's, they may at least have been dreamed of then. The basic lines that guide our society are not so novel that our forebears of the post-Civil War days would not find much that is familiar to them and would not be able to understand the problems of economic growth, stability, and security that concern us today. To declare that we live in a new era implies that our past has lost all meaning for us, that it has ceased to influence the patterns of our present life and our individual and institutional responses to the problems of the day. We find it impossible to deny the effects of the past on the present, and hence, on the future.

In measuring long-term trends in capital formation since 1869 we use averages covering twenty to thirty years in order to free the measures from effects of the long, twenty-year swings noted above. The only exception is the single post-World War II decade, used to give us some idea of the recent levels compared with the past, although there is a persistent question whether the averages for 1946–1955 truly represent the long-term trend levels unaffected by the phasing of the long swing.

The growth in the volume of capital formation can first be summarized in terms of dollar values in constant (1929) prices. In this summary we deal with capital formation, excluding the military items (military construction and munitions), which are studied separately in the detailed discussion, and the inclusion of which modifies the broad long-term trends only slightly. We use Variant III national product, for which our estimates are most detailed, although the results yielded by Variants I and II are not very different from those of III.

1. The annual volume of gross capital formation rose from about $3.5 billion in 1869–1888 to $19 billion in 1929–1955, and $30 billion in 1946–1955. This long-term rise over some three-quarters of a century was thus to about nine times the original level.

2. Capital consumption (depreciation) charges, estimated here largely on the basis of constant economic life spans and straight-line depreciation, also rose rapidly, from an annual level of about $1.5 billion in 1869–1888 to over $14 billion in 1929–1955 and slightly over $19 billion in 1946–1955. The rise here was, therefore, to about thirteen times the initial level.

3. Net capital formation also grew appreciably, from $2.0 billion per year in 1869–1888 to $4.7 billion in 1929–1955 (when the average was greatly reduced by the depression of the 1930's and the war emergency of 1942–1945), and to about $10.5 billion in 1946–1955. The rise was to over five times the initial level.

4. Large and rising volumes of capital formation mean cumulatively enormous additions to the stock of reproducible capital at the disposal of the economy. Even the "nettest" measure of this stock—that adjusted for all cumulated depreciation—grew from $27 billion in 1869 to $419 billion in 1955, or between fifteen and sixteen times its original level. The rise is still striking when the net stock of reproducible wealth is related to the labor force or total population: per member of the labor force, it rose from $2,100 in 1869 to $6,400 in 1955, more than tripling; per capita, it rose from $700 in 1869 to $2,500 in 1955, almost quadrupling.

This record of long-term growth in capital formation and in the stock of reproducible wealth is just as familiar as it is impressive. It is common knowledge that, over the decades since 1869, population and economic product of this country grew at high rates. Population increased from 40 million in 1869 to 166 million in 1955, while the labor force grew from 13 million to 66 million. With more people and workers, there was inducement to accumulate more capital not only to supply the workers with tools, households with residences, and other units with needed buildings, but to provide all with roads, bridges, inventories, and so on. With more labor at hand, there was at least one means of doing it. Net national product in 1929 prices grew from $267 per capita in 1869–1888 to $974 in 1946–1955. That growth was both cause and effect of the growth in capital formation. It was cause in that increased product made possible a larger diversion to capital stock, and it was effect in that the growing volume of capital formation and the growing stock of capital permitted higher total output per worker and per capita.

In this impressive but familiar story, the only point to be noted is the striking rise in capital consumption. Since it grew at an appreciably higher rate than that of gross capital formation, its ratio to the latter also rose—from 0.4 in 1869–1888 to 0.65 in 1946–1955. In other words, in the earlier period it took $1.7 of gross capital formation to provide $1 of net capital formation, i.e., net addition to capital stock; in the recent decade it took almost $3 of gross capital formation to do so. What caused that trend, and what is the significance of the growing share of consumption (replacement) in gross capital formation?

The causes are many and technical, but can be summarized briefly and, we hope, intelligibly. First, given a constant economic life span of a durable good (and a simple depreciation schedule), current depreciation or consumption is a mirror of past gross additions. If such additions grow at a decreasing percentage rate, the ratio of current consumption or depreciation to current gross capital formation will rise. Second, if the average economic life span of durable capital declines over time, either because the rate of obsolescence or economic deterioration of a specific good rises, or (as actually happens) the share of the shorter-lived producers' equipment rises relative to the longer-lived construction component, this, too, will cause the ratio of capital consumption to gross capital formation to rise. The third factor, which is in a way a variant of the second, has to do with the share of depreciable durable capital relative to the nondepreciable net components—net changes in inventories and in claims against foreign countries. If the share of depreciable durable capital in total gross capital formation rises, the result again will be a rise in the ratio of capital consumption to total gross capital formation. In fact, all three of the immediate determinants just noted have operated over the time span covered here. The percentage rate of growth of gross capital formation has declined, in association with the slowing down in the rate of growth of population and of national product. The share of producers' durable equipment in gross durable capital formation has risen, and quite appreciably; and the weight of durable capital formation, subject to depreciation, in gross capital formation has also risen.

While the immediate determinants of the rise in the ratio of capital consumption to gross capital formation can be clearly seen, the significance of the rise is not easy to assay. The estimate of capital consumption is after allowance for maintenance and repair. It does not represent physical deterioration, or a decline in the physical capacity of the capital good to produce. It is largely a measure of obsolescence, reflecting the appearance of new and more efficient capital goods with the passage of time. Consequently, replacement of capital consumed means raising the productive capacity over and above the old to the extent measured by the rate of obsolescence—and this is particularly true of producers' capital equipment. An increasing ratio of capital consumption to gross capital formation does not mean that more new capital must be used for replacement, to make good the ravages of physical deterioration. It is rather a measure of the proportion of new capital that is needed to bring the existing stock to the latest level of efficiency. Net capital formation, then, is what remains for addition to capital stock, after the existing stock has been replaced to compensate for the lag in efficiency behind the ever-rising level set by advancing technology.

Any explanation of the levels of, and trends in, capital formation must relate it to national product. When this relation is considered, a query arises why the volumes and rates of growth in capital accumulated, large as they have been, have not been larger.

5. Gross capital formation accounted for about one-fifth of gross national product, both in current and in constant prices. When the comparison is in constant prices, the trend in the ratio is downward—from 22.6 per cent in 1869–1888 to 21.5 per cent in 1909–1928 and to 17.6 per cent in 1946–1955. When the comparison is in current prices, there is a very mild rise or general long-term stability, the percentages being 20.2 in 1869–1888, 20.9 in 1909–1928, and 21.3 in 1946–1955.

6. With gross capital formation a stable or declining proportion of gross national product, and the ratio of capital consumption to gross capital formation rising appreciably, the ratio of net capital formation to national income (or net national product) shows a distinct downward trend. For volumes in constant prices, the share declines from 14.6 per cent in 1869–1888 to 11.2 in 1909–1928 and to 7.0 per cent in 1946–1955; for volumes in current prices the movement is from 13.0 per

cent in 1869–1888 to 11.0 per cent in 1909–1928 and to 8.7 per cent in 1946–1955.

7. A related measure is the ratio of net capital stock to net national product. This average capital-output ratio rises from 3.2 in 1869–1888 to 3.6 in 1909–1928, but drops to 2.5 in 1946–1955. Even in 1929–1955, when the ratio is raised by underutilization of capital during the depression of the 1930's and the war years, 1942–1945 (military items are excluded here and above), it is 3.3—somewhat lower than in 1909–1928. In other words, in recent decades a larger product could be turned out with less capital investment. And this earlier rise and recent decline in the capital-output ratio is also evident when we relate the grosser capital stock total, net of retirements only, to the appropriate national product total.

In the light of these findings, the query raised above can be amplified by asking why, if real product per capita grew 20 per cent per decade, the long-term net national saving rate was below 15 per cent; why it declined instead of rising; and why the share of gross capital formation in gross national product barely exceeded 20 per cent and at best showed only a very slight rise, even for current prices volumes.

These questions can be answered in two ways. One emphasizes the demand for capital funds and implies that under the existing economic and social conditions larger *ex ante* savings would not have found an outlet because capital investment opportunities were limited. If—to illustrate—technological and other factors determine how much capital is needed per unit of final product at a given time, that is, if they fix the level of the net capital-output ratio at, say, not more than 3 or 4 to 1, a rise in final product (national income) at the rate of 4 per cent per year would mean a ratio of net capital formation to national income of not more than 0.12 or 0.16 (0.04×3, or 0.04×4). Yet there are major flaws in this approach to the questions. The purely technological constraints are clear only if we deal with a single product, and with the minimum capital stock needed to produce it. Even then, the actual ratio can vary within wide limits above the indispensable minimum, since the range of choice is wide—in the intensity of utilization of capital and in the recourse to more or less capital-intensive processes. When we deal with a variety of products, as included in national income, the divergence between the minimum capital-output ratio and the one that may actually be realized is all the wider, because if capital funds are readily available the economy may emphasize the more capital-intensive industries or processes. In particular, when we consider the large stock of new knowledge awaiting productive exploitation and the wide investment opportunities abroad that presumably existed throughout most of the period under discussion, it is difficult to assume that the level of capital formation and the factors behind the stability of the gross capital formation proportion and the decline of the net capital formation proportion are the results of long-run limitations upon the supply of capital investment opportunities.

The alternative approach, which emphasizes the supply of savings, seems more plausible and more fruitful as an analytical lead. Given the limited relative contributions to nationwide savings that, under our institutional conditions, could be made by corporations (in the form of undistributed profits) and by governments, the main question suggested by this approach is why the ultimate consumers in our rapidly growing economy managed to save only a small proportion of their income (at best slightly over 10 per cent), and a proportion which, on a net basis, declined rather than rose, despite rising real income per capita.

The various arguments advanced to answer this question indicate that, among the income groups below the very top, savings reasonably justified by the needs they are to serve (retirement, reserves, etc.) can be but a moderate fraction of income; that the share of the very top income groups in total income has been limited both by the very dynamism of our economy and by public policy (on income and inheritance taxation) which have restricted cumulative concentration of wealth in the same hands, and that these limits on the share in income of the top income groups also held down their share in total savings. Central to all the causes of the low savings-income proportion are the basic features of our economic and social life which, with the free association and mobility among economic groups, made for a strong drive for emulative consumption, and the continuous technological changes in both consumer and producer goods, which stimulated a high and rapidly rising consumption demand. At the same time, many expanding consumer expenditures represented education, training, and preparation for higher earnings in the future, and were in fact, for the individuals concerned, substitutes for money savings of the type used to finance capital formation as defined here. Also, forced saving through credit creation by financial institutions and government is subject to limits of its own, in its possible effect on voluntary saving.

Finally, in recent years, particularly since World War II, monetary savings of individuals and corporations have often been heavily offset by government dissavings, that is, by expenditures on current uses (and on military durables, excluded from capital formation in this summary) financed by borrowing rather than by current revenues.

The analysis of trends in total capital formation is thus linked with the discussion of the factors determining the volume of savings, which leads us to the forces that determine the volume of savings of income groups below the top, the forces that set the share of the very top income groups, and those that limit savings of corporations and governments. The analysis thus indicates the need to examine the whole economic and social structure of income recipients and of a wide range of economic institutions; it can therefore do little more than indicate the directions of further exploration. The conclusion of our discussion—that the limitation on savings available for financing capital formation held down capital formation levels and may have accounted for the decline in the *net* capital formation proportion—cannot, therefore, be more than a reasonable impression. The empirical data are not sufficient to permit us to tell whether the factors adduced spell a net capital formation proportion of 10, 15, or 20 per cent, and unmistakably indicate a declining rather than a constant or slightly rising trend. And, in general, *ex post facto* data can never provide definite proof. They cannot enable us to discriminate properly between two alternative hypotheses each of which refers to *ex ante* assumptions: (1) that would-be savings were greater than would-be capital investment opportunities (and that, therefore, the latter served as a brake); or (2) that would-be savings were smaller than would-be capital investment opportunities (and that, therefore, the former served as a brake). Furthermore, the arguments summarized above deal with long-term factors, on both the demand-for-capital and the supply-of-savings sides. In the short run, the level of capital formation can be below the available supply of savings, because the supply may be offered in different forms and on different conditions from those of the demand for capital funds. In the long run, the meshing of supply and demand for funds is attained, and that is the chief purpose of the complex structure of financial intermediaries. But in the short run, supply and demand may not mesh, and the short run is ever with us. In this sense, capital formation may be limited not merely by the supply of savings or the demand for capital investment but also by the factors that produce a short-term mismatching of the two and by the offsetting forces that facilitate and accelerate their adjustment at the highest possible level of capital investment.

Trends in the Structure of Capital Formation (Chapter 4)

In studying a large aggregate like this country's capital formation, much can be learned by examining its components, if they are affected by different factors and hence behave differently. Our classifications are governed largely by the availability of data, but the data, in turn, reflect commonly observed differences in form, type, and channel of capital formation. The trends in the components, like those in the totals, have to be studied with the aid of averages for twenty to thirty years.

With several classifications to be considered, the summary follows the order of the discussion in Chapter 4 and deals separately with the trends in (1) net changes in claims against foreign countries; (2) structure of domestic capital formation by type of capital good—construction, producers' durables, and net changes in inventories; (3) structure of domestic capital formation by category of user—households, business firms, and governments; (4) shares of selected industry sectors—agriculture, mining, manufacturing, and the regulated industries—in net business durable capital formation.

NET CHANGES IN CLAIMS AGAINST FOREIGN COUNTRIES

1. Gross sources of foreign claims against this country (imports of commodities and services, income on foreign investments, and net unilateral transfers) have ranged over long periods (since 1874) between 5 and 8 per cent of gross national product, excluding war years but including military items throughout, since these may give rise to claims. The trend was slightly downward, from 8 per cent in 1874–1895 to 6.8 per cent in 1946–1955. However, the long-term decline is much sharper if we allow for the supporting effects of unilateral transfers on exports. If we exclude these gifts and grants to other countries, which add to their claims against us, the ratio of foreign inflows to gross national product drops from close to 8 per cent in 1874–1895, to less than 6 per cent in 1923–1928, and to 5 per cent in 1946–1955.

2. Gross sources of claims by the United States against foreign countries (exports, and income on investment abroad) ranged from 5.6 to 7.5 per cent of gross national product, excluding war periods but including military items in gross national product, and the ratio showed

no apparent long-term trend. However, the constancy may have been due in part to the bolstering effect of exports by the proportional increase in unilateral transfers.

3. The net balance of inflows and outflows (net foreign capital investment) changed from negative in 1874–1914, that is, from net imports of capital, to positive, or to net investment abroad, despite large unilateral transfers. Except for war periods, the net foreign balance proportions to gross national product, including military, were quite small—less than 1 per cent.

4. These net balances were also moderate fractions of gross capital formation (excluding military items), rising from about −2 per cent in 1869–1898 to a peak of +8 per cent in 1899–1928, and dropping to +2 per cent in 1946–1955. They were larger fractions of net capital formation, ranging from net foreign investment here of about 3 per cent in 1868–1898 to flow of capital abroad of about 20 per cent in 1919–1948 (a proportion raised by the small volume of net domestic capital formation in the depressed 1930's and through the war years), and dropping to less than 6 per cent in 1946–1955.

These findings suggest three questions discussed in detail in Chapter 4.

The first concerns the small contribution that foreign capital made to capital formation in this country from the 1870's to World War I—surprising in view of the rapid growth of this country during that period and the large investment opportunities that it presumably provided. A brief summary of the discussion in Chapter 4 must suffice here.

The limited proportional contribution of foreign capital to the national product and capital formation in the United States is explained by the following facts: the economic magnitude of all would-be creditor countries was limited relative to that of all would-be debtor countries, even if we assume that all the savings of the former could be channeled into foreign investment; only a portion of the domestic savings of foreign net creditor countries was available for flow abroad, the rest being required at home for uses connected with the needs of members of the community who remained at home and would not be induced to migrate by the greater prospects of growth in the would-be borrower countries; of all savings available for foreign investment, a substantial fraction was channeled with political considerations or advantages in mind, of little importance in respect to the United States—neither a colony nor an active participant in the diplomatic combinations of the Old World. One might add that, in general, a large and rapidly developing country is unlikely to secure a large proportion of its capital formation from abroad. The conditions favoring its rapid growth also favor rapid accumulation of domestic savings, and whatever it secured from the limited pool of capital funds available for economically motivated foreign investment could not be a dominant fraction of its own large domestic savings.

The second question—why the United States shifted to a net creditor position even while its domestic growth and internal need for savings were presumably still high—can also be answered by summarizing the more detailed discussion. It was essentially a matter of a more rapid rise in capital exports than in the inflow of capital from abroad. The rise in capital exports was due partly to the greater stimulus for direct investment abroad—a reflection of the growing reliance on imports of raw materials and on exports of manufactured products. Another factor was the greater availability of savings accessible for portfolio investment abroad—a result largely of the growth of the network of financial institutions that externalized savings and made them more fluid. The rise resulted also from the necessarily greater involvement of the old creditor countries in world wars, which necessitated repatriation of their funds from this country during the war periods, and created conditions (extending into the postwar years) in which lending by this country was stimulated largely on government account and as a matter of national interest.

The third question, concerning the factors limiting capital outflow from the United States, once it became a net creditor, to small proportions of its national product and capital formation, can be answered partly by specific reference to conditions existing since World War I— a combination of pressing needs for capital formation at home and of disturbed conditions in many would-be borrower countries. A more general answer would suggest that, aside from the transient pressures that occur during wars, so long as growth of population and advances in technology assure domestic demand for savings originating in this country, even peaceful conditions do not necessarily mean that large proportions of savings would be available for foreign capital investment by the United States. The very size of the country, and those characteristics of its structure noted above in explaining the limited savings propensities and capital formation proportions also suggest the reasons for the limited proportions (although not the absolute amounts) of savings normally available for investment abroad to total savings or to national product.

Summary of Findings

1. The share of gross construction in domestic gross capital formation declined: for volumes in current prices, it dropped from over 60 per cent in the successive thirty-year periods ending in 1918 to 54 per cent in 1929–1955 (and to 53 per cent in 1946–1955); for volumes in constant prices, it declined from close to 70 per cent to less than 50 per cent in 1929–1955 (and 1946–1955). The share of net changes in inventories also declined: for totals in current prices, from about 15 per cent in 1869–1898 to about 5 per cent in 1929–1955 (and 1946–1955); for totals in constant prices, from about 10 per cent in 1869–1898 to about 6 per cent in 1929–1955 (and 8 per cent in 1946–1955). The share of producers' durable equipment rose, and quite markedly: for volumes in current prices, from somewhat over 20 per cent in 1869–1898 to over 40 per cent in 1929–1955 (and 1946–1955); for volumes in constant prices, from about 20 per cent to almost 45 per cent in 1929–1955 (and almost 46 per cent in 1946–1955).

2. The long-term trends in the structure of domestic net capital formation are a bit different. The share of net construction declined, particularly for volumes in constant prices. The share of net producers' durables rose—even more conspicuously than in the gross totals—from somewhat over 10 per cent in 1869–1898 (for volumes in constant prices) to 37 per cent in 1929–1955 (and to 29 per cent in 1946–1955). But the trends in the share of net changes in inventories differ from the trends in their share in domestic gross capital formation: for net volumes in current prices, the share still declined, although moderately, from over 25 per cent in 1869–1898 to 17 per cent in 1929–1955 (and to 16 per cent in 1946–1955); for volumes in constant prices, it tended to rise. In either case, however, even the thirty-year averages show up-and-down movements in the share of net changes in inventories in the domestic net capital formation total.

3. Within total construction we can distinguish nonfarm residential, government, and "other." This last category (a residual) includes farm construction, business and plant construction, and construction by non-profit institutions, but the business sector dominates it. On the basis of values in constant prices, we find that the share of governments in total construction rose rapidly and markedly, to the point where the share of government construction in total domestic capital formation also rose. The share of nonfarm residential construction in gross construction declined somewhat, from 40 per cent in 1869–1898 to about 30 per cent in 1929–1955 (and 34 per cent in 1946–1955), but its share

in the net total rose from over 50 per cent in 1869–1898 to 64 per cent in 1929–1955 (and 58 per cent in 1946–1955). In either case, the share of nonfarm residential construction in domestic capital formation would show a downward trend—but not a marked one. It is the share of other construction in both gross and net total construction that markedly declined: in gross, from well above 50 per cent in 1869–1898 to below 40 per cent in 1929–1955 (and 1946–1955); in net, from above 40 per cent in 1869–1898 to a negative amount in 1929–1955 (and to 15 per cent in 1946–1955). Obviously, the sharp drop in the rate of growth of other construction accounts largely for the decline in the share of construction in total domestic capital formation.

Some of these findings bear closely upon the allocation of capital formation among major user groups and can best be discussed in the next section. Here we limit our comments to the trends in the share of net changes in inventories in domestic capital formation, and in the share of other—essentially business—construction, relative to those in the share of producers' durable equipment.

Our long-term estimates of net changes in inventories are less reliable than those of the other capital formation components, and our knowledge of the factors that determine allocation of capital formation between them and the other components is equally limited. The one argument advanced in the discussion begins with the obvious statement that net changes in inventories and net durable capital formation, particularly business, serve the same end, that is, facilitate additions to final product. If we assume that the ratios of net changes in inventories and net durable capital formation to additions to final product remain constant (or are subject to similar trends), the share of net changes in inventories in *net* domestic capital formation will remain constant. We know that the share of capital consumption in gross domestic capital formation rose, and that the share of net in gross domestic capital formation declined. It follows that a constant or even slightly rising share of net changes in inventories in *net* domestic capital formation means a declining share in *gross* domestic capital formation. In this explanation of the findings just noted, the unresolved point is whether the ratios of net changes in inventories and of net durable capital formation to additions to final product were constant or moved similarly. There is ground for assuming that the same factors determine both ratios to some extent: expansion of durable capital also means expansion of inventories. Our estimates permit us to calculate the ratios and see how they moved, but in view of the crudity of the inventory estimates, great reliance cannot be placed on this evidence.

The rise in the share of producers' durable equipment and the decline in the share of other construction in domestic capital formation, whether gross or net, mean that *within* durable business capital formation, gross or net, the shift away from construction and toward durable equipment (machinery, tools, etc.) has been marked. No complete explanation of this shift is provided by the data at our disposal, but some forces behind it can be suggested. The trend is apparently the result of a combination of intraindustry and interindustry shifts. Within certain major industrial sectors—agriculture, mining, manufacturing, the regulated industries (particularly the last)—the early phases of expansive growth and capital formation were characterized by substantial shares of construction. The new farm structures, industrial plants, and transportation systems were built, and the initial heavy investment in track, buildings, and so on, was made. In the later phases of their growth these industries could turn out an increasing volume of product with minor additions in construction, and there was a shift to more equipment. Among the industrial sectors, those with a higher ratio of construction to equipment, particularly the utilities, were of far greater weight in total business capital formation between the 1870's and 1914 than in more recent decades, and that interindustry shift contributed to the declining share of construction relative to that of machinery and equipment. Along the same lines, certain recent technological changes may also have contributed to the same result: the modern type industries producing highly fabricated, lighter products tend to have a lower ratio of construction to equipment than the older type industries producing primary metal shapes and other simpler kinds of products. Interestingly enough, there were similar trends away from the heavy construction frame and base to more equipment even within nonfarm residential construction.

STRUCTURE OF DOMESTIC CAPITAL FORMATION, BY CATEGORY OF USER

The distribution of domestic capital formation among households, business firms, and governments is crude, because we have to employ for this purpose the components already distinguished by type of capital good. Thus the share of households is identified with that of nonfarm residential construction, and is too small, in that it excludes farm housing. The share of governments is limited to government construction (local, state, and federal) and is too small, in that it excludes producers' durable equipment flowing to governments, and changes in government inventories. The share of business firms—a sum of "other" construction, producers' durable equipment, and net changes in inventories—is too large, in that it includes most of the items excluded from the other categories, as well as capital formation by nonprofit institutions. Yet, granting these defects in the classification, the broad trends differ little from those that would be revealed by a more accurate classification.

1. The share of the government sector rose, in both gross and net domestic capital formation, in both constant and current prices. The share in the gross totals rose from less than 5 per cent in the early decades to over 15 per cent in 1929–1955; the share in the net totals rose from less than 5 per cent to 24 or 28 per cent in 1929–1955, and to 15 or 13 per cent in 1946–1955. This rise would be somewhat greater if we could include durable equipment flowing to governments and changes in their inventories.

2. With this rise in the share of governments, the share of the private sector—a sum of households and business firms—declined, and the decline would tend to characterize the share of each of the two private user sectors. Of greater interest are the differences in trend between the two private sectors, in the long-term movements in the shares of households and of business firms in total private domestic capital formation. On the basis of the gross totals, the share of households declined: moderately for totals in current prices (from 24 per cent in 1869–1898 to 22 per cent in 1899–1928, to 21 per cent in 1929–1955, and to 21.5 per cent in 1946–1955); and more sharply for totals in constant prices (from 29 per cent in 1869–1898 to 23 per cent in 1899–1928, and to 18 per cent in both 1929–1955 and 1946–1955). The picture changes when we shift to net totals: for totals in current prices, the share of households shows a rise (moving from 30 per cent in 1869–1898 to 29 per cent in 1899–1928, to 40 per cent in 1929–1955, and to 38 per cent in 1946–1955); for totals in constant prices, however, the share of households again dropped, though rather moderately (moving from 38 per cent in 1869–1898 to 30 per cent in 1899–1928, to 34 per cent in 1929–1955, and to 32 per cent in 1946–1955). The decline (or rise in net, in current prices) in the share of the household sector in total private domestic capital formation is matched by a rise (or decline in net, in current prices) in the share of the business sector, although—to repeat—the shares of both private sectors in the totals including governments tended to decline.

Summary of Findings

The marked rise in the share of the government sector in domestic capital formation—even when military items are excluded, as here—is closely associated with the rise in the share of governments in employment and other aspects of economic activity. The underlying factors are discussed in some detail elsewhere. Here we merely add that this trend in the allocation of capital formation is a combination of two variables. One, the rising share of governments in economic activity, is a result of the growing complexity of the domestic structure and of international relations, which compels the governments to assume greater responsibility for facilitating and supervising internal stability and growth and for assuring external security. The other variable, the relation between the volume of government activity and the capital needed for it, is a ratio that cannot be measured precisely, but it is not likely to be lower than the capital-output ratio for the private sector, and its trend may have made for a greater relative draft by governments upon capital investment. Further exploration in this direction calls for the long-needed scrutiny of the capital and income flows in the government sector, involving a functional analysis of government expenditures on both current and capital account.

On the rather disparate trends in the distribution of private capital formation between the household and business sectors, only general comments are appropriate here. First, if gross capital formation by the business sector and by households show the same rates of growth, we would expect the ratio of capital consumption to gross capital formation to rise more rapidly in the business sector, if only because of the shift from longer-lived construction to shorter-lived producers' durable equipment, and because of the reduction in the share of net changes in inventories in gross capital formation. Hence, we would expect the share of business in *net* private capital formation to decline, even though its share in *gross* private capital formation was constant or rising moderately—and this is what we find.

Second, prices of construction have risen more than prices of other goods—partly a reflection of the technological backwardness of that sector compared with industries turning out producers' durable equipment and even most consumer commodities. As a result, the trends in the structure of capital formation in current prices are markedly different from those in the structure of totals in constant prices. More important, the increase in relative prices of construction may be viewed as a causal factor in reducing the demand for its volume in

407

constant prices relative to the demand for other components that have become cheaper. This, clearly, lies behind the greater drop in the share of the household sector (nonfarm residential construction) in the totals in constant prices than in the totals in current prices.

Finally, the volume of both business and household capital formation can be related to the number of ultimate consumers, via the demand for new housing and for additional quantities of other goods for whose production new business capital formation is needed. It was thus possible to show in Chapter 4 that the relative trends in household and in business capital formation can be reduced to trends in the number of ultimate consumers, in their demand for housing and other goods, and in the relevant capital-output ratios that link capital formation with the production of final goods.

SHARES OF SELECTED INDUSTRY SECTORS IN
NET BUSINESS DURABLE CAPITAL FORMATION

For net flow of business construction and producers' durable equipment in 1880–1948, we can draw upon the several monographs to distinguish the shares of agriculture, mining, manufacturing, and the regulated industries. These accounted for about 80 per cent of net durable capital formation in the business sector in 1880, and have dominated that sector throughout the period. The trends summarized below are for shares in the total of these industries (the allocable total) in constant prices, and are observed over three subperiods, 1880–1900, 1900–1922, and 1922–1948.

1. The share of agriculture in the allocable total of net durable capital formation shows no decline, the percentages for the three successive subperiods being 12, 17, and 12. But these are lower than agriculture's share in the allocable *stock* in 1880—32 per cent; hence, the share of agriculture in the allocable stock declined—to 18 per cent in 1948.

2. The share of mining and manufacturing (combined) in the allocable total of net durable capital formation rose, from 38 per cent in 1880–1900 to 47 per cent in 1900–1922, and to 49 per cent in 1922–1948. These shares are appreciably higher than the sector's share in the initial stock in 1880—11 per cent; the sector's share in the allocable stock, therefore, increased—to 39 per cent in 1948.

3. The share of the regulated industries in the allocable total of net durable capital formation declined, dropping from 50 per cent in 1880–1900 to 36 per cent in 1900–1922, then rising to 38 per cent in

1922–1948. These shares are all lower than the share of the sector in the initial stock in 1880—57 per cent; the share of the sector in the allocable stock, therefore, declined—to 44 per cent in 1948.

4. The trends in the shares of the sectors in net durable capital formation are different from the trends in their shares in volume of output or net product originating (also in constant prices). In both totals, the share of agriculture declined (in volume of output, from 36 per cent in 1880 to 10 per cent in 1948, and in net product, from 55 to 14 per cent). In both totals the share of mining plus manufacturing rose (in volume of output, from 59 to 74.5 per cent, and in net product, from 38 to 59 per cent). In both totals the share of the regulated industries rose sharply (in volume of output, from 5 to 15 per cent, and in net product, from 7 to 27 per cent).

5. The initially different distributions of net capital stock and of output, and the divergent trends in the shares of the sectors in net durable capital formation and in output result in wide differences among the several sectors in both the initial average capital-output ratios and their trends. The ratio of net capital stock (durable) to net income originating in 1880 was 1.7 for agriculture, 0.9 for mining and manufacturing combined, and as high as 23.6 for the regulated industries. By 1922, the ratio for agriculture had risen to 2.3, and that for mining and manufacturing to 1.8. While by 1948, the ratio for agriculture had declined to 2.0, and that for mining and manufacturing to 1.0, these terminal ratios were still higher than those in 1880. By contrast, the ratio for the regulated industries declined to 5.6 in 1922, and to 2.5 in 1948. This decline was large enough to dominate the total: the over-all ratio dropped from 3.0 in 1880 to 2.7 in 1922, and then precipitously to 1.6 in 1948.

6. There was clearly convergence among the major sectors with respect to their capital-output ratios: in 1880, they were 1.7, 0.9, and 23.6; in 1948, they were 2.0, 1.0, and 2.5, respectively. Convergence was also observed *within* these sectors in the detailed studies which distinguish regions in agriculture and industries within mining, manufacturing, and the regulated sector.

The few paragraphs above summarize the discussion in Chapter 4, which is, in turn, a summary of the more detailed analysis in the monographs. Upon the many findings presented in the monographs, two general comments are appropriate.

First, the rapidity with which capital-output ratios changed—even those for the major sectors—is impressive. To illustrate: the ratio for manufacturing rose from 0.8 in 1880 to 1.3 in 1900, a rise of more than one-half the initial value in two decades. It then declined from 1.58 in 1922 to 0.98 in 1948. In agriculture the ratio dropped from 1.7 in 1880 to 1.5 in 1900, and then rose to 2.3 in 1922, again, a rise of more than half its value in about two decades. And the speed with which the ratio declined in the regulated industries sector has already been noted. For narrower industrial divisions, the average capital-output ratio obviously changed at even greater rates, and when we shift from average to marginal ratios, both the trends and fluctuations become more prominent. Thus, even if we deal, as in this work, with averages over long periods, the capital-output ratios for separate sectors move quite rapidly. There is somewhat more stability in the nationwide ratios, but this means in essence that secular stability in the capital-output ratio is to be expected for wide aggregates and has little to do with the technological factors that have impact upon specific industries.

Second, the convergence among industries—the reduction in the range of the capital-output ratios—is clearly a significant phenomenon. Sectors that begin their growth with high ratios of capital to output, are likely to experience a rapid decline in their ratios, as extensive expansion of capacity intended for the long future subsides, and as the high ratio of capital per unit of output provides extra incentives for capital saving innovations. On the other hand, the emergence and growth of high capital-output ratio industries may, in and of itself, serve to raise the capital-output ratios in other industries, by facilitating greater mechanization and concentration, and by setting new patterns of business organization that extend the feasible scale of firm operation. It is hardly an accident that the growth of the regulated industries and the reduction in their capital-output ratios coincided with the greater industrialization of agriculture and mechanization of mining and manufacturing and the rise in the capital-output ratios of those sectors, at least to the 1920's. But such convergence has its limits. It is not unlikely that the next decades will show no further convergence, if new sectors with high capital-output ratios loom larger than they did during the recent decades.

Trends in the Share of Internal Financing (Chapter 5)

The attempt to establish meaningful trends in the financing of capital formation encounters two new obstacles. The first, and more obvious, is that our estimates extend back only to 1900, and financing flows are far more sensitive to wars, major depressions, and other disturbances than are capital formation and national product flows. With two world wars, a decade of cold war, and one of the greatest depressions on record—all within some five to six decades—the establishment of long-term trends is difficult, and the results perforce subject to serious qualification.

The second obstacle encountered is even more difficult to overcome. Financing is a process that can best be judged from the standpoint of the individual capital using unit—the household, the business firm, the government agency. Ideally, we should have data for each unit rather than aggregates, and they should cover periods short enough to be unaffected by cancellation of borrowing by repayment. Even then, the units would be found to use not only capital goods but also financial assets, with shifts from one type of asset to another and one type of liability to another. Unfortunately, our data are aggregates for large groups, canceling claims and obligations among units and over substantial time periods. Consequently, we can distinguish between internal and external sources of funds, not for each decision making unit, but only for large industry aggregates; we cannot reduce net changes in sources of funds to the underlying gross borrowing and repayment; and we can associate certain sources of funds with capital formation only by dint of somewhat unrealistic assumptions. More important, our estimates tend to overstate the share of internal financing and understate the share of external financing—as these are viewed by individual economic units; and the long-term movements they show reveal only part of the change that may have occurred in the structure of financing. They must, therefore, be treated as only a partial account of the trends in the relation between capital formation and the financing flows.

For business units, internal funds are capital consumption and depletion allowances plus net undistributed income—a total referred to as gross retention. For households, in connection with nonfarm residential housing, internal funds are the estimated equity shares in the cost of new housing (including land and major alterations), derived by subtracting from total cost the mortgage advances (and sales contracts, which are quite small). For governments, internal funds are derived as the difference between capital outlay and net borrowing, or between additions to assets and net changes in debt. In each case, the basic difference between internal and external financing is that the fund using units have greater discretion in regard to the former than the latter—since external financing involves a decision not only by the user but also by the lender. Unless otherwise indicated, we discuss here financing gross of capital consumption allowances, related, naturally, to gross capital formation or to total uses of funds.

1. For the economy as a whole, the ratio of internal financing to total uses declined, and correspondingly, the ratio of external financing to total uses rose—but the changes were moderate. From 1900 to 1929 the former averaged 0.53; from 1930 through 1955 it averaged 0.42. For selected normal periods, 1900–1909 (or 1901–1910), 1920–1929 (or 1921–1930), and 1945–1955 (or 1946–1956), it averaged 0.60, 0.58, and 0.56, respectively. The trend in the average ratio of gross retention to gross capital formation was also downward: it dropped from 0.72 in the first three decades to 0.61 in the last two and a half; and, over the selected periods, it moved from 0.78 to 0.76 and to 0.77.

2. This decline in the countrywide ratio of internal financing was associated largely with a decline in the ratio of internal financing for households (in connection with nonfarm residential housing) and for the federal government. In nonfarm residential housing, capital formation and total uses of funds are taken as identical, and the ratio of internal financing to that total declined from 0.44 in 1901–1930 to 0.28 in 1931–1955; or, in the three selected periods, from 0.65 to 0.37 to 0.27. For the federal government, the vast noncapital expenditures out of borrowed funds during the depression and World War II, and even in some of the later years, made for the decline in the ratio of internal funds to total uses or to capital formation (excluding military durables). Even in 1900–1929, internal funds were negative, averaging about −$0.2 billion per year; in 1930–1955, they averaged close to −$7 billion. This increase in the federal government's reliance on external financing contributed heavily to the rise in the share of external sources in the countrywide totals and thus to the decline in the share of internal sources.

3. By contrast, the trend in the ratio of internal financing for the business sector—the combined total of agriculture, nonfarm unincorporated business, and corporations—and for state and local governments was upward, though in some cases only moderately so. For the business sector, the ratio of internal sources to total uses rose from 0.59 in 1900–1929 (or 1901–1930) to 0.72 in 1930–1955 (or 1931–1956), but in the latter period the ratio was exaggerated by the peculiar experience of the depression and the war years. The ratio in the selected periods shows but a mild rise, averaging 0.59 in the first decade of the century and in the 1920's, and rising to 0.64 in the post-World War II

years. The movement of the ratio of internal financing to gross capital formation was also upward. For state and local governments, the rise in the ratio of internal financing was more conspicuous: the average ratio to total uses rose from 0.52 in 1900–1929 to 0.80 in 1930–1956, and in the selected periods moved from 0.47 to 0.56 to 0.72. The ratio to gross capital formation also rose, and fairly continuously.

4. Within the business sector proper, the trend in the ratio of internal financing differed for the three major subdivisions. For agriculture, the trend was definitely upward: the ratio to total uses moved from 0.60 in 1900–1929 to 0.91 in 1930–1955, and in the three selected periods, from 0.72, to 0.66, to 0.83. The ratio to gross capital formation reveals similar trends. No such clear trend is observable for nonfarm unincorporated business. True, the average ratio of internal financing to total uses rose from 0.72 in 1900–1929 to 0.81 in 1930–1955, but in the selected periods it was 0.63, 0.78, and 0.63, respectively; and in the ratio to gross capital formation there is similarly no evidence of a rising trend. For both agriculture and nonfarm unincorporated business, the conclusions are affected not only by the fact that our estimates are limited to net aggregates but also by the relatively large volume of entries and exits. Exits from agriculture add to external financing if the retiring farmers, in selling their farms, convert their accumulated savings into debts of the purchasers in the form of mortgages on the hitherto unencumbered farms. Such additions to external financing have no connection with capital formation or uses of funds. Then, too, shifts of unincorporated units to corporate status tend to withdraw those units that have accumulated substantial internal funds, substantial relative to their uses. Internal financing ratios may be understated by these shifts in and out of the two sectors; but the effects on trends cannot even be conjectured.

5. For corporations, the dominant group of the business sector, the ratio of internal financing shows a slight upward trend. The ratio to total uses (nonfinancial corporations) averaged 0.57 in 1901–1929 and 0.67 in 1930–1956; and in the selected periods free from wars and major depressions, it averaged 0.55 (in 1901–1912), 0.55 (in 1923–1929), and 0.61 (in 1946–1956). The average ratio to gross capital formation (all corporations) was 0.91 in 1901–1929 and 0.97 in 1930–1956; in the selected periods, it was 0.85, 0.92, and 0.91, respectively.

6. For business corporations, we can also compare net retention (corporate savings) with net capital formation or net total uses, both unadjusted—as were the gross flows—for effects of changes in valua-

tion of inventories or difference between cost and replacement bases of capital consumption. The ratio of net retention to net capital formation shows a slight upward trend, averaging 0.34 in 1901–1929 and 0.39 in 1930–1956, and in the selected periods, 0.33 (in 1901–1912), 0.28 (in 1923–1929), and 0.37 (in 1946–1956). The ratio of net retention to total uses shows no such rise, averaging 0.22 in 1901–1929 and in 1930–1956, and in the selected periods, 0.22, 0.17, and 0.23, respectively.

7. Among corporations, we have separate data for mining and manufacturing, and the regulated industries. In mining and manufacturing, the average ratio of gross retention to plant and equipment expenditures rose, from 0.88 in 1900–1914 to 1.04 in 1920–1929, and to 1.12 in 1946–1953. For large manufacturing corporations, the ratio of gross retention to total uses shows no distinct trend, averaging 0.70 in 1900–1910, 0.97 in 1920–1929, and 0.67 in 1946–1953, but the samples are too small (particularly in the early years) to warrant much confidence in the results. In the regulated industries, the trend is much more prominent: the ratio of gross retention to total uses averaged, roughly, 0.2 in 1901–1910 and 0.62 in 1941–1950.

Before we make any general comments upon the findings, the reader must be warned of the qualifications, which apply particularly to trends inferred from ratios in which changes over time are neither large nor consistent. With this caution, the following comments are offered.

First, one is impressed by the diversity of the trends in the internal financing ratios in the several sectors. In some, they decline quite markedly, as in nonfarm residential real estate and the federal government; in some, they rise appreciably, as in the agriculture sector, the regulated industries, and state and local governments; in still others, no marked trends are discernible, as in nonfarm unincorporated business, or the trends are only slightly upward, as in mining and manufacturing corporations. In addition, for some sectors, the trends differ as we take the ratio of internal financing to total uses—the more defensible comparison—or as we relate internal financing to capital formation alone. The diversity of trends reflects the differences in complexes of factors that determine the financing of capital formation or total uses in the several sectors—at least as revealed by our data. The forces that may have contributed to diminished reliance by households on equity funds and greater reliance on mortgages in purchasing nonfarm residential housing—the decline in the ratio of the value of house units to average income, the increasing stability of consumer incomes, the growing assistance of government guarantees, and the wider acceptance of consumer credit—are different from the forces that affect the ratios of internal financing of corporations and other business units. They are different also from the factors determining financing by the federal government. There are differences also between the factors determining financing by the federal government and those determining financing by the business sector. Even within the business sector proper, the factors that set the financing ratios for the major industry groups can differ widely.

Second, while disparate complexes of factors affect the financing ratios for the different sectors of the economy, those sectors are parts of a coordinate, operating system. What happens in one, must affect the others. Consequently, there are some lines of association among the different trends, and these too can be discerned. Thus, the factors that made for huge federal government deficits during the last two to two and a half decades and lowered the ratio of internal financing for that sector also made for improvement in the net income position of the agricultural sector. They permitted it and many industries within private business to earn their capital consumption allowances and to effect substantial net savings, which helped raise their internal financing ratios. The same factors, contributing as they did to greater stability of consumer incomes as well as to rising price levels, made possible greater reliance on external financing by households in connection with nonfarm residential housing. In other words, behind the declining shares of internal financing in some sectors and the rising shares in others there were common factors. As a result, the financing ratios for the country as a whole tended to be more stable in the long run than those for the individual sectors.

Finally, there is a seeming contradiction between the marked rise in the ratio of capital consumption to gross capital formation, observed in Chapter 4, and the rather moderate rise in the share of internal financing for the economy, when we exclude the federal government with its use of capital funds to cover current expenditures. Earned capital consumption allowances should represent internal financing; and a marked long-term rise in their ratio to gross capital formation would lead us to expect a sizable rise in the share of internal financing. Yet even for the business sector, the upward trend in the share of internal financing is moderate relative to the rise in its ratio of capital consumption to gross capital formation.

There are essentially two reasons for the difference. One is that the financing ratios cover only the period since 1900—not since 1869—and for that shorter period, the rise in the ratio of capital consumption to gross capital formation was not so large as for the longer period. The second is that our analysis of capital formation deals with totals adjusted for inventory valuation changes and the difference between the cost and replacement bases of capital consumption allowances. In the analysis of financing, however, we emphasized the unadjusted totals, in which the general rise in prices tends to reduce the rise in the ratio of capital consumption allowances to capital formation (both in constant prices). While that reduction in the rise of the ratio of capital consumption should presumably be offset by a rise in the ratio of net undistributed profits, a complete offset apparently did not occur—at least so far as our estimates for corporations indicate. Thus, whereas in the adjusted totals the average ratio of gross retention to gross capital formation rose from 0.72 in 1897–1914 to 0.88 in 1940–1956 (or 0.81 in 1946–1956), in the comparable unadjusted totals (differing somewhat from those utilized above) the ratio rose from 0.71 to 0.83 (or 0.78)—12 instead of 16 (or 7 instead of 9) points. Finally, in relating gross retention to total uses (rather than to gross capital formation), we included changes in financial assets, usually short-term; and external financing is far more dominant in the financing of those assets than it is in the financing of gross capital formation.

Trends in the Structure of External Financing (Chapter 6)

External financing of an economic unit means provision of funds from the outside, either equity in the form of stocks, or debt financing—long-term or short-term. Such financing may flow directly from the lender to the user, or via financial intermediaries (banks, insurance companies, etc.). The detailed discussion of long-term changes in such financing can best be summarized if we deal separately with trends in: (1) distribution of external financing, by category of user of funds; (2) share of equity financing; (3) long-term and short-term debt financing; (4) shares of financial intermediaries.

DISTRIBUTION, BY CATEGORY OF USER OF FUNDS

1. In the distribution of the economy's total external financing, the striking rise in the share of the federal government is the dominating trend: the share rose from an average of 0.08 in the first three decades

of the century to an average of 0.49 in the last two and a half. For the three selected periods (the first decade in the century, the 1920's, and the post-World War II years), the rise was less striking but still marked, the average ratio moving from 0.01, down to −0.09, and up to 0.11. For the selected periods, the average share of the household sector (non-farm residential housing) also rose, moving from 0.17 to 0.33 and to 0.25. The share of state and local governments tended to be stable in those periods, the average share being 0.09, 0.13, and 0.09, respectively. The shares of the other sectors—agriculture, corporations, nonfarm unincorporated business—declined.

2. The average share of households in total private external financing rose markedly, from 0.26 in the first three decades to 0.35 in the last two and a half, and moved from 0.19 to 0.34 to 0.32 in the three selected periods. The average share of corporations shows no distinct trend, remaining at a level close to 0.60. That of agriculture declined markedly; that of nonfarm unincorporated business declined only slightly.

3. Within total external financing for the business sector, corporations were dominant, accounting for two-thirds to almost nine-tenths, disregarding the World War II years. The trend in their average share was upward, from about seven-tenths in the first two decades of the century to close to nine-tenths either in the 1920's or in the post-World War II years. The shares of agriculture and nonfarm unincorporated business declined.

These trends in the distribution of total external financing among users are due to a combination of the trends in the external financing ratios within each sector with the trends in the shares of the sectors in total uses or total financing for the country. Thus, the decline in the share of the business sector in total external financing is a product of the decline in the share of external financing within the business sector (discussed in Chapter 5) and the slight decline in the share of the sector in total uses (which changed from an average of 0.7 in the first decade of the century to somewhat over 0.6 in the 1920's and in the post-World War II years). Much of the discussion in Chapter 5, as well as in Chapter 4 (on the shares of users in gross capital formation), is relevant here in accounting for the trends summarized above.

SHARE OF EQUITY FINANCING

We can study equity financing only in the form of net stock issues—for the corporate sector alone. For the unincorporated sectors, equity funds may be contributed by various informal arrangements, but we cannot gauge their volume or ascertain their precise character.

1. For all nonfinancial corporations, the share of net stock issues in total external financing declined, although not consistently: it averaged 0.35 in the first three decades and 0.27 in 1930–1955, rising from 0.31 in the first period of the century to 0.43 in the 1920's, only to decline sharply to 0.21 in the post-World War II decade. The share in all long-term external financing (i.e., excluding short-term debt financing from the denominator) moved similarly, but the decline was not as marked: the movement was from an average of 0.46 in 1901–1929 to 0.43 in 1930–1955, and in the three selected short periods (1901–1912, 1923–1929, and 1946–1955), from 0.38 to 0.47 and to 0.34.

2. The trends in the shares of net stock issues in either total external or long-term external financing can also be studied separately for the mining and manufacturing corporations and for those in the regulated industries (referred to as public utilities). For both groups these trends were downward, although they were no more consistent over time than those for nonfinancial corporations as a whole.

3. The share of equity financing in external financing—measurable here only for stock issues—can be studied for all business, for the private sector, and for the economy as a whole. In every case, the share of equity financing declined in the long run. For example, the share in total external financing for the country dropped from an average of 0.17 in 1900–1929 (or 1901–1930) to 0.07 in 1930–1955 (or 1931–1956), and moved from an average of 0.12 in the first two decades to 0.20 in the next two, and to 0.07 in the last decade and a half.

In the attempt to explain the trend in the share of equity financing, it is best to emphasize its share in long-term external financing, which excludes the possible effects of a rise in short-term debt (summarized below). The question, then, is why the use of equity funds by corporations declined relative to long-term external financing—a question that may seem all the more puzzling since the large corporations are in the best position to issue stocks, and the weight of the larger firms in the corporate total must have increased.

The answer suggested in the detailed discussion notes the recent disparity in cost in favor of long-term debt relative to equity money (yield of stocks), the tax advantage of deductible payments on fixed debt, as well as the increasing willingness of corporations to assume such debt in view of their stronger position and of the general expectation of rising prices. While all these are relatively recent factors, so is the decline in the share of equity financing in long-term external financing. As to the possible effect of the growing proportion of large corporations in the direction of raising the share of net stock issues, it may have been offset not only by their greater willingness to assume long-term debt obligations, but also by the possibly increasing share of internal financing in total financing within these larger units. Hence, their growth meant less than a proportional contribution to long-term external financing—whether equity or debt.

LONG-TERM AND SHORT-TERM DEBT FINANCING

Short-term debt is limited here to notes and accounts payable, because short-term bonds and notes (maturing within five years) could not be segregated from other bonds and notes before 1919. Consequently, short-term debt is understated and long-term debt overstated, although for most periods and for a definition that limits short-term debt to not much more than two years, the unwarranted shifts in proportions are rather minor.

1. For all nonfinancial corporations, the ratio of short-term debt financing to all external financing rose, averaging 0.22 in the first three decades and 0.38 in 1930–1955, and in selected periods (1901–1912, 1923–1929, and 1946–1955), 0.18, 0.09, and 0.37, respectively. This means that the trend in the ratio of long-term external financing (equity and debt) to total external financing was downward. The ratio of short-term debt financing to all debt financing also rose, from an average of 0.34 in 1901–1929 to 0.52 in 1930–1955 and, in the selected shorter periods, moved from 0.27 to 0.16 to 0.47. For the mining and manufacturing corporations, there were similar movements in the ratio of short-term debt financing to either total external financing or to total debt financing.

2. For agriculture, we classified debt to banks, federal agencies, and others as short-term, and mortgage loans as long-term. On this definition, the ratio of short-term debt financing to external financing or to total debt financing (the two are identical for unincorporated sectors because there are no equity issues) rose: it was roughly 0.3 in the first three decades and somewhat over 0.6 in the last two and a half, and moved from 0.5 in 1900–1914 to 0.6 in 1945–1955. As in the case of corporations, however, the movement was not consistent over time.

3. For nonfarm unincorporated business, the trend in the ratio of changes in short-term debt (debt to banks) to total debt financing or to total external financing is in doubt. The ratio did rise from an aver-

age of 0.43 in the first three decades to 0.56 in the last two and a half, but the movement was not consistent over time and the estimates are not very reliable.

4. For the business sector as a whole, the trend in the ratio of short-term debt financing to total external financing was upward. The same is true for the private sector (business firms and households). The picture changes with the inclusion of governments for which all debt is treated as long-term, since the distinction between long-term and short-term was not possible for the early years, and is much less significant than for the private sector. For the country as a whole, the ratio of short-term debt financing to total debt financing or to total external financing shows little or no rise, averaging 0.23 or 0.21 in the post-World War II decade compared with 0.23 or 0.19 in 1901–1912 or 1900–1914.

The rise or lack of rise in the ratio of short-term debt financing to external financing or to total debt financing in the private sector may be due either to trends in the differential cost and availability of short-term versus long-term credit, or to trends in the ratio of short-lived assets and in the related ratio of such assets to external financing. If it could be shown that either the trend movements or even the changes from period to period in the ratio of short-term debt financing relative to long-term were associated with relevant changes in differential cost and availability, at least a tentative explanation could be claimed. But the comparisons in the detailed discussion do not confirm this hypothesis. The ratio of short-term debt financing generally did not rise when the differential cost of short-term credit declined, nor did it decline when the differential cost rose. The alternative hypothesis seems more relevant: for corporations and for agriculture, there is a much closer association between changes in the ratio of short-term debt financing to total debt financing (or to total external financing) and those in the ratio of changes in short-term assets (inventories and financial claims) to changes in long-term assets (durable real assets). And if we associate internal financing with long-term assets alone, we can also calculate the ratio of changes in short-term assets to external financing and observe that its changes are correlated with those in the ratio of short-term debt financing to external financing. The rationale for these correlations is clear. First, the acquisition of a short-term asset by an economic unit can more easily be financed by short-term than by long-term funds. Second, for an aggregate which includes both borrowers and lenders, the very rise in the relative share of financial claims (classified as short-term assets) means *pari passu* a rise in the weight of short-term debt. Thus, if a manufacturing corporation acquires notes receivable through a sale to another manufacturing corporation, both notes receivable and notes payable in the manufacturing sector rise.

SHARES OF FINANCIAL INTERMEDIARIES

The intermediaries here comprise banks (Federal Reserve, commercial, mutual savings banks including the postal savings system, and savings and loan associations); insurance companies (private life, private and public pension funds, casualty, fire, and so on); and a miscellaneous group ranging from mortgage companies, investment houses, brokerage firms, etc., to government lending institutions, and personal trust departments.

1. The share of financial intermediaries in countrywide external financing rose from 0.44 in 1900–1929 to 0.65 in 1930–1949 and, in selected periods (1901–1912, 1923–1929, and 1946–1949), from 0.48 to 0.49 to 0.68. But their share in countrywide total financing also rose, from 0.21 in the first three decades to 0.38 in the last two and a half, and in three selected decades (the first of this century, the 1920's, and the post-World War II years), from 0.19 to 0.21 to 0.30.

2. The rise in the share of financial intermediaries in external financing was pervasive, occurring in the external financing of most of the major users: state and local and federal governments; households—although not continuously; nonfinancial corporations; and, with less consistency, agriculture, and nonfarm unincorporated business. This was not as true of the share of financial intermediaries in total financing, simply because in some sectors the ratio of external to total financing declined, and that tended to offset the increased importance of financial intermediaries in providing external funds. Thus, for the business sector as a whole, the average share of financial intermediaries in total financing changed from 0.17 in the first three decades to 0.15 in the recent two and a half. It was the household and government sectors that accounted for the rise in the share of financial intermediaries in total financing for the country as a whole.

3. There were distinctive trends in the structure of financial intermediaries, weighted by the size of their assets. In total assets of all intermediaries, the shares accounted for by commercial banks, savings banks, and personal trust departments declined, and it was the drop in the shares of the first two that reduced the share of the banking sector

from an average of somewhat over six-tenths in the first two decades of the century to less than four-tenths in the post-World War II years. The shares of the various groups of insurance and retirement funds rose. The share of the insurance sector as a whole also rose, from an average of almost one-sixth of the total before the 1930's to almost four-tenths in the post-World War II years. Within the miscellaneous group, the shares fluctuated and the long-term trends are not clear. The share of land banks and of the combined group of investment companies, stock brokers, and investment-holding trusts and factors apparently declined; that of government lending institutions rose. But only the latter trend is clearly significant. Finally, we note the rise in the average share of government institutions (Federal Reserve Banks, government lending institutions, government pension and security funds), from 7 per cent in 1901–1922 to 21 per cent in 1913–1939, and to 27 per cent in 1930–1955.

The changing role of financial intermediaries in the financing of this country's economy has been discussed in detail in Raymond Goldsmith's monograph,[1] and we need not go beyond the thumbnail summary above. Some brief general comments, however, are in order.

First, the rise in the shares of financial intermediaries in external and total financing reflects their increased use by individuals and households, the main source of the nation's savings. This long-term shift in what might be called the financial habits of ultimate savers (including also unincorporated enterprises, and even corporations) is a result of far-reaching changes in the pattern of economic and social life. To illustrate: the increase in the proportion of employees and the decline in the proportion of self-employed in our working population meant a shift from savings flowing directly into the saver's business to savings that are generally deposited by the employee-saver in some financial intermediary. Likewise, the increase in urbanization meant easier access of the population to the financial institutions, and the multiplication of facilities also encouraged greater use of financial intermediaries by ultimate savers. We should, therefore, have expected to find many of the trends summarized above even if there had been no marked changes in the distribution of income by size, no decisive increase in the size and diversity of government institutions, no marked shift toward security orientation in the channeling of savings.

Second, these shifts did occur, however, and are clearly reflected in

[1] *Financial Intermediaries in the American Economy since 1900* (Princeton for NBER, 1958).

the trends in the structure of financial intermediaries. It need not be emphasized that the shifts not only meant changes in the relative weights of various types of intermediaries but also contributed to a rise in the shares of all intermediaries in total and external financing. If reduction in the share of upper income groups in income lowered the proportion of savings seeking venture capital investment, it also lowered the share of savings channeled directly through purchase of stocks rather than through intermediaries. Likewise, the quest for security, leading as it did to shifts among intermediaries, also meant a moving away from the direct channeling of savings into investment.

Finally, insofar as there were these distinctive shifts in the movement of ultimate savings through channels other than those prevailing earlier, there may have been shifts in the forms of financing discussed above. If either the ultimate savers or the financial institutions to which they entrust their savings are committed to channel the funds into certain types of investment only (say long-term fixed debt), the resulting effect on differential costs of alternative types of financing may influence the would-be users' choice. Conversely, the pressure of an important user, like the federal government, for marketing its fixed-interest securities may cause the shifting of funds from one type of financing to another, or even between direct and indirect channeling of savings. The trends in the shares and structure of financial intermediaries are, therefore, associated with those in the structure of external financing.

The Long Swings (Chapters 7 and 8)

In addition to the trend movements that can be observed over periods longer than twenty-five or thirty years, there are swings in the growth rate or even in the absolute volume of many important economic components. These swings, approximately twenty years long, are quite distinct from business cycles and must be considered in any discussion of long-term changes in the economy.

The statistical evidence on these swings is of two types. For many economic variables, such alternations in the rate of change are so prominent that continuous annual or quinquennial series show them directly, without any statistical manipulation of the original record. This is true—to cite a few cases—of gross nonfarm residential construction; of gross durable capital expenditures by railroads; of net changes in inventories (a partly conjectural series); of net changes in claims against foreign countries; of net additions to total population; of net immigration; of internal migration of the native born; of stock market prices, and of stock yields. For almost all of these, the evidence extends back to the 1870's; and, for those for which evidence is available for years before the Civil War, there is clear indication of the existence of long swings even in the earlier decades.

For other economic components, the long swings are not so prominent and may be overshadowed either by trend movements or by shorter-term changes associated with business cycles. In such cases the long swings become apparent when the series is smoothed by a moving average and plotted on a ratio scale, which reveals the alternations in the percentage rate of growth. But it must be stressed that the long swings brought to light by this treatment of the series are not statistical illusions—a mere product of the statistical procedures. It is true that a major short rise or decline much above or below the underlying trend—extending over a single year or two, or over a single business cycle—would affect all the ordinates of the moving average in which it is included, and that average would thus stretch out a short change into a long swing. But economic theory leads us to expect that—other factors being absent—such short breaks would be followed by a canceling reaction. Thus, the lack of such a reaction would in itself indicate the existence of a long swing. Likewise, long swings in the percentage rate of growth are no less real than those in the absolute volume of an economic process.

The main difficulty in our discussion of long swings is not in establishing their existence or their wide amplitude in some important economic variables, but in explaining them, in uncovering the links in their transmission. In recent decades, for which data are more plentiful, two major wars and the Great Depression (in large part, a postwar maladjustment) affected the long swings so clearly that it is all too easy to interpret them as war and war-conditioned phenomena. But such an explanation is obviously inapplicable to the decades before World War I. For earlier decades when no major wars occurred, our data are scanty, and cover only two long swings back to the 1870's—not a large sample to rely upon. Some previous studies of these movements have been made, but our detailed discussion in Chapters 7 and 8 and the summary below are, perforce, limited to empirical findings with only suggestions of a few explanatory links.

1. Additions to total population, net immigration, net excess of births over deaths, and net internal migration of the native born dis-

play long swings approximately twenty years in duration. Although some of the series are annual, others are quinquennial or even decennial, and no precise timing study is possible. It is clear, however, that the amplitude of the swings is wide and has widened in recent decades.

2. Nonfarm residential construction and durable capital expenditures by railroads (both gross, in constant prices) display long swings roughly coincident with (or lagging slightly behind) those in population additions, immigration, and net internal migration—and presumably in response to these population movements. Similar swings may characterize other population-sensitive components of capital formation (such as construction of stores, offices, and some public utilities other than railroads), but these components cannot be segregated over a period long enough to serve the present analysis.

3. Until the 1920's, these long swings in population growth and in population-sensitive capital formation were coterminous with opposite swings in other capital formation—total, and in such components as net changes in inventories, net changes in foreign claims, and perhaps "other" private construction and producers' durable equipment combined (excluding capital expenditures by railroads). But the negative association between the long swings in population-sensitive and other capital formation shifted to a positive association beginning with the 1920's, suggesting that the factors that set limits before the 1920's and prevented synchronous acceleration in both population-sensitive and other components of capital formation ceased to be operative after World War I.

4. The inversion of long swings in other capital formation to those in population additions and population-sensitive capital formation before the 1920's, and the difference in timing between long swings in additions to the labor force and those in population affected the long swings in additions to gross commodity product (gross national product, excluding services) and additions to the flow of goods to consumers, total and per capita. In particular, the long swings in additions to flow of goods to consumers per capita tended to be inverted to those in additions to population and in net immigration, although with some lag—at least before the 1920's. There is thus a suggestion of a mechanism by which swings in population additions produced opposite swings in the capacity to add to consumer goods per capita; and the opposite swings induced a reversal in the swings in popula-

tion growth and immigration (the upswing in immigration being a response to the pull of this country as reflected in additions to consumer goods per capita). This, however, is a bare suggestion and there were, most likely, many other factors operating. Moreover, the association ceased after World War I.

5. Gross national product and flow of goods to consumers, total and per capita, all reveal long swings whose relative amplitude tended to widen. There were, naturally, similar swings in net national product, total and per capita. But the long swings in total capital formation, gross and net, become evident only in recent decades, because in the earlier decades the movements in the population-sensitive and in the other components offset each other.

6. It follows that the ratio of gross capital formation to gross national product—whether average or marginal—displays the long swings prominently; and so does the ratio of net capital formation to net national product. These swings, until the recent decades, were inverted to those in gross and net national product.

The findings above relate to real flows—the volume of production in constant prices—and to the population and labor force. For the swings in financial flows the data are even scantier and we must supplement them by some indirect evidence.

7. There are long swings in the structure of capital formation, in current prices, i.e., in the shares of various user sectors, in the apportionment by type of capital good, and in the ratios of capital consumption allowances and net capital formation to gross capital formation for durable types of business capital. Insofar as these components are subject to or represent different types of financing—internal or external, or different types of external financing—long swings in their shares imply corresponding swings in the structure of financing. But our data do not permit us to observe these long swings in the structure of countrywide financing directly, except for the recent decades when the effects of wars dominate the picture (and the period covered is too short for our purpose, anyway).

8. There were clearly marked long swings in stock market prices and stock yields back to the 1880's, when our series begin. This finding can be brought to bear upon long swings in financing by calculating for at least two groups—railroads, and mining and manufacturing corporations—the swings in the ratio of stock yields to bond yields. A

comparison of that ratio with the ratio of net stock or net bond issues to total net issues for the two corporate groups reveals the expected association: in most cases, a long upswing of the differential that makes bonds relatively cheaper is associated with a long upswing in the ratio of net bonds to total net issues, and vice versa. The data are crude and the conclusion necessarily tentative. However, the comparison does suggest that the association is present, and that long swings in the differential cost of bonds and stocks are roughly synchronous with similar movements in the bond-stock ratio in net issues.

9. Finally, for agriculture, mining and manufacturing corporations, and nonfarm residential construction, we can observe financing ratios for time units short enough to reveal whether long swings exist. For agriculture, we have quinquennial data back to 1900, and total uses do reveal swings—although markedly only in recent decades. More important, these swings are related to those in the financing ratios. An upward movement in total uses or in capital formation is associated with a similar movement in the external financing proportion and an opposite movement in the internal financing ratio; a downward movement in total uses or in capital formation is accompanied usually by a decline in the external financing proportion and a rise in the internal.

10. For mining and manufacturing corporations, we observe long swings in plant and equipment expenditures and can study the ratio of gross retention and of net security issues to those expenditures. Here again, even more clearly than in the case of agriculture, long swings in capital formation are accompanied by similar swings in the ratio of net security issues (external financing) to capital formation, and by inverted swings in the ratio of gross retention to capital formation. And the long swings in nonfarm residential construction also appear to be positively associated with swings in the ratio of external to total financing, and negatively associated with swings in the ratio of internal to total financing.

One final general comment on this problem of long swings is appropriate. There is little doubt about the existence of such movements in some major economic flows in the past. And if some important economic flows reveal such swings prominently, the very association between these flows and other processes of the economy is likely to induce similar (or opposite) swings elsewhere. Alternations in gross capital formation are likely to induce swings in capital consumption, in the ratio of the latter to gross capital formation, and hence possibly in the ratio of gross retention or internal funds to capital formation or to total uses. In short, the association among the real flows, and between them and the financial flows, both in space and in time, would lead us to expect that long swings found to be conspicuous in some real flows would be transmitted, though with modification, to other parts of the country's production and its financial framework.

CHAPTER 10

The Past as Prologue

The Structure of a Quantitative Projection

IN this concluding chapter, we attempt to assay prospects for the future on the basis of past trends in population, national product, and capital formation and financing. This is not done in the belief that the primary justification for establishing and analyzing the record of the past lies in the power of prediction that such analysis may bestow—if by prediction one means quantitative estimates of likely future trends. A prior aim of such knowledge is to enrich current generations with the experience of their predecessors and, aside from the direct value of such enrichment of understanding, a vital practical purpose is to contribute to a more intelligent response to current problems. Even if the emergence of such problems cannot be predicted, once they emerge, familiarity with analogous situations in the past should lead to more considered responses than those made in ignorance of the past record and with a view of each current situation as something new under the sun. To be sure, there is an element of implicit prediction in recognizing that a current problem had a counterpart in the past, for such recognition implies similarities in consequences of alternative responses. But this is quite different from a quantitative prediction of trends, in which an explicit forecast, no matter how crude, is made of a specific situation, and probable prospects and problems are inferred.

I stress this point because, with the development of statistical data and of quantitative analysis of economic processes, it has become technically possible to make quantitative projections, extrapolations, and forecasts. Once a statistical bridge from the past has been constructed to provide the take-off point, the very ease with which the relatively simple mathematical operations can be performed tempts the investigator to use his analysis as a direct basis for quantitative projections. Indeed, we considered that approach as a possible use of the empirical findings of this study to gauge future prospects. However, we did not follow it, and our reasons for refraining are stated explicitly below because they may have some relevance to other projections made in recent years.[1]

The essence of a projection is the transfer into the future of some orderly pattern found in the past, with or without modification. The procedure is essentially the same, whatever the series we work with: the birth, death, or net immigration rates used in population projections; the rates of growth of national product per capita, per member of the labor force, or per manhour used in national product extrapolations; the proportion of capital formation to national product, or the capital stock-output ratios used in capital formation projections; the movements of the shares of various types of capital and of shares of various industrial users connected with the apportionment of national product among industries used in projecting components of capital formation; the shares of external and internal financing and of various types of the former used in the projection of trends in financing. The first prerequisite of the procedure is to find some orderly pattern in the past and its explanation—its association with otherwise known, relatively invariant, characteristics of nature or man. Without a modicum of orderly pattern in the past, nothing systematic can be extrapolated into the future.

All this is obvious enough, but it should also be clear from the discussion in the preceding chapters that such an orderly pattern, linked by explanatory hypotheses to some basic, relatively invariant, characteristics of natural and social processes, cannot be established easily. In particular, the possibilities of testing the persistence of these patterns under varying conditions are limited; and in the attempt to support empirically found patterns by explanatory hypotheses, it is rarely possible, in the present state of our knowledge, to assign to such explanatory links empirical coefficients that would necessarily produce the specific trend rates or secular proportions found. For lack of adequate testing and of specific explanation, some major features of the orderly pattern may be sufficiently in doubt to overshadow any apparently precise quantitative projections.

[1] Some of the general arguments in this section have been discussed in greater detail in Simon Kuznets, "Concepts and Assumptions in Long-Term Projections of National Product," *Long-Range Economic Projection* (Studies in Income and Wealth, Vol. 16, Princeton for NBER, 1954), pp. 9–38.

The Past as Prologue

The argument just advanced can be easily illustrated. Some widely used current projections begin with the finding that, since 1870 or 1880, gross national product in constant prices per worker grew at the rate of, say, 2 per cent per year, and was accompanied by a relatively constant proportion of gross capital formation to gross national product of, say, somewhat over 20 per cent. This pattern of rate of growth in per worker product and of a stable gross capital formation proportion is then projected into the future. But in what sense was the rate of growth in per worker product persistent? We know, from the analysis in the present study and others, that not only the annual but also the decadal rate of growth varied; that the movement of the rate revealed long swings; and that because the adjustment for the long swings necessitated the use of two-decade or three-decade averages, the purely statistical persistence of the underlying long-term rate could hardly be tested by the two or two and a half swings in the record back to the 1870's. All these statements apply to the gross capital formation proportion also. Thus there is no statistical basis for claiming a high degree of invariance or persistence in the specific rate of growth or in the specific capital formation proportion: the sample is much too small to permit only a narrow margin of error. Nor is there an analytical basis that can assure us that persistent factors determined an annual rate of growth of per worker product of 2 per cent rather than 2.5 or 1.5 per cent. This is not to argue that analysis of the past and empirical findings are not useful for quantitative projections—if there is a compelling reason for making the projections. It merely emphasizes that the major point of the findings and of the analysis in the preceding chapters is to warn against too facile an extrapolation of past rates, either averaged over a long period or taken from a relatively brief recent period. For if the long-term movements, even when averaged to cancel the business cycles, are a compound of long swings and of underlying trend lines, the rate of the trend lines and their retardation must be carefully established, and the phases of the long swings that would affect the period covered by the projection must be diagnosed, before a reasonable projection is possible. Thus, a projection of the long-term movements over the next twenty-five to thirty years would have to be a compound of projections of the long swings and of the underlying secular rates. For the latter, we would have to decide whether the retardation in the rate of secular growth in per worker product observed in the averages for the two or two and a half successive long swings should be carried into the future. For the long swings, we would have to judge whether or not the movement since World War II is an upward phase of a long swing, to be succeeded by a downward phase, and then in turn by an upward phase—all within the next twenty-five to thirty years.

One obvious implication of these remarks is that the evaluation of empirical and analytical findings for the purpose of extrapolating them into the future is in itself a major task. Moreover, conceiving the extrapolation as a projection of average rates, without close examination of the variety of experience from which these averages have been derived, is a crude and possibly dangerous oversimplification. Since any useful projection involves extrapolating a large number of variables—population, labor force, national product, capital formation, industrial structure, foreign trade, basic price relations, and more—the task of evaluating the findings for the past, of assaying the nature of the orderly patterns that were found, *in close reference to the purposes of the projection that would determine the time scope and character of some of the basic assumptions involved,* becomes formidable indeed. It is not one that can be undertaken in a short postscript to this study, which is essentially and primarily concerned with establishing the long-term record of the past, and providing analytical support for some of the findings.

There is a related consideration in envisaging the task of effective quantitative projection. Extrapolation from the past into the future is inevitably based on a double assumption: (1) that the factors that produced the orderly pattern being extrapolated show no signs of disappearing; (2) that the other forces, which in the past could have produced a major change in the orderly pattern and yet did not, were quite varied and substantial, and that new disturbances in the future may likewise leave the extrapolated pattern unaffected (or modified only within specified margins). So far, we have discussed the difficulties of establishing the orderly pattern and of identifying the factors under (1). But the assumption under (2) has been only implicit in our discussion.

Put explicitly, the comment calls for an analysis of the range of conditions under which the orderly pattern was established and presumably persisted. To illustrate: our economy has been growing at x per cent per decade, when measured in terms of, say, national product per worker, and let us assume that we know the specific patterns that persisted over the last eight to nine decades. But during those decades, extending back to the 1870's, the country was not the battlefield of

432

a major war, certainly not of a war employing atomic weapons. This particular disturbance or condition was not within the range of disturbances or changing conditions under which the economy persisted in growing at *x* per cent per decade; nor was there any war or other disturbance in that period of our past approaching the magnitude of an atomic holocaust in its possible effects on the economy. For this obvious reason all existing projections are explicitly conditioned on the absence of atomic war. If such a stupendous disturbance had occurred in the decades back to the 1870's, and if, in spite of it, the *x* per cent rate of growth per decade in product per worker had been attained, such a limiting condition would not be stipulated in current projections.

The case illustrated by the example is a rather simple one—simple, because we need not examine the decades back to 1870 to be sure that no disturbance approaching the magnitude of an all-out atomic war was among the conditions under which the growth pattern of the economy was attained. But many less obvious and hence more difficult questions arise. Does the cold war of the last fifteen years, if continued for the next two to three decades, constitute a condition for which there is no real analogue within the last eighty or ninety years? And if so, is it likely to modify beyond recognition any projection from the past? What about the rate of technological change already influencing the economy? What about the growing strength of certain organizational elements in economic life—large business corporations, large and strong unions, an increasingly larger government sector? Can we find for all these disturbances and conditions analogues in the past, which did not prevent the past patterns from emerging, so that we can say that their persistence into the future is not likely to invalidate the projection, or at worst will only modify it in ascertainable directions and magnitudes?

Clearly, a serious quantitative projection involves (in addition to an evaluation of the precise character of the orderly pattern found in the past, in reference to the goal and purposes of the projection) a scrutiny of the variable conditions in the past within which the systematic patterns were found, in reference to the new conditions and disturbances that, judging by signs already present, may prevail in the future. Two consequences follow from this second aspect of the logical structure of quantitative (and all) projections. First, all projections are necessarily conditional rather than absolute, in that they are presented as significant, not under any and all circumstances, but only if some disturbances much larger than those in the observable past are ruled out. These large disturbances or catastrophes removed by declaration may be not only the rather unlikely ones, such as planetary cataclysms that would shatter well-established generalizations in the natural sciences, but also the more probable ones, in the realm of human and international affairs. Second, it follows that careful attention to impending changes is required—an assessment of events whose shadows are already upon us. It is indispensable, if the past is to be examined to see whether conditions and disturbances that did occur and were compatible with the orderly pattern found are comparable with those that are likely in the forecastable future.

This second part of the task of making a considered quantitative projection only reinforces the comment above—that it cannot be carried through effectively as a mere postscript to a study like the present one. The results of the study—both our empirical findings and the analytical hypotheses—are raw material for many possible quantitative projections, differing in period of coverage and in emphasis on the various aspects of the economy. Even if the purpose were defined as projecting trends in capital formation and financing, the task would require not only the quantitative projection of population, national product, and industrial structure, but also a host of assumptions based upon a large volume of additional data relating to the current changes foreshadowing future conditions and disturbances. This, then, is a big and separate task to which the present study, one may hope, makes a major contribution, but for which—to use technical terminology—the study is a necessary but not sufficient condition.

Conditions for the Future

To paraphrase the preceding comments: The present study provides a storehouse of findings indispensable for a quantitative projection into the future; but such a projection also involves a series of choices and judgments, which, together with evaluation of the current events that presage the future, is a further and separate step. Whether such a step should be taken depends upon the specific, intended uses of the projection, which would determine its character, and upon a subsequent judgment of the feasibility of the desired prediction on the basis of the findings of this and other studies.

Such seemingly negative comment is forced upon us by the recognition of the requirements of a considered quantitative projection. Yet we should be able to advance toward a projection by noting some current events that suggest the future and may constitute the major conditions under which the past patterns, if projected, could be assumed to operate. In stating these conditions, we will in fact be doing, in a crude and tentative fashion, what would have to be done in detail for a considered projection with the use of all available evidence. The statements that follow, unlike the findings buttressed by empirical evidence and analytical hypotheses in the preceding chapters, are selected broad judgments. Yet they refer to events that are conspicuous and undeniable.

The selection is guided by two criteria. First, we are concerned with conditions that have an apparent bearing upon the topic of interest here—the prospects of demand for and supply of capital. Second, we have in mind a period extending over the next two and a half to three decades—to the mid- or late 1980's—and are therefore concerned with presently observable conditions that seem lasting enough to warrant extrapolation into that longer future. The conditions thus selected for brief mention are: (1) growth of population; (2) changes in science and technology; (3) the position of this country in the concert of nations; (4) the task of governments; (5) savings patterns of the private sector; (6) changes in financing.

GROWTH OF POPULATION

Increase in population is of obvious bearing upon future trends in national product and capital formation. More people mean additional demand for consumer goods and, during the period of formation of family units, increased demand for residential construction. Addition to the number of working-age people means a rise in the labor force ready to man the economic system and waiting to be equipped with capital. For much of the period we have in mind, the future members of the new family units and the future entrants into the labor force are already with us. The infants born today or a year or two ago will, barring catastrophes of the magnitude that we rule out of consideration, be with us and in their early twenties in the quinquennium from 1981 to 1985. With cataclysms removed by assumption, the quantitatively major factor that will affect population numbers over the next thirty years is the birth rate; and for the consumption and capital demanding aspects of population growth, even the birth rate will be of major importance only toward the end of the period, i.e., in the late 1980's.

Some relevant estimates are given in Table 75. The population pro-

TABLE 75

Population Growth and Projections for Selected Age Groups, Excluding Armed Forces Overseas, 1880–1990

A. Volumes and Percentage Changes Per Quinquennium

	Total Population		20–29 Years		10–19 Years		5–9 Years		Under 5 Years	
YEAR	Millions (1)	% Change Per Quinquennium (2)	Millions (3)	% Change Per Quinquennium (4)	Millions (5)	% Change Per Quinquennium (6)	Millions (7)	% Change Per Quinquennium (8)	Millions (9)	% Change Per Quinquennium (10)
				CENSUS ESTIMATES						
1. 1880	50.16		9.17		10.73		6.48			
2. 1890	62.95	12.0	11.42	11.6	13.59	12.5	7.57	8.1		
3. 1900	75.99	9.9	13.86	10.2	15.64	7.3	8.87	8.2		
4. 1910	91.97	10.0	17.24	11.5	18.17	7.8	9.76	4.9		
5. 1920	105.71	7.2	18.36	3.2	20.07	5.1	11.40	8.1		
6. 1930	122.78	7.8	20.70	6.2	23.56	8.3	12.61	5.2		
7. 1940	131.67	3.6	22.68	4.7	24.08	1.1	10.68	−8.0		
8. 1950	150.70	7.0	23.72	2.3	21.74	−5.0	13.20	11.2	16.16	
9. 1955	164.30	9.0	21.91	−7.6	24.37	12.1	17.15	29.9	18.30	13.2
				PROJECTIONS (CENSUS)						
10. 1960	176.91	7.7	21.54	−1.7	30.41	24.8	19.15	11.7	17.93	−2.0
11. 1965	189.36	7.0	24.22	12.4	36.20	19.0	18.73	−2.2	18.88	5.3

PERIOD									
12. 1970	203.69	7.6	30.26	24.9	37.75	4.3	19.68	5.1	21.39	13.3
13. 1975	220.59	8.3	36.10	19.3	38.28	1.4	22.19	12.8	24.60	15.0
EXTRAPOLATIONS									
14. 1980	237.1	(7.5)	37.54	(4.0)	42.11	(10.0)	25.07	(13.0)		
15. 1985	253.7	(7.0)	38.10	(1.5)	46.74	(11.0)	27.58	(10.0)		
16. 1990	272.7	(7.5)	41.15	(8.0)						

B. TOTAL PERCENTAGE GROWTH OVER THIRTY-YEAR PERIODS

		SELECTED AGE GROUPS		
PERIOD	Total Population (1)	20–29 Years (2)	10–19 Years (3)	5–9 Years (4)
PROJECTIONS AND EXTRAPOLATIONS				
17. 1960–1990	54.1	91.0		
18. 1955–1985	54.4	73.9	91.8	60.8
PAST				
19. 1920–1950	42.6	29.2	8.3	15.8
20. 1910–1940	43.2	31.6	32.5	9.4
21. 1900–1930	61.6	49.4	50.6	42.2
22. 1890–1920	67.9	60.8	47.7	50.6
23. 1880–1910	83.4	88.0	69.3	50.6

For an explanation of the figures in parentheses, see note to lines 14 to 16.

(Notes on following page)

437

The Past as Prologue

NOTES TO TABLE 75

SOURCE: Entries for cols. 1, 3, 5, 7, and 9, lines 1 to 8 are from *Historical Statistics of the United States, 1789–1945* (1949), and *Continuation to 1952*, and *1954*, Series B-13, and B-83 through B-86. The entries are for the specific census dates; and no adjustment is made for slight differences in the intercensal intervals in reducing the percentage rates of change to quinquennial units.

Entries for cols. 1, 3, 5, 7, and 9, lines 9 to 13, are from *Current Population Reports*, Series P-25, No. 123 (October 1955) and No. 160 (August 9, 1957). The projection used is Series A, based on the assumption that the 1950–1953 fertility rates remain constant throughout the projection period. The population figures are for July 1 of the given year; and the figures for population under 5 years old are unadjusted for net census undercount. The absolute change from one date to the next as shown in the October 1955 release was assumed to apply to the series excluding armed forces overseas shown in the August 9, 1957 release.

Entries for cols. 1, 3, 5, and 7, lines 14 to 16, are derived by applying the estimated percentage rates of growth shown in parentheses in cols. 2, 4, 6, and 8. The percentage in col. 8, line 14, is based on a rough relation of the percentages in col. 8 to those in col. 10 with a lag of five years; that in col. 8, line 15, is a rough approximation. The percentages in col. 6 are based on those in col. 8, with an appropriate lag; the percentages in col. 4 are based on those in col. 6, again with an appropriate lag. Finally, the percentages in col. 2, lines 14 to 16, are assumed to repeat the pattern in the preceding quinquennia, but not to duplicate the high increase from 1970 to 1975.

jection to 1975 used here, released by the Bureau of the Census in August 1957, assumes that the birth rates of 1950–1953 will continue to 1975 and makes rather conservative assumptions about death rates. Judged by more recent reports, the projection appears to be on the moderate side. Thus, as of January 1, 1958, population excluding armed forces overseas is set at 171.97 million.[2] This leaves only a 4.94 million increase over the two and a half years to mid-1960, if the total of 176.91 million shown in line 10, column 1 is to be attained, compared with a rise of 7.67 million over the two and a half years from mid-1955 to January 1, 1958. But even as derived on the basis of the conservative assumptions used in Table 75, prospective population growth reveals some striking aspects.

If the rates of growth of total population up to 1990 assumed here are realized, the rise over the three decades, 1960–1990, or 1955–1985, will be about 54 per cent. This is larger than the rise from 1920 to 1950 or from 1910 to 1940; it is somewhat below that from 1900 to 1930; and is distinctly below that from 1890 to 1920 or from 1880 to 1910.

More relevant in the present connection, and more striking, are the

[2] See *Current Population Reports*, Bureau of the Census, May 14, 1958, Series P-25, No. 176.

prospective increases in the group 20 through 29 years—the ages when most people enter the labor force, and form new family units. The projected rise of this group from 1955 to 1985 is almost 74 per cent, far higher than that from 1920 to 1950, from 1910 to 1940, from 1900 to 1930, or even from 1890 to 1920. It is exceeded only by the rise from 1880 to 1910, the decades when unrestricted immigration was contributing particularly to this working-age group. The projected rise from 1960 to 1990 is even greater, 91 per cent, and greater than that for any thirty-year span since 1880. Clearly, we are faced during the next thirty years with an exceedingly high relative addition to the age group that makes the largest contribution to new family units and provides the greatest number of new entrants into the labor force.

The rises in prospect for the population groups aged 10 through 19 and 5 through 9 are equally striking. These groups, of course, call particularly upon the services of our educational system. The projected rise from 1955 to 1985 in the 10 through 19 age group is almost 92 per cent, higher than the rise for any thirty-year period since 1880; and that for the group aged 5 through 9 is 61 per cent, also well above any rise during the last three-quarters of the century. With the growth rates in these groups from 1920 to 1950 and from 1910 to 1940 being only small fractions of the impending rise, and the trend in age-specific school attendance rates also likely to rise further, the prospective demand to be made upon an important part of the country's productive system will be unprecedented.

Table 75 was prepared and the above comments written in early 1958. The Bureau of the Census has since published a new set of illustrative projections of population, taking into account the birth rates in recent years, which were much higher than expected. These new projections are utilized in Table 76 and, as in Table 75, it is assumed that throughout the period of projection the recent birth rates continue—in this case, the rates prevailing in 1955–1957 (i.e., Series II). Rather than replace the older estimates in Table 75 by the more recent series, I am showing both, if only to reveal how sharply projections differ when extrapolations are based on the experience of different sets of recent years.

The rates of population growth shown by the new projections only reinforce the conclusions already stated. The projected rate of growth of total population over the next thirty years is higher than that of any thirty-year period since 1890. Only for 1880–1910, when increase in our numbers was so appreciably aided by large net immigration, is

TABLE 76

Recent Revisions in Population Projections for Selected Age Groups, Including Armed Forces Overseas, 1960–1990

A. Volumes and Percentage Changes Per Quinquennium

SELECTED AGE GROUPS

YEAR	Total Population Millions (1)	% Change Per Quinquennium (2)	20–29 Years Millions (3)	% Change Per Quinquennium (4)	10–19 Years Millions (5)	% Change Per Quinquennium (6)	5–9 Years Millions (7)	% Change Per Quinquennium (8)	Under 5 Years Millions (9)	% Change Per Quinquennium (10)
1. 1955 (July 1)	165.27		22.53		24.53		17.15		18.30	
				CENSUS ESTIMATES						
				PROJECTIONS (CENSUS)						
2. 1960	180.13	9.0	22.26	-1.2	30.62	24.8	19.16	11.7	19.99	9.2
3. 1965	195.75	8.7	24.96	12.1	36.48	19.1	20.84	8.8	21.24	6.3
4. 1970	213.81	9.2	30.98	24.1	40.16	10.1	22.09	6.0	24.19	13.9
5. 1975	235.25	10.0	36.79	18.7	43.08	7.3	25.03	13.3	28.11	16.2
6. 1980	259.98	10.5	40.44	9.9	47.27	9.7	28.94	15.6	31.99	13.8
				EXTRAPOLATIONS						
7. 1985	283.38	(9.0)	43.31	(7.1)	54.12	(14.5)	32.85	(13.5)		
8. 1990	310.30	(9.5)	47.34	(9.3)	61.91	(14.4)				

B. Total Percentage Growth over Thirty-Year Periods

SELECTED AGE GROUPS

PERIOD	Total Population (1)	20–29 Years (2)	10–19 Years (3)	5–9 Years (4)
9. 1960–1990	72.3	112.7	102.2	
10. 1955–1985	71.5	92.2	120.6	91.5

The Past as Prologue

NOTES TO TABLE 76

For an explanation of the figures in parentheses, see note to lines 7 and 8.

SOURCE: The census data and projections are from M. Zitter and J. S. Siegel, "Illustrative Projections of the Population of the United States, by Age and Sex, 1960–1980," *Current Population Reports*, Series P-25, No. 187, November 10, 1958. The projection used is Series II, based on the assumption that fertility will remain constant at the 1955–1957 level throughout the projection period.

Entries for cols. 1, 3, 5, and 7, lines 7 and 8, are derived by applying the estimated percentage rates of growth shown in parentheses in cols. 2, 4, 6, and 8. The percentages in col. 4, lines 7 and 8, are based on the rates in col. 6, a decade earlier. The percentages in col. 6, lines 7 and 8, are based on the rates in cols. 8 and 10, a decade earlier. The percentage in col. 8, line 7, is based on the rate in col. 10, a quinquennium earlier. The percentages in col. 2, lines 7 and 8, are assumed to repeat the pattern in the preceding quinquennia, and allow for a trough in the long swing in line 7, twenty years after the trough in the rate of growth shown in line 3.

the rate higher. The projected rates of population growth in the age groups 5 through 9, 10 through 19, and 20 through 29 are even more striking.

Finally, the projected quinquennial rates of change reveal clear signs of a prospective long swing in the important age groups distinguished. Thus, the projection indicates a decline from 1955 to 1960 in the 20 through 29 age group, reflecting the declining birth rate of the 1930's; then the rise resumes, reaching a peak in the quinquennium of 1965–1970, to be followed by another downward phase. In the younger age groups there are similar swings, but naturally with earlier timing. Hence (insofar as the projections are valid), the extraordinarily high rate of secular growth in the age groups from 5 through 19 will be accompanied by a marked long swing. Whatever our inference from these high rates of increase in numbers of school-age youth and of new family makers and new entrants into the labor force concerning the prospective demand for capital in the next two and a half or three decades, we must keep in mind that the population projections suggest long swings that will modify that demand in any one quinquennium or decade.

CHANGES IN SCIENCE AND TECHNOLOGY

In these days of atomic energy, man-made satellites, electronic devices, and other products of burgeoning scientific discovery and technological change, there is little need to stress their urgent effects on present trends in economic product and on the demand for capital. Perhaps less in the focus of public attention is the magnitude of the prospective trend in technological change and its possible impact on the demand for capital.

Our concern here is the potential technological change over the next twenty-five to thirty years, which may differ from the realized change if resources, capital, or entrepreneurial ability are not sufficient. By its nature, the concept of potential technological change is difficult to define precisely, let alone measure. Yet it is extremely useful, for it points to the fact that of the large flow of technological change offered, as it were, to society—even if much of it is not thoroughly tested—only a part is embodied in the productive structure, mainly because of limitations of capital and of entrepreneurial ability.

If potential technological change cannot be precisely defined, it may seem inconsistent to argue that all signs point to an acceleration in the rate of additions to that potential in the coming decades. Yet such signs are fairly prominent and should be noted, for they would have to be evaluated in any considered economic projection.

We begin with the developments in science which, since the late nineteenth century, have been increasingly the dominant source of inventions and major technological changes affecting economic production and consumption. We are witnessing a high rate of additions to scientific work and discovery, resulting in general from two factors. The first is the cumulative impact of the natural science disciplines upon each other, the higher level of attainment in physics giving impetus to chemistry, that in chemistry affecting physics, and so on down the line. There is a similar reciprocal reinforcing effect in the development of pure theory and of technical capacity for experimentation. Advances in experimental method and results, conditioned in part by the general rise in the productive powers of society, permit tests and experiments that lead to reconsideration and revision of theory, which in turn lead to new experiments demanding higher levels of technical performance. The interdisciplinary character of basic research in the natural sciences has advanced rapidly in the past few decades, and advances have been equally rapid in the relation between theoretical work and what might be called experimental and applied technology. This stimulating interdependence may become increasingly effective in the decades to come, accelerating the rate of additions to tested useful knowledge.

Second, the number of scientific workers at various levels has increased enormously throughout the world—and in this connection we must consider the whole world, for science is a transnational complex, available (with some exceptions) to all who have the means to apply it. Even without recourse to figures, we may assume that the number of qualified workers in the field has increased at an exceptionally high rate, considering the increasing number of economically advanced countries that have recognized and emphasized the value of scientific work.

As the pace of scientific research has quickened, greater emphasis has been placed upon the translation of scientific discoveries into practical technological research and application, and a larger flow of resources has been channeled into that development. Indeed, it is sometimes not easy to draw the line between discovery and application, pure and applied research. This does not mean that the transition from the scientific discovery to the practical development is easy, and there are the further steps through the pilot plant to economical and effective mass production of new goods, and their continual improvement. We may reasonably argue that the wider recognition of the value of research and adaptive activity for economic progress and performance has led to the allocation of a rapidly increasing volume of resources to that activity, and that the prospects for the immediate future indicate a much greater addition to input directed toward it.

Of course, greater input of resources is not necessarily assurance of greater output of discovery and new technology ready to be absorbed, on a mass production basis, by the economy's productive system. Yet it would be surprising if this were not the result. Even if the return per unit of such input were somewhat lower than in the past, the huge rise in the input might mean an acceleration in the rate of potential technological change. The impression is particularly strengthened if we recognize that we are at the beginning of another revolution in the supply of industrial power. In the past such revolutions had far-reaching consequences that radically affected the productive structure of the economy—consequences that extended over decades. Steam power, the basis of the modern industrial economy, was introduced in the 1780's, and it was not until the 1880's that its revolutionary impact on the advanced countries of the world began to subside. The introduction of electric power in the last quarter of the nineteenth century, followed by the internal combustion engine, resulted in a series of changes that are still continuing—though at a much slower pace. It seems certain that the development of nonmilitary applications of nuclear physics, of electronics in automation and communications will have an immense impact upon the productive system. These and advances in other fields—rocketry, the biological sciences (promising new sources of cheap food), solar energy (promising unlimited power), and many more—may well dominate the economy of the next two or three decades.

If the rate of additions to potential technological change is likely to be high in the next three decades, it should give momentum to the demand for capital funds (as well as for entrepreneurial ability, private and public). The demand will be not only for resources needed for work on the new inventions and products to the point where economical mass production becomes feasible. The resources needed will be far larger when the basic capital equipment required to satisfy prospective demand is installed, because we can assume that the demand will follow the pattern typical of all successful new products and processes. In the past, the development of new sources of power and its uses, alone, brought to our economy prodigious tasks of capital investment for land transportation—to choose one example. Besides the investment for procuring, refining, and harnessing the raw materials for producing power (coal, oil, water), there was the even greater need of capital to build, equip, and service railroads, electric power plants and power carrying channels, internal combustion motor vehicles and the associated networks of roads, bridges, ferries, and tunnels. There is little reason to assume that the situation will be different, except possibly in degree, in the future. Any major technological change that involves the harnessing of new sources of power, the utilizing of a new complex of natural resources for widespread use, or the creation of new consumer goods with wide markets demands a large framework of material capital equipment that can effectively produce the new power and channel it into useful ends, carry the new sequence of operations with but little input of direct labor, or turn out the new products effectively and cheaply. With increasing volumes of power and larger outputs projected, the economies of scale may set the optimum-size unit at quite a high level, and the resulting indivisibility of initial investment may mean high capital-output ratios for the new producing units, at least in the early years of operation. Thus, if we assume a high rate of potential technological change, the first presumption is of a high rate of demand for capital—unless detailed investigation produces concrete evidence to qualify or invalidate such a presumption.

Of course, technological changes have a ramifying influence. They not only set up new industries and new sectors in the economy, but

444

also affect the established ones—in different ways. Some older industries may be adversely affected if the new technology produces better and effectively competing substitutes; others may be positively stimulated if the changes provide an additional market. The new technology may create demand by some older industries for additional capital, because a new development may, besides providing the basis for an entirely new industry, also serve as a useful addition to the capital equipment of an old industry. New technology may reduce the demand by other established industries for capital, if increases in efficiency outrun the possible rise in the market for the products. Any considered analysis of these effects must specify the likely new technological changes, and then infer their possible effects on the established sectors of the industrial system. All one can say here is that in the past the net effect of new technological changes has been to increase both total output and demand for capital for the economy as a whole, and the greater the rate of technological change, the greater the rise in output and in net demand for capital. While the statement can be nothing more than crude conjecture, it is most reasonable to assume that a projected high rate of potential technological change means a high projected rate of demand for capital—net of any contractions on the part of industries competitively and adversely affected by the new technology.

All this has obvious bearing upon the capital-output ratios. We have already commented upon the variability of those ratios even over long periods, and the difficulty of agreeing upon purely statistical projections into the future to derive amounts of capital formation presumably required by any given projected basket of final goods. But past records do suggest that revolutionary changes in power production result in rises in capital-output ratios, first, because of their high level in the power and closely related industries themselves, and then because of the effect of the extension of the use of power to other industries (manufacturing and agriculture, for example). If the next two or three decades witness a power revolution, it is not unlikely that there will be consequent pressures for raising the capital-output ratios, and these pressures can be responded to without a slowing down in the rate of growth of final output only if the additional savings are forthcoming. It should be emphasized that the capital-output ratios can be raised by a slower growth of output, the denominator of the fraction. If the newly emerging power industries, with their high demands for capital per unit of product (at least in the initial stages),

claim a large part of the limited volume of nationwide capital formation, the rise in the capital-output ratio must be accompanied by a
slowing down in the rate of growth of final output (i.e., of national
product).

POSITION OF THIS COUNTRY IN THE CONCERT OF NATIONS

In dealing with prospects for the future in the position of this country
among other nations, we face a realm of human affairs in which changes
seem to have been fast, furious, and unpredictable. It would be a
hardy prognosticator indeed who, looking back three decades (to the
late 1920's), could assure himself that a fairly thorough and even
highly imaginative study of the situation then would have enabled
him to foresee the shifts on the international scene that have taken
place. He would have had to project the emergence and collapse of
Nazi Germany; the scope and impact of the Second World War;
the broad consequences of the Stalinist regime in the Soviet Union; the
collapse of the overseas empires of Western Europe; the formation of
more than twenty new independent national states; the spread of
Communism to mainland China; the extension of Soviet power to
Eastern and part of Central Europe; and so on, through a long list of
changes, some only now in the making. With such a retrospective
look, one may well ask whether there is any sense in attempting a
projection in this field of low visibility.

Yet, unless we make reasonably realistic assumptions concerning
prospects in international relations, everything else, grounded upon
consideration of domestic factors alone, will be left hanging in the
air. For clearly, problems arising in the relations between this country and others are likely to dominate the scene for decades to come.
If we exclude the contingency of a major world war, it should be
possible at least to secure guidance for thought by considering the
general trends on the international scene and their probable impact
on this country's economy, viewing these trends, both current and
prospective, against a broader historical perspective.

That perspective can best be suggested if we look at the modern
historical process as one dominated by the spread of the industrial
system in a world of sovereign—legally independent—national units,
with widely differing natural and historical heritages. The industrial
system is a complex of economic and social processes based on the
increasing use of technology provided by modern science, and after its
birth at the end of the eighteenth century in Great Britain it spread

446

to other European countries (western, central, and northern), to the North American continent, to some other offshoots of Western Europe across the seas, to Japan, and most recently to Russia, an eastern off-shoot of European civilization. The efforts to introduce it into China, India, and other underdeveloped countries dominate the current scene. The spread of this system, in turn a changing complex reflecting progress in modern technology, and the parallel, if not necessarily simultaneous, spread of the ideas of national independence and national attainments to much of the world would go far to explain the shifts in international relations that have occurred since the early nineteenth century.

The mechanism of the spread, and the relations among the national units involved in it—peaceful flows of goods, men, and capital, or the more warlike types of contact ranging from pressure to outright conflict, or imitation and reaction—already subjects of a vast literature, could be dealt with in detail. But for our purpose, two general features of this process of spread deserve mention.

The first is the inevitable transitoriness of economic leadership. No single nation can retain economic leadership indefinitely, for the simple reason that if industrialization begins in country X—giving it the advantage of leadership—and then spreads to country Y, the shift to Y means a loss of relative (if not absolute) advantage for X. Thus, if the industrial system spreads at all—if industrialization occurs not only in the pioneer state (Great Britain), but also in follower states (United States, Germany, and so on)—its inception in the latter with the higher rates of growth that the newly industrialized nations attain means, *ipso facto*, reduction in the relative superiority of the pioneer state. This conclusion is particularly clear in terms of percentage rates of growth. The quickening of those rates in modern times is part and parcel of the shift from the pre-industrial to the industrial pattern of economic performance, and no country can maintain such quickening for any length of time, relative to other countries that may join in the spread of the industrial system at later dates.

The second general feature to be noted is the increasing diversity of social structure into which the industrial system is fitted, as it spreads from the country of origin to other parts of the world. The system is most likely to spread first to countries whose historical heritage is closest to that of the pioneer country, for this similarity of heritage is likely to make for closer ties and for greater ease in adopting the socially conditioned new ways. Even so, the very fact that the

447

next group of countries are followers will mean that the industrial system is set up within a modified policy and social framework. It is hardly an accident that the United States and Germany were the originators of the protective tariff system and developed corporate structures and economic organizations somewhat different from those in Great Britain. As the system spreads further, it is adopted by countries with a historical background and social structure quite different from those of the pioneer and immediate follower nations. In this sense both Japan and particularly the Soviet Union are, at present, at the end of the line that stretches back to Great Britain; and if China and India manage industrialization, the accompanying social and political structures, in both their internal and external aspects, may be quite different from anything observed so far.

These broad generalizations are advanced because they seem to illuminate much of the recent historical past, and explain the increased international tensions—a compound result of the increasing number of large advanced economies and of the greater divergence in their social and political structures. They also may be useful as a background against which to interpret the obvious changes in the international position of the United States, and to consider the prospective demands upon our economy that these changes and their probable continuation into the future are likely to make.

Of the inferences that can be drawn from the recent trends, viewed against the wider background just suggested, three seem particularly relevant here. First, there is little evidence that the increased international tension, with an apparent division of the world into three camps, two of which are contending for the allegiance of the third, will subside in the foreseeable future. No such relaxation has been observed since World War II or, for that matter, since the 1930's. The forces that generate the tension—the contrast between growth in power and failure of commensurate growth in human welfare within the authoritarian countries, and the gap between aspirations and achievements in the underdeveloped countries of the world—show no signs of abatement. Indeed, a sober and critical estimate of probabilities suggests that the strains are increasing, and that the free part of the world for which this country at present bears the responsibility of leadership may suffer further disturbing losses and shifts in power.

Second, the emergence of this country as a leader has meant continuing claims upon our economy: in the form of outlay for security purposes (much of which in the past was, in a sense, carried for us by other countries then in a leading position); unilateral transfers in the form of economic or military aid; or capital flows abroad under public or private auspices. Given the political structure of the world, no developed country can escape such claims, unless it disregards its security altogether or places the responsibility for it on other shoulders. Since neither alternative is open to a major power like the United States, it is only realistic to assume that such claims will continue and may become a larger proportion of the nation's total product, a point to which we shall return in discussing the prospective role of governments. Of course, there is still another alternative—sacrificing part of the independence of sovereignty by closer union with other countries having similar external problems. While one hesitates to consider this possibility in the present discussion, a more imaginative view of the longer-term implications of this country's position in the world might place heavy emphasis upon it.

Third, the purely economic claims and flows originating in international relations are likely to remain a moderate part of the total nonconsumption claims upon the country's national product. Free movement of private capital investment abroad is not likely to rise relative to governmental loans, grants in aid, military assistance, and especially security expenditures. This is partly a result of political tensions in many capital-hungry countries. Those tensions accompany the continuous search for a social and political organization that can resolve the gap between aspirations and attainments without imposing authoritarianism. It is partly a result of the political cleavages among the more advanced countries of the world. It also results from current technological changes, which exact such pressures on our domestic markets for private capital funds that little is left to flow abroad except to finance indispensable raw material supplies and branch plants.

THE TASK OF GOVERNMENTS

The secular rise in the share of the government sector in national product and in capital formation has been widely discussed. The two questions suggested in the present connection are, first, whether that rise is likely to continue over the next two or three decades; and second, if it does continue, how it will affect the prospective demand for or supply of capital.

The first question is partially answered by the comments just made. Insofar as government activities are affected by the country's international position, the continuation or even rise of the high share of the government sector in the economy is likely. A full answer would depend upon a careful weighing of the many pressures for larger government expenditures on goods—whether at federal or state and local levels—relative to the expected growth of the total national product upon which such government expenditures draw.

The experience of the post-World War II decade and some current projections of government expenditures suggest that the prospect may be for a continuing high share of claims by governments upon the country's gross national product. If we take the latter for the recent decade, from 1948 through 1957, excluding the first two postwar years, and calculate the percentage growth of the product (in 1957 prices) from the first quinquennium (1948–1952) to the second (1953–1957), the rate per year is 3.8 per cent. This is somewhat lower than the rate of 4.4 per cent for the post-World War I decade of 1920 through 1929, although that rate may be somewhat exaggerated by a different mixture of business cycle phases.[3] As a measure of the draft that the governments made upon the gross national product for purposes of consumption, we take government purchases of commodities and services, excluding nonmilitary public construction because the latter represents capital formation.[4] If, then, we calculate the annual percentage share of the draft by governments for consumption, so defined, in gross national product, the arithmetic mean of the shares is 15.1 per cent for 1948–1952 and 17.9 per cent for 1953–1957, which can be compared with 5.7 per cent for 1929.[5] The significant point is that although the second of the two quinquennia was dominated by an economy-minded administration in Washington, and although the share of federal expenditures in national product did decline after

[3] The 1948–1957 totals are from the *Economic Report of the President*, January 1958, Table F-2, p. 118; those for 1920–1929 are Variant III, from the present report, Table R-2.

Inclusion of 1958 only reduces the rate of growth in the post-World War II period. Gross national product (in 1958 prices) grew from 1949–1953 to 1954–1958 at the rate of 3.2 per cent per year (see *Economic Report of the President*, January 1959, Table D-2, p. 140).

[4] A further deduction should be made for producers' equipment (nonmilitary) purchased by governments; but no data are available for these years. The item, however, is small relative to the totals involved.

[5] The calculation is based on totals in current prices, but it would not be significantly different for those in constant prices. For the underlying data, see *Economic Report of the President*, January 1958, Tables F-1, p. 117; and F-32, p. 152.

For 1958 the share of the draft by governments for consumption was 17.7 per cent, slightly higher than the 17.3 per cent for 1953–1957 based on comparable data (see *Economic Report of the President*, January 1959, Table D-1, p. 139, and Table D-32, p. 176.

1953, the rise in the share of state and local expenditures offset that decline; and even in 1957 the share of total government purchases for consumption was three times as high as in 1929. Thus, over the 1948–1957 decade, the relative burden of claims for government consumption continued to be high and even rose somewhat.

That continued high levels of the share of national product claimed by government consumption may prevail in the future is suggested in the recent projection by a panel of the Special Studies Project (in Report IV) of the Rockefeller Brothers Fund.[6] That projection extends to 1967 only, and presents a range of government expenditures from low to high. Even the low projected increase in government purchases of goods (in 1957 dollars) is from $86 billion in 1957 to $127 billion in 1967, or at the rate of 4 per cent per year. (If we use the high projection of gross national product, and assume the same ratio of government purchases of goods and services to gross national product as in the low projection, the rise is from $86 billion in 1957 to about $141 billion in 1967, or at the rate of over 5 per cent per year.) This 4 per cent rate is somewhat higher than the rate of growth of gross national product observed from 1948–1952 to 1953–1957; and if the latter rate persists, the share of government expenditures in gross national product will rise. To be sure, the projection allows for a rise in the share of capital formation within total government purchases of commodities and services; but, on the other hand, the low range projection here is compared with a rate of growth of national product that may well be above the long-term secular level.

It is not unrealistic to assume that the draft by the government sector for current consumption, and not for the purpose of providing capital for the needs already mentioned in discussing population growth and technological change, may remain at the current high levels of its share in gross national product—and may even rise somewhat. This draft, together with private consumption, constitutes a deduction to be made from national product to derive capital formation as a residual, and it thus constitutes also a draft upon the savings of the nation. Hence, a continued high proportional level of government purchases of goods and services for current consumption means, other conditions being equal, that much lower a share for savings and capital formation.

For the problems of savings and capital formation, the high share

[6] *The Challenge to America: Its Economic and Social Aspects* (Rockefeller Brothers Fund, Inc., 1958), p. 71.

of governments in national product and the wider role that governments have been forced to play in the economy and society of recent decades have other implications. Indeed, the mere quantitative weight of the government sector may be less important than the mechanism by which governments secure their share, and the complex of relations among economic groups in the community which the governments may be affecting, often by design, in the process. For example, given one and the same percentage share of government consumption in national product, covering it by proceeds of progressive taxes may have effects on saving and investment in the private sector vastly different from the effects of covering it by sales taxes or deficit financing. The quantitative rise in government activities relative to the rest of the economy, moreover, increases the weight of effects of government policies in securing their share, and carrying through redistributive transfers in the process. Finally, governments can perform additional and important economic functions and, in recent decades, have been pressed into performing them.

The wide field for review thus opened can hardly be surveyed here. But for the problem at hand it is essential to note that, within recent decades, the governments of this country have assumed major responsibility for full employment and economic stability—to an extent unknown in the past; that the increased volume of government expenditures, which involved a rising ratio of taxes to national product, was accompanied by an increasing weight of progressive taxes in the total tax structure; and that the responsibility for full employment, coupled with a pressure for larger government expenditures, for higher consumption levels, and for increased private capital formation, was associated with a marked inflationary trend in the economy.

These changes since the mid-1930's are so conspicuous and well known that they hardly need documentation, and their effect on the consumption and savings patterns of the private sector will be touched upon below. But it may be relevant to observe here, while we are discussing the share and role of governments, that the changes just noted are neither accidental nor capricious assumption by governments of additional responsibilities in the economic sphere, nor can their assumption be viewed as results of ignorance or of narrow interests. On the contrary, the assumption of these additional responsibilities, as well as the broad way in which policy has been shaped, are rooted in powerful underlying factors. The acceptance of responsibility for full employment has been forced by the recognition that government action can and hence must minimize the failure to use resources fully, which the unassisted operation of the private sector can bring about. The increased progressivity of the tax burden and the generally egalitarian trends in our government policy reflect a changed social view of the value of high incomes and large personal savings. They reflect also a different view of the equity of leaving low income groups at a relatively low level in the scale in times when future economic advancement for them may be threatened by external dangers. Clearly, the growing needs of governments for current consumption and capital formation, combined with the aspirations of households for higher levels of living and the needs of the business sector for more capital goods, are likely to generate inflationary trends—if none of the claimant groups can be forced into a position where a shrinking market will lead to a reduction in prices. The burden of the adjustment in these conditions is then carried by those who lose in the attempt to keep their monetary gains commensurate with the real gains in the economy. All these comments are relevant because they indicate that the forces behind recent changes in the role of governments are fairly deep seated. In considering their implications for the savings patterns of the private sector, therefore, we cannot assume that the higher share and the greater role of governments will not continue, at least in the foreseeable future.

SAVINGS PATTERNS OF THE PRIVATE SECTOR

The preceding comments suggest that, because of a larger growth of population in certain strategic age groups, an accelerated rate of potential technological change, and continued pressure upon the economy resulting from international tensions, the prospective demand for capital and the demand by the government sector for current consumption are likely to be large. Whether the continued demand for both will claim a rising proportion of the total projected product is a question that cannot be answered here with assurance. Its considered exploration calls for a detailed analysis of the factors and conditions only briefly noted above. Whatever the probable answer, the demand for capital proportionate to output is not likely to drop, and we may now ask whether the savings patterns in the private sector suggest savings proportions that will match the prospective demand for capital. We are concerned with the private sector alone because, as already indicated, the government sector is not likely to have net savings in the long-term prospect. Indeed, it may be forced to draw upon savings in the private sector.

Much of the discussion in the preceding chapters is applicable here, and three major trends may be stressed. First, the net savings proportion in net national product has, on the whole, declined. This movement is not incompatible with the constant proportion of personal savings to disposable income of individuals and households, because the proportion of disposable income to national product has declined with the rise in the share of direct taxes. Second, capital consumption charges have increased as a proportion of both net and gross national product, contributing to the relative long-term constancy in the gross savings proportion to gross national product. Third, the share of the government sector in gross savings has declined since the 1930's; the share of the corporate sector must have increased in the long run; and the share of individuals and households must have declined. The share of gross private savings in gross private product may have been constant in the long run; but the contribution of corporations must have increased, while that of individuals and households declined (even if the proportion of personal savings to disposable income—both numerator and denominator net or gross of depreciation on individually owned residential housing—is assumed to have remained constant). All these trends are particularly pronounced in the long run since 1870, and for totals in constant prices; they must be qualified for shorter periods, and for totals in current prices, when prices rise significantly. But the trends are sufficiently grounded in long-established patterns of consumer behavior and in factors affecting the structure of capital formation to warrant attention in thinking of the future.

Concerning the savings of individuals and households, we would be inclined to argue that, at best, their ratio to disposable income will remain at the moderate levels that have prevailed in recent years; and that, if the ratio of disposable income to gross private product declines, the ratio of personal savings, even including depreciation on individually owned residential housing, may decline. This prospect is quite compatible with a substantial rise in real income per capita. To use some recent data: per capita disposable income, in 1958 prices, rose from an average of $1,225 for 1939–1941 to an average of $1,688 for 1948–1957, or 38 per cent in slightly more than twelve years.[7] But the ratio of personal savings to disposable income averaged 7.2 per cent in 1939–1941 and 6.8 per cent in 1948–1957 (Table 77). To be sure, the

[7] See *Economic Report of the President*, January 1959, Table D-14, p. 155.

TABLE 77

Structure of Gross Savings in Relation to Gross Product,
1948–1957 Decade Compared with Selected Periods, 1929–1958
(per cent)

Ratios of:	1929	1939–1941	1948–1952	1953–1957	1948–1957	1958
1. Total savings to GNP	16.0	12.9	15.6	14.8	15.2	12.6
2. Government surplus (+) or deficit (−) to GNP	1.0	−2.0	1.1	−0.2	0.5	−2.3
3. Gross private savings to GNP	15.0	14.9	14.5	15.0	14.8	14.9
4. GPP to GNP	95.9	92.1	92.3	91.3	91.8	90.6
5. Gross private savings to GPP	15.7	16.2	15.7	16.5	16.1	16.4
6. Corporate profits before taxes to GPP	10.1	9.7	12.7	11.0	11.8	9.2
7. Taxes to corporate profits before taxes	13.9	35.9	46.8	51.9	49.4	51.1
8. Corporate profits after taxes to GPP	8.7	5.9	6.8	5.3	6.0	4.5
9. Dividends to corporate profits after taxes	66.7	72.4	46.2	57.1	69.5	69.5
10. Undistributed corporate profits to GPP	2.9	1.7	3.7	2.3	3.0	1.4
11. Capital consumption charges to GPP	8.6	8.6	7.1	8.8	8.0	10.0
12. Gross business profits before taxes to GPP	18.7	18.3	19.9	19.8	19.8	19.2
13. Gross business savings to GPP, lines 10 + 11	11.5	10.3	10.8	11.1	10.9	11.4
14. Personal income to GPP	85.7	84.9	86.5	86.4	86.4	89.3
15. Personal taxes to personal income	3.0	3.3	10.4	11.9	11.2	12.2
16. Disposable income to GPP	83.0	82.1	77.5	76.2	76.8	78.5
17. Personal savings to disposable income	5.1	7.2	6.4	7.1	6.8	6.4
18. Personal savings to GPP	4.2	5.8	5.0	5.4	5.2	5.0
19. Gross private savings to GPP, lines 13 + 18, or line 5	15.7	16.2	15.7	16.5	16.1	16.4

Because of rounding, detail will not necessarily add to total.
All entries are arithmetic means of percentages calculated separately for each year.
GNP = gross national product; GPP = gross private product.

Source: See *Economic Report of the President*, January 1959, Appendix Tables D-1, D-3, D-9, D-10, D-13, D-16, and D-56.

Total savings, defined in accordance with the Department of Commerce practice, include gross private domestic investment plus net exports of goods and services. Personal savings are net.

latter was higher than the 5.1 per cent ratio for 1929, but 1929 was in many ways an exceptional year; and the Department of Commerce personal savings estimates for that year may be too low.[8] The ratio of personal savings to personal income was 4.9 per cent in 1929, 6.8 per cent in 1939–1941, 6.0 per cent in 1948–1957, and 5.6 per cent in 1958 (see Table 77).

Several reasons can be adduced for expecting rather low ratios of personal savings to personal and disposable income in the future. First, this country's economy is geared to rising consumption, and our institutions and patterns of social behavior encourage higher consumption per capita. It is unrealistic to assume that these well-established institutions and patterns will be radically changed in the foreseeable future: they have become more rather than less effective in recent decades. Second, technological change at high levels will have an impact on consumer wants just as it will on the demand for capital goods. Third, full employment policy, progressive taxation and, to some extent, rising prices have made for a less unequal distribution of disposable income, which—other conditions remaining the same—contributes to a lower rate of personal savings; and these conditions are likely to prevail in the future. Finally, and perhaps most important of all: if international tensions persist and there is a continued sense of insecurity about the future—not about the economic future (which might make for greater savings propensities) but about life in general in the face of external dangers—the climate will not be favorable for more than a limited accumulation of savings. For savings are essentially a stake in the economic future, and such stakes become less important when noneconomic factors make the future uncertain.

As to the contribution of corporations to the savings of the private sector, the data in Table 77 suggest the limits that may be expected. The decade 1948–1957 was one of strong demand for capital, high levels of demand for consumer goods, and relatively high profits in private business. Yet gross business savings, i.e., undistributed profits plus capital consumption charges, averaged 10.9 per cent of gross private product, somewhat less than in 1929 and somewhat more than in

---

[8] Goldsmith's estimates, for a comparable concept, i.e., excluding consumers' durable goods, yield a much higher ratio of savings to disposable income for 1929 (and other years). Furthermore, the personal savings figures used here and in Table 77 are net, while for our purposes they should be gross of depreciation on residential housing owned by individuals (with a corresponding addition to personal and disposable income), and net of depreciation on housing owned by corporations. Unfortunately, no such annual estimates are readily available.

1939–1941—the latter being years of substantial unemployment and slack in the economy. These savings were not proportionately low because of high dividend disbursements relative to corporate profits after taxes: the percentage of 51.6 in 1948–1957 was lower than that in either 1929 or 1939–1941. Savings were limited partly because capital consumption charges based on original cost were, particularly during 1948–1952, on the low side; and partly because, although corporate profits before taxes in 1948–1957 were somewhat higher relative to gross private product than in 1929 and in 1939–1941, they were, after taxes, distinctly below the 1929 relative level and about the same as that in 1939–1941.

Thus, there was no perceptible rise in the ratio of gross business savings to gross private product in a decade of strong demand for capital funds, compared with earlier periods in which the demand was not strong; nor was there much of a rise in the personal savings proportion to gross private product. As a result, the ratio of total gross private savings to gross private product in 1948–1957 was only slightly higher than that in 1929 (although an upward correction of the personal savings estimate for 1929 might mean a decline from that year), and was about equal to that in 1939–1941. We cannot conclude from this comparison that gross private savings generated were not sufficient, and that the recent inflationary trends were in fact the consequence of insufficient savings. For, as repeatedly indicated in the earlier chapters, we cannot infer imbalances between *ex ante* supply of and demand for savings from *ex post facto* measures of savings and capital formation proportions. But the evidence certainly is consistent with the view that during the 1948–1957 decade a combination of high-level demand for consumer goods and continued high levels of government drafts for current consumption might have kept private savings and capital formation below the proportion required to increase productivity sufficiently to offset inflationary pressures. Unless in the next few years the private sector can generate savings and capital formation in a greater proportion to a rising private product, the pressure of the demand for goods upon the supply of savings will persist.

CHANGES IN FINANCING

In the discussion so far no attention has been directed toward trends in financing. But some conjectures concerning likely trends in financing can be inferred from the comments above. In brief, they amount to a continuation of the trends discussed in Chapters 5 and 6: a moderate rise in the share of internal financing in the business sector; a continued high level and perhaps further rise in the share of external financing in the residential real estate sector; and continuance of external financing in the government sector. And there are no grounds for assuming that, in the channeling of external funds, the share of financial intermediaries, particularly those in the insurance sector, will not continue to rise—given continuance of the trend toward greater equality in the size-distribution of disposable income and a larger proportion of personal savings arising in the lower income groups.

These inferences hardly touch upon the major problems in the area of credit and financing, in response to which changes may occur in financial institutions and in policies bearing upon prospective trends. The preceding discussion has indicated the vastly increased importance of governments and of business corporations in total gross financing. Of total gross savings in Table 77 (understated because they exclude capital formation by governments via public construction), corporate retention plus government surplus or deficit accounts for more than two-thirds. Furthermore, savings of individuals have been increasingly channeled through financial intermediaries. In other words, the whole process of decision concerning the placement of savings has become increasingly depersonalized: it is either in the hands of financial intermediaries, or of business corporations via gross retention, or directly subject to action by governments.

The problem arises how the process of decision is affected by the traditionally conceived instruments of the financial markets via the interest rates, or of the banking system, or of the central bank. There is little question that, despite the rapid adjustment of financial institutions to changing conditions—or perhaps because of such rapid adjustment—there is an acute need to reassess the operation of the financial system, and reconsider the roles of its instruments of adaptation to the changing patterns of savings in the economy. How do interest rates affect saving by individuals or other units, and channel the available savings into capital uses with different periods of pay-off? How does the growth of financial intermediaries, other than commercial banks, affect the relation between central bank policies and the financial stability and growth of a country? How does the large proportion of total savings originating in gross retention by corporations affect the supply of funds to alternative uses? How much of gross retention becomes available for investment in new channels, not set by the corporation's own past experience in a given field? All these questions are clearly made more acute by the large price rises since World War II, with their distorting effects on the comparative economic returns to various groups of the population, and on the supply of productive factors to what are, from the standpoint of society, the more important uses.

Recognition of all these problems will not, of course, tell us much about likely trends in the structure of financing. The broad movements in those trends will be laid down by major technological changes, government drafts, and the persisting patterns of individual and corporate savings. But given the problems and earnest groping toward their solution, some changes should result both in measures intended to regulate and shape the behavior of financial institutions and in the policies pursued by them (also perhaps even in the identity of the institutions). These changes may well affect the trends in the distribution of external financing among types of financial intermediaries and among groups of capital users, the differential prices of various types of external financing, and the distribution of the latter among various types of loan instruments.

Concluding Comments

The above treatment of conditions for the future, far too brief and dogmatic, may carry a sense of firmer conviction than is intended. The discussion reflects conclusions suggested by the record of this country's economy—an economy geared for a long-run rise to increasingly high levels of consumption per capita, and one in which savings and capital formation, though large and sustained, nevertheless have been kept within moderate proportional limits by the secularly high propensity to consume. It is also an economy in which the recently increasing diversion of product to current consumption by governments, combined with high levels of consumer demand, has limited capital formation and savings proportions and brought about, under conditions of full employment, rising price levels which have persisted even through the 1958 recession. Against this background, consideration of the prospective large rise in population numbers—particularly of new family makers, entrants into the labor force, and of the school-age groups—the prospective acceleration of potential technological change and the prospect of continued international competition and strain suggest the following prospects. First, the demand for capital over the coming two and a half to three decades is likely to be large. Second, drains upon the national product for current consumption by governments will continue to be proportionately sizable and may well rise. Third, high levels of consumption and the high secular propensity to consume by individuals and households are likely to continue. Fourth, under the circumstances, the supply of voluntary savings may not be adequate. Finally, inflationary pressures may well continue, with the result that part of the savings needed for capital formation and government consumption will be extracted through this particular mechanism. Yet, extrapolation of inflationary pressures over the next thirty years raises a specter of intolerable consequences, making the policy solutions adopted critically important; and those solutions, in turn, will affect the structure and pattern of financial intermediaries and their role in financing.

In addition to this broad set of prospects for the twenty-five- to thirty-year period as a whole, we should note probable modifications that may be part of the long swings. There are clear signs of long swings in the time pattern of the rates of population growth. We may now be in a downward phase of the long swing, reflecting the currently low rate of family formation and additions to the labor force resulting from the low birth rates of the 1930's. But there may be factors other than demographic. The international political situation is subject to swings and perturbations of its own—and these cannot but affect our country's economy. There are also swings in the pendulum of political leadership at home.

In ending the discussion we must repeat that the prospects just summarized are judgments, and we may well have given too much weight to current events and problems, and too little to the uncertainties of the long-term future. Above all, a major condition for the future is the international situation, which in these days affects even such seemingly domestic factors as the rate of potential technological change made possible by scientific discovery, and the population's propensity to consume and to save. But prognostication of international relations requires far more knowledge of what is happening abroad, or is likely to happen, than I can claim. In particular, little in the present study contributes to our knowledge of trends in the authoritarian economies, or of their stages of development, or of their possible effects on the position and tasks of this country's economy within the next two or three decades. There may well be shifts, particularly within the Soviet Union, that might lead to relaxation of international competition and tension—although it is difficult for a casual observer to discern and evaluate them.

These qualifications, and many others that could be cited, are real. But they should not lead to a denial of the value of orderly speculation on the prospects for the future. The problems suggested are grave enough to warrant much greater attention to the longer-term view than seems to be given it in current projections, and to justify the testing and refining of these speculations in the more considered and careful projection suggested as the next step to which this and other studies can contribute the indispensable materials. Indeed, the one major justification of such hazardous intellectual operations lies in the possibility that they may reveal the magnitude of the problems and generate policies that might limit their impact, if not forestall them altogether. All historical trends—past or prospective—are contingencies, rather than paths that society took or must follow inexorably. Nothing that has happened was inevitable, and nothing in the present outlook is inevitable. But the contingencies must be clearly seen if they are to be acted upon wisely, and a considered long-term projection could not but help us see the paths and choices before us. This additional, if still uncertain, knowledge may lead to a more intelligent response to the challenging prospects for the future.

APPENDIXES

Annual Estimates, 1919–1955

The Basic Concepts and the Compromise Solutions

NATIONAL income or product totals, since they are expressed quantitatively, convey impressions of precision that tend to conceal debatable underlying assumptions. It is important to recognize these assumptions and state them explicitly in defining the concepts.

National income or net national product (terms used interchangeably in discussing the present series) is the *unduplicated* total of all goods produced by the individual members of the nation and by the capital belonging to them. The major difficulties requiring some criteria for solution may be grouped under three heads: (1) the scope implied by all goods; (2) the elimination of duplication; and (3) the reduction of the diverse items to a common denominator so that they can be added and their total compared from year to year and place to place. Of the three groups of problems (debated at length in the national income literature), the second, elimination of duplication, is of interest here.

In estimating the net product of the economy, we do not wish to count the loaf of bread produced and the flour that goes into it and the grain used in making the flour. Where the production relations are clear, as in the example just given, no difficulty arises: national product includes the loaf of bread, but not the flour and grain consumed in its production. But the output of some activities, particularly those under government auspices, is not easily classifiable as *intermediate* product, i.e., of a type used to produce other goods and hence to be excluded, or as *final* product, and hence to be included. Even consumer goods used by households are regarded as final product only because we view their consumption as final use, not as means to produce, that is, to maintain and increase the supply of human beings as if they were tools (which may be the case in a slave economy). In short, final product can be distinguished from intermediate only if we agree on the ultimate purpose of economic activity.

The point of view here is that the purpose of economic activity is the satisfaction of wants of the members of society, present and future, regarded as ultimate consumers. This admits into net product all consumption by households, and all net additions to capital—whether located within the country or represented by claims against other countries—such capital constituting provision for the future. But for technical reasons the concept must be changed somewhat. Instead of recording actual consumption by households, we record flow of goods to them, disregarding changes in household inventories. Furthermore, since consumption of durable capital (construction and equipment) is difficult to estimate, we measure not only *net* additions to the stock of durable capital within the country (net of current consumption) but also *gross* additions. It is in allowing or not allowing for consumption of construction and equipment that we differentiate between net and gross national product.

The concepts can be described most easily in terms of the two final product components—flow of goods to consumers, and gross or net capital formation. The former comprises all commodities and services flowing to ultimate consumers (households) at cost to them, and any services rendered directly by governments. Capital formation includes gross or net additions to the stock of goods within the country in the hands of business and governments (as well as residential construction even if owner occupied) and net changes in claims against foreign countries. In passing from gross to net capital formation, the adjustment for consumption of durable capital must take account of replacement cost. The same concepts, in the income-payments approach, are approximated by adding factor payments *excluding* direct taxes, direct services of governments to ultimate consumers, undistributed profits of business (net or gross of depreciation, and properly adjusted for the effects of changes in inventory valuation and of differences between the cost and replacement bases of depreciation charges), and net or gross savings or losses of governments (defined as the difference between their net or gross capital formation and the excess of their expenditures on goods over current income). If these concepts are followed, all government expenditures on commodities and services cannot be included in final product and treated as if they were flow of goods to consumers or capital formation.

In applying these concepts, particularly to the years of war and disturbance that account for much of the period since 1919, difficult decisions must be made. These decisions, or compromise solutions, are discussed separately for flow of goods to consumers and for capital formation.

FLOW OF GOODS TO CONSUMERS

First, we decided to omit from the services component of the Department of Commerce consumer expenditures series (used either directly or for extrapolation), "services furnished without payment by financial intermediaries except insurance companies." [1] The argument for classifying this item as a final consumer good has always seemed tenuous; and its inclusion as a means of achieving a proper distribution of product by industrial origin is of marginal value, since an industrial distribution of net product is beset with far greater difficulties. The effect of this omission on the estimates is minor: it accounts for only a few percentage points of total services, and for even less of total consumer outlay. Anyone who wishes to retain it can easily reinclude it in the estimates that follow.

A second and far more important and difficult decision is involved in estimating the amount to be added to consumer expenditures to approximate the value of direct services by governments. A proper estimate of this addition would require a functional analysis of all government expenditures on commodities and services and their classification as services to ultimate consumers (health, education, recreation, and the like) or as services to business enterprises and society at large. Such an analysis would also improve the estimate of capital formation under government auspices. But the task is formidable and could be performed only by an agency with full access to government accounts—federal, state, and local. It could not be undertaken here, and for purposes of establishing a national product framework in the study of long-term trends over the last three-quarters of a century, it is not indispensable, since governments have emerged as large producers and spenders only within the last ten to fifteen years. But it is, to my mind, essential to any study of recent changes in national output that attempts to provide fully meaningful results.

[1] Subgroup VII-3, Table 30 of *National Income, 1954 Ed.* (Supplement, *Survey of Current Business,* Department of Commerce) and of *Survey of Current Business,* July 1956.

Appendix A

The rather arbitrary compromise here [2] was to treat direct taxes paid by individuals as a rough approximation to the value of direct services of governments to them (on a nationwide scale, not in the sense of equivalence of direct taxes and services either for any one type of government or for any one group of taxpayers or services recipients). This convention is justified only because, statistically speaking, the relative magnitudes have been small until recent years. Thus, for the 1929–1938 decade, direct taxes and the nontax payments by ultimate consumers were about $2.1 billion per year.[3] For the same decade, total government expenditures on commodities and services were $9.9 billion per year. But we know that of these about $2.6 billion per year was accounted for by gross public construction, and if the 1939 figures are any indication, national security expenditures constituted about one-tenth of total government expenditures.[4] Subtraction of construction and estimated security expenditures alone leaves about $6.3 billion per year in 1929–1938 for other government expenditures on commodities and services. This residual still includes a wide variety of outlays wholly or in part chargeable to business and society at large. Depending upon the interpretation of the dividing line between direct services and outlays representing costs, the volume of direct services of governments to ultimate consumers could have ranged from $1.5 billion to $3.5 billion per year over the 1929–1938 decade. Compared with the crude approximation based on direct tax and nontax payments, a more detailed estimate could make a difference of about $1 billion per year—less than 2 per cent of flow of goods to consumers or slightly more than 1 per cent of national product, gross or net.

The difficulty with this compromise solution arises in its use for years of war and increased direct taxes. Tax payments by ultimate consumers had risen by 1943 to about $18 billion, and by 1955 had climbed to $35 billion.[5] Over the 1946–1955 decade their ratio to total consumer expenditures (Department of Commerce definition) ranged from 10 to 16 per cent, and they loomed large (from 7 to 10 per cent) even as shares in gross national product (Commerce definition). Obviously, this increase in the relative weight of direct taxes does not represent an equivalent increase in the relative importance of direct services of

2 Adopted originally in Simon Kuznets, *National Income and Its Composition, 1919–1938* (New York, NBER, 1941).

3 *National Income, 1954 Ed.*, Table 3.

4 *Ibid.*, Table 2.

5 *Survey of Current Business*, July 1956, Table 3.

governments to ultimate consumers, unless we consider war a net contribution to consumption or to capital formation. Indeed, the nonmilitary part of government expenditures on commodities and services probably declined relative to total consumer expenditures. In 1939, government expenditures, excluding those on national security, were well over one-sixth of personal consumption expenditures (Commerce definition); by 1955, the share had declined to about one-seventh; and in the war years, 1943 and 1944, it was considerably below one-tenth.[6]

Clearly, to use direct tax payments for the war and postwar years as an approximation to the current value of direct services by governments to ultimate consumers would be misleading. Likewise, in the income-payments approach, we would not be justified in continuing to use factor payments including (i.e. gross of) direct taxes. This simple procedure can be retained only if direct taxes are assumed to be payments for services.

As an easy solution, it seemed best to freeze the ratio of direct taxes to total flow of goods to consumers at the average level prevailing during the immediate prewar years. This ratio, 3.6 per cent for both 1929–1938 and 1929–1940, was applied to flow of goods to consumers (consumer expenditures, as estimated by the Department of Commerce, excluding services imputed to financial intermediaries) for all years beginning with 1941. This estimate exaggerates the relative weight of the services of governments to ultimate consumers, at least in comparison with the 1930's. Consequently, under the concept adopted here, it imparts a slight upward bias to the estimates for the 1940's compared with those for the earlier decades.

CAPITAL FORMATION

Among the problems related to the estimation of capital formation, two deserve comment: the omission of some items of government nonmilitary capital formation; and the treatment of that part of military output which is regarded as capital formation.

The concept calls for the inclusion in government nonmilitary capital formation not only of construction (which is covered) but also of net changes in inventories and of additions to the stock of equipment. Our estimates of producers' durables cover the total flow into domestic consumption without deduction of government purchases. Hence they implicitly include additions to government nonmilitary equipment,

---

[6] Table 2 of *National Income, 1954 Ed.* and of *Survey of Current Business*, July 1956.

although their estimation for recent years is based on crude assumptions. But for the early years there are no data on government inventories, and the changes in the latter had to be omitted from our estimates of capital formation. However, they are not of appreciable significance even annually (except in the case of military nondurables, discussed below), let alone from the standpoint of longer-term movements.

The treatment of capital formation covered in military output raises more complicated conceptual questions and involves larger amounts statistically. Theoretically, the concept calls for net additions to inventories and gross and net additions to durable military capital (construction and durable munitions). Statistically, the measurement of net changes in nondurable military inventories is difficult. The results would probably display marked gyrations that would overshadow the net changes not only in total inventories but also in total capital formation, and possibly have erratic effects even upon national product. However, although they would show marked rises during the war years and sharp declines immediately thereafter, the long-term effect would be relatively slight. Therefore, it seemed justifiable to resort to the fiction that all nondurable military goods are consumed during the year in which they are produced, and changes in inventories of such goods are zero.

No such assumption can be adopted for durable munitions and military construction. By definition, they are not consumed within the year and are in fact, additions to the stock of capital within the country and may last for a number of years. Even though they are designed for military purposes, their survival beyond the initial year releases capital resources for other purposes, and while their services cannot be considered final product, the capital stock embodied in them, like other types of capital that serve a protective purpose, should be included.

The decision to include gross and net capital formation embodied in military construction and durable military goods raises still further questions. How are they to be distinguished from nondurable goods? What rate of consumption (i.e., what life period and depreciation curve) should be assumed for them? How should their current values be adjusted to a constant price basis comparable with that for other commodities and services?

The present estimates of these items differ from our earlier estimates

470

on all three counts.[7] First, recent work (largely on the estimation of government wealth) has permitted a much clearer separation between durable and nondurable military output, yielding appreciably lower totals for the former. Thus, in Table R-6 durable munitions are $8.5 billion and $18.4 billion for 1942 and 1943, respectively, whereas the earlier estimates were $30.0 billion and $53.4 billion.[8] There are corresponding reductions in the gross value of durable munitions for preceding years, but the totals are significant only for 1918 and 1919.

Because of this narrower definition of durable munitions, changes in two other aspects of the estimates became advisable and feasible. The exclusion of all but relatively durable munitions warranted the use of a life of nine years (derived largely from a combination of wealth estimates and gross production) rather than the five years for the war periods and the ten years for the nonwar periods set in the earlier study. Also, with the inclusion of additional war and nonwar years, it became exceedingly difficult to adjust the cost of military construction and munitions to levels comparable with normal, peacetime output.[9] Instead, it seemed best to accept the price adjustment used in the Department of Commerce national income accounts.[10]

These changes in the treatment of durable military output may seem arbitrary, and there is no denying a large element of personal judgment in the procedures. Only two extenuating comments can be made here. First, the changes reflect observations over a longer period and bring the present estimates into closer agreement with the Commerce estimates. Second, given the concept, one errs less in making a rough allowance for the inclusion of durable capital designed for military purposes than in either omitting it altogether or including under final product all military outlay by governments.

The Three Variants

The statistical estimation of the totals and components corresponding to the basic concepts just discussed is based partly upon the work on national income carried out originally at the National Bureau of Economic Research and reported in a series of volumes extending back

[7] See Simon Kuznets, *National Product since 1869* (New York, NBER, 1946).

[8] *Ibid.*, Table I-9, p. 42.

[9] Originally attempted in Simon Kuznets, *National Product in Wartime* (New York, NBER, 1945).

[10] See *National Income, 1954 Ed.*, p. 157.

to the early 1920's and forward to the most recent, *National Product since 1869*. It also relies heavily upon the national income work of the Department of Commerce, which has provided an increasingly valuable and detailed set of estimates for the years since 1929. These source materials, used in different combinations, yielded three sets of continuous and comparable estimates, each corresponding to the basic concepts followed here. The detailed results will be of interest only to investigators for whom we provide the reference tables and notes at the end of each appendix. However, the three sets of estimates, called Variants I, II, and III, are briefly described here.

There are three variants of flow of goods to consumers, of net national product (national income), and of gross national product. But in all the variants of national product, capital formation and its components (gross and net) are identical. The variants differ, therefore, only in the measure of flow of goods to consumers. Variant I is based on the original estimates of national income derived by the income-payments method in *National Income and Its Composition, 1919–1938*. It approximates services (and hence total flow of goods to consumers) by subtracting from national income independently derived estimates of cost of commodities to consumers and of net capital formation, and it is extrapolated forward from the 1930's by appropriate items in the Commerce national income accounts. Variant II retains all the commodity flow series of Variant I but measures the services component directly, to yield a new total of flow of goods to consumers. Variant III takes as its base the Commerce commodity flow and services estimates for the years beginning with 1929 but uses only those components that reflect the concepts underlying Variants I and II. These components of flow of goods to consumers are then extrapolated back to 1919 by the commodity components of Variant I and the services component of Variant II.

These three measures are *statistical* variants of what is intended to be one and the same concept of flow of goods to consumers and of net and gross national product. The discrepancies among them are to be ascribed to differences in estimating procedure. In considering these purely statistical discrepancies, we deal with the estimates in current prices, averaged for decades. Since identical indexes are applied to the three in adjusting for price changes, the differences among the variants in 1929 prices are similar, and since our interest is in long-term movements, decade averages will suffice. Furthermore, the annual

Appendix A

movements of many of the series are identical for all variants because they are based on the same estimates, either incorporated directly or used as extrapolators.

Table A-1 groups all commodity flows to consumers together. It properly emphasizes the services component, which is derived differently for each variant. Two questions are of interest. What is the relative difference in level among the three variants? More important,

TABLE A-1

COMPARISON OF THE THREE VARIANTS, DECENNIAL AVERAGES,
CURRENT PRICES, 1919–1955

	Absolute Figures (billions of dollars)				Indexes (Variant I = 100)			
	1919–1928	1929–1938	1939–1948	1946–1955	1919–1928	1929–1938	1939–1948	1946–1955
Commodity flow to consumers								
Variant I	42.3	37.7	78.7	137.6	100.0	100.0	100.0	100.0
Variant II	42.3	37.7	78.7	137.6	100.0	100.0	100.0	100.0
Variant III	40.6	36.1	75.2	132.6	96.2	95.7	95.6	96 4
Services								
Variant I	21.4	22.1	33.9	61.0	100.0	100.0	100.0	100.0
Variant II	26.5	27.3	42.8	76.2	123.6	123.6	126.0	124.8
Variant III	25.5	26.1	40.9	73.4	119.1	118.3	120.5	120.3
Flow of goods to consumers								
Variant I	63.7	59.8	112.6	198.7	100.0	100.0	100.0	100.0
Variant II	68.8	65.0	121.5	213.8	107.9	108.7	107.8	107.6
Variant III	66.2	62.2	116.1	206.0	103.9	104.1	103.1	103.7
Net national product (national income)								
Variant I	72.2	61.3	121.5	214.2	100.0	100.0	100.0	100.0
Variant II	77.2	66.5	130.3	229.3	107.0	108.5	107.3	107.1
Variant III	74.6	63.7	124.9	221.6	103.4	104.0	102.9	103.4
Gross national product								
Variant I	82.1	71.1	144.0	260.0	100.0	100.0	100.0	100.0
Variant II	87.2	76.3	152.9	275.1	106.2	107.3	106.1	105.8
Variant III	84.6	73.5	147.5	267.3	103.0	103.4	102.4	102.8

Because of rounding, detail will not necessarily add to total.

SOURCE: Calculated from Tables R-1, R-3, and R-9.

what is the difference among them in the broad movements over the three and a half decades since 1919?

In general, the direct estimates of services are higher than the estimate derived as a residual (compare Variants II and III with Variant I). This accords with the general finding that national product estimates derived by the flow-of-income approach are somewhat lower than those obtained by the final-product approach. Consequently, the estimate of services derived as a residual will be lower than that derived directly. But while the excess of the direct estimates is a fairly substantial proportion of the lower estimate of services, the difference is only between 7 and 8.5 per cent of net national product and somewhat less of gross national product in Variant II, and about 6 per cent of net national product and 5 per cent of gross national product in Variant III. The estimate of services in Variant II is larger because the Commerce ratio of services to consumer commodity flow is applied to the National Bureau's somewhat higher estimate of the latter. Variants I and III are preferable to Variant II because the latter is somewhat hybrid, and hence its over-all levels are likely to be more affected by inconsistency in component structure.

For the present purposes, it is the comparative *movement* of the three variants over time that is more relevant. The movement of the decade averages in Variants II and III is not significantly different from that in Variant I. The similarity between Variants I and II is to be expected in view of their predominantly common structure. But even Variants I and III, estimated independently, reflect reliance on a common set of basic data for an overwhelming proportion of the over-all totals.

The discrepancies in movement over the decades among the variants would have to be large indeed to affect the secular trends materially. From 1919–1928 to 1946–1955, the national product totals about tripled. A difference of a few percentage points in a rise of over 200 per cent can hardly be significant, in view of the general margin of error that attaches to the estimates.

One may conclude that the statistical discrepancies among the three variants (in terms of decennial averages) are of little significance in an analysis of long-term movements. That conclusion would clearly be true for shorter-period averages for the two variants of most interest here—I and III.

Appendix A

Comparison with the Department of Commerce Totals, 1929 to 1955

The concepts underlying the three variants differ from those underlying the Commerce estimates. We therefore compare our estimates with those of the Commerce Department to demonstrate the effects of the conceptual differences on the level of the two sets of series and, particularly, on their movement during the recent decades.

In this comparison we use Variant III, in which the flow of goods to consumers is essentially the Commerce estimate. Using Variant III rather than I or II minimizes the statistical differences and reveals the conceptual differences more clearly.

GROSS NATIONAL PRODUCT

Table A-2 provides an indication of the major sources of difference between the two sets of estimates of gross capital formation.

First, our estimates of gross construction totals are consistently larger than the Commerce estimates because they include public construction. In fact, the difference between columns 1 and 2, entered in column 3, is exactly equal to the volume of public construction. Since public construction (including military) increases appreciably in the 1940's and early 1950's, the shortage in the Commerce estimates grows accordingly.

Second, our series on gross producers' durables is consistently larger than the Commerce series—also to be expected. Our series includes durable munitions as well as other types of durable equipment sold to governments; the Commerce series is limited to private durable equipment. In the World War II years and most later years, durable munitions account for the dominant proportion of the difference (compare columns 6 and 7). But there is always a residual difference assignable partly to statistical discrepancies, partly to the inclusion here of nonmilitary producers' durables purchased by governments.

It would be comforting to be able to assert that this residual difference (i.e., the difference between columns 6 and 7) represents a fair approximation to the annual flow of nonmilitary producers' durables to governments. But this cannot be claimed even for 1929 to 1933 for which years we have independent estimates of total producers' durables by the National Bureau and of private producers' durables by the Department of Commerce. All that can be said is that the average level seems reasonable. Thus, for 1929–1938 the residual difference

Appendix A

TABLE A-2

Gross Capital Formation: Major Sources of Difference between NBER Estimates and Department of Commerce Estimates, Current Prices, 1929–1955

(billions of dollars)

| | Construction | | | Producers' Durables | | | Durable Munitions, Included in (4), Excluded from (5) |
	NBER (total) (1)	Commerce (private) (2)	Shortage, Commerce: Public, Signs Reversed, Included in (1), Excluded from (2), (2) − (1) (3)	NBER (total) (4)	Commerce (private) (5)	Shortage, Commerce (5) − (4) (6)	(7)
1929	11.2	8.7	−2.5	7.5	5.8	−1.6	0.2
1930	9.0	6.2	−2.9	5.8	4.5	−1.3	0.2
1931	6.6	4.0	−2.7	3.7	2.8	−0.9	0.3
1932	3.7	1.9	−1.9	2.1	1.6	−0.5	0.3
1933	3.1	1.4	−1.6	2.2	1.6	−0.6	0.2
1934	3.9	1.7	−2.2	3.3	2.3	−1.0	0.3
1935	4.5	2.3	−2.2	4.2	3.1	−1.1	0.4
1936	6.8	3.3	−3.5	5.9	4.2	−1.7	0.5
1937	7.5	4.4	−3.1	6.6	5.1	−1.5	0.5
1938	7.4	4.0	−3.4	5.3	3.6	−1.7	0.5
1939	8.6	4.8	−3.8	5.8	4.2	−1.6	0.4
1940	9.1	5.5	−3.6	7.0	5.5	−1.4	0.3
1941	12.4	6.6	−5.8	10.2	6.9	−3.3	1.9
1942	14.4	3.7	−10.7	14.8	4.3	−10.4	8.5
1943	8.6	2.3	−6.3	23.8	4.0	−19.7	18.4
1944	5.8	2.7	−3.1	26.4	5.4	−20.9	20.2
1945	6.2	3.8	−2.4	21.0	7.7	−13.4	12.8
1946	12.7	10.3	−2.4	14.2	10.7	−3.5	2.7
1947	17.5	14.0	−3.4	19.6	16.7	−2.9	1.8
1948	22.7	17.9	−4.8	22.9	19.1	−3.8	2.2
1949	23.9	17.5	−6.4	22.4	17.8	−4.6	2.5
1950	29.7	22.7	−7.0	26.0	21.1	−4.9	2.5
1951	32.8	23.3	−9.4	32.0	23.2	−8.8	5.9
1952	34.6	23.7	−10.9	35.2	23.1	−12.1	8.9
1953	37.2	25.8	−11.4	37.1	24.3	−12.8	9.4
1954	39.8	27.9	−11.9	33.1	22.4	−10.7	7.0
1955	45.2	32.7	−12.5	33.0	23.7	−9.3	5.6

Because of rounding, detail will not necessarily add to total.

Source, by Column

(1), (4), and (7) Tables R-4 and R-6.
(2) and (5) Tables 2 and 31 in *National Income, 1954 Ed.* (Supplement, *Survey of Current Business*) and in *Survey of Current Business*, July 1956.

averages about $0.85 billion. Its ratio to public construction during that decade (0.85 to 2.6) or to total government outlay on goods and services (0.85 to 9.9) seems quite moderate. However, these are merely plausibilities, and not much weight can be placed on the difference derivable from columns 6 and 7 of Table A-2.

The sum of the shortages in the Commerce series on gross construction and gross producers' durables and of the minor differences in the other two components of gross capital formation (net changes in inventories and in claims against foreign countries) is shown in Table A-3 (column 1). Columns 2 to 4 indicate the two sources of difference between our estimate of the flow of goods to consumers and the Commerce series on consumer expenditures: the latter includes imputed services of financial intermediaries, and excludes the volume of direct services of governments to ultimate consumers. The net difference (column 4) indicates again a shortage in the Commerce estimates, small in the early years but increasing as our estimate of government services to ultimate consumers increases.

All these shortages in capital formation and flow of goods to consumers are more than offset by the inclusion in the Commerce national product series of total government expenditures on commodities and services (column 5). Fairly substantial even in the 1930's, they rise to great heights during the war years of the 1940's and, after a brief contraction in 1946–1948, rise again to levels not much below those of World War II. These expenditures, largely excluded from Variant III, more than outweigh the shortages previously described and produce a consistent excess in the Commerce gross national product total (column 6).

Three aspects of the comparison deserve emphasis. First, columns 6 and 7 indicate that the excess of the Commerce totals over those in Variant III is largely accounted for by the *conceptual* differences in the treatment of government. Second, the excess constitutes a fairly substantial fraction of the total in Variant III even in the 1930's, and rises to as much as 49 per cent in the 1940's and almost 18 per cent in subsequent years (column 8). It follows that the Commerce concept yields a greater rise in gross national product after the 1930's than ours does. Third, the sizable relative excess of the Commerce series is not limited to the World War II years but will persist so long as government expenditures on commodities and services are heavily dominated by those for war and preparation for war, and so long as ultimate con-

TABLE A-3

GROSS NATIONAL PRODUCT: SOURCES OF DIFFERENCE BETWEEN VARIANT III AND DEPARTMENT OF COMMERCE ESTIMATES, CURRENT PRICES, 1929–1955

(dollar amounts in billions)

	Gross Capital Formation, Shortage, Commerce (1)	Flow of Goods to Consumers Excess, Commerce: Imputed Services of Financial Intermediaries (2)	Shortage, Commerce: Tax and Nontax Payments by Individuals[a] (3)	Net Difference (Shortage), Commerce (2) + (3) (4)	Excess, Commerce: Government Expenditures on Commodities and Services (5)	Total Excess, Commerce (1) + (4) + (5)	Excess, Commerce, Due to Treatment of Government (7)	(6) as % of GNP, Variant III (8)
1929	−4.1	1.3	−2.6	−1.4	8.5	3.0	1.7	2.9
1930	−4.2	1.1	−2.5	−1.4	9.2	3.6	2.5	4.1
1931	−3.6	1.0	−1.9	−0.8	9.2	4.8	3.8	6.7
1932	−2.4	0.9	−1.5	−0.6	8.1	5.1	4.3	9.5
1933	−2.4	0.8	−1.5	−0.7	8.0	5.0	4.3	9.7
1934	−3.5	0.8	−1.6	−0.8	9.8	5.5	4.9	9.3
1935	−3.7	0.8	−1.9	−1.1	10.0	5.2	4.8	7.7
1936	−5.6	0.8	−2.3	−1.4	11.8	4.8	4.4	6.2
1937	−4.7	0.9	−2.9	−2.0	11.7	4.9	4.2	5.7
1938	−5.4	0.8	−2.9	−2.0	12.8	5.3	4.9	6.7
1939	−5.7	0.8	−2.4	−1.6	13.3	6.0	5.4	7.1
1940	−5.3	0.8	−2.6	−1.8	14.1	7.0	6.4	7.5
1941	−9.4	0.9	−2.9	−2.1	24.8	13.3	12.8	11.8
1942	−21.3	0.9	−3.2	−2.3	59.7	36.2	35.4	29.4
1943	−26.2	0.9	−3.6	−2.6	88.6	59.7	59.0	45.0
1944	−24.3	1.2	−3.9	−2.7	96.5	69.5	68.6	49.0
1945	−15.9	1.3	−4.3	−3.0	82.9	63.9	62.7	42.7
1946	−5.9	1.5	−5.2	−3.7	30.9	21.3	19.9	11.3
1947	−6.5	1.5	−5.9	−4.4	28.6	17.7	16.4	8.3
1948	−8.8	1.7	−6.3	−4.6	36.6	23.2	21.6	9.9
1949	−11.1	1.9	−6.4	−4.6	43.6	27.9	26.2	12.2
1950	−11.9	2.0	−6.9	−4.9	42.0	25.2	23.3	9.7
1951	−18.3	2.2	−7.4	−5.2	62.8	39.3	37.1	13.6
1952	−23.1	2.5	−7.8	−5.3	77.5	49.1	46.7	16.6
1953	−24.3	2.8	−8.2	−5.4	84.4	54.7	52.0	17.7
1954	−22.7	3.0	−8.4	−5.4	76.5	48.4	45.5	15.5
1955	−21.9	3.4	−8.9	−5.6	76.8	49.3	46.0	14.4

Because of rounding, detail will not necessarily add to total.
a Through 1940. For description of estimate for 1941–1955, see text.

SOURCE, BY COLUMN

(1) Difference between col. 5 of Table R-4 and the sum of gross private domestic investment and net foreign investment given in Table 2 of *National Income, 1954 Ed.*, and of *Survey of Current Business*, July 1956.

(2) Group VII-3 of Table 30 in the above two sources.
(3) 1929–1940 from *Survey of Current Business*, July 1956, Table 3. *Ibid.*, Table 2.
(5) Col. 5 minus col. 3, signs reversed, and minus cols. 3 and 6 of Table A-2, with signs reversed.
(7)
(8) For gross national product, Variant III, see Table R-1, col. 9.

sumption and capital formation continue to be a smaller proportion of total government expenditures than in the nonwar years before the 1940's.

NET NATIONAL PRODUCT AND NATIONAL INCOME

All the conceptual (and minor statistical) disparities between the gross national product totals in Variant III and in the Commerce series apply also to a comparison of net national product and national income in the two sets of estimates. But there are additional sources of difference, some accentuating and others reducing the difference in *level*, and all contributing to a marked difference in *movement* from the 1930's to the 1940's and later years.

In the concept underlying Variant III, net national product and national income are identical. In the conceptual structure of the Commerce series, the difference between gross and net national product is capital consumption charges, and there is a further difference between net national product and national income in that the latter is net of business taxes and business transfer payments (excluding subsidies to business and the surplus of government enterprises).

The sources of difference between net national product, Department of Commerce definition, and net national product (or national income), Variant III, lie not only in those already stated above in the comparison of gross national product, but also in the measurement of capital consumption (Table A-4). Our series on capital consumption is consistently and appreciably larger than that recorded in the Commerce income accounts, partly because it includes consumption charges on government construction and munitions, even though as indicated in footnote 1, Chapter 3, it does not allow for depreciation of nonmilitary producers' equipment purchased by governments (column 4). But there are other sources of difference in the capital consumption item. We include depletion charges, excluded by the Department of Commerce on the ground that they do not represent depreciation of reproducible capital. The logic of this exclusion has always seemed doubtful, partly because, with changing technology, reproducibility (and substitutability) is a relative rather than an absolute term; partly because, like much of depreciation proper (on reproducible goods), which represents loss in competitive position because of obsolescence, depletion of natural resources also means loss in competitive position. Finally, a third factor causing shortage in the Commerce estimates of capital consumption in all years except the 1930's is the use of the

Appendix A

TABLE A-4

CAPITAL CONSUMPTION: SOURCES OF DIFFERENCE BETWEEN NBER ESTIMATES AND DEPARTMENT OF COMMERCE ESTIMATES, CURRENT PRICES, 1929–1955

(dollar amounts in billions)

	Total Capital Consumption			Difference (Shortage), Commerce, Due to Scope		Difference Due Largely to Basis of Depreciation Valuation		Price Index, Construction and Producers' Durables
	NBER (1)	Commerce (2)	Total Difference (Shortage), Commerce (2) − (1) (3)	Depreciation, Public Construction, and Munitions (4)	Depletion (5)	NBER Depreciation (6)	Difference, Commerce (2) − (6) (7)	(1929 = 100.0) (8)
1929	11.1	8.6	−2.5	−1.4	−0.5	9.2	−0.6	100.0
1930	10.6	8.5	−2.1	−1.3	−0.5	8.8	−0.2	96.4
1931	9.8	8.2	−1.6	−1.3	−0.5	8.0	0.2	89.7
1932	8.6	7.6	−1.0	−1.2	−0.4	7.0	0.6	80.8
1933	8.3	7.2	−1.2	−1.4	−0.4	6.5	0.6	78.3
1934	9.1	7.1	−2.0	−1.7	−0.4	7.1	0.1	83.6
1935	9.2	7.2	−1.9	−1.7	−0.4	7.0	0.2	84.2
1936	9.7	7.5	−2.2	−1.9	−0.4	7.4	0.1	84.8
1937	10.8	7.7	−3.0	−2.1	−0.5	8.3	−0.5	93.0
1938	11.1	7.8	−3.3	−2.1	−0.5	8.5	−0.7	94.8
1939	11.2	7.8	−3.4	−2.3	−0.5	8.5	−0.6	93.6
1940	11.8	8.1	−3.6	−2.3	−0.5	8.9	−0.8	96.2
1941	13.6	9.0	−4.5	−2.8	−0.6	10.2	−1.2	103.5
1942	16.5	10.2	−6.4	−3.9	−0.8	11.9	−1.7	112.9
1943	19.6	10.9	−8.7	−5.7	−0.8	13.1	−2.2	120.6
1944	23.2	12.0	−11.2	−7.5	−0.9	14.8	−2.8	126.4
1945	25.5	12.5	−12.9	−9.0	−0.9	15.6	−3.0	129.2
1946	27.5	11.7	−15.8	−11.0	−0.9	15.6	−4.0	141.0
1947	35.4	14.1	−21.3	−13.2	−1.2	21.1	−6.9	165.8
1948	41.4	16.5	−24.9	−14.8	−1.5	25.1	−8.6	182.2
1949	44.0	18.4	−25.6	−15.2	−1.6	27.2	−8.8	185.4
1950	46.9	20.5	−26.4	−15.9	−1.7	29.3	−8.8	190.1
1951	52.5	23.5	−29.1	−16.5	−2.0	34.0	−10.5	205.6
1952	51.2	23.9	−27.3	−15.7	−2.0	33.5	−9.6	209.0
1953	51.9	26.5	−25.4	−13.8	−2.1	36.0	−9.5	214.0
1954	52.1	28.8	−23.4	−12.5	−2.2	37.5	−8.7	213.8
1955	54.9	31.3	−23.6	−12.6	−2.4	40.0	−8.7	217.6

Because of rounding, detail will not necessarily add to total.

SOURCE, BY COLUMN
(1) Table R-8, col. 3.
(2) *Survey of Current Business*, July 1956, Table 4.
(3) Table R-6, col. 6, and annual series underlying Table R-31, cols. 2 and 3.
(5) Estimated by the procedure described in the notes to Table R-8, col. 3.
(6) Col. 1 minus the sum of cols. 4 and 5, with signs reversed.
(8) Arithmetic average of price index of private new construction and of private producers' durable equipment (*Survey of Current Business*, July 1956, Table 41), each shifted to a 1929 base.

original cost rather than the reproduction cost basis in calculating depreciation charges (column 7). When current prices are greatly in excess of original cost, the shortage in the Commerce estimates of capital consumption is fairly substantial. This is evident in the inverse relation between the movement of that shortage in column 7 and the movement of the price index of durable capital goods in column 8 (unweighted average of the Commerce price indexes for construction and producers' durables, each shifted to a 1929 base).

Since our capital consumption estimates are larger than those of the Department of Commerce, the reduction in passing from gross to net national product is larger in Variant III than in the Commerce series. The shortage in the Commerce estimates of capital consumption must, therefore, be *added* to the excess of its estimates of gross national product to derive the total excess of the Commerce estimates of net national product over those in Variant III. Therefore, the sign of the entries in column 3 of Table A-4 is reversed in column 2 of Table A-5. The sum of columns 1 and 2 is, then, the total excess of the Commerce net national product totals (column 3).

It is not surprising that the relative excess is appreciably greater than that in gross national product shown in Table A-3. Nor is it surprising that the relative magnitude of the excess rises significantly from the 1930's to the mid-1940's. What should be emphasized is that the relative level remains high after World War II. The average excess for 1946–1955 is almost 27 per cent of the level in Variant III, or more than twice as large as the average of 11.2 per cent for 1929–1938 (column 4). For gross national product, the corresponding excess is 12.9 per cent for 1946–1955 and 6.8 per cent for 1929–1938. The relative excess of the Commerce net national product series increases because depreciation on government capital is not deducted and because the replacement cost basis for business capital is not used. These omissions form an increasing proportion of gross national product because of the bulge in government capital that occurred during the war years and because of the continued inflation of prices of durable capital goods. As a result, the discussion above concerning the effects of the conceptual structure of the Commerce estimates on the rise in gross national product totals after the 1930's applies with even greater force to the rise in the net national product totals.

When the net national product totals in Variant III are compared with the Commerce national income totals, the level of the discrepancy is markedly different (columns 5 to 7 of Table A-5). National income,

TABLE A-5

NET NATIONAL PRODUCT AND NATIONAL INCOME: SOURCES OF DIFFERENCE BETWEEN VARIANT III
AND DEPARTMENT OF COMMERCE ESTIMATES, CURRENT PRICES, 1929–1955
(dollar amounts in billions)

	Gross National Product, Excess, Commerce (1)	Capital Consumption, Shortage (signs reversed) Commerce (2)	*Net National Product*		*National Income*			
			Total Excess, Commerce (1) + (2) (3)	(3) as % of NNP, Variant III (4)	Business Taxes, Transfer Payments, and Surplus of Government Enterprises, Commerce (5)	Statistical Discrepancy, Commerce (6)	Excess, Commerce (3) − (5) − (6) (7)	(7) as % of NNP, Variant III (8)
1929	3.0	2.5	5.5	6.1	7.7	0.3	−2.5	−2.8
1930	3.6	2.1	5.7	7.4	7.8	−1.0	−1.1	−1.5
1931	4.8	1.6	6.4	10.3	7.6	0.8	−2.0	−3.3
1932	5.1	1.0	6.1	13.6	7.6	0.8	−2.2	−5.0
1933	5.0	1.2	6.2	14.4	7.7	0.9	−2.5	−5.8
1934	5.5	2.0	7.5	14.9	8.2	0.7	−1.4	−2.7
1935	5.2	1.9	7.1	12.2	8.4	−0.2	−1.1	−1.9
1936	4.8	2.2	7.0	10.2	9.2	1.1	−3.3	−4.9
1937	4.9	3.0	8.0	10.6	9.7	−0.2	−1.5	−1.9
1938	5.3	3.3	8.7	12.6	9.4	0.5	−1.2	−1.8
1939	6.0	3.4	9.4	12.7	9.3	1.2	−1.1	−1.5
1940	7.0	3.6	10.6	13.0	10.0	0.8	−0.2	−0.3
1941	13.3	4.5	17.8	18.0	11.7	0.4	5.8	5.8
1942	36.2	6.4	42.5	39.9	12.1	−0.8	31.2	29.3
1943	59.7	8.7	68.5	60.5	13.1	−1.7	57.2	50.5
1944	69.5	11.2	80.7	68.0	14.0	2.8	63.9	53.9
1945	63.9	12.9	76.8	61.9	15.3	4.5	57.1	46.0
1946	21.3	15.8	37.1	23.1	17.1	0.9	19.1	11.9
1947	17.7	21.3	39.1	21.8	19.6	1.4	18.1	10.1
1948	23.2	24.9	48.1	24.9	21.3	−2.1	28.9	15.0
1949	27.9	25.6	53.6	28.9	22.6	0.1	30.9	16.7
1950	25.2	26.4	51.7	24.3	24.4	0.2	27.1	12.7
1951	39.3	29.1	68.3	28.9	26.4	1.3	40.6	17.2
1952	49.1	27.3	76.4	31.2	29.4	2.0	45.0	18.4
1953	54.7	25.4	80.0	31.2	32.0	2.6	45.4	17.7
1954	48.4	23.4	71.8	27.6	31.8	1.8	38.2	14.7
1955	49.3	23.6	72.9	25.4	33.7	1.8	37.4	13.0

Because of rounding, detail will not necessarily add to total.

SOURCE, BY COLUMN
(1) Table A-3, col. 6.
(2) Table A-4, col. 3, signs reversed.
(4) and (8) For net national product, Variant III, see Table R-1, col. 6.
(5) and (6) *Survey of Current Business*, July 1956, Table 4.

as measured by the Department of Commerce, can best be described
as the sum of final products, weighted by factor payments, plus undistributed profits of private enterprise (i.e., return to the factor of
enterprise). Final products are defined to include consumer outlay net
of direct taxes, private capital formation, and government purchases

of commodities and services. National income, as measured in Variant III, is the sum of final products, weighted by factor incomes. But here final products, while excluding government purchases of commodities and services, include an estimate of direct services of governments to ultimate consumers (approximated by the full total of direct taxes through 1940 and by a constant fraction of total consumer outlay for later years). They also include capital formation by governments. When our estimates of government services to ultimate consumers and public capital formation outweigh government purchases of goods measured at factor cost (i.e., reduced by business taxes, etc.), our estimates of national income are larger than the Commerce totals. This was the case through most of the 1930's, although by only a few percentage points. But in periods of large war and postwar government expenditures, government services to ultimate consumers plus public capital formation fall far short of government purchases even on a factor cost basis. This explains the shift in columns 7 and 8 from small negative entries in the 1930's to large positive ones in the 1940's and later years.

It is particularly to be noted that the upward trend after the 1930's in the excess of the Commerce estimates over those in Variant III is just as conspicuous in the comparison of national income as in the comparison of net national product. The only element that moderates this upward trend is the statistical discrepancy (column 6). Since that tends to rise from the 1930's to the 1940's (although it drops again after 1945), its subtraction tends to reduce, but to only a small degree, the increasing effects of the conceptual differences between the Commerce national income totals and those in Variant III. The average excess of the Commerce national income series over net national product, Variant III, is 14.7 per cent for 1946–1955, compared with an average shortage of 3.2 per cent for 1929–1938 (column 8). If we apply these percentages to the decade averages in Table A-1, we find that, whereas net national product, Variant III, rises from an index of 100 for 1929–1938 to 348 for 1946–1955, the derived rise for the Commerce national income totals would be from an index of 100 to 412.

NATIONAL PRODUCT IN CONSTANT PRICES

The comparisons in Tables A-2 to A-5 are for totals in current prices. With the indexes applied to adjust for changes in prices quite similar for both sets of estimates, the differences between the two and the movement of these differences over time are only slightly affected by the deflation. There is little need, therefore, to repeat the comparisons in detail.

Yet from many standpoints, the national product totals in constant prices are more meaningful than those in changing current prices. It seemed useful, therefore, to present a brief comparison of the two sets of series in constant prices (Table A-6). Because the Commerce tables show constant price estimates for gross national product alone, and those for other totals can be approximated only roughly, we limit the comparison to gross and net national product.

Three findings can be clearly perceived. First, the Commerce totals show a greater rise from the average level of the 1930's than do the totals in Variant III. This is particularly marked in columns 3 and 4, where the difference in the estimation of capital consumption is added to the difference in treatment of the government sector.

Second, with the Commerce totals in the 1930's already in excess of those in Variant III, the disparity in the trends just observed serves to increase the difference in levels. Thus, for net national product the excess in the Commerce estimates, which is about 7 per cent during 1929–1938, grew to about 22 per cent during 1951–1955.

The third and most interesting finding is the variation in the difference which stems largely from the fluctuations in the proportionate weight of government expenditures, the latter in turn due largely to fluctuations in the relative magnitude of expenditures on defense. The difference in the indexes was moderate in 1939–1941, increased markedly in 1942-1945, the years of heavy military outlays, decreased in 1946–1950 when defense expenditures became relatively moderate, and then rose again in 1951–1955.

These differences in trend and movement are clearly associated with the differences in concept. The concept underlying the Variant III estimates views national product as a contribution either to consumption by ultimate consumers or to capital formation. From this point of view, the great effort during World War II and the defense effort of 1951–1955 was translated into but moderate gains because so much of it went into currently consumed nondurable munitions and into a highly depreciable stock of durable military goods. In the Commerce concept, all government expenditures on goods are final product, and the measures are therefore fully affected by any productive effort that finds its outlet in sales to governments, regardless of whether the product is added to the capital stock of the country or is consumed—in the office or on the battlefield.

Appendix A

TABLE A-6

NATIONAL PRODUCT IN 1929 PRICES: VARIANT III AND DEPARTMENT OF COMMERCE ESTIMATES COMPARED, 1939–1955

	Gross National Product		Net National Product	
	Variant III (1)	Commerce (2)	Variant III (3)	Commerce (4)
Average value, 1929–1938 (billions of dollars)	87.3	91.4	76.6	82.2
Indexes		(1929–1938 = 100.0)		
1939	118.8	120.6	120.5	122.4
1940	129.4	131.6	132.1	134.3
1941	144.6	151.8	148.0	156.6
1942	140.4	171.3	140.8	178.1
1943	139.6	190.9	137.4	200.1
1944	145.0	205.5	139.9	215.3
1945	149.1	201.5	142.1	210.7
1946	174.0	179.1	171.6	187.8
1947	175.8	177.9	171.0	185.6
1948	181.9	186.9	175.9	194.3
1949	176.4	184.9	168.1	190.7
1950	197.9	202.8	191.4	209.0
1951	204.5	216.8	197.4	223.6
1952	206.4	225.1	201.2	232.7
1953	211.9	233.9	207.5	240.9
1954	213.5	230.5	209.6	235.6
1955	231.6	247.2	229.3	252.6
Averages of indexes				
1939–1941	130.9	134.7	133.5	137.8
1942–1945	143.5	192.3	140.0	201.0
1946–1950	181.2	186.3	175.6	193.5
1951–1955	213.6	230.7	209.0	237.1

SOURCE, BY COLUMN

(1) and (3) For Variant III, see Table R-2, cols. 9 and 6, respectively.

(2) and (4) The current price series, shown for 1929–1948 in Table 4 of *National Income, 1954 Ed.* and for 1949–1955 in Table 4 of *Survey of Current Business*, July 1956, were converted to 1929 prices by the price index implicit in gross national product, Table 41, of the same sources.

TABLE R-1

FLOW OF GOODS TO CONSUMERS, NET NATIONAL PRODUCT, AND GROSS NATIONAL PRODUCT,
THREE VARIANTS, CURRENT PRICES, 1919–1955

(billions of dollars)

| | Flow of Goods to Consumers | | | Net National Product | | | Gross National Product | | |
	Variant I (1)	Variant II (2)	Variant III (3)	Variant I (4)	Variant II (5)	Variant III (6)	Variant I (7)	Variant II (8)	Variant III (9)
1919	53.6	56.9	54.7	64.2	67.4	65.2	74.0	77.2	75.0
1920	62.2	66.3	63.7	74.2	78.3	75.7	85.3	89.4	86.8
1921	56.6	61.3	58.9	59.4	64.2	61.8	68.7	73.5	71.1
1922	56.1	60.8	58.4	60.7	65.4	63.0	69.5	74.2	71.8
1923	62.2	67.2	64.6	71.6	76.7	74.1	81.2	86.3	83.7
1924	65.5	71.3	68.6	72.1	77.9	75.2	81.8	87.6	85.0
1925	65.7	70.8	68.3	76.0	81.2	78.6	86.0	91.1	88.5
1926	71.0	76.8	74.0	81.6	87.4	84.6	92.0	97.8	95.0
1927	70.8	76.7	73.9	80.1	85.9	83.1	90.4	96.2	93.4
1928	73.2	79.4	76.5	81.7	87.9	85.0	92.2	98.5	95.5
1929	77.2	83.7	80.3	87.2	93.7	90.3	98.4	104.9	101.5
1930	72.8	75.9	72.3	77.3	80.4	76.9	87.9	91.0	87.5
1931	60.7	63.5	62.2	60.3	63.0	61.7	70.1	72.8	71.5
1932	48.0	52.5	49.9	42.9	47.3	44.8	51.5	55.9	53.4
1933	46.6	50.7	47.1	42.2	46.2	42.6	50.5	54.6	51.0
1934	51.9	55.1	52.7	49.5	52.8	50.3	58.7	61.9	59.5
1935	53.6	59.9	57.4	54.4	60.7	58.2	63.6	69.8	67.3
1936	58.6	66.7	64.0	62.9	71.0	68.3	72.5	80.7	77.9
1937	64.7	72.2	69.3	70.5	77.9	75.1	81.3	88.7	85.8
1938	63.4	69.6	66.7	65.5	71.7	68.8	76.6	82.8	79.9
1939	66.6	72.2	69.2	71.2	76.8	73.8	82.5	88.1	85.1
1940	70.9	76.8	73.7	79.1	84.9	81.8	90.8	96.7	93.6
1941	81.0	87.4	83.9	96.0	102.4	99.0	109.6	116.0	112.5
1942	89.3	96.6	92.0	103.7	111.0	106.5	120.2	127.5	123.0
1943	100.4	108.6	103.2	110.4	118.6	113.2	130.0	138.2	132.8
1944	109.6	118.6	112.6	115.8	124.8	118.7	138.9	147.9	141.9
1945	121.6	131.4	124.7	121.1	130.8	124.2	146.6	156.3	149.6
1946	146.2	157.2	150.3	156.3	167.4	160.5	183.8	194.9	188.0
1947	164.2	176.4	169.3	174.0	186.1	179.0	209.4	221.5	214.5
1948	176.5	189.7	182.2	187.0	200.2	192.8	228.4	241.6	234.1
1949	178.8	192.3	185.2	178.9	192.4	185.3	222.9	236.5	229.3
1950	191.6	206.0	198.9	205.6	219.9	212.9	252.5	266.8	259.8
1951	205.9	221.5	213.6	228.8	244.4	236.5	281.4	297.0	289.0
1952	215.5	232.0	223.6	237.0	253.6	245.2	288.2	304.8	296.4
1953	226.8	244.4	235.9	247.6	265.1	256.7	299.5	317.0	308.6
1954	232.3	250.5	241.9	250.5	268.7	260.1	302.6	320.9	312.2
1955	248.9	268.2	259.6	276.0	295.3	286.7	331.0	350.2	341.6

Gross and net capital formation are identical for all three variants.

SOURCE, BY COLUMN

(1) Table R-3, sum of cols. 1–4.
(2) Table R-3, cols. 1–3 plus Table R-9, col. 1.
(3) Table R-9, sum of cols. 2–5.
(4) Col. 1 plus Table R-4, col. 7.
(5) Col. 2 plus Table R-4, col. 7.

(6) Col. 3 plus Table R-4, col. 7.
(7) Col. 1 plus Table R-4, col. 5.
(8) Col. 2 plus Table R-4, col. 5.
(9) Col. 3 plus Table R-4, col. 5.

FLOW OF GOODS TO CONSUMERS, NET NATIONAL PRODUCT, AND GROSS NATIONAL PRODUCT,
THREE VARIANTS, 1929 PRICES, 1919–1955

(billions of dollars)

	Flow of Goods to Consumers			Net National Product			Gross National Product		
	Variant I (1)	Variant II (2)	Variant III (3)	Variant I (4)	Variant II (5)	Variant III (6)	Variant I (7)	Variant II (8)	Variant III (9)
1919	49.7	53.8	52.2	58.7	62.8	61.1	67.8	71.9	70.3
1920	51.3	55.8	54.2	59.4	63.8	62.2	68.5	73.0	71.4
1921	54.1	58.9	57.0	56.7	61.5	59.6	65.5	70.3	68.4
1922	56.5	61.2	59.2	61.1	65.8	63.9	70.4	75.1	73.2
1923	61.2	66.3	64.3	70.4	75.5	73.5	80.0	85.0	83.0
1924	65.3	71.0	69.0	71.9	77.6	75.6	81.6	87.3	85.2
1925	64.0	69.0	67.1	74.3	79.3	77.3	84.3	89.3	87.4
1926	68.9	74.6	72.5	79.2	84.9	82.8	89.8	95.5	93.4
1927	70.7	76.5	74.2	80.1	85.9	83.6	90.6	96.4	94.2
1928	72.5	78.6	76.3	81.1	87.2	84.9	91.9	98.0	95.7
1929	76.9	83.4	80.3	86.9	93.4	90.3	98.0	104.5	101.4
1930	74.9	78.0	75.9	79.5	82.6	80.5	90.5	93.7	91.5
1931	69.1	71.9	73.2	69.4	72.2	73.5	80.2	83.0	84.3
1932	62.1	66.9	66.4	56.0	60.8	60.3	66.4	71.2	70.7
1933	62.4	67.2	65.0	55.6	60.4	58.2	65.7	70.5	68.3
1934	65.2	69.2	68.6	61.1	65.0	64.4	71.3	75.2	74.6
1935	66.1	73.7	73.1	68.3	76.0	75.4	78.8	86.4	85.8
1936	71.8	81.6	80.8	76.0	85.8	85.0	86.9	96.7	95.8
1937	76.7	85.4	84.4	85.0	93.7	92.7	96.2	104.9	103.9
1938	77.0	84.3	83.0	79.4	86.6	85.4	90.6	97.9	96.7
1939	81.5	87.9	87.0	86.8	93.2	92.3	98.2	104.6	103.7
1940	85.7	92.4	91.7	95.2	101.9	101.2	107.0	113.7	113.0
1941	91.6	98.6	97.9	107.0	114.1	113.3	119.9	127.0	126.2
1942	89.9	97.5	96.2	101.6	109.2	107.8	116.4	124.0	122.6
1943	92.2	100.3	98.8	98.6	106.7	105.2	115.3	123.4	121.9
1944	95.2	103.7	102.2	100.1	108.6	107.1	119.7	128.1	126.6
1945	101.5	110.4	109.1	101.3	110.2	108.8	122.7	131.6	130.2
1946	113.4	123.1	122.3	122.5	132.2	131.4	143.0	152.7	151.9
1947	115.5	125.4	124.9	121.5	131.4	130.9	144.1	154.0	153.5
1948	117.7	127.9	127.5	124.9	135.1	134.7	149.0	159.2	158.8
1949	120.8	131.0	130.7	118.8	129.0	128.7	144.0	154.2	154.0
1950	127.9	138.5	138.7	135.8	146.4	146.6	162.0	172.6	172.8
1951	128.8	139.9	139.8	140.2	151.3	151.2	167.6	178.7	178.6
1952	132.9	144.3	144.0	143.0	154.4	154.0	169.2	180.6	180.2
1953	138.6	150.1	150.0	147.4	159.0	158.8	173.6	185.1	185.0
1954	140.9	152.6	152.6	148.8	160.6	160.5	174.8	186.5	186.4
1955	150.7	162.9	163.1	163.2	175.3	175.6	189.8	202.0	202.2

Gross and net capital formation are identical for all three variants. The price index used in calculating net changes in claims against foreign countries in 1929 prices is that implicit in gross national product excluding such changes, Variant I. Strictly speaking, for Variants II and III we should have computed the index implicit in those variants. But the difference is negligible and has been disregarded.

SOURCE, BY COLUMN

(1) Table R-3, sum of cols. 5–8.
(2) Table R-3, cols. 5–7, plus Table R-10, col. 1.
(3) Table R-10, sum of cols. 2–5.
(4) Col. 1 plus Table R-5, col. 7.
(5) Col. 2 plus Table R-5, col. 7.

(6) Col. 3 plus Table R-5, col. 7.
(7) Col. 1 plus Table R-5, col. 5.
(8) Col. 2 plus Table R-5, col. 5.
(9) Col. 3 plus Table R-5, col. 5.

Appendix A

TABLE R-3

COMPONENTS OF FLOW OF GOODS TO CONSUMERS, VARIANT I, 1919–1955
(billions of dollars)

	Current Prices				1929 Prices			
	Perish-ables (1)	Semi-durables (2)	Durables (3)	Services (4)	Perish-ables (5)	Semi-durables (6)	Durables (7)	Services (8)
1919	24.4	10.1	5.42	13.7	19.9	7.50	4.98	17.3
1920	26.9	11.7	6.24	17.3	21.0	6.52	4.92	18.9
1921	21.8	9.52	5.05	20.2	21.8	7.84	3.99	20.4
1922	21.1	9.82	5.50	19.7	22.6	8.86	5.08	19.9
1923	22.7	11.1	7.00	21.4	23.5	9.76	6.64	21.3
1924	23.4	10.5	7.02	24.5	25.3	9.03	6.92	24.1
1925	25.0	11.0	7.98	21.7	25.1	9.95	7.78	21.2
1926	26.6	11.5	8.32	24.6	26.3	10.0	8.64	24.0
1927	26.3	11.7	7.94	24.9	26.8	11.2	8.20	24.5
1928	26.9	11.8	8.15	26.4	26.7	11.2	8.40	26.2
1929	28.0	12.1	8.77	28.4	28.0	11.8	8.76	28.4
1930	25.9	10.5	6.76	29.6	27.5	10.6	6.93	29.9
1931	21.2	8.80	5.17	25.6	26.2	10.5	5.73	26.6
1932	17.8	6.54	3.44	20.3	25.9	9.51	4.28	22.4
1933	17.8	6.35	3.49	19.0	26.9	8.65	4.20	22.6
1934	20.9	7.38	4.02	19.6	27.5	8.92	4.92	23.9
1935	23.2	7.85	4.88	17.7	28.8	9.65	6.07	21.6
1936	26.1	8.64	6.02	17.8	32.2	10.6	7.49	21.5
1937	28.2	9.06	6.61	20.9	33.7	10.6	7.88	24.5
1938	27.1	8.89	5.43	21.9	34.4	10.7	6.46	25.4
1939	27.8	9.47	6.37	23.0	35.7	11.8	7.64	26.4
1940	29.5	9.95	7.42	24.0	37.4	12.2	8.77	27.3
1941	34.0	11.8	9.22	25.9	39.8	13.1	10.1	28.5
1942	39.8	14.8	6.65	28.1	40.6	13.5	6.52	29.4
1943	45.2	17.9	6.30	31.1	41.3	14.6	5.61	30.7
1944	49.7	19.8	6.46	33.6	44.0	14.4	5.12	31.7
1945	55.5	22.5	7.74	36.0	47.8	15.0	5.79	32.8
1946	64.9	24.9	15.2	41.2	50.9	15.3	11.2	36.1
1947	73.0	25.8	19.7	45.8	50.2	14.5	13.3	37.5
1948	77.8	26.9	21.2	50.6	50.5	14.3	13.8	39.2
1949	77.1	25.5	22.5	53.7	51.5	14.3	14.5	40.4
1950	80.5	25.8	27.3	58.0	53.0	14.5	17.6	42.8
1951	89.8	27.7	25.9	62.6	54.5	14.3	15.7	44.3
1952	94.5	28.2	25.4	67.3	56.1	15.0	15.5	46.2
1953	97.5	28.2	28.5	72.7	58.3	15.1	17.3	48.0
1954	99.5	28.0	28.0	76.7	59.1	15.0	17.4	49.4
1955	103.7	29.4	34.0	81.7	62.2	15.8	21.0	51.7

Appendix A

SOURCE, BY COLUMN

(1–3) 1919–1933: Simon Kuznets, *National Product since 1869* (New York, NBER, 1946), Table I-5.

1934–1951: The 1929–1933 ratio of the given series to the Commerce series in *National Income, 1954 Ed.* (Supplement, *Survey of Current Business*, Department of Commerce), Table 30, applied to the Commerce series for 1934 to 1951. Of the nondurable commodities, subgroups II-1, II-3, II-4, V-5, IX-3, and one-half of XII-2 were considered semidurable and the balance perishable.

(4) 1919–1938: Net national product, given in Simon Kuznets, *National Income and Its Composition, 1919–1938* (New York, NBER, 1941), Table 1, minus cols. 1–3 and Table R-4, col. 7.

1939–1951: The 1929–1938 ratio of the given series to the Commerce series in *National Income, 1954 Ed.*, Table 30, excluding subgroup VII-3, applied to the Commerce series for 1939 to 1951.

(5–7) 1919–1933: *National Product since 1869*, Table I-5.

1934–1951: The procedure is the same as that for cols. 1–3. The Commerce series for the major groups are given in *National Income, 1954 Ed.*, Table 40; those for the subgroups were obtained by letter.

(8) 1919–1938: Col. 4 divided by the price index given in *National Product since 1869*, Table I-4B, col. 4.

1939–1951: The procedure is the same as that for col. 4; the source is the same as that for cols. 5–7.

(1–8) 1952–1955: Estimated by the procedure indicated for 1951, from data in *Survey of Current Business*, July 1956, or (for cols. 5 and 6) obtained by letter from the Department of Commerce.

TABLE R-4

Gross and Net Capital Formation, Current Prices, 1919–1955
(billions of dollars)

	Gross Construction (1)	Gross Producers' Durables (2)	Net Changes in: Inventories (3)	Net Changes in: Claims against Foreign Countries (4)	Gross Capital Formation (1)+(2)+ (3)+(4) (5)	Net Producers' Durables and Construction (6)	Net Capital Formation (3)+(4)+(6) (7)
1919	6.40	6.19	3.95	3.82	20.4	2.78	10.6
1920	6.73	6.30	7.27	2.84	23.1	1.92	12.0
1921	6.36	4.02	0.15	1.61	12.2	1.10	2.86
1922	8.02	4.14	0.60	0.64	13.4	3.33	4.57
1923	9.73	5.80	3.05	0.48	19.1	5.92	9.45
1924	10.8	5.44	−0.89	0.99	16.3	6.51	6.62
1925	11.9	5.92	1.75	0.68	20.3	7.89	10.3
1926	12.6	6.40	1.55	0.44	21.0	8.52	10.5
1927	12.4	5.92	0.45	0.72	19.5	8.06	9.22
1928	12.0	6.35	−0.34	1.01	19.0	7.78	8.45
1929	11.2	7.48	1.70	0.77	21.1	7.53	10.0
1930	9.04	5.76	−0.35	0.69	15.1	4.19	4.53
1931	6.63	3.73	−1.24	0.20	9.32	0.60	−0.44
1932	3.74	2.09	−2.51	0.17	3.48	−2.77	−5.12
1933	3.08	2.19	−1.52	0.15	3.89	−3.08	−4.45
1934	3.92	3.35	−0.93	0.43	6.77	−1.86	−2.36
1935	4.53	4.17	1.28	−0.05	9.93	−0.45	0.78
1936	6.80	5.86	1.35	−0.09	13.9	2.97	4.23
1937	7.50	6.61	2.37	0.06	16.5	3.34	5.77
1938	7.38	5.31	−0.59	1.11	13.2	1.59	2.11
1939	8.57	5.81	0.62	0.89	15.9	3.14	4.65
1940	9.08	6.95	2.40	1.51	19.9	4.24	8.15
1941	12.4	10.2	4.69	1.27	28.6	9.06	15.0
1942	14.4	14.8	1.72	0.08	30.9	12.6	14.4
1943	8.65	23.8	−0.96	−1.87	29.6	12.8	9.98
1944	5.78	26.4	−1.16	−1.69	29.3	8.99	6.14
1945	6.23	21.0	−1.28	−1.07	24.9	1.81	−0.55
1946	12.7	14.2	5.95	4.84	37.6	−0.66	10.1
1947	17.5	19.6	−0.81	8.94	45.2	1.59	9.72
1948	22.7	22.9	4.25	1.96	51.9	4.32	10.5
1949	23.9	22.4	−2.68	0.53	44.2	2.26	0.12
1950	29.7	26.0	7.40	−2.20	60.9	8.76	14.0
1951	32.8	32.0	10.5	0.23	75.4	12.2	22.9
1952	34.6	35.2	3.05	−0.16	72.8	18.7	21.6
1953	37.2	37.1	0.37	−2.02	72.6	22.4	20.8
1954	39.8	33.1	−2.12	−0.41	70.4	20.8	18.2
1955	45.2	33.0	4.29	−0.47	82.0	23.3	27.1

Because of rounding, detail will not necessarily add to total.
The series are identical for all three variants.

490

Source, by Column

(1) 1919–1951: In all years the estimates are the sum of (1) the cost of oil and gas wells drilled, and (2) all other new construction.

1. 1919–1928: Estimated by multiplying the 1929 price series described in the notes to Table R-5 by the price index for petroleum pipe lines. The latter is calculated from *Construction and Building Materials, Statistical Supplement, May 1954* (Department of Commerce), pp. 33 and 82, and adjusted to a 1929 base.

   1929–1951: *Ibid.*, Table 24.

2. 1919 and 1920: Sum of (a) new private nonfarm residential construction including additions and alterations and excluding nonhousekeeping, and (b) other new construction. (a) is from Leo Grebler, David M. Blank, and Louis Winnick, *Capital Formation in Residential Real Estate: Trends and Prospects* (Princeton for NBER, 1956), Appendix B, Table B-6; (b) is from *Construction and Building Materials, Statistical Supplement, May 1954*, Tables 2 and 3.

   1921–1951: *Ibid.*

   1952–1955: *Survey of Current Business*, July 1956, Table 31.

(2) 1919–1933: Kuznets, *National Product since 1869*, Table I-6. Excludes munitions produced in government owned plants.

1934–1951: Sum of (1) munitions, (2) private producers' durables, and (3) government purchases of producers' durables, excluding munitions. (1) is from Table R-6, col. 4; (2) is the Commerce series for private producers' durables given in *National Income, 1954 Ed.*, Table 2; (3) was extrapolated from 1933 by applying to public construction excluding military (series underlying Table R-30, col. 2) the 1929–1933 ratio of (3) to the latter. For 1929 to 1933, (3) was estimated by subtracting from col. 2 the series described under (1) and (2).

1952–1955: Estimated by the procedure indicated for 1934–1951, (2) being taken from *Survey of Current Business*, July 1956, Table 2.

(3) 1919–1928: *National Product since 1869*, Table I-11.

1929–1951: Sum of (1) the Commerce series on net changes in business inventories, and (2) net changes in monetary metals. (1) is from *National Income, 1954 Ed.*, Table 2, and (2) is the sum of the changes in gold and silver stocks. For 1897 to 1932, the series on gold, excluding imports and exports, is from Raymond W. Goldsmith, *A Study of Saving in the United States*, Vol. I (Princeton, 1955), Table K-3, col. 11; and for 1933 to 1951, from *Federal Reserve Bulletin* (Board of Governors of the Federal Reserve System, February 1954), p. 221, or *Survey of Current Business*, 1942 Supplement, p. 72. The stocks of silver bullion and coin are from appropriate years of the *Annual Report of the Director of the Mint* (Bureau of the Mint), and changes in them are derived by the procedure described in Simon Kuznets, *Commodity Flow and Capital Formation*, Volume I (New York, NBER, 1938), Note A to Table VII-11.

1952–1955: Estimated by the procedure indicated for 1929–1951. (1) is from *Survey of Current Business*, July 1956, Table 2. For (2) the series on gold is from *Federal Reserve Bulletin*, August 1956, p. 905, and the stocks of silver bullion and coin are from the *Annual Report of the Director of the Mint*, 1952, 1953, 1954, and 1955. Where calendar year figures for 1955 were not available for the latter, fiscal year figures were used.

(4) Balance on goods and services, and net unilateral transfers.

1919–1944: From *Balance of International Payments of the United States, 1946–1948* (Bureau of Foreign and Domestic Commerce), Table XXIII.

1945–1952: From *National Income, 1954 Ed.*, Table 11, adjusted for United States territories and possessions.

1953–1955: From *Survey of Current Business*, July 1956, Table 2.

(6) Col. 1 plus col. 2 minus Table R-8, col. 3.

GROSS AND NET CAPITAL FORMATION, 1929 PRICES, 1919–1955

(billions of dollars)

	Gross Construction (1)	Gross Producers' Durables (2)	Net Changes in:		Gross Capital Formation (1)+(2)+ (3)+(4) (5)	Net Producers' Durables and Construction (6)	Net Capital Formation (3)+(4)+(6) (7)
			Inventories (3)	Claims against Foreign Countries (4)			
1919	6.30	5.45	2.82	3.50	18.1	2.61	8.93
1920	5.41	5.31	4.21	2.28	17.2	1.55	8.05
1921	6.34	3.55	−0.04	1.54	11.4	1.10	2.60
1922	8.77	4.18	0.31	0.65	13.9	3.65	4.62
1923	9.65	5.78	2.82	0.47	18.7	5.90	9.20
1924	10.8	5.44	−0.93	0.98	16.2	6.53	6.58
1925	12.1	5.96	1.60	0.67	20.3	8.01	10.3
1926	12.8	6.54	1.18	0.44	20.9	8.68	10.3
1927	12.7	6.09	0.42	0.72	19.9	8.25	9.38
1928	12.3	6.50	−0.38	1.01	19.4	7.97	8.60
1929	11.2	7.47	1.70	0.77	21.1	7.52	9.99
1930	9.35	6.08	−0.52	0.71	15.6	4.40	4.59
1931	7.46	4.12	−0.67	0.23	11.1	0.79	0.34
1932	4.84	2.47	−3.22	0.22	4.31	−3.08	−6.09
1933	3.67	2.70	−3.24	0.20	3.33	−3.76	−6.80
1934	4.21	3.88	−2.60	0.52	6.02	−2.09	−4.17
1935	5.03	4.86	2.88	−0.07	12.7	−0.53	2.28
1936	7.30	6.83	1.04	−0.11	15.0	3.29	4.22
1937	7.54	7.18	4.70	0.07	19.5	3.52	8.29
1938	7.38	5.58	−0.63	1.31	13.6	1.68	2.37
1939	8.68	6.10	0.88	1.06	16.7	3.32	5.26
1940	9.06	7.14	3.32	1.78	21.3	4.42	9.51
1941	11.6	9.36	5.97	1.40	28.4	8.12	15.5
1942	12.1	12.0	2.17	0.08	26.4	9.40	11.6
1943	6.93	19.1	−1.18	−1.66	23.2	9.28	6.43
1944	4.65	22.5	−1.18	−1.46	24.5	7.56	4.93
1945	4.84	18.7	−1.47	−0.90	21.2	2.14	−0.23
1946	8.49	11.2	6.13	3.76	29.6	−0.83	9.06
1947	9.67	13.5	−0.68	6.15	28.6	0.55	6.02
1948	11.3	14.6	4.13	1.28	31.3	1.76	7.16
1949	12.0	13.6	−2.74	0.34	23.3	0.41	−1.99
1950	14.4	15.4	5.62	−1.41	34.0	3.64	7.85
1951	14.7	17.7	6.28	0.14	38.8	4.99	11.4
1952	15.0	19.5	1.81	−0.10	36.3	8.36	10.1
1953	15.7	20.6	−0.16	−1.17	35.0	10.2	8.86
1954	16.9	18.2	−0.95	−0.24	33.9	9.10	7.91
1955	18.6	17.8	3.02	−0.27	39.1	9.73	12.5

Because of rounding, detail will not necessarily add to total.

The series are identical for all three variants. The price index used in calculating net changes in claims against foreign countries in 1929 prices is that implicit in gross national product excluding such changes, Variant I. Strictly speaking, for Variants II and III, we should have computed the index implicit in those variants. But the difference is negligible and has been disregarded.

Appendix A

Source, by Column

(1) 1919–1952: In all years the estimates are the sum of (1) the cost of oil and gas wells drilled, and (2) all other new construction.

1. 1919–1928: Extrapolation of estimate for 1929 by the series on cost in 1935 prices, described in Kuznets, *National Income and Its Composition, 1919–1938,* p. 645.

   1929–1952: Series in current prices (see notes to Table R-4) divided by the price index for petroleum pipe lines calculated from *Construction and Building Materials, Statistical Supplement, May 1954,* pp. 33 and 82, and adjusted to a 1929 base.

2. 1919–1920: Sum of (a) new private nonfarm residential construction including additions and alterations and excluding nonhousekeeping, and (b) other new construction. (a) is from Grebler, Blank, and Winnick, *Capital Formation in Residential Real Estate,* Appendix B, Table B-6; (b) is from *Construction and Building Materials,* Tables 15 and 16, adjusted to a 1929 base.

   1921–1952: *Construction and Building Materials,* Tables 15 and 16, adjusted to a 1929 base.

1953–1955: In all years the estimates are the sum of (1) private construction including the cost of oil and gas wells drilled, and (2) public construction.

1. Current price series (see notes to Table R-4) converted to 1929 prices by the price index implicit in the series in current and 1947 prices given in the *Economic Report of the President,* January 1956, pp. 165 and 168, adjusted to a 1929 base.

2. Extrapolation of the estimate for 1952 by the 1947–1949 price series in *Construction Review,* October 1956, p. 18.

(2) 1919–1933: Kuznets, *National Product since 1869,* Table I-6.

1934–1951: Sum of (1) munitions, and (2) producers' durables, excluding munitions. (1) is from Table R-7, col. 2; for (2) the sum of the series described under (2) and (3) in the notes to Table R-4, col. 2, was divided by the price index calculated by extrapolating that implicit in producers' durables excluding munitions (computed for 1929 to 1933 from Tables R-4 through R-7) by that implicit in the Commerce series on private producers' durables given in *National Income, 1954 Ed.,* Table 41.

1952–1955: Estimated by the procedure indicated for 1934–1951, the price index for (2) being extrapolated by that given in *Survey of Current Business,* July 1956, Table 41.

(3) The series in current prices (see notes to Table R-4, col. 3) converted to 1929 prices. For (1) the Commerce series in 1947 prices (Table 41 of *National Income, 1954 Ed.* or of the *Survey of Current Business,* July 1956) were adjusted to a 1929 price base. For (2) constant price series of silver were estimated by the procedure described in Kuznets, *Commodity Flow and Capital Formation,* Vol. I, Note A to Table VII-11; those for gold for 1934 and later years were estimated by multiplying changes in current prices by 0.59057, the ratio of the price of gold in 1929 to that in the given year.

(4) Table R-4, col. 4 divided by the price index implicit in gross national product excluding changes in claims against foreign countries (Table R-1, col. 7 minus Table R-4, col. 4, divided by Table R-2, col. 1 plus Table R-5, cols. 1–3).

(6) Col. 1 plus col. 2 minus Table R-8, col. 6.

493

MILITARY GOODS: GROSS OUTPUT AND CONSUMPTION, CURRENT PRICES, 1914–1955
(billions of dollars)

	Gross Military Output (1)	Durable Military Output (2)	Gross Construction (3)	Gross Munitions (4)	Consumption of:	
					Construction (5)	Munitions (6)
1914	0.32	0.12	0.02	0.10	*	0.01
1915	0.32	0.11	0.02	0.09	*	0.02
1916	0.46	0.19	0.02	0.17	*	0.03
1917	6.13	1.52	0.61	0.91	0.02	0.10
1918	16.5	3.80	1.56	2.25	0.08	0.32
1919	9.68	2.42	1.09	1.33	0.16	0.56
1920	2.04	0.53	0.16	0.36	0.24	0.68
1921	1.27	0.38	0.05	0.33	0.20	0.69
1922	0.58	0.14	0.02	0.12	0.19	0.62
1923	0.45	0.09	0.02	0.08	0.21	0.63
1924	0.46	0.10	0.01	0.10	0.21	0.62
1925	0.49	0.11	0.01	0.10	0.20	0.60
1926	0.48	0.10	0.01	0.09	0.21	0.53
1927	0.48	0.11	0.01	0.10	0.20	0.36
1928	0.58	0.17	0.02	0.16	0.19	0.20
1929	0.62	0.19	0.02	0.17	0.19	0.14
1930	0.63	0.19	0.03	0.16	0.18	0.12
1931	0.79	0.29	0.04	0.25	0.17	0.12
1932	0.78	0.29	0.03	0.26	0.15	0.13
1933	0.65	0.23	0.04	0.20	0.16	0.14
1934	0.85	0.35	0.05	0.30	0.17	0.17
1935	0.95	0.39	0.04	0.36	0.17	0.19
1936	1.20	0.53	0.03	0.50	0.18	0.23
1937	1.19	0.51	0.04	0.47	0.18	0.29
1938	1.33	0.58	0.06	0.52	0.12	0.34
1939	1.25	0.50	0.12	0.38	0.06	0.54
1940	2.21	0.70	0.38	0.32	0.05	0.55
1941	13.8	3.50	1.62	1.88	0.10	0.66
1942	49.4	13.5	5.02	8.48	0.28	1.10
1943	79.7	21.0	2.55	18.4	0.50	2.50
1944	87.5	21.0	0.84	20.2	0.57	4.32
1945	73.8	13.5	0.69	12.8	0.61	5.74
1946	18.5	2.90	0.19	2.71	0.74	7.30
1947	10.9	2.00	0.20	1.80	0.92	8.78
1948	11.0	2.40	0.16	2.24	1.03	9.79
1949	13.2	n.a.	0.14	2.46	1.02	10.1
1950	14.0	n.a.	0.18	2.49	1.04	10.7
1951	33.4	n.a.	0.89	5.90	1.15	10.7
1952	46.1	n.a.	1.39	8.88	1.24	9.44
1953	48.9	n.a.	1.31	9.37	1.32	7.16
1954	40.7	n.a.	1.03	6.95	1.38	5.54
1955	38.6	n.a.	1.30	5.58	1.47	5.05

The output of military goods before 1914 is considered negligible.

n.a. = not available except as sum of cols. 3 and 4.

* Less than $5 million.

NOTES TO TABLE R-6

SOURCE, BY COLUMN

(1) 1914–1938: Kuznets, *National Product since 1869*, Table I-9, and an unpublished extension of that table for 1914 to 1918.

1939–1951: *National Income, 1954 Ed.*, Table 2. Government sales were deducted.

1952–1955: *Survey of Current Business*, July 1956, Table 2. Government sales were deducted.

(2) 1914–1938: Estimated by the following steps:

1. For 1941 to 1945, *The Budget of the United States Government*, 1947 (79th Cong., 2d sess., H.Doc. 411), Table B, p. 752, shows expenditures on nonmunitions, and total expenditures for military activities. From these the ratio of nonmunitions to total expenditures was calculated for each year.

2. For 1914 to 1948, the ratio of military pay to gross military output (col. 1) was calculated. Military pay for 1914 to 1918 is from Willford Isbell King, *The National Income and Its Purchasing Power* (New York, NBER, 1930), Table CXXIII, p. 364; for 1919 to 1938, from Kuznets, *National Income and Its Composition, 1919–1938*, Table G-2, p. 812; and for 1939 to 1948, from *National Income, 1951 Ed.*, Table 14.

3. For 1941 to 1945, the ratio of military pay (see step 2) to nonmunitions (see step 1) was calculated.

4. Since the ratio in step 2 is almost identical for 1919 and 1941, it was assumed that the ratio of military pay to nonmunitions is the same for both years. Hence, dividing military pay in 1919 by the 1941 ratio of military pay to nonmunitions yielded the estimate of nonmunitions for 1919. (The revision of the Department of Commerce series on military pay, shown in *National Income, 1954 Ed.*, raises the 1941 ratio from 43.3 per cent to 43.4 per cent, but the difference seemed too slight to warrant recalculation of our estimates.)

5. The ratio of nonmunitions to gross military output was calculated for 1919, and for 1941 to 1945. For 1918, the year of biggest military output in World War I, the ratio was assumed the same as for 1944, the year of biggest military output in World War II. For 1917, it was assumed to be at the 1919 level. Gross military output in 1917 and 1918 was then multiplied by these ratios to yield nonmunitions in those years.

6. Munitions in 1917–1919 were calculated by subtracting nonmunitions from gross military output.

7. For 1941 to 1945, the ratio of expenditures on durable military assets (see notes to 1939–1950) to munitions was calculated. For 1941 to 1944, there is little change in this ratio, it being identical in 1941 and 1944. The level for these years was assumed to apply in each year, 1917 to 1919. Multiplying munitions by this ratio yielded the estimate of expenditures on durable military assets in these years.

8. The ratio of expenditures on durable military assets to gross military output excluding military pay was calculated annually for 1917 to 1919, and for 1939 to 1948, when it declined from 58 per cent in 1939 to 26 per cent in 1945. For all the years from 1938 back to 1922, and for 1914 to 1916, it was assumed to be 60 per cent (slightly higher than in 1939). For 1921 and 1920, when military output was at somewhat higher levels, the ratio was assumed to be lower. For those years, it was interpolated along a straight line between 1919 and 1922. Multiplying gross military output excluding military pay by these ratios yielded the estimates of expenditures on durable military assets for 1920 to 1938, and 1914 to 1916.

495

Appendix A

(2) 1939–1948: Expenditures on durable military assets given by Raymond W. Goldsmith, "The Growth of Reproducible Wealth of the United States of America from 1805 to 1950," *Income and Wealth, Series II* (International Association for Research in Income and Wealth, Cambridge, England, Bowes and Bowes, 1952), Table III, col. 1, p. 312. This series was not used beyond 1948 because it seemed out of line with the Commerce series on munitions purchased.

(3) 1914: *Historical Statistics of the United States, 1789–1945* (Dept. of Commerce, 1949), Series H-28, p. 169. Calendar year estimate is the average of two fiscal year figures.

1915–1953: *Construction and Building Materials, Statistical Supplement, May 1954,* Table 3.

1954–1955: *Survey of Current Business,* July 1956, Table 31.

(4) 1914–1948: Col. 2 minus col. 3. Includes munitions produced in government owned plants, not covered in Table R-4.

1949–1955: The Commerce series on munitions purchased in 1948–1953, obtained by letter, was related to col. 1. Its percentage in 1954 and 1955 was estimated by inspection of the movement in prior years in relation to the movement in col. 1. Durable munitions were then estimated as a percentage of munitions purchased, the level and movement of the percentage being assumed to follow that in prior years in relation to the changes in the volume of munitions purchased.

(5) Table R-7, col. 3 multiplied by the implicit price index for military construction (col. 3 divided by Table R-7, col. 1).

(6) Table R-7, col. 4 multiplied by the implicit price index for munitions (col. 4 divided by Table R-7, col. 2).

TABLE R-7

(billions of dollars)

	Gross Construction (1)	Gross Munitions (2)	Consumption of:	
			Construction (3)	Munitions (4)
1914	0.03	0.17	ᵃ	0.01
1915	0.03	0.15	ᵃ	0.03
1916	0.03	0.25	ᵃ	0.05
1917	0.77	1.11	0.02	0.13
1918	1.71	2.14	0.09	0.31
1919	1.05	1.17	0.15	0.49
1920	0.12	0.31	0.18	0.57
1921	0.05	0.29	0.19	0.61
1922	0.02	0.12	0.19	0.63
1923	0.01	0.08	0.19	0.63
1924	0.01	0.10	0.19	0.62
1925	0.01	0.10	0.19	0.61
1926	0.01	0.09	0.19	0.54
1927	0.01	0.10	0.19	0.37
1928	0.02	0.16	0.19	0.21
1929	0.02	0.17	0.19	0.14
1930	0.03	0.17	0.20	0.13
1931	0.05	0.28	0.20	0.13
1932	0.05	0.30	0.20	0.15
1933	0.05	0.24	0.20	0.17
1934	0.06	0.35	0.20	0.19
1935	0.04	0.41	0.20	0.23
1936	0.03	0.58	0.21	0.27
1937	0.04	0.51	0.19	0.32
1938	0.07	0.54	0.13	0.36
1939	0.14	0.26	0.06	0.38
1940	0.41	0.22	0.05	0.38
1941	1.59	1.23	0.09	0.43
1942	4.14	6.40	0.24	0.83
1943	1.97	14.3	0.39	1.95
1944	0.67	17.0	0.45	3.65
1945	0.55	11.6	0.48	5.18
1946	0.13	2.18	0.50	5.88
1947	0.11	1.23	0.50	6.01
1948	0.08	1.40	0.51	6.11
1949	0.07	1.52	0.51	6.25
1950	0.09	1.48	0.51	6.33
1951	0.40	3.42	0.52	6.18
1952	0.61	5.18	0.55	5.51
1953	0.57	5.72	0.58	4.37
1954	0.45	4.18	0.60	3.33
1955	0.55	3.30	0.62	2.98

ᵃ Less than $5 million.

(Notes on following page)

Appendix A

Source, by Column

(1) 1914: Derived by dividing the current price figure (Table R-6, col. 3) by an index obtained by extrapolating that implicit in the estimate for 1915 by the cost of construction index described in Kuznets, *National Product since 1869*, Table IV-4, notes to line 1.

1915–1953: From *Construction and Building Materials, Statistical Supplement, May 1954*, Table 16, converted to a 1929 base.

1954 and 1955: Extrapolated from 1953 by the series in 1947–1949 prices in *Construction Review*, October 1956, p. 18.

(2) Table R-6, col. 4 divided by the following price index: The munitions price index for 1939 to 1953 described in *National Income, 1954 Ed.*, p. 157, was provided by the Department of Commerce, together with an extension through 1955. For 1929 to 1938 it was assumed to be the same as that for private producers' durables (*ibid.*, Table 41). It was adjusted to a 1929 base and extrapolated back to 1919 by the index implicit in producers' durables (Table R-4, col. 2 divided by Table R-5, col. 2). It was extrapolated from 1919 to 1914 by the price index for producers' durables given by William H. Shaw in *Value of Commodity Output since 1869* (New York, NBER, 1947), p. 294, adjusted to include passenger cars for business use and converted to a 1929 base (see notes on the adjustment of consumers' durables, Table R-13, cols. 1–3 and 5–7).

(3) Estimated from col. 1, assuming a twenty-year life terminating at the middle of the given year.

(4) Estimated from col. 2, assuming a nine-year life terminating at the middle of the given year.

TABLE R-8

CAPITAL CONSUMPTION, 1919–1955

(billions of dollars)

	Current Prices			1929 Prices		
	Non-military (1)	Military (2)	Total (1) + (2) (3)	Non-military (4)	Military (5)	Total (4) + (5) (6)
1919	9.09	0.72	9.81	8.50	0.64	9.14
1920	10.2	0.92	11.1	8.42	0.76	9.18
1921	8.40	0.88	9.29	7.99	0.79	8.79
1922	8.02	0.81	8.83	8.47	0.82	9.29
1923	8.77	0.84	9.62	8.71	0.82	9.53
1924	8.89	0.83	9.72	8.85	0.81	9.66
1925	9.12	0.80	9.93	9.22	0.80	10.0
1926	9.72	0.74	10.5	9.89	0.74	10.6
1927	9.74	0.57	10.3	9.97	0.57	10.5
1928	10.2	0.39	10.6	10.4	0.40	10.8
1929	10.8	0.34	11.1	10.8	0.34	11.1
1930	10.3	0.31	10.6	10.7	0.32	11.0
1931	9.47	0.29	9.76	10.5	0.33	10.8
1932	8.32	0.28	8.60	10.0	0.35	10.4
1933	8.05	0.30	8.34	9.76	0.37	10.1
1934	8.78	0.34	9.12	9.79	0.40	10.2
1935	8.78	0.37	9.15	9.98	0.43	10.4
1936	9.27	0.41	9.68	10.4	0.48	10.8
1937	10.3	0.47	10.8	10.7	0.50	11.2
1938	10.6	0.46	11.1	10.8	0.48	11.3
1939	10.6	0.60	11.2	11.0	0.45	11.5
1940	11.2	0.60	11.8	11.4	0.43	11.8
1941	12.8	0.75	13.6	12.4	0.53	12.9
1942	15.1	1.38	16.5	13.7	1.06	14.8
1943	16.6	3.00	19.6	14.4	2.33	16.7
1944	18.3	4.89	23.2	15.5	4.10	19.6
1945	19.1	6.35	25.5	15.7	5.66	21.4
1946	19.5	8.04	27.5	14.2	6.38	20.5
1947	25.7	9.70	35.4	16.1	6.52	22.6
1948	30.5	10.8	41.4	17.5	6.62	24.1
1949	32.9	11.2	44.0	18.5	6.76	25.3
1950	35.2	11.7	46.9	19.3	6.85	26.2
1951	40.7	11.8	52.5	20.7	6.70	27.4
1952	40.5	10.7	51.2	20.1	6.05	26.2
1953	43.4	8.48	51.9	21.2	4.94	26.1
1954	45.2	6.92	52.1	22.0	3.93	26.0
1955	48.4	6.52	54.9	23.0	3.60	26.6

Because of rounding, detail will not necessarily add to total.

(Notes on following page)

Appendix A

Source, by Column

(1) Sum of estimates for (1) nonfarm residential construction, (2) government non-military construction, and (3) business construction and equipment.

    1. Grebler, Blank, and Winnick, *Capital Formation in Residential Real Estate*, Appendix E, Table E-2, extended through 1955 by the procedure indicated in notes 4 and 5 to that table.

    2. Sum of separate estimates for sewer and highway construction, and all other government nonmilitary construction, derived by multiplying the series in 1929 prices (see notes to col. 4) by the price index for the given type of construction. The latter, shown through 1952 in *Construction and Building Materials, Statistical Supplement, May 1954*, Table 10 or p. 82, and calculated for 1953–1955 from the current price series in *Survey of Current Business*, July 1956 and the constant price series in *Construction Review*, May and October 1956, were adjusted to a 1929 base.

    3. Sum of estimates for (a) business construction (including farm residential, which cannot be segregated from farm business), (b) depletion, and (c) business equipment, including capital outlays charged to current expense.

        a. The series in 1929 prices, described in the notes to col. 4, multiplied by the price index implicit in gross construction excluding nonfarm residential and government construction calculated from the series underlying Table R-30, cols. 4 and 9.

        b. The series in 1929 prices (see notes to col. 4) multiplied by the price index implicit in producers' durables excluding munitions, calculated from Tables R-4 through R-7.

        c. From total capital consumption by business, in 1929 prices (see notes to col. 4), were deducted the estimated depreciation on business construction, in 1929 prices (see item a, above), and estimated depletion in 1929 prices (see item b, above). The balance was multiplied by the price index implicit in producers' durables excluding munitions, calculated from Tables R-4 through R-7.

(2) Table R-6: col. 5 plus col. 6.

(4) Sum of estimates for (1) nonfarm residential construction, (2) government non-military construction, and (3) business construction and equipment.

    1. Estimates underlying col. 1 converted to 1929 prices by the index implicit in gross construction, for which see notes to Table R-30, col. 6.

    2. Sum of separate estimates for sewer and highway construction, and all other government nonmilitary construction. The life of sewers and highways was assumed to be twenty-five years, that of other government construction, fifty years. Depreciation, therefore, was calculated for each year as the average of gross construction for the twenty-five or fifty years terminating at the middle of the given year. The construction series, except that for sewers, are those given for 1915–1952 in *Construction and Building Materials, Statistical Supplement, May 1954*, Table 16, and for 1953–1955 in *Construction Review*, October 1956, Table 4, adjusted to a 1929 base. Sewer construction is the current price series given for 1915–1952 in *Construction and Building Materials, Statistical Supplement, May 1954*, Table 3, and for 1953–1955 in *Construction Review*, May and October 1956, converted to 1929 prices by the price index indicated for sewers and water supply (see notes to col. 1, item 2). The construction series for prior years are described in the notes to Table R-30.

(4) 3. Sum of estimates of (a) depreciation charges including accidental damage to fixed capital, (b) depletion, and (c) capital outlays charged to current expense.

    a. From the Commerce series given for 1929–1951 in *National Income, 1954 Ed.,* Table 4, and for 1952–1955 in *Survey of Current Business,* July 1956, Table 4, we deducted the estimate of depreciation on account of persons other than unincorporated enterprises (shown for 1933 and later years in the same sources, Table 6), most of which is depreciation on nonfarm residences. The 1933–1935 ratio of the resulting series to Solomon Fabricant's series on accounting measures of business depreciation, provision for fire and marine losses, and depreciation charges on farm dwellings, given in *Capital Consumption and Adjustment* (New York, NBER, 1938), Table 29, p. 160, and Table 26, p. 145, was calculated and applied to the latter annually back to 1919, yielding annual estimates on an original cost basis for the entire period. To convert to 1929 prices we used Fabricant's price index given for 1919 to 1935 (*ibid.,* Table 35, p. 183), and extended through 1955 by the price index implicit in preliminary estimates of business depreciation, on original cost and 1929 price bases. These estimates, calculated separately for business construction and for business equipment, are described below.

    Preliminary Estimate of Depreciation on Business Construction. Depreciation was calculated for each year as the average of the annual construction for the fifty years terminating at the middle of the given year. The calculation was carried through in current prices (original cost basis) and in 1929 prices. The construction series underlying these calculations are those described in the notes to Table R-30, cols. 4 and 9.

    Preliminary Estimate of Depreciation on Business Equipment. Depreciation was calculated for each year as the average of the annual flow for the thirteen years terminating at the middle of the given year. The calculation was carried through in current prices (original cost basis) and in 1929 prices. The flow series for 1919 to 1955 are those for producers' durables in Tables R-4 and R-5, minus munitions, Tables R-6 and R-7. For our constant price series on flow for the years before 1919, we used Shaw's series on output in 1913 prices in *Value of Commodity Output since 1869,* recomputed to a 1929 base, adjusted to include passenger cars for business use, and raised by the ratio described in Kuznets, *National Product since 1869,* Table II-4, notes to col. 3 (see also notes to col. 1). This series does not take account of changes in finished inventories, but the depreciation estimates based on it differ only slightly, at least for 1919–1928, from those based on the flow after inventories. For our current price series on flow for these years we multiplied the constant price series by the price index implicit in the series on output.

    b. Estimated at 8 per cent of the series calculated under (a). This is the average percentage for 1919–1935 that depletion is of business depreciation (including fire and marine losses and depreciation charges on farm dwellings) derived from Fabricant, *Capital Consumption and Adjustment,* Table 30, p. 166.

    c. For each year, 1929 to 1955, capital outlays charged to current expense (Table 4 of *National Income, 1954 Ed.,* or of *Survey of Current Business,* July 1956) were calculated as a per cent of private producers' durables (same sources, Table 2). The percentages range from 8 to 16, being low in prosperous years and high in depression years. Similar percentages and fluctuations in them were assumed for the years before 1929. These percentages, applied to producers' durables in 1929 prices, excluding munitions (Table R-5, col. 2 minus Table R-7, col. 2) yielded the estimates of capital outlays charged to current expense, in 1929 prices.

(5) Table R-7: col. 3 plus col. 4.

Services, Variant II, and Components of Flow of Goods to
Consumers, Variant III, Current Prices, 1919–1955
(billions of dollars)

	Variant II Services (1)	Variant III			
		Perish- ables (2)	Semi- durables (3)	Durables (4)	Services (5)
1919	16.9	23.9	8.72	5.72	16.3
1920	21.4	26.4	10.1	6.58	20.6
1921	25.0	21.3	8.21	5.33	24.1
1922	24.4	20.6	8.47	5.81	23.5
1923	26.4	22.2	9.59	7.38	25.5
1924	30.3	23.0	9.05	7.41	29.2
1925	26.8	24.5	9.51	8.42	25.9
1926	30.4	26.1	9.94	8.77	29.3
1927	30.8	25.7	10.1	8.37	29.7
1928	32.6	26.3	10.2	8.60	31.4
1929	34.8	27.2	10.4	9.21	33.4
1930	32.7	25.1	8.91	7.16	31.2
1931	28.3	21.2	7.70	5.48	27.7
1932	24.7	17.1	5.64	3.65	23.5
1933	23.0	17.0	5.21	3.47	21.4
1934	22.8	20.3	6.32	4.21	21.8
1935	24.0	22.6	6.73	5.11	23.0
1936	25.9	25.4	7.40	6.30	24.9
1937	28.3	27.4	7.76	6.92	27.2
1938	28.2	26.4	7.61	5.69	27.0
1939	28.6	27.0	8.11	6.67	27.4
1940	29.9	28.7	8.52	7.77	28.7
1941	32.3	33.1	10.1	9.66	31.1
1942	35.4	38.7	12.6	6.97	33.8
1943	39.3	43.9	15.3	6.60	37.3
1944	42.6	48.4	17.0	6.76	40.4
1945	45.7	54.0	19.3	8.10	43.4
1946	52.2	63.2	21.3	15.9	49.9
1947	58.0	71.0	22.1	20.6	55.7
1948	63.8	75.7	23.1	22.2	61.3
1949	67.2	75.0	21.9	23.6	64.7
1950	72.4	78.3	22.1	28.6	69.9
1951	78.2	87.4	23.7	27.1	75.4
1952	83.9	91.9	24.2	26.6	80.9
1953	90.2	94.9	24.2	29.8	87.1
1954	94.9	96.9	24.0	29.4	91.7
1955	101.0	100.9	25.2	35.7	97.7

Appendix A

SOURCE, BY COLUMN

(1) 1919–1928: To the decade average given in Table R-18, col. 1, we applied the ratios of the annual estimates in Variant I (Table R-3, col. 4) to their decade average.

1929–1955: The flow of commodities to consumers (Table R-3, cols. 1–3) multiplied by the ratio of services in Variant III (col. 5) to the Commerce series on consumer expenditures on commodities (Table 30 of *National Income, 1954 Ed.*, or of *Survey of Current Business*, July 1956).

(2–4) 1919–1928: The 1929–1931 ratio of the given series to Table R-3, col. 1, 2, or 3, applied to the latter for 1919 to 1928.

1929–1955: From same sources as col. 1; for the distribution of nondurables between perishables and semidurables, see the notes to Table R-3, cols. 1–3.

(5) 1919–1928: The 1929–1931 ratio of the given series to col. 1 applied to the latter for 1919 to 1928.

1929–1955: Sum of the Commerce series on services excluding subgroup VII-3 (same sources as col. 1) and estimated services of governments. For 1929 to 1940, the latter is assumed equal to personal tax and nontax payments (Table 3 of same sources). For 1941 and the later years, it is estimated at 3.6 per cent of personal consumption expenditures excluding subgroup VII-3 (Table 30 of same sources). This constant percentage is the average for the years 1929–1940 (and also for the shorter period, 1929–1938).

TABLE R-10

SERVICES, VARIANT II, AND COMPONENTS OF FLOW OF GOODS
TO CONSUMERS, VARIANT III, 1929 PRICES, 1919–1955
(billions of dollars)

	Variant II Services (1)	Variant III Perishables (2)	Variant III Semi-durables (3)	Variant III Durables (4)	Variant III Services (5)
1919	21.4	19.6	6.62	5.37	20.7
1920	23.4	20.6	5.75	5.30	22.5
1921	25.2	21.5	6.92	4.29	24.3
1922	24.7	22.2	7.82	5.47	23.8
1923	26.4	23.1	8.61	7.15	25.4
1924	29.8	24.9	7.97	7.45	28.7
1925	26.2	24.7	8.78	8.38	25.2
1926	29.7	25.8	8.83	9.30	28.6
1927	30.3	26.3	9.91	8.83	29.2
1928	32.3	26.2	9.89	9.04	31.2
1929	34.8	27.2	10.4	9.21	33.4
1930	33.0	26.5	9.36	7.45	32.6
1931	29.5	26.5	9.27	6.40	31.0
1932	27.3	24.8	8.22	4.86	28.5
1933	27.4	24.7	7.44	4.72	28.2
1934	27.9	26.5	7.81	5.38	28.9
1935	29.3	27.7	8.44	6.63	30.3
1936	31.3	31.0	9.29	8.18	32.2
1937	33.3	32.5	9.27	8.60	34.0
1938	32.7	33.2	9.37	7.05	33.4
1939	32.8	34.5	10.3	8.35	33.9
1940	34.0	36.1	10.7	9.57	35.3
1941	35.6	38.4	11.5	11.0	36.9
1942	37.0	39.1	11.8	7.12	38.1
1943	38.7	39.8	12.8	6.13	40.0
1944	40.2	42.5	12.6	5.59	41.5
1945	41.7	46.1	13.2	6.32	43.4
1946	45.7	49.1	13.4	12.2	47.6
1947	47.4	48.4	12.7	14.6	49.3
1948	49.4	48.7	12.5	15.1	51.3
1949	50.6	49.6	12.6	15.9	52.6
1950	53.4	51.1	12.7	19.2	55.6
1951	55.4	52.6	12.6	17.1	57.5
1952	57.6	54.2	13.2	16.9	59.7
1953	59.5	56.2	13.2	18.9	61.7
1954	61.1	57.1	13.1	19.0	63.3
1955	63.9	60.0	13.8	22.9	66.4

SOURCE, BY COLUMN

(1) Table R-9, col. 1 divided by the price index implicit in services, Variant I, calculated from Table R-3, cols. 4 and 8.

(2–4) 1919–1928: The 1929–1931 ratio of the given series to Table R-3, col. 5, 6, or 7 applied to the latter for 1919 to 1928.

1929–1955: The 1947 price series given in Table 40 of *National Income, 1954 Ed.*, or of *Survey of Current Business*, July 1956, and obtained by letter for the subgroups classified as semidurables (see notes to Table R-3, cols. 1–3), converted to a 1929 base.

(5) 1919–1928: Table R-9, col. 5 divided by the price index implicit in services, Variant I, calculated from Table R-3, cols. 4 and 8.

1929–1955: Table R-9, col. 5 divided by the price index implicit in the Commerce series on services (given in Table 41 of the sources indicated in the notes to cols. 2-4), and adjusted to a 1929 base.

APPENDIX B

Estimates for Overlapping Decades, 1869–1953

HERE, the estimates in the three variants presented in Appendix A for 1919–1955 are carried back to 1869 in the form of averages for decades overlapping at five-year intervals. These decade series merit presentation because they constitute the basis for the estimates for shorter time intervals in Appendix C, and may be more acceptable to technical purists than the more hazardous estimates in Appendix C. It is at this stage that some basic assumptions underlying their estimation can be most clearly seen and appraised. The comments below deal briefly with selected aspects of the decade estimates and are relevant also to the more continuous series based on them.

Constant Price Valuation Base

The choice of the year to be used as the price base for valuation in constant prices is made early in the procedure and is of wide effect upon the interpretation of the results. The procedure involves the following steps:

1. Securing estimates of flow of finished products, at producers' current prices, by the narrowest categories that production statistics permit
2. Obtaining a price index for each of these categories, with some selected year or period as base
3. Dividing the current price volumes by these price indexes to obtain volumes at producers' constant prices
4. Allowing for transportation and distributive margins (as percentages of the volumes in constant prices under step 3) to obtain flow at final cost to consumers, in constant prices

5. Multiplying the results under step 4 by price indexes to obtain flow to consumers (at cost to them) in current prices

The series for steps 1 and 2 are taken from William H. Shaw for the most part,[1] but whereas he used 1913 as the base year for his constant price volumes, we use 1929. As will be seen below, differences in base years can significantly affect the volumes in constant prices. The effect of the choice of the base year can best be demonstrated by a simple arithmetical illustration quoted here, with minor changes, from an earlier discussion of the problem: [2]

Assume that at point I, say 1869, and at point II, say 1929, national product consists of two finished products, A and B, and that their quantities and prices are as follows:

	I	II
1. Quantity of A (units)	1,000	10,000
2. Price per unit of A	$10	$5
3. QPA, (1) × (2)	$10,000	$50,000
4. Quantity of B (units)	2,000	4,000
5. Price per unit of B	$15	$20
6. QPB, (4) × (5)	$30,000	$80,000
7. National product, current prices, (3) + (6)	$40,000	$130,000

The price adjustment corresponding to our procedure, on the assumption that we have complete price information and that the prices listed above reflect quality changes, can be set up as follows:

Price adjustment, using II as base year, complete information

	I	II
1. Price index for A	200.0	100.0
2. QPA, 1929 prices	$5,000	$50,000
3. Price index for B	75.0	100.0
4. QPB, 1929 prices	$40,000	$80,000
5. National product, 1929 prices, (2) + (4)	$45,000	$130,000

Percentage rise from I to II equals 189 or [(900, % rise in quantity production of A, × 0.11, weight of A at I, with quantities weighted by prices of II) + (100, % rise in quantity production of B, × 0.89, weight of B at I, with quantities weighted by prices of II)].

---

[1] See his *Value of Commodity Output since 1869* (New York, NBER, 1947).

[2] Simon Kuznets, "Long-Term Changes in the National Income of the United States of America since 1870," *Income and Wealth, Series II* (International Association for Research in Income and Wealth, Cambridge, England, Bowes and Bowes, 1952), pp. 44–46.

Appendix B

If we use I (i.e., the earlier year) as the base for the price indexes, the rise in national product in constant prices is appreciably greater.

Price adjustment, using I as base year, complete information

	I	II
1. Price index for A	100.0	50.0
2. QPA, 1869 prices	$10,000	$100,000
3. Price index for B	100.0	133.3
4. QPB, 1869 prices	$30,000	$60,000
5. National product, 1869 prices, (2) + (4)	$40,000	$160,000

Percentage rise from I to II equals 300 or [(900 × 0.25, weight of A at I, with quantities weighted by prices of I) + (100 × 0.75, weight of B at I, with quantities weighted by prices of I)].

The choice of the base year has this effect so long as the implicit assumption of the illustration is kept, viz., that there is a negative correlation between the proportional changes in quantities and the proportional changes in prices. Because in the illustration the greater growth in the quantity of A is combined with a price decline in A, whereas the lesser growth of B is associated with a price rise in B, the percentage rise in national product in prices of II is much smaller than that in national product in prices of I. Yet this implication is, on the whole, valid: among the several products, greater growth would be exhibited by relatively new products subject to rapid technical improvement and, correspondingly, to a rapid downward (or lesser upward) price movement.

The effects of the shift from the 1913 to the 1929 price base can be most easily measured by comparing the Shaw series and our recalculation of his constant price series to a 1929 price base, before our adjustments for scope. The current price volumes are identical, and so are the minor group price indexes. The only difference is that in converting the minor groups to constant prices, Shaw used the minor group price indexes on a 1913 price base, whereas we used them on a 1929 price base.

The results in Table B-1 are illuminating. For every major group, the volumes in 1929 prices tend, on the whole, to rise less than the volumes in 1913 prices. This tendency is not observed or is quite minor in the early years. The divergence becomes marked in the last decade, 1919–1928. For this decade, the rise from 1869 in the 1929 price-based series is almost 4 per cent less than that in the 1913 price-based series for perishable commodities, over 20 per cent less for semidurable

Appendix B

TABLE B-1

Movement in 1913 Price Series Compared with That in 1929 Price Series, Major Groups of Finished Products, 1869–1928

(amounts in millions of dollars, at producers' prices)

	1869 (1)	1879 (2)	1889 (3)	1889–1898 (4)	1899–1908 (5)	1909–1918 (6)	1919–1928 (7)
Perishables							
Absolute figure							
1. Current prices	1,594	1,996	2,906	3,043	5,124	9,338	16,529
2. 1913 prices	1,129	2,304	3,291	3,868	6,058	7,943	10,469
3. 1929 prices	1,769	3,629	5,143	6,030	9,451	12,356	15,775
Index (1869 = 100)							
4. 1913 prices	100	204	291	343	537	704	927
5. 1929 prices	100	205	291	341	534	698	892
Semidurables							
Absolute figure							
6. Current prices	665	828	1,133	1,139	1,810	3,288	6,967
7. 1913 prices	420	810	1,185	1,345	2,014	2,770	4,152
8. 1929 prices	757	1,425	2,093	2,356	3,536	4,640	5,842
Index (1869 = 100)							
9. 1913 prices	100	193	282	320	480	660	989
10. 1929 prices	100	188	276	311	467	613	772
Consumers' durables							
Absolute figure							
11. Current prices	263	304	499	511	872	1,821	4,997
12. 1913 prices	220	366	609	699	1,029	1,858	4,430
13. 1929 prices	335	630	1,074	1,233	1,816	2,629	4,751
Index (1869 = 100)							
14. 1913 prices	100	166	277	318	468	845	2,014
15. 1929 prices	100	188	321	368	542	785	1,418
Producers' durables							
Absolute figure							
16. Current prices	291	313	543	534	1,100	2,238	4,297
17. 1913 prices	178	328	615	678	1,227	1,853	2,907
18. 1929 prices	318	591	1,103	1,231	2,208	3,140	4,100
Index (1869 = 100)							
19. 1913 prices	100	184	346	381	689	1,041	1,633
20. 1929 prices	100	186	347	387	694	987	1,289

Source: Calculated from William H. Shaw, *Value of Commodity Output since 1869* (New York, NBER, 1947), by procedure described in the text.

commodities, almost 30 per cent less for consumers' durables, and over 20 per cent less for producers' durables. The reason for these differences is that the rapidly growing commodities, whose prices declined particularly markedly from 1913 to 1929, are assigned lower weights when 1929 prices are used than when multiplied by 1913 prices. The major conclusion is that the rates of growth of volumes in constant prices can be affected substantially by a shift in the price base. Over long periods and for categories within which technological advances produce substantial differential price changes, the use of more recent year bases yields lower rates of growth than does the use of earlier year bases.

In other words, if we use an early year price base, we assign to the rapidly growing *new* goods, which in the course of time become cheaper mass-production necessities, the prices of earlier years when these goods may have been rare, high-priced, luxury products (although quite inefficient by modern standards). For instance, if we multiply the number of automobiles by the prices of 1900, their fast increasing number will be assigned enormous weights, and the rate of growth in the resulting total will be far greater than in a total in which the number is assigned the much lower relative prices of current years. (The same can be said of household electrical appliances, radio and television sets, and much of producers' durable equipment.)

But in the nature of the case, recent year price weights should be used, since our historical records, insofar as they involve measurement, necessarily represent an observer of today looking backward rather than an observer of a century ago looking forward. Only the observer of today has weights to apply to the goods that were not in existence a century or half a century ago. Any judgment of growth must be made from the standpoint of a later phase, because in the earlier phase of the economy the subsequent stages cannot be seen even in embryo. There is no need to defend the use of the 1929 price base rather than of the 1913. Our only justification for retaining the 1929 price base (instead of shifting to a later one) is that the limitations of the price data and the relatively minor price-differential trends since 1929 make recalculation to a more recent year base seem hardly worth while.[3]

[3] Actually, a more recent year base is used when we employ the Commerce totals in constant prices to extrapolate our series. A comparison of the effect of the 1939 and the 1947 price bases in the two price adjustment calculations by the Department of Commerce (see *National Income, 1951* and *1954 Eds.*) does not reveal the expected shifts. The more recent year price base yields a somewhat lower rate of growth

Appendix B

None of these comments touches upon the effect of omissions of new products from the price data or of the failure of prices to allow for quality changes. In general, if prices of older commodities are used as substitutes for prices of new commodities (at least to represent trends), price declines are underestimated and price rises overestimated. Hence the rate of growth in volumes in constant prices is underestimated. The failure of prices to reflect quality changes also results in a downward bias in the rate of growth. This downward bias is naturally greater for goods in which quality improvements have been more substantial, and here again it is the newer commodities that are subject to more pronounced technological changes. But the bias associated with quality changes exists only to the extent that newer commodities enter the comparison. In comparing two points of time in which the newer goods exist only at one point, their inclusion at the later point is based upon current or recent relations between the newer and older goods—for already established qualities of the newer goods. Therefore, the quality bias is, by its nature, limited: quality change is small in the older goods that exist throughout the period of comparison; and the weight of quality changes in the newer goods is limited for any long-term comparison because at the earlier terminus of the period such new goods were either nonexistent or quite small in relative volume.

Long after the calculations used in this volume had been completed, it became possible to check the price indexes used in converting flow of goods to consumers to 1929 prices with the consumer price indexes computed by Clarence Long and by Albert Rees in their studies dealing with movement of real wage rates from the 1870's to World War I.[4] In Table B-2 we compare the quinquennial and decennial arithmetic means of the price indexes implicit in our conversion of the annual estimates of flow of goods to consumers from current to 1929 prices (Variant I) with the averages of the consumer price indexes computed by Long and by Rees for purposes of adjusting current wage rates for changes in purchasing power. The Long and Rees indexes, to the base of 1860 and 1914 respectively, have been

from 1929 to 1949 in producers' durable equipment and in nondurable consumer commodities, but not in consumers' durable commodities (due allowance being made for the slight revisions in the current price totals).

4 See Clarence D. Long, *Wages and Earnings in the United States, 1860–1890* (Princeton for NBER, 1960); and Albert Rees, *Real Wages in Manufacturing, 1890–1914* (Princeton for NBER, 1961).

Appendix B

TABLE B-2

PRICE INDEX IMPLICIT IN FLOW OF GOODS TO CONSUMERS (VARIANT I) COMPARED
WITH LONG AND REES CONSUMER PRICE INDEXES, 1869-1913

	Implicit Price Index, Kuznets (1929 = 100) (1)	Consumer Price Indexes, Long and Rees (1929 = 100) (2)	Difference between (1) and (2) as % of (2) (3)
	AVERAGES FOR SUCCESSIVE QUINQUENNIA		
1. 1869–1873	78.7	74.4	+5.8
2. 1874–1878	65.8	64.6	+1.9
3. 1879–1883	59.6	58.8	+1.4
4. 1884–1888	53.9	55.3	−2.5
5. 1889–1893	52.7	52.7	0
6. 1894–1898	46.8	48.6	−3.7
7. 1899–1903	50.5	49.3	+2.4
8. 1904–1908	55.5	52.6	+5.5
9. 1909–1913	61.5	55.2	+11.4
	AVERAGES FOR OVERLAPPING DECADES		
10. 1869–1878	72.2	69.5	+3.9
11. 1874–1883	62.7	61.7	+1.6
12. 1879–1888	56.8	57.1	−0.5
13. 1884–1893	53.3	54.0	−1.3
14. 1889–1898	49.8	50.7	−1.8
15. 1894–1903	48.7	49.0	−0.6
16. 1899–1908	53.0	51.0	+3.9
17. 1904–1913	58.5	53.8	+8.7

Averages are calculated from annual series.

SOURCE, BY COLUMN

(1) Calculated from series underlying Tables R-25 and R-26.

(2) Annuals for 1869–1890 are the estimates (on an 1860 price base) by Ethel D. Hoover, as given in Clarence D. Long, *Wages and Earnings in the United States, 1860–1890* (Princeton for NBER, 1960), Table B-1, p. 156. Annuals for 1890–1913 are the estimates (on a 1914 price base) by Albert Rees, *Real Wages in Manufacturing, 1890–1914* (Princeton for NBER, 1961), Table 43. The Rees series was extended back through 1889 by the movement in the Hoover index, which was extended forward through 1893 by the movement in the Rees series. The two series were spliced at 1889–1893, the mid-point of the period covered. On the basis of the movement in this spliced series, the entry in col. 1 for 1889–1893 was extended backward and forward.

shifted to a 1929 base, by a simple splicing with the 1889–1893 quin-quennium.

The new consumer price indexes show less decline from the 1870's to the 1890's, and consequently less rise from the 1890's to World War I than the price index implicit in our estimates of flow of goods to consumers. But the differences are relatively minor. In particular, the long-term trends in the flow of goods to consumers in constant prices would be relatively little affected by the substitution of the Long and Rees indexes for ours. Thus from 1869–1878 to 1904–1913, the use of the Long and Rees indexes would mean a reduction in the total growth of less than 5 per cent (the difference between +3.9 in line 10 and +8.7 in line 17); and if, for the purpose of gauging long-term trends, we use averages for three decades, as we do in Chapters 3 and 4, the effect of the differences in the two sets of price indexes would be even smaller.

The effect on rates of growth over shorter periods is more marked. But with specific reference to the long swings discussed in Chapter 7, it should be noted that in many of the components studied, the amplitude of alternations in the rate of growth is far wider than the differences in the movements of price indexes for the corresponding periods. In particular, there is no association between the price differentials in Table B-2 and the swings in flow of goods to consumers in constant prices observed in Chapter 7. One may, therefore, assume that differences between the price indexes in Table B-2 would not have a significant effect on the analysis in the substantive chapters. Thus even if the new price indexes turned out to be preferable for our purposes (and this would depend upon their availability for price adjustment of the separate components of flow of goods to consumers), the resulting revisions would be relatively minor.

Freight Charges and Distributive Margins

The estimates in Variant I in Tables R-11 through R-19 (at the end of this appendix) differ little from the decade averages previously published.[5] For the flow of goods to consumers they are almost identical, and for national product they are slightly larger primarily because of the upward revision in the basic series on construction. But the differences are quite minor, which means that, for the decades before 1919–1928, the previously published series and the present

[5] Simon Kuznets, *National Product since 1869* (New York, NBER, 1946).

estimates in all three variants are similar, because the basic component series employed in Variant I are also used to extrapolate Variants II and III back of 1929. The discussion in the earlier source is fully applicable here, not only to the decade estimates, their derivation, and their limitations, but also to the comparison with Martin's estimates of realized national income and with general indexes of output.[6]

Most of the new work in the field (largely in the National Bureau's studies of productivity) starts with the 1900's and cannot be used for testing the estimates for earlier periods. There is, however, one important exception: Harold Barger's study of productivity in distribution yields results that, however approximate, are of great value in testing the validity of some major crude assumptions underlying the extrapolations back from 1919–1928.[7]

To pass from the flow of commodities into domestic consumption at producers' prices to the cost to ultimate users we assume a constant spread for freight charges and distributive margins. These constant percentage markups are applied to the volumes in constant prices, but the resulting estimates of cost to ultimate users are then converted back to current prices by means of essentially wholesale or producers' prices, for lack of others. In effect, a constant relative spread is assumed for commodity flows in both constant and current prices. Whatever error is thus introduced into the commodity flow totals also affects the services component, because the latter is based on ratios to the former (trends in such ratios having been derived from budget data).

Barger's study gives the results of a careful sifting of the available data for the past and these should reveal any trends in the ratio of freight charges plus distribution costs to either producers' value or final cost to users. The relevant data are summarized in Table B-3. Column 1 of part A is the percentage of retail value made up of freight charges and value added in distribution (based upon charges and margins derived from samples and related to volumes in current prices). The trend in the percentage is a combination of two factors: movement in the relative charges and margins for individual store types, and movement in the shares of commodities flowing through distributive channels (which rose with urbanization and growth of the country). The percentages can be viewed as affecting the total flow

---

[6] *Ibid.*, particularly pp. 59–90.
[7] Harold Barger, *Distribution's Place in the American Economy since 1869* (Princeton for NBER, 1955).

TABLE B-3

ESTIMATED EFFECT OF TRENDS IN FREIGHT CHARGES PLUS VALUE ADDED BY
DISTRIBUTION, 1869–1929

A. BASED ON COSTS IN CURRENT PRICES

	Freight Charges Plus Value Added, All Consumables, as Per Cent of Retail Value (1)	Trend in (1) (Difference from 1919–1929) (2)	(2) × 0.8 (To apply to GNP) (3)	GNP, Variant I, Current Prices (1919–1928 = 100.0) (4)	(4) Adjusted by (3) (5)
1869–1879	31.9	−5.4	−4.3	8.68	8.31
1879–1889	34.2	−3.1	−2.5	13.2	12.9
1889–1899	35.5	−1.8	−1.4	15.8	15.6
1899–1909	36.5	−0.8	−0.6	27 1	26.9
1909–1919	36.5	−0.8	−0.6	49 2	48.9
1919–1929	37.3	0.0	0.0	100.0	100.0

B. BASED ON NET OUTPUT OF DISTRIBUTION

	Output of Finished Goods (1899 = 100) (1)	Net Output of Distribution (1899 = 100) (2)	(2) as Per Cent of (1) (3)	Trend in (3) (Difference from 1919–1929) × 35% (4)	(4) × 0.8 (To apply to GNP) (5)
1869–1879	37.0	33.0	89	−3.15	−2.5
1879–1889	58.5	55.0	94	−1.4	−1.1
1889–1899	85.0	83.0	98	0.0	0.0
1899–1909	122.5	123.5	101	1.05	0.8
1909–1919	171.0	169.0	99	0.35	0.3
1919–1929	255.5	250.5	98	0.0	0.0

SOURCE, BY COLUMN

Part A

(1) Harold Barger, *Distribution's Place in the American Economy since 1869* (Princeton for NBER, 1955), Table 18, last line, reduced to per cent of retail value.
(4) For gross national product, Variant I, see Table R-11, col. 7.

Part B

(1) and (2) Barger, *op. cit.*, Table 10.

of goods to consumers, because their effect on commodity components of flow of goods to consumers applies also to the services component.

The trend in these percentages (column 2) indicates that in assuming a constant spread we *overestimate* the flow of goods to consumers in current prices by about 5 per cent in 1869–1878, and by rapidly decreasing percentages thereafter, with the result that by the first decade of the twentieth century the overestimate is insignificant. When applied to gross national product, the percentage must be reduced, because much of capital formation does not go through retail channels, and the small segment that does probably has not risen in relative weight. We therefore multiplied the percentage overstatement in column 2 by 0.8 (the average share of flow of goods to consumers in gross national product) to secure the approximate overstatement in gross national product in the earlier decades (column 3).

The assumption of a constant spread between flow at producers' prices and cost to ultimate users appears to result in an overestimate of gross national product in the earlier decades and a corresponding underestimate in the rate of growth. To gauge the underestimate in the rate of growth, we compared the rate of growth in the index of gross national product in current prices, Variant I (column 4), with that in the index adjusted by the percentages in column 3 (column 5). The unadjusted rate of growth per decade (based on column 4) is 63.0 per cent; the adjusted rate (based on column 5), 64.5 per cent, is only slightly different.

However, the trends in the volumes in constant prices are far more significant, and since the sample margins used by Barger are necessarily related to volumes in current prices, we do not know whether a trend in the margins would be apparent if the numerator (value added in distribution) and the denominator (total product, or product at producers' prices) were both adjusted for relevant price changes. Such an adjustment, if possible, might remove completely any rise in distributive margins (or in margins plus freight charges). This presumption is supported by the fact that distributive costs rose most rapidly from 1869 to 1899 when producers' prices (the denominator) were declining. Whatever the case, one could perhaps get a better approximation to distributive charges in constant prices by allowing only for the change in the proportion of commodities flowing through retail channels. In part B of Table B-2, therefore, we compare Barger's index of net output of distribution (column 2, essentially an index of the volume of commodities sold through retail outlets weighted by constant distributive margins) with the output of finished goods (column 1). The increasing ratio of net output of distribution to output of finished goods (column 3) is some measure of the increasing weight of distribution—changes in unit margins being eliminated. If we multiply the trend in the ratio by the average weight of freight and distributive charges in the final value of commodities (column 1 of part A), we get the approximate effect of this trend on flow of goods to consumers (column 4); and if we multiply it further by 0.8, we get the effect on gross national product (column 5). The results, which reflect the effect of trends in distribution alone, suggest an overstatement of gross national product of about 2.5 per cent in the earliest decade, which disappears completely by the beginning of the twentieth century.

It is difficult to draw firm conclusions, but any bias in the rates of growth introduced by the assumption of a constant spread between volume in producers' prices and in cost to final users appears to be minor. There is, therefore, no convincing reason for revising our estimates in the light of these findings, particularly since those for the earlier decades probably suffer from a downward bias because of the greater weight of items that had to be omitted for lack of reliable and continuous data.

Omissions and Undercoverage in Earlier Decades

Some discussion of the possible omissions from the estimates for the earlier decades is provided in *National Product since 1869*.[8] It suggests that the undercoverage is in the neighborhood of 5 per cent for 1869–1878, continues at about 4 per cent to the end of the century, and then dwindles to practically zero by 1919–1928. Barger's more recent study contains estimates for some of the omitted items—federal liquor taxes and state gasoline taxes (neither of which has a significant effect on the trend), and firewood.[9]

Firewood is only one of several omitted products that declined rapidly in importance as the economy grew and urbanization proceeded. Their inclusion in our totals would have raised the levels of the earlier decades more than those of the recent decades, and thus would have reduced somewhat the rates of growth. A list of the products omitted should include horses sold to the urban population (which, if used for pleasure, would be an addition to consumers' durables), hay for those horses (an addition to consumers' perishables), various items produced within the household, whether urban or rural, and others.

If it were possible to approximate these items acceptably and continuously, the effort might be warranted. But such an approximation is hardly feasible.[10] Monographs on the pattern of life both in the

---

[8] Pp. 59–62.

[9] Barger, *op. cit.*, Table B-1, p. 128.

[10] Barger's series on the value of firewood (based on Shaw's series in *Value of Commodity Output since 1869*, p. 103) requires further checking before it can be accepted. The total for domestic use, at producers' prices, is $587 million for 1869, or 40 per cent of the producers' value of all finished *food* flowing into domestic consumption ($1,372 million, according to Shaw, pp. 30–31). If we add other fuel and

earlier decades and today might yield clues to their relative weights.

Those weights, however, should not be exaggerated, since we accept the current concept of consumers' goods and disregard the fact that many of them offset difficulties of urban life. Hazarding a guess, let us set the maximum allowance for the total value of commodities omitted in the earlier decades at the high level of 20 per cent of gross national product as given. This, added to the possible 5 per cent shortage associated with the 1870 Census, would mean a total shortage of about 25 per cent for 1869–1878. As they now stand, the estimates of gross national product in 1929 prices yield an average rate of increase per decade (from 1869–1878 to 1939–1948) ranging from 42.3 per cent for Variant I to 42.9 per cent for Variant III; if we assume a 25 per cent shortage in the level for 1869–1878, the rate of increase per decade drops to 37 per cent. Even a larger reduction would not change materially the characteristics of the long-term trends. However, it is a qualification that must be borne in mind for any inferences based upon the specific pattern of movement of the rates of growth over time.

The Three Variants Compared

Table B-4 indicates the similarities and divergences among the three variants. The series by which the level for the 1919–1928 decade is extrapolated back for each component of the flow of goods to consumers and of capital formation is the same for the three variants. Hence, differences in level and movement for the decade before 1919–1928 must originate in the sources of difference for recent decades, discussed in Appendix A, i.e., essentially in the estimates of the services component.

The small relative excess of the national product totals in Variants II and III over that in Variant I, in current prices, which ranges in 1919–1928 from 3 to 7 per cent, becomes still smaller as we go back; in 1869–1878 it ranges from 1 to 5 per cent. The reason is the more rapid rise in the services component from 1869–1878 to 1919–1928 than in the over-all totals. Since the services component accounts for the excess of Variants II and III over Variant I in 1919–1928, its ex-

---

lighting products ($79 million), the total value of fuel and lighting products in 1869 is almost half the value of food (both at producers' prices). In 1909, the total value of food is $5.7 billion, whereas fuel and lighting products, including firewood, amount to only $526 million, or less than 10 per cent of the value of food.

Appendix B

TABLE B-4

COMPARISON OF THE THREE VARIANTS, DECADE AVERAGES, 1869–1928, AND
RATES OF GROWTH, 1869–1948

	Flow of Goods to Consumers		Net National Product		Gross National Product	
	Variant II	Variant III	Variant II	Variant III	Variant II	Variant III

A. DECADE AVERAGES AS RELATIVES OF VARIANT I
(Variant I for each decade = 100)
Based on Values in Current Prices

1869–1878	106.1	101.6	105.3	101.4	104.9	101.3
1879–1888	106.4	102.1	105.6	101.8	105.1	101.7
1889–1898	106.7	102.5	105.8	102.2	105.2	101.9
1899–1908	107.3	103.2	106.3	102.8	105.6	102.5
1909–1918	107.3	103.2	106.4	102.8	105.7	102.5
1919–1928	107.9	103.9	107.0	103.4	106.2	103.0

Based on Values in 1929 Prices

1869–1878	106.8	103.2	105.8	102.7	105.2	102.4
1879–1888	106.5	103.1	105.6	102.6	105.0	102.4
1889–1898	106.5	103.1	105.4	102.6	104.8	102.3
1899–1908	107.1	103.6	106.0	103.1	105.4	102.8
1909–1918	107.6	104.2	106.6	103.6	105.8	103.2
1919–1928	108.4	105.2	107.4	104.6	106.5	104.0

B. RATE OF GROWTH PER DECADE, BASED ON VALUES IN 1929 PRICES
(per cent)

1869–1878 to 1919–1928:			
Variant I	50.2	48.8	49.8
Variant II	50.7	49.3	50.2
Variant III	50.8	49.4	50.3
1869–1878 to 1939–1948:			
Variant I	43.1	41.2	42.3
Variant II	43.4	41.6	42.5
Variant III	43.9	42.0	42.9

SOURCE: Calculated from Tables R-11 and R-12.

trapolation back by a trend more strongly marked than those for the other components carries it to relatively lower levels in the earlier decades and reduces the percentage excess.

From the standpoint of long-term trends, the most important result is that the totals in Variants II and III show higher rates of growth than those in Variant I, again because of the greater weight assigned to the services component. Therefore we compare the rates of growth in the three variants, for totals in 1929 prices.

For the first five decades, 1869–1878 to 1919–1928, the decade rates of growth are slightly lower for the totals in Variant I than for those in Variants II and III, but the differences are so small that no great significance can be attached to them. Even when the period is extended to seven decades, 1869–1878 to 1939–1948, the differences in the decennial rates of growth for the totals in the three variants are still small.

Since all the estimates for the earlier decades probably suffer from a downward bias, the rates of growth are overstated, although, we hope, not by a wide margin. This suggests that the variant yielding the lowest rate of growth is to be preferred. But there are no compelling reasons for preferring any one of the three variants in the study of long-term trends: they yield almost identical results. To be consistent with earlier publications in the field and lacking convincing reasons to the contrary, we retain Variant I throughout. Since Variant III is linked to the most recent set of historical series (the Commerce series), we retain it also. Variant II, however, being in a sense a hybrid and for our purposes of little additional value, is not used in the analysis or in the later appendixes. But it can easily be refined along the lines in Appendix C by anyone desiring to do so.

Appendix B

TABLE R-11

FLOW OF GOODS TO CONSUMERS, NET NATIONAL PRODUCT, AND GROSS NATIONAL PRODUCT,
THREE VARIANTS, CURRENT PRICES, AVERAGES PER YEAR FOR OVERLAPPING DECADES,
1869–1953

(billions of dollars)

	Flow of Goods to Consumers			Net National Product			Gross National Product		
	Variant I (1)	Variant II (2)	Variant III (3)	Variant I (4)	Variant II (5)	Variant III (6)	Variant I (7)	Variant II (8)	Variant III (9)
1. 1869–1878	5.68	6.03	5.78	6.56	6.90	6.65	7.13	7.48	7.22
2. 1874–1883	7.20	7.65	7.34	8.36	8.81	8.49	9.08	9.54	9.22
3. 1879–1888	8.60	9.15	8.78	9.88	10.4	10.1	10.8	11.4	11.0
4. 1884–1893	9.37	9.98	9.58	10.8	11.5	11.1	12.0	12.7	12.3
5. 1889–1898	9.98	10.6	10.2	11.6	12.3	11.8	13.0	13.7	13.2
6. 1894–1903	12.3	13.2	12.7	14.5	15.4	14.9	16.2	17.1	16.6
7. 1899–1908	17.2	18.4	17.7	19.9	21.2	20.5	22.3	23.5	22.8
8. 1904–1913	22.9	24.7	23.8	26.3	28.0	27.1	29.4	31.1	30.2
9. 1909–1918	31.5	33.8	32.5	35.7	38.0	36.8	40.4	42.7	41.4
10. 1914–1923	47.9	51.4	49.4	54.3	57.8	55.8	62.0	65.5	63.5
11. 1919–1928	63.7	68.8	66.2	72.2	77.2	74.6	82.1	87.2	84.6
12. 1924–1933	65.2	70.1	67.3	70.1	75.1	72.3	80.1	85.0	82.2
13. 1929–1938	59.8	65.0	62.2	61.3	66.5	63.7	71.1	76.3	73.5
14. 1934–1943	70.0	76.5	73.2	76.3	82.8	79.5	88.6	95.0	91.7
15. 1939–1948	112.6	121.5	116.1	121.5	130.3	124.9	144.0	152.9	147.5
16. 1944–1953	173.7	187.0	179.6	185.2	198.5	191.2	225.2	238.4	231.1

Gross and net capital formation are identical for all three variants.

SOURCE

Lines 1–10, by column:
(1) Table R-13, sum of cols. 1–4.
(2) Table R-13, cols. 1–3 plus Table 18, col. 1.
(3) Table R-18, sum of cols. 2–5.
(4) Col. 1 plus Table R-14, col. 8.
(5) Col. 2 plus Table R-14, col. 8.
(6) Col. 3 plus Table R-14, col. 8.
(7) Col. 1 plus Table R-14, col. 5.
(8) Col. 2 plus Table R-14, col. 5.
(9) Col. 3 plus Table R-14, col. 5.
Lines 11–16: Averages of annual estimates in Table R-1.

Appendix B

TABLE R-12

FLOW OF GOODS TO CONSUMERS, NET NATIONAL PRODUCT, AND GROSS NATIONAL PRODUCT, THREE VARIANTS, 1929 PRICES, AVERAGES PER YEAR FOR OVERLAPPING DECADES, 1869–1953

(billions of dollars)

	Flow of Goods to Consumers			Net National Product			Gross National Product		
	Variant I	Variant II	Variant III	Variant I	Variant II	Variant III	Variant I	Variant II	Variant III
	(1)	(2)	(3)	(4)	(5)	(6)	(7)	(8)	(9)
1. 1869–1878	8.02	8.57	8.28	9.49	10.0	9.74	10.5	11.0	10.7
2. 1874–1883	11.6	12.4	12.0	13.7	14.5	14.1	15.1	15.9	15.5
3. 1879–1888	15.2	16.2	15.7	17.8	18.8	18.2	19.7	20.7	20.2
4. 1884–1893	17.6	18.7	18.1	20.8	22.0	21.4	23.4	24.6	24.0
5. 1889–1898	20.2	21.5	20.8	24.0	25.3	24.6	27.3	28.6	27.9
6. 1894–1903	25.2	26.9	26.1	30.0	31.7	30.8	34.0	35.7	34.8
7. 1899–1908	32.1	34.4	33.3	37.6	39.9	38.8	42.4	44.7	43.6
8. 1904–1913	39.0	41.9	40.6	45.0	47.9	46.6	50.8	53.7	52.4
9. 1909–1918	43.8	47.2	45.7	50.2	53.6	52.0	57.2	60.6	59.1
10. 1914–1923	50.4	54.4	52.8	56.8	60.9	59.2	65.2	69.3	67.6
11. 1919–1928	61.4	66.6	64.6	69.3	74.4	72.4	79.0	84.2	82.2
12. 1924–1933	68.7	73.7	72.0	73.4	78.4	76.7	83.9	88.9	87.2
13. 1929–1938	70.2	76.2	75.1	71.7	77.7	76.6	82.5	88.4	87.3
14. 1934–1943	79.8	87.1	86.1	85.9	93.2	92.3	98.1	105.4	104.4
15. 1939–1948	98.4	106.7	105.7	106.0	114.2	113.3	123.5	131.8	130.9
16. 1944–1953	119.2	129.4	128.9	125.5	135.7	135.2	149.5	159.7	159.2

Gross and net capital formation are identical for all three variants. The price index used in calculating net changes in claims against foreign countries in 1929 prices is that implicit in gross national product excluding such changes, Variant I. Strictly speaking, for Variants II and III we should have computed the index implicit in those variants. But the difference is negligible and has been disregarded.

SOURCE

Lines 1–10, by column:
(1) Table R-13, sum of cols. 5–8.
(2) Table R-13, cols. 5–7 plus Table R-19, col. 1.
(3) Table R-19, sum of cols. 2–5.
(4) Col. 1 plus Table R-15, col. 8.
(5) Col. 2 plus Table R-15, col. 8.
(6) Col. 3 plus Table R-15, col. 8
(7) Col. 1 plus Table R-15, col. 5.
(8) Col. 2 plus Table R-15, col. 5.
(9) Col. 3 plus Table R-15, col. 5.
Lines 11–16: Averages of annual estimates in Table R-2.

Appendix B

TABLE R-13

COMPONENTS OF FLOW OF GOODS TO CONSUMERS, VARIANT I, AVERAGES PER YEAR FOR
OVERLAPPING DECADES, 1869-1953

(billions of dollars)

	Current Prices				1929 Prices			
	Perish-ables (1)	Semi-durables (2)	Durables (3)	Services (4)	Perish-ables (5)	Semi-durables (6)	Durables (7)	Services (8)
1. 1869–1878	2.57	1.17	0.47	1.47	3.47	1.55	0.69	2.33
2. 1874–1883	3.36	1.38	0.55	1.91	5.24	2.13	0.97	3.26
3. 1879–1888	3.96	1.62	0.68	2.33	6.88	2.76	1.38	4.18
4. 1884–1893	4.22	1.75	0.80	2.60	7.77	3.24	1.75	4.82
5. 1889–1898	4.54	1.77	0.82	2.85	8.98	3.67	1.98	5.53
6. 1894–1903	5.66	2.04	0.97	3.67	11.3	4.41	2.36	7.12
7. 1899–1908	7.64	2.82	1.38	5.32	14.1	5.50	2.91	9.63
8. 1904–1913	10.0	3.66	1.88	7.41	16.6	6.57	3.48	12.4
9. 1909–1918	13.9	5.12	2.66	9.74	18.5	7.30	3.99	14.1
10. 1914–1923	20.0	8.42	4.55	14.9	20.5	7.90	4.70	17.3
11. 1919–1928	24.5	10.9	6.86	21.4	23.9	9.19	6.55	21.8
12. 1924–1933	23.9	10.1	6.70	24.5	26.5	10.3	6.98	25.0
13. 1929–1938	23.6	8.61	5.46	22.1	29.1	10.2	6.27	24.7
14. 1934–1943	30.2	10.6	6.29	23.0	35.1	11.6	7.15	25.9
15. 1939–1948	49.7	18.4	10.6	33.9	43.8	13.9	8.78	32.0
16. 1944–1953	76.0	25.5	20.0	52.2	51.7	14.7	13.0	39.9

Appendix B

SOURCE

Lines 1–10, columns 1–3 and 5–7: Kuznets, *National Product since 1869*, Table II-8 adjusted for 1899–1908 through 1914–1923 as indicated below.

Perishables. Adjusted to exclude gasoline and lubricating oils for business use of passenger cars. It was assumed that the item was negligible for the years before 1904. For 1904, 1909, 1914, and 1919, the percentage that gasoline and lubricating oils constituted of the output of fuel and lighting products (manufactured) in current prices was calculated from Shaw, *Value of Commodity Output since 1869*, Table II-1, p. 112, and for 1919, 1921, and 1923 from Kuznets, *Commodity Flow and Capital Formation*, Vol. I, Table I-4, p. 82. Annual percentages were interpolated along a straight line and applied to the value of fuel and lighting products for domestic consumption (Shaw, Tables I-1 and I-2, pp. 33 and 66) to yield annual estimates of the output of gasoline and lubricating oils for domestic consumption. It was assumed that 30 per cent was for business use of passenger cars (see notes to *National Product since 1869*, Table I-1, col. 2). This was converted to constant prices by the price index for group 5a (Shaw, Table IV-1, pp. 290–291) adjusted to a 1929 base. The average value in 1929 prices was calculated for 1904–1913, 1909–1918, and 1914–1918. Its percentage of the output of all perishable commodities for domestic consumption in 1929 prices (*National Product since 1869*, Table II-1, col. 2) was calculated for these same periods and applied to the series on final flow (*ibid.*, col. 5, that for 1914–1918 being estimated by subtracting from the total for 1914–1923—the average for which is shown in line 14—the total for 1919–1923 as calculated from the annual estimates for those years) to yield the amount by which the latter was adjusted. The adjusted series in 1929 prices was converted to current prices by multiplying by the price index implicit in Shaw's series on the output of perishable commodities for domestic consumption excluding gasoline for business use of passenger cars. The estimates for 1914–1923 were derived by averaging the estimate for 1914–1918 obtained by this procedure with the average of the annual series for 1919–1923 shown in Table R-3.

Semidurables. Adjusted to exclude tires and tubes for business use of passenger cars. It was assumed that the item was negligible for the years before 1904. Of the total destined for domestic consumption in 1929 prices (values in current prices in Shaw, Tables I-1 and I-2, pp. 39 and 67, deflated by the price index for group 11, *ibid.*, Table IV-1, pp. 290–291, adjusted to a 1929 base), 30 per cent was assumed to represent the amount for business use of passenger cars (see notes to *National Product since 1869*, Table I-1, col. 2). The average value was calculated for 1904–1913, 1909–1918, and 1914–1918. Its percentage of the output of all semidurable commodities for domestic consumption in 1929 prices (*ibid.*, Table II-2, col. 2) was calculated for these same periods and applied to the series on final flow (*ibid.*, col. 5, that for 1914–1918 being estimated by subtracting from the total for 1914–1923—the average for which is shown in line 14—the total for 1919–1923 calculated from the annual estimates for those years) to yield the amount by which the latter was adjusted. The adjusted series in 1929 prices was converted to current prices by multiplying by the price index implicit in Shaw's series on the output of semidurable commodities excluding tires and tubes for business use of passenger cars. The estimates for 1914–1923 were derived by averaging the estimate for 1914–1918 obtained by this procedure with the average of the annual series for 1919–1923 shown in Table R-3.

Durables. Adjusted to exclude 30 per cent of the output of passenger cars—the amount assumed to be used for business purposes (see *National Product since 1869*, notes to Table I-1, col. 2). The total value of motor vehicles and accessories for domestic consumption in current prices is shown in Shaw, Tables I-1 and I-2, pp. 47–48 and 68. Thirty per cent of the total was taken, and deflated by the price index for group 20a, *ibid.*, Table IV-1, pp. 292–293, adjusted to a 1929 base. The average value in 1929 prices was calculated for 1899–1908, 1904–1913, 1909–1918, and 1914–1918. Its percentage of the output of all consumers' durable commodities for domestic consumption in 1929 prices (*National Product since 1869*, Table II-3, col. 2) was calculated for those same periods and applied to the series on final flow (*ibid.*, Table II-6, line 6) to yield the amount by which the latter was adjusted. The adjusted series in 1929 prices was converted to current prices by multiplying by the price index implicit in Shaw's series on the output of consumers' durables destined for domestic consumption excluding motor vehicles and accessories used for business purposes. The estimates for 1914–1923 were derived by averaging the estimate for 1914–1918 obtained by this procedure with the average of the annual series for 1919–1923 shown in Table R-3.

Lines 1–10, columns 4 and 8: Extrapolated from 1919–1928 by the procedure described in *National Product since 1869*, notes to Table II-7, cols. 2 and 5.

Lines 11–16: Averages of annual estimates in Table R-3.

GROSS AND NET CAPITAL FORMATION, CURRENT PRICES, AVERAGES PER YEAR
FOR OVERLAPPING DECADES, 1869–1953

(billions of dollars)

	Gross Construction (1)	Gross Producers' Durables (2)	Net Changes in:		Gross Capital Formation (1) + (2) + (3) + (4) (5)	Net Construction (6)	Net Producers' Durables (7)	Net Capital Formation (3) + (4) + (6) + (7) (8)
			Inventories (3)	Claims against Foreign Countries (4)				
1. 1869–1878	0.80	0.36	0.38	−0.09	1.45	0.45	0.14	0.88
2. 1874–1883	0.97	0.46	0.46	a	1.88	0.51	0.18	1.16
3. 1879–1888	1.33	0.55	0.39	−0.04	2.23	0.72	0.21	1.28
4. 1884–1893	1.89	0.58	0.26	−0.08	2.67	1.12	0.16	1.47
5. 1889–1898	2.14	0.62	0.23	0.02	3.00	1.24	0.13	1.62
6. 1894–1903	2.37	0.84	0.48	0.19	3.88	1.26	0.23	2.16
7. 1899–1908	3.18	1.29	0.40	0.22	5.08	1.70	0.44	2.76
8. 1904–1913	4.11	1.66	0.57	0.08	6.42	2.19	0.46	3.30
9. 1909–1918	4.37	2.77	0.79	0.99	8.91	1.72	0.78	4.28
10. 1914–1923	5.83	4.53	1.82	1.93	14.1	1.52	1.12	6.40
11. 1919–1928	9.69	5.65	1.76	1.32	18.4	3.90	1.48	8.46
12. 1924–1933	9.34	5.13	−0.14	0.58	14.9	3.11	1.42	4.97
13. 1929–1938	6.38	4.66	−0.04	0.34	11.3	−0.22	1.43	1.50
14. 1934–1943	8.32	8.68	1.19	0.33	18.5	0.70	4.04	6.27
15. 1939–1948	11.8	16.6	1.54	1.49	31.4	1.05	4.74	8.82
16. 1944–1953	22.3	25.7	2.56	0.94	51.5	5.76	2.27	11.5

Because of rounding, detail will not necessarily add to total.
a Less than $5 million.
The series are identical for all three variants.

SOURCE, BY COLUMN

(1) Lines 1–8 (and 1864–1873, see notes to Table R-15, col. 1): Sum of (1) the cost of oil and gas wells drilled, and (2) all other new construction.

1. Averages of annual estimates derived by multiplying the 1929 price series described in the notes to Table R-15 by the price index for petroleum pipe lines. The latter was derived for 1915 and later years from *Construction and Building Materials, Statistical Supplement, May 1954*, pp. 33 and 82, and was extrapolated back from 1915 by the cost of construction index described in Kuznets, *National Product since 1869*, Table IV-4, notes to line 1.

2. Estimated by multiplying the 1929 price series described in the notes to Table R-15 by the price index. The latter was derived by extrapolating the price index implicit in the estimate for 1915 (see notes to Table R-30, col. 10) by the cost of construction index indicated under item 1.

Line 9: Average of 1909–1913, derived by the method indicated for lines 1–8, and of 1914–1918, the average of the annual estimates described in the notes to Table R-30, col. 5.

Line 10: Average of annual estimates described in the notes to Table R-30, col. 5.

(2) Lines 1–6: From *National Product since 1869*, Table II-13.

Lines 7–10: Table R-15, col. 2, lines 7–10, multiplied by the price index implicit in Shaw's series on output of producers' durable commodities destined for domestic consumption adjusted to include passenger cars used for business (see notes to Table R-15) and converted to a 1929 base. The estimate for 1914–1923 was derived by averaging that for 1914–1918 obtained by this procedure with the average of the annual series for 1919–1923 shown in Table R-4.

(3) Lines 1–10: From *National Product since 1869*, Table II-15.

(4) Lines 1–10: Averages of annual estimates derived as follows:

1869–1896: Based on C. J. Bullock, J. H. Williams, and R. S. Tucker, "The Balance of Trade of the United States," *Review of Economic Statistics*, July 1919. We distributed the totals given there for fiscal periods ending June 30, 1850–1873, 1874–1895, and 1896–1914, by calendar years.

(4) Four components were estimated separately and then summated: (1) the net balance of goods, to which freight charges, commissions, fees for ships chartered, etc. were added, (2) investment income, (3) tourists' expenditures, and (4) immigrants' funds and remittances.

1. *Net Balance of Goods.* To distribute this item annually, we used the export-import balance for merchandise and silver. The annual merchandise balance is the calendar year total of monthly figures reported in various issues of *Monthly Summary of Foreign Commerce* (Dept. of Commerce). The annual silver balance is the average of the balance for pairs of fiscal years given in *Historical Statistics of the United States, 1789–1945*, Series M-50

2. *Investment Income.* Bullock, Williams, and Tucker give estimates for the periods 1870–1873 and 1874–1895, and annual estimates for 1869, 1878, 1883, 1890, and 1895 (*op. cit.*, pp. 223 and 226). Annual figures for the intervening years were interpolated along a straight line and adjusted by the ratio of the given total for the period to the sum of the preliminary annual estimates. The estimate for 1896 was derived by the same procedure: interpolating annual figures along a straight line between those given for 1895, 1900, 1908, and 1913 (*ibid.*, pp. 230 and 251), and adjusting by the ratio of the total given for 1896–1914 to the sum of the preliminary annual estimates for that period.

3. *Tourists' Expenditures.* These were carried at $37 million annually, 1869–1873 (Bullock, Williams, and Tucker, p. 223) and $35 million annually, 1874–1895 (*ibid.*, p. 227). For 1896–1914 a preliminary annual series was derived by multiplying the number of American citizens returning to the United States (given for fiscal years in *Statistical Abstract, 1916*, Dept. of Commerce, p. 111, and averaged for calendar years) by an average expenditure of $500 (see Bullock, Williams, and Tucker, p. 230). The preliminary figure for 1896 was adjusted by the ratio of the given total for 1896–1914 (*ibid.*, p. 231) to the sum of the preliminary annual estimates for that period.

4. *Immigrants' Funds and Remittances.* Funds brought in were estimated annually by multiplying the number of immigrants (given for fiscal years in *Statistical Abstract, 1916*, p. 727, and averaged for calendar years) by $50 for 1869–1873 (Bullock, Williams, and Tucker, p. 223); $20 for 1874–1895 (*ibid.*, p. 227); and $25 for 1896 (*ibid.*, p. 232). Immigrants' remittances in 1869–1873 were negligible; in 1874–1895 they were carried at $20 million per year (*ibid.*, p. 227); for 1896 they were extrapolated from the 1907 figure (*ibid.*, p. 231) by annual data on international money orders (given for fiscal years in *Statistical Abstract, 1916*, p. 726, and averaged for calendar years). In every case the annual estimates were adjusted to the given totals for the periods.

1897–1918: From Goldsmith, *A Study of Saving*, Vol. I, Table K-1, p. 1079.

(1–4) Lines 11–16: Averages of annual estimates in Table R-4.

(6) Col. 1 minus Table R-16, col. 3.

(7) Col. 2 minus Table R-16, col. 6.

Appendix B

TABLE R-15

Gross and Net Capital Formation, 1929 Prices, Averages Per Year
for Overlapping Decades, 1869–1953

(billions of dollars)

	Gross Con-struction (1)	Gross Producers' Durables (2)	Net Changes in: Inven-tories (3)	Net Changes in: Claims against Foreign Countries (4)	Gross Capital Formation (1) + (2) + (3) + (4) (5)	Net Con-struction (6)	Net Producers' Durables (7)	Net Capital Formation (3) + (4) + (6) + (7) (8)
1. 1869–1878	1.67	0.48	0.44	−0.14	2.46	0.98	0.18	1.46
2. 1874–1883	2.15	0.75	0.62	ᵃ	3.52	1.19	0.31	2.11
3. 1879–1888	2.98	1.03	0.56	−0.07	4.50	1.70	0.39	2.58
4. 1884–1893	4.36	1.24	0.40	−0.15	5.84	2.65	0.35	3.25
5. 1889–1898	5.25	1.42	0.39	0.04	7.10	3.08	0.30	3.81
6. 1894–1903	5.67	1.82	0.84	0.40	8.73	3.06	0.48	4.78
7. 1899–1908	6.68	2.56	0.60	0.42	10.3	3.61	0.86	5.49
8. 1904–1913	7.82	3.06	0.80	0.13	11.8	4.20	0.86	5.99
9. 1909–1918	7.32	3.79	0.91	1.40	13.4	3.07	1.01	6.40
10. 1914–1923	6.81	4.64	1.33	2.03	14.8	1.88	1.15	6.40
11. 1919–1928	9.70	5.48	1.20	1.23	17.6	3.98	1.45	7.85
12. 1924–1933	9.71	5.34	−0.41	0.59	15.2	3.10	1.43	4.72
13. 1929–1938	6.80	5.12	−0.06	0.38	12.2	−0.37	1.54	1.50
14. 1934–1943	7.99	8.20	1.66	0.44	18.3	0.41	3.63	6.13
15. 1939–1948	8.74	13.4	1.81	1.15	25.1	0.53	4.04	7.53
16. 1944–1953	11.1	16.7	1.77	0.66	30.2	2.11	1.77	6.31

Because of rounding, detail will not necessarily add to total.

ᵃ Less than $5 million.

The series are identical for all three variants. The price index used in calculating net changes in claims against foreign countries, in 1929 prices, is that implicit in gross national product excluding such changes, Variant I. Strictly speaking, for Variants II and III we should have computed the index implicit in those variants. But the difference is negligible and has been disregarded.

SOURCE, BY COLUMN

(1) Lines 1–8 (and 1864–1873, see below): Sum of (1) the cost of oil and gas wells drilled, and (2) all other new construction.

    1. Averages of annual estimates extrapolated from the 1919 figure (see notes to Table R-5, col. 1) by the number of wells drilled. The latter series is given or estimated as follows:

        1859–1869 (years before 1869 are not used in this table but are needed to extend total construction back to 1864, see notes to Table R-30, col. 1): The number of producing wells drilled in 1859 and 1869 is given in *Petroleum and Natural Gas Production* (Works Progress Administration, July 1939), p. 321. Annual estimates were interpolated between those for 1859 and 1869 by production, as reported in *Mineral Resources of the United States, 1912* (Geological Survey), Pt. II, p. 367. While the WPA figures fail to cover dry wells and thus lead to an underestimate, the use of production as an interpolator tends to overestimate the series in the intervening years since a rise in production may be due in part to increased production of old wells. But the annual estimates are used primarily to establish the level for the decade and it has been assumed that the averaging of the annuals cancels whatever error may attach to the estimate for a given year.

        1870: Straight-line interpolation between estimates for 1869 and 1871.

        1871–1888: The number of oil wells completed in Pennsylvania, New York, and Northern West Virginia in 1872–1888, as reported in *Mineral Resources of the United States, 1892*, p. 627, was assumed to be the total, since activity in other fields was negligible. For 1871 the number was estimated by the change from 1871 to 1872 in the number of drilling wells in the Pennsylvania and New York oil fields, *ibid., 1889 and 1890*, p. 307. To the number of oil wells was added the number of gas wells. The latter was estimated by straight-line interpolation be-

Appendix B

(1) tween the figure for 1884 (assumed to be zero, since it was negligible before 1885) and the WPA figure for 1889 (see below).

1889–1898: The number of producing wells drilled in 1889 is given in *Petroleum and Natural Gas Production*, pp. 321 and 322. The number of dry wells is not given. But, since the WPA series on the number of natural gas wells drilled in 1902 is much higher than that shown by Barger (see below), it was assumed that the overstatement in the former would offset the omission of dry wells. Annual interpolation between the WPA figure for 1889 and Barger's for 1899 was by the number of wells completed in the Appalachian Field as reported for 1892–1899 in *Census of Mines and Quarries, 1902* (Special Reports of the Census Office), p. 733, and extended from 1889 to 1892 by the number of wells completed in Pennsylvania, New York, and Northern West Virginia as reported in *Mineral Resources of the United States, 1892*, p. 627.

1899–1913: Given in *The Mining Industries, 1899–1939*, by Harold Barger and Sam H. Schurr (New York, NBER, 1944), Table 18, p. 195.

1914–1918: Given in *Mineral Resources of the United States, 1922*, Part II, p. 416.

2. 1864–1873 (not used in this table, but necessary for the estimate of total construction for that decade—see notes to Table R-30, col. 1): Extrapolation of estimate for 1869–1878 by procedure described in Kuznets, *National Product since 1869*, Table II-14, notes to col. 4.

1869–1913: Estimated by the procedure described in Table II-5, notes to col. 7, *ibid.*; the revised ratio of new construction in 1919–1933 to cost of materials consumed is 1.54056.

Line 9: Average of 1909–1913, derived by the method indicated for lines 1–8, and of 1914–1918, the average of the annual estimates described in the notes to Table R-30, col. 10.

Line 10: Average of the annual estimates described in the notes to Table R-30, col. 10.

(2) Lines 1–10: *National Product since 1869*, Table II-4, col. 5 adjusted for 1899–1908 through 1914–1923 to include passenger cars used for business. The average output of the latter for domestic consumption in 1929 prices (see notes to estimates of consumers' durables, Table R-13) for 1899–1908, 1904–1913, 1909–1918, and 1914–1918 as a percentage of the output of producers' durable commodities for domestic consumption (*ibid.*, col. 2) was calculated for these same periods and applied to the series on final flow (*ibid.*, Table II-6, line 10) to yield the amount by which the latter was adjusted. The estimate for 1914–1923 was derived by averaging that for 1914–1918 obtained by this procedure, with the average of the annual series for 1919–1923 shown in Table R-5.

(3) Lines 1–10: From *National Product since 1869*, Table II-13.

(4) Lines 1–10: Table R-14, col. 4 divided by the index implicit in gross national product excluding net changes in foreign claims (Table R-11, col. 7 minus Table R-14, col. 4, divided by Table R-12, col. 1 plus Table R-15, cols. 1–3).

(1–4) Lines 11–16: Averages of annual estimates in Table R-5.

(6) Col. 1 minus Table R-17, col. 3.

(7) Col. 2 minus Table R-17, col. 6.

Appendix B

TABLE R-16

CAPITAL CONSUMPTION, CURRENT PRICES, AVERAGES PER YEAR FOR OVERLAPPING DECADES, 1869–1953

(billions of dollars)

	Construction			Producers' Durables			Total
	Non-military (1)	Military (2)	Total (1) + (2) (3)	Non-military (4)	Military (5)	Total (4) + (5) (6)	Total (3) + (6) (7)
1. 1869–1878	0.35		0.35	0.22		0.22	0.57
2. 1874–1883	0.45		0.45	0.28		0.28	0.73
3. 1879–1888	0.61		0.61	0.34		0.34	0.95
4. 1884–1893	0.78		0.78	0.42		0.42	1.20
5. 1889–1898	0.90		0.90	0.48		0.48	1.39
6. 1894–1903	1.11		1.11	0.61		0.61	1.72
7. 1899–1908	1.48		1.48	0.85		0.85	2.33
8. 1904–1913	1.92		1.92	1.20		1.20	3.11
9. 1909–1918	2.64	0.01	2.65	1.94	0.05	1.99	4.64
10. 1914–1923	4.21	0.11	4.32	3.04	0.36	3.40	7.72
11. 1919–1928	5.58	0.20	5.79	3.62	0.55	4.17	9.96
12. 1924–1933	6.04	0.19	6.23	3.42	0.30	3.71	9.94
13. 1929–1938	6.44	0.17	6.60	3.04	0.19	3.22	9.83
14. 1934–1943	7.44	0.18	7.62	3.98	0.66	4.64	12.3
15. 1939–1948	10.3	0.49	10.7	7.69	4.13	11.8	22.6
16. 1944–1953	15.6	0.96	16.5	15.0	8.40	23.4	39.9

Because of rounding, detail will not necessarily add to total.

The series are identical for all three variants.

SOURCE, BY COLUMN

(1) Lines 1-10: Averages of annual estimates for (1) nonfarm residential construction, (2) government construction excluding military, and (3) business construction.

1. 1869–1888: The annual series in 1929 prices underlying Table R-17, col. 1, multiplied by the index of the cost of nonfarm residential construction. The latter was calculated for 1889 (from the annual series underlying Table R-30, cols. 1 and 6) and extrapolated back to 1869 by the cost of construction index described in Kuznets, *National Product since 1869*, Table IV-4, notes to line 1.

1889–1923: Given in Grebler, Blank, and Winnick, *Capital Formation in Residential Real Estate*, Appendix E, Table E-2, pp. 384–385.

2. Estimated separately for (a) sewer and highway construction and (b) all other government construction. For both (a) and (b) the annual estimates in 1929 prices underlying Table R-17, col. 1 were multiplied by the price index calculated

(1) for the given type of construction from the estimates described in the notes to Table R-30, col. 2 or col. 7.

3. Sum of (a) estimated depreciation on "other" construction, and (b) depletion. For both (a) and (b) the annual estimates in 1929 prices underlying Table R-17, col. 1 were multiplied by the appropriate price index. For (a) the price index was calculated from the annual series underlying Table R-30, cols. 4 and 9; for (b) the price index is that implicit in output of producers' durables (see notes to Table R-14, col. 2) excluding munitions (Tables R-6 and R-7).

Lines 11–16: Averages of annual estimates derived by deducting from Table R-8, col. 1, annual estimates of consumption of business equipment and of capital outlays charged to current expense described in the notes to Table R-8, col. 1.

(2) Lines 9–16: Averages of annual estimates given in Table R-6, col. 5. The volume of military construction before 1909–1918 is considered negligible.

(4) Lines 1–10: Averages of annual estimates of consumption of business equipment and of capital outlays charged to current expense derived by multiplying the series underlying Table R-17, col. 4 by the price index for producers' durables (see notes to Table R-14, col. 2) excluding munitions (Tables R-6 and R-7).

Lines 11–16: Averages of annual estimates of consumption of business equipment and of capital outlays charged to current expense described in the notes to Table R-8, col. 1.

(5) Lines 9–16: Averages of annual estimates given in Table R-6, col. 6. The volume of munitions before 1909–1918 is considered negligible.

CAPITAL CONSUMPTION, 1929 PRICES, AVERAGES PER YEAR FOR OVERLAPPING DECADES, 1869–1953

(billions of dollars)

	Construction			Producers' Durables			
	Non-military (1)	Military (2)	Total (1) + (2) (3)	Non-military (4)	Military (5)	Total (4) + (5) (6)	Total (3) + (6) (7)
1. 1869–1878	0.69		0.69	0.30		0.30	0.99
2. 1874–1883	0.96		0.96	0.45		0.45	1.41
3. 1879–1888	1.28		1.28	0.64		0.64	1.93
4. 1884–1893	1.71		1.71	0.89		0.89	2.59
5. 1889–1898	2.17		2.17	1.12		1.12	3.29
6. 1894–1903	2.61		2.61	1.34		1.34	3.95
7. 1899–1908	3.08		3.08	1.69		1.69	4.77
8. 1904–1913	3.62		3.62	2.20		2.20	5.82
9. 1909–1918	4.23	0.01	4.24	2.72	0.05	2.78	7.02
10. 1914–1923	4.82	0.10	4.92	3.14	0.34	3.49	8.41
11. 1919–1928	5.54	0.19	5.72	3.50	0.53	4.03	9.76
12. 1924–1933	6.41	0.20	6.60	3.60	0.31	3.91	10.5
13. 1929–1938	6.98	0.19	7.17	3.36	0.21	3.57	10.7
14. 1934–1943	7.41	0.18	7.58	4.04	0.53	4.57	12.2
15. 1939–1948	7.88	0.33	8.21	6.30	3.08	9.37	17.6
16. 1944–1953	8.46	0.51	8.97	9.42	5.55	15.0	23.9

Because of rounding, detail will not necessarily add to total.
The series are identical for all three variants.

SOURCE, BY COLUMN

(1) Lines 1–9: Averages of annual series for (1) nonfarm residential construction, (2) government construction excluding military, and (3) business construction.

1. 1869–1888: Depreciation for 1889 (see below) is 2.167 per cent of the value of structures in 1929 prices as of the middle of the year. It was assumed that this rate applies for each year back to 1869. The value of structures at the end of 1889 is given in Grebler, Blank, and Winnick, *Capital Formation in Residential Real Estate*, Appendix D, Table D-1, p. 360. Subtracting gross construction and depreciation during the year yields the estimate of value of structures at the beginning of 1889. Value at the middle of 1889 is estimated by straight-line interpolation between the value at the beginning and at the end of the year. Value of structures at the beginning of 1889 and of each prior year is computed successively as:

$$\frac{2.02167 \text{ (stock at end of year)} - 2 \text{ (gross construction during year)}}{1.97833}$$

For gross construction annually back to 1869, see Table R-30, notes to col. 6.

1889–1918: Grebler, Blank, and Winnick, Appendix E, Table E-2, p. 384.

(1) 2. Estimated by the procedure indicated in the notes to Table R-8, col. 4.

    3. Sum of (a) estimated depreciation on other construction, and (b) depletion.

        a. 1869–1876: For 1879–1888, depreciation on nonfarm residential construction is 37.8 per cent of depreciation on other construction, both in 1929 prices. Depreciation on nonfarm residential construction in 1929 prices for 1869–1878 divided by this percentage yielded a preliminary estimate of depreciation on other construction in 1929 prices for that decade. Interpolating between (or extrapolating from) the log of the decade average of this estimate and that of the estimate for 1877–1886, both centered at their mid-points, gave a preliminary series of annuals for 1869–1881. The ratio of the decade estimate for 1869–1878 to the sum of the annuals for those years and the ratio of the final figures for 1877–1879 (see below) to those just calculated were computed and centered at the mid-points of the respective periods. Annual ratios were interpolated between (or extrapolated from) them and applied to the preliminary annual series on depreciation for 1869–1876 to yield the final annuals for those years.

        1877–1918: Average depreciation per year for 1919–1928 (see below) is 3.898 per cent of the value of real estate improvements excluding residential and tax exempt for December 31, 1922, as shown in Kuznets, *National Product since 1869*, Table IV-5, Part B, p. 218. This percentage was applied to the corresponding wealth series shown (*ibid.*) for June 1 of 1880, 1890, and 1900, to yield estimates of the average annual depreciation for the decades ending June 1 of 1886, 1896, and 1906, respectively. (The wealth estimate for 1912 was not used in these computations because of the relatively small increase between it and the estimate for 1922.) Preliminary annual estimates of depreciation (on a calendar year basis) were derived by extrapolating from or interpolating between the logs of these decade estimates centered at their mid-points. The ratios of the decade estimates for 1877–1886, 1887–1896, 1897–1906 and of the final figures for 1919–1921 to averages of the preliminary annuals for those periods were calculated and centered at the mid-point of the given periods. Annual ratios were then extrapolated from or interpolated between these points along a straight line. The preliminary annuals were adjusted by these ratios and checked against the series derived directly from the wealth estimates. Since the average of the adjusted annuals for 1877–1886 constituted a higher percentage of the wealth estimate for 1880 than the averages for 1887–1896 and 1897–1906 constituted of the wealth estimates for 1890 and 1900, respectively, the 1877–1886 average was adjusted to the percentage for those later decades, and the annuals for 1877–1891 were recomputed.

        b. 7.016 per cent of the sum of the estimates under (a) and those underlying col. 4. This is the average percentage calculated from the corresponding series for 1919–1928.

(1) Lines 10–16: Average of annual estimates underlying the series in Table R-31, cols. 6, 7, and 9, and described in the notes to lines 1–9, above, or to Table R-8, col. 4.

(2) Averages of annual estimates in Table R-7, col. 3.

(4) Depreciation on business equipment plus capital outlays charged to current expense as estimated for 1919 and later years (see notes to Table R-33, col. 5) extrapolated by applying to a preliminary series on depreciation of business equipment the 1919–1921 ratio of the final to the preliminary series. The latter was calculated by the procedure outlined in the notes to Table R-8, col. 4.

(5) Averages of annual estimates in Table R-7, col. 4.

Appendix B

TABLE R-18

SERVICES, VARIANT II, AND COMPONENTS OF FLOW OF GOODS TO CONSUMERS,
VARIANT III, CURRENT PRICES, AVERAGES PER YEAR FOR OVERLAPPING
DECADES, 1869–1953

(billions of dollars)

	Variant II Services (1)	Perish- ables (2)	Semi- durables (3)	Durables (4)	Services (5)
			Variant III		
1. 1869–1878	1.82	2.52	1.01	0.50	1.75
2. 1874–1883	2.36	3.29	1.19	0.58	2.28
3. 1879–1888	2.88	3.88	1.39	0.72	2.78
4. 1884–1893	3.21	4.13	1.51	0.85	3.10
5. 1889–1898	3.52	4.44	1.53	0.86	3.39
6. 1894–1903	4.54	5.54	1.76	1.02	4.37
7. 1899–1908	6.58	7.49	2.43	1.46	6.34
8. 1904–1913	9.16	9.80	3.16	1.98	8.82
9. 1909–1918	12.0	13.7	4.41	2.81	11.6
10. 1914–1923	18.4	19.6	7.26	4.80	17.8
11. 1919–1928	26.5	24.0	9.39	7.24	25.5
12. 1924–1933	29.4	23.3	8.67	7.05	28.3
13. 1929–1938	27.3	23.0	7.37	5.72	26.1
14. 1934–1943	29.5	29.4	9.05	6.59	28.2
15. 1939–1948	42.8	48.4	15.7	11.1	40.9
16. 1944–1953	65.4	74.0	21.9	20.9	62.9

SOURCE, BY COLUMN

(1) Lines 1–11: The flow of commodities to consumers, Table R-13, cols. 1–3, multiplied by the ratio of services to flow of commodities. The ratio was calculated for 1929–1938 from Table R-9, col. 1, and Table R-3, cols. 1–3, and extrapolated by the ratio underlying Table R-13, cols. 1–4.

Lines 12–16: Averages of annual estimates in Table R-9, col. 1.

(2–4) Lines 1–10: Table R-13, cols. 1–3, respectively, multiplied by the 1929–1931 ratio of the series in Variant III (Table R-9, cols. 2–4, respectively) to that in Variant I (Table R-3, cols. 1–3, respectively).

Lines 11–16: Averages of annual estimates in Table R-9, cols. 2–4, respectively.

(5) Lines 1–10: Col. 1 multiplied by the 1929–1931 ratio of the series in Variant III to that in Variant II (Table R-9, cols. 5 and 1, respectively).

Lines 11–16: Averages of annual estimates in Table R-9, col. 5.

Appendix B

TABLE R-19

SERVICES, VARIANT II, AND COMPONENTS OF FLOW OF GOODS TO CONSUMERS, VARIANT III, 1929 PRICES, AVERAGES PER YEAR FOR OVERLAPPING DECADES, 1869–1953

(billions of dollars)

		Variant II Services (1)	Variant III			
			Perish-ables (2)	Semi-durables (3)	Durables (4)	Services (5)
1.	1869–1878	2.87	3.41	1.36	0.74	2.77
2.	1874–1883	4.03	5.16	1.88	1.05	3.88
3.	1879–1888	5.18	6.76	2.43	1.48	4.99
4.	1884–1893	5.96	7.64	2.86	1.88	5.74
5.	1889–1898	6.83	8.83	3.24	2.13	6.58
6.	1894–1903	8.81	11.1	3.90	2.54	8.48
7.	1899–1908	11.9	13.9	4.86	3.14	11.5
8.	1904–1913	15.3	16.3	5.80	3.75	14.7
9.	1909–1918	17.4	18.1	6.44	4.29	16.8
10.	1914–1923	21.4	20.1	6.97	5.06	20.6
11.	1919–1928	26.9	23.5	8.11	7.06	25.9
12.	1924–1933	30.0	25.8	9.01	7.56	29.7
13.	1929–1938	30.7	28.1	8.89	6.85	31.3
14.	1934–1943	33.3	33.9	10.1	7.80	34.3
15.	1939–1948	40.2	42.3	12.1	9.59	41.7
16.	1944–1953	50.1	49.9	12.8	14.2	52.0

SOURCE, BY COLUMN

(1) Lines 1–11: Table R-18, col. 1 divided by the price index implicit in services, Variant I, calculated from Table R-13, cols. 4 and 8.

Lines 12–16: Averages of annual estimates in Table R-10, col. 1.

(2–4) Lines 1–10: Table R-13, cols. 5–7, respectively, multiplied by the 1929–1931 ratio of the series in Variant III (Table R-10, cols. 2–4, respectively) to that in Variant I (Table R-3, cols. 5–7, respectively).

Lines 11–16: Averages of annual estimates in Table R-10, cols. 2–4, respectively.

(5) Lines 1–10: Table R-18, col. 5 divided by the price index implicit in services, Variant I (see note to col. 1).

Lines 11–16: Averages of annual estimates in Table R-10, col. 5.

Annual Estimates and Quinquennial Moving Averages for the Years before 1919

A CLOSE study of long-term trends in many aspects of the economy, in this and several other countries, reveals alternations in the rate of growth that extend over periods much longer than those associated with business cycles, and yet short enough so that several can be observed within the total period covered in our series (a span of over eight decades). These long swings in the rate of secular growth, which in this country averaged somewhat over twenty years in length, are naturally of considerable interest in any analysis of secular movements. Yet overlapping decade averages, like those in Appendix B, while revealing such swings, do not permit adequate study of them. For this purpose we need annual estimates, or at least measures that represent the changing level of economic performance over shorter periods and in more continuous succession.

We therefore devoted much effort to deriving annual estimates for the period before 1919, the initial year of the annual series in Appendix A. The effort was only partly successful. For the early years of the period, 1869–1888, the derived annual series, even for the comprehensive aggregates—gross and net national product—did not seem sufficiently reliable as *annual* measures to warrant presentation. For the next twenty years, 1889–1908, acceptable annual estimates could be derived only for the broad aggregates—national product, capital formation, and flow of goods to consumers.

For the specific uses of our study of secular trends in capital formation and financing these annual estimates are of interest only as raw material in the calculation of five-year or more complicated moving averages, which serve to cancel the short-term fluctuations while still revealing the underlying secular movements and any longer swings in them with sufficient accuracy. The limitations of the annual series are greatly reduced by the averaging process and therefore have only minor bearing upon the moving averages. We discuss these five-year moving averages in the last section of this appendix and give them fully in the reference tables following it, since they constitute the basis for much of the analysis of long-term movements in the economy at large, and in capital formation. But it seemed unwarranted to publish the annual estimates themselves, except for the aggregates in those years for which the estimates were within margins of tolerance as *annual* estimates.[1]

We present the annual estimates for 1889–1908 alone, and only for the wider aggregates. These estimates, if acceptable, together with those in Appendix A, provide an annual series on national product, flow of goods to consumers, and capital formation, extending from 1889 through 1955. Their derivation and reliability are now discussed briefly.

Extension of the Annual Estimates to 1909

The first and quite distinct step in deriving the annual estimates for the years before 1919 was the utilization of the earlier work of the National Bureau covering the years back to 1909. This was possible only for the most aggregative totals—gross and net national product. Table R-20 summarizes the results of this effort, and provides a description of the procedure.

Table R-20 shows gross national product only in 1929 prices, because annual estimates for the earlier years are based essentially upon the relation of annual flow of finished commodities to gross national product in constant prices. And we needed the extension to 1909 to widen the period over which the relation could be studied.

The calculations in Table R-20 and, more particularly, the detailed notes describing their derivation, indicate that the estimates used here for 1909–1918 are probably subject to a wider margin of error than those for the years beginning with 1919. Yet it seemed preferable to make full use of the earlier work at the National Bureau on the *direct*

---

[1] Annual estimates underlying the published five-year moving averages are available in mimeographed form in the files of the National Bureau of Economic Research.

estimates of national income for 1909–1918 rather than substitute indirectly derived annual estimates.

Derivation of the Annual Estimates by Regression

The procedure involved the following steps:

1. In Shaw's *Value of Commodity Output since 1869* and the work embodied in Kuznets' *National Product since 1869* we have *annual* series from 1869 through the recent years on the output of finished commodities and construction materials destined for domestic consumption. These are available in both current and constant prices, but we thought the relation to the national product aggregates would be more stable if the two variables were expressed in constant prices. At least, the difference in short-term movements between the prices of finished commodities (at producers' door) and prices of other components of national product would not complicate the relation.

2. As indicated above, the series described under step 1 (see Table R-21, column 1) covers output destined for domestic consumption. Since the balance of commodity foreign trade enters the national product totals, we added this item, also in constant prices, to the annually estimated output of finished commodities. This gave us the independent variable in the regression (Table R-21, column 6).

3. We accepted the levels of national product indicated by the averages for overlapping decades in Appendix B, and used the annual series of total output of finished commodities for what it revealed concerning the year-to-year fluctuations, not the interdecade movements. For 1909–1938, the period for which they were compared in regression analysis, both variables were expressed in terms of annual deviations from the lines connecting the successive overlapping decade averages. Thus the dependent variable—the annual ratio of the output of finished commodities to gross national product—was expressed as the absolute deviation from the ratio calculated from the lines connecting the successive overlapping decades (1909–1918, 1914–1923, etc.); and the independent variable—the actual annual value of output of finished commodities—was expressed as the percentage deviation from the annual value estimated from the lines connecting the successive overlapping decades.

4. The period for which the regression could be examined extended beyond 1938. But it seemed best to exclude the years of World War II and its aftermath, characterized by exceptional conditions, and there

was some advantage in limiting the regression to the thirty years closest to the period for which it was to be extrapolated.

5. The scatter of the two variables described under step 3 was studied separately for Variants I and III, and a smooth freehand regression curve drawn for each. The relationship could not be effectively described by a simple mathematical function, and there was no sufficient advantage in trying to find and fit a more complicated one.

The relation suggested by the regression curves can be seen clearly from Table C-1, which shows, for selected values of X (deviations of

TABLE C-1

SELECTED VALUES, REGRESSION OF GROSS NATIONAL PRODUCT (Y) ON INDEX OF FINISHED COMMODITY OUTPUT (X), BOTH VARIABLES IN 1929 PRICES AND IN TERMS OF ANNUAL PERCENTAGE DEVIATIONS FROM LINES CONNECTING OVERLAPPING DECADE AVERAGES, BASED ON 1909–1938

Selected Values of X (1)	Corresponding Values of Y	
	Variant I (2)	Variant III (3)
−23.5	−21.5	−21.5
−20.0	−18.1	−18.2
−12.5	−11.2	−11.1
−10.0	−8.9	−8.8
−7.5	−6.6	−6.6
−5.0	−4.4	−4.4
−2.5	−2.2	−2.2
−1.5	−1.3	−1.3
−1.0	−0.9	−0.9
−0.5	−0.4	−0.4
0.0	0.0	0.0
0.5	0.4	0.4
1.0	0.9	0.9
1.5	1.3	1.3
2.5	2.1	2.1
5.0	4.0	4.2
7.5	5.8	6.1
10.0	7.7	7.9
12.5	9.9	10.2
20.0	16.3	17.5

For derivation, see text.

finished commodity output from its interdecade lines), the estimated values of Y (deviations of gross national product from its interdecade lines). The relation is, of course, positive, and is progressively damped as the deviation from the interdecade lines increases—either positively or negatively. Thus when the deviation of X is within the range of 1.0 per cent, that for Y is one decimal point less, i.e., within the range of 0.9 per cent. When the deviation of X is around 20 per cent, that for Y is reduced somewhat more sharply, to between 16 and 18 per cent. Finally, the damping of the percentage deviations is somewhat more conspicuous for large *positive* deviations than for large *negative* deviations (compare the reduction from $+20$ to either $+16.3$ or $+17.5$ with that from -20 to -18.1 or -18.2). These results accord with expectations. The commodity part of aggregate output is somewhat more sensitive to short-term changes, particularly those associated with business cycles, than the services component. This differing sensitivity of the two broad components of national product is more marked when the short-term fluctuations are of wider amplitude. The difference in the extent of damping between the large positive and large negative deviations may be due to the historical peculiarities of the period, perhaps to what happened in the depression of the 1930's compared with the more prosperous decades. The effect of the depression on all components of national product may have been more widespread than the effect of the better times.

Given the regression function of Y and X, and given the annual series of finished commodity output back to 1869, we estimated annual values of gross national product in 1929 prices back to 1869 in Variants I and III. But before using these annual estimates, we tested them for reliability. We know in advance, from the derivation of the series on finished commodity output, that the estimates for the years before 1889 are on a much weaker basis than those for 1889 and later years, so that there is a prima facie case against placing too much reliance upon the *annual* estimates of national product for 1869–1888. But how much confidence can we place in the estimates of national product for the years beginning with 1889?

A Test of the Regression Estimates

To test the regression relation we calculated the *estimated* annual values of gross national product for 1909–1938 and compared them with the *actual* annual values (Table C-2). A study of columns 3 to 6 leads us to some broad conclusions.

1. The average difference over the period between the estimated and actual values of gross national product is somewhat over 2 per

Appendix C

TABLE C-2

ANNUAL VALUES ESTIMATED BY REGRESSION COMPARED WITH ACTUAL VALUES, GROSS
NATIONAL PRODUCT, 1929 PRICES, 1909–1938

(amounts in billions of dollars)

	Estimated Values (1)	Actual Values (2)	Percentage Difference $\frac{(1) - (2)}{(2)} \times 100$ (3)	5-Year Moving Average of (3) (4)	Year-to-Year Percentage Change in: Estimated Values in (1) (5)	Actual Values in (2) (6)
			A. VARIANT I			
1909	50.3	52.1	−3.45			
1910	52.0	52.8	−1.35		+3.4	+1.2
1911	53.4	52.6	1.54	0.97	+2.6	−0.3
1912	55.8	53.4	4.54	1.75	+4.6	+1.6
1913	58.4	56.4	3.56	1.63	+4.6	+5.6
1914	55.5	55.2	0.43	1.68	−5.1	−2.1
1915	58.0	59.1	−1.92	0.77	+4.6	+7.1
1916	65.4	64.2	1.77	1.12	+12.7	+8.7
1917	64.8	64.8	a	1.21	−0.9	+0.9
1918	65.0	61.8	5.31	1.07	+0.3	−4.7
1919	68.4	67.8	0.87	0.81	+5.2	+9.8
1920	66.7	68.5	−2.60	1.02	−2.4	+1.1
1921	65.8	65.5	0.48	−0.32	−1.5	−4.5
1922	71.1	70.4	1.03	−0.88	+8.1	+7.5
1923	78.9	80.0	−1.38	−0.51	+10.9	+13.6
1924	80.0	81.6	−1.95	−0.97	+1.4	+2.0
1925	83.7	84.3	−0.73	−1.59	+4.6	+3.3
1926	88.2	89.8	−1.82	−1.31	+5.4	+6.5
1927	88.8	90.6	−2.07	−1.25	+0.6	+0.9
1928	91.9	91.9	0.03	−1.85	+3.5	+1.3
1929	96.4	98.0	−1.63	−2.11	+5.0	+6.7
1930	87.1	90.5	−3.78	−1.98	−9.7	−7.6
1931	77.7	80.2	−3.10	−1.43	−10.8	−11.4
1932	65.4	66.4	−1.41	−0.17	−15.8	−17.3
1933	67.5	65.7	2.77	0.79	+3.2	−1.0
1934	74.6	71.3	4.66	1.95	+10.5	+8.5
1935	79.6	78.8	1.04	1.82	+6.7	+10.5
1936	89.2	86.9	2.69	0.81	+12.1	+10.3
1937	94.2	96.2	−2.05		+5.6	+10.7
1938	88.6	90.6	−2.29		−6.0	−5.8

a Less than +0.005.

(continued)

TABLE C-2 (concluded)

	Estimated Values (1)	Actual Values (2)	Percentage Difference $\frac{(1) - (2)}{(2)} \times 100$ (3)	5-Year Moving Average of (3) (4)	Year-to-Year Percentage Change in:	
					Estimated Values in (1) (5)	Actual Values in (2) (6)
			B. VARIANT III			
1909	51.8	53.8	−3.61			
1910	53.6	54.4	−1.44		+3.4	+1.1
1911	55.1	54.3	1.50	0.94	+2.8	−0.2
1912	57.6	55.1	4.47	1.76	+4.6	+1.6
1913	60.4	58.2	3.78	1.70	+4.8	+5.5
1914	57.2	57.0	0.51	1.85	−5.2	−2.1
1915	60.0	61.1	−1.76	1.04	+4.8	+7.2
1916	67.8	66.3	2.25	1.46	+13.1	+8.6
1917	67.2	66.9	0.40	1.56	−1.0	+0.8
1918	67.4	63.7	5.88	1.33	+0.4	−4.8
1919	71.0	70.3	1.06	0.93	+5.3	+10.3
1920	69.3	71.4	−2.95	1.06	−2.4	+1.6
1921	68.5	68.4	0.28	−0.36	−1.1	−4.2
1922	73.9	73.2	1.02	−1.06	+7.8	+7.0
1923	82.0	83.0	−1.24	−0.48	+10.9	+13.5
1924	83.2	85.2	−2.42	−0.92	+1.5	+2.7
1925	87.3	87.4	−0.06	−1.53	+5.0	+2.5
1926	91.6	93.4	−1.92	−1.29	+5.0	+7.0
1927	92.3	94.2	−2.02	−0.81	+0.7	+0.8
1928	95.7	95.7	−0.02	−0.80	+3.7	+1.7
1929	101.4	101.4	−0.03	−1.07	+6.0	+6.0
1930	91.5	91.5	−0.03	−1.20	−9.8	−9.8
1931	81.6	84.3	−3.24	−0.32	−10.8	−7.9
1932	68.8	70.7	−2.71	0.90	−15.7	−16.2
1933	71.4	68.3	4.42	0.62	+3.8	−3.3
1934	79.1	74.6	6.06	1.02	+10.9	+9.2
1935	84.6	85.8	−1.43	0.84	+6.9	+15.0
1936	94.6	95.8	−1.21	−0.48	+11.9	+11.6
1937	100.2	103.9	−3.61		+5.8	+8.5
1938	94.5	96.7	−2.24		−5.6	−7.0

SOURCE, BY COLUMN

(1) See text for derivation.
(2) Table R-22, col. 1, and Table R-2, col. 7.

cent (2.08 per cent for Variant I and 2.12 per cent for Variant III). This, offhand, does not seem to be a substantial discrepancy, but it must be remembered that the estimated values are based on deviations from decade averages, and as proportions of these deviations, the differences between the estimated and the actual values would loom much larger.

2. The range in the percentage differences is fairly substantial: from about −4 per cent to over +5 per cent for Variant I, and from about −3.5 per cent to over +6 per cent for Variant III. The largest percentage differences are due to the failure of the independent variable (total finished commodity output) to time properly the *turns* in the dependent variable (gross national product). For eleven years gross national product changes the direction of its movement from that in the preceding year (for example, column 6 of Table C-2 shows that 1911 is marked by a decline in gross national product from 1910, whereas 1910 shows an increase over 1909). For Variant I, the average difference for those years between the estimated and the actual values is 2.44 per cent, whereas for the other eighteen years—those in which the change in gross national product is in the same direction as in the preceding year—the average difference is only 1.78 per cent. A similar calculation for Variant III yields an average difference of 2.26 per cent for the eleven years of turns in gross national product and 1.95 per cent for the other eighteen years. The reason is, perhaps, that finished commodity output, being more quickly responsive to short-term changes, particularly those associated with business cycles, may, even in annual series, show a lead over the more comprehensive and less quickly responsive gross national product series. This seems to be the case in 1916–1918, when the decline in the estimated series appears in 1917, but in the actual series not until 1918; and during the 1930's, when the estimated series rises in 1933, but the actual series not until 1934.

3. This suggests the desirability of comparing the successive year-to-year percentage changes in the estimated and actual series (columns 5 and 6). By and large, there is similarity in direction of change: for both Variants I and III, of the twenty-nine pairs of signs, twenty-four are the same in the actual and estimated series, and only five are opposite. But the significance of this finding is greatly reduced by the fact that both series reveal a strong upward secular trend: of the twenty-nine changes, only nine are negative; and agreement of sign is, therefore, accounted for in large part by the identical upward secular

trend, and only in part by similarity of annual fluctuations. If we recognize only those cases where there is close agreement—roughly those in which the percentage change from year to year is of the same sign for both series, and in which the change in the estimated series is not more than about a third larger or smaller than that in the actual series—we find only thirteen in Variant I and only twelve in Variant III.

4. It is important that the percentage differences between the estimated and the actual series still persist, though greatly reduced in amplitude, when expressed as five-year moving averages (column 4). In general, the estimated series are somewhat higher than the actual series from 1911 through about 1919, because during that war-dominated decade commodity output tended to rise more than the services component of gross national product. By contrast, the estimated series are somewhat short of the actual series during the 1920's and the first few years of the 1930's, reflecting the fact that during this period the rise in commodity output was at a somewhat lower rate and the cyclical decline at a somewhat higher rate than the rise and decline in the services component. Again in 1933–1936, the estimated series are somewhat higher than the actual series, suggesting that the recovery was more marked in the commodity component than in the services component. Perhaps if a more flexible regression curve had been fitted, these persistent differences between the estimated and the actual series, which are present even in the five-year moving averages, might have been reduced; but they probably could not have been completely eliminated.

In trying to appraise the significance of this finding for the validity of moving averages of the annual estimates for the years before 1909, we may find some consolation in the fact that the disturbances in prices and other aspects of the economy have been particularly large since World War I, and that in the less disturbed decades between the 1870's and World War I, there was less opportunity for persistent differences between the estimated and the actual series. If such an assumption is warranted, the differences between the moving averages of the estimated series and of the actual series may have been, for those earlier decades, within a somewhat narrower range than the ± 2 per cent shown by the moving averages for 1909–1938 in column 4. But even so, some differences, possibly within a range of ± 1 per cent, should be allowed for.

Another way of testing the reliability of the estimated series as an indicator of short-term changes is to calculate its fluctuations during business cycles and phases, and compare the results with those for the actual series (Table C-3). Similar measures are shown also for finished commodity output.

TABLE C-3

CHANGE PER YEAR IN ANNUAL ESTIMATES DURING REFERENCE CYCLE PHASES, FINISHED COMMODITY OUTPUT, ESTIMATED AND ACTUAL GROSS NATIONAL PRODUCT, 1929 PRICES, 1911-1938

(percentages of average value for each reference cycle)

Successive Reference Cycles and Phases	Finished Commodity Output (1)	Gross National Product, Variant I		Gross National Product, Variant III	
		Estimated Values (2)	Actual Values (3)	Estimated Values (4)	Actual Values (5)
1. 1911–1914					
Expansion, 1911–1913	+5.2	+4.5	+3.5	+4.6	+3.5
Contraction, 1913–1914	−6.9	−5.3	−2.2	−5.4	−2.2
Differential	−12.2	−9.7	−5.7	−10.0	−5.7
2. 1914–1919					
Expansion, 1914–1918	+3.3	+3.8	+2.6	+3.9	+2.6
Contraction, 1918–1919	+4.8	+5.3	+9.7	+5.5	+10.2
Differential	+1.4	+1.5	+7.1	+1.6	+7.6
3. 1919–1921					
Expansion, 1919–1920	−4.5	−2.5	+1.1	−2.5	+1.6
Contraction, 1920–1921	−2.9	−1.5	−4.5	−1.1	−4.3
Differential	+1.6	+1.0	−5.6	+1.4	−5.9
4. 1921–1924					
Expansion, 1921–1923	+8.7	+8.8	+9.7	+8.7	+9.4
Contraction, 1923–1924	+0.6	+1.5	+2.2	+1.5	+2.9
Differential	−8.1	−7.3	−7.5	−7.1	−6.6
5. 1924–1927					
Expansion, 1924–1926	+5.3	+4.8	+4.7	+4.8	+4.6
Contraction, 1926–1927	−0.1	+0.7	+0.9	+0.7	+0.8
Differential	−5.4	−4.1	−3.8	−4.1	−3.8
6. 1927–1932					
Expansion, 1927–1929	+4.6	+4.5	+4.2	+5.1	+4.0
Contraction, 1929–1932	−14.0	−12.0	−12.0	−12.1	−11.3
Differential	−18.6	−16.5	−16.2	−17.1	−15.3
7. 1932–1938					
Expansion, 1932–1937	+8.1	+7.2	+7.5	+7.4	+7.8
Contraction, 1937–1938	−8.4	−7.0	−7.0	−6.6	−8.5
Differential	−16.5	−14.2	−14.5	−14.0	−16.3

SOURCE, BY COLUMN

(1) Calculated from Table R-21, col. 6.

(2)–(5) Calculated from Table C-2, cols. 1 and 2.

Appendix C

5. In five of the seven complete reference cycles distinguished during the period of comparison, the estimated series shows results that are satisfactorily similar to those for the actual series. In four of them, the series estimated by regression shows a closer approximation to the cyclical behavior of the actual series than is shown by finished commodity output; and in that sense the estimate is a better approximation than the independent variable.

6. In two cases, 1914–1919 and 1919–1921, however, the estimated series does not follow closely the behavior of the actual series during the reference cycles. This is particularly conspicuous in the very short cycle, 1919–1921, which is missed completely by the estimated series.

The Annual Estimates, 1889–1908

Two conclusions emerge from the tests discussed in the preceding section. First, gauged by the short-term changes in the annual series on gross national product, the procedure by which the series was derived for 1869–1908 is only moderately successful. For the test period, 1909–1938, the series misses a few of the turns of the actual series and provides close agreement in year-to-year changes in only about a third of the cases. Second, even when the series is cumulated into five-year moving averages, the percentage differences remain. However, the differences are narrow, and they may be assumed to be even narrower (perhaps within the range of ±1 per cent) for the less disturbed decades preceding World War I.

The regression procedure yielded gross national product in 1929 prices in two variants—I and III. We thought it useful to supplement this series by its counterpart in current prices, and by three other broad aggregates—net national product, flow of goods to consumers, and capital formation. The supplementary series were based upon the alternative series of annual estimates derived by components and used exclusively for the calculation of the moving averages given in the reference tables at the end of this appendix (discussed briefly in the next section). From those series we have an annual estimate of capital consumption (a cumulative series little affected by annual variations) which was applied directly as a subtrahend to gross national product in 1929 prices to obtain net national product, and was added later to net national product in current prices to yield gross national product in current prices. From the component series we also computed the annual ratio of flow of goods to consumers to gross national product in

1929 prices to derive the division of gross national product into flow of goods to consumers and gross capital formation. From the latter we subtracted capital consumption to arrive at net capital formation. And lastly, having derived from the component series the annual implicit price index for flow of goods to consumers and net capital formation, we converted the 1929 price series to current prices. Thus, the annual series in Tables R-22 and R-23 are basically estimates of gross national product derived by regression, but converted to current prices and distributed between the two major components by price indexes and ratios yielded by the component series described below.

The annual series in Tables R-22 and R-23 other than gross national product in 1929 prices are subject to a somewhat wider margin of error than that series. However, this additional qualification is a minor one. If the annual estimates of gross national product are acceptable despite the qualifications suggested by the tests in Tables C-2 and C-3, there is little ground for rejecting the annual estimates of net national product, or such broad components as flow of goods to consumers and capital formation.

The Estimates by Components

The regression procedure used to establish the relation between the total output of finished commodities and gross national product can be extended to components only if: (1) there is an annual index going back to 1869 for some part of the component; (2) the annual measure of the total value of this component, as it enters national product for the years since 1919, is not subject to a wide margin of error; (3) the relation between the two may be expected to be simple and not too variable over time. While requirement (1) would have to be satisfied for any method of securing annual estimates of a component, requirements (2) and (3) would raise much more serious difficulties than were encountered in the regression for gross national product. In view of the limited success of that procedure in estimating gross national product, its laboriousness if applied to the several components of national product, and the obvious doubts about its validity in estimating these narrow groups, we thought it best not to extend the procedure beyond those cases where it promised sufficient advantages over the alternative and cruder method—that of finding annual indexes by which annual values could be directly interpolated as variations around the basic levels provided by the overlapping decade averages in Appendix B.

Appendix C

The procedure in general was to find, for each component of flow of goods to consumers and of capital formation, annual series or indexes which, though limited in their coverage, would provide some indication of annual fluctuations around lines connecting the overlapping decade averages. We realized that the series available as annual interpolators were most frequently the more sensitive indexes and would yield annual values exaggerating the short-term changes compared with those reflected in more comprehensive and hence more accurate measures. It was decided accordingly that, while the resulting annual estimates might be good indicators of the timing of short-term movements (although with some bias toward a lead), they would not be acceptable measures of the amplitude of short-term changes. For this reason, the annual estimates of the various components are not shown. Nevertheless, the five-year moving averages calculated from them should be fairly acceptable approximations to those that would be yielded by the true series, if such were available, and they should be useful, therefore, for the study of the long swings in the rate of secular growth.

The details of the derivation of the annual series that underlie the five-year moving averages will be found in the copious notes to Tables R-25 through R-34, which contain those averages. It is impossible to summarize them here. But we call attention to two aspects of these estimates.

First, we found it desirable to distribute gross construction among three major types: nonfarm residential, government (military and nonmilitary), and all other. This distribution of a major component of capital formation is of value in relating our estimates to those derived for various use sectors (agriculture, manufacturing, etc.—see discussion in Appendix D); and is of obvious utility in apportioning capital formation among the three major groups of users—households, business firms, and governments.

Second, the annual series underlying the moving averages in Tables R-25 through R-34 are directly comparable with the annual series in Tables R-1 through R-10 in Appendix A. Indeed, for the years beginning with 1919 they are identical with the latter, except for the greater detail given for construction. But we did not think it desirable to reconcile the gross national product totals derived by adding the annual estimates of components with those shown for 1909–1918 in column 7 of Table R-20. Such a reconciliation would have distorted the time pattern of movement of the components and introduced breaks between 1909–1918 and the subsequent or preceding years. Therefore, the gross national product totals derived from components differ from those shown in Table R-20. The differences, however, would not seriously affect the validity of the five-year moving averages.[2]

No real test of the reliability of the annual series underlying the moving averages appears to be at hand. However, two feasible comparisons do convey an impression that the short-term fluctuations in the underlying annual series conform reasonably to what one would expect.

The first comparison is between five-year moving averages of the annual estimates of gross national product derived by regression and those of the annual totals derived by adding components (see Table R-24). The differences between the two sets of averages are minor, mostly well within 1 per cent. But the time pattern reveals a systematic source of the differences. The differences in columns 3 and 6 fluctuate in sign, reflecting the business cycles which both underlying annual series record. Because the totals derived as the sum of components are more sensitive to cyclical fluctuations than the totals derived by regression, the former tend to exceed the latter during reference expansions and to fall short of them during reference contractions. These differences are sufficiently marked to remain even in the five-year moving averages. Thus, the signs are positive from 1871 to 1873, a period of reference expansion, and then decline to negatives in 1876 and 1877, toward the trough point in the reference contraction. Similar movement is found in the 1880's and subsequent decades. In other words, the differences between the annual measures based on components and those derived by regression are largely in cyclical sensitivity; and much of the latter is removed when the annual series are re-

[2] The differences can be seen from the following comparison:

Gross National Product, Variant I, 1929 Prices
(billions of dollars)

	Estimate in Table R-20	Estimate by Adding Components
1909	52.1	52.0
1910	52.8	52.6
1911	52.6	53.7
1912	53.4	56.5
1913	56.4	59.1
1914	55.2	54.0
1915	59.1	55.6
1916	64.2	64.3
1917	64.8	62 5
1918	61.8	61.4

TABLE C-4

Change Per Year in Annual Estimates during Reference Cycle Phases, Gross National Product, Flow of Goods to Consumers, and Gross Capital Formation, 1929 Prices, 1870–1919

(percentages of average value for each reference cycle)

SUCCESSIVE REFERENCE CYCLES AND PHASES	VARIANT I				VARIANT III		Component Series, Gross Capital Formation (7)
	Gross National Product		Flow of Goods to Consumers		Component Series		
	Regression Series (1)	Component Series (2)	Regression Series (3)	Component Series (4)	Gross National Product (5)	Flow of Goods to Consumers (6)	
1. 1870–1878							
Expansion, 1870–1873	+8.9	+8.6	+7.9	+7.7	+8.7	+7.8	+11.8
Contraction, 1873–1878	+6.7	+6.1	+7.0	+6.4	+6.1	+6.4	+5.0
Differential	−2.2	−2.6	−0.8	−1.2	−2.6	−1.4	−6.8
2. 1878–1885							
Expansion, 1878–1882	+6.7	+7.5	+7.1	+7.9	+7.5	+7.8	+6.2
Contraction, 1882–1885	+2.3	+1.8	+3.2	+2.7	+1.8	+2.7	−1.3
Differential	−4.4	−5.7	−3.9	−5.2	−5.6	−5.1	−7.5
3. 1885–1888							
Expansion, 1885–1887	+4.4	+4.4	+2.0	+2.0	+4.3	+2.0	+12.1
Contraction, 1887–1888	−1.3	−1.9	+1.0	+0.4	−1.8	+0.4	−9.5
Differential	−5.7	−6.2	−1.0	−1.6	−6.1	−1.6	−21.6
4. 1888–1891							
Expansion, 1888–1890	+4.8	+5.6	+0.8	+1.6	+5.4	+1.5	+17.3
Contraction, 1890–1891	+5.9	+4.7	+8.4	+7.2	+4.8	+7.2	−2.5
Differential	+1.2	−0.9	+7.6	+5.6	−0.6	+5.7	−19.7
5. 1891–1894							
Expansion, 1891–1892	+7.0	+9.5	+2.1	+4.5	+9.4	+4.5	+22.7
Contraction, 1892–1894	−2.9	−4.5	+0.3	−1.3	−4.4	−1.3	−12.9
Differential	−9.9	−14.1	−1.8	−5.8	−13.8	−5.8	−35.6

	(1)	(2)	(3)	(4)	(5)	(6)	(7)
6. 1894–1896							
Expansion, 1894–1895	+8.8	+11.9	+8.5	+11.6	+11.8	+11.5	+12.6
Contraction, 1895–1896	+2.9	−2.4	+4.8	−0.5	−2.2	−0.3	−8.0
Differential	−5.9	−14.3	−3.7	−12.1	−14.0	−11.8	−20.6
7. 1896–1900							
Expansion, 1896–1899	+5.4	+6.4	+5.7	+6.6	+6.4	+6.7	+5.5
Contraction, 1899–1900	+4.9	+3.4	+2.5	+0.9	+3.4	+1.0	+10.8
Differential	−0.4	−3.0	−3.2	−5.7	−3.0	−5.7	+5.4
8. 1900–1904							
Expansion, 1900–1903	+5.1	+5.5	+5.4	+5.8	+5.5	+5.9	+4.4
Contraction, 1903–1904	−1.2	−1.5	+1.4	+1.1	−1.3	+1.3	−9.4
Differential	−6.3	−7.0	−4.0	−4.7	−6.8	−4.6	−13.8
9. 1904–1908							
Expansion, 1904–1907	+6.2	+6.4	+5.5	+5.7	+6.4	+5.8	+8.5
Contraction, 1907–1908	−7.6	−10.5	−3.8	−6.8	−10.3	−6.7	−21.9
Differential	−13.7	−16.8	−9.3	−12.5	−16.7	−12.5	−30.4
10. 1908–1911							
Expansion, 1908–1910		+6.6		+5.8	+6.7	+5.8	+9.6
Contraction, 1910–1911		+2.1		+5.0	+2.0	+4.8	−7.8
Differential		−4.5		−0.7	−4.6	−1.0	−17.4
11. 1911–1914							
Expansion, 1911–1913		+4.8		+2.9	+4.7	+2.9	+11.3
Contraction, 1913–1914		−9.0		−1.4	−8.7	−1.3	−35.8
Differential		−13.8		−4.3	−13.4	−4.2	−47.1
12. 1914–1919							
Expansion, 1914–1918		+3.1		+1.6	+3.1	+1.8	+7.6
Contraction, 1918–1919		+10.4		+5.1	+10.5	+5.4	+27.8
Differential		+7.4		+3.4	+7.4	+3.6	+20.1

SOURCE, BY COLUMN

(1) and (3) For the annual series underlying the computations, see Table R-22 and its notes. (2), (4), (5), (6), and (7) Calculated from the annual series underlying Tables R-26 and R-29.

duced to five-year averages. The differences between those averages show cycles, but their duration and amplitude are not significant enough to affect materially the study of long swings in the rate of secular growth. One can argue that for the purpose at hand the totals derived by adding components are not much inferior to those derived by regression.

The second comparison is of the changes per year during reference cycles and their phases in the annual series derived by adding components (Table C-4). It is limited to the broader aggregates that we would expect to reflect the occurrence of cycles in general business, an expectation that cannot be entertained with respect to some narrow components (within flow of goods to consumers or within capital formation). For comparative purposes we also show similar measures for two totals derived by regression—gross national product (derived directly) and flow of goods to consumers (derived indirectly).

The consistency with which the annual series record the reference cycles is marked if, in view of the strong upward trend in the series, we consider only the difference between the rate of change in each expansion and subsequent contraction. The World War I cycle is an exception, due to a much earlier downturn of output than the reference chronology allows for. Of the other eleven reference cycles, the various annual series record downturns in ten, and the one instance of an upturn in those cycles—in gross capital formation—is also due to an earlier downturn and can hardly be considered an exception, in view of the tendency of capital formation to lead general business conditions. Only in the short 1888–1891 cycle is there a true exception—the upturn in flow of goods to consumers. This finding is hardly a genuine test, but it does suggest that the annual fluctuations in the underlying series are not erratic, at least with respect to timing.

The second finding—to be expected from our discussion of the two sets of national product totals in Table R-24—is the wider amplitude in response to reference cycles of totals derived by adding components than of totals derived by regression (compare columns 2 and 1; columns 4 and 3). The amplitude of reference cycle changes in a true estimate of gross national product would probably be closer to the amplitude of cycle changes in the series derived by regression than to that of cycle changes in the series derived by adding components. But as already indicated in the discussion of Table R-24, the greater sensitivity of the totals derived by adding components should be reflected in only minor degree in the five-year moving averages.

TABLE R-20

NATIONAL PRODUCT, VARIANTS I AND III, 1929 PRICES, 1909–1918

(amounts in billions of dollars)

	Net National Product, Variant I, Current Prices, 1909–1918, Preliminary (1)	National Income, Current Prices (2)	Price Index, Net National Product, Variant I (1929 = 100) (3)	*Net National Product, Variant I, 1929 Prices* Preliminary (1) ÷ (3) (4)	Final (5)	Capital Consumption, 1929 Prices (6)	Gross National Product, Variant I, 1929 Prices (5) + (6) (7)
			A. VARIANT I				
1909	31.0	30.5	56.1	55.3	46.2	5.92	52.1
1910	32.8	32.3	58.8	55.7	46.6	6.16	52.8
1911	32.3	31.8	58.5	55.2	46.2	6.40	52.6
1912	34.8	34.2	62.2	55.9	46.8	6.64	53.4
1913	36.3	35.7	61.3	59.2	49.5	6.89	56.4
Average, 1909–1918				60.1	50.2		57.2
1914	35.0	34.5	60.9	57.5	48.1	7.12	55.2
1915	38.5	37.9	62.1	62.0	51.8	7.31	59.1
1916	47.0	46.3	69.3	67.8	56.7	7.54	64.2
1917	56.7	55.8	83.2	68.1	56.9	7.88	64.8
1918	60.1	59.2	94.1	63.9	53.4	8.32	61.8
1919	64.2	69.8	109.4				
1920	74.2	69.7	125.1				
1921	59.4	53.8	104.8				
1922	60.7	62.0	99.4				
1923	71.6	69.7	101.7				

(continued)

	Net National Product, Variant III, Current Prices, 1909–1918, Preliminary (1)	National Income, Current Prices (2)	Price Index, Net National Product, Variant III (1929 = 100) (3)	Net National Product, Variant III, 1929 Prices Preliminary (1) ÷ (3) (4)	Final (5)	Capital Consumption, 1929 Prices (6)	Gross National Product, Variant III, 1929 Prices (5) + (6) (7)
			B. VARIANT III				
1909	31.9	30.5	55.2	57.8	47.8	5.92	53.8
1910	33.7	32.3	57.9	58.2	48.2	6.16	54.4
1911	33.2	31.8	57.5	57.8	47.9	6.40	54.3
1912	35.8	34.2	61.1	58.6	48.5	6.64	55.1
1913	37.4	35.7	60.3	62.0	51.3	6.89	58.2
Average, 1909–1918				62.9	52.0		59.1
1914	36.1	34.5	59.9	60.2	49.8	7.12	57.0
1915	39.6	37.9	61.0	64.9	53.7	7.31	61.1
1916	48.4	46.3	68.1	71.0	58.8	7.54	66.3
1917	58.3	55.8	81.8	71.3	59.0	7.88	66.9
1918	61.9	59.2	92.5	66.9	55.4	8.32	63.7
1919	65.2	69.8	106.7				
1920	75.7	69.7	121.7				
1921	61.8	53.8	103.7				
1922	63.0	62.0	98.6				
1923	74.1	69.7	100.9				

Because of rounding, detail will not necessarily add to total.

SOURCE, BY COLUMN (A AND B)

(1) 1909–1918: Col. 2 multiplied by the 1919–1923 ratio of col. 1 to col. 2. The use of 1919 for splicing the series in col. 1 (and col. 3) reduces the average discrepancy for 1909–1918 (from 19.6 to 5.4 per cent for Variant I, with a similar reduction for Variant III), but yields almost identical estimates in cols. 5 and 7.

1919–1923: Table R-1, col. 4 or col. 6.

(2) 1914–1921: Income payments–business savings aggregate in Simon Kuznets, *National Product in Wartime* (New York, NBER, 1945), Appendix Table III-9, p. 141, adjusted to include imputed rent.

1909–1913 and 1922–1923: Unpublished extensions of the series for 1914–1921.

(3) 1909–1918: Series for 1919–1923 extrapolated by a composite index of (1) cost of living (weighted 85), (2) wholesale prices of metals (weighted 7.5), and (3) wholesale prices of building materials (weighted 7.5). (1) is the BLS index back to 1913 (*Historical Statistics of the United States, 1789–1945*, Series L-41), extrapolated to 1909 by the Federal Reserve Bank of New York index (*ibid.*, Series L-36). (2) and (3) are the BLS wholesale price indexes (*ibid.*, Series L-21 and L-22, respectively).

1919–1923: Implicit price index obtained by dividing Table R-1, col. 4 or col. 6 by Table R-2, col. 4 or col. 6.

(4) The figure for 1909–1918 is an average of the annual estimates.

(5) The annual estimates in col. 4 multiplied by the ratio of the final decade average, given in Table R-12, col. 4 or col. 6, to the decade average in col. 4.

(6) Sum of the annual series underlying Table R-31, col. 10 and Table R-33, col. 5.

	Output Destined for Domestic Consumption, 1929 Prices (1)	Exports, Current Prices (2)	Imports, Current Prices (3)	Balance of Exports over Imports		Finished Commodity Output, 1929 Prices (6)
				Current Prices (4)	1929 Prices (5)	
1869	3.77	0.34	0.44	−0.10	−0.10	3.67
1870	3.76	0.40	0.46	−0.06	−0.06	3.69
1871	3.81	0.46	0.57	−0.11	−0.13	3.68
1872	4.87	0.47	0.66	−0.19	−0.21	4.66
1873	5.08	0.57	0.60	−0.03	−0.03	5.05
1874	5.09	0.57	0.56	0.01	0.01	5.10
1875	5.15	0.51	0.50	0.01	0.01	5.16
1876	5.49	0.59	0.43	0.16	0.22	5.70
1877	5.99	0.62	0.48	0.14	0.20	6.18
1878	6.38	0.74	0.43	0.31	0.47	6.85
1879	7.19	0.77	0.51	0.25	0.41	7.60
1880	8.45	0.89	0.70	0.19	0.28	8.73
1881	8.74	0.83	0.67	0.16	0.24	8.98
1882	9.43	0.77	0.75	0.02	0.02	9.45
1883	9.45	0.80	0.69	0.11	0.16	9.61
1884	9.66	0.75	0.63	0.12	0.19	9.85
1885	9.77	0.69	0.59	0.10	0.17	9.94
1886	10.4	0.71	0.66	0.05	0.08	10.5
1887	10.9	0.72	0.71	0.01	0.01	10.9
1888	10.7	0.69	0.73	−0.03	−0.06	10.7
1889	11.1	0.83	0.77	0.06	0.09	11.2
1890	11.8	0.86	0.82	0.03	0.06	11.9
1891	12.4	0.97	0.83	0.14	0.24	12.7
1892	13.7	0.94	0.84	0.10	0.18	13.8
1893	13.2	0.88	0.78	0.10	0.18	13.3
1894	12.5	0.83	0.68	0.15	0.30	12.8
1895	14.0	0.82	0.80	0.02	0.05	14.1
1896	13.7	1.01	0.68	0.32	0.66	14.4
1897	14.6	1.10	0.74	0.36	0.73	15.4
1898	14.6	1.26	0.64	0.62	1.22	15.9
1899	16.1	1.28	0.80	0.48	0.87	17.0
1900	16.6	1.48	0.83	0.65	1.10	17.7
1901	18.5	1.47	0.88	0.59	1.01	19.5
1902	19.1	1.36	0.97	0.39	0.63	19.7
1903	20.0	1.48	1.00	0.49	0.78	20.8
1904	19.6	1.45	1.04	0.42	0.66	20.3
1905	20.8	1.63	1.18	0.45	0.71	21.5
1906	23.3	1.80	1.32	0.48	0.74	24.1
1907	23.9	1.92	1.42	0.50	0.73	24.6
1908	21.3	1.75	1.12	0.64	0.96	22.2
1909	23.6	1.73	1.48	0.25	0.36	24.0
1910	24.5	1.87	1.56	0.30	0.41	24.9
1911	24.8	2.09	1.53	0.56	0.82	25.6
1912	26.2	2.40	1.82	0.58	0.80	27.0
1913	27.5	2.48	1.79	0.69	0.94	28.5

(continued)

	Output Destined for Domestic Consumption, 1929 Prices (1)	Exports, Current Prices (2)	Imports, Current Prices (3)	*Balance of Exports over Imports*		Finished Commodity Output, 1929 Prices (6)
				Current Prices (4)	1929 Prices (5)	
1914	26.1	2.11	1.79	0.32	0.45	26.6
1915	25.3	3.55	1.78	1.78	2.44	27.7
1916	28.3	5.48	2.39	3.09	3.45	31.7
1917	28.2			3.28	2.66	30.9
1918	28.3			3.12	2.26	30.6
1919	29.3			4.02	2.76	32.0
1920	28.8			2.95	1.82	30.6
1921	27.8			1.98	1.93	29.7
1922	31.2			0.72	0.71	31.9
1923	35.2			0.38	0.36	35.5
1924	34.8			0.98	0.95	35.7
1925	36.9			0.68	0.63	37.5
1926	39.4			0.38	0.36	39.7
1927	39.0			0.68	0.68	39.7
1928	39.9			1.04	1.02	41.0
1929	42.4			0.84	0.84	43.2
1930	37.3			0.78	0.86	38.2
1931	32.7			0.33	0.44	33.1
1932	26.9			0.29	0.42	27.3
1933	27.9			0.23	0.33	28.2
1934	30.9			0.48	0.61	31.5
1935	33.6			0.24	0.28	33.9
1936	38.6			0.03	0.04	38.6
1937	41.0			0.27	0.29	41.3
1938	37.0			1.13	1.37	38.4

Because of rounding, detail will not necessarily add to total.

SOURCE, BY COLUMN

(1) From Shaw's series, given in *Value of Commodity Output since 1869*, Tables I-1 and I-2, for 1869, 1879, and 1889–1938, interpolated for 1870–1878 and 1880–1888, and converted to 1929 prices as described in the notes to Kuznets, *National Product since 1869*, Tables II-1 to II-5, col. 2.

An additional adjustment was made in the data for 1904–1938 to eliminate the value of gasoline and tires and tubes for passenger cars used for business purposes. The procedure for 1904–1918, described in the notes to Table R-13, cols. 5 and 6, was followed for the later years also, except that for gasoline for 1929–1938 the Commerce estimate of producers' value was used, since there was no NBER series.

(2) and (3) Calendar year totals of monthly figures reported in various issues of *Monthly Summary of Foreign Commerce* (Dept. of Commerce).

(4) 1869–1915: Col. 2 minus col. 3.

1916–1938: From *Historical Statistics of the United States, 1789–1945*, Series M-55, pp. 243–244.

(5) Col. 4 divided by the BLS wholesale price index, Series L-15 (*ibid.*, pp. 233–234), shifted to a 1929 base.

(6) Col. 1 plus col. 5. Since the Shaw series is available only through 1939 and the calculation of the estimates in Table R-22, col. 1 calls for an average for 1934–1943, we estimated the latter by applying to the 1929–1938 decade average the percentage change from 1929–1938 to 1934–1943 in the sum of Table R-13, cols. 5–7 (or Table R-19, cols. 2–4) and Table R-15, cols. 1 and 2.

ANNUAL ESTIMATES OF NATIONAL PRODUCT AND MAJOR COMPONENTS,
VARIANTS I AND III, REGRESSION SERIES, 1929 PRICES, 1889–1918
(billions of dollars)

	Gross National Product (1)	Net National Product (2)	Flow of Goods to Consumers (3)	Gross Capital Formation (4)	Net Capital Formation (5)
A. VARIANT I					
1889	22.9	20.2	17.6	5.25	2.60
1890	24.2	21.4	17.3	6.95	4.14
1891	25.7	22.7	18.8	6.89	3.90
1892	27.5	24.4	19.2	8.37	5.23
1893	26.9	23.6	19.9	7.02	3.74
1894	26.0	22.6	19.3	6.72	3.34
1895	28.5	25.0	21.1	7.40	3.92
1896	29.3	25.7	22.1	7.19	3.60
1897	31.2	27.5	23.2	7.99	4.26
1898	32.4	28.5	24.1	8.21	4.35
1899	34.6	30.6	26.2	8.31	4.31
1900	36.2	32.0	26.9	9.32	5.18
1901	39.5	35.2	29.4	10.1	5.78
1902	40.2	35.7	29.9	10.3	5.85
1903	42.3	37.6	31.8	10.5	5.88
1904	41.8	37.0	32.2	9.58	4.78
1905	44.4	39.4	33.7	10.7	5.77
1906	49.1	43.9	36.8	12.3	7.08
1907	50.5	45.0	38.1	12.4	6.92
1908	46.9	41.2	36.7	10.2	4.49
1909	52.1	46.2	39.7	12.4	6.46
1910	52.8	46.6	40.5	12.2	6.09
1911	52.6	46.2	41.5	11.1	4.66
1912	53.4	46.8	41.1	12.3	5.63
1913	56.4	49.5	42.9	13.5	6.58
1914	55.2	48.1	45.4	9.85	2.73
1915	59.1	51.8	46.3	12.9	5.56
1916	64.2	56.7	47.3	16.9	9.36
1917	64.8	56.9	48.7	16.1	8.21
1918	61.8	53.4	47.6	14.1	5.79
B. VARIANT III					
1889	23.4	20.8	18.2	5.25	2.60
1890	24.8	22.0	17.8	6.96	4.14
1891	26.2	23.3	19.3	6.89	3.91
1892	28.3	25.1	19.8	8.41	5.28
1893	27.5	24.2	20.5	7.02	3.74
1894	26.6	23.2	19.9	6.72	3.34
1895	29.1	25.7	21.7	7.40	3.93
1896	30.0	26.4	22.8	7.19	3.60
1897	32.0	28.2	24.0	7.99	4.27
1898	33.2	29.3	24.9	8.21	4.35
1899	35.4	31.4	27.1	8.31	4.31
1900	37.1	33.0	27.8	9.32	5.18
1901	40.6	36.3	30.5	10.1	5.82
1902	41.2	36.8	30.9	10.3	5.86
1903	43.4	38.8	32.9	10.5	5.89

(continued)

	Gross National Product (1)	Net National Product (2)	Flow of Goods to Consumers (3)	Gross Capital Formation (4)	Net Capital Formation (5)
			B. VARIANT III (concluded)		
1904	42.9	38.1	33.3	9.57	4.77
1905	45.7	40.7	34.9	10.7	5.76
1906	50.7	45.4	38.3	12.3	7.12
1907	52.2	46.7	39.7	12.5	6.96
1908	48.3	42.6	38.1	10.2	4.48
1909	53.8	47.8	41.4	12.4	6.46
1910	54.4	48.2	42.1	12.2	6.07
1911	54.3	47.9	43.2	11.1	4.67
1912	55.1	48.5	42.8	12.3	5.66
1913	58.2	51.3	44.7	13.5	6.61
1914	57.0	49.8	47.1	9.84	2.72
1915	61.1	53.7	48.2	12.9	5.55
1916	66.3	58.8	49.4	16.9	9.36
1917	66.9	59.0	50.8	16.0	8.16
1918	63.7	55.4	49.6	14.1	5.73

Because of rounding, detail will not necessarily add to total.

Source, by Column

(1) 1869–1873 (not shown): Table R-21, col. 6 divided by its 1869–1878 ratio to Table R-12, col. 7 or col. 9.

1874–1908 (1874–1888 not shown): Derived by the following procedure. For 1909–1938:

1. Decade averages of Table R-21, col. 6 were computed and centered at the middle of the decade, and interpolated logarithmically along a straight line for the intervening years.

2. Percentage deviations of the annuals in Table R-21, col. 6 from those derived in step 1 were computed.

3. The ratios of the decade averages of Table R-21, col. 6 to the decade averages of gross national product in Table R-12, col. 7 or col. 9 were computed, centered at the middle of the decade, and interpolated along a straight line.

4. The ratio of Table R-21, col. 6 to gross national product, Table R-2, col. 7 or col. 9, or Table R-20, col. 7, was computed annually for 1909–1938.

5. Absolute deviations of the annual ratios in step 4 from those derived in step 3 were computed.

6. A freehand smooth curve was fitted to the deviations derived in steps 2 and 5, with those in step 2 as the independent variable.

For 1874–1908, after steps 1–3 had been carried through for these years:

7. Deviations corresponding to those computed in step 5 were read from the curve described in step 6 for the points derived in step 2.

8. These deviations were added to the ratios derived in step 3.

9. The adjusted ratios were then applied to the series in Table R-21, col. 6 to yield annual estimates of gross national product, Variant I or Variant III.

1909–1918: Table R-20, col. 7.

(2) and (5) Cols. 1 and 4, respectively, minus the annual series on capital consumption underlying Table R-29, col. 5.

(3) and (4) Col. 1 distributed between flow of goods to consumers and gross capital formation on the basis of the corresponding distribution of the annual series underlying Table R-26, col. 3 or 6.

ANNUAL ESTIMATES OF NATIONAL PRODUCT AND MAJOR COMPONENTS,
VARIANTS I AND III, REGRESSION SERIES, CURRENT PRICES, 1889–1918
(billions of dollars)

	Gross National Product (1)	Net National Product (2)	Flow of Goods to Consumers (3)	Gross Capital Formation (4)	Net Capital Formation (5)
A. VARIANT I					
1889	12.0	10.7	9.59	2.43	1.13
1890	12.4	11.1	9.25	3.17	1.86
1891	12.9	11.6	9.91	3.03	1.73
1892	13.3	12.0	9.76	3.57	2.23
1893	13.3	11.9	10.3	2.94	1.56
1894	12.0	10.6	9.30	2.72	1.33
1895	12.9	11.5	9.95	2.98	1.60
1896	12.9	11.5	10.1	2.82	1.43
1897	13.9	12.4	10.7	3.20	1.71
1898	14.8	13.2	11.4	3.42	1.80
1899	16.4	14.5	12.5	3.82	2.00
1900	17.9	16.0	13.5	4.40	2.48
1901	19.4	17.4	14.7	4.70	2.73
1902	20.4	18.3	15.5	4.87	2.79
1903	21.6	19.4	16.6	5.02	2.86
1904	21.7	19.4	17.1	4.54	2.26
1905	23.6	21.2	18.3	5.34	2.88
1906	26.7	24.0	20.2	6.52	3.82
1907	28.6	25.7	21.9	6.75	3.81
1908	26.4	23.4	21.1	5.24	2.28
1909	30.4	27.2	23.6	6.81	3.64
1910	31.6	28.2	24.8	6.78	3.43
1911	31.3	27.7	25.1	6.18	2.61
1912	33.0	29.2	26.0	7.02	3.28
1913	35.0	31.1	27.2	7.88	3.91
1914	34.6	30.5	29.1	5.54	1.44
1915	38.3	33.9	30.6	7.75	3.33
1916	47.2	42.2	35.4	11.9	6.80
1917	59.3	52.8	45.5	13.8	7.31
1918	65.9	57.4	51.2	14.7	6.20
B. VARIANT III					
1889	12.2	10.9	9.79	2.43	1.12
1890	12.6	11.3	9.45	3.18	1.87
1891	13.2	11.8	10.1	3.03	1.73
1892	13.6	12.3	.10.0	3.58	2.25
1893	13.5	12.1	10.6	2.94	1.56

(continued)

TABLE R-23 (concluded)

	Gross National Product (1)	Net National Product (2)	Flow of Goods to Consumers (3)	Gross Capital Formation (4)	Net Capital Formation (5)
		B. VARIANT III (concluded)			
1894	12.3	10.9	9.57	2.72	1.33
1895	13.2	11.8	10.2	2.98	1.60
1896	13.2	11.8	10.4	2.82	1.43
1897	14.2	12.7	11.0	3.20	1.72
1898	15.1	13.5	11.7	3.42	1.80
1899	16.7	14.9	12.9	3.82	2.00
1900	18.3	16.4	13.9	4.41	2.49
1901	19.9	18.0	15.2	4.71	2.75
1902	20.9	18.8	16.0	4.87	2.79
1903	22.1	20.0	17.1	5.03	2.87
1904	22.2	19.9	17.7	4.54	2.26
1905	24.2	21.7	18.9	5.33	2.88
1906	27.5	24.8	20.9	6.54	3.84
1907	29.4	26.5	22.6	6.77	3.84
1908	27.1	24.1	21.9	5.24	2.27
1909	31.3	28.1	24.5	6.81	3.64
1910	32.4	29.0	25.6	6.77	3.42
1911	32.2	28.6	26.0	6.19	2.62
1912	33.9	30.2	26.9	7.04	3.30
1913	36.1	32.1	28.2	7.89	3.93
1914	35.7	31.6	30.2	5.53	1.44
1915	39.6	35.2	31.9	7.75	3.32
1916	48.6	43.5	36.7	11.9	6.81
1917	60.4	53.9	46.6	13.8	7.27
1918	66.7	58.2	52.1	14.6	6.14

Because of rounding, detail will not necessarily add to total.

SOURCE, BY COLUMN

(1) and (4) Cols. 2 and 5, respectively, plus the annual series on capital consumption underlying Table R-29, col. 2.

(2) Col. 3 plus col. 5.

(3) Col. 3 of Table R-22 multiplied by the price index implicit in the annual series underlying col. 1 (or 4) of Tables R-25 and R-26.

(5) Col. 5 of Table R-22 multiplied by the price index implicit in the annual series underlying cols. 3 and 6 of Table R-29.

TABLE R-24

COMPARISON OF FIVE-YEAR MOVING AVERAGES OF GROSS NATIONAL PRODUCT,
VARIANTS I AND III, ESTIMATED BY REGRESSION AND ESTIMATED BY COMPONENTS,
1929 PRICES, 1869–1922

(billions of dollars)

Year on Which Moving Average Is Centered	Variant I			Variant III		
	Re-gression Series (1)	Com-ponent Series (2)	Difference (2) − (1) (3)	Re-gression Series (4)	Com-ponent Series (5)	Difference (5) − (4) (6)
1871	8.74	8.90	+0.16	8.96	9.11	+0.15
1872	9.34	9.47	+0.13	9.58	9.70	+0.12
1873	9.96	10.1	+0.13	10.2	10.3	+0.12
1874	10.8	10.9	+0.08	11.1	11.2	+0.08
1875	11.4	11.4	+0.01	11.7	11.7	+0.01
1876	12.2	12.1	−0.05	12.4	12.4	−0.05
1877	13.1	13.1	−0.06	13.4	13.4	−0.06
1878	14.5	14.5	ᵃ	14.8	14.8	−0.01
1879	15.7	15.7	ᵃ	16.1	16.1	−0.02
1880	16.9	17.0	+0.05	17.4	17.4	+0.01
1881	18.0	18.1	+0.09	18.5	18.5	+0.03
1882	18.9	19.0	+0.11	19.4	19.5	+0.05
1883	19.5	19.5	+0.04	20.0	20.0	−0.01
1884	20.1	20.2	+0.07	20.6	20.7	+0.04
1885	20.8	20.8	+0.02	21.3	21.3	ᵃ
1886	21.2	21.3	+0.02	21.8	21.8	+0.02
1887	21.8	21.8	−0.02	22.3	22.3	−0.01
1888	22.6	22.6	+0.03	23.1	23.1	+0.04
1889	23.4	23.4	ᵃ	23.9	24.0	+0.01
1890	24.5	24.6	+0.13	25.0	25.1	+0.11
1891	25.4	25.6	+0.12	26.0	26.1	+0.09
1892	26.1	26.2	+0.10	26.7	26.7	+0.06
1893	26.9	27.1	+0.17	27.5	27.7	+0.13
1894	27.6	27.6	ᵃ	28.3	28.3	−0.03
1895	28.4	28.2	−0.15	29.0	28.9	−0.16
1896	29.5	29.2	−0.29	30.2	29.9	−0.30
1897	31.2	30.9	−0.23	31.9	31.7	−0.25
1898	32.7	32.3	−0.46	33.5	33.0	−0.48
1899	34.7	34.6	−0.19	35.6	35.4	−0.24
1900	36.5	36.4	−0.15	37.5	37.3	−0.19

(continued)

TABLE R-24 (concluded)

Year on Which Moving Average Is Centered	Variant I			Variant III		
	Re-gression Series (1)	Com-ponent Series (2)	Difference (2) − (1) (3)	Re-gression Series (4)	Com-ponent Series (5)	Difference (5) − (4) (6)
1901	38.5	38.6	+0.03	39.6	39.5	−0.02
1902	40.0	40.0	ᵃ	41.1	41.0	−0.04
1903	41.6	41.8	+0.15	42.8	42.9	+0.12
1904	43.5	43.8	+0.26	44.8	45.0	+0.24
1905	45.6	45.9	+0.28	47.0	47.2	+0.22
1906	46.5	46.6	+0.04	47.9	47.9	ᵃ
1907	48.6	48.6	+0.04	50.1	50.1	−0.02
1908	50.3	50.2	−0.05	51.9	51.8	−0.10
1909	51.0	50.9	−0.03	52.6	52.5	−0.06
1910	51.6	52.1	+0.54	53.2	53.7	+0.54
1911	53.4	54.8	+1.31	55.1	56.4	+1.30
1912	54.1	55.2	+1.09	55.8	56.9	+1.09
1913	55.3	55.8	+0.42	57.1	57.5	+0.39
1914	57.7	57.9	+0.21	59.5	59.7	+0.18
1915	60.0	59.1	−0.87	61.9	61.0	−0.87
1916	61.0	59.6	−1.47	63.0	61.6	−1.41
1917	63.5	62.3	−1.22	65.7	64.5	−1.17
1918	65.4	64.9	−0.51	67.7	67.3	−0.45
1919	65.7	65.1	−0.53	68.1	67.7	−0.45
1920	66.8	66.7	−0.06	69.4	69.4	−0.01

In this and the following tables showing five-year moving averages, the dates in the title cover the earliest and latest years included in the averages.

ᵃ Less than $0.005 billion.

SOURCE, BY COLUMN

(1) and (4) Calculated from the annual series described in the notes to Table R-22, col. 1.

(2) and (5) Table R-26, cols. 3 and 6, respectively.

Year on Which Moving Average Is Centered	Variant I			Variant III		
	Flow of Goods to Consumers (1)	Net National Product (2)	Gross National Product (3)	Flow of Goods to Consumers (4)	Net National Product (5)	Gross National Product (6)
1871	5.31	6.13	6.64	5.38	6.20	6.71
1872	5.49	6.34	6.88	5.56	6.41	6.96
1873	5.70	6.59	7.17	5.78	6.67	7.25
1874	5.85	6.82	7.44	5.94	6.92	7.53
1875	5.98	6.90	7.53	6.08	7.00	7.63
1876	6.06	6.95	7.58	6.18	7.06	7.70
1877	6.20	7.14	7.78	6.33	7.27	7.91
1878	6.72	7.77	8.44	6.85	7.91	8.58
1879	7.18	8.34	9.04	7.33	8.48	9.18
1880	7.76	9.02	9.77	7.91	9.17	9.92
1881	8.34	9.66	10.5	8.50	9.81	10.6
1882	8.81	10.1	11.0	8.97	10.3	11.2
1883	8.83	10.1	11.0	9.01	10.3	11.2
1884	8.91	10.1	11.1	9.10	10.3	11.3
1885	8.86	10.1	11.1	9.06	10.3	11.3
1886	8.86	10.0	11.1	9.06	10.2	11.3
1887	8.97	10.1	11.3	9.18	10.3	11.5
1888	9.12	10.5	11.7	9.33	10.7	11.9
1889	9.37	10.8	12.1	9.58	11.0	12.3
1890	9.58	11.2	12.5	9.79	11.4	12.7
1891	9.80	11.5	12.8	10.0	11.7	13.1
1892	9.74	11.5	12.8	9.96	11.7	13.1
1893	9.90	11.6	13.0	10.1	11.9	13.2
1894	9.88	11.5	12.9	10.1	11.8	13.1
1895	10.0	11.5	12.9	10.3	11.8	13.2
1896	10.2	11.7	13.2	10.5	12.0	13.5
1897	10.8	12.5	14.1	11.2	12.8	14.4
1898	11.5	13.3	15.0	11.8	13.7	15.3
1899	12.5	14.6	16.4	12.9	15.0	16.8
1900	13.5	15.8	17.7	13.9	16.2	18.1
1901	14.6	17.2	19.2	15.0	17.6	19.6
1902	15.5	18.1	20.2	16.0	18.6	20.7
1903	16.5	19.2	21.4	17.0	19.7	21.9
1904	17.6	20.6	22.9	18.2	21.2	23.5
1905	18.9	22.1	24.6	19.5	22.7	25.2
1906	19.7	22.7	25.4	20.4	23.4	26.1
1907	21.0	24.3	27.2	21.7	25.0	27.9
1908	22.3	25.7	28.7	23.0	26.4	29.5
1909	23.3	26.4	29.6	24.1	27.2	30.4
1910	24.4	27.5	30.9	25.2	28.4	31.7
1911	25.9	29.5	33.1	26.9	30.4	34.0
1912	26.9	30.0	33.8	27.9	31.0	34.7
1913	27.7	30.7	34.7	28.8	31.8	35.7
1914	29.7	33.5	37.7	30.8	34.6	38.9
1915	33.0	37.4	42.2	34.2	38.6	43.4
1916	37.5	42.3	48.0	38.7	43.5	49.2
1917	42.5	49.2	56.0	43.7	50.3	57.2
1918	49.2	57.7	65.9	50.4	58.9	67.1
1919	53.4	61.1	70.2	54.9	62.6	71.6
1920	55.9	63.1	72.6	57.5	64.8	74.3

(continued)

Year on Which Moving Average Is Centered	Variant I			Variant III		
	Flow of Goods to Consumers (1)	Net National Product (2)	Gross National Product (3)	Flow of Goods to Consumers (4)	Net National Product (5)	Gross National Product (6)
1921	58.1	66.0	75.8	60.1	68.0	77.7
1922	60.5	67.6	77.3	62 9	70.0	79.7
1923	61.2	68.0	77.5	63.8	70.5	80.0
1924	64.1	72.4	82.1	66.8	75.1	84.8
1925	67.0	76.3	86.3	69.9	79.1	89.1
1926	69.3	78.3	88.5	72.3	81.3	91.5
1927	71.6	81.3	91.8	74.6	84.3	94.8
1928	73.0	81.6	92.2	75.4	84.0	94.6
1929	71.0	77.3	87.8	73.0	79.4	89.9
1930	66.4	69.9	80.0	68.2	71.7	81.9
1931	61.1	62.0	71.7	62.4	63.3	73.0
1932	56.0	54.5	63.7	56.8	55.3	64.6
1933	52.2	49.9	58.9	53.8	51.5	60.5
1934	51.8	50.4	59.4	54.2	52.8	61.8
1935	55.1	55.9	65.3	58.1	58.9	68.3
1936	58.4	60.6	70.5	62.0	64.1	74.1
1937	61.4	64.9	75.3	65.3	68.8	79.2
1938	64.8	69.8	80.7	68.6	73.6	84.5
1939	69.3	76.4	88.1	72.6	79.7	91.4
1940	74.2	83.1	95.9	77.1	86.0	98.8
1941	81.6	92.1	106.6	84.4	94.9	109.4
1942	90.2	101.0	117.9	93.1	103.8	120.7
1943	100.4	109.4	129.1	103.3	112.3	131.9
1944	113.4	121.5	143.9	116.6	124.6	147.0
1945	128.4	135.5	161.8	132.0	139.1	165.3
1946	143.7	150.8	181.4	147.8	155.0	185.6
1947	157.5	163.5	198.2	162.4	168.3	203.1
1948	171.5	180.4	219.4	177.2	186.1	225.1
1949	183.4	194.9	238.9	189.8	201.3	245.3
1950	193.7	207.5	254.7	200.7	214.5	261.7
1951	203.7	219.6	268.9	211.4	227.3	276.6
1952	214.4	233.9	284.8	222.8	242.3	293.2
1953	225.9	248.0	300.5	234.9	257.0	309.5

SOURCE, BY COLUMN

All entries are averages of annual series.

(1) and (4) 1871–1916: Calculated from the annual series for 1869–1918 derived as the sum of those described in the notes to Table R-27, cols. 1–4, and 5–8, respectively.

1917–1953: Calculated from the annual series for 1915–1918 described above, and those for 1919–1955 in Table R-1, cols. 1 and 3, respectively.

(2) and (5) 1871–1916: Calculated from the annual series for 1869–1918 derived as the sum of the series underlying col. 1 or 4, and that described in the notes to Table R-29, col. 3.

1917–1953: Calculated from the annual series for 1915–1918 described above, and that for 1919–1955 in Table R-1, cols. 4 and 6, respectively.

(3) and (6) 1871–1916: Calculated from the annual series for 1869–1918 derived as the sum of the series underlying col. 1 or 4, and that described in the notes to Table R-29, col. 1.

1917–1953: Calculated from the annual series for 1915–1918 described above, and that for 1919–1955 in Table R-1, cols. 7 and 9, respectively.

FIVE-YEAR MOVING AVERAGES OF FLOW OF GOODS TO CONSUMERS,
NET NATIONAL PRODUCT, AND GROSS NATIONAL PRODUCT,
VARIANTS I AND III, 1929 PRICES, 1869–1955
(billions of dollars)

Year on Which Moving Average Is Centered	Variant I			Variant III		
	Flow of Goods to Consumers (1)	Net National Product (2)	Gross National Product (3)	Flow of Goods to Consumers (4)	Net National Product (5)	Gross National Product (6)
1871	6.78	8.08	8.90	7.00	8.30	9.11
1872	7.22	8.59	9.47	7.45	8.82	9.70
1873	7.70	9.15	10.1	7.94	9.40	10.3
1874	8.26	9.88	10.9	8.53	10.1	11.2
1875	8.75	10.3	11.4	9.03	10.6	11.7
1876	9.28	10.9	12.1	9.57	11.2	12.4
1877	10.0	11.8	13.1	10.3	12.1	13.4
1878	11.1	13.1	14.5	11.4	13.5	14.8
1879	12.0	14.3	15.7	12.4	14.6	16.1
1880	13.1	15.5	17.0	13.4	15.9	17.4
1881	14.0	16.5	18.1	14.4	16.9	18.5
1882	14.7	17.3	19.0	15.2	17.7	19.5
1883	15.2	17.7	19.5	15.6	18.1	20.0
1884	15.7	18.2	20.2	16.2	18.7	20.7
1885	16.1	18.7	20.8	16.6	19.2	21.3
1886	16.4	19.0	21.3	16.9	19.6	21.8
1887	16.8	19.4	21.8	17.3	20.0	22.3
1888	17.1	20.1	22.6	17.6	20.6	23.1
1889	17.5	20.8	23.4	18.1	21.3	24.0
1890	18.1	21.8	24.6	18.6	22.3	25.1
1891	18.6	22.6	25.6	19.2	23.2	26.1
1892	18.9	23.0	26.2	19.5	23.6	26.7
1893	19.7	23.8	27.1	20.4	24.4	27.7
1894	20.3	24.3	27.6	20.9	24.9	28.3
1895	21.0	24.7	28.2	21.6	25.4	28.9
1896	21.7	25.6	29.2	22.4	26.3	29.9
1897	23.2	27.2	30.9	23.9	28.0	31.7
1898	24.2	28.4	32.3	25.0	29.2	33.0
1899	25.8	30.6	34.6	26.7	31.4	35.4
1900	27.2	32.2	36.4	28.1	33.2	37.3
1901	28.8	34.3	38.6	29.8	35.2	39.5
1902	30.0	35.5	40.0	31.1	36.6	41.0
1903	31.5	37.1	41.8	32.6	38.3	42.9
1904	33.0	39.0	43.8	34.3	40.2	45.0
1905	34.7	40.9	45.9	36.0	42.2	47.2
1906	35.5	41.3	46.6	36.9	42.7	47.9
1907	37.0	43.2	48.6	38.5	44.6	50.1
1908	38.3	44.5	50.2	39.9	46.1	51.8
1909	39.3	45.0	50.9	40.9	46.6	52.5
1910	40.3	45.9	52.1	42.0	47.6	53.7
1911	42.2	48.4	54.8	43.9	50.0	56.4
1912	43.1	48.5	55.2	44.8	50.2	56.9
1913	43.7	48.9	55.8	45.5	50.6	57.5
1914	44.7	50.8	57.9	46.6	52.6	59.7
1915	45.4	51.7	59.1	47.4	53.7	61.0

(continued)

Year on Which Moving Average Is Centered	Variant I			Variant III		
	Flow of Goods to Consumers (1)	Net National Product (2)	Gross National Product (3)	Flow of Goods to Consumers (4)	Net National Product (5)	Gross National Product (6)
1916	45.9	51.9	59.6	47.9	53.9	61.6
1917	47.0	54.3	62.3	49.2	56.4	64.5
1918	48.6	56.5	64.9	50.9	58.9	67.3
1919	49.9	56.5	65.1	52.4	59.0	67.7
1920	51.8	57.8	66.7	54.4	60.4	69.4
1921	54.6	61.2	70.4	57.4	64.0	73.2
1922	57.7	63.9	73.2	60.7	66.9	76.2
1923	60.2	66.9	76.3	63.3	70.0	79.4
1924	63.2	71.4	81.2	66.4	74.6	84.4
1925	66.0	75.2	85.3	69.4	78.6	88.6
1926	68.3	77.3	87.6	71.8	80.8	91.2
1927	70.6	80.3	90.9	74.1	83.8	94.4
1928	72.8	81.4	92.2	75.9	84.4	95.3
1929	72.8	79.4	90.3	76.0	82.6	93.4
1930	71.1	74.6	85.4	74.4	77.9	88.7
1931	69.1	69.5	80.2	72.2	72.6	83.3
1932	66.7	64.3	74.8	69.8	67.4	77.9
1933	65.0	62.1	72.5	69.2	66.4	76.7
1934	65.5	63.4	73.8	70.8	68.7	79.0
1935	68.4	69.2	79.8	74.4	75.1	85.7
1936	71.4	74.0	84.7	78.0	80.6	91.4
1937	74.6	79.1	90.1	81.7	86.1	97.2
1938	78.5	84.5	95.8	85.4	91.3	102.6
1939	82.5	90.7	102.4	88.8	97.0	108.7
1940	85.1	94.0	106.4	91.1	100.0	112.4
1941	88.2	97.8	111.4	94.3	104.0	117.5
1942	90.9	100.5	115.7	97.3	106.9	122.1
1943	94.1	101.7	118.8	100.8	108.4	125.5
1944	98.4	104.8	123.4	105.7	112.1	130.6
1945	103.6	108.8	129.0	111.4	116.7	136.8
1946	108.7	114.1	135.7	117.2	122.6	144.2
1947	113.8	117.8	140.6	122.9	126.9	149.7
1948	119.1	124.7	148.4	128.8	134.5	158.2
1949	122.2	128.2	153.3	132.3	138.4	163.5
1950	125.6	132.5	158.4	136.1	143.0	168.9
1951	129.8	137.0	163.3	140.6	147.9	174.1
1952	133.8	143.1	169.4	145.0	154.2	180.6
1953	138.4	148.5	175.0	149.9	160.0	186.5

SOURCE, BY COLUMN

All entries are averages of annual series.

(1) and (4) 1871–1916: Calculated from the annual series for 1869–1918 derived as the sum of those described in the notes to Table R-28, cols. 1–4, and 5–8, respectively.

1917–1953: Calculated from the annual series for 1915–1918 described above, and those for 1919–1955 in Table R-2, cols. 1 and 3, respectively.

(2) and (5) 1871–1916: Calculated from the annual series for 1869–1918 derived as the sum of the series underlying col. 1 or 4, and that described in the notes to Table R-29, col. 6.

1917–1953: Calculated from the annual series for 1915–1918 described above, and that for 1919–1955 in Table R-2, cols. 4 and 6, respectively.

(3) and (6) 1871–1916: Calculated from the annual series for 1869–1918 derived as the sum of the series underlying col. 1 or 4, and that described in the notes to Table R-29, col. 4.

1917–1953: Calculated from the annual series for 1915–1918 described above, and that for 1919–1955 in Table R-2, cols. 7 and 9, respectively.

FIVE-YEAR MOVING AVERAGES OF COMPONENTS OF FLOW OF GOODS TO CONSUMERS,
VARIANTS I AND III, CURRENT PRICES, 1869–1955

(billions of dollars)

Year on Which Moving Average Is Centered	Variant I				Variant III			
	Perishables (1)	Semidurables (2)	Durables (3)	Services (4)	Perishables (5)	Semidurables (6)	Durables (7)	Services (8)
1871	2.33	1.17	0.47	1.33	2.29	1.01	0.50	1.59
1872	2.43	1.20	0.48	1.38	2.38	1.03	0.51	1.64
1873	2.53	1.22	0.50	1.44	2.48	1.06	0.53	1.72
1874	2.63	1.21	0.50	1.50	2.58	1.05	0.53	1.78
1875	2.75	1.18	0.49	1.55	2.70	1.02	0.51	1.85
1876	2.81	1.17	0.47	1.61	2.76	1.01	0.49	1.92
1877	2.84	1.19	0.47	1.70	2.78	1.03	0.50	2.02
1878	3.08	1.30	0.50	1.84	3.02	1.12	0.53	2.19
1879	3.30	1.39	0.54	1.95	3.24	1.20	0.56	2.33
1880	3.61	1.49	0.58	2.08	3.53	1.29	0.61	2.48
1881	3.92	1.60	0.63	2.20	3.84	1.38	0.67	2.62
1882	4.20	1.64	0.67	2.29	4.12	1.42	0.70	2.73
1883	4.20	1.62	0.68	2.34	4.12	1.39	0.72	2.78
1884	4.18	1.63	0.70	2.40	4.09	1.41	0.74	2.85
1885	4.08	1.62	0.72	2.43	4.00	1.40	0.76	2.90
1886	4.01	1.64	0.74	2.47	3.93	1.41	0.78	2.94
1887	4.00	1.69	0.77	2.51	3.92	1.46	0.81	2.99
1888	4.04	1.74	0.80	2.54	3.96	1.50	0.85	3.02
1889	4.18	1.78	0.83	2.59	4.09	1.54	0.87	3.08
1890	4.25	1.84	0.86	2.64	4.16	1.59	0.90	3.14
1891	4.42	1.85	0.86	2.68	4.33	1.59	0.91	3.19
1892	4.42	1.79	0.84	2.70	4.33	1.55	0.88	3.21
1893	4.54	1.76	0.82	2.78	4.45	1.52	0.87	3.31
1894	4.53	1.72	0.80	2.84	4.44	1.48	0.84	3.38
1895	4.62	1.69	0.77	2.92	4.53	1.46	0.82	3.48
1896	4.66	1.70	0.78	3.03	4.56	1.47	0.82	3.61
1897	4.93	1.82	0.85	3.24	4.83	1.57	0.89	3.86
1898	5.22	1.93	0.90	3.43	5.11	1.67	0.95	4.08
1899	5.72	2.08	0.98	3.73	5.60	1.79	1.03	4.44
1900	6.18	2.22	1.06	4.02	6.06	1.91	1.12	4.79
1901	6.66	2.40	1.16	4.38	6.52	2.06	1.22	5.22
1902	7.06	2.51	1.22	4.71	6.92	2.17	1.29	5.60
1903	7.45	2.66	1.31	5.08	7.30	2.29	1.39	6.05
1904	7.84	2.88	1.44	5.48	7.68	2.49	1.52	6.53
1905	8.34	3.10	1.56	5.92	8.17	2.67	1.64	7.05
1906	8.64	3.23	1.61	6.25	8.46	2.79	1.69	7.44
1907	9.16	3.46	1.72	6.69	8.97	2.98	1.81	7.97
1908	9.75	3.61	1.82	7.10	9.55	3.11	1.92	8.46
1909	10.2	3.71	1.87	7.47	10.0	3.20	1.97	8.90
1910	10.7	3.86	1.96	7.84	10.5	3.32	2.07	9.34

(continued)

Year on Which Moving Average Is Centered	Variant I				Variant III			
	Perish-ables (1)	Semi-durables (2)	Durables (3)	Services (4)	Perish-ables (5)	Semi-durables (6)	Durables (7)	Services (8)
1911	11.4	4.09	2.15	8.32	11.2	3.53	2.26	9.91
1912	11.8	4.17	2.23	8.71	11.6	3.60	2.36	10.4
1913	12.0	4.24	2.31	9.15	11.8	3.66	2.44	10.9
1914	12.8	4.56	2.58	9.81	12.5	3.93	2.72	11.7
1915	14.3	5.19	2.90	10.6	14.0	4.48	3.06	12.6
1916	16.6	6.18	3.16	11.6	16.2	5.33	3.34	13.8
1917	19.0	7.35	3.79	12.4	18.6	6.34	3.99	14.8
1918	21.9	8.88	4.55	13.8	21.5	7.65	4.80	16.5
1919	23.3	9.66	4.88	15.6	22.9	8.33	5.15	18.5
1920	23.6	10.1	5.20	17.0	23.1	8.74	5.49	20.2
1921	23.4	10.5	5.84	18.5	22.9	9.02	6.16	22.0
1922	23.2	10.5	6.16	20.6	22.7	9.09	6.50	24.6
1923	22.8	10.4	6.51	21.5	22.3	8.97	6.87	25.6
1924	23.8	10.8	7.16	22.4	23.3	9.31	7.56	26.7
1925	24.8	11.2	7.65	23.4	24.3	9.63	8.07	27.9
1926	25.6	11.3	7.88	24.4	25.1	9.76	8.31	29.1
1927	26.6	11.6	8.23	25.2	26.0	10.0	8.68	29.9
1928	26.7	11.5	7.99	26.8	26.1	9.91	8.42	31.0
1929	25.7	11.0	7.36	27.0	25.1	9.46	7.76	30.7
1930	24.0	9.95	6.46	26.0	23.4	8.58	6.82	29.4
1931	22.1	8.85	5.53	24.6	21.5	7.58	5.79	27.4
1932	20.7	7.91	4.58	22.8	20.2	6.76	4.79	25.1
1933	20.2	7.38	4.20	20.4	19.7	6.32	4.38	23.5
1934	21.2	7.35	4.37	18.9	20.5	6.26	4.55	22.9
1935	23.3	7.86	5.00	19.0	22.6	6.68	5.20	23.6
1936	25.1	8.36	5.39	19.6	24.4	7.16	5.65	24.8
1937	26.5	8.78	5.86	20.3	25.8	7.52	6.14	25.9
1938	27.7	9.20	6.37	21.5	27.0	7.88	6.67	27.0
1939	29.3	9.83	7.01	23.2	28.5	8.42	7.34	28.3
1940	31.6	11.0	7.02	24.6	30.8	9.40	7.35	29.6
1941	35.2	12.8	7.19	26.4	34.3	10.9	7.54	31.6
1942	39.6	14.8	7.21	28.6	38.6	12.7	7.55	34.3
1943	44.8	17.4	7.27	31.0	43.6	14.9	7.62	37.2
1944	51.0	20.0	8.46	34.0	49.6	17.1	8.87	41.0
1945	57.6	22.2	11.1	37.5	56.1	19.0	11.6	45.3
1946	64.2	24.0	14.0	41.5	62.4	20.5	14.7	50.1
1947	69.7	25.1	17.3	45.5	67.8	21.5	18.1	55.0
1948	74.6	25.8	21.2	49.9	72.6	22.1	22.2	60.3
1949	79.6	26.3	23.3	54.2	77.5	22.6	24.4	65.4
1950	83.9	26.8	24.5	58.4	81.7	23.0	25.6	70.4
1951	87.9	27.1	25.9	62.9	85.5	23.2	27.2	75.6
1952	92.4	27.6	27.0	67.5	89.9	23.6	28.3	81.0
1953	97.0	28.3	28.4	72.2	94.4	24.3	29.7	86.5

SOURCE, BY COLUMN

All entries are averages of annual series.

(1) 1871–1916: Calculated from the annual series for 1869–1918 derived by multiplying the 1929 price series (see notes to Table R-28, col. 1) by the price index implicit in output for domestic consumption. Output for domestic consumption, in current and 1929 prices, was estimated by the method described in the notes to Kuznets, *National Product since 1869*, Table II-1, cols. 1 and 2, except that a further adjustment was made for 1904–1918 to exclude gasoline and lubricating oils consumed by passenger cars used for business (see notes to Table R-13, cols. 1–3).

1917–1953: Calculated from the annual series for 1915–1918 described above, and that for 1919–1955 in Table R-3, col. 1.

(2) 1871–1916: Calculated from the annual series for 1869–1918 derived by multiplying the 1929 price series (see notes to Table R-28, col. 2) by the price index implicit in output for domestic consumption. Output for domestic consumption, in current and 1929 prices, was estimated by the method described in the notes to *National Product since 1869*, Table II-2, cols. 1 and 2, except that a further adjustment was made for 1904–1918 to exclude tires and tubes for passenger cars used for business (see notes to Table R-13, cols. 1–3).

1917–1953: Calculated from the annual series for 1915–1918 described above, and that for 1919–1955 in Table R-3, col. 2.

(3) 1871–1916: Calculated from the annual series for 1869–1918 derived by multiplying the 1929 price series (see notes to Table R-28, col. 3) by the price index implicit in output for domestic consumption. Output for domestic consumption, in current and 1929 prices, was estimated by the method described in the notes to *National Product since 1869*, Table II-3, cols. 1 and 2, except that a further adjustment was made for 1899–1918 to exclude passenger cars used for business (see notes to Table R-13, cols. 1–3).

1917–1953: Calculated from the annual series for 1915–1918 described above, and that for 1919–1955 in Table R-3, col. 3.

(4) 1871–1916: Calculated from the annual series for 1869–1918 derived by multiplying the 1929 price series (see notes to Table R-28, col. 4) by a price index obtained as follows.

1. The implicit annual price index for services, 1919–1941, was derived from Table R-3, cols. 4 and 8.

2. The implicit decade average price index for services, 1869–1878 through 1934–1943, was derived from Table R-13, cols. 4 and 8, centered at the mid-point for each decade, and interpolated along a straight line.

3. Deviations of the annual indexes derived in step 1 from those derived in step 2 were computed.

4. The implicit annual price index for consumer commodities was derived for 1919–1941 from Table R-3, cols. 1–3 and 5–7, and for 1869–1918 from the annual series underlying cols. 1–3 of the present table and cols. 1–3 of Table R-28.

5. The implicit decade average price index for consumer commodities was derived for 1869–1878 through 1914–1923 from decade averages of the annual series underlying cols. 1–3 of the present table, and cols. 1–3 of

(Notes on following page)

Appendix C

(4)   Table R-28, and for 1914–1923 through 1934–1943 from Table R-13, cols. 1–3 and 5–7, and interpolated along a straight line.

6. Deviations of the annual indexes derived in step 4 from those derived in step 5 were computed.

7. The regression line of deviations in step 3 on deviations in step 6 for 1919–1941 was computed, yielding the equation, $y = 0.633464 + 0.107464x$.

8. By means of the equation in step 7 and deviations in step 6 for 1869–1918, deviations corresponding to those in step 3 were derived.

9. Deviations in step 8 were subtracted from the indexes described in step 2 for 1869–1918, yielding a preliminary annual price index for services. This price index was adjusted as follows: The annual 1929 price series (see notes to Table R-28, col. 4) was multiplied by the preliminary price index just described, yielding a preliminary series in current prices. Ten-year averages of this series were computed for the overlapping decades, and a preliminary implicit price index for the decades derived; the ratio of the price index for decades described in step 2 to this preliminary index was computed, interpolated along a straight line, and applied to the preliminary price index to yield the final annual price index by which the 1929 price values were converted to current prices.

1917–1953: Calculated from the annual series for 1915–1918 described above, and that for 1919–1955 in Table R-3, col. 4.

(5)–(7) 1871–1916: Calculated from the annual series for 1869–1918 derived by multiplying the Variant I estimate (see notes to cols. 1–3) by the 1929–1931 ratio of the Variant III to the Variant I estimate. See notes to lines 1–10, Table R-18, cols. 2–4.

1917–1953: Calculated from the annual series for 1915–1918 described above, and those for 1919–1955 in Table R-9, cols. 2–4.

(8) 1871–1916: Calculated from the annual series for 1869–1918 derived as follows: the 1929–1931 ratio of the Variant III to the Variant II estimate (see notes to Table R-18, col. 5, lines 1–10) applied to the Variant II estimate derived annually by the procedure for 1919–1928 outlined in the notes to Table R-9, col. 1.

1917–1953: Calculated from the annual series for 1915–1918 described above, and that for 1919–1955 in Table R-9, col. 5.

FIVE-YEAR MOVING AVERAGES OF COMPONENTS OF FLOW OF GOODS TO CONSUMERS,
VARIANTS I AND III, 1929 PRICES, 1869–1955
(billions of dollars)

Year on Which Moving Average Is Centered	Variant I				Variant III			
	Perish- ables (1)	Semi- durables (2)	Durables (3)	Services (4)	Perish- ables (5)	Semi- durables (6)	Durables (7)	Services (8)
1871	2.83	1.38	0.60	1.98	2.78	1.22	0.64	2.35
1872	3.06	1.44	0.62	2.10	3.01	1.27	0.67	2.50
1873	3.28	1.51	0.67	2.24	3.22	1.33	0.72	2.67
1874	3.58	1.56	0.72	2.40	3.52	1.37	0.77	2.86
1875	3.84	1.62	0.75	2.53	3.77	1.43	0.81	3.02
1876	4.11	1.71	0.78	2.68	4.04	1.51	0.84	3.18
1877	4.43	1.86	0.85	2.86	4.36	1.64	0.91	3.41
1878	5.00	2.06	0.91	3.14	4.92	1.82	0.98	3.73
1879	5.46	2.22	0.99	3.37	5.37	1.96	1.07	4.02
1880	5.96	2.39	1.08	3.62	5.86	2.11	1.16	4.32
1881	6.39	2.55	1.17	3.85	6.28	2.25	1.26	4.59
1882	6.80	2.64	1.23	4.04	6.69	2.33	1.32	4.82
1883	6.99	2.70	1.30	4.17	6.87	2.38	1.40	4.96
1884	7.18	2.82	1.40	4.31	7.06	2.49	1.50	5.14
1885	7.28	2.89	1.49	4.42	7.16	2.55	1.60	5.26
1886	7.36	2.97	1.58	4.52	7.24	2.62	1.70	5.38
1887	7.41	3.10	1.67	4.62	7.28	2.74	1.80	5.50
1888	7.40	3.20	1.76	4.70	7.28	2.83	1.89	5.59
1889	7.58	3.30	1.81	4.81	7.46	2.92	1.95	5.73
1890	7.80	3.44	1.88	4.95	7.67	3.03	2.02	5.89
1891	8.15	3.49	1.90	5.08	8.01	3.08	2.04	6.05
1892	8.39	3.50	1.89	5.17	8.24	3.09	2.03	6.15
1893	8.85	3.59	1.93	5.38	8.70	3.17	2.08	6.41
1894	9.14	3.64	1.96	5.54	8.99	3.21	2.11	6.60
1895	9.52	3.71	2.00	5.76	9.36	3.28	2.15	6.86
1896	9.83	3.85	2.07	6.00	9.66	3.39	2.23	7.15
1897	10.4	4.10	2.25	6.42	10.2	3.62	2.42	7.65
1898	10.9	4.24	2.32	6.76	10.7	3.74	2.50	8.05
1899	11.6	4.49	2.43	7.28	11.4	3.96	2.62	8.67
1900	12.2	4.72	2.54	7.75	12.0	4.17	2.73	9.23
1901	12.9	5.01	2.66	8.32	12.6	4.42	2.86	9.90
1902	13.3	5.20	2.70	8.79	13.1	4.59	2.91	10.5
1903	13.8	5.45	2.84	9.35	13.6	4.81	3.06	11.1
1904	14.4	5.68	3.04	9.94	14.1	5.02	3.27	11.8
1905	15.1	5.86	3.16	10.6	14.9	5.18	3.40	12.6
1906	15.3	5.99	3.17	11.0	15.1	5.29	3.41	13.1
1907	15.8	6.23	3.34	11.6	15.6	5.50	3.59	13.8
1908	16.4	6.37	3.45	12.1	16.1	5.62	3.72	14.4
1909	16.8	6.56	3.47	12.5	16.5	5.79	3.74	14.9
1910	17.1	6.84	3.58	12.8	16.8	6.03	3.85	15.3

(continued)

Year on Which Moving Average Is Centered	Variant I				Variant III			
	Perish-ables (1)	Semi-durables (2)	Durables (3)	Services (4)	Perish-ables (5)	Semi-durables (6)	Durables (7)	Services (8)
1911	17.9	7.16	3.79	13.3	17.6	6.32	4.08	15.9
1912	18.4	7.31	3.80	13.6	18.1	6.45	4.09	16.2
1913	18.6	7.45	3.80	13.9	18.3	6.58	4.10	16.5
1914	18.8	7.61	4.02	14.3	18.5	6.72	4.33	17.0
1915	18.9	7.58	4.18	14.7	18.6	6.70	4.50	17.6
1916	19.1	7.46	4.17	15.2	18.8	6.58	4.49	18.1
1917	19.3	7.46	4.43	15.8	18.9	6.59	4.77	18.9
1918	19.8	7.32	4.66	16.8	19.5	6.46	5.02	20.0
1919	20.4	7.30	4.50	17.7	20.0	6.44	4.85	21.1
1920	21.1	7.58	4.57	18.6	20.7	6.69	4.92	22.1
1921	21.8	8.10	5.12	19.6	21.4	7.14	5.52	23.3
1922	22.8	8.40	5.51	20.9	22.5	7.41	5.93	24.9
1923	23.7	9.09	6.08	21.4	23.3	8.02	6.55	25.5
1924	24.6	9.52	7.01	22.1	24.1	8.40	7.55	26.3
1925	25.4	10.0	7.63	23.0	25.0	8.82	8.22	27.4
1926	26.0	10.3	7.99	24.0	25.6	9.08	8.60	28.6
1927	26.6	10.8	8.35	24.8	26.1	9.57	8.95	29.5
1928	27.0	11.0	8.18	26.6	26.4	9.68	8.77	31.0
1929	27.0	11.1	7.60	27.1	26.6	9.77	8.18	31.5
1930	26.8	10.7	6.82	26.7	26.3	9.44	7.39	31.3
1931	26.9	10.2	5.98	26.0	25.9	8.94	6.53	30.7
1932	26.8	9.64	5.21	25.1	25.8	8.42	5.76	29.8
1933	27.0	9.44	5.04	23.4	26.0	8.24	5.60	29.4
1934	28.2	9.47	5.39	22.4	26.9	8.24	5.95	29.6
1935	29.8	9.68	6.11	22.8	28.5	8.45	6.70	30.7
1936	31.3	10.1	6.56	23.4	30.2	8.84	7.17	31.8
1937	32.9	10.7	7.11	23.9	31.8	9.33	7.76	32.8
1938	34.7	11.2	7.65	25.0	33.5	9.78	8.35	33.8
1939	36.2	11.7	8.17	26.4	34.9	10.2	8.92	34.7
1940	37.6	12.2	7.90	27.4	36.3	10.7	8.62	35.5
1941	39.0	13.0	7.73	28.5	37.6	11.4	8.44	36.9
1942	40.6	13.6	7.22	29.5	39.2	11.9	7.89	38.4
1943	42.7	14.1	6.63	30.6	41.2	12.4	7.24	40.0
1944	44.9	14.6	6.84	32.1	43.3	12.7	7.47	42.1
1945	46.8	14.8	8.20	33.8	45.2	12.9	8.96	44.4
1946	48.7	14.7	9.84	35.5	47.0	12.9	10.7	46.6
1947	50.2	14.7	11.7	37.2	48.4	12.9	12.8	48.9
1948	51.2	14.6	14.1	39.2	49.4	12.8	15.4	51.3
1949	51.9	14.4	15.0	40.8	50.1	12.6	16.4	53.3
1950	53.1	14.5	15.4	42.6	51.2	12.7	16.8	55.4
1951	54.7	14.7	16.1	44.4	52.8	12.8	17.6	57.4
1952	56.2	14.8	16.7	46.1	54.2	12.9	18.2	59.6
1953	58.0	15.0	17.4	47.9	56.0	13.2	19.0	61.7

All entries are averages of annual series.

(1)–(3) 1871–1916: Calculated from the annual series for 1869–1918 derived by interpolating between or extrapolating from the decade averages in Table R-13, cols. 5–7, on the basis of the annual series on output for domestic consumption in 1929 prices, described in the notes to Table R-27, cols. 1–3. The ratios of the decade averages of flow to the decade averages of output were computed and centered at the mid-points of the decades. Annual ratios were interpolated along a straight line, and applied to the annual output figures.

1917–1953: Calculated from the annual series for 1915–1918 described above, and those for 1919–1955 in Table R-3, cols. 5–7.

(4) 1871–1916: Calculated from the annual series for 1869–1918 derived as follows.

1. For the period from 1869 to 1943 the decade averages in Table R-13, col. 8, were centered at the mid-points of the decades and annual estimates were interpolated along a straight line.

2. For 1919–1941 deviations of the annual estimates in Table R-3, col. 8, from those derived in step 1 were computed.

3. Step 1 was carried through for consumer commodities from the decade averages in Table R-13, cols. 5–7.

4. For 1869–1941 step 2 was carried through for consumer commodities, from the annual series underlying cols. 1–3 of the present table.

5. For 1919–1941 the regression line of deviations in step 2 on deviations in step 4 was computed, yielding the equation, $y = -18.809 + 0.304053x$.

6. By means of the equation in step 5 and the deviations for 1869–1918 in step 4, deviations for 1869–1918 corresponding to those in step 2 were derived.

7. Deviations derived in step 6 were subtracted from the estimates in step 1, yielding a preliminary annual series for services in 1929 prices. The ratios of the decade averages in Table R-13, col. 8 to the ten-year averages of the preliminary annual series were computed, and centered at the mid-points of the decades. Annual ratios were interpolated along a straight line between those points, and applied to the preliminary annual series to yield the final annual series for services.

1917–1953: Calculated from the annual series for 1915–1918 described above, and that for 1919–1955 in Table R-3, col. 8.

(5)–(7) 1871–1916: Calculated from the annual series for 1869–1918 derived by multiplying the Variant I estimate (see notes to cols. 1–3) by the 1929–1931 ratio of the Variant III to the Variant I estimate. See notes to Table R-19, lines 1–10, cols. 2–4.

1917–1953: Calculated from the annual series for 1915–1918 described above, and those for 1919–1955 in Table R-10, cols. 2–4.

(8) 1871–1916: Calculated from the annual series for 1869–1918 derived by dividing the current price series (see notes to Table R-27, col. 8) by the price index implicit in the Variant I estimate.

1917–1953: Calculated from the annual series for 1915–1918 described above, and that for 1919–1955 in Table R-10, col. 5.

TABLE R-29

FIVE-YEAR MOVING AVERAGES OF CAPITAL FORMATION AND CAPITAL CONSUMPTION,
CURRENT AND 1929 PRICES, 1869–1955

(billions of dollars)

Year on Which Moving Average Is Centered	Current Prices			1929 Prices		
	Gross Capital Formation (1)	Capital Consumption (2)	Net Capital Formation (3)	Gross Capital Formation (4)	Capital Consumption (5)	Net Capital Formation (6)
1871	1.34	0.51	0.82	2.11	0.81	1.30
1872	1.40	0.55	0.85	2.25	0.88	1.37
1873	1.47	0.58	0.89	2.40	0.95	1.45
1874	1.59	0.62	0.97	2.63	1.02	1.62
1875	1.55	0.63	0.92	2.70	1.10	1.60
1876	1.52	0.63	0.89	2.83	1.18	1.65
1877	1.58	0.64	0.94	3.07	1.26	1.81
1878	1.72	0.67	1.06	3.36	1.34	2.02
1879	1.86	0.70	1.16	3.66	1.43	2.23
1880	2.01	0.76	1.26	3.94	1.53	2.42
1881	2.13	0.82	1.31	4.14	1.64	2.51
1882	2.22	0.88	1.34	4.31	1.75	2.57
1883	2.18	0.93	1.25	4.36	1.86	2.50
1884	2.21	0.98	1.23	4.50	1.97	2.52
1885	2.24	1.02	1.22	4.71	2.09	2.62
1886	2.26	1.07	1.19	4.83	2.22	2.62
1887	2.31	1.14	1.17	4.98	2.35	2.63
1888	2.56	1.20	1.36	5.54	2.50	3.05
1889	2.69	1.25	1.44	5.90	2.66	3.24
1890	2.92	1.29	1.63	6.53	2.82	3.71
1891	3.04	1.33	1.72	6.93	2.97	3.96
1892	3.10	1.34	1.76	7.22	3.12	4.10
1893	3.06	1.36	1.71	7.33	3.25	4.08
1894	3.01	1.37	1.63	7.35	3.37	3.98
1895	2.91	1.40	1.51	7.23	3.49	3.74
1896	3.00	1.45	1.55	7.43	3.61	3.82
1897	3.22	1.54	1.69	7.76	3.73	4.03
1898	3.48	1.64	1.84	8.09	3.86	4.22
1899	3.89	1.76	2.13	8.73	4.00	4.73
1900	4.23	1.88	2.35	9.20	4.15	5.06
1901	4.56	1.99	2.58	9.71	4.30	5.41
1902	4.71	2.08	2.63	9.95	4.46	5.49
1903	4.91	2.19	2.72	10.3	4.63	5.65
1904	5.29	2.33	2.96	10.8	4.82	5.94
1905	5.67	2.50	3.17	11.2	5.02	6.15

(continued)

Year on Which Moving Average Is Centered	Current Prices			1929 Prices		
	Gross Capital Formation (1)	Capital Consumption (2)	Net Capital Formation (3)	Gross Capital Formation (4)	Capital Consumption (5)	Net Capital Formation (6)
1906	5.69	2.66	3.02	11.1	5.24	5.82
1907	6.14	2.84	3.30	11.6	5.47	6.16
1908	6.42	3.02	3.40	11.9	5.70	6.20
1909	6.35	3.20	3.15	11.7	5.94	5.71
1910	6.48	3.36	3.12	11.8	6.17	5.59
1911	7.11	3.56	3.55	12.6	6.40	6.18
1912	6.84	3.74	3.09	12.0	6.64	5.40
1913	6.94	3.96	2.98	12.0	6.87	5.15
1914	8.05	4.26	3.80	13.1	7.10	6.05
1915	9.22	4.80	4.42	13.7	7.35	6.31
1916	10.5	5.71	4.79	13.6	7.64	6.00
1917	13.5	6.86	6.63	15.3	8.04	7.29
1918	16.7	8.19	8.47	16.4	8.41	7.94
1919	16.7	9.04	7.68	15.2	8.66	6.58
1920	16.7	9.51	7.23	14.9	8.94	5.98
1921	17.6	9.73	7.90	15.9	9.19	6.68
1922	16.8	9.71	7.11	15.5	9.29	6.21
1923	16.2	9.48	6.76	16.1	9.46	6.65
1924	18.0	9.71	8.30	18.0	9.83	8.19
1925	19.2	10.0	9.23	19.2	10.1	9.15
1926	19.2	10.2	9.03	19.4	10.3	9.03
1927	20.2	10.5	9.70	20.3	10.6	9.71
1928	19.2	10.6	8.54	19.4	10.8	8.57
1929	16.8	10.5	6.35	17.4	10.9	6.58
1930	13.6	10.1	3.48	14.3	10.8	3.49
1931	10.6	9.69	0.90	11.1	10.7	0.41
1932	7.72	9.29	−1.57	8.08	10.5	−2.43
1933	6.68	9.00	−2.32	7.50	10.4	−2.89
1934	7.60	8.98	−1.38	8.28	10.4	−2.11
1935	10.2	9.42	0.79	11.3	10.6	0.76
1936	12.1	9.97	2.10	13.4	10.8	2.60
1937	13.9	10.4	3.50	15.5	11.0	4.48
1938	15.9	10.9	4.98	17.2	11.3	5.93
1939	18.8	11.7	7.14	19.9	11.7	8.18
1940	21.7	12.8	8.87	21.3	12.4	8.86
1941	25.0	14.5	10.4	23.2	13.5	9.67
1942	27.7	16.9	10.7	24.7	15.1	9.60

(continued)

Year on Which Moving Average Is Centered	Current Prices			1929 Prices		
	Gross Capital Formation (1)	Capital Consumption (2)	Net Capital Formation (3)	Gross Capital Formation (4)	Capital Consumption (5)	Net Capital Formation (6)
1943	28.7	19.7	9.00	24.7	17.1	7.65
1944	30.5	22.5	8.02	25.0	18.6	6.37
1945	33.3	26.2	7.08	25.4	20.2	5.24
1946	37.8	30.6	7.19	27.0	21.6	5.39
1947	40.7	34.8	5.99	26.8	22.8	4.00
1948	47.9	39.0	8.89	29.4	23.7	5.62
1949	55.5	44.1	11.4	31.2	25.1	6.09
1950	61.0	47.2	13.8	32.7	25.8	6.90
1951	65.2	49.3	15.9	33.5	26.2	7.24
1952	70.4	50.9	19.5	35.6	26.4	9.22
1953	74.6	52.5	22.1	36.6	26.5	10.1

The series are identical for Variants I and III.

(Notes on following page)

Appendix C

SOURCE, BY COLUMN

All entries are averages of annual series.

(1) 1871–1916: Calculated from the annual series for 1869–1918 derived as the sum of the series described in the notes to Table R-30, col. 5, Table R-33, col. 1, and Table R-34, cols. 1 and 3.

1917–1953: Calculated from the annual series for 1915–1918 described above, and that for 1919–1955 in Table R-4, col. 5.

(2) 1871–1916: Calculated from the annual series for 1869–1918 derived as the sum of the series described in the notes to Table R-31, col. 5, and Table R-33, col. 2.

1917–1953: Calculated from the annual series for 1915–1918 described above, and that for 1919–1955 in Table R-8, col. 3.

(3) 1871–1916: Calculated from the annual series for 1869–1918 derived by subtracting capital consumption (see notes to col. 2) from gross capital formation (see notes to col. 1).

1917–1953: Calculated from the annual series for 1915–1918 described above, and that for 1919–1955 in Table R-4, col. 7.

(4) 1871–1916: Calculated from the annual series for 1869–1918 derived as the sum of the series described in the notes to Table R-30, col. 10, Table R-33, col. 4, and Table R-34, cols. 2 and 4.

1917–1953: Calculated from the annual series for 1915–1918 described above, and that for 1919–1955 in Table R-5, col. 5.

(5) 1871–1916: Calculated from the annual series for 1869–1918 derived as the sum of those described in the notes to Table R-31, col. 10, and Table R-33, col. 5.

1917–1953: Calculated from the annual series for 1915–1918 described above, and that for 1919–1955 in Table R-8, col. 6.

(6) 1871–1916: Calculated from the annual series for 1869–1918 derived by subtracting capital consumption (see notes to col. 5) from gross capital formation (see notes to col. 4).

1917–1953: Calculated from the annual series for 1915–1918 described above, and that for 1919–1955 in Table R-5, col. 7.

TABLE R-30

FIVE-YEAR MOVING AVERAGES OF GROSS CONSTRUCTION, BY TYPE OF CONSTRUCTION, CURRENT AND 1929 PRICES, 1869–1955

(billions of dollars)

YEAR ON WHICH MOVING AVERAGE IS CENTERED	CURRENT PRICES					1929 PRICES				
	Nonfarm Residential (1)	Government		Other (4)	Total (5)	Nonfarm Residential (6)	Government		Other (9)	Total (10)
		Excluding Military (2)	Military (3)				Excluding Military (7)	Military (8)		
1871	0.22	0.06		0.50	0.77	0.47	0.11		0.92	1.50
1872	0.22	0.06		0.52	0.81	0.49	0.12		0.97	1.58
1873	0.23	0.06		0.56	0.86	0.51	0.13		1.05	1.69
1874	0.25	0.07		0.59	0.90	0.55	0.13		1.13	1.82
1875	0.26	0.07		0.54	0.87	0.62	0.14		1.06	1.82
1876	0.28	0.06		0.48	0.83	0.71	0.14		0.99	1.84
1877	0.29	0.06		0.47	0.82	0.75	0.15		1.00	1.90
1878	0.30	0.07		0.47	0.83	0.79	0.15		1.01	1.95
1879	0.31	0.07		0.52	0.91	0.82	0.16		1.14	2.12
1880	0.33	0.08		0.59	1.00	0.84	0.17		1.27	2.29
1881	0.35	0.08		0.68	1.11	0.87	0.18		1.42	2.47
1882	0.40	0.09		0.74	1.23	0.99	0.19		1.52	2.70
1883	0.48	0.09		0.75	1.32	1.18	0.20		1.52	2.90
1884	0.57	0.10		0.74	1.40	1.41	0.21		1.47	3.09
1885	0.67	0.10		0.73	1.50	1.68	0.22		1.44	3.33

Year								
1886	0.73	0.10	0.74	1.56	1.83	0.23	1.45	3.51
1887	0.79	0.11	0.70	1.60	2.02	0.24	1.36	3.62
1888	0.83	0.11	0.86	1.81	2.12	0.25	1.72	4.09
1889	0.81	0.12	0.98	1.91	2.09	0.27	2.01	4.37
1890	0.81	0.12	1.18	2.11	2.09	0.28	2.53	4.90
1891	0.79	0.13	1.30	2.22	2.09	0.30	2.84	5.22
1892	0.75	0.13	1.43	2.31	2.01	0.32	3.21	5.54
1893	0.72	0.14	1.41	2.27	2.00	0.33	3.24	5.57
1894	0.72	0.14	1.35	2.21	2.02	0.34	3.14	5.51
1895	0.70	0.14	1.25	2.09	1.98	0.36	2.95	5.30
1896	0.70	0.15	1.20	2.05	1.98	0.37	2.90	5.25
1897	0.70	0.16	1.19	2.04	1.95	0.39	2.82	5.16
1898	0.65	0.17	1.28	2.10	1.77	0.41	2.98	5.16
1899	0.65	0.18	1.43	2.26	1.72	0.43	3.30	5.46
1900	0.63	0.20	1.64	2.47	1.61	0.46	3.68	5.75
1901	0.64	0.22	1.82	2.68	1.58	0.50	3.98	6.05
1902	0.66	0.25	1.96	2.87	1.59	0.55	4.26	6.40
1903	0.82	0.28	1.95	3.04	1.91	0.61	4.17	6.69
1904	0.93	0.31	2.05	3.29	2.10	0.65	4.21	6.96
1905	1.03	0.35	2.15	3.54	2.23	0.71	4.23	7.18
1906	1.13	0.40	2.18	3.71	2.38	0.79	4.19	7.35
1907	1.25	0.43	2.32	4.00	2.55	0.83	4.34	7.72
1908	1.22	0.46	2.53	4.22	2.41	0.88	4.69	7.97
1909	1.19	0.50	2.56	4.25	2.30	0.95	4.73	7.99
1910	1.20	0.53	2.56	4.30	2.31	0.99	4.73	8.03

(continued)

TABLE R-30 (concluded)

YEAR ON WHICH MOVING AVERAGE IS CENTERED	CURRENT PRICES					1929 PRICES				
	Nonfarm Residential (1)	Government Excluding Military (2)	Military (3)	Other (4)	Total (5)	Nonfarm Residential (6)	Government Excluding Military (7)	Military (8)	Other (9)	Total (10)
1911	1.22	0.55	a	2.75	4.51	2.31	1.01		4.98	8.31
1912	1.17	0.58		2.60	4.35	2.23	1.06	0.01	4.66	7.95
1913	1.21	0.62	0.01	2.34	4.17	2.28	1.12	0.01	4.16	7.58
1914	1.26	0.64	0.01	2.27	4.17	2.34	1.12	0.02	3.92	7.40
1915	1.19	0.66	0.13	2.21	4.19	2.15	1.09	0.17	3.55	6.96
1916	1.04	0.68	0.44	2.05	4.22	1.81	1.02	0.52	2.98	6.32
1917	1.09	0.73	0.66	2.30	4.77	1.66	0.95	0.72	2.92	6.24
1918	1.07	0.82	0.69	2.83	5.41	1.38	0.87	0.74	3.08	6.05
1919	1.19	0.99	0.69	2.98	5.85	1.31	0.92	0.74	2.99	5.96
1920	1.64	1.19	0.58	3.12	6.52	1.76	1.08	0.59	3.07	6.50
1921	2.38	1.37	0.27	3.42	7.45	2.49	1.21	0.25	3.34	7.30
1922	3.06	1.57	0.05	3.64	8.32	3.18	1.39	0.04	3.58	8.19
1923	3.85	1.76	0.02	3.72	9.36	4.05	1.61	0.02	3.84	9.52
1924	4.50	1.88	0.01	4.21	10.6	4.70	1.75	0.01	4.34	10.8
1925	4.83	2.03	0.01	4.61	11.5	4.99	1.88	0.01	4.70	11.6
1926	4.90	2.20	0.01	4.82	11.9	5.09	2.09	0.01	4.93	12.1
1927	4.61	2.32	0.01	5.07	12.0	4.77	2.24	0.01	5.18	12.2
1928	3.96	2.46	0.02	5.02	11.4	4.08	2.45	0.02	5.11	11.7
1929	3.22	2.56	0.02	4.46	10.3	3.34	2.66	0.02	4.57	10.6
1930	2.37	2.44	0.03	3.68	8.52	2.49	2.72	0.03	3.79	9.02

Year										
1931	1.56	2.27	0.03	2.88	6.74	1.66	2.61	0.04	3.00	7.30
1932	1.00	2.21	0.04	2.04	5.28	1.13	2.57	0.04	2.17	5.91
1933	0.81	2.08	0.04	1.44	4.38	0.98	2.43	0.05	1.59	5.04
1934	0.81	2.26	0.04	1.30	4.41	1.00	2.52	0.04	1.44	5.01
1935	1.06	2.50	0.04	1.57	5.16	1.23	2.60	0.04	1.67	5.55
1936	1.35	2.85	0.04	1.78	6.03	1.52	2.89	0.05	1.84	6.29
1937	1.75	3.16	0.06	1.99	6.96	1.90	3.19	0.06	2.03	7.19
1938	2.14	3.37	0.13	2.23	7.86	2.24	3.38	0.14	2.24	7.99
1939	2.52	3.50	0.45	2.52	8.98	2.50	3.42	0.45	2.49	8.86
1940	2.50	4.01	1.44	2.41	10.4	2.41	3.71	1.27	2.39	9.78
1941	2.29	4.10	1.94	2.29	10.6	2.15	3.62	1.65	2.26	9.69
1942	1.93	3.80	2.08	2.24	10.1	1.74	3.23	1.76	2.16	8.88
1943	1.56	3.50	2.14	2.28	9.48	1.32	2.84	1.78	2.09	8.03
1944	1.65	3.11	1.86	2.93	9.54	1.20	2.39	1.49	2.33	7.40
1945	2.56	2.62	0.89	4.08	10.2	1.56	1.90	0.68	2.77	6.92
1946	4.07	2.80	0.42	5.69	13.0	2.22	1.81	0.31	3.46	7.79
1947	5.52	3.61	0.28	7.18	16.6	2.89	2.13	0.19	4.06	9.27
1948	7.80	4.63	0.17	8.68	21.3	3.89	2.58	0.09	4.61	11.2
1949	9.18	5.90	0.31	9.91	25.3	4.33	3.08	0.15	4.86	12.4
1950	10.1	7.16	0.55	10.9	28.7	4.59	3.55	0.25	5.10	13.5
1951	10.8	8.24	0.78	11.8	31.6	4.75	3.95	0.35	5.32	14.4
1952	11.8	9.17	0.96	12.9	34.8	5.06	4.27	0.42	5.58	15.3
1953	12.6	10.0	1.18	14.1	37.9	5.22	4.54	0.52	5.89	16.2

Because of rounding, detail will not necessarily add to total.
ᵃ Less than $0.005 billion.
The series are identical for Variants I and III.

(Notes on following page).

Appendix C

All entries are averages of annual series.

(1) Calculated from the annual series for 1869–1955 described below.

1869–1883: Estimated by the following steps.

1. Decade averages of construction excluding government were calculated for 1864–1873, 1869–1878, 1874–1883, 1879–1888, and 1884–1893 by deducting from the decade averages of gross construction (Table R-14, col. 1, and extension indicated in its notes) decade averages of government construction (computed from the annual series underlying cols. 2 and 3, and extension indicated in their notes).

2. The ratio of the decade average of nonfarm residential construction for 1884–1893 (calculated from the annuals underlying col. 1) to the decade average of construction excluding government (step 1) was calculated (42.7 per cent). The ratio for 1879–1888 was assumed to be 42 per cent (slightly lower than for 1884–1893); for 1874–1883, 37 per cent (appreciably lower than for 1879–1888); for 1869–1878, 33 per cent (appreciably lower than for 1874–1883); and for 1864–1873, 33 per cent (the same as for 1869–1878).

3. The decade averages of construction excluding government (step 1) were multiplied by the ratios assumed in step 2, to yield decade averages of nonfarm residential construction.

4. Interpolating along a straight line between the logs of the decade averages (step 3) centered at their mid-points, yielded a preliminary annual series. Those for 1879–1883 were discarded because the decade average for 1879–1888 derived by averaging them with the series for 1884–1888 was appreciably higher than that estimated in step 3. We replaced them by estimates obtained by averaging: (a) a series in which the percentage change from year to year was assumed to be the same as that from 1877 to 1878, and (b) a series in which the percentage change from year to year was assumed to be the same as that from 1884 to 1885.

5. Finally, the annual series estimated in step 4 was adjusted by the ratio of the decade average (step 3) to the decade average of the preliminary series.

1884–1888: By letter from David M. Blank (Institute for Urban Land Use and Housing Studies, Columbia University).

1889–1952: Grebler, Blank, and Winnick, *op. cit.*, Appendix B, Table B-6, p. 338.

1953–1955: From *Survey of Current Business*, July 1956, Table 31.

(2) Calculated from the annual series for 1869–1955 described below.

1869–1914: Sum of separate estimates for federal, state, and local governments described below.

Federal government: Sum of separate estimates for (1) military and naval construction, (2) conservation and development, (3) nonresidential building, and (4) other public construction. Each series was carried back through 1819 since it was needed for the estimate of capital consumption. We assumed that before 1915 the volume of residential building, highway construction, and construction for sewage disposal and water supply was negligible.

1. *Historical Statistics of the United States, 1789–1945*, Series H-28, adjusted to a calendar year basis by averaging pairs of fiscal years. While this construction

(2)   is financed from military and naval funds, we have not treated it as military (see Table R-6, col. 3) although most of it for 1861–1865 and for 1898 undoubtedly falls in that category.

2. The 1915 figure extrapolated by *Historical Statistics*, Series H-29 and H-31. The latter were adjusted to a calendar year basis by averaging pairs of fiscal years.

3. *Ibid.*, Series H-30, adjusted to a calendar year basis by averaging pairs of fiscal years.

4. The 1915 figure extrapolated by *Historical Statistics*, Series H-32, adjusted for 1819–1882 and 1903–1915 as follows.

1819–1882: Net expenditures for lighthouse service (*ibid.*, Series K-172) were deducted. The balance was adjusted to a calendar year basis by averaging pairs of fiscal years.

1903–1915: The series as shown includes expenditures on the Panama Canal which should not properly be included in the series for continental United States. A series excluding these expenditures was calculated by subtracting nonresidential building (see above) from Goldsmith's fiscal year estimate of public building underlying the calendar year series shown in *A Study of Saving in the United States*, Vol. I, Table R-27, col. 11, p. 619. Calendar year estimates were derived by averaging pairs of fiscal years.

State and local governments:

1869–1901: The annual series in 1929 prices underlying col. 7 multiplied by the price index derived by extrapolating that implicit in the estimate for 1902 by the cost of construction index described in Kuznets, *National Product since 1869*, Table IV-4, notes to line 1.

1902–1914: Sum of estimates of construction of (1) highways, (2) sewers, (3) public service enterprises including water supply systems, and (4) all other.

1. Highways: Sum of separate estimates for states, counties, and local governments.

State governments: Outlays on highways are reported for 1915–1919 in *Financial Statistics of States* (Bureau of the Census). They were assumed to be for fiscal years, although some states report on a calendar year basis. Outlays for 1902 and 1913 were calculated as the difference between operation alone and operation including outlays as reported in the *Census of Wealth, Debt and Taxation* for those years. Estimates for 1903–1912 and for 1914 were interpolated along a straight line. Calendar year estimates were derived by averaging pairs of fiscal years. The resulting outlay series for 1915–1919 is somewhat lower than the construction series for those years shown in *Construction and Building Materials, Statistical Supplement, May 1954*, Table 3. This could be attributed to our procedure in deriving the calendar year series for outlay and to its exclusion of federal aid. To adjust the outlay series upward did not seem warranted, and it was used as a continuation of the construction series without splicing with the latter.

Counties: Total outlay is reported for fiscal years 1902 and 1913 in *Census of Wealth, Debt and Taxation, 1902* and *1913*. Estimates for 1904–1912 were derived as the product of outlay by cities of 100,000 and over (described below) and the ratio of county outlay to the latter, the ratio

(Notes continue on following page)

(2) being interpolated along a straight line between those for 1902 and 1913. Total outlay for 1903 was estimated as a straight-line interpolation between that for 1902 and that for 1904. Outlay on highways is reported for 1902 (*ibid.*). Its ratio to total outlay was computed for that year and estimated for 1941 from data for selected counties reported in *Financial Statistics of Counties: 1941* (Bureau of the Census), Table 27. Annual ratios for 1903–1913 were interpolated along a straight line between those for 1902 and 1941. Highway outlay for 1903–1913 was estimated as the product of this ratio and total outlay. This outlay series was used as a continuation of the construction series reported for 1915 and later years in *Construction and Building Materials, Statistical Supplement, May 1954*, Table 3. Since the latter series is for calendar years, a fiscal year estimate for 1916 was derived by averaging pairs of calendar years. Fiscal year figures for 1914 and 1915 were interpolated along a straight line between those for 1913 and 1916. The fiscal year series for 1902–1915 was then adjusted to a calendar year basis by averaging pairs of years.

Local governments: Total capital outlay for 1902 is reported in *Census of Wealth, Debt and Taxation* for that year. The *Census* for 1913 reports outlay for all local governments of 2,500 and over. Total outlay for all local governments in that year was derived by substituting for the census figure for cities of 2,500–8,000 an estimate of outlay for all minor civil divisions, calculated as follows.

a. Outlay by cities of 25,000 and over is reported for 1902 in *Financial Statistics of Cities* (Bureau of the Census).

b. Outlay by cities of 30,000 and over, and by cities of 100,000 and over is reported for 1904–1913 (*ibid.*).

c. It was assumed that the change in outlay from 1902 to 1904 by cities of 100,000 and over was the same, proportionately, as the change from the 1902 outlay by cities of 25,000 and over to the 1904 outlay by cities of 30,000 and over.

d. For 1902 and 1913, outlay by cities of 25,000 (or 30,000) to 100,000 was calculated by subtracting outlay by cities of 100,000 and over from that by cities of 25,000 (or 30,000) and over.

e. The ratio of outlay by all minor civil divisions in 1902 to the outlay by cities of 8,000–25,000 was calculated from the *Census of Wealth, Debt and Taxation* and extrapolated to 1913 by the change in the ratio of outlay by cities of 25,000 (or 30,000) to 100,000 to that by cities of 100,000 and over.

f. Outlays by all minor civil divisions in 1913 were estimated by multiplying outlay by cities of 8,000–30,000 as reported in the *Census* for 1913, by the ratio calculated in step e.
   The ratio of total outlay to that by cities of 100,000 and over was computed for 1902 and 1913, interpolated along a straight line for the intervening years, and held at the 1913 level for 1915–1919. Outlay by cities of 100,000 and over as reported in *Financial Statistics of Cities, 1904* through *1912* and *1915* through *1919* was then multiplied by this ratio to yield total outlay for those years. Outlay for 1903 was estimated by straight-line interpolation between that for 1902 and that for 1904.

(2)   The ratio of highway outlay to total outlay by cities of 30,000 and over was computed for 1904–1913 and 1915–1919 from the same source. Total outlay by all local governments was multiplied by this ratio to yield highway outlay in those years. For 1915–1919, the estimates so derived were replaced by the estimates of highway construction given in *Construction and Building Materials, Statistical Supplement, May 1954*, Table 3. While the former are slightly higher, on the average, than the latter, the difference is too small to warrant adjustment of the series for 1904–1913. The estimate for 1914 was interpolated along a straight line between those for 1913 and 1915. Highway outlay in 1902 and 1903 was estimated by multiplying the expenditures by 148 cities (of 30,000 and over) on street paving and on bridges other than toll, as reported in *Financial Statistics of Cities, 1905*, Table 5, pp. 170–171, by the 1904–1905 ratio of highway outlay by all local governments to highway expenditures by these cities.

2. Sewers: Estimates cover cities alone. Expenditures by states and counties are negligible.

Financial Statistics of Cities reports outlay on sewers and sewage disposal for 1904–1912 and 1915–1919, by cities of 30,000 and over. Outlay for 1913 was assumed to be the same percentage of outlay for sanitation (*ibid.*) as in 1912. All local government construction of sewers in 1915 and later years is reported in *Construction and Building Materials, Statistical Supplement, May 1954*, Table 3. Outlay for 1904–1913 was adjusted by the 1915–1918 average ratio of construction to outlay. Construction in 1914 was interpolated along a straight line between that for 1913 and 1915. Construction in 1902 and 1903 was estimated by multiplying the expenditures on sanitation by 148 cities (of 30,000 and over), as reported in *Financial Statistics of Cities* for 1905, Table 5, pp. 164–165, by the 1904–1905 ratio of sewer construction by all local governments to sanitation expenditures by these cities.

3. Public service enterprises including water supply: Sum of separate estimates for state and local governments. Construction by counties was negligible.

State governments: Outlay for public service enterprises is reported for 1913 in *Census of Wealth, Debt and Taxation* for that year, and for 1915–1919 in *Financial Statistics of States*. (Expenditures on water supply are not available separately, and any such expenditures are included in "all other" construction by states.) It was interpolated for 1914 along a straight line between the figures for 1913 and 1915. For 1902 it was estimated as the same percentage of outlay on other than highway as in 1913. Outlay on other than highway was derived for both years by deducting highway outlay (see above) from total outlay as reported in *Census of Wealth, Debt and Taxation*. Estimates for 1903–1912 were interpolated along a straight line between those for 1902 and 1913. Pairs of years were averaged to yield a calendar year series. This series was used in place of a construction series, since no construction series was available.

Local governments: Outlay by cities of 30,000 and over on (a) water supply systems, and on (b) municipal service enterprises, and public service enterprises excluding water supply systems is reported for 1904–1913 and 1915–1919 in *Financial Statistics of Cities*, Table 9. Outlay for 1914 was interpolated along a straight line between that for 1913 and 1915. Outlay in 1902 and 1903 was estimated as the product of payments by 148 cities of 30,000 and over for the given type of outlay (i.e., waterworks, or electric

(Notes continue on following page)

Appendix C

(2)   light and power, gas works, etc., as shown in *Financial Statistics of Cities, 1905*, Table 6, pp. 198–199) and the 1904–1905 ratio of outlay by all cities of 30,000 and over to expenditures by those cities.

    a. Water supply systems: *Construction and Building Materials, Statistical Supplement, May 1954*, Table 3, shows construction for 1915 and later years. Construction for 1902–1914 was estimated by applying to the outlay series for cities of 30,000 and over (described above) the 1915–1918 ratio of the construction to the outlay series.

    b. Municipal service enterprises, etc.: From the construction series for 1915 and later years (*ibid.*, Table 3) was deducted the outlay by states (see above) to yield an estimate of construction by cities. The latter was extrapolated back to 1902 by applying to the outlay series for cities of 30,000 and over (described above) the 1915–1918 ratio of the construction to the outlay series.

  4. All other construction: Estimated by the following steps.

    a. From total outlay by states and local governments was deducted their outlay on highways. The latter is described above, as is total outlay by counties and cities. Total state outlay is shown for 1902 and 1913 in *Historical Statistics of the United States, 1789–1945*, Series P-198, and for 1915–1918 in *Financial Statistics of States*. Straight-line interpolation between these figures yielded the annual estimates for 1903–1912 and 1914. The resulting series—assumed to be for fiscal years (see notes on state highway outlays)—was adjusted to a calendar year basis by averaging pairs of fiscal years.

    b. Construction by state and local governments for 1915 and later years is given in *Construction and Building Materials, Statistical Supplement, May 1954*, Table 5. Federal aid (*ibid.*) was added, and highway construction (*ibid.*) deducted.

    c. State and local construction other than highway, as derived in step b, was extrapolated from 1915 to 1902 by multiplying the outlay series described in step a by the 1915–1918 ratio of the construction to the outlay series.

    d. From state and local construction other than highway was deducted sewer, water supply, and public service enterprise construction described above.

1915–1952: *Construction and Building Materials, Statistical Supplement, May 1954*, Table 3.

1953–1955: From *Survey of Current Business*, July 1956, Table 31.

(3) Calculated from the annual series in Table R-6, col. 3.

(4) Calculated from the annual series derived as the difference between that underlying col. 5 and those underlying cols. 1–3.

(5) Calculated from the annual series for 1869–1955 derived as the sum of (1) the cost of oil and gas wells drilled, and (2) all other new construction.

  1. 1869–1918: Calculated by multiplying the 1929 price series underlying col. 10 by the price index for petroleum pipe lines. The latter was computed for 1915 and later years from *Construction and Building Materials, Statistical Supplement, May 1954*, pp. 33 and 82 and was extrapolated from 1915 by the cost of con-

Appendix C

(5)   struction index described in *National Product since 1869*, Table IV-4, notes to line 1.

1919–1955: Described in the notes to Table R-4, col. 1.

2. 1869–1914: A preliminary series was calculated by multiplying the 1929 price series underlying col. 10 by the price index. The latter was derived by extrapolating the price index implicit in the estimate for 1915 by the cost of construction index indicated above. For 1869–1913 the preliminary series was adjusted by the ratios of the final decade averages underlying Table R-14, col. 1 to the ten-year averages of the preliminary series. The ratios were centered at the mid-point of each overlapping decade and estimated annually by straight-line interpolation between these mid-points. No adjustment was made in the estimate for 1914.

1915–1918: Sum of new private nonfarm residential construction given in col. 1, and other new construction shown in *Construction and Building Materials, Statistical Supplement, May 1954*, Tables 2 and 3.

1919–1955: Described in the notes to Table R-4, col. 1.

(6) Calculated from the annual series for 1869–1955 described below.

1869–1888 (1864–1868 also estimated, for computation of 1864–1873 decade): A preliminary series was calculated by dividing the series underlying col. 1 by the annual price index derived by extrapolating the index implicit in the estimate for 1889 by the cost of construction index described in *National Product since 1869*, Table IV-4, notes to line 1. The preliminary series was then adjusted to the level of the decade estimates derived by dividing the decade estimates in current prices (see notes to col. 1) by the decade averages of the annual price index.

1889–1952: Grebler, Blank, and Winnick, *op. cit.*, Appendix B, Table B-6.

1953–1955: Col. 1 divided by the price index derived by extrapolating that for 1952 by the index implicit in the 1947–1949 price series for all private residential nonfarm building (including nonhousekeeping), *Construction Review*, September 1956.

(7) Calculated from the annual series for 1869–1955 described below.

1819–1914 (1819–1868 estimated for calculation of depreciation): Sum of separate estimates for federal government, and state and local governments.

Federal government: Sum of separate estimates for (1) military and naval construction, (2) conservation and development, (3) nonresidential building, and (4) other public construction. For each type of construction, the series in current prices as described in the notes to col. 2 was deflated by the annual price index derived by extrapolating that implicit in the estimate for 1915 by the cost of construction index described in *National Product since 1869*, Table IV-4, notes to line 1. The latter, available only back to 1840, was extended to 1810 by the Warren and Pearson wholesale price index of building materials given in *Historical Statistics of the United States, 1789–1945*, Series L-10.

State and local governments:

1819–1901: Extrapolated from 1902 by the following procedure:

1. Decade averages of net national product per capita in 1929 prices as shown for 1874–1883, 1884–1893, 1894–1903, and 1899–1908 in Kuznets' paper in *Income and Wealth, Series II* (International Association for Research in Income

(Notes continue on following page)

(7)   and Wealth, 1952), Table 4, p. 55, were centered at the end of 1878, 1888, 1898, and 1903, respectively. (The net national product series from which they were calculated differs slightly from that in Table R-12, col. 4, but the effect on the per capitas is negligible.) In *National Income in the United States, 1799–1938* by Robert F. Martin (National Industrial Conference Board, 1939), Table 1, is shown per capita realized income in 1926 prices. Since the series shows practically no change from 1902 to the end of 1903 (estimated by averaging the estimates for 1903 and 1904), it was assumed that the 1929 price series figure for 1902 was identical with that for the end of 1903 (i.e., the mid-point of the decade average for 1899–1908). The 1929 price figure for the end of 1878 (i.e., the mid-point of the decade average for 1874–1883) was extrapolated to the end of 1868, 1858, 1848, and 1838 by the change in the Martin series from 1869 to 1879, 1859 to 1869, 1849 to 1859, and 1839 to 1849, respectively. The figure for the end of 1808 was estimated on the assumption that there was a 50 per cent increase in per capita income between 1808 and 1838. Estimates for the end of 1818 and 1828 were interpolated along a logarithmic straight line between those for 1808 and 1838.

2. Urban and rural population as of the end of 1818, 1828, 1838, etc., and for July 1, 1902 were estimated. The end-of-year figures were derived by averaging pairs of July 1 figures (for 1818 and 1819, 1828 and 1829, etc.). The July 1 figures were estimated as follows.

Urban, rural, and total population as of census dates are given for 1800 and later years in *Historical Statistics of the United States, 1789–1945*, Series B-16, B-17, and B-13. From these series the ratio of urban to total population was computed. The ratio as of July 1 for any given year was derived by interpolating along a straight line between the ratios for the census dates. Applying these ratios to total population as of July 1 (*ibid.*, Series B-31) yielded a breakdown of the total into urban and rural.

Since in the later years construction in urban areas accounts for a much higher proportion of total public construction than that in rural areas, it was assumed that this was true in the years before 1902. To reflect this differential, we weighted urban population 3 and rural population 1.

3. Multiplying the weighted index of population derived in step 2 by the per capitas derived in step 1 yielded the index by which total public construction in 1902 in 1929 prices was extrapolated back to the end of 1898, 1888, 1878, etc. The ratio of construction to total population as of these dates was calculated, and annual ratios as of July 1 were interpolated along a straight line between them. These ratios, multiplied by total population as of July 1 (*ibid.*, Series B-31), yielded the estimate of public construction for each year from 1901 through 1819.

1902–1914: Sum of the components underlying col. 2 each converted to 1929 prices by a price index derived for each series by extrapolating that implicit in the estimate for 1915 by the cost of construction index described in *National Product since 1869*, Table IV-4, notes to line 1.

1915–1952: The series in *Construction and Building Materials, Statistical Supplements, May 1954*, Table 16, adjusted to a 1929 price base.

1953–1955: The 1952 figure extrapolated by the 1947–1949 price series given in *Construction Review*, September 1956, Table 4, p. 11.

(8) Calculated from the annual series in Table R-7, col. 1.

(9) Calculated from the annual series derived as the difference between that underlying col. 10 and those underlying cols. 6–8.

(10) Calculated from the annual series for 1869–1955 derived as the sum of (1) the cost of oil and gas wells drilled, and (2) all other new construction.

    1. 1869–1918: Described in the notes to Table R-15, col. 1.

    1919–1955: Described in the notes to Table R-5, col. 1.

    2. 1869–1913: Interpolations between or extrapolations from the series underlying Table R-15, col. 1, by the annual series on output of construction materials for domestic consumption described in *National Product since 1869*, Table II-5, notes to col. 2. The ratios of the decade averages of gross construction to the decade averages of output were computed and centered at the midpoints of the decades. Annual ratios were interpolated along a straight line and applied to the annual output figures. The resulting estimates for 1909–1913 when averaged with those for 1914–1918 yielded a figure for 1909–1918 below that shown in Table R-15, col. 1. They were adjusted by the relative difference between the two estimates for the quinquennium.

    1914: Extrapolation of the figure for 1915 by the 1914–1915 change in Shaw's series on output of construction materials in constant prices as calculated from *Value of Commodity Output since 1869*, p. 77.

    1915–1918: Sum of new private nonfarm residential construction (col. 6), and other new construction given in *Construction and Building Materials, Statistical Supplement, May 1954*, Tables 15 and 16, and adjusted to a 1929 price base.

    1919–1955: Described in the notes to Table R-5, col. 1.

TABLE R-31

FIVE-YEAR MOVING AVERAGES OF DEPRECIATION ON CONSTRUCTION, BY TYPE OF CONSTRUCTION, CURRENT AND 1929 PRICES, 1869–1955
(billions of dollars)

YEAR ON WHICH MOVING AVERAGE IS CENTERED	CURRENT PRICES					1929 PRICES				
	Nonfarm Residential (1)	Government		Other (4)	Total (5)	Nonfarm Residential (6)	Government		Other (9)	Total (10)
		Excluding Military (2)	Military (3)				Excluding Military (7)	Military (8)		
1871	0.06	0.03		0.21	0.31	0.13	0.06		0.37	0.56
1872	0.06	0.03		0.23	0.33	0.14	0.06		0.40	0.61
1873	0.07	0.03		0.25	0.35	0.15	0.06		0.44	0.65
1874	0.07	0.03		0.26	0.37	0.16	0.07		0.48	0.70
1875	0.07	0.03		0.28	0.38	0.17	0.07		0.52	0.76
1876	0.07	0.03		0.28	0.39	0.18	0.07		0.57	0.82
1877	0.07	0.03		0.29	0.40	0.19	0.08		0.61	0.88
1878	0.08	0.04		0.31	0.42	0.20	0.08		0.65	0.93
1879	0.08	0.04		0.33	0.45	0.22	0.08		0.70	0.99
1880	0.09	0.04		0.35	0.48	0.23	0.08		0.73	1.05
1881	0.10	0.04		0.38	0.51	0.24	0.09		0.78	1.10
1882	0.10	0.04		0.41	0.55	0.26	0.09		0.82	1.16
1883	0.11	0.04		0.43	0.59	0.27	0.10		0.86	1.23
1884	0.12	0.05		0.46	0.63	0.30	0.10		0.91	1.30
1885	0.13	0.05		0.48	0.66	0.32	0.10		0.95	1.38
1886	0.14	0.05		0.51	0.70	0.35	0.11		1.00	1.47
1887	0.15	0.05		0.54	0.75	0.39	0.11		1.06	1.56
1888	0.17	0.05		0.56	0.78	0.42	0.12		1.11	1.65
1889	0.18	0.06		0.58	0.81	0.46	0.12		1.17	1.75
1890	0.19	0.06		0.59	0.84	0.49	0.13		1.23	1.85

Year										
1891	0.20	0.06		0.60	0.86	0.53	0.14		1.29	1.95
1892	0.21	0.06		0.60	0.86	0.56	0.14		1.34	2.04
1893	0.22	0.06		0.60	0.88	0.59	0.15		1.39	2.13
1894	0.22	0.06		0.61	0.90	0.62	0.16		1.44	2.22
1895	0.23	0.07		0.62	0.92	0.65	0.16		1.49	2.31
1896	0.24	0.07		0.64	0.95	0.68	0.17		1.54	2.39
1897	0.25	0.08		0.67	1.00	0.71	0.18		1.59	2.48
1898	0.27	0.08		0.71	1.06	0.73	0.19		1.65	2.57
1899	0.29	0.09		0.75	1.12	0.76	0.20		1.71	2.66
1900	0.31	0.09		0.79	1.19	0.78	0.21		1.76	2.75
1901	0.32	0.10		0.84	1.26	0.80	0.22		1.82	2.84
1902	0.34	0.11		0.87	1.32	0.81	0.23		1.88	2.92
1903	0.35	0.12		0.92	1.38	0.83	0.24		1.94	3.01
1904	0.38	0.13		0.98	1.48	0.86	0.26		1.99	3.11
1905	0.41	0.14		1.04	1.59	0.89	0.27		2.06	3.21
1906	0.44	0.15		1.10	1.69	0.92	0.29		2.12	3.32
1907	0.47	0.16		1.16	1.79	0.95	0.30		2.18	3.44
1908	0.50	0.18		1.21	1.89	0.98	0.32		2.25	3.56
1909	0.52	0.19		1.26	1.97	1.02	0.34		2.32	3.68
1910	0.54	0.20		1.30	2.05	1.04	0.36		2.39	3.80
1911	0.56	0.22	a	1.36	2.14	1.07	0.39	a	2.46	3.92
1912	0.58	0.23	a	1.42	2.23	1.10	0.41	a	2.53	4.04
1913	0.59	0.25	a	1.48	2.32	1.12	0.44	a	2.60	4.17
1914	0.62	0.27		1.58	2.47	1.15	0.46		2.68	4.29
1915	0.66	0.31	0.01	1.76	2.74	1.17	0.49	0.01	2.76	4.43
1916	0.74	0.36	0.02	2.04	3.16	1.19	0.51	0.02	2.84	4.56
1917	0.84	0.44	0.05	2.39	3.72	1.20	0.54	0.05	2.93	4.72
1918	1.00	0.54	0.10	2.84	4.49	1.21	0.56	0.09	3.01	4.87
1919	1.10	0.62	0.14	3.12	4.97	1.22	0.58	0.13	3.09	5.01
1920	1.16	0.66	0.17	3.25	5.24	1.22	0.60	0.16	3.16	5.15

(continued)

TABLE R-31 (concluded)

YEAR ON WHICH MOVING AVERAGE IS CENTERED	CURRENT PRICES					1929 PRICES				
	Nonfarm Residential (1)	*Government*		*Other* (4)	*Total* (5)	*Nonfarm Residential* (6)	*Government*		*Other* (9)	*Total* (10)
		Excluding Military (2)	*Military* (3)				*Excluding Military* (7)	*Military* (8)		
1921	1.22	0.72	0.20	3.33	5.48	1.24	0.63	0.18	3.23	5.28
1922	1.27	0.76	0.21	3.35	5.59	1.28	0.66	0.19	3.28	5.41
1923	1.26	0.77	0.20	3.26	5.49	1.33	0.70	0.19	3.33	5.56
1924	1.33	0.81	0.20	3.31	5.65	1.40	0.75	0.19	3.41	5.74
1925	1.42	0.86	0.21	3.43	5.92	1.47	0.79	0.19	3.49	5.95
1926	1.49	0.89	0.20	3.51	6.10	1.55	0.85	0.19	3.58	6.17
1927	1.57	0.94	0.20	3.61	6.32	1.62	0.90	0.19	3.68	6.40
1928	1.62	0.97	0.20	3.71	6.50	1.67	0.97	0.19	3.78	6.61
1929	1.63	1.00	0.19	3.74	6.56	1.70	1.04	0.20	3.86	6.79
1930	1.58	0.99	0.18	3.73	6.48	1.72	1.11	0.20	3.92	6.94
1931	1.51	1.02	0.17	3.66	6.36	1.71	1.18	0.20	3.95	7.04
1932	1.43	1.08	0.17	3.62	6.29	1.69	1.25	0.20	3.96	7.10
1933	1.36	1.14	0.16	3.55	6.22	1.68	1.31	0.20	3.95	7.15
1934	1.33	1.23	0.17	3.54	6.26	1.67	1.38	0.20	3.94	7.18
1935	1.38	1.37	0.17	3.62	6.54	1.65	1.44	0.20	3.94	7.23
1936	1.44	1.47	0.16	3.77	6.85	1.65	1.50	0.19	3.96	7.29
1937	1.49	1.54	0.14	3.84	7.01	1.65	1.57	0.16	3.98	7.36
1938	1.57	1.63	0.12	3.94	7.26	1.66	1.65	0.13	4.00	7.44
1939	1.68	1.73	0.10	4.05	7.55	1.68	1.73	0.10	4.03	7.54
1940	1.77	1.91	0.12	4.10	7.90	1.70	1.81	0.11	4.07	7.69
1941	1.87	2.12	0.20	4.19	8.38	1.71	1.89	0.17	4.11	7.87
1942	2.00	2.30	0.30	4.39	8.98	1.72	1.96	0.24	4.15	8.07
1943	2.12	2.47	0.41	4.62	9.62	1.72	2.01	0.33	4.19	8.24
1944	2.27	2.66	0.54	4.97	10.4	1.71	2.05	0.41	4.19	8.36
1945	2.51	2.86	0.67	5.62	11.7	1.70	2.08	0.46	4.20	8.45

Year	(1)	(2)	(3)	(4)	(5)	(6)	(7)	(8)	(9)	(10)
1946	2.83	3.12	0.77	6.38	13.1	1.70	2.10	0.49	4.25	8.54
1947	3.11	3.41	0.86	7.14	14.5	1.72	2.12	0.50	4.30	8.65
1948	3.44	3.72	0.95	7.91	16.0	1.76	2.16	0.51	4.38	8.80
1949	3.81	4.06	1.03	8.74	17.6	1.81	2.20	0.51	4.49	9.01
1950	4.11	4.38	1.09	9.31	18.9	1.86	2.25	0.52	4.57	9.20
1951	4.36	4.65	1.15	9.80	20.0	1.92	2.31	0.53	4.64	9.40
1952	4.64	4.95	1.22	10.3	21.1	1.98	2.37	0.55	4.70	9.61
1953	4.93	5.33	1.31	10.8	22.4	2.05	2.44	0.57	4.77	9.84

Because of rounding, detail will not necessarily add to total.
ᵃ Less than $5 million.

The series are identical for Variants I and III.

SOURCE, BY COLUMN

All entries are averages of annual series.

(1) Calculated from the annual series for 1869–1955 described below.

1869–1888: See notes to Table R-16, col. 1.

1889–1952: Given in Grebler, Blank, and Winnick, *op. cit.*, Appendix E, Table E-2, pp. 384–385.

1953–1955: Col. 5 multiplied by the price index implicit in gross construction, Table R-30, cols. 1 and 6.

(2) Calculated from the annual series for 1869–1955 estimated separately for (1) sewer and highway construction, and (2) all other government construction excluding military. For both (1) and (2), the annual estimates in 1929 prices underlying col. 7 were multiplied by the price index calculated for the given type of construction from the series described in the notes to Table R-30, col. 2 or 7.

(3) Calculated from the annual series in Table R-6, col. 5.

(4) Calculated from the annual series for 1869–1955 estimated as the sum of (1) estimated depreciation on "other" construction, and (2) depletion. For both (1) and (2) the annual estimates in 1929 prices underlying col. 9 were multiplied by the appropriate price index. The price index for (1) was calculated from the series underlying Table R-30, cols. 4 and 9; that for (2) before 1919 is the index implicit in output

of producers' durables (see notes to Table R-14, col. 2), excluding munitions (Tables R-6 and R-7), and for 1919–1955, the index implicit in flow of producers' durables, excluding munitions (Tables R-4 to R-7).

(5) Calculated from the annual series for 1869–1955 estimated as the sum of those underlying cols. 1–4.

(6) Calculated from the annual series for 1869–1955 described below.

1869–1888: See notes to Table R-17, col. 1.

1889–1952: Given in Grebler, Blank, and Winnick, *op. cit.*, Appendix E, Table E-2, pp. 384–385.

1953–1955: Calculated by the procedure indicated for preceding years in notes to Table E-2, *ibid.*, p. 385.

(7) Calculated from the annual series for 1869–1955 described in the notes to Table R-8, col. 4.

(8) Calculated from the annual series in Table R-7, col. 3.

(9) Calculated from the annual series for 1869–1955 estimated as the sum of (1) estimated depreciation on "other" construction, and (2) depletion.

1869–1918: Described in the notes to Table R-17, col. 1.

1919–1955: Described in the notes to Table R-8, col. 4.

(10) Calculated from the annual series for 1869–1955 estimated as the sum of those underlying cols. 6–9.

TABLE R-32

Five-Year Moving Averages of Net Construction, by Type of Construction, Current and 1929 Prices, 1869–1955

(billions of dollars)

YEAR ON WHICH MOVING AVERAGE IS CENTERED	CURRENT PRICES					1929 PRICES				
	Nonfarm Residential (1)	*Government* *Excluding Military* (2)	*Military* (3)	*Other* (4)	*Total* (5)	*Nonfarm Residential* (6)	*Government* *Excluding Military* (7)	*Military* (8)	*Other* (9)	*Total* (10)
1871	0.16	0.02		0.28	0.46	0.34	0.05		0.54	0.93
1872	0.16	0.03		0.29	0.48	0.35	0.06		0.57	0.97
1873	0.17	0.03		0.31	0.51	0.36	0.06		0.61	1.04
1874	0.18	0.03		0.33	0.54	0.40	0.07		0.65	1.11
1875	0.19	0.03		0.26	0.49	0.45	0.07		0.54	1.06
1876	0.21	0.03		0.20	0.44	0.53	0.07		0.42	1.02
1877	0.22	0.03		0.17	0.42	0.56	0.07		0.39	1.03
1878	0.22	0.03		0.16	0.41	0.58	0.08		0.36	1.02
1879	0.23	0.03		0.20	0.46	0.60	0.08		0.45	1.13
1880	0.24	0.04		0.24	0.52	0.62	0.09		0.54	1.24
1881	0.25	0.04		0.30	0.59	0.63	0.09		0.64	1.37
1882	0.30	0.04		0.34	0.68	0.74	0.10		0.70	1.54
1883	0.37	0.05		0.32	0.73	0.91	0.11		0.65	1.67
1884	0.45	0.05		0.28	0.78	1.11	0.11		0.57	1.79
1885	0.54	0.05		0.24	0.83	1.35	0.11		0.48	1.95

1886	0.59	0.05	0.23	0.86	1.48	0.12	0.45	2.04
1887	0.64	0.06	0.16	0.85	1.63	0.13	0.30	2.06
1888	0.66	0.06	0.30	1.02	1.69	0.13	0.61	2.44
1889	0.63	0.06	0.40	1.10	1.63	0.14	0.84	2.61
1890	0.62	0.06	0.60	1.28	1.60	0.16	1.30	3.05
1891	0.59	0.07	0.70	1.36	1.56	0.16	1.55	3.28
1892	0.54	0.07	0.83	1.44	1.45	0.18	1.87	3.50
1893	0.51	0.07	0.80	1.39	1.41	0.18	1.85	3.44
1894	0.50	0.07	0.74	1.31	1.40	0.19	1.70	3.29
1895	0.47	0.08	0.62	1.16	1.33	0.20	1.46	2.99
1896	0.46	0.08	0.56	1.10	1.30	0.20	1.36	2.86
1897	0.44	0.08	0.51	1.04	1.24	0.21	1.23	2.68
1898	0.37	0.09	0.57	1.03	1.03	0.22	1.33	2.58
1899	0.36	0.10	0.69	1.14	0.96	0.23	1.60	2.80
1900	0.33	0.10	0.84	1.28	0.84	0.25	1.92	3.00
1901	0.32	0.12	0.98	1.42	0.78	0.28	2.16	3.22
1902	0.32	0.14	1.08	1.56	0.78	0.32	2.38	3.48
1903	0.46	0.16	1.03	1.66	1.08	0.36	2.23	3.67
1904	0.56	0.18	1.07	1.81	1.24	0.40	2.22	3.85
1905	0.62	0.21	1.11	1.95	1.35	0.44	2.18	3.96
1906	0.69	0.24	1.09	2.02	1.46	0.50	2.07	4.03
1907	0.78	0.26	1.16	2.20	1.60	0.52	2.16	4.28
1908	0.72	0.28	1.32	2.33	1.42	0.56	2.44	4.42
1909	0.66	0.32	1.31	2.28	1.29	0.61	2.41	4.31
1910	0.66	0.32	1.27	2.25	1.27	0.63	2.34	4.24

(continued)

TABLE R-32 (concluded)

YEAR ON WHICH MOVING AVERAGE IS CENTERED	CURRENT PRICES					1929 PRICES				
	Nonfarm Residential (1)	Government		Other (4)	Total (5)	Nonfarm Residential (6)	Government		Other (9)	Total (10)
		Excluding Military (2)	Military (3)				Excluding Military (7)	Military (8)		
1911	0.65	0.33	a	1.39	2.37	1.24	0.62	0.01	2.52	4.39
1912	0.60	0.35	0.01	1.18	2.12	1.13	0.65	0.01	2.13	3.91
1913	0.61	0.37	0.01	0.86	1.85	1.16	0.68	0.02	1.56	3.41
1914	0.64	0.37	0.01	0.69	1.71	1.19	0.66	0.02	1.24	3.11
1915	0.53	0.35	0.13	0.44	1.45	0.98	0.60	0.17	0.79	2.54
1916	0.31	0.32	0.42	0.02	1.06	0.62	0.51	0.49	0.14	1.76
1917	0.25	0.29	0.61	−0.09	1.05	0.45	0.41	0.66	−0.01	1.52
1918	0.06	0.28	0.59	−0.01	0.92	0.16	0.31	0.65	−0.06	1.18
1919	0.09	0.38	0.55	−0.14	0.88	0.09	0.34	0.61	−0.10	0.95
1920	0.49	0.52	0.40	−0.13	1.28	0.54	0.47	0.43	−0.09	1.35
1921	1.16	0.65	0.07	0.09	1.97	1.25	0.58	0.07	0.12	2.01
1922	1.80	0.81	−0.16	0.29	2.74	1.90	0.72	−0.15	0.30	2.78
1923	2.59	0.99	−0.18	0.47	3.87	2.72	0.91	−0.17	0.50	3.96
1924	3.16	1.08	−0.19	0.90	4.95	3.31	1.00	−0.18	0.93	5.06
1925	3.41	1.17	−0.20	1.18	5.57	3.52	1.09	−0.18	1.21	5.64
1926	3.41	1.31	−0.19	1.32	5.84	3.54	1.24	−0.18	1.35	5.94
1927	3.04	1.38	−0.19	1.46	5.70	3.15	1.34	−0.18	1.49	5.80
1928	2.33	1.49	−0.18	1.31	4.95	2.41	1.48	−0.18	1.33	5.05
1929	1.59	1.56	−0.17	0.72	3.69	1.64	1.62	−0.17	0.71	3.80
1930	0.79	1.45	−0.15	−0.06	2.04	0.77	1.61	−0.16	−0.13	2.08

Year										
1931	0.05	1.25	−0.14	−0.79	0.37	−0.05	1.43	−0.16	−0.95	0.26
1932	−0.44	1.13	−0.13	−1.58	−1.01	−0.57	1.32	−0.16	−1.78	−1.19
1933	−0.55	0.95	−0.12	−2.11	−1.84	−0.70	1.11	−0.15	−2.36	−2.10
1934	−0.52	1.03	−0.13	−2.23	−1.85	−0.66	1.14	−0.16	−2.50	−2.17
1935	−0.32	1.14	−0.13	−2.05	−1.38	−0.42	1.16	−0.16	−2.27	−1.68
1936	−0.09	1.38	−0.12	−1.99	−0.82	−0.13	1.39	−0.14	−2.12	−1.00
1937	0.26	1.61	−0.08	−1.85	0.06	0.26	1.61	−0.09	−1.95	−0.17
1938	0.57	1.74	0.01	−1.71	0.61	0.58	1.73	0.01	−1.76	0.56
1939	0.84	1.76	0.35	−1.53	1.43	0.82	1.69	0.34	−1.54	1.32
1940	0.72	2.10	1.32	−1.69	2.46	0.71	1.90	1.15	−1.68	2.09
1941	0.42	1.98	1.74	−1.90	2.23	0.44	1.73	1.48	−1.84	1.81
1942	−0.07	1.50	1.78	−2.15	1.07	0.02	1.27	1.51	−1.99	0.81
1943	−0.56	1.03	1.73	−2.33	−0.14	−0.39	0.82	1.45	−2.09	−0.21
1944	−0.62	0.44	1.32	−2.04	−0.90	−0.51	0.34	1.08	−1.86	−0.95
1945	0.04	−0.24	0.22	−1.54	−1.51	−0.14	−0.18	0.22	−1.43	−1.53
1946	1.24	−0.32	−0.36	−0.70	−0.14	0.52	−0.29	−0.18	−0.79	−0.75
1947	2.41	0.20	−0.59	0.04	2.07	1.17	a	−0.32	0.24	0.62
1948	4.36	0.91	−0.78	0.77	5.27	2.14	0.42	−0.41	0.24	2.38
1949	5.37	1.84	−0.72	1.17	7.66	2.52	0.88	−0.36	0.37	3.41
1950	6.02	2.78	−0.54	1.59	9.84	2.73	1.30	−0.27	0.53	4.29
1951	6.41	3.60	−0.37	2.03	11.7	2.83	1.64	−0.19	0.68	4.96
1952	7.15	4.22	−0.27	2.60	13.7	3.08	1.90	−0.13	0.88	5.72
1953	7.64	4.70	−0.13	3.32	15.5	3.17	2.10	−0.06	1.12	6.33

Because of rounding, detail will not necessarily add to total.
a Less than $5 million.

SOURCE: All entries are averages of annual series calculated by subtracting the series underlying Table R-31, cols. 1–10, from those underlying Table R-30, cols. 1–10, respectively.

FIVE-YEAR MOVING AVERAGES OF GROSS AND NET PRODUCERS' DURABLES,
CURRENT AND 1929 PRICES, 1869–1955

(billions of dollars)

Year on Which Moving Average Is Centered	Current Prices			1929 Prices		
	Gross Producers' Durables (1)	Capital Consumption (2)	Net Producers' Durables (3)	Gross Producers' Durables (4)	Capital Consumption (5)	Net Producers' Durables (6)
1871	0.39	0.21	0.18	0.46	0.24	0.22
1872	0.40	0.22	0.18	0.48	0.27	0.22
1873	0.40	0.24	0.16	0.49	0.29	0.20
1874	0.41	0.25	0.16	0.51	0.32	0.19
1875	0.37	0.25	0.12	0.50	0.34	0.16
1876	0.33	0.24	0.09	0.49	0.36	0.13
1877	0.33	0.24	0.09	0.54	0.38	0.16
1878	0.38	0.24	0.14	0.64	0.41	0.24
1879	0.45	0.26	0.19	0.77	0.44	0.33
1880	0.53	0.28	0.25	0.91	0.48	0.43
1881	0.58	0.31	0.28	1.01	0.53	0.48
1882	0.60	0.33	0.27	1.04	0.58	0.46
1883	0.55	0.34	0.21	1.00	0.63	0.37
1884	0.53	0.35	0.18	1.00	0.67	0.32
1885	0.52	0.36	0.16	1.02	0.71	0.31
1886	0.52	0.37	0.15	1.05	0.75	0.30
1887	0.56	0.39	0.17	1.13	0.79	0.34
1888	0.61	0.41	0.20	1.24	0.84	0.40
1889	0.64	0.44	0.20	1.32	0.90	0.42
1890	0.64	0.45	0.19	1.36	0.96	0.40
1891	0.65	0.47	0.18	1.42	1.02	0.40
1892	0.63	0.48	0.15	1.40	1.07	0.33
1893	0.61	0.48	0.14	1.43	1.12	0.31
1894	0.60	0.47	0.13	1.47	1.15	0.32
1895	0.58	0.48	0.10	1.44	1.18	0.25
1896	0.58	0.50	0.08	1.42	1.21	0.20
1897	0.66	0.53	0.12	1.54	1.25	0.29
1898	0.75	0.58	0.17	1.66	1.29	0.37
1899	0.84	0.64	0.20	1.75	1.34	0.41
1900	0.97	0.69	0.28	1.97	1.40	0.57
1901	1.10	0.72	0.38	2.23	1.46	0.77
1902	1.16	0.76	0.40	2.34	1.54	0.80
1903	1.22	0.80	0.42	2.47	1.62	0.85
1904	1.36	0.85	0.50	2.72	1.71	1.01
1905	1.48	0.91	0.57	2.94	1.81	1.13
1906	1.47	0.98	0.49	2.88	1.92	0.96
1907	1.54	1.05	0.48	2.97	2.03	0.94
1908	1.64	1.13	0.50	3.10	2.14	0.95
1909	1.62	1.23	0.39	2.98	2.26	0.72
1910	1.65	1.31	0.33	2.97	2.37	0.60

(continued)

Year on Which Moving Average Is Centered	Current Prices			1929 Prices		
	Gross Producers' Durables (1)	Capital Consumption (2)	Net Producers' Durables (3)	Gross Producers' Durables (4)	Capital Consumption (5)	Net Producers' Durables (6)
1911	1.85	1.42	0.43	3.24	2.48	0.76
1912	1.92	1.51	0.41	3.31	2.60	0.71
1913	1.96	1.64	0.32	3.24	2.70	0.54
1914	2.28	1.79	0.49	3.57	2.80	0.76
1915	2.83	2.06	0.76	3.94	2.92	1.02
1916	3.69	2.56	1.14	4.34	3.07	1.27
1917	4.56	3.14	1.42	4.81	3.32	1.50
1918	5.42	3.70	1.72	5.27	3.54	1.73
1919	5.57	4.07	1.50	5.09	3.65	1.44
1920	5.45	4.27	1.18	4.86	3.80	1.06
1921	5.29	4.25	1.04	4.85	3.90	0.95
1922	5.14	4.12	1.02	4.85	3.88	0.97
1923	5.07	3.99	1.08	4.98	3.90	1.08
1924	5.54	4.06	1.49	5.58	4.08	1.50
1925	5.90	4.09	1.81	5.96	4.13	1.83
1926	6.01	4.10	1.91	6.10	4.16	1.94
1927	6.42	4.16	2.26	6.51	4.22	2.29
1928	6.38	4.11	2.27	6.53	4.22	2.32
1929	5.85	3.91	1.94	6.05	4.06	1.98
1930	5.08	3.66	1.43	5.33	3.89	1.44
1931	4.25	3.33	0.92	4.57	3.66	0.91
1932	3.42	3.00	0.43	3.85	3.41	0.44
1933	3.10	2.78	0.33	3.61	3.24	0.37
1934	3.53	2.72	0.81	4.15	3.21	0.94
1935	4.44	2.87	1.56	5.09	3.32	1.77
1936	5.06	3.12	1.94	5.66	3.49	2.17
1937	5.55	3.38	2.18	6.11	3.68	2.43
1938	6.11	3.66	2.45	6.56	3.88	2.69
1939	6.98	4.14	2.84	7.07	4.18	2.89
1940	8.61	4.94	3.67	8.04	4.74	3.30
1941	12.3	6.16	6.14	10.7	5.65	5.09
1942	16.4	7.94	8.47	14.0	7.08	6.94
1943	19.2	10.0	9.20	16.3	8.82	7.50
1944	20.0	12.0	8.02	16.7	10.2	6.46
1945	21.0	14.6	6.42	17.0	11.7	5.27
1946	20.8	17.5	3.34	16.1	13.1	2.98
1947	20.0	20.2	−0.20	14.3	14.1	0.19
1948	21.0	23.0	−2.01	13.7	14.9	−1.28
1949	24.6	26.4	−1.83	15.0	16.1	−1.14
1950	27.7	28.3	−0.60	16.2	16.6	−0.46
1951	30.5	29.3	1.20	17.4	16.8	0.55
1952	32.7	29.8	2.86	18.3	16.8	1.53
1953	34.1	30.2	3.94	18.8	16.6	2.14

Because of rounding, detail will not necessarily add to total.
The series are identical for Variants I and III.

(Notes on following page)

Appendix C

All entries are averages of annual series.

(1) Calculated from the annual series for 1869–1955 described below.

1869–1918: The 1929 price series underlying col. 4 multiplied by the price index implicit in output for domestic consumption. Output for domestic consumption, in current and 1929 prices, was derived by the method described in the notes to *National Product since 1869*, Table II-4, cols. 1 and 2, except that a further adjustment was made for 1899–1918 to include passenger cars used for business (see notes to Table R-13, cols. 1–3).

1919–1955: Table R-4, col. 2.

(2) Calculated from the annual estimates underlying Table R-16, col. 6.

(3) Calculated from the annual series derived by subtracting that underlying col. 2 from that underlying col. 1.

(4) Calculated from the annual series for 1869–1955 described below.

1869–1918: Interpolations between or extrapolations from the decade averages in Table R-15, col. 2, by the annual series on output for domestic consumption in 1929 prices, described in the notes to col. 1. The ratios of the decade averages of flow to the decade averages of output were computed and centered at the midpoints of the decades. Annual ratios were interpolated along a straight line and applied to the annual output figures.

1919–1955: Table R-5, col. 2.

(5) Calculated from the annual estimates underlying Table R-17, col. 6.

(6) Calculated from the annual series derived by subtracting that underlying col. 5 from that underlying col. 4.

FIVE-YEAR MOVING AVERAGES OF NET CHANGES IN INVENTORIES
AND IN CLAIMS AGAINST FOREIGN COUNTRIES,
CURRENT AND 1929 PRICES, 1869–1955
(billions of dollars)

Year on Which Moving Average Is Centered	Net Changes in Inventories		Net Changes in Claims against Foreign Countries	
	Current Prices (1)	1929 Prices (2)	Current Prices (3)	1929 Prices (4)
1871	0.35	0.39	−0.18	−0.24
1872	0.35	0.40	−0.16	−0.22
1873	0.37	0.43	−0.15	−0.21
1874	0.39	0.46	−0.11	−0.16
1875	0.37	0.47	−0.06	−0.09
1876	0.37	0.50	−0.01	−0.01
1877	0.40	0.57	0.03	0.06
1878	0.45	0.66	0.06	0.10
1879	0.44	0.66	0.06	0.10
1880	0.45	0.68	0.04	0.07
1881	0.43	0.65	0.01	0.02
1882	0.40	0.60	−0.02	−0.03
1883	0.34	0.51	−0.03	−0.06
1884	0.33	0.51	−0.06	−0.10
1885	0.29	0.47	−0.06	−0.12
1886	0.27	0.44	−0.09	−0.17
1887	0.25	0.42	−0.10	−0.19
1888	0.26	0.43	−0.11	−0.22
1889	0.24	0.41	−0.10	−0.20
1890	0.25	0.43	−0.09	−0.17
1891	0.24	0.41	−0.06	−0.13
1892	0.21	0.37	−0.05	−0.09
1893	0.24	0.44	−0.05	−0.10
1894	0.22	0.42	−0.03	−0.05
1895	0.23	0.46	0.01	0.03
1896	0.27	0.54	0.10	0.22
1897	0.37	0.72	0.16	0.34
1898	0.38	0.71	0.26	0.56
1899	0.47	0.87	0.31	0.66
1900	0.47	0.83	0.32	0.65
1901	0.50	0.86	0.28	0.56
1902	0.42	0.70	0.26	0.51
1903	0.44	0.72	0.21	0.40
1904	0.47	0.75	0.17	0.32
1905	0.49	0.75	0.16	0.30
1906	0.35	0.54	0.16	0.30
1907	0.50	0.75	0.10	0.19
1908	0.53	0.76	0.04	0.07
1909	0.46	0.65	0.02	0.03
1910	0.54	0.75	a	0.01

(continued)

Year on Which Moving Average Is Centered	Net Changes in Inventories		Net Changes in Claims against Foreign Countries	
	Current Prices (1)	1929 Prices (2)	Current Prices (3)	1929 Prices (4)
1911	0.76	1.06	−0.01	−0.02
1912	0.57	0.78	ᵃ	ᵃ
1913	0.47	0.66	0.35	0.54
1914	0.67	0.85	0.93	1.33
1915	0.63	0.71	1.58	2.03
1916	0.60	0.59	1.98	2.39
1917	1.39	1.14	2.77	3.13
1918	2.81	1.94	3.02	3.09
1919	2.54	1.60	2.75	2.60
1920	2.54	1.57	2.22	2.00
1921	3.01	2.02	1.88	1.69
1922	2.04	1.28	1.31	1.18
1923	0.93	0.75	0.88	0.86
1924	1.21	1.00	0.65	0.64
1925	1.18	1.02	0.66	0.66
1926	0.50	0.38	0.77	0.76
1927	1.02	0.90	0.73	0.72
1928	0.60	0.48	0.73	0.73
1929	0.04	0.11	0.68	0.69
1930	−0.55	−0.62	0.57	0.59
1931	−0.78	−1.19	0.40	0.42
1932	−1.31	−2.05	0.33	0.37
1933	−0.98	−1.37	0.18	0.22
1934	−0.47	−1.03	0.12	0.15
1935	0.51	0.56	0.10	0.12
1936	0.70	1.08	0.29	0.35
1937	1.00	1.78	0.38	0.45
1938	1.23	1.86	0.70	0.82
1939	1.90	2.85	0.97	1.12
1940	1.77	2.34	0.97	1.12
1941	1.69	2.23	0.38	0.53
1942	1.34	1.82	−0.14	0.03
1943	0.60	0.86	−0.66	−0.51
1944	0.85	0.89	0.06	−0.04
1945	0.35	0.32	1.83	1.18
1946	1.39	1.39	2.59	1.77
1947	1.09	1.07	3.04	2.13
1948	2.82	2.49	2.81	2.02
1949	3.72	2.52	1.89	1.30
1950	4.50	3.02	0.07	0.05
1951	3.72	2.16	−0.72	−0.44
1952	3.83	2.52	−0.91	−0.56
1953	3.21	2.00	−0.57	−0.33

ᵃ Less than $0.005 billion.

Appendix C

The series are identical for Variants I and III. The price index used in calculating net changes in claims against foreign countries in 1929 prices is that implicit in gross national product excluding such changes, Variant I. Strictly speaking, for Variant III we should have computed the index implicit in that variant. But the difference is negligible and has been disregarded.

SOURCE, BY COLUMN

All entries are averages of annual series.

(1) Calculated from the annual series for 1869–1955 described below.

1869–1918: The 1929 price series underlying col. 2 multiplied by the BLS wholesale price index for all commodities, given in *Historical Statistics of the United States, 1789–1945*, Series L-15, adjusted to a 1929 base.

1919–1955: Table R-4, col. 3.

(2) Calculated from the annual series for 1869–1955 described below.

1869–1918: A preliminary series was derived by applying to annual changes in commodity output for 1869–1918 the regression line of annual changes in inventories (Table R-5, col. 3) on annual changes in commodity output (derived from Table R-21, col. 1) for 1919–1938. The regression equation is $y = 0.4462 + 0.306228x$. The final annual series was then calculated by computing the ratios of the decade averages in Table R-15, col. 3 to the decade averages of the preliminary annual series, interpolating along a straight line, and applying the resulting annual ratios to the preliminary series.

1919–1955: Table R-5, col. 3.

(3) Calculated from the annual estimates described in the notes to Table R-14, col. 4, or given in Table R-4, col. 4.

(4) Calculated from the annual series for 1869–1955 described below.

1869–1918: The series in current prices underlying col. 3 divided by the price index implicit in gross national product excluding net changes in claims against foreign countries, Variant I (series underlying Table R-25, col. 3, minus that underlying col. 3 in the present table divided by the sum of the series underlying Table R-26, col. 1, Table R-30, col. 10, Table R-33, col. 4, and col. 2 in the present table.

1919–1955: Table R-5, col. 4.

Changes in Net Durable Capital, Sector Estimates,
Compared with Commodity Flow Totals of Net
Construction and Equipment

Nature of the Comparison

IN the preceding appendixes we presented estimates of durable capital
formation (construction plus producers' durable commodities), gross
and net, in current and in 1929 prices. For the years since 1919, the
estimates are based on the *annual* volume of construction and of flow
of producers' durable commodities into domestic consumption. For
the earlier years they are based on the flow of construction materials
and of producers' durable commodities, available decennially and
interpolated annually. The underlying information, particularly for
the decades before 1919, is given in the censuses of production (chiefly
that of manufactures), and the data relate exclusively to the flow of
commodities without indicating the industry that is the ultimate user
of the capital good in question.

In the monographs on real capital accumulation and its financing
in the major sectors of the economy an attempt has been made to
prepare estimates of additions to capital for a period long enough to
permit analysis of secular trends. In some of those sectors—agriculture,
mining, manufacturing—the estimates are based upon the value of
capital held by enterprises as reported in current prices either in the
relevant censuses of production, or in corporate balance sheets. The
current price values must be converted to constant prices before changes
in real capital stock can be properly measured. In another sector—
residential real estate—the basic estimates relate to the gross volume of

capital additions, which are then reduced by an appropriate charge for capital consumption. In the regulated industries (utilities) sector a somewhat similar method is used: capital expenditures net of capital consumption are estimated.

The point to be noted is that for the years before 1919, the two sets of series—the total based on flow of commodities, and the sector estimates—are independent of each other. In some cases the primary source of the data is identical for both sets: thus, the *Census of Manufactures* is the source of the data not only for flow of producers' durable commodities and construction materials but also for capital held by manufacturing enterprises. However, the information on commodity production is quite distinct from that on capital. For other sectors—for instance, agriculture and mining—the data on capital come from a primary source different from that for total construction and flow of producers' durable commodities. Likewise, nonfarm residential and government construction estimates before 1919 are quite independent of the series on total construction: from 1919 on, total construction is, in effect, a summation of parts, whereas before 1919 it is an extrapolation based on the flow of all construction materials.

Although we show the two sets of estimates for the entire period 1880–1948, we limit our analysis to the comparison for 1880–1922, for two reasons. First, only in the earlier period are the sector estimates relatively independent of those derived from the flow of construction materials and producers' durable equipment; from 1919 on, this is not true of the estimates of nonfarm residential and government construction—quantitatively important sectors in recent years. Second, and perhaps more important, the estimates of capital formation for the years since 1919 do not need the careful checking of level and movement that the estimates for the earlier years do, since the available data provide a more solid foundation. Furthermore, a check of the level and movement in the earlier periods is a test of both sets of estimates, although, obviously, agreement of the totals provides no assurance that the sector estimates are free from significant errors.

The two sets of estimates can be compared effectively only for *net* volumes, in constant prices, and for construction and producers' durable equipment *combined*. Net volumes must be used because in several sectors capital additions are derived as differences between capital stock at two points of time. Since capital stock is given net of accumulated capital consumption, the differences represent net capital additions. We could have estimated capital consumption and derived gross capital additions, but in so doing we would only have added a further conjectural element to the comparison. We combine construction and producers' durable equipment because the underlying data on gross capital expenditures for several sectors do not distinguish the two. The same is true of the capital stock data for other sectors.

Finally, it seemed best to compare totals in constant prices since our main interest is in real capital accumulation. Besides, the price series used in the two sets of estimates are essentially the same. Keeping the prices in the comparison does not affect the results if the original data are in current prices, whereas a spurious element of similarity is introduced if the price element is added to the comparison where the original data do not require it.

Results of the Comparison

The detailed comparison is presented in Table R-35, although full information on the derivation of the sector estimates is not given there. It is available in the occasional papers and monographs already published by the National Bureau. A summary is given in Table D-1.

The periods distinguished in this table (and in Table R-35) are dictated largely by the censuses from which the data on capital stock for several sectors are derived. More periods could have been set up. For example, we could have taken account of the Census for 1904. But this further detail would hardly have been useful. In general, comparisons of the type made here are significant only for relatively long periods; and besides, we are interested in the longer-term movements alone.

The total of the sector estimates is narrower in scope than the total based on flow of construction materials and producers' durable equipment. The sector total excludes and the commodity flow total includes the following items: nonhousekeeping residential construction; construction and equipment for several industrial divisions included in the censuses of wealth in "other industrial" (trade, the construction industry, the finance and service industries); durable capital accumulation for such nonprofit institutions as trade unions, benevolent societies, etc.; and finally, producers' durable equipment flowing to governments. The total of sector estimates should, therefore, be smaller than the total derived from flow of construction materials and producers' durables, except for periods—if any—when net durable capital formation in the missing sectors can be assumed to be negative.

Appendix D

TABLE D-1

NET CONSTRUCTION AND EQUIPMENT, SECTOR TOTALS COMPARED WITH
COMMODITY FLOW TOTALS,
1929 PRICES, 1880–1948
(billions of dollars)

	1880–1890 (1)	1890–1900 (2)	1900–1912 (3)	1912–1922 (4)	1922–1930 (5)	1930–1940 (6)	1940–1948 (7)
1. Total, sectors	22.7	25.6	48.9	29.8	46.3	5.2	33.9
2. Total, direct estimate of net construction and producers' durables	23.0	33.8	60.7	29.8	54.0	7.5	41.3
3. Difference, line 2 minus line 1	0.3	8.2	11.8	ª	7.7	2.4	7.4
4. Line 1, per year	2.27	2.56	3.89	2.98	6.39	0.52	3.87
5. Line 2, per year	2.30	3.38	4.82	2.98	7.44	0.75	4.72
6. Difference, line 5 minus line 4	0.03	0.82	0.94	ª	1.06	0.24	0.85

Because of rounding, detail will not necessarily add to total.
ª Less than $0.05 billion.

SOURCE, BY LINE

1. Table R-35, line 8. For 1880–1890, we added an arbitrary allowance of $0.2 billion for lines 5b and 5c. Line 5d was omitted throughout.

2. Table R-35, line 9.

The two series move similarly, and the former is smaller than the latter, the positive difference presumably reflecting in part net capital formation in the missing sectors. Since the similarity in the pattern of movement may be due in part to the use in the two series of identical time periods with differing duration, we reduced the changes in each series to an annual basis (lines 4 and 5). Even then, the similarity persists—as it should, because the omissions from the sector estimates are a relatively small fraction of the total.

Yet there are some perceptible differences. Of these, the most important is in the movement from 1880–1890 to 1890–1900. In the earlier decade the two totals are practically identical, and net capital formation assignable to the missing sectors is negligible. In 1890–1900, the total based on commodity flow is about $8 billion larger than the sector total. The sector total rises about 13 per cent from the first to the second decade; the total based on commodity flow rises 47 per cent.

We checked further by comparing the difference between the two

TABLE D-2

DIFFERENCE BETWEEN SECTOR TOTALS AND COMMODITY FLOW TOTALS
OF NET CONSTRUCTION AND EQUIPMENT COMPARED WITH ESTIMATES
OF NET CAPITAL FORMATION FOR MISSING SECTORS,
1929 PRICES, 1880–1922

(billions of dollars)

	1880–1890 (1)	1890–1900 (2)	1900–1912 (3)	1912–1922 (4)	Total 1880–1922 (5)
1. Difference, Table D-1, line 3	0.3	8.2	11.8	a	20.3
		VALUATION A			
2. Real estate improvements, other industrial	2.81	1.49	4.17	−2.62	5.85
3. Equipment, other industrial	2.20	0.84	2.34	−0.58	4.80
4. Equipment, tax exempt	0.52	0.77	1.24	−0.28	2.26
5. Total, lines 2, 3, and 4	5.53	3.10	7.76	−3.48	12.91
		VALUATION B			
6. Real estate improvements, other industrial	2.56	1.61	4.68	−1.23	7.62
7. Equipment, other industrial	2.18	1.15	2.32	−0.91	4.74
8. Equipment, tax exempt	0.52	0.77	1.24	−0.28	2.26
9. Total, lines 6, 7, and 8	5.26	3.54	8.25	−2.42	14.62

Because of rounding, detail will not necessarily add to total.
a Less than $0.05 billion.

SOURCE: Lines 2–4 and 6–8 calculated from Simon Kuznets, *National Product since 1869* (New York, NBER, 1946), Tables IV-5 and IV-6, pp. 218–219.

series with an independent estimate of net capital formation for the missing sectors (Table D-2). From the wealth estimates originally presented in *National Product since 1869* (particularly Tables IV-5 and IV-6, pp. 218–219) we took the following items to represent the missing sectors: "other industrial" real estate improvements and equipment, and "tax exempt" equipment. The allowance is too large because some tax exempt equipment is included under the nonprofit institutions (religious bodies, hospitals, etc.) covered under the sector estimates in Table R-35; and it is too small because some nonhousekeeping residential construction may be included under "residential" in the wealth estimates, and because construction by some nonprofit institutions is missing from the sector estimates in Table R-35. But these discrepancies in scope are minor compared with the margin of error involved in the procedures employed in dividing the total value of real estate into land and improvements and in adjusting the successive estimates for changes in valuation.

Two aspects of the comparison in Table D-2 are of interest. The first concerns the order of magnitudes. For the period from 1880 to 1922 as a whole, the difference between the sector totals and the totals based on commodity flow is larger than net capital accumulation in the missing sectors suggested by the wealth data. These totals are $20.3 billion, and between $12.9 billion and $14.6 billion, depending upon the basis of valuation assumed in passing from current to constant prices. The difference is substantial, but can easily arise out of faulty adjustment of the wealth data for changes in prices. However, a difference of almost $6 billion (the difference in column 5 between line 1 and Valuation B, line 9—more acceptable than Valuation A, line 5) is not large in terms of the aggregate for 1880–1922 which in Table D-1, line 2, amounts to $147.3 billion. It can, in fact, be interpreted as evidence of substantial agreement between the two sets of estimates with respect to order of magnitude.

It is in the pattern of movement from period to period that differences emerge, especially from 1880–1890 to 1890–1900. The census of wealth data suggest that net capital formation in the missing sectors is over $5 billion in 1880–1890 compared with only about $3.5 billion in 1890–1900, as contrasted with the negligible amount in the earlier decade and the $8.2 billion in the later decade suggested by the difference between the sector and the commodity flow totals in Table D-1. And there is disagreement in the succeeding periods. The difference in Table D-1 suggests net capital formation in the missing sectors of $11.8 billion for 1900–1912 and practically zero for 1912–1922, whereas the census of wealth figures in Table D-2 (Valuation B) show only $8.2 billion for 1900–1912 and a disinvestment of $2.4 for 1912–1922.

Which of the two patterns is more acceptable—that suggested by the capital stock data or that indicated by the commodity flow data? We definitely favor the latter, for two major reasons. First, in observing movements over time, records of flows are generally more reliable than net changes in successive large totals that represent stocks. A small relative error in the estimate of a large stock can mean a damaging error in the derived net change. Hence, even if we could assume that the capital stock and the flow data are subject to the same relative error, there is ground for preferring the latter. Second, while evaluation of relative error margins is largely a matter of judgment, the strong impression here is that the capital stock data, which require major adjustments before successive totals of *reproducible* capital in constant prices can be secured, are subject to wider margins of error than the flow data, even though the latter were interpolated between successive census totals on the basis of rather small samples of annual series.

TABLE D-3

SECTOR TOTALS OF CHANGES IN NET DURABLE CAPITAL COMPARED WITH
NET CHANGES IN THE EARLIER ESTIMATES OF VALUE OF
REAL ESTATE IMPROVEMENTS AND VALUE OF EQUIPMENT,
1929 PRICES, 1880–1922

(billions of dollars)

	1880–1890 (1)	1890–1900 (2)	1900–1912 (3)	1912–1922 (4)	Total 1880–1922 (5)
1. Sector total, Table D-1	22.7	25.6	48.9	29.8	127.1
Earlier Estimates					
		VALUATION A			
2. Real estate improve-ments, total	21.2	19.9	47.8	1.08	89.9
3. Real estate improve-ments, other industrial	2.81	1.49	4.17	−2.62	5.85
4. Line 2 minus line 3	18.4	18.4	43.6	3.70	84.1
5. Equipment, total	6.93	8.34	18.1	2.63	36.0
6. Equipment, other industrial + tax exempt	2.72	1.62	3.58	−0.86	7.05
7. Line 5 minus line 6	4.21	6.72	14.5	3.49	28.9
8. Line 4 plus line 7	22.6	25.1	58.2	7.19	113.0
		VALUATION B			
9. Real estate improve-ments, total	20.0	20.5	50.6	9.66	100.8
10. Real estate improve-ments, other industrial	2.56	1.61	4.68	−1.23	7.62
11. Line 9 minus line 10	17.5	18.9	46.0	10.9	93.2
12. Equipment, total	6.91	8.79	18.1	2.12	35.9
13. Equipment, other industrial + tax exempt	2.70	1.92	3.56	−1.19	7.00
14. Line 12 minus line 13	4.21	6.87	14.5	3.31	28.9
15. Line 11 plus line 14	21.7	25.7	60.5	14.2	122.1

Because of rounding, detail will not necessarily add to total.

SOURCE: Lines 2, 3, 5, 6, 9, 10, 12, and 13, calculated from Kuznets, *National Product since 1869*, Tables IV-5 and IV-6, pp. 218–219.

It is not unlikely that further work and revision of the capital stock estimates would yield a somewhat different picture of relative magnitudes in 1880–1890 and 1890–1900—in the omitted sectors and perhaps even in some of the covered sectors. In this connection Table D-3 is of at least suggestive value. It presents a comparison of the totals yielded by the rough estimates based on capital stock data in *National Product since 1869* with the totals based on the sector estimates in Table R-35. For the entire period 1880–1922, the estimate based on the more recent and detailed work is not much different from that of the older series (Valuation B)—about $127 billion compared with $122 billion. Nor is there much difference in the totals for the first two decades. But in the last two periods substantial revisions appear: for 1900–1912 a reduction from $60.5 billion to $48.9 billion; and for 1912–1922 an increase from $14.2 billion to $29.8 billion. While many of our flow estimates have also been revised, none of the changes in the comprehensive totals has been as large as those shown in Table D-3. The table thus illustrates the marked modifications in net changes derivable from capital stock data resulting from changes in detail of procedure.

But it should be emphasized that this comment applies to net changes for relatively short periods. The longer the period of comparison, the higher, usually, the ratio of the intervening flow to the terminal stock figures and the narrower, therefore, the effect of errors in the latter upon possible errors in the former. For this reason we can attach some weight to the agreement of the commodity flow and the sector totals over the entire span from 1880 to 1922. For a study of the movement over the shorter periods, the estimates based on flow data are preferable.

TABLE R-35

Change in Value of Buildings and Equipment, Sector Estimates, Compared with Net Construction and Net Producers' Durables, Commodity Flow Totals, 1929 Prices, 1880–1948

(millions of dollars)

	June 1, 1880–June 1, 1890 (1)	June 1, 1890–June 1, 1900 (2)	June 1, 1900–Dec. 31, 1912 (3)	Dec. 31, 1912–Dec. 31, 1922 (4)	Dec. 31, 1922–Apr. 1, 1930 (5)	Apr. 1, 1930–Apr. 1, 1940 (6)	Apr. 1, 1940–Dec. 31, 1948 (7)
1. Agriculture (change in reproducible wealth)	726	1,476	4,677	1,883	150	−1,969	5,030
2. Mining, total (change in reproducible wealth)	464	734	1,855	1,849	928	−1,470	599
a. Metals	149	194	265	−72	−2	−302	−41
b. Anthracite coal	25	33	49	8	−24	−76	−20
c. Bituminous coal	60	151	426	145	−131	−239	69
d. Petroleum and natural gas	159	301	1,036	1,756	1,030	−742	583
e. Other nonmetallic minerals	70	55	79	13	54	−111	7
3. Manufacturing, total (change in reproducible wealth)	2,585	3,168	8,133	6,749	5,001	−1,695	9,437
a. Food, liquors, and tobacco	433	843	n.c.	n.c.	n.c.	−500	603
b. Textiles, clothing, and leather	492	550	n.c.	n.c.	n.c.	−1,136	261
c. Rubber products	14	28	n.c.	n.c.	n.c.	−143	181
d. Forest products	319	107	n.c.	n.c.	n.c.	−365	193
e. Paper, printing, and publishing	260	287	n.c.	n.c.	n.c.	−101	515
f. Chemicals, and petroleum refining	162	215	n.c.	n.c.	n.c.	1,203	3,905
g. Stone, clay, and glass products	111	174	n.c.	n.c.	n.c.	−308	−16
h. Metals and metal products	751	928	n.c.	n.c.	n.c.	−170	3,428
i. Miscellaneous	43	36	n.c.	n.c.	n.c.	−175	367

4. Nonfarm residential construction (net)	12,321	12,943	14,995	7,602	22,293	−1,321	3,526
5. Private nonprofit institutions, and proprietary hospitals, total (change in reproducible wealth)	n.a.	n.a.	n.a.	n.a.	n.a.	730	328
a. Religious bodies	530	563	597	227	920	226	325
b. Secondary schools and higher educational institutions	n.a.	183	323	386	381	284	36
c. Private nonprofit hospitals	n.a.	111	292	402	305	287	15
d. Proprietary hospitals	n.a.	n.a.	n.a.	n.a.	n.a.	−67	−48
6. Government construction (net)	1,160	1,956	6,045	8,334	7,527	13,418	11,192
7. Transportation and other public utilities, total (change in reproducible wealth)	4,692	4,495	12,005	2,398	8,798	−2,606	3,712
a. Telephones	67	333	733	−33	1,209	91	1,929
b. Local bus lines	0	0	[a]	12	99	140	154
c. Electric light and power	100	497	2,327	709	3,420	61	1,024
d. Steam railroads	3,807	1,506	5,212	817	2,605	−1,579	−21
e. Electric railways	290	1,557	1,737	−429	−771	−1,002	−812
f. Other	427	602	1,995	1,322	2,236	−317	1,438
8. Total of above sectors [b]	22,478	25,335 [c] / 25,629 [d]	48,922	29,830	46,303	5,154 [c] / 5,087 [d]	33,824
9. Net construction and net producers' durables	22,981	33,785	60,710	29,849	53,955	7,534	41,273
10. Difference (line 9 minus line 8)	503	8,450 [c] / 8,156 [d]	11,788	19	7,652	2,380 [c] / 2,447 [d]	7,449

Because of rounding, detail will not necessarily add to total.

n.a. = not available; n.c. = not calculated.

[a] Less than $0.5 million.

[b] Excludes government equipment, nonhousekeeping residential construction, "other" nonprofit institutions, "other" industrial, as well as subgroups for which it is indicated that data are not available for the given period.

[c] Comparable with entry for preceding period.

[d] Comparable with entry for following period.

(Notes on following page)

Appendix D

For those wealth series for which the value for the given census date was not reported, it was interpolated along a logarithmic straight line between the two dates closest to the given date. In estimating net construction and net producers' durables for a fraction of a year, the total for the year was pro-rated on the basis of the number of months covered (for example, the period from June 1 through December 31 was assigned 7/12 of the total for the given calendar year).

For agriculture, mining, and manufacturing, specific references are to the earlier Occasional Papers; but the series are identical with those in the later monographs.

SOURCE, BY LINE

1. Change in value estimated separately for machinery and equipment and for buildings. For the value of machinery and equipment, we used Alvin S. Tostlebe's series in *The Growth of Physical Capital in Agriculture, 1870–1950* (Occasional Paper 44, New York, NBER, 1954), Table G-1, p. 91. For the value of buildings, Tostlebe supplied special computations for the census dates 1880, 1890, 1900, 1910, 1920, 1930, 1940, and 1950.

2. Change in value estimated from special tabulations provided by Israel Borenstein (for census dates 1880, 1890, 1909, 1919, 1929, 1940, and 1948) underlying his series in *Capital and Output Trends in Mining Industries, 1870–1948* (Occasional Paper 45, New York, NBER, 1954), or revisions of them. The series for nonmetallic minerals for 1880, 1890, and 1909 was first raised by the proportionate difference between the entry for 1919 comparable with those for the later years and the entry for 1919 comparable with those for the earlier years.

3. Change in value estimated from special calculations provided by Daniel Creamer (for census dates 1880, 1890, 1900, 1909, 1914, 1919, 1929, 1937, and 1948) underlying his series in *Capital and Output Trends in Manufacturing Industries, 1880–1948* (Occasional Paper 41, New York, NBER, 1954), or revisions of them.

4. Calculated from the annual series described in Table R-32, notes to col. 6. For cols. 1 and 2, the use of Grebler's estimate of value as of June 1, 1890 (rather than the value arrived at by pro-rating net construction) yields slightly different results: $12,466 million for col. 1, and $12,798 million for col. 2.

5. Change in value estimated from NBER series (mimeographed) prepared by Robert Rude. His series for religious bodies were estimated for December 31, 1870, 1890, 1906, 1916, 1922, 1928, 1936, 1947, and 1948; those for educational institutions, for June 30, 1890, 1906, 1916, 1926, 1928, 1936, and 1948; and those for hospitals, for December 31, 1890, 1906, 1910, 1916, 1923, 1928, 1935, and for September 30, 1946 and 1948 for private nonprofit hospitals, and for December 31, 1928 and 1935, and September 30, 1946 and 1948 for proprietary hospitals.

6. Calculated from the annual series described in Table R-32, notes to cols. 7 and 8.

7. Change in value estimated from the annual series, January 1, 1880 through January 1, 1949, in Melville J. Ulmer, *Capital in Transportation, Communications, and Public Utilities: Its Formation and Financing* (Princeton for NBER, 1960), Table B-1, pp. 235–236; Table C-1, pp. 256–257; Table D-1, pp. 320–321; Table E-1, pp. 374–375; Table F-1, pp. 405–406; Table G-1, p. 440; Table H-1, pp. 452–453.

8. Calculated from the annual series described in Table R-32, notes to col. 10, and in Table R-33, notes to col. 6.

Estimates of Population and of the Labor Force: Census and Mid-Censal Dates, and Quinquennial Moving Averages

SINCE population and labor force are two important variables in our analysis of trends in national product and capital formation, and since long swings in the rate of secular growth are a major component in long-term changes, we need continuous estimates of these two variables—either acceptable annual estimates, or annual approximations that yield acceptable five-year moving averages. For the purpose at hand, the available annual series on population suffer from three defects: (1) they make no allowance for the known underenumeration of the group 0 to 4 years of age; (2) for the decades before 1900, they are based on straight-line interpolation between the decennial census figures; and (3) before 1920 the annual registration of births and deaths was only partial. For labor force, annual estimates are available only for the recent decades. We thought it advisable, therefore, to derive new and consistent series on population and on labor force, sufficiently continuous to serve our purpose.

In this task, we had the invaluable assistance of the staff of the University of Pennsylvania Study of Population Redistribution and Economic Growth, directed by Dorothy S. Thomas and the author. The detailed notes to Tables R-36 and R-38 describe the procedures used, aimed at securing an adequate population series and, indirectly, a series on labor force. The technically-minded reader is directed to these notes, and will find additional information in the full report of the study.[1] Here we give only a brief sketch of the procedures and comment upon the character of the estimates.

Estimates of Population, Census and Mid-Censal Dates

The annual estimates of population are the sum of separate estimates for the native born white, the nonwhite, and the foreign born. Before such annual estimates of native born could be attempted, several steps were necessary: (1) adjustment of each census total from 1870 to 1950 for the underenumeration of the age group 0 to 4 years; (2) adjustment of the census total for 1870 for the underenumeration which may have affected all age groups; and (3) estimation of the mid-censal population (the population as of the mid-point between two census dates) for the period from 1870 to 1940.

1. The general method followed in adjusting for underenumeration of the age group 0 to 4 years was to work back from the age group 10 to 14 years in the next census year, applying to the latter a "reverse survival" or "revival" ratio secured from life tables. The principle underlying this adjustment was that there was much less, if any, tendency to undercount the age group 10 to 14 years than to undercount the age group 0 to 4 years. Comparison of the native born 0 to 4 group in one census with the native born 10 to 14 group in the next census (10 years later) in many cases showed the latter to be larger than the former, whereas deaths during the intercensal interval would have made it smaller. Unless there had been a major overcount of the 10 to 14 years group, which seemed unlikely, this result was due to the usual tendency to undercount the 0 to 4 group. The adjustment for the latter was made separately for whites and nonwhites. For 1950, for which no life tables were available at the time of computation, the undercount was assumed proportional to that established for 1940.

2. The adjustment for underenumeration in the 1870 Census followed the same procedure. A revival ratio was applied to the number of native born reported in the 1880 Census. This was done separately for whites and nonwhites, by age group and by sex. The ratio estimated in this case for each 1880 group 14 years of age and over was the 1880–1890 census survival rate modified by the trend from 1870 to 1890 in

[1] *Population Redistribution and Economic Growth, United States, 1870–1950*, Vols. I and II (American Philosophical Society, Philadelphia, 1957 and 1960). A third volume is in preparation.

the life table survival rates. For the 10 to 14 group in 1880 the revival ratio was taken from the life tables (see discussion under step 1 above), because the census survival rates for this age group are misleading owing to the census undercount of the 0 to 4 group in the initial of the two censuses. This adjustment, and that for underenumeration of the 0 to 4 group, add some 2.39 million to the 1870 total of native born compared with the usual adjustment of 1.26 million which excludes the correction for underenumeration of the 0 to 4 group.[2]

3. Mid-censal population was estimated in two distinct steps. First, mid-censal population was estimated for the age groups 0 to 4 and 5 to 9. For this purpose reverse survival or revival ratios were applied to the groups 5 to 9, and 10 to 14 years of age, respectively, in the census totals for the terminal date of the interval, the ratios being derived from appropriate life tables.

Second, for each age group 5 years and over, the number of deaths and disappearances during the census interval was estimated as the difference between the number of persons in the given age group at the beginning of the interval and the number in the group 10 years older at the next census. The estimates were made separately for males and females, for native whites, and nonwhites. Since the native born population of the United States could be reasonably assumed to be a closed group, these differences were treated as deaths. From appropriate life tables, the ratio of deaths during the first five years to those during the entire intercensal period, for each age, sex, and race group, was used to apportion the deaths during the intercensal interval between the first and the second half of that interval. These calculations, carried through for each decade from 1870 through 1940, were subject to only two modifications: (1) for 1870–1880 the revised 1870 figures were used; (2) for the 1910–1920 decade a special adjustment was made to take account of the influenza epidemic of 1918, not reflected in the life tables for 1920.

The above calculations were carried through for the native born white and total nonwhite. For foreign born whites an annual series was available from the detailed work on the census data on foreign born and on the annual series of immigration and emigration prepared by Simon Kuznets and Ernest Rubin.[3]

[2] See *Historical Statistics of the United States, 1789–1945,* Series B-2 for 1870 and note 11 to that figure.

[3] In connection with *Immigration and the Foreign Born* (Occasional Paper 46, New York, NBER, 1954).

Appendix E

Estimates of the Labor Force, Census and Mid-Censal Dates

Here too, we used the detailed work on estimates of the gainfully occupied and the labor force, by states, for the period since 1870, prepared by the University of Pennsylvania Study of Population Redistribution and Economic Growth. One conclusion of that study, of major importance to us, is that the shift from the gainfully occupied concept, followed in the censuses before 1940, to the labor force concept, adopted in the Census of 1940, has no significant effect on long-term trends. For our purpose, then, the two concepts are sufficiently similar to permit treatment of the resulting totals as a continuous and comparable series.

Another specific result of the Pennsylvania study utilized is the estimate of the number in the labor force 10 to 13 years of age in 1940 and 1950. The Censuses for those two years omitted that age group from the labor force count, whereas the earlier censuses had covered it in the totals of gainfully occupied. We therefore added that age group to the 1940 and 1950 totals to secure a series fully comparable in age coverage.

Having this series of the gainfully occupied or labor force for ages 10 and over for each census year, we could proceed to the subsequent calculations, which were relatively simple.

1. The procedures described in the first section of this appendix yielded population by age and sex for each census year, and for the mid-point of each intercensal interval, separately for native white and total nonwhite. We could, therefore, obtain population 10 years of age and over, separately for males and females, and for native born whites and all nonwhites.

2. For foreign born whites, we had annual series, but no age distribution except for the census years. For the mid-censal foreign born population 10 years of age and over, we interpolated between the number at the beginning and end of the intercensal interval on the basis of the annual series for total foreign born whites, male and female separately.

3. The sum of the results under (1) and (2) gave us total population, 10 years of age and over, male and female separately, at the census dates and at the mid-points of the intercensal intervals, 1870 to 1940.

4. For each census year, we had total labor force or gainfully occupied 10 years of age and over, separately for males and females. We calculated the ratio of this series to total population, 10 years of age and over, male and female separately, and estimated the ratio for the

mid-point of the intercensal interval by straight-line interpolation. The application of this interpolated ratio to population 10 years of age and over, male and female separately, gave us the mid-censal estimate of the labor force.

The Annual Series and the Five-Year Moving Averages

The estimating procedures described above yielded series on native born white, and total nonwhite population, male and female separately, for census dates, 1870 to 1950, and at roughly quinquennial intervals from 1870 to 1940, supplemented by an annual series on foreign born white population from 1869 through 1940. We also had series on the labor force, male and female separately, for census dates, 1870 to 1950, and at roughly quinquennial intervals from 1870 through 1940.

The next question was whether we could interpolate between the quinquennial estimates to derive acceptable *annual* approximations. This would have been possible for population, and perhaps for labor force, from 1920 on, since the available annual series on population for those years is based on a sufficiently comprehensive area of registration of births and deaths to warrant confidence in the annual changes shown. But any attempt to do so for the decades before 1920, and particularly before 1900, would run into serious difficulties. And since five-year moving averages suffice for our purposes, the time expenditure for making annual estimates did not seem warranted.

We decided therefore, that it was sufficient to estimate native born and total nonwhite population, annually, by straight-line logarithmic interpolation between the totals given at roughly quinquennial intervals, and then to add the annual series on foreign born whites estimated by Kuznets and Rubin. This was done for all the intervals from 1870 through 1940.

For the years after 1940, we estimated the annual total population directly, rather than by components, by interpolation between and extrapolation from the adjusted census totals for 1940 and 1950, using the annual estimates of the Census Bureau as an index. For the labor force also for the years after 1940, we made annual interpolations between and extrapolations from the census totals for 1940 and 1950, on the basis of the Census Bureau annual series on the labor force.

The procedure for the years beginning with 1920 could have been refined easily, but was not, because we felt that little effect on the five-year moving averages could be anticipated. To check on our decision, we calculated five-year moving averages of the available annual population series from 1920 to 1940 and compared them with five-year moving averages of the series derived by our procedure (shown in Table R-37). Our estimates are consistently larger than those derived from the current annual series, because of our adjustment for the underenumeration of the 0 to 4 group. But the excess ranges from 0.4 million to 0.8 million, or from slightly over 0.3 per cent to slightly over 0.7 per cent of the totals. This variation of about one-half of 1 per cent did not seem significant enough to warrant changes in the already established procedure, which could be followed for the full period covered.

The fact remains that the underlying annual series of population and labor force are not true annual estimates, but rather quinquennial series. Yet the resulting five-year moving averages should be reliable enough for a study of long swings in the rate of secular growth. They also permit us to calculate five-year moving averages of product and flow of goods per capita, and per member of the labor force (see Table R-40).

POPULATION EXCLUDING ARMED FORCES OVERSEAS, CENSUS AND MID-CENSAL DATES,
1870–1950

(millions)

| | Native White | | Foreign White | | Nonwhite | | Total |
	Male (1)	Female (2)	Male (3)	Female (4)	Male (5)	Female (6)	Population (7)
June 1, 1870	14.79	14.58	2.94	2.55	2.94	2.95	40.75
June 1, 1875	16.73	16.57	3.46	2.98	3.27	3.31	46.32
June 1, 1880	18.85	18.43	3.52	3.04	3.46	3.41	50.71
June 1, 1885	21.15	20.63	4.61	3.84	3.72	3.65	57.61
June 1, 1890	23.63	22.99	4.95	4.17	3.98	3.90	63.63
June 1, 1895	26.23	25.52	5.43	4.59	4.35	4.27	70.39
June 1, 1900	28.82	28.03	5.52	4.70	4.67	4.62	76.36
May 8, 1905	31.61	30.76	6.37	5.11	4.95	4.89	83.70
Apr. 15, 1910	34.82	33.90	7.52	5.82	5.20	5.12	92.39
Feb. 22, 1915	38.19	37.34	8.18	6.46	5.45	5.39	101.01
Jan. 1, 1920	41.20	40.48	7.53	6.18	5.56	5.50	106.45
Feb. 15, 1925	45.16	44.51	7.73	6.54	5.94	5.94	115.82
Apr. 1, 1930	48.63	48.07	7.50	6.48	6.28	6.34	123.30
Apr. 1, 1935	51.17	50.86	6.69	5.91	6.49	6.62	127.74
Apr. 1, 1940	53.74	53.62	6.01	5.41	6.69	6.90	132.37
Apr. 1, 1950	62.25	63.07	5.18	4.98	7.74	8.08	151.30

Estimates include the armed forces stationed in the United States at the time of enumeration.

SOURCE, BY COLUMN

(1), (2), (5),

and (6) 1870–1940: From "Midcensal Estimates of the Native White and Total Nonwhite Population of the United States, 1870–1940," unpublished memorandum by Everett S. Lee (Study of Population Redistribution and Economic Growth, University of Pennsylvania), Table II-B for 1870 and 1875, and Table I for later dates.

While the basic data are the census totals by race, nativity, age, and sex, several adjustments and additional calculations had to be made. The adjustments were designed to correct the 1870 Census total for the undercount and all census totals for underenumeration of the age group 0 to 4 years. The additional calculations were needed to estimate mid-censal population totals for a study of movement by five-year intervals, and entailed estimating deaths and births during a given intercensal period and distributing them between the halves of that period. It is impossible here to give a detailed description of the procedures employed, but the notes below will be useful to technicians as a more specific indication of what was done.

1. Adjustment of the Age Group 0 to 4 Years for Underenumeration, Census Dates

"Reverse survival" or "revival" ratios were applied to the age group 10 to 14 years at the following census and the resulting estimate was substituted for the enumerated age group 0 to 4 years. This is not a correction for underenumeration *per se* but for underenumeration relative to the enumerated 10–14 age

(Notes continue on following page)

(1), (2), (5), and (6)   group at the following census. For native whites, the survival ratios were obtained from a series of life tables for native whites, prepared by Dorothy Thomas and the University of Pennsylvania staff in connection with the Kuznets-Rubin study, *Immigration and the Foreign Born* (see pp. 65–68 of Occasional Paper 46, New York, NBER, 1954). For nonwhites, the survival ratios from the life tables for Negroes centering around census years were averaged to approximate decade ratios for the period 1900–1940. For the period before 1900, the 1900–1910 ratio of Negro to native white ratios, multiplied by the native white ratios for 1870–1880, 1880–1890, and 1890–1900, respectively, yielded ratios for all nonwhites for those decades.

2. Deriving Mid-Censal Population

a. Estimating the Age Groups 0 to 4, and 5 to 9 Years

The 0–4 and 5–9 age groups at mid-censal dates were estimated by applying reverse survival or revival ratios to the age groups 5–9, and 10–14, respectively, at the terminal census. The reverse survival ratios were derived in the following manner. For each of the life tables of the United States from 1900 through 1950 the ratios of the L_x's in the 0–4 age group to those in the 5–9 group, and of those in the 5–9 age group to those in the 10–14 group were obtained. In establishing the ratio to be used in computing a given mid-censal population, the ratios from the life tables centering around the initial and the terminal censuses were weighted 3 and 1 in favor of the latter. For example, in computing the ratio used in estimating the 1935 0–4 age group from the 1940 enumerated 5–9 age group, the reverse survival ratio from the 1940 life table was given a weight of 3 and that from the 1930 life table a weight of 1.

For the period 1870–1900, the English life tables for 1871–1880, 1881–1890, and 1891–1900 were used to establish a trend. The United States ratio for total whites for the 1900–1910 decade (as estimated by averaging the 1900 and 1910 ratios) was divided by the English ratio for 1901–1910. The resulting dividend, multiplied by the English ratios for 1871–1880, 1881–1890, and 1891–1900, yielded estimates that were assumed to represent the ratios that would have been found in United States decade life tables for native whites, had these existed. These decade ratios were assumed to apply to 1875, 1885, and 1895, respectively, and those for the census years were interpolated between them or extrapolated from them. Here again, the resulting ratios were weighted 3 and 1 in favor of the second census year. For nonwhites, the corresponding ratios were obtained by dividing the 1900–1910 ratio for Negroes by that for native whites, and multiplying the dividend by the native white revival ratios for 1880–1875, 1890–1885, and 1900–1895.

b. Estimating the Age Groups 10 Years and Over

i. Apportioning Deaths between the Two Halves of Each Intercensal Period from 1870 to 1910, and from 1920 to 1940

Here, a method was needed that would take account of the uneven distribution of deaths during an intercensal period and yield mid-censal estimates in which

(1), (2), (5), and (6)

the biases were to some extent proportional to those of both the preceding and following censuses. From life tables the proportion of deaths that occurred in each group in the first five years of the intercensal period was established and on that basis the total number of deaths for that age group was distributed between the two halves of the period.

The life tables used were those for the United States including or centered around the census years 1900, 1910, 1920, 1930, 1940, and 1950. (It should be noted that those for 1900, 1910, and 1920 were based on the mortality rates in those years—only ten states and the District of Columbia in 1900, the coverage increasing in 1910 and 1920. For the last three census years the mortality in all the states is covered, that in Texas in 1930 having been estimated.) The deaths in a given age group in the first five years of an intercensal period and those in the entire period were obtained by subtracting from the sum of the L_x's in the given age group the sum of those in the groups 5 and 10 years older. The proportional distribution of the deaths computed from these data was calculated for each census year and the proportions for contiguous census years averaged (except those for 1910 and 1920) to approximate the proportion that would have been obtained from decade life tables (e.g., the proportion used for 1900–1910 was the average of those for 1900 and 1910).

The total number of deaths for a given age group was estimated as the difference between the number of persons in the given age group at the beginning of the intercensal period and the number in the group 10 years older at the end of the period. Multiplying that number by the proportion established from the life tables yielded the number of deaths occurring in the first five and last five years of the period. The estimated deaths for the first five-year period were then subtracted from the population at the beginning of the period, yielding the number surviving to the mid-censal point. This procedure was followed for each age group 5–14 and over, resulting in a mid-censal population estimate for ages 10 and over.

Because there were no United States life tables for the years before 1900, and because very few states recorded the number of deaths during that period, the 1900–1910 proportions were used in distributing the number of deaths for the intercensal periods before 1900. (Proportions computed from the English life tables for 1871–1880, 1881–1890, and 1891–1900 showed trends for some age groups too different from those in the United States life tables to warrant their use as extrapolators of the United States ratios. Furthermore, such extrapolation of the United States trend, besides being a doubtful procedure, would make relatively little difference in the resulting mid-censal estimates.)

ii. Apportioning Deaths between the Two Halves of the 1910–1920 Intercensal Period

Because of the influenza epidemic of 1918, a year not included in the 1919–1921 life table, the method em-

(Notes continue on following page)

621

(1), (2), (5), and (6)

ployed for the other decades could not be used in estimating the mid-censal population aged 10 and over between 1910 and 1920. Instead, an attempt was made to distribute among the age cohorts of the 1910 Census and persons born after that date the number of deaths occurring each year from April 15, 1910 to January 1, 1920. For example, the group aged 5–14 at the 1910 Census was assigned the following proportions of the deaths occurring in 1910 and succeeding years:

1910 $\quad$ $0.45747D_5 + 0.70834(D_6 \ldots \ldots D_{14})$
$\quad\quad\quad$ $+ 0.25087D_{15}$

1911 $\quad$ $0.04253D_5 + 0.74913D_6 + D_7 \ldots \ldots D_{14}$
$\quad\quad\quad$ $+ 0.95747D_{15} + 0.25087D_{16}$

1912 $\quad$ $0.04253D_6 + 0.74913D_7 + D_8 \ldots \ldots D_{15}$
$\quad\quad\quad$ $+ 0.95747D_{16} + 0.25087D_{17}$

and so on.

The underlying assumption was a rectangular distribution of deaths for each year of age and for each calendar year. Since the deaths were recorded by 5-year age groups, it was further assumed that one-fifth of the deaths in each 5-year age group could be assigned to each included single year of age. Because the deaths of native whites in 1912 and 1913 were not reported separately, they were estimated by straight-line interpolation between those for 1911 and 1914. Furthermore, the proportion of native white deaths in the registration states between April 15, 1910 and January 1, 1915 to those between April 15, 1910 and January 1, 1920 was assumed to apply to all native white population.

An important factor in the distribution of deaths among age groups over a long period is migration. In-migration increases the number of deaths in most age groups simply because the population is increased by migration, while out-migration has the opposite effect. For nonwhites, the rather small amount of in-migration, probably increasing in the war years, made the proportion of deaths occurring in an age cohort of 1910 in the registration states of 1910 much too high for the second half of the period. For nonwhites, therefore, the proportion of deaths in 1910–1915 to those in 1910–1920 was estimated by adjusting the native white proportions by the 1900–1910 ratio of nonwhite to native white.

iii. A Check on the Method Used for All Intercensal Periods except 1910–1920

It was assumed that the average of the proportions established from life tables for each end of the decade adequately represented proportions for the entire intercensal interval. A crude check on this assumption for the periods from 1900 to 1940 was made on the basis of the distribution of the deaths of native whites in the registration states following the procedure employed for the period 1910–1920. The proportion of deaths occurring in the first five years of each intercensal period was quite close to that obtained by using life tables. The largest difference was just over 4 percentage points, but the proportions derived from the registration states data

(1), (2), (5), and (6)   were much more irregular than those obtained from the life tables, partly because of the smoothing of life table values and partly because of the unavoidably crude distribution of deaths. In addition, deaths of native whites had to be estimated for those years when they were not presented separately.

c. Special Adjustment for 1870 and 1875

The 1870 population was computed as follows. Reverse survival ratios were applied to the more complete enumeration of 1880, using the 1880–1890 census survival ratios adjusted for the effect of changing mortality. The life tables for native whites computed by Dorothy Thomas and the University of Pennsylvania staff were used to estimate the effect of changing mortality. The ten-year survival ratios computed from those tables for each age group for 1870–1880 were divided by the ratios for 1880–1890. The resulting adjustment was applied to the census survival ratios for 1880–1890. The adjusted ratios were then applied to the appropriate 1880 populations to yield 1870 populations for the age groups 5–9 through 50–54. For ages 55 and over in 1870 the 1880–1890 census survival ratios were used without adjustment because of the unreliability of the life tables for the upper age groups. The age group 0–4 was estimated by the life table survival ratio referred to under b-i above. The adjustment applied to the native white census survival ratios was applied also to the nonwhite census survival ratios.

The 1875 population was computed as follows. The ratios of five- to ten-year reverse survival ratios were obtained from life tables and applied to the ten-year reverse survival ratios used above to approximate five-year reverse census survival ratios. The resulting five-year reverse survival ratios were then multiplied by the appropriate age groups in the 1880 Census to yield an estimated 1875 population for each age group except the 0–4 group which was estimated by the life table survival ratio referred to under b-i above.

1950: *Census of Population, 1950.* Numbers of nonwhite males and nonwhite females, as reported, were adjusted for underenumeration of children under 5 by applying to the 1950 enumeration of the 0–4 group the 1940 ratio of the adjusted 0–4 group to the enumerated 0–4 group, computed from the University of Pennsylvania Study (cited) and extrapolated to 1950 by the similar ratio computed for 1940 and 1950 from *Current Population Reports* (Census Bureau, Series P-25, No. 98). The numbers of native white males and native white females, as reported, were adjusted for underenumeration of children under 5 by the same procedure, except that the 1940 University of Pennsylvania ratio was the ratio of native whites adjusted to total whites enumerated, and the extrapolating ratio was the ratio of total whites adjusted to total whites enumerated.

(3) and (4)   1870–1940: From worksheets underlying the estimates given in Simon Kuznets and Ernest Rubin, *Immigration and the Foreign Born,* Table B-6.

1950: *Census of Population, 1950,* Vol. II, Table 35.

(7) Sum of cols. 1–6.

TABLE R-37

FIVE-YEAR MOVING AVERAGES OF TOTAL POPULATION, JULY 1, 1869–1955
(millions)

Year on Which Moving Average Is Centered (July 1)	Native White		Foreign White		Nonwhite		Total Population Excluding Armed Forces Overseas (7)	Armed Forces Overseas (8)	Total Population Including Armed Forces Overseas (9)
	Male (1)	Female (2)	Male (3)	Female (4)	Male (5)	Female (6)			
1871	15.2	15.0	3.10	2.69	3.02	3.03	42.0	0	42.0
1872	15.6	15.4	3.22	2.77	3.08	3.10	43.1	0	43.1
1873	16.0	15.8	3.32	2.85	3.14	3.17	44.2	0	44.2
1874	16.4	16.2	3.39	2.91	3.20	3.23	45.3	0	45.3
1875	16.8	16.6	3.43	2.95	3.26	3.28	46.2	0	46.2
1876	17.2	16.9	3.43	2.96	3.31	3.32	47.1	0	47.1
1877	17.6	17.3	3.41	2.96	3.35	3.35	48.0	0	48.0
1878	18.0	17.7	3.43	2.97	3.39	3.37	48.9	0	48.9
1879	18.4	18.1	3.51	3.03	3.43	3.40	49.9	0	49.9
1880	18.9	18.5	3.67	3.13	3.47	3.43	51.1	0	51.1
1881	19.3	18.9	3.88	3.27	3.52	3.46	52.4	0	52.4
1882	19.8	19.3	4.12	3.43	3.57	3.51	53.7	0	53.7
1883	20.2	19.8	4.33	3.59	3.62	3.56	55.1	0	55.1
1884	20.7	20.2	4.49	3.72	3.67	3.61	56.4	0	56.4
1885	21.2	20.7	4.60	3.82	3.73	3.66	57.7	0	57.7
1886	21.7	21.1	4.69	3.90	3.78	3.71	58.9	0	58.9
1887	22.2	21.6	4.76	3.97	3.83	3.75	60.1	0	60.1
1888	22.7	22.1	4.83	4.04	3.88	3.80	61.3	0	61.3
1889	23.2	22.5	4.93	4.13	3.94	3.86	62.6	0	62.6
1890	23.7	23.0	5.05	4.22	4.00	3.92	63.9	0	63.9
1891	24.2	23.5	5.17	4.33	4.06	3.98	65.2	0	65.2
1892	24.7	24.0	5.28	4.42	4.13	4.05	66.6	0	66.6
1893	25.2	24.5	5.37	4.50	4.20	4.13	68.0	0	68.0
1894	25.7	25.0	5.43	4.56	4.28	4.20	69.2	0	69.2
1895	26.3	25.5	5.45	4.60	4.35	4.27	70.5	0	70.5

Year									
1896	26.8	26.0	5.42	4.60	4.41	4.34	71.6	0	71.6	71.6
1897	27.3	26.5	5.41	4.61	4.48	4.42	72.8	0	72.8	72.8
1898	27.8	27.0	5.43	4.63	4.55	4.48	74.0	0	74.0	74.0
1899	28.3	27.6	5.46	4.65	4.61	4.55	75.2	a	75.2	75.2
1900	28.9	28.1	5.52	4.68	4.67	4.61	76.4	0.01	76.4	76.4
1901	29.4	28.6	5.62	4.73	4.73	4.67	77.8	0.01	77.8	77.8
1902	30.0	29.2	5.77	4.80	4.79	4.73	79.2	0.02	79.2	79.2
1903	30.5	29.7	5.95	4.89	4.85	4.79	80.8	0.02	80.7	80.8
1904	31.1	30.3	6.17	5.01	4.90	4.84	82.4	0.02	82.3	82.4
1905	31.7	30.9	6.44	5.16	4.96	4.89	84.1	0.03	84.1	84.1
1906	32.3	31.5	6.65	5.31	5.01	4.94	85.8	0.03	85.7	85.8
1907	33.0	32.1	6.87	5.45	5.06	4.99	87.5	0.04	87.5	87.5
1908	33.6	32.7	7.11	5.60	5.11	5.04	89.3	0.05	89.2	89.3
1909	34.3	33.4	7.31	5.73	5.16	5.09	91.0	0.05	91.0	91.0
1910	35.0	34.1	7.45	5.84	5.21	5.14	92.7	0.06	92.7	92.7
1911	35.6	34.7	7.66	5.98	5.26	5.19	94.5	0.06	94.5	94.5
1912	36.3	35.4	7.89	6.13	5.31	5.24	96.4	0.06	96.3	96.4
1913	37.0	36.1	7.99	6.25	5.36	5.30	98.1	0.07	98.1	98.1
1914	37.7	36.8	8.04	6.34	5.41	5.34	99.7	0.07	99.7	99.7
1915	38.4	37.5	8.08	6.40	5.45	5.38	101.2	0.07	101.2	101.2
1916	39.0	38.2	8.02	6.40	5.48	5.42	102.6	0.07	102.5	102.6
1917	39.6	38.8	7.87	6.34	5.50	5.44	103.7	0.08	103.6	103.7
1918	40.3	39.5	7.74	6.28	5.53	5.47	104.9	0.08	104.8	104.9
1919	40.9	40.2	7.66	6.28	5.57	5.52	106.2	0.08	106.1	106.2
1920	41.6	40.9	7.57	6.27	5.62	5.57	107.6	0.09	107.5	107.6
1921	42.3	41.6	7.52	6.30	5.67	5.64	109.2	0.09	109.1	109.2
1922	43.1	42.4	7.56	6.37	5.74	5.71	111.0	0.09	110.9	111.0
1923	43.9	43.2	7.61	6.44	5.82	5.80	112.8	0.09	112.7	112.8
1924	44.6	44.0	7.63	6.47	5.89	5.88	114.5	0.09	114.4	114.5
1925	45.3	44.7	7.67	6.50	5.96	5.96	116.2	0.10	116.2	116.2
1926	46.1	45.4	7.68	6.52	6.03	6.04	117.9	0.10	117.8	117.9
1927	46.7	46.1	7.64	6.51	6.10	6.12	119.4	0.10	119.3	119.4
1928	47.4	46.8	7.60	6.50	6.16	6.20	120.8	0.10	120.7	120.8
1929	48.1	47.5	7.53	6.48	6.22	6.27	122.2	0.10	122.0	122.2
1930	48.7	48.1	7.43	6.42	6.28	6.34	123.4	0.11	123.3	123.4

(continued)

TABLE R-37 (concluded)

Year on Which Moving Average Is Centered (July 1)	Native White		Foreign White		Nonwhite		Total Population Excluding Armed Forces Overseas (7)	Armed Forces Overseas (8)	Total Population Including Armed Forces Overseas (9)
	Male (1)	Female (2)	Male (3)	Female (4)	Male (5)	Female (6)			
1931	49.2	48.7	7.30	6.34	6.33	6.41	124.3	0.11	124.5
1932	49.8	49.3	7.15	6.24	6.38	6.47	125.3	0.12	125.4
1933	50.3	49.9	6.98	6.13	6.42	6.52	126.2	0.12	126.3
1934	50.8	50.4	6.81	6.00	6.46	6.58	127.1	0.13	127.2
1935	51.3	51.0	6.65	5.88	6.50	6.64	127.9	0.14	128.1
1936	51.8	51.5	6.51	5.77	6.54	6.69	128.9	0.14	129.0
1937	52.3	52.1	6.37	5.67	6.58	6.75	129.8	0.15	129.9
1938							130.7	0.16	130.9
1939							131.7	0.18	131.9
1940							132.7	0.34	133.0
1941							133.5	0.81	134.3
1942							133.9	1.88	135.8
1943							134.0	3.33	137.3
1944							135.4	3.55	138.9
1945							137.3	3.49	140.8
1946							139.6	3.10	142.7
1947							142.8	2.10	144.9
1948							146.5	0.70	147.2
1949							149.2	0.63	149.8
1950							151.6	0.75	152.4
1951							154.1	0.91	155.0
1952							156.6	1.05	157.6
1953							159.2	1.15	160.3

Because of rounding, detail will not necessarily add to total.
a Less than 0.005 million.

Appendix E

The description of the series in a given column applies to the annual estimates underlying the five-year moving averages.

(1) and (2) Logarithmic straight-line interpolation of Table R-36, cols. 1 and 2, respectively.

(3) and (4) Calculated from Kuznets and Rubin, *Immigration and the Foreign Born*, Table B-6.

(5) and (6) Logarithmic straight-line interpolation of Table R-36, cols. 5 and 6, respectively.

(7) 1869: Extrapolated from 1870 with the Census Bureau estimate (given in *Historical Statistics of the United States, 1789–1945*, Series B-31) as index.

1870–1939: Sum of cols. 1–6.

1940–1949: Interpolated between the 1940 and 1950 entries in Table R-36, col. 7, by the series on population residing in the United States, adjusted for the 0–4 undercount, as given in *Current Population Reports*, Series P-25, No. 98.

1950–1955: Extrapolated from the 1950 entry in Table R-36, col. 7, by the series in *Current Population Reports*, Series P-25, No. 146.

(8) 1869–1939: The number in the armed forces overseas was assumed to be negligible in 1900 and earlier census years, since the number of soldiers, sailors, and marines alone, excluding officers, reported in *Census of Occupations, 1900* is larger than the total number in the armed forces reported in Solomon Fabricant, *The Trend of Government Activity since 1900* (New York, NBER, 1952), Table B-5. The armed forces overseas in 1910, 1920, and 1930 were estimated by subtracting from the total armed forces (*ibid.*), the number resident in the United States. The latter are given for 1910 in *Census of Occupations, 1910;* for 1920 and 1930 they were derived by adding to the number of soldiers, sailors, and marines reported in *Census of Occupations, 1920* and *1930*, the estimated number of officers. The latter were derived on the basis of the ratio of officers to soldiers, sailors, and marines, computed for 1910 and 1940 and interpolated along a straight line. For the 1940 ratio, the number of soldiers, sailors, and marines was taken from *Census of Population, 1940*, Vol. III, Part 1; and the number of officers was derived by subtracting the former from the total armed forces in the United States given in *Census of Population, 1950*, Vol. II, Part 1. The armed forces overseas in 1940 is given in *Current Population Reports*, Series P-25, No. 98. Interpolations between 1900, 1910, 1920, 1930, and 1940 were made along a straight line.

1940–1955: Derived as the difference between total population including and total population excluding armed forces overseas, given in *Current Population Reports*, Series P-25, Nos. 98 and 146.

(9) Sum of cols. 7 and 8.

TABLE R-38

LABOR FORCE, TEN YEARS OLD AND OVER, EXCLUDING ARMED FORCES OVERSEAS,
CENSUS AND MID-CENSAL DATES, 1870–1950

(numbers in millions)

| | Male, 10 Years and Over | | | Female, 10 Years and Over | | | |
	Population (1)	Ratio, Labor Force to Population (2)	Labor Force (3)	Population (4)	Ratio, Labor Force to Population (5)	Labor Force (6)	Total (7)
June 1, 1870	14.85	.748	11.11	14.44	.131	1.90	13.01
June 1, 1875	16.83	.768	12.92	16.54	.139	2.30	15.22
June 1, 1880	18.74	.787	14.74	18.03	.147	2.65	17.39
June 1, 1885	21.88	.780	17.06	20.75	.158	3.29	20.35
June 1, 1890	24.35	.773	18.82	23.06	.170	3.91	22.73
June 1, 1895	27.15	.786	21.35	25.74	.179	4.61	25.96
June 1, 1900	29.70	.800	23.75	28.25	.188	5.32	29.07
May 8, 1905	33.27	.806	26.82	31.30	.211	6.60	33.42
Apr. 15, 1910	37.03	.813	30.09	34.55	.234	8.08	38.17
Feb. 22, 1915	40.51	.797	32.30	38.12	.223	8.48	40.78
Jan. 1, 1920	42.29	.782	33.06	40.45	.211	8.55	41.61
Feb. 15, 1925	46.24	.772	35.70	44.72	.216	9.66	45.36
Apr. 1, 1930	49.95	.762	38.08	48.77	.220	10.75	48.83
Apr. 1, 1935	52.87	.743	39.30	52.23	.227	11.85	51.15
Apr. 1, 1940	55.29	.724	40.05	55.16	.233	12.88	52.92
Apr. 1, 1950			43.72			16.54	60.26

Estimates include armed forces stationed in the United States at the time of enumeration.

SOURCE, BY COLUMN

(1) and (4) Sum of native white, foreign white, and nonwhite population.

  Native white and nonwhite:

   1870, 1875, and later mid-censal dates: For source see notes to Table R-36, cols. 1, 2, 5, and 6.

   1880 and later census dates: *Census of Population* for respective years.

  Foreign white:

   Census dates: *Census of Population* for respective years.

   Mid-censal dates: Interpolated with total foreign white population as index. See notes to Table R-36, cols. 3 and 4, for derivation of the latter.

(2) and (5) 1870: Ratio of labor force (gainfully occupied) to population 10 years and over, both as reported in the *Census Compendium, 1870*.

   1880 and later census dates: Ratio of col. 3 to col. 1, or col. 6 to col. 4.

   Mid-censal dates: Straight-line interpolation between ratios for census dates.

(3) and (6) 1870, 1875, and later mid-censal dates: Col. 1 times col. 2, or col. 4 times col. 5.

Appendix E

(3) and (6) 1880, 1890, 1900, 1910, 1920, 1930: *Census of Occupations* for respective years.

1940 and 1950: Labor force 14 years and over, reported in *Census of Population, 1940*, Vol. III, Part 1, and *1950*, Vol. II, Part 1, plus an estimate of labor force, 10 to 13 years old, by Ann Miller, of the staff of the University of Pennsylvania Study of Population Redistribution and Economic Growth. This estimate was derived separately for male and female, as follows:

1. Participation rates (i.e. gainful workers as a percentage of population) were computed for 10- to 13-year-olds by state, 1930.

2. Participation rates were computed for 14- to 15-year-olds by state, 1930, 1940, 1950.

3. The ratio of the rate obtained in step 1 to that obtained in step 2 for 1930 was computed for each state.

4. The ratio derived in step 3, multiplied by the participation rates for 14- to 15-year-olds for the given state as derived in step 2, yielded the estimated participation rates for 10- to 13-year-olds in 1940 and 1950.

5. The participation rates for 10- to 13-year-olds computed in step 4 was applied to population aged 10–13 for each state in 1940 and 1950 to derive estimates of 10- to 13-year-olds in the labor force in those years.

Originally the procedure called for deriving the ratios obtained in step 3 for the four Censuses 1900 through 1930 and extrapolating, on the basis of these four points, the ratios for 1940 and 1950. When the ratios were computed, however, it appeared that the simpler procedure of using just the 1930 ratios with no further adjustments would yield equally adequate results.

The basic assumption underlying the procedure is that participation rates for the two age groups move together. There seems no reason to doubt the general validity of this assumption, although the relationship between the two is not likely to be as direct as this method implies.

As estimated by this procedure, the total number of workers aged 10–13 in all states combined is 132,800 for 1940 and 201,300 for 1950.

(7) Sum of cols. 3 and 6.

TABLE R-39

FIVE-YEAR MOVING AVERAGES OF TOTAL LABOR FORCE, TEN YEARS OLD AND OVER, JULY 1, 1869–1955

(millions)

Year on Which Moving Average Is Centered (July 1)	Male (1)	Female (2)	Total Excluding Armed Forces Overseas (3)	Armed Forces Overseas (4)	Total Including Armed Forces Overseas (5)
1871			13.50	0	13.50
1872	11.84	2.06	13.90	0	13.90
1873	12.20	2.14	14.34	0	14.34
1874	12.56	2.22	14.78	0	14.78
1875	12.93	2.30	15.22	0	15.22
1876	13.29	2.37	15.66	0	15.66
1877	13.66	2.44	16.10	0	16.10
1878	14.03	2.51	16.54	0	16.54
1879	14.41	2.59	17.00	0	17.00
1880	14.82	2.68	17.50	0	17.50
1881	15.24	2.79	18.03	0	18.03
1882	15.68	2.90	18.58	0	18.58
1883	16.14	3.03	19.17	0	19.17
1884	16.59	3.16	19.74	0	19.74
1885	17.01	3.28	20.29	0	20.29
1886	17.41	3.41	20.82	0	20.82
1887	17.78	3.54	21.32	0	21.32
1888	18.13	3.66	21.80	0	21.80
1889	18.52	3.79	22.31	0	22.31
1890	18.93	3.92	22.85	0	22.85
1891	19.37	4.06	23.43	0	23.43
1892	19.85	4.19	24.04	0	24.04
1893	20.35	4.33	24.69	0	24.69
1894	20.85	4.47	25.33	0	25.33
1895	21.35	4.61	25.97	0	25.97
1896	21.84	4.76	26.60	0	26.60
1897	22.33	4.90	27.23	0	27.23
1898	22.81	5.04	27.85	0	27.85
1899	23.32	5.21	28.53	a	28.53
1900	23.86	5.39	29.25	a	29.25
1901	24.42	5.60	30.03	0.01	30.03
1902	25.02	5.84	30.86	0.01	30.87
1903	25.64	6.10	31.74	0.02	31.75
1904	26.27	6.37	32.64	0.02	32.66
1905	26.91	6.64	33.55	0.03	33.58
1906	27.55	6.93	34.48	0.03	34.52
1907	28.21	7.22	35.43	0.04	35.47
1908	28.86	7.51	36.37	0.05	36.42
1909	29.48	7.76	37.24	0.05	37.29
1910	30.06	7.97	38.03	0.06	38.08

(continued)

Year on Which Moving Average Is Centered (July 1)	Male (1)	Female (2)	Total Excluding Armed Forces Overseas (3)	Armed Forces Overseas (4)	Total Including Armed Forces Overseas (5)
1911	30.59	8.14	38.73	0.06	38.79
1912	31.08	8.26	39.34	0.06	39.41
1913	31.52	8.34	39.86	0.07	39.92
1914	31.89	8.40	40.30	0.07	40.37
1915	32.21	8.46	40.67	0.07	40.74
1916	32.47	8.49	40.96	0.07	41.04
1917	32.67	8.52	41.18	0.08	41.26
1918	32.86	8.55	41.41	0.08	41.49
1919	33.12	8.62	41.74	0.08	41.82
1920	33.45	8.73	42.18	0.09	42.27
1921	33.86	8.88	42.74	0.09	42.83
1922	34.33	9.08	43.41	0.09	43.50
1923	34.85	9.29	44.14	0.09	44.23
1924	35.35	9.51	44.86	0.09	44.95
1925	35.84	9.72	45.56	0.10	45.66
1926	36.32	9.94	46.26	0.10	46.36
1927	36.79	10.15	46.94	0.10	47.04
1928	37.24	10.37	47.61	0.10	47.71
1929	37.65	10.58	48.24	0.10	48.34
1930	38.02	10.80	48.82	0.11	48.93
1931	38.34	11.02	49.36	0.11	49.48
1932	38.62	11.24	49.86	0.12	49.98
1933	38.86	11.46	50.32	0.12	50.45
1934	39.08	11.68	50.76	0.13	50.89
1935	39.29	11.89	51.17	0.14	51.31
1936	39.47	12.10	51.57	0.14	51.71
1937	39.63	12.31	51.94	0.15	52.09
1938	39.94	12.56	52.50	0.16	52.66
1939	40.42	12.86	53.27	0.18	53.46
1940	40.94	13.39	54.33	0.34	54.67
1941	41.46	14.37	55.83	0.81	56.64
1942	41.56	15.40	56.96	1.88	58.83
1943	41.07	16.32	57.39	3.33	60.72
1944	40.94	16.70	57.63	3.55	61.18
1945	41.06	16.82	57.87	3.49	61.37
1946	41.26	16.56	57.82	3.10	60.93
1947	41.93	16.30	58.22	2.10	60.33
1948			59.20	0.70	59.91
1949			60.29	0.63	60.92
1950			61.06	0.75	61.81
1951			61.74	0.91	62.65
1952			62.37	1.05	63.42
1953			63.08	1.15	64.23

Because of rounding, detail will not necessarily add to total.
ᵃ Less than 0.005 million.

(Notes on following page)

Appendix E

SOURCE, BY COLUMN

The description of the series in a given column applies to the annual estimates underlying the five-year moving averages.

(1) and (2) 1870–1939: Logarithmic straight-line interpolation of Table R-38, cols. 3 and 6, respectively.

1940–1949: Interpolation between the 1940 and 1950 estimates in Table R-38, cols. 3 and 6, with the sum of civilian labor force and armed forces in the United States as index. The former is the annual average given in *Current Population Reports*, Series P-50, Nos. 2, 13, 19, 31, and 40, and the latter is for July 1, derived as the difference between the population series including armed forces and that excluding them, given in *Current Population Reports*, Series P-25, No. 98.

(3) 1869: Extrapolation from 1870 with total population (series underlying Table R-37, col. 7) as index.

1870–1949: Sum of cols. 1 and 2.

1950–1955: Extrapolation of 1950 total in Table R-38, col. 7 by the index described in the above notes to cols. 1 and 2, 1940–1949. The sources of the underlying data are *Current Population Reports*, Series P-50, Nos. 40 and 45; Series P-57, No. 138; and Series P-25, No. 146.

(4) Table R-37, col. 8.

(5) Sum of cols. 3 and 4.

FIVE-YEAR MOVING AVERAGES OF NATIONAL PRODUCT AND FLOW OF GOODS
TO CONSUMERS, VARIANTS I AND III, 1929 PRICES, PER CAPITA
AND PER MEMBER OF LABOR FORCE, 1869–1955
(dollars)

Year on Which Moving Average Is Centered	Per Capita			Per Member of Labor Force	
	Gross National Product (1)	Net National Product (2)	Flow of Goods to Consumers (3)	Gross National Product (4)	Net National Product (5)
		A. VARIANT I			
1871	211	192	161	657	597
1872	219	199	167	679	616
1873	228	207	174	703	637
1874	241	218	182	737	668
1875	247	224	189	751	679
1876	256	231	196	771	696
1877	272	246	208	809	731
1878	295	268	226	871	790
1879	314	285	241	921	837
1880	332	302	255	969	881
1881	345	314	266	1,003	913
1882	354	322	274	1,024	930
1883	354	320	275	1,018	921
1884	358	323	278	1,024	924
1885	360	324	279	1,024	921
1886	361	323	279	1,021	915
1887	362	323	280	1,022	911
1888	369	328	278	1,037	922
1889	374	331	280	1,049	930
1890	384	340	282	1,074	951
1891	391	346	285	1,090	963
1892	393	346	284	1,089	959
1893	399	351	291	1,097	966
1894	399	350	293	1,092	959
1895	400	351	298	1,086	952
1896	407	357	303	1,096	960
1897	425	373	318	1,135	998
1898	436	383	326	1,156	1,018
1899	459	406	343	1,209	1,069
1900	475	421	355	1,242	1,100
1901	495	440	370	1,282	1,139
1902	504	448	378	1,294	1,150
1903	517	460	390	1,316	1,170
1904	531	472	401	1,340	1,192
1905	545	485	412	1,364	1,215
1906	543	481	413	1,349	1,197
1907	556	493	423	1,372	1,218
1908	563	499	429	1,380	1,224
1909	559	494	431	1,366	1,207
1910	561	495	434	1,367	1,205

(continued)

Year on Which Moving Average Is Centered	Per Capita			Per Member of Labor Force	
	Gross National Product (1)	Net National Product (2)	Flow of Goods to Consumers (3)	Gross National Product (4)	Net National Product (5)
A. VARIANT I, CONCLUDED					
1911	579	511	446	1,411	1,246
1912	572	503	447	1,400	1,231
1913	569	499	446	1,397	1,225
1914	581	509	449	1,434	1,258
1915	584	511	449	1,450	1,270
1916	580	506	448	1,451	1,265
1917	601	523	453	1,510	1,315
1918	619	539	463	1,564	1,362
1919	613	532	470	1,558	1,350
1920	620	537	481	1,578	1,367
1921	644	560	499	1,643	1,429
1922	658	575	519	1,680	1,466
1923	675	592	533	1,723	1,509
1924	708	622	551	1,804	1,586
1925	733	646	568	1,866	1,646
1926	743	656	579	1,890	1,667
1927	761	672	591	1,932	1,706
1928	763	673	602	1,932	1,705
1929	739	650	596	1,869	1,644
1930	693	605	577	1,749	1,527
1931	645	559	556	1,624	1,408
1932	597	513	532	1,499	1,289
1933	574	491	514	1,436	1,230
1934	579	498	515	1,448	1,244
1935	622	540	534	1,552	1,346
1936	656	573	553	1,637	1,429
1937	693	608	574	1,729	1,518
1938	732	645	600	1,818	1,603
1939	776	687	625	1,912	1,693
1940	799	706	640	1,943	1,716
1941	828	728	656	1,968	1,730
1942	852	740	670	1,971	1,715
1943	865	741	685	1,962	1,682
1944	887	754	708	2,024	1,720
1945	915	772	735	2,112	1,782
1946	949	798	761	2,237	1,881
1947	969	812	785	2,336	1,958
1948	1,008	847	809	2,477	2,081
1949	1,023	855	815	2,515	2,103
1950	1,038	869	824	2,560	2,142
1951	1,053	883	837	2,604	2,185
1952	1,075	907	849	2,671	2,255
1953	1,091	926	862	2,723	2,311

(continued)

Year on Which Moving Average Is Centered	Per Capita			Per Member of Labor Force	
	Gross National Product (1)	Net National Product (2)	Flow of Goods to Consumers (3)	Gross National Product (4)	Net National Product (5)
		B. VARIANT III			
1871	216	197	166	673	613
1872	224	204	172	695	632
1873	233	212	179	720	654
1874	247	224	188	755	686
1875	253	230	195	770	698
1876	263	238	203	790	715
1877	278	252	215	829	751
1878	302	275	233	892	811
1879	321	293	248	942	858
1880	340	310	263	991	904
1881	353	322	274	1,026	936
1882	362	330	282	1,047	954
1883	362	329	283	1,042	945
1884	367	332	287	1,048	948
1885	369	333	287	1,048	945
1886	370	332	288	1,046	939
1887	371	332	288	1,046	936
1888	377	337	287	1,061	946
1889	382	340	289	1,073	954
1890	393	349	291	1,098	975
1891	400	355	294	1,114	987
1892	402	355	293	1,113	983
1893	407	360	299	1,122	990
1894	408	360	302	1,117	984
1895	409	360	307	1,111	977
1896	417	366	313	1,122	986
1897	435	384	328	1,163	1,025
1898	446	394	337	1,185	1,046
1899	470	417	354	1,239	1,099
1900	487	433	367	1,273	1,131
1901	507	452	383	1,315	1,171
1902	517	461	392	1,328	1,184
1903	531	474	404	1,351	1,205
1904	546	487	415	1,376	1,229
1905	560	501	428	1,403	1,254
1906	559	498	430	1,389	1,237
1907	573	510	439	1,413	1,259
1908	580	516	446	1,422	1,266
1909	577	512	449	1,408	1,249
1910	579	512	452	1,409	1,247
1911	597	529	464	1,454	1,290
1912	590	521	465	1,443	1,275
1913	586	516	464	1,441	1,269
1914	599	527	467	1,479	1,303
1915	602	530	468	1,497	1,317

(continued)

Year on Which Moving Average Is Centered	Per Capita			Per Member of Labor Force	
	Gross National Product (1)	Net National Product (2)	Flow of Goods to Consumers (3)	Gross National Product (4)	Net National Product (5)
	B. VARIANT III, CONCLUDED				
1916	600	525	467	1,500	1,314
1917	621	544	474	1,562	1,368
1918	641	561	485	1,621	1,418
1919	637	555	493	1,618	1,411
1920	644	561	505	1,641	1,429
1921	670	586	525	1,709	1,494
1922	686	602	546	1,750	1,536
1923	703	619	561	1,793	1,579
1924	736	651	579	1,876	1,657
1925	762	676	597	1,940	1,719
1926	773	686	609	1,966	1,743
1927	791	702	620	2,006	1,780
1928	789	699	628	1,997	1,770
1929	765	677	622	1,935	1,710
1930	720	633	604	1,817	1,596
1931	670	584	580	1,687	1,470
1932	622	538	557	1,561	1,350
1933	608	526	548	1,521	1,316
1934	621	539	556	1,551	1,347
1935	668	586	580	1,667	1,462
1936	708	624	604	1,765	1,557
1937	748	663	628	1,865	1,653
1938	784	698	652	1,947	1,733
1939	823	735	673	2,030	1,811
1940	844	751	685	2,053	1,826
1941	874	773	702	2,076	1,838
1942	899	787	717	2,080	1,824
1943	914	790	734	2,072	1,793
1944	939	806	760	2,143	1,839
1945	971	828	791	2,241	1,911
1946	1,009	858	820	2,378	2,022
1947	1,032	876	848	2,488	2,109
1948	1,074	913	875	2,640	2,244
1949	1,091	923	883	2,682	2,270
1950	1,107	938	893	2,730	2,312
1951	1,122	953	907	2,777	2,358
1952	1,146	978	920	2,847	2,431
1953	1,163	997	934	2,903	2,490

SOURCE: Averages of annual series calculated from the annual aggregates underlying Table R-26, and the annual series on population and labor force underlying Tables R-37 and R-39.

Index

(Page numbers in **boldface** type refer to tables, charts, and figures.)

Index

Index

Index

Lightning Source UK Ltd.
Milton Keynes UK
UKOW01f1036130617

303166UK00001B/23/P

9 780691 625560